South Africa
Lesotho
Swaziland

www.baedeker.com

Verlag Karl Baedeker

SIGHTSEEING HIGHLIGHTS ★ ★

Even if visitors to South Africa are spoilt for choice, it would be a shame to overlook any of the major sights. On the one hand there are natural phenomena such as big-game parks, a flowering semi-desert and whales along rugged rocky cliffs, on the other hand old Cape Dutch wine towns and large cities bursting with life: here we have compiled a list of the sights that should be on every holiday list.

1 ★★ Cape Town
»South Africa's mother city« and one of the most beautiful cities in the world, colourful and lively at the foot of the famous Table Mountain. The surrounding area (the Cape peninsula with classy seaside towns and even classier vineyards, a magnificent botanical garden, Blouberg beach and the former prison settlement of Robben Island) is just as much worth visiting. ▸ page 229

2 ★★ Cape of Good Hope
Although it is not the continent's southern-most point, the weather-beaten Cape of Good Hope is nonetheless very impressive. ▸ page 257

Cape Town
A unique mix of cultures makes this town at the foot of Table Mountain particularly attractive.

3 ★★ Stellenbosch
Enchanting, wonderfully situated Cape Dutch town and probably South Africa's most famous wine town, located just east of Cape Town. ▸ page 473

4 ★★ Paarl
After Stellenbosch, Paarl is the most famous place in the arc of wine towns around Cape Town. It is also of historical interest as the »cradle« of Afrikaans. ▸ page 419

5 ★★ West Coast National Park
A bare coastal landscape on the Atlantic north of Cape Town and a mecca for birdwatchers and windsurfers. Countless daisies come into bloom here in springtime. ▸ page 505

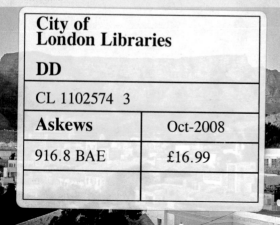

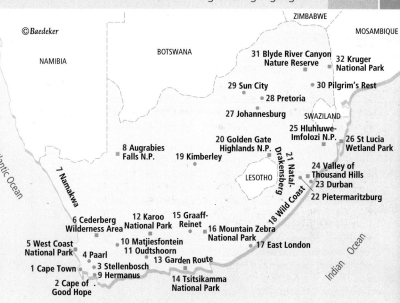

©Baedeker

ZIMBABWE

MOSAMBIQUE

NAMIBIA

BOTSWANA

31 Blyde River Canyon
Nature Reserve

32 Kruger
National Park

29 Sun City

30 Pilgrim's Rest

28 Pretoria

27 Johannesburg

SWAZILAND

25 Hluhluwe-
Imfolozi N.P.

26 St Lucia
Wetland Park

20 Golden Gate
Highlands N.P.

8 Augrabies
Falls N.P.

19 Kimberley

21 Natal-
Drakensberg

LESOTHO

24 Valley of
Thousand Hills

18 Wild Coast

23 Durban

22 Pietermaritzburg

Atlantic Ocean

7 Namakwa

6 Cederberg
Wilderness Area

12 Karoo
National Park

15 Graaff-
Reinet

16 Mountain Zebra
National Park

5 West Coast
National Park

4 Paarl

10 Matjiesfontein

11 Oudtshoorn

17 East London

Indian Ocean

1 Cape Town

3 Stellenbosch

13 Garden Route

2 Cape of
Good Hope

9 Hermanus

14 Tsitsikamma
National Park

6 ✶✶ Cederberg Wilderness Area

A bizarre rocky landscape with San rock drawings where the land becomes semi-desert. The valley of the Olifants River is a well-known fruit-growing region and is becoming a source of excellent wines.
► page 263

7 ✶✶ Namakwa

There is hardly any rain in the hinterland of the northern Atlantic coast, but during the spring many square miles are covered by colourful flowers. Adventurers enjoy a trip to the Richtersveld Park. ► page 397

8 ✶✶ Augrabies Falls National Park

Even landscapes that are almost desert can contain a lot of water, and this one is aptly called »place of big noise«. Extreme living conditions form the basis for some interesting fauna and flora. ► page 202

9 ✶✶ Hermanus

Huge whales and playful dolphins come tantalizingly close in this popular holiday town. Attractive trips to the Hemel-en-Aarde Valley and to Cape Agulhas, the continent's southernmost point.
► page 315

10 ✶✶ Matjiesfontein

Dining and sleeping in the Lord Milner Hotel is almost exciting enough in itself, but the Great Karoo has yet more impressive experiences in store.
► page 386

11 ✶✶ Oudtshoorn

Ostrich feathers, ostrich eggs, ostrich steaks … everything here involves these strange, impressive birds. Fantastic excursion over the Swartberg Pass to Prince Albert. ► page 413

12 ✶✶ Karoo National Park

From Beaufort West the Great Karoo can be experienced in all its glory, the best months are the »rainy« autumn months from February to March.
► page 205

Swartberg Pass
An adventurous drive over the pass between Oudtshoorn and Prince Albert, which was opened in 1888

BAEDEKER'S BEST TIPS

From the many tips in this travel companion we have compiled those that are particularly interesting: experience South Africa at its best.

⚠ On two wheels
A particularly nice way to get to know Cape Town – with the wind in your hair. ▶ **page 232**

⚠ Jazz in Cape Town
Cape Town is a real mecca for jazz lovers. ▶ **page 242**

Sabi Sabi
Wilderness meets luxury in the Kruger National Park.

⚠ Long Street
This is the colourful heart of Cape Town. ▶ **page 245**

⚠ Kagga Kamma
See springboks in a picturesque rocky landscape during the day and spend the night in comfortable caves.
▶ **page 262**

⚠ Rooibos tea
Find out how the basic ingredient for this popular drink is »made«.
▶ **page 265**

⚠ Rafting on Great Fish River
You needn't be a canoe freak to enjoy some wet fun here.
▶ **page 268**

⚠ Bunny Chow
Much better than a burger: this Indian version. ▶ **page 283**

⚠ Temple of Understanding
Magnificently colourful Indian world.
▶ **page 284**

⚠ Strandloper Trail
Explore this diverse coastal landscape on shanks' pony. ▶ **page 294**

⚠ Adventure at Storms River
Experience the jungle from above or abseil 100m/300ft into a canyon.
▶ **page 302**

⚠ Edwardian shopping
A »British« atmosphere can still be experienced in Grahamstown.
▶ **page 310**

⚠ Kwandwe Game Reserve
Enjoy a safari in a very private, luxurious atmosphere.
▶ **page 313**

⚠ Hermanus Wine Route
A pleasurable alternative to whale-watching in the idyllic hinterland of Hermanus. ▶ **page 317**

Legendary cape: the Cape of Good Hope ▶ page 257

BACKGROUND

PRACTICALITIES

*Excursion into the
land of the Zulu*
▶ **page 295**

TOURS

SIGHTS
FROM A to Z

PRICE CATEGORIES

▶ **Hotels**
2 people in a double room
with a bath, breakfast included:
Budget: up to ZAR 500
Comfortable:
ZAR 500 – ZAR 1000
Luxury: more than ZAR 1000

▶ **Restaurants**
Prices for a main course:
Inexpensive: ZAR 25 – ZAR 60
Mid-range: ZAR 40 – ZAR 80
Expensive: ZAR 60 – ZAR 100

Experience exotic animals in the wild, e.g. in the Kruger National Park.
► page 355

The Natal Drakensberg mountains, the »Alps of South Africa«, hold magnificent scenery in store.
► page 401

Cape Town is worth a visit if only because of its spectacular location.
► page 229

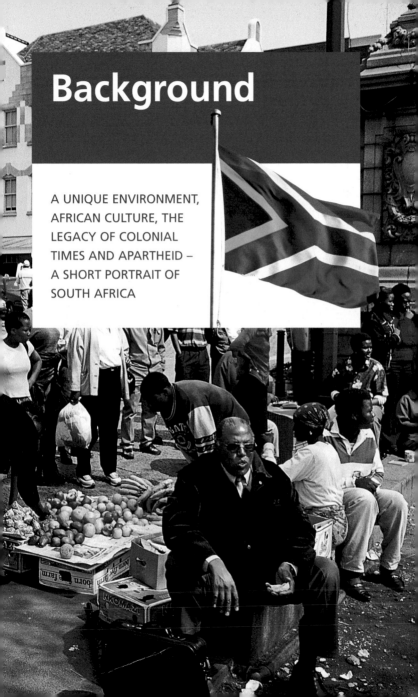

Background

A UNIQUE ENVIRONMENT,
AFRICAN CULTURE, THE
LEGACY OF COLONIAL
TIMES AND APARTHEID –
A SHORT PORTRAIT OF
SOUTH AFRICA

A WORLD IN ONE COUNTRY

This is the slogan that South Africa uses to attract visitors. Does it keep this promise? It most certainly does, since the country at the Cape of Good Hope, the southernmost of the African continent, is undeniably one of the most beautiful travel destinations in the world.

South Africa is a country full of spectacular contrasts: sub-Saharan Africa coupled with European and Asian elements. The combination of adventure and excellent infrastructure is also second to none in the world. The coexistence of tradition and modernity and the mix of people of all skin colours, who usually offer visitors a kind, open and friendly welcome, are equally fascinating. Although race relations have largely relaxed since the abolition of apartheid, Nelson Mandela's vision of a »rainbow nation« is still far from being fulfilled. It is still primarily black people who are affected by poverty, inadequate education, meagre living conditions and unemployment, the result of which is violence and crime. Visitors do not usually experience much of this, not least because it is advisable not to wander around quite so casually as at home, particularly in the larger cities.

Wild animals
Adventure, but in moderation: that is South Africa's recipe for success as a holiday destination.

A Unique Environment and a Diverse Culture

South Africa as a travel destination also has plenty of »bright sides«, quite literally in fact: one of the strongest impressions of the country is its bright sunshine, both in summer and in winter. South Africa gets 2800 to 3800 hours of sunshine a year. London in contrast gets 1500. And with the seasons reversed, it provides a wonderful opportunity to take a holiday in warm conditions at a time when the northern hemisphere is in the grip of winter. The country's real treasure, and its most important asset for tourism, however comes from its spectacular and very diverse landscapes. Inhospitable semi-deserts in the west and north, savannahs, craggy mountains, seemingly never-ending gentle green hills and lush, sub-tropical forests in the east, along with picturesque vineyards and a jagged, rocky coastline in the south frequented by whales and dolphins. Famous nation-

The heritage of the colonial era
Beautiful houses in the Cape Dutch style, such as the Steenberg Country Hotel, are part of the kaleidoscope of South African sights.

Traditional and modern
A smile for a stranger: a Zulu girl in traditional »make up« and denim jacket

Giant's Castle in the uKhahlamba Drakensberg Park
Fans of stunning landscapes and impressive hiking tours get their money's worth in South Africa.

All of the smells and colours of Africa
Take different landscapes in different climate zones as well as a colourful ethnic mix, and the result is a very special, interesting culinary culture.

Neat hospitality
The many beautiful and stylish guesthouses, such as the Matoppo Inn in Beaufort West, are among the many treats of a South African holiday.

Gentle beaches, wild cliffs
More than 2000 miles of coastline along the Indian Ocean and the Atlantic, here in Clifton near Cape Town, make South Africa a mecca for holidaymakers who like to while away their days on the beach.

al parks and private game reserves provide exciting encounters with a fantastic flora and fauna. Of course everyone wants to experience the Big Five: elephants, lions, rhinoceroses, leopards and buffaloes; but giraffes and hippopotamuses should not be forgotten, nor indeed the smaller animals. The uniqueness of the vegetation at the Cape has caused it to be classified as a »botanical province« in its own right; the bizarre succulents in the semi-desert are no less impressive. South Africa is assumed to be the »cradle of mankind«, since it was here that the remains of the earliest humans were found. Many rock paintings recall the San, the oldest inhabitants. Everywhere there are signs and evidence of the conflict-laden history between black peoples and the Europeans who started settling at the Cape in 1652 and who determined the country's fate for over 300 years. Cities brimming with activity, rich in tradition like Cape Town, South Africa's »mother city«, or modern like Johannesburg, the country's economic powerhouse, and idyllic towns from the colonial period such as Stellenbosch, Graaff-Reinet and Paarl all offer a wealth of culture that is vibrant and definitely worth experiencing.

Holidaying in South Africa

Although for visitors from Europe it takes a good ten hours to reach South Africa by plane, it is only two zones east of Greenwich Mean Time, so jetlag is not a problem. As one of the most popular travel destinations worldwide, the country boasts an excellent tourist infrastructure. However, there are certain times of the year when the

Kalahari
Unforgettable impressions are guaranteed in South Africa.

beaches and the game reserves have many visitors, not least because South Africans themselves like to travel in their own country. This is mainly relevant in the summer holidays between the beginning of December and mid-January, the period around Easter, and two weeks in July. The climate in South Africa is such that there is a rewarding destination for every season. There are innumerable opportunities for sporting activities of a more or less adventurous kind. The restaurant and hotel sectors range from good to excellent, and the pleasant level of prices deserves a mention, since it allows even visitors on a budget to enjoy a relatively luxurious stay. Discover South Africa, its beauty and hospitality – you will want to come again.

Facts

Where can the Great Escarpment be found and where is the Karoo? How many white people live in South Africa and how many Indians? What is special about the protea, South Africa's national flower? Which seasons are the best for travelling to which parts of the country? Read here about the country and its people, its economy and politics, its society and everyday life.

Natural Environment

Landscapes

South Africa's **coast** is almost 3000km/1900mi long. It borders the Atlantic in the south-west and the Indian Ocean in the south and south-east. The coast is exposed to two ocean currents: in the west the cold Benguela current, which flows from Antarctica northwards to Angola, and the warm Agulhas current, which flows southwards from the equatorial region. **South Africa's southernmost point** and thus the most southerly point of the African continent is Cape Agulhas (Cape of Needles), not the famous, more westerly Cape of Good Hope near Cape Town. The **interior** largely consists of an extensive, undulating plateau, the **highveld**, which rises to elevations between 1200m and 1753m (3900–5750ft) above sea level. It descends towards the Kalahari basin in the north and north-west and the Limpopo depression in the north-east. Towards the coast it falls off relatively steeply at the **Great Escarpment**; both along the Atlantic and the Indian Oceans there are only narrow strips of coastal plain between the highveld and the sea.

The coast and the interior

The interior plateau (Northern Cape, Free State, Gauteng) is part of a very old and stable massif of the earth's crust; it consists of magma rocks dating from the Palaeozoic era as well as of younger sedimentary rocks dating from the Mesozoic. Interminable erosion processes over the course of the earth's history have largely levelled the surface forms; a **peneplain** has formed, from which individual mesas and **extensive ridges** (e.g. Witwatersrand) rise, and into which rivers such as the Vaal and Orange have cut. The Palaeozoic rocks of the highveld also contain the most valuable **deposits of precious and non-ferrous metals as well as bituminous coal**, which have made South Africa one of the most important mining countries in the world. The diamond deposits, at Kimberley for example, go back to Mesozoic intrusions. Mining has led to a great reshaping of the earth's surface in the region. One famous feature is the »Big Hole« near Kimberley, the result of diamond mining, while large areas of the Witwatersrand near Johannesburg are shaped by slag heaps and open-cast mines.

Central high plateau

Towards the north the central plateau gradually falls away to the dry **Kalahari Basin**, which displays the characteristic traits of a sand desert with dunes and continues into Botswana. In the north-east (towards Zimbabwe and Mozambique) the plateau merges into the moister **lowveld**, also called the **bushveld**, via the **middelveld** (600–1200m/2000–3900ft above sea level) along the Limpopo river.

← *Swellendam has a very attractive townscape with its Cape Dutch, Georgian and Victorian buildings (here the Reformed Church).*

Little Karoo: landscape at the Swartberg Pass

Great Escarpment The Great Escarpment, a prominent fault scarp, forms the boundary of the central plateau. In the east and the south-east (Mpumalanga, KwaZulu-Natal) it is particularly prominent in the shape of the **Drakensberg mountains**, an impressive range consisting of quartzite, dolomite, diabase, basalt and granite. It reaches heights of more than 2300m/7500ft (in Gauteng), more than 3000m/10,000ft in the Natal/Lesotho border region and around 3500m/11,500ft in Lesotho itself. In the border region between Lesotho and the province of KwaZulu-Natal, the Drakensberg range displays its mountainous character most strikingly. This is also where the highest mountain of the Republic of South Africa, **Injesuti** (3408m/11,182ft), is located. The landscape is shaped by sharp ridges and steep rock walls, deep canyons and hundreds of high waterfalls. All this provides great natural attractions for tourists. Nature reserves and national parks have been set up in order to protect these landscapes and their flora and fauna. The Great Escarpment is a **traffic obstruction** that is difficult to overcome. Thus in 250km/155mi there is just a single mountain pass over the Drakensberg range in KwaZulu-Natal. The main crossing for roads and railways from the coast to the plateau lies in the west in the area of the Great Karoo, where the Great Escarpment is lower for a length of 80km/50mi.

Cape Ranges In the Western Cape and Eastern Cape provinces the Great Escarpment is fronted by the Cape Ranges. They are made up of several parallel mountain formations. The folds and faults in these ranges indicate great tectonic movements during the Mesozoic era (**Owart-**

berg range, Langberge, Baviaanskloofberge, Tsitsikammaberge amongst others). They too reach heights of between 1500m/5000ft and more than 2000m/6500ft; the highest elevation is the Seweweekspoort Peak (2326m/7632ft). The most famous mountain however is **Table Mountain** near Cape Town (1087m/3566ft), one of several foothills that fall off very steeply towards the sea.

Karoo

The name Karoo, a Khoikhoi word for a stony desert area, is now applied to three geographical areas. The **Great Karoo**, a very dry, stony semi-desert, lies at between 600m and 900m (2000–3000ft) between the Great Escarpment and the northern Cape Ranges. The **Little Karoo** is a dry depression between two mountain ranges running parallel to each other from east to west north of Cape Agulhas. The **Upper Karoo** on the other hand lies north of the Great Escarpment and makes up the lowest (900–1200m/3000–4000ft) and driest part of the central plateau: it is an almost waterless semi-desert to desert.

Western Coastal Terraces

Between the interior plateau and the Atlantic west coast lies the dry, terraced landscape of **Namakwa** (formerly Namaqualand). The hostile, sparsely populated narrow coastal plain is traversed by dry riverbeds and covered by a salt crust in some areas.

Natural Regions

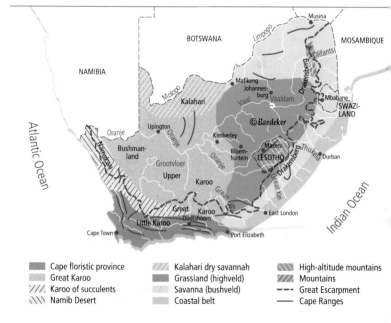

Cape floristic province	Kalahari dry savannah	High-altitude mountains
Great Karoo	Grassland (highveld)	Mountains
Karoo of succulents	Savanna (bushveld)	--- Great Escarpment
Namib Desert	Coastal belt	— Cape Ranges

KwaZulu-Natal Coastal Plain Between the Great Escarpment and the Indian Ocean in the northern part of KwaZulu-Natal lies **South Africa's only wide coastal plain**. The southern extension of the Maputo coastal plain in Mozambique, it is crossed by many rivers that flow from the Drakensberg range into the Indian Ocean. The flat coast has many beautiful sandy beaches.

Rivers

The mountains of the Great Escarpment form the most important watershed. The **Orange River** (2400km/1500mi in length) flowing from the Drakensberg range into the Atlantic from east to west, with its biggest tributary, the **Vaal**, and the **Limpopo**, which forms a large stretch of South Africa's northern border, are the biggest river systems. Their highly variable water flow make them just as unnavigable as the numerous shorter rivers that flow from the escarpment into the Indian Ocean, usually with a steep downward gradient. However, the severe water shortage in the interior means that all rivers are of great significance for supplying drinking water and water for domestic use, as well as for energy generation and irrigation.

Orange River While only smaller rivers flow into the Atlantic from the Cape region, the Orange River, which flows into the Atlantic near Oranjemund at the border to Namibia, is **South Africa's most significant river** by far. It has its source at an elevation of 3000m/10,000ft in the Drakensberg range, then flows through Lesotho, and forms the border between the provinces of Free State and Northern Cape. After its confluence with the Vaal River it flows through the province of

Wide open prairie in Free State

Northern Cape, occasionally in deep gorges, and then forms the border with Namibia until it reaches the sea. Fluctuations in water volume, frequent rapids and sandbanks mean this river is not suitable for navigation. The longest of the Orange River's tributaries, which also has the greatest volume of water, is the **Vaal River** (1250km/775mi), which has its source in the northern Drakensberg range. It is the most important watercourse for the Witwatersrand industrial agglomeration. The water shortage in the central plateau is demonstrated by the fact that the Orange River with its 2340km/1450mi length has a catchment area of around one million sq km/400,000 sq mi, but not a single permanently flowing tributary on the whole 1200km/750mi stretch between the Vaal confluence and the Atlantic. It is only every few years that the **Molopo** in particular, coming from the Kalahari basin, with its Nossob and Auob tributaries, has enough water even to reach the Orange River.

The most significant South African river flowing into the Indian   **Limpopo**
Ocean is the Limpopo (1600km). Its source is in the Witwatersrand. It follows a semi-circle along the borders of Botswana and Zimbabwe through Mozambique before flowing into the ocean to the northeast of Maputo. Because of its canyon and its formidable (948m/3110ft) waterfalls, the **Tugela River** is the most famous of the numerous short but voluminous rivers that flow with a steep downhill gradient from the Natal-Drakensberg range into the Indian Ocean

Climate

What every visitor to South Africa remembers is the **bright sun-**   **Sunny paradise**
shine: with up to 3480 hours of sunshine each year »sunny South Africa« is climatically one of the most attractive regions in the world. Despite this, the climate is surprisingly varied. It ranges from the south-east coast on South Africa's »weather side«, which is damp all year round with summery warm temperatures, to the warm-temperate eastern interior plateau (highveld) with its more or less regular summer rain, to the semi-desert and desert climate of the north-western highlands and the Atlantic coast. Finally the Cape Province has a typical Mediterranean climate with rainfall in winter and a dry period during the summer months. The determining climatic factors are the country's location below the subtropical ridge, the surrounding oceans with the warm Agulhas current in the east and the cold Benguela current in the west, its altitude, and the flat relief of the central plateau, which is sheltered from maritime influences by the 5000km/3000mi-long Great Escarpment.
Both the southern Atlantic **St Helena High** and the **Mascarene High** over the southern Indian Ocean are responsible for bringing good

South Africa Climatic Regions

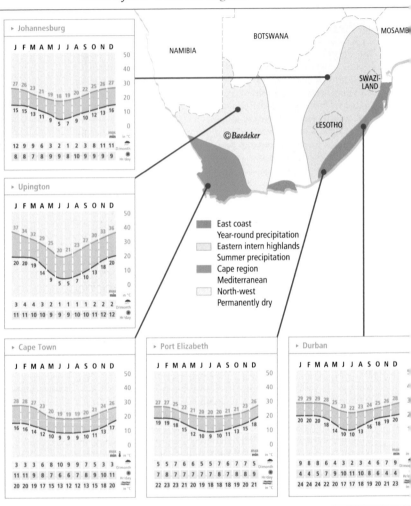

weather. Usually they are connected by a ridge of high pressure over the interior, but during the summer tropical disturbances frequently enter this area from the north-east. They bring heavy rains and thunderstorms to the eastern highlands, the Drakensberg range, and the adjoining coastal zones. Highland lows during the winter months are much rarer. Their rainfall can affect the entire south-eastern part of the country. Their dark rain clouds, driven inland from the ocean by the strong south-eastern winds, have given these weather conditions the name **Black South-Easter**. In the desert-like north-west and the Atlantic Namib desert, high pressure is dominant, inhibiting rainfall all year round. Cape Province receives its necessary precipitation from low-pressure areas coming from the Westerlies.

In South Africa, which lies in the southern hemisphere, the seasons are opposite to those in the northern hemisphere. When Europe is treated to the summer sun, it is winter in South Africa; when autumn makes its entrance north of the equator, South Africa is experiencing the beginning of spring, and when spring brings out the buds in the northern hemisphere, the leaves at the Cape start turning red.

Inverted seasons

Generally speaking the sea is warmest from February to March, and coolest in June and July. The Indian Ocean coast has the highest water temperatures. Pleasant swimming temperatures of 20°C/68°F are exceeded all year round along the northern part of the coast (Durban maximum 24°C/75°F, minimum 21°C/70°F) and between November and April (Port Elizabeth maximum 22°C/72°F in February, minimum 18°C/64°F in August) in the south. The waters of the Cape Town beaches hardly reach 20°C/68°F even in March. In addition currents reduce the already low water temperatures in individual bays quite significantly (e.g. False Bay 19°C/66°F, Table Bay 10°C/50°F at the same time). Bathing in the Atlantic is only for the more hardy, since its maximum water temperature is 17°C/63°F.

Water temperatures

South Africa's climate make this country an all-year-round destination, with just a few reservations. One of the areas disadvantaged by excessive humidity is the northern coast along the **Indian Ocean** (Natal) between the months of November and April. Conditions around the **Cape** are somewhat muggy in January and February, but constant air movement here provides refreshment. Similar conditions exist along the Atlantic coast. During the summer months there is also frequently a bothersome coastal fog. The **highland climate** is not stressful at all; the altitude and low humidity mean the nights are pleasantly cool. With respect to the seasons, spring and autumn are the most favourable times to go.

When to go

South-East Coast: Humid All Year Round

The northern section of the south-east coast has a tropical climate in summer with a rainy season lasting from October to March. Rainfall is particularly plentiful in the shadow of the Great Escarpment (the record is held by Pietermaritzburg, where 167 litres per sq m (6.57in) fell on 23 December 1978). The Transvaal Escarpment, South Africa's most humid region, experiences annual rainfalls of over 3000 litres per sq m (118in). Summer temperatures of over 30°C/86°F are relatively rare, but the high humidity of 70–80% away

Northern section

from the sea-breeze often causes oppressively sultry conditions. With lows around 21°C/70°F even the nights are not very refreshing. The winter weather (June to August) on the other hand is ideal. Blue skies are common and the sun shines around 70 to 75% of the time. The temperatures of 23°C/73°F during the day and 17°C/63°F at night are also very pleasant. This is equally true of the sea with temperatures between 20 and 22°C (68–72°F).

Southern section Towards the south the amount of rainfall becomes less and the summer precipitation maximum peters out. While the annual mean rainfall is 1015 litres per sq m (40in) in Durban, it is only 625 litres per sq m (25in) in Port Elizabeth. The temperatures also drop. The southern coastal areas usually register 25–26°C/77–79°F on summer days, with a night-time low of 18°C/64°F. During winter the corresponding temperatures lie at 20°C/68°F during the day and 9°C/48°F during the night. The amount of sunshine is a fantastic 2800 hours annually (in comparison: London receives 1500 hours per year). This means an average of 80% sunshine (9 hours a day) for Port Elizabeth during the summer and still 60% (7 hours a day) during the winter.
A special feature of the south-east coast is the extreme variability of temperature. If the wind does not come from the sea as it normally does, but instead blows as a trade wind from the mountains along the edge of the plateau down towards the coast, then temperatures of up to 35°C/95°F are possible all year round and can even exceed 40°C/104°F in spring (absolute maximums Durban 42.0°C/107.6°F in September, Port Elizabeth 40.7°C/105.3°F in March).

Mediterranean Cape Province

The area in a radius of approximately 300km/190mi around Cape Town is favoured by a **Mediterranean climate**, dry in summer and damp in winter, with 3000 hours of sunshine a year. Particularly during the summer months the sun demonstrates what it is capable of by shining 11 hours a day (80% of the possible time). However even in winter there are still 50 to 60% more hours of sunshine than Britain experiences during its summer. The western Cederberg and Swartberg ranges profit most from the winter rains. Precipitation in Cape Town is comparatively modest with 520 litres per sq m (20in) per year. Wintry cold spells with snowfalls at higher elevations can give the 1100m/3900ft Table Mountain a white cap. Significantly more snow falls at the highest elevations (Matroosberg 2250m/7380ft), which not only allows winter sports, but is also of great importance for the water supply.
The influence of the oceans means the temperatures are very balanced and pleasant all year round. One exception is the area where the sea breeze blows: the low water temperatures mean a warm pullover should always be at hand. Away from this area summer days generally record 25–26°C/77–79°F, and 18°C/64°F even in July, the

An »artwork« in the sand of the Kalahari. A tour in the Kgalagadi Transfrontier Park leaves indelible impressions.

coolest month. During the summer temperatures rarely drop below 15°C/59°F at night, and during winter hardly ever below 8°C/46°F. For that reason night frosts are only an issue in the highlands. At the other end of the scale it can sometimes get unbearably hot. If the wind comes from the hot highlands, 40°C/104°F is quite possible (absolute maximums Cape Town 40.7°C/105.3°F in March, Oudtshoorn 44°C/111.2°F in January).

One special feature is the **Cape Doctor**. During summer there is often a strong south-easterly wind that can blow for weeks. It not only raises dust, but also provides the necessary air exchange in the Table Mountain basin. A spectacular sign of this dry trade-wind is the **table cloth**, the cloud cover over Table Mountain.

Desert-Like North-West

The north-western interior and the adjoining Atlantic coast are **extremely dry and hot**. The annual precipitation in the highlands is well below 200 litres per sq m (8in) and in the Namib desert even less than 100 litres per sq m (4in). Here, the life-giving water often stays away for years. The number of hours of sunshine – 3800 hours a year, a figure exceeded in few other regions on earth – is correspondingly high. During summer temperatures of 35–37°C/95–97°F are recorded regularly and occasionally even temperatures of over 40°C/104°F (absolute maximum Upington 43°C/109°F in December), while the thermometer quickly drops to around 20°C/68°F on clear nights. During winter values between 21°C/70°F during the day and 4°C/39°F during the night are normal. Slight frost down to -5°C/23°F is no rarity in the interior (absolute minimum Upington -7.9°C/-17.8°F in June). In the area affected by the sea breeze, the cold Benguela current (maximum 17°C/63°F) and frequent coastal fog cause a palpable reduction of the air temperatures down to an average of 22°C/72°F on summer days and 18°C/64°F on winter days.

Eastern Interior: Summer Humidity

Not least because of the **healthy climate**, the eastern highlands (1000–1800m/3280–5900ft) are where the white population is concentrated. Little rainfall, a lot of sunshine, and predominantly pleasant temperatures are the notable features. The summer rainfalls (October to April) usually occur in the form of heavy showers or thunderstorms (annual amount: Johannesburg 811 litres per sq m or 32in). Despite that, this period is still dominated by the sun. In Johannesburg it shines a full 8 hours a day on average in January (12 days of rain) or 60% of the possible time, while it hardly takes a break during the winter with sunshine 80 to 90% of the time. The daytime temperature reaches 25–28°C/77–82°F on average during the summer, depending on the altitude. In extreme cases it can even reach 35°C/95°F, while temperatures generally drop to 14–17°C/57–63°F at night. Temperatures of 20°C/68°F during the day and 6°C/43°F during the night are normal during the winter months. During that time cold spells coming from the south mean slight night frost is no rarity and on the heights of the Drakensberg mountains there is snowfall (absolute minimum Johannesburg -5.6°C/22°F in July). Above 1500m/4900ft it is even possible to have a slight frost in summer. The »black frost« is feared in this connection, because it can cause severe damage to the sensitive maize and wheat crops. Here dry, cold air from Antarctic latitudes comes to rest under cloudless conditions when the ground can radiate its heat back into space at night. The constant wind that can sometimes reach storm force is typical of the plateaux.

Flora and Fauna

Mecca for nature lovers   South Africa possesses an **extremely varied flora and fauna**, both on land and in the water. The country only covers 4% of the African landmass and around 0.8% of the entire earth's landmass, but it is home to almost 10% of all higher plants (22,600 of the 250,000 species), 8% of all bird species (718 of 9000), 5.8% of all mammalian species (227 of 3927; 43 of them marine mammals), and 4.6% of all reptile species (286 of 6214). In comparison, the United States, a country that is seven times larger than South Africa, only has around 15,000 plant species. Australia, whose total area is six times larger than South Africa, only has 656 bird species and 224 mammalian species.In addition South Africa has many endemic plants and animals, i.e. species that exist nowhere else on earth: 25% of the plants and reptiles, 15% of the mammals, and 6% of the birds. The flora differs so much from other regions in the world that the South African landscape was named as **one of the earth's six floristic provinces**. The great biodiversity in South Africa, which unlike Europe was not robbed of almost all its life during an ice age 10,000 years ago, can be attributed to the extreme variety of habitats, from evergreen rainforest to extremely dry deserts and cold high mountain regions. It is with some justification that South Africa advertises itself as »a world in one country«.

The enormous wealth of plants and animals requires adequate nature conservation policies. Humans were far too irresponsible with the natural environment here in the past. In 1880 the last bluebuck (blue antelope) was killed; a short while later the zebra-like quagga met with the same fate. Despite intensive efforts by the state to conserve the natural environment, the list of plant and animal species, most of them endemic, that are threatened by extinction is by no means short. Some of the most endangered species are the riverine rabbit, the roan antelope, and the African wild dog; 1500 plant species are on the endangered species list. Jan van Riebeeck was the first to issue hunting bans in 1656. The first game reserve, the Kruger National Park, was created in 1898. In addition, there are 22 further national parks and several hundred regional and private game reserves; the most important are marked on the map on p.148. Overall a total of 72,000 sq km/28,000 sq mi is under protection, spread over 580 reserves. In actual fact that only makes up 5.8% of South Africa's total area. In recent times more and more game reserves have been set up. This is necessary because many parks are unsustainable in the long term. Remote, small reserves lack the tourists and thus the financial means to secure their upkeep. In addition new reserves are needed in order to provide migrating animal herds with the space they require and to make sure that they do not have to limit themselves to just one area.

Nature conservation

? DID YOU KNOW ...?

■ South Africa's natural environment holds quite a number of records. While Europe is home to only one kingfisher, there are ten species in South Africa. The northern hemisphere has two species of heather; South Africa has around 500. South Africa is home to the largest land mammal (elephant), the second-largest (white rhinoceros), the tallest (giraffe), the fastest (cheetah), and the smallest (Etruscan shrew), the largest bird in the world (ostrich) and the largest flying bird (kori bustard), as well as the largest reptile in the world, the leatherback sea turtle. And the world's largest marine mammal, the blue whale, swims past its coasts.

Flora

The plant world in particular is distinguished by its extreme diversity. A total of 22,600 native flowering plant species have been recorded, including 730 tree species. The main vegetation zones are forest, savannah, bush and grass steppes, dry savannahs and desert steppes.

Only around 1.5% of South Africa's area is forested, but this figure is increasing, particularly in KwaZulu-Natal, thanks to afforestation

Forests

The protea (here with a sunbird) come in many different shapes and colours.

programmes for the production of timber. Forests are mainly limited to the coastal regions and are developed to different degrees. In the Cape Ranges and along the coastline of the three Cape provinces the forests are predominantly open deciduous forests, which also penetrate to greater heights, where it is drier in the form of riparian forests along river channels. In the savannah areas most of the rivers are also accompanied by tall, dense riparian forests. In the moister areas of the east coast there are also remains of evergreen forests (e.g. Ficus species) alongside palm trees of the *phoenix* genus. The largest existing evergreen rainforests are located in the Tsitsikamma National Park on a stretch of around 175km/110mi between George and Humansdorp along the coast west of Port Elizabeth. The up to 40m/130ft tall trees, some of them ancient, include ironwoods, yellowwoods, stinkwoods and Kamassi boxwoods; at lower levels ferns and lianas dominate. In the subtropical zone of KwaZulu-Natal there are still some evergreen rainforests along the inaccessible windward mountain slopes exposed to the south-east trade winds. With a few exceptions, the formerly extensive forests in the hot humid coastal plain of KwaZulu-Natal have been cleared for agriculture. Besides different species of palm trees they are often made up of mahogany, ebony, ironwood, strelitzia and mangroves (on the coast) amongst other species; orchids are also common.

Savannah The **bushveld** is the typical form of vegetation in the regions of the central plateau up to an elevation of about 1000m/3300ft that do not get a lot of precipitation and are dry in winter. Particularly in Limpopo and Mpumalanga provinces, as well as at the lower elevations (up to approximately 800m/2625ft) of the Eastern Cape province and the uplands of Natal, savannahs are the natural form of vegetation; however, large areas have been cleared for agriculture, particularly pasture. The characteristic features of this type of vegetation are an under-storey made up of grasses and shrubs that grow up to 1m/3ft high, and lone-standing trees, usually not very tall but deeply rooted, that are well adapted to the long winter drought: for example the widespread acacia species, stem succulents such as spurges (euphorbias), adansonia digitata (baobab), leaf succulents such as aloes, fever trees, mopanes and fig trees. In particularly arid locations, such as along the border of the Karoo and the Kalahari, thorn bushes and thorn trees are dominant (e.g. camel thorn). The common name for these landscapes is **thornveld** (thorn savannah).

Towards the south-west the savannah turns with increasing altitude and more severe climate conditions (winter coldness and dryness) into a bush and grass steppe (**grassveld**). It covers the eastern part of the plateau in Gauteng and the Free State. With the exception of some acacias (e.g. camel thorns along the southern border of the Kalahari) and introduced willow and eucalyptus species, the dry frosts that last for several months during the winter prevent the growth of almost any trees. The plateau looks like an endless grass landscape that could otherwise only support a macchia-like shrub vegetation: low shrubs, whose leaves and branches are protected from evaporation by hairs or a layer of wax. In moister locations the grass can grow to a height of over 1m/3ft; in other areas it grows 40–60cm/16–24in tall. However, the natural grass vegetation in the pastoral areas has often been extensively replaced by grazing grasses. Grass vegetation can also be found in the higher altitudes of the Drakensberg range. Up to an elevation of about 1400m/4600ft species-rich mountain meadows predominate; at higher altitudes there are alpine meadows, as far as the soil and relief allow.

Bush and grass steppe

The bush and grass steppe turn into Karoo vegetation with the increasing aridity that exists towards the west. This type of vegetation is also known as dry savannah, desert steppe, or semi-desert. It covers the majority of Northern Cape province, where the average amount of annual precipitation drops from around 400mm/16in to below 120mm/5in and in some years it does not even rain at all. Besides perennial dry grasslands that cover the ground only scantily, shrub-like tamarisks, acacias and other low plants grow in protected and moister areas, such as along the banks of rivers that occasionally carry water. Their small leaves, woody stems and far-branching root systems allow them to survive several months of extreme aridity. Otherwise succulents are common. They are able to absorb water from the surrounding humidity (particularly from dew) and store it in tubers, stems or leaves.

Dry savannah, desert steppe, semi-desert

Goegap Nature Reserve (Northern Cape) in the spring: kokerbooms and flowers in bloom

Desert   Desert can be found in the north-west of Northern Cape province in a 120km/75mi-wide belt parallel to the coast and on the Namibian border (along the lower course of the Orange River). The annual precipitation here lies below 100–120mm/4–5in and even that amount is uncertain. This area has practically no vegetation. The exceptions are plants adapted to extreme aridity, such as »living stones« and some creeping plants that live on sand dunes off the nightly dew. Thorn bushes are able to exist in somewhat moister depressions and wadis (riverbeds); the kokerboom, a species of aloe, can also occasionally be found here.

Desertification   Both the deserts and the desert steppes are increasing in size at the expense of the grass steppes and savannahs. This desertification is generally attributed to pasture management based on the European model. Excessive livestock numbers strain the grassland so much that it can no longer regenerate itself, particularly in the frequently occurring dry years. The clearing of trees for fire and construction wood has accelerated this development and has particularly led to severe erosion damage as a consequence of the sporadically occurring torrential rainfalls.

Cape flora   In the south-west Cape with Cape Town at its centre the prevailing climate is Mediterranean. The summers are hot and dry while the winters are cool to warm and moist. Over the history of the earth a plant world has developed here that is quite unique. It is by far the **smallest of the six floristic provinces in the world**, but it has the

The red disa, a famous orchid species that grows at the Cape

greatest diversity; many of the 8500 plant species can only be found here. In 2004 the floristic province was included on UNESCO's list of World Heritage Sites with eight protected areas. In South Africa the Cape vegetation is called **fynbos**, which is Afrikaans for »fine bush«. Its principal characteristic is its adaptation to summer-time aridity; the main species are sclerophyllous evergreens (amongst them around 600 erica species), 400 species of leucadendrons (amongst them 85 protea species), numerous aster, strawflower and geranium species, as well as a wealth of bulb and rhizome plants, such as lilies, irises, gladioli, freesias and terrestrial orchids. Native trees on the other hand are rather more rare and usually confined to mountain terrain that is difficult to access. One such tree is the **clanwilliam cedar**, which only occurs in the Cederberg mountains.

The protea, **South Africa's national flower**, is a whole genus of   Protea
shrubs that usually reach a height of 1–3m/3–10ft, less often up to
5m/16ft; the flowers resemble thistles and occur in many colours
from red and pink to yellow, white, silver and greenish (▶ photographs p.30, 199). The different protea species grow in all the hill
and mountain regions that are not too dry or too moist in the southern Cape, in Free State, KwaZulu-Natal, Gauteng, all the way to the
north-east.

The wealth and beauty of South Africa's flora can be experienced in   Botanical
the many botanical gardens, which are usually also research and na-   gardens
ture conservation centres. The Kirstenbosch National Botanical Garden is located south of Cape Town at Table Mountain at an elevation
between 100m and 1000m (330–3300ft). This side of Table Mountain receives particularly high precipitation and as a consequence this
area has favourable growth conditions for more than 1400 plant species. Further botanical gardens worth seeing are: Karoo National
Botanical Garden near Worcester (semi-desert and arid flora), Free
State National Botanical Garden in Bloemfontein, Natal National
Botanical Garden in Pietermaritzburg with the subtropical flora of
KwaZulu-Natal, Lowveld National
Botanical Garden near Nelspruit
with lowland flora, Witwatersrand
National Botanical Garden in Roo-
depoort near Johannesburg with
highveld flora, Harold Porter Na-
tional Botanical Garden near
Betty's Bay with the flora of the
winter rain area, Pretoria Botanical
Garden and Municipal Botanical
Garden Durban.

? DID YOU KNOW ...?

■ Proteas are fire-adapted plants. A thick bark
makes them resistant to the frequent grass
fires during the dry period. Many species of
proteaceae even require exposure to fire
before they will open their fruits, after which
their seeds reach their full germination
capacity.

Fauna

The big-game fauna (elephants, rhinoceroses, giraffes, antelopes, ze-   Big game
bras, hippopotamuses, lions, leopards, cheetahs, etc.), once very rich,
has largely been displaced by the expansion of agricultural land and
relegated to the large national parks. Baboons and guenons can still
be found in the moister mountain areas, while various species of antelope, such as the eland, oryx, springbok, waterbuck, impala, kudu,
blue wildebeest and sable antelope can still be found in savannahs,
steppes, and semi-deserts that are not being used for agriculture. The
smaller mammals worth mentioning are hyenas, jackals, bat-eared
foxes, aardwolves, Cape foxes and various wild cats.

The bird world is represented in South Africa with over 850 species.   Birds
That figure includes several species that occur nowhere else in the
world, such as the sunbird, which is a significant pollinator for plants

Lions have been re-introduced to many reserves.

with long pipe-shaped flowers in the south-west region of the Cape. Other birds characteristic of the area are weavers and the long-legged secretary bird. The blue crane is considered the national bird of South Africa. The largest bird in the world, the ostrich, is now being bred in Little Karoo (Oudtshoorn). One of the largest flying birds, the gompou, a kind of great bustard that can reach 20kg/44lb, can also be found there and in the Kalahari.

Reptiles and amphibians

In the category of reptiles and amphibians there are around 300 snake species (pythons, mambas, boomslangs and bitis amongst others) and 200 lizards (including geckos, monitor lizards and chameleons). Crocodiles no longer live anywhere but in reserves; and the twelve species of turtle, including the leatherback sea turtle of northern Natal that can weigh up to 500kg/1100lb, have also become severely reduced in numbers.

Insects

Amongst the insects of South Africa there are around 800 (often very colourful) species of butterfly. The termite mounds are distinctive features in arid areas. Several insect species have been wiped out in order to fight plagues; for example the tsetse fly, which is responsible for transmitting sleeping sickness. The anopheles mosquito responsible for transmitting the malaria pathogen on the other hand still lives in areas that are moist and warm (►Practicalities, Health).

Animal welfare and national parks

The spread of the Bantu peoples and settlement by whites has caused the habitats of many animal species to become very much smaller; in particular, the large animals that were widely distributed and common until the 18th century, such as the black and white rhinoceroses, elephants, and various species of antelope, have at times even been threatened with extinction. These days numerous initiatives and organizations have guaranteed the conservation of vulnerable animal species since a legal basis for the creation of game reserves in national parks was created by the National Parks Act in 1926. At this time there are 23 national parks, several further game reserves and a lake area in different types of landscape, which stand under the supervision of the National Parks Board and are amongst the country's biggest tourist attractions. The most important ones are as follows. The **Kruger National Park** (approx. 450km/280mi east of Johannesburg) is one of the most famous reserves in the world. It is home to 137 mammal species, 493 bird species, 112 reptile species and 49 fish species; among the mammalian species in the park are the »big five« (elephant, rhinoceros, buffalo, lion and leopard) as well as the cheetah, giraffe, hippopotamus, baboon, impala, kudu, wildebeest and the African wild dog. The **Kgalagadi Transfrontier Park** (Northern Cape province) together with the protected areas in Botswana provides a habitat not just for gemsbok antelope, wildebeest, gazelles and zebras, but also for lions, leopards, hyenas and vultures. The **Addo Elephant National Park** north of Port Elizabeth is the last retreat of the approximately 300 elephants still living on the Cape. The **Hluhluwe-Imfolozi Game Park** in Zululand north of Durban is a retreat for black and white rhinoceroses. The **Mountain Zebra National Park** in Great Karoo is home to the mountain zebra, which has become very rare. The **Augrabies Falls National Park** is a refuge for monkeys, antelopes, various wild cat species and birds (including ospreys).

Special bird protection areas have been set up, particularly along the Atlantic coast. Penguins, cormorants, pelicans and gannets are all at home here. The **Tsitsikamma National Park** on the Indian Ocean even has an underwater educational trail for snorkellers.

Impala antelopes are only around 1m/3ft tall. Here two males.

State and Society

Constitution South Africa's constitution was signed by president Nelson Mandela in Sharpeville on 10 December 1996. It came into effect on 4 February 1997. This constitution, South Africa's first that was the product of an assembly elected by the entire population, is meant to promote the development of a society based on democratic values, social justice and human rights on the basis of a separation of powers, federal structures, and a bill of rights. In addition constitutionally anchored, independent national institutions (such as the South African Human Rights Commission and the Commission for the Promotion and Protection of the Rights of Cultural, Religious and Linguistic Communities) further strengthen democracy in South Africa.

Legislature The legislature of the Republic of South Africa consists of two chambers. The **National Assembly** gets its 360 to 400 members from a direct general election that takes place every five years. The **National Council of Provinces** consists of 90 delegates, ten from each province. The National Council represents the interests of the provinces at the national level. In addition every province has a parliament with 30 to 90 members, a government and optionally its own constitution.
The municipalities are the lowest administrative level and possess both legislative and executive powers. In accordance with the principle of »co-operative governance« embedded in the constitution, all three levels of government – central, provincial and municipal – work closely together.
As traditional leaders still play a significant role in the political and social lives of the black population in rural areas, special **Houses of Traditional Leaders** have been set up, which represent the interests of the various ethnic groups at all three levels of government. Houses of Traditional Leaders exist in six provinces: Eastern Cape, Free State, KwaZulu-Natal, Mpumalanga, North West and Limpopo.

Since 2000 South Africa has had a new coat of arms. It depicts two ears of wheat around a shield with two human figures, taken from the rock drawings in Linton. The coat of arms is flanked by two tusks. Above it is a protea, a secretary bird with open wings and the rising sun. The tusks are joined by the motto »diverse people unite«, which is written in the language of the Khoikhoi.

South Africa's president and head of government is Thabo Mbeki. **President**
He was elected as Nelson Mandela's successor by the National Assembly on 14 June 1999. The deputy president and the ministers are
determined by the president, who also assigns the latter their responsibilities.

South Africa's national anthem is a combination of »Stem van Suid- **National anthem**
Afrika« (»The Call of South Africa«), which was written by the poet
and politician C. J. Langenhoven (1873–1932) and set to music by
M. L. de Villiers, and »Nkosi, Sikelel' i-Afrika«. The first verse and
the refrain of black South Africa's anthem was composed by Enoch
Mankayi Sontonga (1860–1904) in 1897; verses two to eight were
penned by Sek Mqhayi (1875–1945). The first verse is usually sung
in Xhosa or Zulu, the second in SeSotho, followed by an Afrikaans
and an English verse of the »Stem van Suid-Afrika«.

Nkosi, sikelel' i-Afrika   *Lord, bless Africa*
Malupakam'upondo Iwayo   *May her spirit rise up high*
Yiva imitandazo yetu   *Hear thou our prayers*
Usisikelele.   *Lord bless us*
Yihla Moya, Yihla Moya,   *Your family.*
Yihla Moya Oyingewele.

Uit die blou van onse hemel, uit die diepte van ons see,   **»Stem van Suid-**
Oor ons ewige gebergtes waar die kranse antwoord gee.   **Afrika«**
Deur ons ver-verlate vlaktes met die kreun van ossewa –
Ruis die stem van ons geliefde, van ons land Suid-Afrika.
Ons sal antwoord op jou roepstem, ons sal offer wat jy vra:
Ons sal lewe, ons sal sterwe – ons vir jou, Suid-Afrika.

Ringing out from our blue heavens, from our deep seas breaking round,
Over everlasting mountains, where the echoing crags resound,
From our plains where creaking wagons, cut their trails into the earth,
Calls the spirit of our country, of the land that gave us birth.
At thy call we shall not falter, firm and steadfast we shall stand,
At thy will to live and perish, O South Africa, dear land.

Since the founding of the Union of South Africa in 1910 South Afri- **Capitals**
ca has had three »capitals«: Pretoria is the seat of government and
the administrative capital, Cape Town is the seat of parliament, and
the centrally located Bloemfontein is the judicial capital.

The courts of law are independent. South Africa's highest court, the **Judiciary**
Constitutional Court of South Africa, has its seat in Bloemfontein.

The South African Police Service (SAPS) was fundamentally restruc- **Police and army**
tured after the end of the apartheid era and is under the control of

the Secretary for Safety and Security. The government has formed several special units to support the police and to fight crime. The South African National Defence Force (SANDF, approx. 80,000 soldiers) unified the previous army with the former Homelands forces and guerrilla forces.

Parties   The most significant organization of South Africa's black population and by far the country's largest party (70% of votes in the 2004 election) is the African National Congress (ANC, ▶ Baedeker Special p.42) founded in 1912. The more radical Pan Africanist Congress (PAC) that broke away from the ANC in 1959 is one of the smallest of the twelve parties represented in parliament. The third-largest force (7%) is M. Buthelezi's (▶ Famous People) Inkatha Freedom Party (IFP), which was created as a Zulu cultural organization in 1928. It participates in the Mbeki government. With 12% of the vote the Democratic Alliance (DA) forms the largest opposition party. Its tradition goes back to the grand old lady of South African liberalism Helen Suzman, who spoke out for 36 years against the oppression of blacks. The New National Party (NNP) emerged from the former National Party, mostly made up of Boers, which was founded in 1912 and governed from 1948 to 1994. With only 1.65% of the votes in the 2004 election it has finally lost its dominant position. The United Democratic Movement (UDM, 2.3%) formed in 1997, which was the first expressly cross-racial party, mainly targets upwardly mobile blacks and whites in the economic centres. Other parties represented in the National Assembly are: Independent Democrats, African Christian Democratic Party, Freedom Front Plus, United Christian Democratic Party, Minority Front and Azanian People's Organization.

Administrative divisions   The historical regions still play an important role in the everyday life of South Africa (▶ History). After the abolition of apartheid the territory was also re-structured. **Nine provinces** replaced the former four provinces, four »independent« states and six autonomous homelands. For a long time their responsibilities were a matter of dispute. With the constitution of 1997 a compromise solution was found in the form of a presidential democracy with federal elements.

Provinces

Western Cape   The Western Cape stretches along the Indian and Atlantic Oceans in a wide arc around Cape Town, the provincial capital, which is home to around 10% of the country's population. The inhabitants, the majority of them coloureds, speak English and Afrikaans. The province has a broad spectrum of secondary manufacturing industries, a strong service sector (tourism, transport) and a profitable agricultural sector (intensive fruit and vegetable cultivation).

Facts and Figures South Africa

Pretoria •

South Africa

© *Baedeker*

Location
► southern Africa
latitude 22°–35° south
longitude 17°–33° east

Geography
► area 1.219 million sq km/470,000 sq mi
(cf UK 95,000 sq mi,
USA 3.8 million sq mi)
► north-south extent approx. 1100km/
680mi (Limpopo – Cape Agulhas)
► east-west extent approx. 1500km/
930mi (Oranjemund – Richards Bay)
► neighbouring states: Namibia,
Botswana, Zimbabwe, Mozambique,
Swaziland;
Lesotho an enclave

Population
► population: 46.4 million
► population density: 2–520 per sq km
(5–1350 per sq mi)
► largest conurbations: Johannesburg
approx. 3.2 million (with Soweto 4.2–6
million), Durban 3.1 million, Cape Town
2.9 million, Pretoria 1.9 million, Port
Elizabeth 1 million, East London
700,000
► ethnic composition: black 79%, white
10%, coloured 8.5%, Asian 2.5%
► language groups:
Zulu 23.8%, Xhosa 17.6%, Afrikaans
13.3%, Sepedi 9.4%, English 8.2%,
Tswana 8.2%, Sotho 7.9 %, Tonga
4.4 %, Swati 2.7%, Venda 2.3%,
Ndebele 1.6%, other 0.5%

Constitution and government
► parliamentary democracy with a
head of state who is also head of
government
► two-chamber parliament: National
Assembly (with directly elected
representatives) and National Council
(represents provinces)

Economy
► gross domestic product approx. 600
billion US-$ (13,000 US-$ per person)
► main business sectors: mining (gold,
coal, diamonds, platinum, etc), textiles,
chemical products, automobile manufacture, food
► principal trading partners: USA,
Germany, UK

National flag
► after the end of apartheid, South Africa
chose a new flag. It displays a
horizontal Y in six colours, some of
them taken from the political parties of
the country. The flag represents the
effort to establish unity and reconciliation.

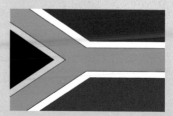

Eastern Cape The Eastern Cape province is mainly made up of land intensively cultivated by white farmers in the hinterland of the central south coast around Port Elizabeth, as well as the former homelands of Transkei and Ciskei, where the prevailing economy is subsistence agriculture. The Umzimkulu district is an exclave in KwaZulu-Natal. The province, which is home to around 14% of the country's population, is characterized by a large Xhosa population. The per capita GDP is one of the lowest in the country.

Northern Cape Northern Cape province is South Africa's largest province, but, largely on account of its aridity, only 1.8% of the population live there. The main sources of income are extensive pastoralism and mining. The province does not have a large economic, cultural and administrative centre. The regional language is Afrikaans.

North-West North-West province, which is to a large extent semi-arid, is home to 8.5% of the total population, the majority of whom are Tswana.

Provinces

Province	Capital	Population million (2004)	Area in 1000 km²	Persons/ km²
Western Cape	Cape Town	4.75	129.4	36.7
Northern Cape	Kimberley	0.82	361.8	2.3
Eastern Cape	Bisho	7.40	169.6	43.6
Free State	Bloemfontein	2.74	129.5	21.2
North West	Mafikeng	3.80	116.3	32.7
KwaZulu-Natal	Pietermaritzburg	9.76	92.1	106.0
Mpumalanga	Nelspruit	3.25	79.5	40.9
Gauteng	Johannesburg	9.42	17.0	554.1
Limpopo	Polokwane	5.42	123.9	43.7

Animal husbandry, maize, sunflower and peanut cultivation, and mining (platinum) are all economically significant. The GDP here is below the national average.

Free State

Free State (formerly Orange Free State) includes the former home-lands of Quaqua and Thaba Nchu (Bophuthatswana). The province has a broad secondary industrial sector and is well endowed with natural resources. The region is home to around 6% of the country's population. The main languages are Southern Sotho and Afrikaans. The areas around Bloemfontein, Welkom (gold mining), and Sasol-burg (coal chemicals) are the province's economic centres.

Gauteng

The multi-ethnic and multi-lingual province of Gauteng, formerly PWV (Pretoria-Witwatersrand-Vereeniging), is South Africa's stron-gest economic area. It is home to almost 20% of the country's popu-lation. The province is sub-divided into three differently structured districts. The metropolitan area of Pretoria is South Africa's adminis-trative centre, its transport and service centre, as well as the main lo-cation for electrical engineering and automobile construction. Wit-watersrand and Johannesburg play the most significant role as min-ing and financial centres. Secondary industry (particularly metallurgy, chemicals) and energy production are prevalent around the towns of Vereeniging and Vanderbijlpark in the south. More than one third of the South African GDP is generated in this province, even though it is the country's smallest with just 1.4% of the total area. It is also the core of white settlement in South Africa. Over 40% of this population group are concentrated here.

Limpopo

The province of Limpopo (formerly Northern Province) consists of areas dominated by agriculture in the north of the old province of Transvaal, the north of Kruger National Park, as well as in the for-mer homelands Lebowa, Venda, and Gazankulu. The economy is not very developed; 12% of the country's population generate just 6% of the total GDP. The per capita GDP and annual income are the lowest in the entire country. The population is ethnically and linguistically very diverse. The main languages spoken here are Northern Sotho (Sepedi, more than 50%), Tsonga and Venda.

Mpumalanga

The province of Mpumalanga (formerly Eastern Transvaal) which in-cludes the former homelands of KaNgwane, KwaNdebele, as well as a part of Bophuthatswana, includes the agriculturally attractive east-ern part of South Africa. There are no large towns or centres; the provincial capital is Nelspruit. Mpumalanga's economy is character-ized by energy generation, mining and agriculture; it is one of the country's most important fruit and vegetable growing regions. The per capita GDP is above the national average and amounts to 8.2% of South Africa's total GDP. The main languages spoken in this prov-ince are Swati, Zulu and Ndebele.

Pin from the anti-apartheid movement of the 1980s

AFRICAN NATIONAL CONGRESS

When the South African State President F. W. de Klerk announced that the government would turn away from its apartheid policies, the time had finally come for the country's oldest political party, the ANC, which had been prohibited for three decades, and for its legendary leader Nelson Mandela, who had been imprisoned for 29 years.

In 1912 black intellectuals and those with a political interest founded the »South African Native National Congress« in Bloemfontein, renamed the »**African National Congress**« in 1923, in order to fight against racism and ethnic rivalries, for the black majority's right to participate in politics and for the improvement of their living conditions. The blacks were not just denied the right to vote: after 1913 they were confined to reserves and prohibited from acquiring real estate outside them. Until the Second World War the ANC, which was dominated by urban middle-class members, restricted its activities to petitions, protests and assemblies.

Escalation

Inspired by the **Atlantic Charter** of 1941, in which Roosevelt and Churchill announced the war aim to be a liberal world order, in 1943 the ANC demanded full rights of citizenship for black South Africans. The government under J. C. Smuts however issued a firm denial. From that point onwards the ANC became more radical. In 1944, with the involvement of Nelson Mandela, the ANC Youth League was founded, which demanded tougher methods. The goal was no longer integration into the whites' political system, but rather liberation from this system. The ANC responded to the apartheid laws, which became increasingly oppressive after 1948, with boycotts, strikes and, following Gandhi, peaceful resistance, i.e. civil disobedience. In 1952, when white South Africa was celebrating the 300th anniversary of Jan van Riebeeck's landing, tens of thousands of blacks participated in a counter-demonstration for the first time. On 26 June 1955, 3,000 representatives of all of the races of South Africa – blacks, coloureds, Indians and also whites of the new Liberal Party – came together in Soweto to hold a people's congress against apartheid. The **Freedom Charter** was passed, demanding for equality for all races; until the 1990s this charter was the basis of the ANC's political programme.

After the congress the South African government had 156 leaders of the various movements arrested and put on trial for high treason. The five-year trial ended with the acquittal of all the accused. One of them, the head of the ANC **Albert Luthuli**, was awarded the Nobel Peace Prize in 1960. The congress alliance of 1955 disintegrated again quickly, particularly because of disagreements regarding the question of how to proceed further. Tension also arose within the ANC: the pluralists demanded equality, while the African nationalists, contrary to the ANC's policies so far, sought a South Africa free from white rule. In 1959 the African nationalists separated from the ANC and founded the **Pan Africanist Congress** (PAC).

The war ...

For 1960 the ANC and the PAC planned big campaigns against the hated pass laws. The PAC called for a peaceful demonstration in front of the

Cape Town, 1990: under police protection ANC followers wait for Nelson Mandela, who has just been released from prison.

Sharpeville police station to take place on 21 March 1960. The police officers, who felt threatened, shot into the crowd, killing 69 demonstrators. The international community reacted with horror and outrage. All over the country strikes and demonstrations took place, which cost yet more lives. The government's reaction was tough. On 8 April 1960 it prohibited the ANC and the PAC, which then continued their work underground and in exile. Both parties founded fighting organizations, the ANC the **Umkhonto we Sizwe** (»Spear of the Nation«). At its head was Mandela, who rose to be the president of the ANC and the leader of the black movement after Luthuli was exiled and Sobukwe convicted. Although this organization achieved some spectacular attacks it broke apart again by

1963. Nelson Mandela, who had been arrested in 1962 and sentenced to five years in prison, was sentenced to life imprisonment for sabotage in 1963 on account of material found in the Umkhonto headquarters. For some

Nelson Mandela was given his freedom when he was released from the Victor Verster Prison near Paarl.

time it seemed as if the government had broken the blacks' resistance. Activists were sometimes imprisoned without having been sentenced, and many died in police custody. The executions reached record numbers. At the beginning of the 1970s many new organizations were created, including those that wanted to create a »black consciousness« movement on the model of the Black Panthers in the United States. When the government sought to introduce Afrikaans, the »language of the white oppressors«, as the teaching language in schools,

20,000 students demonstrated in **Soweto** on 16 June 1976. The police shot randomly at the unarmed children and young people, killing two of them (photograph p.82). There were bloody uprisings all over the country. This time it took the government until the end of 1977 to get the situation under control again. It prohibited and persecuted all of the radical oppositional organizations; the leader of the black consciousness movement **Steve Biko** died in prison as the result of torture in 1977.

... and its end

Sympathy for the ANC and Nelson Mandela grew all over the world. In early 1990 President Frederik de Klerk, »Africa's Gorbachev«, in the face of heavy resistance from his own ranks and the whites of the extreme right, legalized the activities of the ANC, the PAC and the Communist Party; he released Mandela from prison and started a dialogue with his one-time enemy. For their efforts to achieve reconciliation between the white and non-white population Mandela and de Klerk received the Nobel Peace Prize in 1992. At the first free parliamentary election in South Africa, in April 1994, the ANC was the strongest party with 62% of the vote; in the most recent elections in 2004 it received almost 70%.

The province of KwaZulu-Natal is located south of Mpumalanga. It   **KwaZulu-Natal** is home to 21% of the population, not least because of the natural water supply. The majority of the inhabitants are Zulu. The creation of this province represented an extension and consolidation of the old Zulu kingdom. Greater Durban is the centre of population, as well as the economic and administrative focus. Approx. 80% of South Africa's Asian community live here. The infrastructure in the Zulu villages is poor. In addition the Zulu population is growing rapidly and there are not many jobs.

Education and Economy

Until the beginning of the 1990s education and training were dependent on a person's membership of one of the officially fixed racial groups. The lack of qualified workers led to a first levelling of opportunities during the 1980s by increased spending on the school system of the blacks and the introduction of compulsory education for coloureds (1980). School attendance had already become obligatory for Indians in 1965, while the same became true for blacks only after the abolition of apartheid. Since 1996 compulsory education has generally required nine years of school attendance. New universities with subsidiary locations in black townships made it easier for the black population to pursue higher education. Accordingly black students have made up the largest group at South African universities since 1995.

Although racial segregation was officially abolished in South African schools in 1990 and the »White Paper on Education and Training« has proclaimed equality and non-discrimination since 1995, the con-

Black and white in one classroom is still not to be taken for granted.

sequences of racial discrimination are still very apparent. 22% of blacks aged 20 or older have no education and only 5% have completed higher education; on the other hand only 1% of whites of the same age group have no educational qualification and 30% have finished some form of post-secondary education. Literacy amongst the black population is just over 80%, while almost 100% of the white community are able to read and write. The figures for coloureds and Asians are 90 to 95%.

The education situation of younger blacks and their prospects of obtaining better jobs have improved. Besides a growing number of private schools and colleges there are 24 higher education facilities and 26,000 state schools, approximately half of which, however, are in urgent need of renovation. A lack of equipment, large classes and poorly trained teachers are further weaknesses of the school system, even though the state spends around 23% (2004) of its budget on education.

Population

Population groups
The historically determined composition of the population means that South Africa differs demographically from all other African states. The four main ethnic groups are blacks, coloureds, whites, and Asians. During the apartheid era a person's membership of one of these groups was officially determined; it then affected, among other things, political rights, education and career choice.

Whites
Whites, who were politically, economically and culturally dominant until 1994, make up nearly 10% of the total population. 90% of them live in urban settlements. Besides the metropolitan agglomerations, they mainly live in rural small and mid-sized towns; only around 10% of them are farmers living in rural areas. Approximately 55% of the whites, as descendants of the Dutch settlers who came to South Africa after 1652, speak Afrikaans. Some 35% of the white population are of British descent and speak English. The British came to South Africa after 1795. The remaining white population has German, French, Portuguese, Italian or some other ancestry.

Coloureds
»Coloureds« (in Afrikaans »kleurlinge«) make up nearly 9% of the population. The majority of them are descendants of relationships between whites and the indigenous Cape population (Khoikhoi and San) but also of relationships between whites and Malay slaves as well as between whites and members of the Bantu peoples. They mainly settle around Cape Town and in the south of the country. 80% of them speak Afrikaans and are Christians.

The approximately 200,000 Cape Malays are also considered coloureds. They are descendants of slaves who were brought to the Cape from what was then Batavia and the East Indies by the Dutch East India Company 350 years ago. 60,000 of them live in Cape Town alone. Many of them have names such as February, April or September, which denote the date the slaves came to their new owners. They are devout Muslims. A further independent group is formed by the Griqua, who speak a modified Afrikaans. They are mainly descendants of Europeans and Khoikhoi, and they even had their own state for a while.

Asians

The Asians in South Africa (2.5% of the total population) are primarily of Indian origin. These days they mainly live as traders in the Durban region. From 1860 onwards they were brought to Natal by British colonists to work as contracted labourers on the sugar cane plantations. Most of them speak English, but Indian languages are also still spoken, particularly Tamil, Hindi, Gujarati, and Urdu.

The small Chinese community is descended from people who were brought to South Africa for the mining industry at the end of the 19th century. The majority of them had returned to China by 1910, after more and more blacks started to work in mining. After 1920 there was another influx of Chinese people to South Africa. Their descendants now primarily live in Johannesburg and the surrounding areas and make their living as merchants. They speak English and

Colourful mix: café in Cape Town's Long Street

Afrikaans without having given up their native languages. Most of the Asians are Hindus (70%), 20% are Muslims, and around 10% are Christians.

Khoikhoi and San

The original inhabitants of the land are the San and Khoikhoi. The old names bushmen and Hottentots respectively were the product of colonial rule and, since they are perceived to be discriminatory, are no longer used. Both the San and the Khoikhoi were pushed back by immigrating Bantu peoples and by whites. Today there are still an estimated 55,000 San and Khoikhoi living in South Africa, particularly in the impassable areas of the Northern Cape (► Baedeker Special p.90).

»A world in one country«: a Xhosa village in Transkei ...

Blacks The blacks started moving to the south of the continent from central Africa from the 11th century onwards. With a proportion of 79% of the total population they are South Africa's largest population group. Like the whites they are not a homogeneous group. Today a distinction is made between nine Bantu peoples, which are in turn subdivided into many more ethnic groups; there are 200 amongst the Zulu alone. Numerically the Zulu people is the largest (9.2 million), followed by the Xhosa (7.2 million), the Northern Sotho (3.7 million), the Southern Sotho (3.1 million), the Tswana (3.3 million), the Swazi (1.0 million), the Ndebele (0.6 million), the Tsonga (1.8 million) and the Venda (0.9 million).

The blacks live partly in tribal units in primarily rural settlements, especially in the area of the ten former homelands (▶ map p.78), partly in the urban »black« settlements, or else in the former townships. i.e. black districts of »white« towns. The proportion of black people living in urban areas that were declared white by the racial segregation laws steadily increased because of worker migration. The failure of the »grand apartheid«, which aspired to achieve a separation of white and black living areas, can be seen by the fact that there were 8.4 million blacks living in »white« areas when only 4.5 million whites lived there, and that there were more blacks living in »white« areas than there were living in the black homelands. The largest »black« town in a »white« area was Soweto near Johannesburg. Today between two and four million people live there (the estimates vary considerably). Since the original tribal areas do not correspond to any national borders, a large number of Swazi, Southern Sotho and Tswana live outside South Africa in Swaziland, Lesotho and Botswana.

... the V & A Waterfront shopping centre in Cape Town at Christmas time

The population of South Africa is 47.39 million (2006), which implies an average population density of 38 inhabitants per sq km/97 per sq mi. The population density varies greatly from province to province. The fast-growing urban areas of the industrial and mining areas and the ports (Cape Town, Durban, Johannesburg, and Witwatersrand with 520 inhabitants per sq km/1330 per sq mi) are densely populated, but so are some of the traditional Bantu centres of population, where some live as subsistence farmers, while others commute to work or have seasonal jobs in the conurbations. Approximately 40% of blacks live in these rural areas of the former homelands. The semi-arid to arid areas of the central and northern Cape where white farmers engage in extensive pastoralism are on the other hand very sparsely populated (a little over two inhabitants per sq km/five per sq mi, a figure which is declining).

Population density

The social structure largely corresponds to membership of ethnic groups. The whites and large numbers of coloureds and Indians have the same kind of employment, lifestyle, standard of living and social relationships as Europeans do; white beggars are however no longer rare in the cities. Part of the black population still live in clan or tribal units, which also provides social protection, and traditional villages, while the urban blacks often live in neighbourhoods divided on tribal lines, but are more strongly Europeanized. Many villages have large percentages of women, children and old men because of worker migration.

Social structure

Since 1994 South Africa has officially recorded a loss of population due to emigration, although the estimated number of illegal immi-

Migration

A township near Cape Town

grants of two to five million actually causes an excess of immigrants over emigrants. The officially recruited migrant workers, most of whom work in mining, do not have immigrant status; generally speaking they have to return to their native countries (Lesotho, Swaziland, Botswana, Namibia, Malawi and Mozambique amongst others) after 24 months. Amongst the whites there was a net increase in population during the 1970s, caused by immigrants from Europe (particularly Great Britain) as well as from Zimbabwe after the latter obtained independence. During the 1980s white immigration decreased because of the political and economic problems, and since the late 1990s many white people have packed their bags (often heading for Australia or New Zeeland) in order to get away from the growing social tensions.

Languages

A large proportion of South Africa's population are bilingual. They either speak Afrikaans and English, or one of the two in combination with one of the black languages. The population's composition is also manifest in the linguistic situation: with the end of the apartheid era eleven languages replaced English and Afrikaans, which had been the two official languages until then. Besides Afrikaans, which is also the mother tongue of most of the coloureds, and English, which is spoken by some 36% of whites as well as by most of the Asian community, the other official languages are Zulu, Xhosa, Northern Sotho, Southern Sotho, Tswana, Tsonga, Swati, Venda and Ndebele. Zulu, Xhosa, Swati, and Ndebele are all Nguni languages; Northern Sotho, Southern Sotho and Tswana are part of the Sotho language group; the Tsonga have links to both language groups and the Venda have their own language.

Afrikaans Afrikaans is a product of the dialects of Dutch 17th-century immigrants (from western Brabant, Zeeland and southern Holland).

Through contact with Bantu and Khoisan languages, German, English, French, Portuguese and Malay, new words were added and others changed their meaning. A similar thing happened with the pronunciation, spelling and grammar. Afrikaans is spoken by about 90% of coloureds and 54% of whites, who are very attached to their »taal« (»language«); in 1975 they erected a very pompous monument to it on a hill near Paarl. Grammar school teacher Arnoldus Pannevis published the first newspaper in Afrikaans (*Die Patriot*) in Paarl in 1876; he also wrote a grammar book and a dictionary. In 1925 this language, which had once been considered an inferior Creole, became an official language of South Africa.

Zulu is spoken by more than ten million Zulus living in South Africa. 7.6 million of them live in the province of KwaZulu-Natal, 1.9 million in Gauteng. Click consonants are typical of this language. There is a rich literature of myths, legends, riddles, proverbs and dance and ceremonial songs that have been handed down orally.   **Zulu**

Religions

South Africa is a country that has freedom of religion. The congregations largely finance themselves from membership contributions. Around 80% of the population are Christian. The approximately 4000 independent churches of the blacks, the African Independent Churches, have the most members (ten million). Since 1960 their

Open-air service of one of the African Independent Churches

membership percentage has increased from 20% to 30%. Next are the five big Christian churches: the two Dutch Reformed Churches (approx. 10%), Catholics (approx. 10%, 80% of them black), Anglicans, Methodists and Lutherans, whose membership proportion has dropped from 60% to 45% during the same period. In addition there are numerous other churches and breakaway denominational groups.

Reformed churches On the »white« side of the spectrum are the reformed churches of Dutch Calvinist origin, the smaller Nederduitsch Hervormde Kerk van Afrika, whose members were almost exclusively Boers, and the Nederduitsch Gereformeerde Kerk. As the »established church« the latter greatly contributed to the justification and stabilization of apartheid. It was also closely linked to the power elite; over half the government ministers came from pastors' families and many cabinet members were theologians. Within the Nederduitsch Gereformeerde Kerk were four independent churches, each representing the members of a particular race.

African Independent Churches The African offshoot of Christianity arose from the late 19th century as a reaction to colonialism. The most significant are the Zionist churches (Zion Christian Church, ZCC) and the Nazareth Baptist Church. The Zion Christian Church was founded by Engenas B. Lekganyane, the son of a farm labourer in Zion City Moria in Transvaal in 1910. Zulu Jesaiah Shembe, who is now worshipped as a Messiah, founded the Nazareth Baptist Church in 1911. Its centre is Ekuphakameni north-east of Durban. The Zionist church has always placed importance on the traditional beliefs: shamans are taken seriously, prophecies, initiation and cleansing rites, taboos and exorcisms are intertwined with Christian thought.

Further faith communities Around 100,000 Jews, descendants of German, British and eastern European immigrants from the last two centuries, live in South Africa. There are also over 500,000 Hindus, and approx. 700,000 Muslims.

Economy

South Africa is a newly industrialized country (NIC). This classification is however only valid in its full sense for the white residential and economic areas; the former homelands of the blacks are better classed as developing countries shaped by an agricultural economy and society. In 2007 South Africa had a per capita income of about US$ 13,000, which was higher than that of some eastern European states, making it the richest African state after the petroleum exporter Libya. Despite this, more than 50% of households live below the

Grinding mill in a gold mine in Randfontein

poverty line, a figure in which the black community is massively over-represented. While housing, water, electricity and schools are taken for granted by white South Africans, black South Africans have a lot of catching up to do: they lack flats and houses, access to clean drinking water (32% of households have access to water in their homes and 29% in their yards), and electricity supply (30% of households have no electric light, 25% heat their homes with wood).

The number of unemployed people is high, between 20 and 40% depending on the province. Around 30% of blacks are unemployed, while the figures are 5% for whites, 10% for Indians and 17% for coloureds. Despite relatively favourable economic statistics (growth since 1990 of 2–3% per year) the rate of inflation is high (over 9% a year since 1990). In addition the willingness to invest is dampened by high interest rates and the extremely large amount of violent crime, which, besides the large number of AIDS infections and deaths amongst the black population, will probably continue to burden the employment situation for a long time to come.

Unemployment and inflation

Since the end of the 19th century the basis of South Africa's economy has been mining. Mining contributes approx. 50% to the foreign exchange income and over 8% of the country's GDP. Around half a million people are employed in more than 900 deep and open-cast mines. South Africa is considered to be one of the countries most richly endowed with natural resources in the world. The use of these natural resources is becoming increasingly diversified. South Africa is

Mining

the globally most important producer of gold, platinum, chromium, manganese and vanadium, and is one of the most significant producers of diamonds, bituminous coal, iron ore, nickel, uranium and phosphate. In addition there are further ores, so that South Africa is self-sufficient and has great significance as an exporter, sometimes even dominating the market in almost all natural resources, with the exception of petroleum, natural gas and bauxite. Overall 50% of export revenue is generated by mining products (gold alone 25%). The great foreign demand and the rich deposits mean the mining sector will continue to be of great significance in the future. During the 1980s the mining and export of bituminous coal, iron ore and platinum increased, while gold mining declined, since the low world market price of those years meant the expenses of many mines were no longer covered. The mined amount decreased gradually from around 1000 tons (1970) to approx. 272 tons a year in 2007.

Industry Another significant economic pillar is the country's industry; mining and industry together generate 40% of South Africa's GDP and provide work for almost half of those in gainful employment. The wage transfers of the foreign migrant workers also make them a significant economic factor for the small neighbouring states. The most important industrial regions are located at Witwatersrand and around Johannesburg and Pretoria (around 50% of the total production), as well as in Durban, Pietermaritzburg, Richards Bay, Cape Town, Port Elizabeth and East London. Some of the industry is closely connected to the mining sector (raw material processing, semi-finished goods), while other areas of industry are aimed at the manufacture of consumer goods for the domestic market and for export. The

Large-scale cereal cultivation near Bredasdorp in the Overberg

country's growing isolation from the 1960s onwards, due to sanctions and trade boycotts, resulted in a well-developed industrial sector becoming increasingly extended, so that South Africa is self-sufficient in most areas.

An important foundation for South Africa's industrialization is the favourable energy situation due to the rich deposits of high-quality coal, which covers 77% of the primary energy requirement and is also made into fuel (it must not be forgotten, however, that approx. 50% of the energy requirement of private households is met with wood); 30% is exported. Since OPEC cut off the supply of petroleum from 1973 onwards, its proportion has dropped to only 10% of primary energy. During the 1980s crude oil and natural gas deposits were found close to the coast in the Indian Ocean off Mossel Bay. The plentiful deposits of uranium are used in Africa's only nuclear power station, Koeberg near Cape Town, and covers 6% of the total energy requirement. The generation of hydro-electricity is somewhat difficult on account of the greatly fluctuating amounts of water in the rivers, but South Africa is involved in the Cabora Bassa hydro-electric power station in Mozambique and in the Lesotho Highland Project. Currently South Africa is an exporter of electricity and supplies almost all its neighbours. The use of the extremely plentiful solar energy (220 W/sq m, in Europe only 100 W/sq m) is only slowly getting off the ground.

In the agricultural sector there are highly mechanized, specialized **Agriculture** farms producing goods for the global market (cereals, potatoes, vegetables, fruit, tobacco; in the south-western Cape and along the Indian Ocean also wine, citrus fruits and sugar cane amongst other things). On the other hand there are small, traditional subsistence farms in the former homelands with agriculture and horticulture as well as animal husbandry. Until 1991 the land ownership laws prohibited the Bantu population from acquiring land in the »white« areas, which meant that the fast population increase in the black districts caused a rapid decline in the availability of agriculturally usable areas. With the land reform introduced in 1997, the old land distribution is due to be abolished.

The greatly fluctuating amounts of precipitation and the frequent years of drought make artificial irrigation with the help of reservoirs and river water important for intensive agriculture. As a result agricultural activity has been extended far into the semi-arid regions; however, the dry climate means that more than two-thirds of the usable agricultural area in Northern Cape province and in Free State to the west can only be used as extensive livestock grazing grounds.

Despite the fluctuating yields caused by the weather South Africa is self-sufficient in almost all agricultural products. Agriculture only contributes 4% to GDP. However, almost 10% of those gainfully employed work in agriculture. This figure is relatively high because of the low degree of mechanization in Bantu agriculture.

The huge sugar terminal at the port of Durban. South Africa produces around 2.5 million tons of sugar annually, of which more than 1 million tons are exported.

Transport South Africa's transport infrastructure is well developed and is up to European standards in many parts of the country. The road network is relatively dense (366,000km/227,000mi, of which 66,000km/40,000mi are surfaced). Of the 9600km/6000mi of motorway, 2400km/1500mi are toll roads. Trains run on a total of 30,400km/19,000mi of track and are of particular significance for workers commuting in the industrial areas and for freight transport (raw material transports), as well as for transit traffic from the neighbouring land-locked countries to South African ports. Private motorization has greatly increased over the past 30 years. Despite the peripheral location, the maritime traffic connections are very good; the most significant ports are Richards Bay (over 80 million tons annual turnover), Saldanha Bay (deepwater port for iron ore export and crude oil import), Durban, Cape Town and Port Elizabeth. The international airport of Johannesburg is the transport hub for the whole of southern Africa.

Tourism Nine out of ten non-African tourists come to South Africa first and foremost to experience its nature and wild animals. Accordingly the national parks are amongst the most significant attractions, the top one being the Kruger National Park, the largest »zoo« in the world. While domestic tourism has been developing strongly for a long time now, international tourism only started really growing from the 1980s onwards. The number of foreign tourists is currently approx. 6.5 million, of whom 1.5 million (24%), and thus the largest single group, come from Great Britain, followed by 15% from Germany. The infrastructure is very good. Currently more than 1200 hotels and 2000 guesthouses offer around 50,000 rooms. Tourism contributes around 7% to GDP. Eleven tourists create one job. Around 750,000 people work in the tourism industry, which has become the fourth most important foreign exchange earner.

During the 1980s South Africa fell into a recession as a result of domestic political tensions and foreign political pressure resulting from its apartheid policies, but now the country has positive economic data to present. Despite this change for the better, poverty, unemployment, AIDS and high crime rates are a serious burden. The ANC's programme has a free-market orientation, laying the foundation for more stability and strict financial discipline. The government's economic programme for »Growth, Employment, and Redistribution« was meant to reduce the employment problem, lower the rate of inflation, and stimulate foreign investment on the basis of stronger economic growth. However, crime is the main factor behind the reticence of potential investors. In addition, the emigration of qualified experts, unfavourable demographical developments caused by the low life-expectancy of the (young) black population because of AIDS (12% or more of the country's population are infected), and the inadequate qualification of many blacks all constrain South Africa's economic development. In this regard the positive discrimination in favour of black employees on the basis of the »Affirmative Action Program« remains problematical. This fact lies at the roots of the »Black Economic Empowerment« programme of 2003, which was aimed at raising the qualifications of black skilled workers and leaders long-term and supporting »black« enterprises through national support measures.

Although South Africa's economy has broadened its spectrum, mining, and in particular the mining of gold, platinum and coal, still brings the bulk of hard cash into the country. Dependency on the price of gold places a strain on South Africa's economy time and again. The last gold crisis of 1999 led to mass dismissals and closings of gold mines. If the industrial and service sectors are not strengthened, South Africa's economy will continue to be at the mercy of the development of the price of gold (at the moment at least there is an upward trend).

The elections of 1999 and 2004 have stabilized the political situation. The economic and social structures need considerable improvement. Society is still divided by the great disparity of affluence between blacks and whites, which is the main cause of the high crime rate and the revival of racist thinking on both sides, as well as violent conflicts. On the other hand a new, influential and well-off black elite has developed, which has slowly been acquiring political and economic power. The social boundaries are no longer identical to the ethnic boundaries. Thabo Mbeki's government has committed itself to improving the lives of all and to reducing social disparities. This is a great challenge – maybe too great.

History

Who was Jan van Riebeeck; who was Cecil Rhodes? What led to the apartheid era and what was the job of the »Truth and Reconciliation Commission«? Stages in the emergence of the state of South Africa, from Australopithecus and the Khoisan to the immigration of black Bantu tribes, from Anglo-Dutch colonization to the vision of a »rainbow nation«.

Early History

3.5 million years	First hominids in South Africa
100,000 years	Earliest remains of Homo sapiens
50,000 years	Earliest evidence for the Khoisan
From 1000 BC onwards	Spread of the Bantu peoples
After 1000 AD	Immigration of the Bantu peoples to South Africa

Discoveries of bones in caves in Taung, Sterkfontein and Makapan prove that hominids, early forms of human (Australopithecus, »southern ape«) were living in South Africa as much as 3.5 million years ago. Developmentally they stand between humans and apes. Further excavations in Sterkfontein, Kromdraai and Swartkrans have brought to light remains of younger relatives of Australopithecus, extinct subspecies or the next level of development, who were already using stone tools and making fire 1.5 million years ago. In the Klasies River Caves on the south coast between Cape Town and Port Elizabeth approximately 80,000-year-old bones of modern humans (Homo sapiens) were discovered. In early 1994 two pieces of jawbone around 100,000 years old were found in the same caves. These are the hitherto oldest known remains of Homo sapiens, who possibly spread across the globe from Africa.

The Cradle of Mankind

Further items from Fish Hoek and the area of the Echo Caves are around 75,000 and 50,000 years old. This evidence includes bones and tools that resemble stone-age pieces in Europe, as well as rock paintings, which are estimated to date back to 28,000 BC. They were probably created by the San (►Baedeker Special p.90), who, together with the Khoikhoi are amongst the oldest-known inhabitants of the southern African continent. Because of their kinship the San and Khoikhoi are grouped together under the term »Khoisan«. There are various speculations as to their origin. According to an earlier theory they originally lived in East Africa and then migrated south-west until they reached the Cape. Recently it has been thought that all Khoisan were hunters and gatherers and had a Neolithic culture in modern-day northern Botswana in around 500 BC. Then the Khoikhoi started keeping livestock, which they either bought or stole from black tribes. After that they lived as nomadic pastoralists. At the beginning of the 17th century the San and Khoikhoi inhabited the entire coastal area from Namibia to East London.

San and Khoikhoi

← *The former president Frederik de Klerk is sworn in before being questioned by the Truth and Reconciliation Commission in Cape Town in 1997.*

Finds from Early History

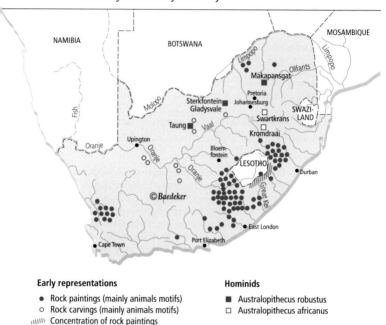

Early representations

● Rock paintings (mainly animals motifs)
○ Rock carvings (mainly animals motifs)
⁄⁄⁄⁄⁄⁄ Concentration of rock paintings

Hominids

■ Australopithecus robustus
□ Australopithecus africanus

Black peoples of South Africa The largest native ethnic group in Africa is formed by the Bantu. The term was chosen by the German linguist W. H. Bleek (1827–75) and means »human« in the languages of the blacks. They contain a large number of ethnic groups, such as Sotho, Tswana and Zulu. Their area of origin is in modern-day Cameroon and Nigeria. In search of grazing grounds and places to settle, the Bantu, who planted crops and raised livestock, migrated south in individual groups, displacing the Khoisan peoples from their settlements within just a few centuries from 1000 BC onwards. The oldest evidence of settlement to be found in the north-east of South Africa and in Natal dates from the second to the fifth century AD and comes from farming peoples with an iron-age culture. The ephemeral nature of the main materials used, grass, wood and clay, means that archaeologists can base their theories only on a few remains from this time. What is certain however is that the peoples in western and central Africa were familiar with the extraction and processing of iron and other metals. They used steel to make hoes, axes, blades for knives, spears and razors amongst other things, while softer metals were used to make bracelets and pearls. A large number of fired pottery goods have also survived. In 1932 the remains of a mine and a trading centre estimated to date back to 1200 AD were discovered on Mapungubwe hill near the mining town of Musina; glass beads and ivory carvings were found, as well as gold items, including an approximately 15cm/6in-long rhinoceros made of thin hammered gold leaf. It is thought to be a symbol of rule and is regarded as one of the most significant pieces of evidence of African heritage. In 1997 it was declared a »cultural treasure«. It is kept in the Mapungubwe Museum in Pretoria (►p. 457).

From the 11th century onwards the Bantu peoples then pushed forwards in waves into South Africa. The Nguni, who include the Xhosa, the Zulu, the Swazi and the Ndebele, spread all the way to the east coast. The Sotho moved west around 500 years ago; the Northern Sotho (Pedi) settled in the modern-day provinces of Limpopo and Mpumalanga, the Southern Sotho (Basotho) in Lesotho and in Free State, die Western Sotho (Tswana) moved west all the way to Botswana. The Ovambo-Herero made their way to modern-day Namibia. Around 300 years ago the fourth Bantu group, the Venda, appeared in the modern-day province of Limpopo, and the Tsonga moved out of the Portuguese region along the east coast to the north-east of South Africa during the 19th century. The people lived in self-contained communities with their herds and planted cereals and vegetables. Contact between the Bantu and the Khoisan peoples led to the clicking consonants being absorbed into the Xhosa and Zulu languages.

The Age of Discovery · First Settlements

1488	Bartolomeu Dias circumnavigates the Cape of Good Hope.
1497 / 1498	Vasco da Gama discovers the sea route to India.
1652	Founding of the Dutch colony at the Cape by the Dutch East India Company
18th century	The »Trekboers« spread into the interior. 1779: start of the Xhosa Wars

Phoenicians are said to have been the first to sail around Africa's southern tip at the behest of the Egyptian pharaoh Necho (ruled 609–594 BC). The Carthaginians too supposedly achieved this around 520 BC, this time from the east, as can be gathered from the reports of the Greek historian Herodotus (490–420 BC). In 1291 one of the brothers Vadino and Ugolino Vivaldi from Genoa is said to have sailed around the Cape. However there is no certain evidence of any such navigation before the end of the 15th century.

First attempts

The Portuguese expeditions
In search of a sea route to India the Portuguese started undertaking expeditions along the West African coast from the 15th century onwards. In 1485 **Diego Cão** reached the Namibian coast north of modern-day Swakopmund, where he set up a cross (Cape Cross). Three years later, in 1488, **Bartolomeu Dias** (or Diaz) landed in Walvis Bay and then in Angra Pequena. He subsequently sailed round the »Cape of Storms«, which was soon renamed the »Cape of Good Hope«. On 3 February he and his men made landfall near modern-day Mossel Bay, »which we called Angra dos Vaqueiros, because we saw so many cows there which were being looked after by their herdsmen,« reported the historian João de Barros. The final destination of this excursion was the mouth of the Great Fish River.

On 8 July 1497 **Vasco da Gama** set off on an expedition. On 22 November he sailed around the Cape of Good Hope and on Christmas Day reached the south-east coast, which he named »Terra do Natal« (»Natal« means »Christmas«). On 20 May 1498 he finally reached Kolkata on the Malabar coast. Thus the Portuguese opened up the sea route to India. From then they regularly undertook expeditions to Asia, Mossel Bay and Mombasa becoming important stopover bases where they took on water and food supplies and engaged in bartering. However, they were not interested in founding settlements. In 1503 a navigating error led to the discovery of Table Bay by **Antonio de Saldanha**. For more than a century the bay was named after him (today a bay 100km/602mi further north bears that name). It was only during the course of the 16th century that the Portuguese were faced with competition from the English and the Dutch, who had started founding trading companies and bases.

The landing of ships of the English **Honourable East India Company** at the Cape in 1605 remained without consequences, although their crews declared the land around Saldanha Bay »until the kingdom of the next Christian prince« a British possession. The abduction to England of the Khoikhoi chief Xhoré on the instructions of the East India Company in 1613 also remained without consequence. He was allowed to return home six months later.

First settlements
In 1647 the Dutch *Nieuw Haerlem* was shipwrecked in Table Bay on its way home from the east. The survivors built a fort at the foot of Table Mountain, where they lived for more than a year until they were rescued. As soon as they returned home Leendert Janszen and **Jan van Riebeeck** (►Famous People) pressured the **Dutch East India Company** (Vereenigde Oost-Indische Compagnie, VOC) to set up a permanent base on the Cape. In 1650 the VOC agreed to the plan. Leadership of the endeavour was entrusted to Riebeeck, and on Christmas Eve 1651 he set sail from Texel with five ships, the *Drommedaris*, the *Reijger*, the *Goede Hoop*, the *Walvis*, and the *Oliphant*. On 6 April 1652 the first two ships landed at the Cape. With 90 people, amongst them eight women, Riebeeck laid the foundation stone for Cape Town as the first permanent settlement of the VOC in

South Africa. Initially it was only a supply base for merchant vessels on their way to India. Passing ships of the company had to »supply herbs, meat, water, and other necessary victuals so that they could heal their sick«. To ensure a better food supply the first nine »Vryburgers«, former VOC employees, were allowed to settle as farmers in the vicinity of Cape Town in 1657.

When Jan van Riebeeck left South Africa in 1662, Cape Town was a place with four roads and 200 white inhabitants. In 1666 construction of the Castle of Good Hope was begun in Cape Town. It is the oldest building in South Africa. The colony grew rapidly. In 1679 **Stellenbosch** was founded by Simon van der Stel (later governor of the Cape colony) as the second settlement on the Cape. Settlers from Holland, Germany and France all came to South Africa, and became »Boers« (Dutch »boeren«, »free citizens«); amongst the French were numerous Huguenots who had left their homes after the revocation of the Edict of Nantes in 1685. In around 1700 there were approximately 1100 whites (402 men, 224 women, 521 children) living on the Cape; by 1707 the number of colonists had already grown to

Jan van Riebeeck lands in Table Bay on 6 April 1652.
A painting by Charles Davidson Bell.

Colonization

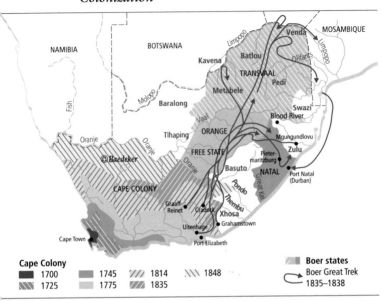

Cape Colony

■ 1700	■ 1745	▨ 1814	▧ 1848
▨ 1725	■ 1775	▨ 1835	

Boer states

Boer Great Trek 1835–1838

803 adults and 820 children. In 1743 the number had further increased to approximately 4000. **Slaves** were brought to the Cape as labourers from East and West Africa and Madagascar as well as Holland's colonies in the East Indies. Right from the start marriages took place between settlers, slaves and natives; the offspring of these marriages were the ancestors of the »coloureds«. Table Bay as well as the neighbouring Stellenbosch, Paarl, Drakenstein, Franschhoek and Roodezand (now Tulbagh) were all colonized. The expansion was to the detriment of the native population, who were driven away from their grazing land and water sources, exterminated or forcibly integrated as labourers. Until 1795 the colony was governed by officers of the Dutch East India Company, who were not personally allowed to own any land. Everything from food prices to the trading of ivory, hides, leather, ostrich eggs and slaves was controlled by the VOC.

Departure into the country's interior At the beginning of the 18th century the cultivation of wine and wheat was barely profitable as a result of overproduction and fixed VOC prices. More and more farmers acquired flocks of sheep and herds of cattle, which required less capital and work. In the search of new grazing grounds the »Trekboers«, semi-nomadic livestock farmers, advanced with their herds along the east coast into unsettled land. In 1779, at the Great Fish River; they came across the Xhosa, whom they called »Kaffirs«; the latter were making their way to the south of the country. The result was a total of nine bloody wars (**Xhosa Wars**) lasting until 1878. »Equipped with rifles and ideologically armed with a very narrow, Calvinistic interpretation of the Bible, the Boers pushed forward«. Their Christian duty included »subjugating the black ›pagans‹ and treating them as slaves.« (T. Roth).

First British Occupation

1795	Republican efforts British rule.
1802	The Cape Colony becomes Dutch again.
1816–28	Reign of the Zulu chief Shaka: military dictatorship and wars of conquest

In 1782 the Dutch East India Company paid its last-ever dividends. Wars, corrupt officials and increasing conflicts between the VOC administration at the Cape and their subjects led to its downfall. Discontent about tributes, land distribution and prices for agricultural products, the experience that the company could not guarantee adequate protection of the frontier regions, and the influence of republican ideas from Europe following the French Revolution all contributed to the uprising of the Boers in Swellendam and Graaff-Reinet (1795); they formed **revolutionary national assemblies**, and declared their territory a free republic. By the end of the century France and Britain had established themselves as Europe's leading powers and were competing for mastery of the world's oceans. The Cape, lying in the path of many sea routes, became a tempting prize: **in July 1795 the British landed** in Muizenberg. Six weeks later they forced both of the independent republics to capitulate. With that the reign of the Dutch East India Company, whose existence lasted formally until 1798, was broken. The government was taken over by a British major-general, James Craig. At the time the colony's population was around 18,000 whites, 15,000 Khoikhoi and 22,000 slaves. Approximately 5000 of the colonists lived in Cape Town, a further 1000 in Stellenbosch, while the rest lived as nomadic Trekboers in the countryside. In 1799 the third war between the Boers and Xhosa broke out on the eastern border. The Xhosa received help from many of the Khoikhoi.

The last years of the VOC

After the **Treaty of Amiens in 1802** the Cape Colony had to be returned to the Netherlands. As a result of the French Revolution numerous reforms were implemented. Legislative and executive powers were given to a political council consisting of four members, of whom at least two had to be citizens of the colony. The central gov-

Dutch interlude

Boer Republics and the British Conquest of South Africa

1839–54	Founding of the republics of Natal, Transvaal and Orange Free State
1865 and 1894	British annexation of the Ciskei (British Kaffraria) and the Transkei
1856	Natal becomes a British crown colony.
1860	Founding of the Zuid-Afrikaansche Republiek
1866	Diamonds discovered at the Orange River
1886	Gold discovered at Witwatersrand
1896	The Jameson Raid fails.
1899–1902	Boer War. Under the Treaty of Vereeniging, Transvaal and Orange Free State become British crown colonies.

Founding In 1839 the Boers founded the **Natalia Republic** with Pietermaritzburg as the capital. However, by 1842 it was annexed by the British. Once again the Boers set off on a trek northwards from Natal, where they founded several small independent states. Although the British occupied the land between the Orange River, the Vaal, and the Drakensberg mountains in 1848 as sovereign territory, in 1852 the settlers were able to sign the Sandrivier Treaty with the British government, in which Great Britain recognized the independence of the Boer state of **Transvaal** (from 1857 the South African Republic) as well as that of **Orange Free State** in 1854.

Cape Colony After the eighth frontier war between the Boers and the Xhosa, the Cape Colony got a constitution in 1853 and with it a limited amount of self-administration. All male British subjects aged 21 or over »with an income of at least 50 pounds a year or whose property yielded at least 25 pounds a year, irrespective of class and skin colour« received the right to vote. This meant that blacks (who in Natal outnumbered whites by 19 to one) were disfranchised. However the Cape Colony became bigger too: Ciskei (located to the west of the Great Kei River), which had been declared British sovereign territory in 1847, was annexed to the Cape Colony as **British Kaffraria** in 1865, and the same thing happened in 1871 with **Basutoland** (modern-day Lesotho), which had been annexed two years earlier.

Nongqawuse By the mid-19th century the Xhosa had survived eight frontier wars and one cattle plague introduced from Europe, to which thousands of animals fell victim. In their despair they clung to the **prophecies of the 16-year-old Xhosa girl Nongqawuse**. She promised her people the resurrection of all of their herds and the downfall of the whites. On 18 February 1857 two suns would rise and a storm would banish the white settlers into the ocean. As a sacrifice Nongqawuse demanded the slaughter of all cattle and the burning of all provisions. At least 200,000 cattle were slaughtered and as a result more than 40,000 Xhosa starved to death and a further 30,000 fled to other areas in search of food. Nongqawuse was captured and brought to Robben Island. Around 1898 she died somewhere in the Eastern Cape, where she was living in exile. The depopulated area was resettled with 2300 veterans of the Crimean War and 4000 German immigrants.

After the ninth war between Boers and Xhosa (1877–78) the Cape Colony annexed most of the areas between Kaffraria and Natal. Under **prime minister Cecil Rhodes** the annexation of the entire area between the Great Kei River and Natal to the Cape Colony took place in 1894. In 1885 the area south of the Molopo River was placed under British protection as British Bechuanaland and in 1895 became part of the Cape Colony.

The British defeat the Zulu in the Battle of Ulundi in 1879.

Natal   From 1856 onwards Natal was a colony in its own right, subordinate to the British crown with limited self-administration. After a Zulu rebellion in 1879 their ruler Cetshwayo was subdued in the Battle of Ulundi, and Zululand became a British crown colony in 1887. In 1897 the land was incorporated into Natal. The same thing happened with Tsongaland, which was annexed in 1895. In 1893 Natal received its own government; non-whites were excluded almost completely from the franchise. This particularly affected **Indians**, who had been brought into the country as workers for the sugar-cane plantations from 1860 onwards. After their contracts expired they had the choice of returning to India or of remaining in the country. Many decided to stay. Furthermore many self-employed Indians, particularly merchants, also migrated to South Africa. Around 1870 the number of Indians living in Natal was already 30,159; by 1904 that number had risen to 100,918, while the number of whites living in Natal was 97,109. In 1894 they founded the Natal Indian Congress. The lawyer Mohandas K. Gandhi (► Famous People) was one of the founding members.

Orange Free State   When Orange Free State was founded in 1854 all non-white inhabitants were excluded from citizenship. Around 3000 Griqua (Khoikhoi) subsequently migrated east under their chief Adam Kok, where they founded **East Griqualand** (1861–63). Through battles with the Basotho the Boer state increased its territory by adding parts of the Sotho lands; after the British annexation in 1868 the Boers had to retreat to the area west of the Caledon; Basutoland came under the administration of the Cape Colony (it was at that time that the borders of modern Lesotho were determined).

After the discovery of **diamonds** at the Orange River in 1866 the area became a very valuable colonial possession, witnessing the immigration of adventurers and fortune-hunters from all around the world. A vehement dispute about mining rights ensued between the British colonial government at the Cape, the Boers, and the Griqua and Tswana, a Bantu people living here. In 1871 Great Britain occupied the diamond fields and declared the area to be the crown colony of **Griqualand West**. After several years and the payment of compensation to the Orange Free State (90,000 pounds sterling, an absurdly small sum), this area was finally incorporated into the Cape Colony in 1884.

Transvaal   After the Voortrekkers had crossed the Vaal and defeated the Ndebele under the leadership of Mzilikazi in 1837, several Boer republics had formed between the Vaal and the Limpopo by 1844 (Potchefstrom, Soutpansberg, Utrecht, Lydenburg). They were recognized by the British in 1852 and by 1860 had united under their president Marthinus Pretorius (1818–1901) to form the **Zuid-Afrikaansche Republiek** (South African Republic); Pretoria was made the capital. The constitution of 1860 stated that there could be no equality between

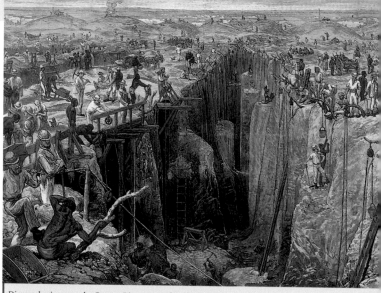
Diamond miners on the Orange River. A woodcut from 1872.

whites and non-whites either in the state or in the church. Domestic and external political problems (frontier wars with African tribes) provided the British with a pretext for occupying the Transvaal. After several unsuccessful negotiations and skirmishes, the Boers defeated the British garrison at **Amajuba Hill** in 1881. The Pretoria Convention of August 1881 granted self-government to Transvaal; it did however remain under British suzerainty. **Paul Kruger** (► Famous People) became its first president.

In 1886 the largest gold deposits in the world were found at the **Witwatersrand**, 50km/30mi from the Boer capital of Pretoria. Gold seekers from all around poured into the country. The gold-seeker camp E'Goli (»City of Gold«) became the **future Johannesburg**, which rapidly developed into a city. Soon there were two »outlanders« for every one of the approximately 85,000 Transvaal inhabitants, which led to serious tensions. The gold was tempting for the British too: under Cecil Rhodes, prime minister of the Cape Colony, dreams of a unified South Africa under British rule revived. A putsch was intended to topple the government in Pretoria, after which Transvaal was to be incorporated into the empire. The British banked on the support of the discontented outlanders. The coup was organized by the adventurer **Dr Leander Starr Jameson**, head of the British administration in Rhodesia, who had already led the occupation of that country. The putsch failed in December 1896 and Cecil Rhodes had to resign. Anti-British sentiment in the Boer republics reached its climax and in 1897 Transvaal and Orange Free State

Gold rush

◄ Jameson Raid

The main British army under Frederick Roberts opens fire on the Paardeberg Boer camp in February 1900.

signed a defence pact. The new governor of the Cape Colony, Sir Alfred Milner, continued to pursue the goal of a unified South Africa, while the Boer republics tried to maintain their independence. On 11 October 1899 war finally broke out.

Guerilla war 1899–1902

After initial victories (around 52,000 Boers were fighting almost 450,000 heavily armed British soldiers under the supreme command of Lord Roberts and later Lord Kitchener) the Boers succumbed. After the fall of Bloemfontein, Johannesburg and Pretoria the war appeared to be over. In actual fact a two-year-long, gruelling guerrilla war broke out in which 34,000 Boers, 22,000 British and 15,000 blacks lost their lives. The British pursued a »scorched earth policy«: the farms of the fighting Boers were burned down and their wives and children were detained in concentration camps, where many of them, including 22,000 children, died of malnutrition and poor hygiene. Barbed wire fences were set up all across the land in order to stop the Boer commandos. On 31 May 1902 the **Treaty of Vereeniging** was finally signed and the Boer republics of Transvaal and Orange Free State became British colonies. Now all four colonies (Cape Colony, Natal, Transvaal, and Orange Free State) and the High Commission territories of Basutoland, Bechuanaland, Swaziland and Southern Rhodesia were under British rule.

? DID YOU KNOW ...?

■ that British soldiers wore khaki uniforms for the first time on 20 October 1899 at the Battle of Talana Hill?

Union of South Africa

1910	Founding of the Union of South Africa, as part of the British Empire
From 1911	First racial segregation laws
1950	Introduction of the »Book of Life«

Reconstruction

The land had been greatly ravaged by the war. A large number of agricultural businesses (at least 30,000 farmsteads) had been destroyed and large areas were depopulated. Many of the Boers who had lost their property moved to the towns in search of a new existence. However all the important positions in the areas of economy, administration, and culture were filled by British people. On the labour market the Boers had to compete with the cheaper black workers. As a result nationalistic Boer organizations developed, demanding amongst other things that white people should get better jobs and higher wages. The coming years were dedicated to reconstruction, which included the repatriation and resettlement of the civilian population, as well as the construction of roads, railway lines and public buildings. Profits from the gold mines did the rest. The labour shortage was made good by bringing in workers from abroad. A total of 62,000 Chinese migrated to South Africa. Between 1903 and 1907 the value of gold production increased by almost 120%. Reconciliation between the Boers and the British made progress: Transvaal was granted domestic self-administration in 1906, Orange Free State in 1907. Nothing however changed about the voting rights; almost 80% of the population continued to be excluded from political participation. Only in the Cape Colony were 15% of the voters non-white.

Union of South Africa

Through the union of the colonies of Natal, Cape Colony, Transvaal, and Orange Free State, as fostered by Great Britain, the Union of South Africa, a state within the British Empire with 1.2 million white and 4.6 million non-white inhabitants, was created on 31 May 1910. Pretoria (Transvaal) became the seat of government, Cape Town (Cape Colony) the seat of parliament, and Bloemfontein (Orange Free State) the seat of the supreme court. In the constitution of 1910 the franchise was reserved exclusively to whites. Only in Cape Colony did the more liberal law of 1853 remain in effect; this made the right to vote subject to property, income and education, which meant that some wealthier blacks and coloureds were enfranchised. The blacks lost this right in 1936, the coloureds in 1956.

Domestic political conflict

At the first elections the South African Party, a union of several groups (Botha's party Het Volk, the Orangia-Union, and the Afrikaner-Bond of the Cape Province), was victorious. The Boer general Louis Botha (►Famous People) became the first prime minister. The

GLITTERING STONES

Everything started in the year 1866, when the 15-year-old Boer Erasmus Jacob found a magnificent pebble in the bed of the Orange River near Hopetown. It turned out to be a 21-carat diamond, which went down in history as the Eureka Diamond.

A short while later the 83.5-carat »Star of Africa« was found (1 carat equals 0.2g). A real diamond fever only began in 1869 however with the discovery of five volcanic deposits near **Kimberley**. Usually diamonds were found on the surface of the earth, and mostly in rivers. This was not the case in Kimberley, where they were discovered in a blue-black ore, kimberlite, in a volcanic shaft reaching far into the earth's interior.

Diamond tycoons

The further down the diamond miners dug, the greater the investment and effort involved. For that reason individual claims eventually joined together into associations. It was during these days that the adventurer **Cecil Rhodes** came on the scene. He bought everything he could get his hands on. In 1880 he acquired the claims of the **De Beer family**, on whose land two large mines had been discovered. Thus he founded the De Beers Mining Company Ltd. His most acrimonious rival was **Barney Barnato**, a Londoner who was interested in

setting up a monopoly himself. But in 1888 Rhodes successfully bought the Barnato Diamond Mining Company, and by doing so created De Beers Consolidated Mines Ltd. Almost all of the diamond mining in South Africa was now in the hands of a single company, and in exchange Barnato had received the biggest cheque in banking history: 5,338,650 pounds. At Kimberley South Africa's industrialization began; in 1885 the railway from the ports of Cape Town, Port Elizabeth and East London reached this town in the country's interior. Furthermore the country now also had a source of foreign currency. However the first forms of apartheid also originated in the diamond mines in Kimberley: the black workers were accommodated in strictly guarded camps and had to subject themselves to strip searches, while the white workers were not subjected to this procedure. The year Cecil Rhodes died, in 1902, **Ernest Oppenheimer** (1880–1957), the son of a Jewish tobacconist from Friedberg in Germany, came to South Africa, commis-

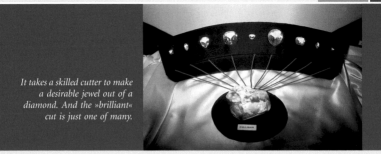

It takes a skilled cutter to make a desirable jewel out of a diamond. And the »brilliant« cut is just one of many.

sioned by the London diamond trader Anton Dunkelsbuehler. By 1929 he had successfully managed to unite the other companies into cartels, including those in the then German colony of South West Africa which in 1912 had delivered 1 million carats, approx. 20% of the total African diamond production. The cartels controlled almost the entire international trade for decades under the umbrella of the De Beers company. Today the South African company **Anglo American Corporation** (founded in 1917) handles more than 60% of the world trade via the Diamond Trading Company in London, which was founded by Oppenheimer (as the Central Selling Organisation) in 1930. Ernest Oppenheimer was also the richest and most powerful man in South Africa, its secret ruler, without whom the country's economy did not function. The Oppenheimer family were, like other significant business representatives, opponents of apartheid. Thus they tried to improve the black workers' training and living conditions. They supported black trade unions and were amongst the first to pay black workers the same as white workers. The end of apartheid met with strong approval, because it also marked the end of the serious restrictions to which the South African industry had been subjected for years.

South African diamonds

South Africa is the world's fifth-largest diamond producer. There are large deposits in the kimberlite shafts in Kimberley, Cullinan (Pretoria) and Postmasburg, where the stones are mined above and below ground (down to a depth of 3000m/9800ft). However, it is the flood plains of the Namakwa and the oceans floor off South Africa's west coast that are considered to be the richest source of jewel diamonds in the world. Most of the diamonds are used in industry for different purposes; only around a quarter are made into jewellery. The kimberlite shaft of Pretoria gave the world some of its most beautiful gem-quality diamonds, including the Transvaal Blue (25 carats), the Premier Rose (139 carats) and the famous **Cullinan**, the biggest rough diamond ever found (3106 carats, approx. 600g). It was given to King Edward VII for his 66th birthday. The gem-cutter Joseph Asscher from Amsterdam split the stone into 105 pieces (9 larger ones and 96 smaller ones), of which the largest piece adorns the sceptre of the British crown jewels. While Asscher was splitting the diamond a doctor and two nurses were present, because he was under such stress that he suffered a nervous breakdown after completing the work and was ordered bed rest for three months.

discord between Botha, who advocated the incorporation of South Africa into the British Empire, and James B. M. Hertzog (1866–1942), who strove for an independent state, led to the withdrawal of Hertzog and other Boer nationalists from the government and to the founding of the National Party (NP).

First race laws Right after the founding of the Union of South Africa racial segregation laws were passed: the Mines and Works Act of 1911 regulated the working conditions of black mine workers; Job Reservation prohibited blacks from getting jobs requiring qualifications. In 1977 158,000 positions were still on this list. The Native Labour Act declared breaches of contract (i.e. strikes) to be criminal acts. The Native Land Act of 1913 prohibited black inhabitants from acquiring land outside certain areas. This laid the groundwork for the homeland policies (see below). 70% of the population were assigned 7.5% of the land, which had the least fertile soils and absolutely no natural resources. In 1914 the Riotous Assemblies Act created the legal basis for prohibiting political assemblies and strikes.

Industrialization Between the two World Wars the Union of South Africa changed from being a colony to being a powerful industrialized country. In 1920 the Union of South Africa, as a member of the League of Nations, obtained the mandate over the former German South-West Africa (Namibia), which had been occupied by South African troops in 1914–15. In 1922 the jobs and wages of white workers were threatened by competition from blacks; and after several walkouts the South African Communist Party (SACP) was formed. In 1924 the opposition National Party came to power. Its goals were the »creation of national Christianity and the protection of the Boer race and culture«. In 1925 Afrikaans became the country's second official language next to English.

Further racial laws In the following years the rights of the black population were limited even further. The Natives Urban Act (1923) provided the basis for setting up residential areas for blacks in the towns; Soweto became the most famous township. In 1950 another law, the Group Areas Act, allowed residential areas to be fixed for coloureds and Asians too. In order to better control the immigration of blacks into the towns, the particularly hated Pass Laws, in effect since the early 19th century, were tightened. Non-white men were required to have their pass, the Book of Life, on them at all times. The borders that they crossed and their employer had to be entered into this book. If a black person did not have a pass on him, the police could arrest him and temporarily loan him out as a slave to a white farmer. In 1952 the Pass Law was also extended to women. The Immorality Act of 1927 made sexual relations between members of different races punishable; in 1949 the Prohibition of Mixed Marriages Act was introduced, forbidding interracial marriages.

In 1933 a grand coalition between the National Party and the South African Party took over the government. The parties merged a year later. Out of protest a group surrounding the minister and newspaper proprietor D. F. Malan, leader of the nationalists in the Cape Province, left the National Party and formed the »Purified National Party«. Nationalistic groupings formed all over the country; one of them was the Afrikaner Broederbond, a secret society to which all prime ministers, most Boer members of parliament, and higher officials belonged after 1948. In 1936 the grand coalition between the NP and SAP passed the Representation of Natives Act. The newly created council only possessed an advisory function, but it served as the basis for the abolition of the more liberal voting rights of the blacks that were still in effect in the Cape Province. That same year the reservations in which blacks could acquire land were increased in size to about 13% of the country's total area.

Purified National Party

After the Second World War broke out Hertzog attempted to take a neutral course in his foreign policies. Once the pro-British forces had asserted themselves he resigned his party positions in favour of J. C. Smuts (1870–1950) and on 6 September 1939 the Union of South Africa entered the war on the side of Great Britain. A total of 186,218 white soldiers fought as volunteers in the forces, initially in East and North Africa, and from 1943 also in Italy; in addition 24,975 women and 123,131 non-whites assisted the troops as non-combatants.

Second World War

Apartheid and Resistance

1909	First Native National Conference
1912	Founding of the South African Native National Congress (from 1923 African National Congress, ANC)
1960	Sharpeville Massacre
1961	Republic of South Africa leaves the Commonwealth
1970s	Establishment of the homelands

During the 19th century there had already been resistance to the dominance of the whites. In 1909 the first »National South African Native Conference« was held to make suggestions for improving the constitution; it had no success. In 1912 black intellectuals founded the South African Native National Congress (in 1923 renamed African National Congress; ► Baedeker Special p.42) to fight against ra-

Prehistory

Provinces and Homelands *up to 1993–1994*

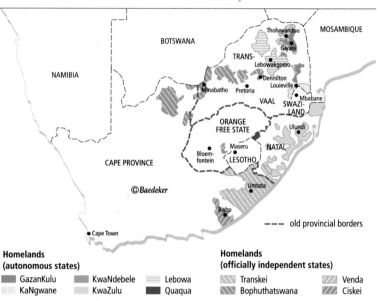

Homelands
(autonomous states)

- GazanKulu
- KaNgwane
- KwaNdebele
- KwaZulu
- Lebowa
- Quaqua

Homelands
(officially independent states)

- Transkei
- Bophuthatswana
- Venda
- Ciskei

--- old provincial borders

©Baedeker

cial segregation and racial rivalries. They demanded the vote for blacks and abolition of the race laws. In 1913–14 M. K. Gandhi led the march of the Indians from Natal to Transvaal organized by the Natal Indian Congress, which had been founded in 1894; he achieved some improvements for the Indian community. After the First World War the Industrial and Commercial Workers Union founded in 1917 became the vehicle for a protest movement of the black population. The question whether change could be achieved without violence was disputed within the ANC. While the younger members became more radical, the older member in particular advocated that they should at least make use of the small opportunities for participation open to them.

1948–61 For a long time the land that had been made available to the blacks had been unable to feed the people. More and more of them went to the cities where they filled the slums to bursting-point. Riots and strikes by black workers as well as their increasing politicization stoked a fear of the black majority on the part of many of the whites. In 1948 the National Party won 40% of the votes. They formed a union with the Afrikaaner Party, which gave them a governing majority that they kept until 1994. The governments of D. F. Malan (1948–54), J. E. Strijdom (1954–58) and H. F. Verwoerd (1958–66) are considered to be the »architects of apartheid«. The term apartheid comes from Dutch and means »being apart«, »separation«. Its central lie was its promise »to create a world in which blacks and whites lived separately, but were equal« (R. Malan); in actual fact apartheid was meant to ensure that »the white man will always be the boss«. The pillars of the racial segregation policies were the Land Act of 1913, which prohibited blacks from acquiring land, the Population Registration Act of 1950, which divided the people of the Union of South Africa into whites, blacks, Indians and coloureds, and the Group Areas Act passed in the same year, which stated that people were only allowed to live and work in the areas they had been assigned to. Hundreds of further laws ensured the implementation of apartheid in everyday life.

According to the »pure idea«, which was never honestly realized, all **Homelands** black South Africans were supposed to return to their »traditional« settlement areas and gain their political rights there »in self-determination«. Pretoria set up ten »homelands« for the Bantu peoples, who together made up 75% of South Africa's total population. The areas, 13% of the total land, were primarily located in the northern and eastern Transvaal, in the eastern Cape Province and in Natal. They were very fragmented: the Zulu for example were distributed across ten regions. Neither were they economically viable. The law also permitted forced resettlement: around 3.5 million people were resettled in homelands. In the rest of South Africa, 87% of the total land area, blacks were only allowed to live and work temporarily as »guest workers«. In this way the dream of a 100% white South Africa was to be realized. The Pass Laws served as a monitoring system; every violation was punished: 1.2 million in ten years. Economically and politically the homelands remained dependent on Pretoria (two fifths of the budget went into the homelands); the only exception was Bophuthatswana because of its platinum mines.

Political structures were supposed to be determined by a mixture of modern and more traditional elements. The parliaments were formed from elected and appointed representatives. In the administration the chiefs, being traditional authorities, played a significant role. However, for many years there were mounting reports on the lack of financial control, corruption, mismanagement and high levels of debt. The Ciskei, Venda, Lebowa, Gazankulu and Quaqua were all among South Africa's poorhouses.

Only four homelands accepted the »independence« offered by Pretoria. These were the TBVC states Transkei (1976), Bophuthatswana (1977), Venda (1979) and Ciskei (1981). As a result their inhabitants lost their South African citizenship. These states were not internationally recognized, however, which basically made their inhabitants stateless. Buthelezi, the prime minister of the Kwazulu homeland and of the largest Zulu group (►Famous People), rejected independence and was thus a crucial factor in the failure of the homelands policies.

The Reservation of Separate Amenities Act of 1953 introduced racial segregation to hospitals, schools, churches, beaches, public transport, public toilets and park benches, to mention a few. The Bantu Education Act of the same year regulated the schooling of blacks, which was to cost only one twentieth of the amount for the education of a white person. In 1956 the coloureds also lost their right to vote.

Growing resistance From 1949 onwards the ANC organized walkouts, acts of public disobedience, and protest marches. Its membership quickly increased to more than 100,000. In 1955 several other organizations joined the ANC. They passed the »Freedom Charter« for a non-racist, democratic South Africa, which was the fundamental document of ANC policies until the 1990s. Three months later the largest police raid in the history of South Africa took place. Over 156 activists were arrested.

PAC and Sharpeville In 1959 the government passed a regulation on the consumption of alcoholic beverages. Bars were set up for black people in which the beer served had a low alcohol content. Brewing beer privately, which had traditionally been a woman's job, was prohibited. This led to new unrest. That same year a group of blacks separated from the ANC and formed the Pan Africanist Congress (PAC); they thought the ANC was too moderate and allowed its policies to be influenced too much by white intellectuals and communists. Not long after-

Only whites were allowed to sit on this bench in Durban (1962).

wards, on 21 March 1960, the PAC called a demonstration against the detested Pass Laws in Sharpeville near Vereeniging. 15,000 demonstrators peacefully assembled in front of the commissariat and demanded to be arrested. The police shot into the crowd: 69 Africans died and at least 180, amongst them women and children, were wounded, mostly by shots in the back. The massacre triggered global outrage; there were demonstrations against the apartheid regime at the UN and in many European countries. The government declared a state of emergency and passed emergency laws, one of them being the »Unlawful Organizations Act«, with which it banned the ANC and the PAC and arrested their leaders. Both organizations continued their work underground and outside South Africa until 1990.

In 1961 the French, Belgian, and a short while later the British colonies further north in Africa became independent. London, too, condemned apartheid ever more loudly. At that point the governing party revived an old plan: the question of leaving the Commonwealth. In October 1960 52.3% voted for this in a referendum (only whites had the right to vote). On 15 March 1961 South Africa withdrew from the British Commonwealth.

Republic of South Africa 1961–89

1961	Nobel Peace Prize for the ANC leader A. Luthuli
1976	Student riots in Soweto
1977 onwards	Increasing international ostracism of South Africa
1984	Nobel Peace Prize for Bishop Desmond Tutu

The developments between 1961 and 1984 were determined by Verwoerd's successors J. B. Vorster (1966–78) and P. W. Botha (1978–84) after Verwoerd's assassination in 1966. Both continued the apartheid policies that had made the Boers rich. The black population worked 15 hours more a week on average for wages that amounted to only a sixteenth of what whites earned. The »privileged« blacks lived in the townships, all the others in the overpopulated slums. More than 500,000 miners with short-term work contracts lived in hostels. More than two million people were forcibly relocated in 20 years, and four million were arrested for violations of the Pass Laws; there were more than 7000 political prisoners. The ANC became more influential, its leader Albert Luthuli (1898–1967) was awarded the Nobel Peace Prize in 1961. The leadership of the movement was mainly in the hands of Nelson Mandela (► Famous People), who had gone into hiding. In 1963 he was sentenced to life imprisonment in the Rivonia trial together with the other leaders of

A photograph that went around the world: the student revolt in Soweto, 1976.

the ANC. In 1966, after bloody confrontations, the UN formally declared South Africa's mandate over South-West Africa to be ended. However, despite this fact the South African army continued to fight against the South West Africa People's Organization (SWAPO) until Namibia finally became independent on 21 March 1990. In 1972 the ANC and the PAC were given observer status at the UN, and in 1974 South Africa was expelled from the United Nations. In 1975 the Portuguese colonies of Angola and Mozambique became independent and in 1980 Robert Mugabe became the first elected prime minister of Zimbabwe, formerly Rhodesia.

In 1976 the government of South Africa decided to introduce Afrikaans alongside English as the teaching language in black schools. Since many teachers and students hardly spoke any Afrikaans and Afrikaans was detested as the language of the oppressors, riots broke out at several schools in Soweto, the black township approximately 20km/12mi south-west of Johannesburg. The police caused a bloodbath: 23 people died and 220 were injured. The rebellion spread to other towns and lasted more than eight months.

Steve Biko In September 1977 the founder of the South African Students' Organization, Steve Biko, died in police custody in Port Elizabeth after having been tortured. He was the leader of a new generation of blacks, the Black Consciousness Movement, which, having broken with the non-violent policies of the earlier organizations, aimed at promoting »black consciousness« on the model of the Black Power movement and the Black Panthers.

Homelands According to official statistics there were 19 million blacks living in the homelands (► p. 79) in 1978; in reality the figure was no more than nine million; the rest lived in the surroundings of industrial conurbations. There was nothing in the homelands: seven out of ten families lived below the poverty line; in some homelands half the children died of malnutrition before the age of five.

As a reaction to the death of Steve Biko and the prohibition of numerous black organizations, the UN Security Council imposed an arms embargo on South Africa in 1977. Sweden was the first industrialized nation to prohibit investment in the country in 1979. More and more South African companies began to exert pressure on the government to bring about reforms. Another important reason for a change of the circumstances was the economy's growing need for qualified black skilled labour, which could not be met because of the apartheid policies.

International ostracism

Pieter W. Botha, prime minister since 1978, had promised the creation of a »clean« administration as well as the abolition of several particularly hurtful apartheid laws. Already in 1979 a new employment law permitted the formation of black unions; in 1985 they joined together to become the Congress of South African Trade Unions (Cosatu). In 1984 a constitution was approved as a result of a referendum amongst the white population in the previous year; it gave Indians and coloureds the right to vote; a white veto remained in existence, however. The black majority continued to be excluded from the vote, which led to bloody riots all over the country. Broadly based grass-roots movements formed, including the United Democratic Front in 1983, which has a similar philosophy to the ANC and in which more than 600 anti-apartheid organizations came together. In 1984 the black Anglican bishop Desmond Tutu received the Nobel Peace Prize (► Famous People). In 1985 the prohibition on interracial relationships was lifted and in 1986 the Pass Laws were abolished. That same year blacks were given full land ownership rights; hotels, restaurants, and some cinemas and theatres were now open to blacks. In 1985 Botha offered Mandela, who had been in prison since 1962, his freedom if he »unconditionally rejected violence as a political weapon«. Mandela refused: »It was only then, when all other forms of resistance were no longer open to us, that we turned to armed struggle. Let Botha ... renounce violence. Let him say that he will dismantle apartheid.«

Reforms 1985–86

Neither Botha nor the National Party were seriously willing to share power. It was this background that really fuelled the riots. Sebokeng was the first township to explode. The uprising quickly spread. The economy found itself in a serious recession; the price of gold had fallen dramatically. 37% of the working population participated in strikes. Once again a state of emergency was declared, which this time lasted until 1990. Hundreds of UDF leaders went to prison. In 1986 within a period of three months more than 20,000 activists were arrested and ANC quarters bombed. In addition organizations belonging to the anti-apartheid movement were banned from holding meetings or engaging in any other activities, and the security laws and press censorship were tightened significantly. While the sanctions against South Africa were increased and international capital

Setbacks

was removed from the country, Botha stopped the reforms. The white hardliners organized themselves around the Conservative Party (CP), which had been formed in 1982, and the Afrikaaner Weerstandsbeweging (Afrikaaner Resistance Movement, AWB), which had come into existence in 1973. In 1986 war broke out between the followers of the UDF/ANC and the conservative Inkatha Freedom Party led by Buthelezi, the president of the KwaZulu homeland (▶Famous People). In the towns of the eastern Cape many followers of the ANC and the Pan Africanist Congress (PAC) attacked each other; many white people used the black-on-black violence to their advantage. The whole country was in turmoil and the total death toll passed 3000. The secret services were granted absolute powers; explosives and bombs were used to fight opponents; murderers in the service of the state were active as far away as Europe. From mid-1987 the miners started striking for better safety regulations. It became the most significant strike of black workers; 40 mines were closed for several months. Once again the police got involved, and many were injured and arrested. 40,000 workers were sacked and sent back to their homelands. On 18 July 1988, on his 70th birthday, Nelson Mandela had been in prison for 26 years. In Cape Town, Johannesburg and London people sang for his release.

The Turning Point

1990	New policies under President de Klerk
1994	The ANC wins in the first free elections; Nelson Mandela becomes president.
1994–99	Truth and Reconciliation Commission

De Klerk becomes president In 1989 the ANC, the UDF and Cosatu formed a coalition against racial segregation. Their central demand was »one man – one vote«. The pressure from foreign countries also continued to increase. Tough sanctions paralysed the country's economy; banks and foreign capital withdrew. Botha quickly lost influence in his own party too. On 15 August 1989, three weeks before the end of his mandate, Botha was replaced as state president by Frederik de Klerk (▶Famous People). The ensuing parliamentary elections were boycotted by the Indians and the coloureds out of solidarity for the 21 million blacks who were not allowed to vote.

The turning point In a historic speech at the opening of parliament on 2 February 1990 de Klerk initiated a turnaround: he lifted the ban on the ANC, PAC, UDF and the Communist Party, relaxed the state of emergency, and announced the release of Nelson Mandela and other political prisoners. In June the state of emergency was declared over and in October racial segregation in schools, hospitals, and other public institutions was abolished.

After talks between de Klerk, Mandela, and other representatives of black organizations, the »Convention for a Democratic South Africa« (Codesa) convened in Johannesburg in December 1991 for the purpose of discussing a new constitution. Issues such as the future of the homelands and violence amongst blacks, to which over 15,000 people had fallen victim since the 1980s, were also addressed. In a referendum in 1992 de Klerk won 68.7% of the votes of the white eligible voters for the continuation of his reforms.

On 10 April 1993 Chris Hani, one of the leaders of the ANC and the secretary-general of the Communist Party, was shot by an extreme right-wing white person. The violent confrontations in the black townships intensified. In July it became known that secret payments had been made by the government to the conservative Zulu party, the Inkatha Freedom Party. On 6 December 1993 a transitional constitution was passed. It was effective from the day of the first free elections on 27 April 1994 until 1997. At the same time a Transitional Executive Council (TEC) was formed, in which all organizations participating in the negotiation process were represented, except for members of the Freedom Alliance (Conservative Party, Afrikaaner Volksfront, and Inkatha Freedom Party as well as the governments of the homelands Bophuthatswana, Ciskei and Kwazulu). In addition all homeland inhabitants were awarded the vote. **Transitional Executive Council**

On 1 March 1994 South Africa handed over to Namibia twelve uninhabited islands off the coast of that country, and the port exclave of Walvis Bay. South Africa had governed the 1124 sq km/440 sq mile area with its nearly 40,000 inhabitants for 84 years. **1994**

In March president Lucas Mangope's refusal to allow the approximately 2.5 million inhabitants of the Bophuthatswana homeland to participate in the elections in April led to serious unrest. The conflict worsened when a 5000-man private army of white right-wing extremists came to Mangope's »aid«. With the support of the homeland army and police who had abandoned Mangope, and following the invasion of South African troops, Mangope's government fell. Until the elections in April 1994 a transitional president appointed by South Africa's government took over the homeland's administration. Corrections to the transitional constitution, such as more rights of self-determination for the new provinces and the recognition of the kingdom of KwaZulu, cleared the way for Inkatha, the Conservative Party and the Afrikaaner Volksfront to participate in the parliamentary elections in April after all.

18 political parties participated in the first free election on 27 April 1994. 22.7 million South Africans had the right to vote. As was expected, the ANC and Nelson Mandela were victorious. They won **The first elections**

A truly historic moment: South Africa's new president Nelson Mandela, flanked by his deputy president Thabo Mbeki (left) and the former president F.W. de Klerk, 9 May 1994

62.7% of the votes; de Klerk's National Party (NP) got 20.4% and Buthelezi's Inkatha Freedom Party (IFP) 10.5% of the votes. After 342 years the dominance of the white minority in South Africa was finally over.

On 27 April 1994 the transitional constitution, which gave equal rights to all South Africans, came into effect. The four TBVC states (Transkei, Bophuthatswana, Venda, Ciskei) were reincorporated into the territory of the state. On 9 May 1994 Nelson Mandela was elected president in the National Assembly with no dissenting votes. In May the UN Security Council lifted the last sanctions on South Africa, including the weapons embargo. South Africa rejoined the international community and became the 53rd member of the Organization of African Unity (OAU), the 109th member of the Non-Alignment Movement (NAM), and the 51st member of the Commonwealth of Nations. In all the republic has diplomatic relations with 153 countries and is a member of ten international organizations.

New legal system   The Constitutional Court was inaugurated in Bloemfontein. With this step South Africa completed the transition from a constitutional system on the British model to a continental European one, in which the legislative and the executive are no longer above the constitution but have to subordinate themselves to it. The death penalty was abolished.

New constitution   On 8 May 1996 South Africa's new constitution was passed with an overwhelming majority; President Nelson Mandela signed it in December. In June de Klerk's National Party left the government of national unity. De Klerk had previously announced that the time had come to build a strong, constructive opposition in order to promote a real multi-party democracy. The National Party renamed itself the New National Party, trying to give itself a new image, but after it received only 1.65% of the votes in the 2004 elections it disbanded in 2005.

In February 1997 South Africa's new constitution came into effect. According to the preamble the constitution is designed to establish a society based on democratic values, social justice and fundamental human rights. Nelson Mandela relinquished the post of ANC president. Thabo Mbeki became his successor and presidential candidate for the 1999 elections.

The »Truth and Reconciliation Commission« set up in 1994 and chaired by Desmond Tutu officially ended its work when the final report was handed over to Nelson Mandela. Even though leading figures under the old regime such as P. W. Botha refused to appear before it and remained unchallenged, it made a significant contribution to the recording of the crimes of apartheid as well as initiating a process of reconciliation between the various ethnic groups.

Truth and Reconciliation Commission

After Mandela had relinquished the leadership of the ANC it was uncertain whether the organization would maintain its importance. However, in the second democratic elections in 1999 it almost won a two-thirds majority in the National Assembly (the requirement for changes to the constitution); in 2004 it did achieve this necessary majority.

Stabilizing the political situation

The development of the economy is made hugely more difficult by the spread of AIDS (approx. ten per cent of the South African population is infected with HIV). Skilled labour is in short supply and businesses have to battle with a high mortality rate amongst their employees; many jobs including management jobs would basically have to be given to two people. Until 2003 President Mbeki together with his health minister hindered effective prevention and treatment with »white« medications. Intense national education programmes have only recently become available, too late for the generation of 20 to 50-year-olds. The »Black Economic Empowerment« programme, estimated to cost 50 billion rand, is designed to fight poverty and under-development. The aim is to promote education and thus increase job opportunities for the black population. Another goal is to promote the development of »black« businesses. In 2003 Mbeki said about the programme: »It is not about making whites poorer and blacks richer. It is not about getting rid of the current group of leaders and replacing them with others who happen to be black, which would change nothing but skin colour in the management and cause the loss of the many years of experience of the previous managers«. Mbeki lost the presidency of the ANC to his rival Jacob Zuma in 2007. Thus Zuma will probably be the candidate for the presidency in the next national elections, in 2009.

Current problems and goals

Arts and Culture

Millennia-old rock drawings created by the San, evidence of powerful kingdoms, and beautiful architecture from Holland and England all document the country's eventful history. The lively, robust cultural scene, from the traditional African music and its influences on jazz and pop to theatre and film, is no less interesting.

Folk Art · Visual Arts

The earliest surviving evidence of South African art comes from the **Drawings** rock drawings and engravings of the San (previously called Bush-**of the San** men). Both the origin of this ancient hunter-gatherer people and the origin of their art are mysterious. Some of the world-famous pictures could be 30,000 years old and thus be amongst the oldest known drawings (►Baedeker Special p.90). They are difficult to date, since for religious reasons the San kept to certain subjects and their own artistic canon. More recent pictures can be recognized by the fact that they also show Europeans and the animals they introduced. The rock paintings are distributed over thousands of locations, often in caves, from the Limpopo to the Cape (► map p.60). Drawings on sandstone or granite can primarily be found in mountainous regions and in river valleys, engravings or carvings in the open field. They are usually located in remote areas and are not easily accessible. In addition they are threatened by the effects of weathering, vandalism and ignorance. San drawings are protected national monuments. There are large numbers of them in the Eastern and North-Eastern Cape and in the southern Drakensberg mountains. They display regionally varying styles. More than 700 rock drawings with animal motifs can be viewed in just a single cave in the Giant's Castle (►Natal Drakensberg mountains). Copies can be found in some museums.

Until a few years ago apartheid and the boycott of South African cul-**Folk art** ture created a false impression. It appeared as if there was significant tribal art in western and central Africa, but hardly any in southern Africa. The acquisition and return of collections from foreign countries now show a rich tradition in wood sculpting and glass-bead art. Three museums in particular have exhibits of sculptures, mostly beautifully made applied art such as head supports, spoons, pots and staffs, and glass-bead art: the Johannesburg Art Gallery (Brenthurst and Horstmann collections), the South African National Gallery in Cape Town (glass beads of the Eastern Cape and a collection of traditional art acquired in the United States in 1994–95), and the museum in Ulundi (KwaZulu-Natal province) with a collection of Zulu glass beads. Works like the **Lydenburg Heads** (right), richly ornamented terracotta heads (c. 1500 AD, in the South African Museum in Cape Town, but rarely exhibited), named after the place of their discovery, confirm that South African history did not begin with its colonization by whites, as South African school books still taught up until the mid-20th century.

← *In the Ndebele museum village of Botshabelo near Middelburg (Mpumalanga province)*

*A ranger explains the roc[k]
drawings in the Cederber[g]
Wilderness Are[a]*

SAN ART

Before the film trilogy *The Gods Must Be Crazy* was released in the early 1980s, hardly anyone outside Africa had ever heard of the San. Even though these films were lowbrow entertainment cinema, they did bring this dying people into the world's consciousness.

South Africa and the entire world owe thanks to **Africa's oldest people**, who have populated this continent for 40,000 years, because they have left behind a priceless heritage: more than 60,000 **rock drawings and carvings**, spread across South Africa, Lesotho, Namibia and Zimbabwe. In the Natal Drakensberg mountains alone 35,000 of these drawings have been found at some 600 locations; in the year 2000 the uKhahlamba Drakensberg Park was declared a UNESCO World Heritage Site on account of the San rock drawings there (and its landscape).

Animals and people

The San were hunters and gatherers and thus extremely familiar with the behaviour of animals. The depiction of mammals, particularly larger ones like the common eland, was a central motif of their drawings. The artists depicted people just as often, either naked or in ornate gowns. However, unlike the animals, which were shown in a very life-like manner, humans were portrayed in a stylized form. The drawings show the San hunting, gathering, at dances, at ritual festivals and in family life, at meetings with the Khoikhoi, other blacks and the white settlers. All of the works are relatively small: rarely larger than around 30cm/1ft; only in two cases were humans depicted lifesize. Unfortunately the majority of the rock drawings **cannot be dated with certainty**. Since the pigments usually consist of mineral substances that are millions of years old, radio-carbon dating has not proved to be very helpful. In recent times scientists have had some success by bombarding the drawings with atomic particles. A painted stone from Namibia is estimated to be around 28,000 years old, while paintings depicting horses or meetings with white people in the south-western Cape show that this art was still practised during the 19th century. White settlers once found a bag with ten pigments on a belt of a San, including **metal and plant colours** as well as a mixture of quicklime and blood from hunted animals. Unfortunately almost all of the rock drawings are exposed to weathering; quite a

number however have also already fallen victim to visitors' stupidity and even vandalism.

Shamanic art

It is likely that the rock drawings were created by medicine men and women. A central rite of the San was dancing into a trance, during which the shaman experienced different hallucinations: transformations into animals, death at the hand of another and many other things. Thus these rock drawings are also a **symbolic art**, which not only illustrates reality but also trance images, the world of spirits, gods and ancestors.

The San today

In the past the San were referred to in English as Bushmen. This term goes back to the Dutch colonists, who insulted the nomads as »bosjesman«, which means basically »bandit« or »vagrant«. The San are rarely taller than 1.50m/5ft, have yellow skin, pronounced cheek bones and slanted eyes. Modern anthropology combines the San and the Khoikhoi as **Khoisan**, owing to their linguistic and ethnic kinship. The Khoikhoi were called »Hottentots« by the colonists, because of the click sounds in their language.

When the Dutch landed in South Africa at the beginning of the 17th century, the San and the Khoikhoi inhabited the coastal region of Namibia all the way to modern-day East London. Since they were shy and peaceful (the ethnologist Elizabeth Marshall called them the »peaceful people«) and tended to avoid confrontations, they withdrew from the white and black migrants all the way into the pathless Kalahari. The Khoikhoi died out or merged with other ethnic groups. In the Kalahari and in some remote areas of Namibia there are still a few San families living as hunters and gatherers. While the women gather tubers, berries and water, the men devote themselves to hunting. Their most important weapons are the bow and poison arrows. The San live in small family groups; larger organizational structures are absent. Apart from hunting dogs they do not keep any animals; they do not have houses, but rather grass huts with a fire pit.

Modern times are proving tough for the San, but they themselves do not consider this to be dramatic, seeing themselves as part of the generation of »rainbow children«, with a firm sense of the future.

History of the folk art

Africa's art is mainly religious in origin. Ancestor figures, spirits and animal figures as well as fetishes are probably the most widespread forms of expression. In addition there are sacred containers as well as emblems of rank and dignity (staffs, sceptres, pipes and fronds). Sculpture served as a medium for making contact with the spirit world. It was meant to be so beautiful that the spirit would like it and be invited to stay in the figure. That way it would participate in life and impart fertility, wealth, children, advice or protection; similarly with the animal figures and the fetishes, objects fitted with magical substances and sanctified by a medicine man, which protected their supplicant in all kinds of situations. The mask made the dead souls or the various protective spirits tangible and mythical processes comprehensible. Both the ancestor figure and the mask were sanctified and in the moment when the initiated slipped into the costume the divine power entered him. One of the most popular materials was wood, which is particularly perishable (especially in South Africa's climate). The wood was treated with an adze or a knife. Another popular material was clay, which was only fired for a short time and is thus quite fragile.

Several other techniques and materials in folk art also have a long tradition. They remain alive in the craftwork of some parts of the country. They include pottery, plaiting, weaving, carvings, leatherwork and forgework; a lot of attention is sometimes also still given to body art, hair, and clothing even today. Clothes were artistically decorated by embroidery, dyeing, appliqué and perforating. The Zulus and Ndebele in particular are famous for their imaginative and decorative beadwork. Originally the beads were made of a mixture of clay and goat's milk, which was then pierced and dried. Subsequently they were strung on grass, animal hair or string. From the 17th century onwards Portuguese merchants also brought colourful glass beads into the country. Over the centuries the women developed patterns based on horizontal, vertical or diagonal lines, depending on the threading technique used.

 DON'T MISS

- South Africa is home to **more than 300 museums**; amongst the most important are:
- Cape Town: South African Museum, District Six Museum, Gold of Africa Museum, South African National Gallery, Robben Island
- Johannesburg: MuseuMAfrica, Apartheid Museum, South African National Museum of Military History
- Pretoria: National Cultural History Museum, Transvaal Museum, Mapungubwe Museum, Voortrekker Monument Museum
- Bloemfontein: Anglo-Boer War Museum, National Museum

Ndebele art

The colourful art of the Ndebele that can be seen on wall paintings, bead art and clothing has also become known outside South Africa through exhibitions and publications. The geometric design of painted walls in the forecourt with symbols can be found in their settlement area north-east of Pretoria. In the past they used earth paints, but since 1945 they have been using synthetic paints. The ar-

The South African Museum in Cape Town. One department is devoted to the native peoples and their culture.

tist Esther Mahlangu, whose works have been seen from Washington to Paris, has taken over their shapes and colours (▶Baedeker Special p.460).

Artistically crafted products made by Afrikaans-speaking whites come mainly in the form of architecture (▶p. 94), furniture and silverware. Furniture and objects of utility can best be viewed in the Cultural History Museum and at Groot Constantia in Cape Town. Since its refurbishment in 1995 the Cultural History Museum in Pretoria has developed a focus on »white domestic culture«. In Pretoria and numerous small towns there are small museums dedicated to the Afrikaner way of life. **»White« craftwork**

So far South Africa's visual arts have not produced an internationally significant artist. For a long time they only used traditional forms. Thus landscapes were a common subject of South African painting ever since the early representations of the Cape by Thomas Bowler (1812–69) and Thomas Baines (1820–75). Amongst the most famous names of the first half of the 20th century are Jacob Hendrik Pierneef (1886–1957) and Irma Stern (1904–66), to whom is dedicated an entire museum in Cape Town, exhibiting portraits and landscapes. She and Maggie Laubser (1866–1973), who both studied in Weimar and Berlin before returning to South Africa, brought modern art movements into the country. The best insight into the increasingly »political« art of recent times can be gained from the National Gallery in Cape Town and the Johannesburg Art Gallery. Many further museums, in Pretoria and Stellenbosch for example, display South African **Visual arts**

Africanus 95   artistic creations. There are plenty of private art galleries, but few of them have anything exceptional on display. The biennial hosted for the first time in Johannesburg in 1995 has the goal of re-establishing the interrupted connection between South Africa's visual arts and the rest of the art world. European painting can best be seen in the Johannesburg Art Gallery and, in Cape Town, in the William Fehr collection (Rust en Vreugd, Castle of Good Hope) and in the Old Town House.

Art by black
South Africans
The art of black South Africans was neglected until the 1990s. After decades of eurocentric purchasing policy on the part of the large museums and private collections (of which there are several of significance in South Africa), there was much catching up to do, which caused a sharp increase in prices. Amongst the rediscovered artists were Gerard Sekoto (1913–93), the »father« of township art who died in exile in Paris, and Ernest Macoba (born 1910). Township art developed during the late 1950s and 1960s in the overpopulated outskirts of South African cities. The young black artists particularly addressed subjects from their everyday lives through expressive representational art. This art also received attention in other countries and was exhibited in museums, art galleries, and private collections.

Most recently sculptors from the north, particularly from Venda, have attracted more interest. Jackson Hlungwani creates large powerful wood sculptures motivated by mythology and Christianity. Often the transition from colourful images with a naïve tendency to »Airport Art«, the mass art targeted at tourists, is quite fluid.

The most comprehensive collection of black art is in the museum of Fort Hare University in remote Alice in Eastern Cape province. This is where most of the leading black politicians in southern Africa went to study.

Architectural Styles

Cape Dutch style   There is no uniform South African architecture, since native traditions were ignored and architectural styles from Europe and America were used as models instead. Thus the architectural style known as Cape Dutch was also created on a European model. Good examples can particularly be found in Stellenbosch, Paarl, Franschoek and Tulbagh near Cape Town, as well as in Cape Town itself. The houses possess simple, symmetrical, rectangular outlines, usually in the shape of a T, H, or U; further typical features are thick, whitewashed walls, a rounded gable, and a large, rectangular vestibule, which can be reached by an elevated veranda that runs the entire length of the house. The roofs were originally thatched, but after the mid-18th century they were frequently replaced by flat roofs (one example is the Rust-en-Vreugd house in Cape Town).

Towards the end of the 18th century two European artists were commissioned by the Dutch East India Company to come to Cape Town. Anton Anreith (1754–1822), a skilful German sculptor and wood carver, arrived in South Africa in 1776. Amongst other things he created the lectern of the Groote Kerk in Cape Town and the gable of the wine cellar of Groot Constantia. In 1783 Louis Michel Thibault (1750–1815) came to the country as a military engineer. Groot Constantia and the Koopmans de Wet House, both in Cape Town, are two examples of buildings constructed to his plans. Both artists maintained the Cape Dutch tradition, which they refined a good deal with new ideas and elements.

After South Africa became a British colony, neo-classical English   **British styles**
Georgian-style architecture gradually asserted itself. It was subsequently replaced by the exuberance and opulence of the Victorian era. The discovery of gold and diamonds also attracted many architects from outside South Africa towards the end of the 19th century. The dominant architect at the turn of the century and in the first years of the 20th century was Sir Herbert Baker (1862–1946), who became Cecil Rhodes's »house architect«. It was for Rhodes that he built the Groote Schuur in the traditional Cape Dutch style in 1890. His most famous buildings include the Rhodes Memorial in Cape Town (1905–08), the station (1908), Government House, and the

Palmiet Estate, a Cape Dutch estate straight from a picture book.

Union Buildings in Pretoria (from 1905 and 1910–13), as well as the Supreme Court in Johannesburg (1911). J. M. Solomon, a successor, designed the campus of the University of Cape Town.

Modernism After 1925 it was mainly foreign architectural movements that established themselves in South Africa. One such was the »international style«, characterized by asymmetrical compositions, simple cubic shapes, white plasterwork, and the absence of ornamentation. Examples include House Munro in Pretoria (McIntosh, 1932), House Harris in Johannesburg (Hanson, Tomkin and Finkelstein, 1933), and Casa Bedo in Johannesburg (Cowin and Ellis, 1936). In its room arrangement Casa Bedo is reminiscent of Mies van der Rohe, with its wide eaves and the hipped roof it goes back to Baker and Frank Lloyd Wright. For two decades it was the model for many houses.

Today the influence of Louis Kahn (1901–74) and the American school dominates the field of architecture. The skylines of South Africa's cities with their modern business buildings resemble those in the rest of the world. Amongst the most impressive are the Carlton Centre (Skidmore, Owings Merrill, 1966–72) in Johannesburg, the Standard Bank (Philip Dowson, 1971) and the Diamond Building (Helmut Jahn, 1984).

Music · Theatre · Dance

The change Largely unknown not too long ago, now successful on the world's stages: in the shadow of the cultural boycott against South Africa lifted in 1991, theatre, jazz, ethno-pop, and contemporary dance developed, though hardly noticed by the outside world at first. The jazz bars and art galleries in Johannesburg and Cape Town were already places where whites, blacks, and coloureds could meet unselfconsciously before this was normal; they thus contributed to the change. Unbounded energy and joie de vivre are particularly characteristic of South African stagecraft and music. The combination of African verve, rhythm, and natural body control with »European« discipline and technique created art which is receiving increasing attention in Europe.

The change that took place between 1990 and 1995 also involved art. After years of cultural atrophy caused both by the boycott and the rigid and often ridiculous censorship, international superstars are performing at the Cape again, as are Africa's own great musicians, such as Manu Dibango and Salif Keita. The singer Miriam Makeba (▶Famous People), the pianist Abdullah Ibrahim, and the trumpeter Hugh Masekela have returned home after many years in exile.

Most recently a kind of rollback can be observed; »eurocentric« art forms and institutions are being reduced. Theatre, orchestra, ballet companies etc. are being closed or disbanded, including three out of

Abdullah Ibrahim, formerly Dollar Brand, is one of biggest names in jazz.

four symphony orchestras, including the Cape Town Philharmonic Orchestra and the State Theatre in Pretoria (now converted into the »Spoornet State Theatre«, an entertainment and culture centre). Even theatres famous for their anti-apartheid work have not escaped this trend. Some speak of »cultural murder« and once again there is an exodus of artistic creative people, though for a different reason. Members of the former State Theatre Ballet and other disbanded companies have gone independent with a great deal of idealism and formed the »South African Ballet Theatre«; it remains to be seen how other artists and the country as a whole react to this new situation.

In the remote university town of Grahamstown there are ten days in June and July, the days of the national art festival, where everything that counts in South African art can be seen and heard as at no other time: theatre and cabaret, opera and jazz, dance and visual arts. During that time the small town is completely overrun. Accommodation must be booked well in advance.

National art festival

South African melodies and singers are well known around the world, though often the listeners are unaware of the artists' country of origin. Ethno-pop (tribal music combined with pop music) and jazz in particular have had international success. South Africa was and is one of the big jazz nations of the world. It is said that more jazz records are sold per capita in South Africa than in any other country. The influence of the township rhythms, and sometimes the penny whistle, makes it unmistakable. Besides »veterans« such as Miriam Makeba and the equally significant singer Dorothy Masuka, as well as the African Jazz Pioneers, a traditional group of the older generation, younger groups made their big breakthrough during the

Ethno-pop and jazz

mid-1990s. Amongst them are the fusion group Bayete, who makes much use of Zulu sounds, and Tananas, who combine numerous stylistic elements and musical traditions. Some young musicians like the saxophonist McCoy Mrubata and the drummers Vusi Khumalo and Lulu Gontsana often perform in Europe. Even before the return of Abdullah Ibrahim (formerly Dollar Brand), one of the most significant jazz pianists in the world, an independent jazz scene and music developed in Cape Town through musicians such as the saxophonist Winston Mankunku and Basil »Mannenberg« Coetzee. It was in Cape Town that Marimba bands such as Amampondo, which uses the traditional sounds of the Eastern Cape (Xhosa music), emerged. Several bands and musicians who make use of the musical tradition of the Zulus and sometimes develop it into ethno-pop are quite successful internationally, for instance Ladysmith Black Mambazo (who became famous in Europe and America through their participation in the *Graceland* album by Paul Simon) and Mahlathini and the Mahotella Queens, who sing *a cappella*. Johnny Clegg, the »white Zulu«, who initially combined good beats and catchy tunes with Juluka, South Africa's first mixed-race duo, then later also with Savuka, is particularly popular in France (► Famous People). Everyone has heard of the Soul Brothers, David Masondo and Moses Ngwenya, who have sold over ten million records with their tender ballads. They sing in Zulu about beautiful women, street gangs, conflict in the community, but mainly about love. After the buyback of

Joseph Shabalala, leader of the Ladysmith Black Mambazo group, dances with Zulu women at the festival of the sugar harvest.

the rights to their own music, they founded the first record company run solely by blacks. Good jazz and ethno-pop are available in every music shop; in big shopping centres more cheaply even than in smaller shops.

The musicians can be heard in a large number of bars, particularly **Music bars** in Johannesburg, the cultural centre of South Africa. »Kippie's« at the Market Theatre, named after the saxophonist Kippie Moeketsi, is a musical centre with a long tradition. Meeting places also developed in Yeoville, Melville, Rosebank, and Orange Grove. In Cape Town there are now jazz bars in the harbour district and along the waterfront; the student quarter Observatory and Long Street in the city centre, which turns into one big party at the weekends, have intimate bars tucked away that are also popular places for socializing. Events and locations are announced in the *Weekly Mail* newspaper amongst other places.

Music and dance also shape stage productions more in South Africa **Theatre** than elsewhere. The musicals *Sarafina* (1988; staged for over a year on Broadway in New York and made into a movie with Whoopi Goldberg), and *Township Fever* by Mbongeni Ngema (►Famous People) used catchy music to draw the world's attention to apartheid and the rule of injustice.
South Africa's most significant playwright is Athol Fugard (born 1932). After Shakespeare he is the most-played dramatist in the United States. *Time* magazine called him the greatest living playwright in the English language. His plays, such as *The Island* (1974), *The Road to Mecca* (1985), and *Boesman and Lena* (1969) are performed on stages all around the world. Almost all of them are set in Fugard's home in Eastern Cape province and in the Karoo steppe, but they are placeless and timeless. His autobiographically inspired works portray victims (often of racist mania) and desperate people. Many see Fugard's *Sizwe Bansi Is Dead* (1973) as the beginning of black protest theatre.
Another form of resistance on stage was political cabaret, which engendered an internationally successful artist in Pieter-Dirk Uys (born 1945, ►Baedeker tip p.385). His reputation in South Africa is almost legendary and he is able to get away with anything. In the guise of his fictitious character Evita Bezuidenhout, the »most famous female South African«, he can criticize whoever he wants, be they members of the old government or the new. According to Nelson Mandela, Uys made the transition at the Cape easier by using puns and gently biting mockery to bring Afrikaners to change their way of thinking.
The Market Theatre in Johannesburg with its three stages was for many years at the centre of non-racist theatrical life and a meeting place for intellectuals and artists. It is located in an art district (secured by guards) together with Kippie's jazz bar, galleries, a flea market on Saturdays, and the Museum Africa next door, with training fa-

cilities for actors and artists, the seat of various artist unions, and stages for contemporary dance (Dance Factory). It took over the tradition of the Space Theatre in Cape Town, which later closed down, where many of South Africa's significant actors trained during the 1970s. After the change of regime, the Market Theatre lost its dominant position. The financially and technically better equipped Johannesburg Civic Theatre had freed itself of its stigma dating back to the apartheid era. In addition many whites avoided the »Market« in the city centre because of their fear of crime. In Cape Town too the relationship shifted between the Nico Malan Theatre, a venue with an opera house in the city centre which had been boycotted by blacks and coloureds until a few years ago, and the independent Baxter near the university. The »Nico« increased in standing not least because the country's probably most daring director, Marthinus Basson, staged remarkable productions of predominantly Afrikaans plays. The Market and the Baxter, like many other stages that were often popular theatres shaped by the British influence, received no financial support from the old government; today their future, under the new »black« cultural policies, is once again uncertain.

Dance and ballet As in the rest of Africa, dance has an old and deep-seated tradition in South Africa. It began with tribal dances and the »Gumboot« dance of the mine workers, which are not just kept alive for foreign visitors. The University of Cape Town, which was the first university in the world to offer ballet as a subject, trained dancers who went to leading British ballet troupes. The choreographer John Cranko (1927–73) received his first training in Cape Town; he emigrated at the age of 19. In his will he stated that his works should be performed in his home country only after the abolition of apartheid: by 1990 the time had come.

Contemporary dance became the most exciting stage movement alongside and maybe ahead of jazz in South Africa during the mid-1990s. It veritably exploded: in 1993 there were two dance festivals in South Africa, the annual »Dance Umbrella« in Johannesburg in the theatre of the University of Witwatersrand (February and March) with around 100 world premiere performances, and at the national art festival in Grahamstown; by 1994 there were already six festivals. In Soweto alone there are 300 to 400 dance groups. The most significant independent groups in contemporary dance, such as the Free Flight Dance Company and Moving Into Dance in Johannesburg, now perform regularly in Europe. Dance, even more perhaps than theatre, has become a reflection of the South African soul.

Musical theatre The first »African« opera was performed for the first time in 1995 at the first African opera festival in Cape Town. With *Enoch, Prophet of God* the composer Roelof Temmingh and the librettist Michael Williams have attempted to provide a counterweight to the classical European arts of opera, orchestral music and ballet, since political

Carmen South African style: scene with the leading actor Pauline Malefane

change also led to a reorientation of governmental sponsorship of the arts; it was the first time the interests of black South Africans were to be taken into account. *Enoch* was based on actual events, a battle between the police and a religious sect that took place in 1921. The opera combines traditional African sounds with contemporary music and choral sounds. Bizet's opera *Carmen*, which was made into a movie by Mark Dornford-May under the title *U-Carmen e-Khayelitsha* in the Cape Town township of Khayelitsha, is a real hit. Everything is spoken and sung in Xhosa, which turned out to be a perfect operatic idiom. The classical love story set in the gruelling everyday life in a township won the Golden Bear at the Berlin Film Festival in 2005.

»White« choral music has a long and rich tradition amongst black South Africans. Handel's *Messiah* has been translated into Zulu. Interest in classical music, which had previously been focused around Johannesburg, Cape Town and Durban increased for a little while after the end of apartheid; subsequently there has been a dramatic drop in audience numbers.

Classical music

Famous People

Nelson Mandela and Desmond Tutu are probably the most famous names in South Africa's recent history. The strong personalities who shaped the face of South Africa include power-hungry imperialists and apartheid politicians, no less than fearless leaders of the resistance and famous musicians and writers.

Louis Botha (1862–1919)

The Bothas, more than any other family, are associated with South African apartheid policies. Pieter Willem Botha was South Africa's state president from 1984 to 1989, Roelof Frederik Botha was the country's foreign minister from 1977 to 1994. The first person with this old Boer name who came to prominence was Louis Botha, the first prime minister of the Union of South Africa when it was created in 1910, and a father of apartheid. He was born in Greytown, Natal, on 27 September 1862. As a farmer in the Boer republic of Transvaal he got elected to parliament in 1897. In the Boer Wars, in which he was significantly involved as a general, he appeared to be liberal and balanced. Botha was one of the signatories of the peace treaty of Vereeniging of 1902. The Boers together with Botha countered the anglicization of South Africa with the formation of the first Afrikaner party: Het Volk (The People). From it emerged the first self-administration government of the Boer republic, of which Louis Botha became the prime minister. Under him South Africa's four colonies joined together to form the Union of South Africa. Botha became the guarantor of apartheid enforcement. In addition he sought reconciliation with the British government, which was particularly inconvenient for many of his political allies when the First World War broke out, because this meant that South Africa was forced to implement the commands of the British allies, like the order to occupy German South-West Africa (modern Namibia). Only after Botha had put down a mutiny by the Boer forces could the order be carried out on 9 July 1915. Louis Botha died while still in office in Rusthof, Transvaal, on 28 August 1919.

Politician

Gatsha Mangosuthu Buthelezi (born 1928)

His hostility to Nelson Mandela and the ANC pushed the country into a bloody civil war prior to the first democratic elections in 1994. The two men had not always been enemies however. As a student Buthelezi was a member of the ANC youth league, which was not prohibited at the time, and during Mandela's incarceration he repeatedly pleaded for his release. Buthelezi was born in Mahlabatini, Natal, on 27 August 1928. He is related to the Zulu royal family through his mother, crown princess Magogo. From 1972 he was the head of government of the KwaZulu homeland and as such he resolutely opposed the South African government, which wanted to give KwaZulu an »independence« that would have made the Zulus foreigners in their own country. In 1975 he revived a traditional Zulu cultural organization as a »national cultural liberation movement«: Inkatha yeNkululeko yeSizwe. The ANC served as his model; he even

Politician

← *Revered as »Madiba«, which means father: Nelson Mandela at the first democratic elections in Oshlange near Durban in 1994*

With the Treaty of Vereeniging of 1902 the Boer Wars came to an end and South Africa became British. At the front, from the left: Christian de Wet, Louis Botha and Lord Kitchener.

took over its colours of black, gold and green and thus addressed the black population. It looked almost as if the ANC, prohibited in 1961, would be able to get a foothold in South Africa again via Inkatha. The exiled leadership of the ANC saw it that way, but Buthelezi did not. Their views were too far apart: Buthelezi rejected armed struggle and criticized the 1976 Soweto student uprising. The tensions heightened after 1983. Verbal attacks turned ever more frequently into bloody confrontations between the militant followers of the two camps. The struggle spilled over from Natal to the townships of Johannesburg. The ensuing civil war claimed over 15,000 lives before its end in 1994.

In the West, Buthelezi was the darling of European liberals and business for a long time, because he associated resistance to apartheid with the commitment to non-violence and with a free market economy. Outside South Africa he met many leading statesmen. His opponents, particularly black African politicians, accused him of collaboration and tribalism. Then however he increasingly put off old friends, including British conservative politicians, when he started closing ranks with white right-wing extremists after 1992. The agreement between President de Klerk and Nelson Mandela was a heavy blow for Buthelezi: he feared a defeat in the elections of April 1994, since many Zulus also wanted to vote for the ANC, for whom victory seemed almost a foregone conclusion. He called for a boycott of the elections and to that end he also used King Goodwill Zwelithini, the highest Zulu authority, who traditionally was required to remain neutral. Shortly before the election Mandela and de Klerk were able to bring the Inkatha king to participate in the election, when he was given the concession that the Zulu monarchy would be anchored in the constitution as a constitutional monarchy. The Inkatha Freedom Party (IFP) won 10.5% of the votes at the first elections of 1994. Buthelezi became the minister of home affairs; in the subsequent elections of 1999 and 2004 the IFP lost a proportion of their votes, but remained the third-strongest party.

Johnny Clegg (born 1953)

Musician

Johnny Clegg is a phenomenon in South Africa's music world. He has been called the »white« Zulu. He was born in Rochester, England in 1953. His mother was a cabaret singer, his stepfather a journalist from South Africa. Shortly after his birth his family emigrated to Zimbabwe. His stepfather familiarized him with African Kwela music from a very early age and he learned the language of the Ndebele before he learned English. In the late 1950s the family moved to South Africa. At the age of 14 Johnny ran away from home and became friends with a Zulu, who instructed him in Zulu music and their dances. The apartheid state was unhappy about this: he was arrested for the first time when he was 15 years old. From 1970 he performed with the Zulu Sipho McHunu. Their music was full of Western and black African stylistic elements. In 1976 they brought out their first record called *Woza Friday*. A little while later, ignoring apartheid, they founded Juluka, a band consisting of both black and white musicians. In South Africa their seven records won them two platinum and five gold awards. In 1986 Clegg formed Savuka, a band that brings the languages and musical traditions of Europe and the Zulu together with a captivating beat. Their songs describe African village life, unemployment, imprisonment and tribal battles. Savuka's records also rapidly conquered the charts.

Mohandas Karamchand Gandhi (1869–1948)

Peaceful revolutionary

Mohandas K. Gandhi, the most significant leader of the Indian liberation movement, who was later also known as Mahatma (»great soul«), spent his »apprenticeship« in South Africa. Gandhi was born in Porbandar in India on 2 October 1869. After reading law in London (1888–91) he returned to India to practise. In 1893 he went to the British crown colony of Natal for professional reasons. There the elegant young man experienced what it meant not to be part of the white class: on a train ride from Durban to Pretoria he was thrown out of the first class compartment in Pietermaritzburg, because it was taboo for non-whites. Gandhi's conclusions from that memorable night changed world history. In 1884 he became one of the founders of the Indian National Congress. It offered the first organ-

Gandhi as a lawyer in Johannesburg, around 1894

ized resistance and was a model for actions by black South Africans. Soon Gandhi was the political leader of the Indian community in South Africa. In 1906 he was able to convince the British Colonial Secretary to abolish the registration of Indians. However, the new government of Transvaal immediately passed a law requiring the registration of fingerprints. During a mass rally Gandhi subsequently called on his fellow-countrymen to resist passively and non-violently. There were numerous arrests, and Gandhi was not spared. Gandhi later drew on his experiences in the Transvaal in India's fight for independence. In 1914 he returned to his home country and became the leader of the national resistance to the British. However, after India obtained its independence he did not succeed in preventing the partition of the country. On 30 January 1948, Gandhi was shot by a fanatical Hindu.

Nadine Gordimer (born 1923)

Author Political commitment is definitely her thing, but Nadine Gordimer strongly resists the label of being a political author. She was born in Springs near Johannesburg on 20 November 1923; her father was a watchmaker, a Lithuanian immigrant, and her mother was English. Her literary success started in 1952 with the publication of her second collection of stories *The Soft Voice of the Serpent and Other Stories*. Her novels and stories, written in English and following the European literary tradition, are neither instructive nor sensational. It is rather that Gordimer in her quiet, shy manner voices the country's inner conflict (*The Conservationist*, 1974) and represents the question of the possibilities of white commitment (*Burger's Daughter*, 1979). She describes the effects of the policies on the people, the feelings of guilt of white liberals, the penetration of all areas of life by the ideology of racial discrimination. This places her amongst the ranks of renowned South African authors such as Alan Paton, Athol Fugard, Breyten Breytenbach, André Brink and John Coetzee. Censorship in South Africa persecuted her and some of her books were banned. Despite that, she remained in the country. There are voices who re-

proached her for this and for the fact that she is a member of the privileged upper class, does not speak an African language, and only became a member of the ANC after it had been permitted as a party again. Her work has won her numerous prizes, including the Nobel Prize for Literature in 1991.

Frederik Willem de Klerk (born 1936)

With his parliamentary speech on 2 February 1990 state president de Klerk, »Africa's Gorbachev«, surprised the entire world. He announced three important measures: the readmission of the ANC (►Baedeker Specialp.42), the PAC (Pan Africanist Congress) and the Communist Party, the release of Nelson Mandela and other political prisoners, as well as the introduction of the full right to vote for non-whites. This speech marked the end of the apartheid state.

Politician

He was the son of a conservative family of politicians of Huguenot origin. He was born in Johannesburg on 18 March 1936 and studied law. As a convinced supporter of apartheid he was a member of the National Party, which came to power in 1948, being elected into the purely white parliament in 1972. At the end of the 1980s South Africa was internationally isolated and sanctions were paralysing the economy. The position of President Botha had become untenable. In February 1989 de Klerk initially became leader of the National Party and on 15 August 1989, after Botha's resignation, he became president. Until then de Klerk had at most been considered a mediator between apartheid opponents and supporters. During his first months in office he had spoken of a careful convergence and he had also had many talks with Mandela when the latter was in prison, but nothing looking like fundamental change occurred. Instead an affair of the de Klerk family caused headlines: his wife Marike forbade her son to marry a coloured woman. During the election campaign of 1990 de Klerk created the image of a »new South Africa«, which however no one really believed at first. On 2 February the new parliamentary year began with de Klerk's extraordinary speech. First he limited the influence of the police and the army, then he annulled 46 apartheid laws, and in December the negotiations between the government and 19 largely black organizations began. In March 1992 de Klerk allowed the whites to vote on his policies. More than 85% participated, of whom 68.7% were in favour of his reforms. In 1993 de Klerk and Nelson Mandela were awarded the Nobel Peace Prize, a daring decision, since the peace that had been created at the time was still very fragile. In 1994 South Africa's first free elections took place and de Klerk became one of Nelson Mandela's two deputy presidents in the government of national unity. Just two years later de Klerk pushed his party to leave the government out of protest against the new constitution; in August 1997 he resigned as chairman of the National Party. De Klerk's autobiography *The Last Trek. A New Beginning* was published in 1999.

Paul »Ohm« Kruger (1825–1904)

President of Transvaal South Africa's history towards the end of the 19th century was shaped by two men: Cecil Rhodes, the prime minister of the Cape Colony, and his opponent Paul Kruger, nicknamed »Ohm« meaning »uncle«, the president of Transvaal. Kruger was born in Vaalbank near Colesberg (Cape Province) on 10 October 1825. The progenitor of the family, Jacob Kruger from Berlin, had come to the Cape in 1713 as a mercenary of the Dutch East India Company. Paul Kruger was a real Voortrekker. As a boy he participated in the »Great Trek« (1834–40) to Natal. In 1864 he became commander general of the Boer Transvaal republic, which had been sovereign since 1852. Under his leadership Transvaal and the second sovereign Boer republic, Orange Free State, rose up against the British rule and achieved independence in 1881. In 1883 Kruger was elected president of Transvaal.

He was an ardent nationalist and an unwavering Calvinist. He compared the history of the Boers to that of the old Israelites. This point of view became part of the growing Boer nationalism. In 1895 Cecil Rhodes planned a revolt by the »uitlanders« (»foreigners«) of Johannesburg who had flooded into the country after the discovery of gold at the Witwatersrand; the goal was to topple the Transvaal republic and bring it back into the British Empire. The plan was to support the rebels with a 660-man army, which was led by one of Rhodes's confidants, Dr Jameson.

However, the »Jameson Raid« of December 1895 failed. The German emperor Wilhelm II subsequently sent a congratulatory telegram, the »Kruger telegram«, which caused great offence to the British. Great Britain decided to take tougher measures. Kruger offered negotiations, but to no avail. On 9 October 1899 he gave Great Britain an ultimatum, again to no avail. He wanted the British to withdraw their troops from the borders. On the 11 October he declared war on Britain. In October 1900, when the Afrikaners' defeat in the »Boer War« (1899–1902) became inevitable, he travelled to Europe, where he unsuccessfully pleaded for the support of Germany and other states. He never returned to South Africa and died in Switzerland on 14 July 1904. His mortal remains were brought to Pretoria.

Besides the Kruger telegram there are two terms that mention his name: the Kruger National Park and the krugerrand. Kruger, who loved nature, founded the Sabie Game Reserve in 1898, which later became the Kruger National Park, to protect wildlife. The krugerrand is a gold coin containing an ounce (31.1g) of pure gold (plus 2.8g of alloy metal) that has been minted since 1967. Originally a popular object for investors, it was displaced by similar coins such as the Canadian »Maple Leaf« and the American »Eagle« because of South Africa's internationally despised apartheid policies.

Miriam Makeba (born 1932)

For all Africans she is »Mama Afrika« and together with Winnie Mandela she was one of the most famous and most renowned female representatives of the anti-apartheid movement: the singer Miriam **Singer**

(actually Zenzile) Makeba was born in Prospect near Johannesburg on 4 March 1932. In 1959 the 27-year-old nurse appeared in the film *Come Back Africa*, which was filmed in Sophiatown, a black suburb of Johannesburg (after its demolition it became »Tri-omf«, a white residential area). Her public rejection of apartheid caused her to be banished from South Africa. Her exile began in the United States, where, supported by Harry Belafonte, she achieved international fame with her songs *Pata Pata*, *Westwinds* and *The Click Song*. In 1968 she married the American civil rights activist Stokely Carmichael and later the musician Hugh Masekela. For a time she represented Guinea, where she lived during the 1980s, as a special envoy for the UN. In 1987 she achieved a triumphant comeback on Paul Simon's Graceland tour. That same year the American James Hall published a book about the most famous singer of the black continent: here Miriam Makeba vividly describes her life, her career as a singer and her battle against apartheid (*Miriam Makeba: My Story*, 1988). Today she is living in South Africa again.

Nelson Mandela (born 1918)

First black president

He spent more than a quarter of a century behind bars as the number one enemy of the state (as prisoner number 0 221 141 011). Then he, a man who had never voted before, became head of state after the free elections of 1994 as the first black president. Rolihlahla Mandela (thus the name given to him at his birth, which means »shaker of trees«, colloquially »troublemaker«) was born in Mvezo, a tiny village near Umtata, the capital of Transkei, on 18 July 1918. His father was chief and advisor of Jongintaba, king of the Thembu, a Xhosa tribe. On his first day of school Mandela was given a »civilized« name by his teacher: Nelson. He was educated in the village primary school, the Clarkebury Institute, the Wesleyan College and the University of Fort Hare, which, until 1960, was the only higher education facility for blacks. He fled from a planned, traditional wedding and went to Johannesburg, where he worked in a law office. In correspondence courses he studied law, first at the University of South Africa and then at the University of the Witwatersrand. His politicization did not come about on a specific day, »a steady accumulation of a thousand slights, a thousand indignities (…) produced in me an anger, a rebelliousness, a desire to fight the system that imprisoned my people.« In 1944 he became a member of the African National Congress (▶ Baedeker Special p.42) and founded the ANC's Youth League together with Oliver Tambo and others.

After completing his studies Mandela opened South Africa's first black law practice together with Tambo in 1952. He quickly became a symbolic figure of the oppression of the black majority. After he called for the non-violent infringement of the race laws in 1925 the government banned him from all political activity. Despite that he continued to remain active for the ANC. Between 1956 and 1961 he stood trial for high treason, but was acquitted. On 14 June 1958 Mandela married the black social worker Winnie Nomzamo Madikizela. After the Sharpeville massacre of 1961 the ANC was banned and Mandela went into hiding. He organized a general strike that was put down with much bloodshed. This also marked the end of non-violent resistance for Mandela. He founded the ANC's military wing, the »Umkhonto we Sizwe« (»the spear of the nation«), which performed acts of sabotage. In 1962 Mandela was arrested and sentenced to five years in prison. In the »Rivonia trial« in 1964 this was extended to life. Mandela spent most of his time on Robben Island. Not just in South Africa but in other countries too many people spoke out for his release. In 1985 president Botha offered Mandela freedom under certain conditions, which he rejected: »There is no freedom in apartheid«.

On 11 February 1990 the time had finally arrived. Caving in to internal and external pressure, President Frederik de Klerk announced Mandela's release after 28 years in prison. Both, de Klerk and Mandela (first vice-president of the ANC, which had been permitted again, and after July 1991 its president), worked for the abolition of apartheid, the creation of a democratic state, and the reconciliation of all South Africans. They were awarded the Nobel Peace Prize for their efforts in December 1993. This made Mandela South Africa's third Nobel Prize winner after Albert Luthuli (around 1898 to 1967, Zulu chief and president of the ANC from 1952), and Desmond Tutu. As expected the ANC emerged from the 1994 elections as the strongest party. On 10 May 1994 Nelson Mandela became de Klerk's successor and was thus proclaimed South Africa's first black state president. At the centre of his policies was the convergence of the divided society, the reconciliation of South Africa's various racial groups. Mbeki won the 1999 elections, thus taking over the presidency from Mandela. The symbolic figure of reconciliation and one of the most impressive political personalities of the 20th century relinquished his position. It was the beginning of a new era. Now the »global elder statesman« is honoured as »Madiba«, no longer accompanied by his wife Winnie whom he married in 1958. She lost her reputation as a anti-apartheid activist through criminal machinations and political failure, and had to surrender all of her political offices. In 1992 Winnie and Nelson Mandela divorced. On his 80th birthday Nelson Mandela married Graça Machel, the former First Lady of Mozambique.

Thabo Mbeki (born 1942)

From very early on politics influenced Thabo Mbeki's life, in which normal family structures were not possible. He was born in the village of Mbewuleni in Transkei on 18 June 1942. His mother, Epainette Moerane, was working as a teacher in Durban when she met Govan Mbeki during the 1930s. Both had had progressive upbringings and became members of the Communist Party. When Thabo was ten years old he was sent to school in Queenstown. After the 1960 Sharpeville massacre he went to Johannesburg; Soweto was a stronghold of the opposition. There he met Nelson Mandela in 1961. His first important position was that of secretary of the African Students' Organization. In 1962 he went into exile in Britain, where he studied at the University of Sussex. There he established the student division of the ANC and became a confidant of Oliver Tambo. While Mandela and his own father were sentenced to life imprisonment in

Politician

1964, Mbeki worked in exile for the democratic liberation of South Africa. During the 1970s Mbeki became the second secretary of the Revolutionary Council, which was led by Tambo in Lusaka (Zambia). In 1975 he represented the ANC in Swaziland, becoming Tambo's political secretary at the ANC headquarters in Lusaka in 1978. In 1984 he was given diplomatic duties as the leader of ANC Department of Information.

Thabo Mbeki is considered a thinker and strategist. He was the initiator of the talks between the ANC's leadership and the South African government, which began in Groote Schuur in 1991. In the years prior to the first democratic elections Mbeki proved to be an adept negotiator for all political groups. In 1994 he was elected one of the two deputy presidents of South Africa. That same year he became the vice president of the ANC, and its president in 1997. In his famous speech at the introduction of the new constitution in May 1996 the visionary Mbeki called the African Renaissance the key concept for the future of the black continent. Since being elected president of South Africa in 1999 he has been faced with difficult challenges. Crime, AIDS, social injustice and unemployment are hurdles which make it difficult for Mbeki's election slogan »a better life for all« to become reality. He lost the chair of the ANC in 2007.

Mbongeni Ngema (born 1955)

Dramatist The composer, author, director and choreographer Mbongeni Ngema is one of the most popular artists in South Africa. His songs and musicals are not just part of black contemporary culture, they were also messages from the oppressed majority of his home country that went all around the world. Ngema grew up in a village in Zululand. He came to the theatre more by chance than anything else: at an amateur production in a gold mine he stepped in for one of the actors who had fallen ill. He started writing plays, which he performed with amateurs in churches, hospitals, and on football pitches in the townships. Gibson Kente, the great black theatre figure, became one of his first teachers. Together with Percy Mtwa, an actor colleague, he developed a South African version of the New Testament: *Woza Albert!*. This play was staged at the legendary Market Theatre in Johannesburg and was a global success. Ngema founded his own troupe, the Committed Artists. His next play, *Asinamali*, was taken from everyday life in South Africa: a rent strike in a township near Durban. This play also became a global success, was performed on Broadway, and earned numerous prizes for its author. The next production was the famous *Sarafina* (1988), his first musical, which addresses the story of the student riots in Soweto. It played on Broadway for two years and was made into a film with Whoopi Goldberg and Leleti Khumalo (now Ngema's wife). His *Magic at 4* is a musical about the conflicts of an emerging society, and *Music of Freedom* is a song about the hope that everyone can live peacefully together.

Jan van Riebeeck (1619–77)

The story of modern South Africa began in 1652 with the founding of Cape Town by Jan Anthoniszoon van Riebeeck. Van Riebeeck was born in Culemborg near Rotterdam on 21 April 1619. In 1639 he went into the service of the Dutch East India Company (Vereenigde Oostindische Compagnie, VOC). He was soon promoted to the position of merchant until he was called back home in 1647 under suspicion of having lined his own pockets in Japan. On his way home he was on one of five ships that were bringing the survivors and cargo of the stranded *Nieuw Haerlem* back to Holland. When the VOC decided to set up a supply base at the Cape of Good Hope, van Riebeeck made himself available. On 6 April 1652 he anchored in Table Bay, which was an excellent natural harbour. On board were his wife, his four-month-old son, and 90 men, women and children. He was not supposed to found a colony, but merely set up a permanent supply base for travellers on their way to East India. In order to guarantee the supply of »Kaapstad«, van Riebeeck suggested settling farmers as free citizens. The company was to leave them land that they could cultivate themselves, and buy their products at fixed prices. The VOC accepted the proposal and nothing stood in the way of flourishing trade at the Cape. However, politically the situation intensified dramatically: after cruel conflicts between the native inhabitants and the settlers, the blacks – who were known as »Hottentots« – withdrew into the interior. Under van Riebeeck slavery also found its way into this part of the world; from 1657 slaves were taken from East Africa, Madagascar, India and the East Indies. When van Riebeeck left the Cape on 7 May 1662 to become a commander and president in Malacca, Cape Town was a place with four roads and around 200 white inhabitants.

Founder of Cape Town

Cecil Rhodes (1853–1902)

The greatest adversary of Paul Kruger (see above) was Cecil John Rhodes, a British-South African diamond king, statesman, pioneer of British imperialism, »representative of God and the devil« (Mark Twain) and a »great villain« (R. Rotberg). The son of a minister, he was born in Bishop's Stortford (near Hertford) in England on 5 July 1853. In 1870 he moved to his brother's farm in Natal in order to cure a lung problem. From 1878 onwards he earned himself a fortune in the diamond business; in 1880 he founded De Beers Consolidated Mines Ltd. (▶ Baedeker Special p.74). In between he studied law at the University of Oxford. Rhodes was not just a sharp businessman, but also a ruthless, power-hungry politician. Determined to realize his dream of travelling from Cairo to the Cape in a sleeper-car, he initiated the conquest of Bechuanaland (modern Botswana) in 1884; in 1889 he founded the British South Africa Company, which, with royal consent, acquired the areas of Northern and

Diamond merchant

Cecil Rhodes in a portrait by G. F. Watts, 1898
(National Portrait Gallery, London)

Southern Rhodesia (modern Zambia and Zimbabwe), which were named after him in 1895. At all costs he wanted to include the Boer republics of Transvaal and Orange Free State in a British colonial empire between the Cape and the Mediterranean. Then gold was found at the Witwatersrand in Transvaal, which attracted British fortune-seekers. When they demanded the right to vote in elections, the Boers refused. Rhodes, who had been the prime minister of the Cape Colony since 1890, mobilized against the Boers. In addition he planned the revolt of the »outlanders« living in Transvaal, the »Jameson Raid« (▶ p. 71). After it failed, Rhodes had to resign. He died in Muizenburg on 26 March 1902.

Shaka (around 1789 to 1828)

»Black Napoleon of South Africa«   Every year on 22 September thousands of Zulus in traditional dress, armed with a spear and shield, assemble in Stanger approx. 70 km/45mi north of Durban. The occasion is the anniversary of the death of the legendary Zulu king and »black Napoleon of South Africa«, Shaka (Chaka). He was born as the son of chief Senzangakona. Like every other boy he had to tend his father's sheep when he was six. When one of the sheep was torn apart by a wild dog, the father cast out the boy and his mother. Thereupon he was exposed to the ridicule of other children, which is said to have given Shaka the ambition to achieve fame and power. Under Dingiswayo, chief of the Mtetwa, Shaka was promoted from warrior to regiment commander.

After his father's death in 1815 Dingiswayo helped him become chief of the Zulu, who at that time were a small ethnic group; after Dingiswayo's death Shaka also took over the chieftainship of the Mtetwa. In next to no time Shaka unified over 100 Zulu tribes into a powerful nation that was politically and militarily tightly organized. The impis (regiments) steamrollered the autocrats of the neighbouring tribes. Shaka's wars and the unparalleled terror of his rule caused a huge diaspora amongst the neighbouring peoples (▶ History). In 1824 Shaka peacefully approached Europeans in modern-day Durban. However, he developed more and more into a bloodthirsty despot. When his mother died in 1827 he forced the Zulu people into cruel obsequies. He also tried to abolish the old tribal council. On 25 September 1828 he was murdered by his half-brothers Dingane and Mhlangane. There is now a tombstone at the place where he died; thousands of Zulus come here once a year to honour the man who made their people into proud warriors. In 1986 South African television produced a ten-part series about Shaka's life with the title *Shaka Zulu*.

Joe Slovo (1926–95)

For decades he, the »red devil«, the »bringer of terror«, was the worst enemy of the apartheid government. The black population on the other hand respected Joe Slovo, the leader of the South African Communist Party (SACP). He was born in a Jewish ghetto in Lithuania on 23 May 1926. When he was nine years old his family emigrated to South Africa. At the age of 16 he became a member of South Africa's Communist Party. In the Second World War he fought in northern Africa on the side of the allies. After the ANC was banned in 1960 he played a decisive part in establishing the ANC's military wing, Umkhonto we Sizwe (▶ Baedeker Special p.42). In 1963 he went into exile in Mozambique, and set up an ANC operational centre in Maputo in 1977. He suffered the probably hardest blow of his life when his wife Ruth First, a politician and author, was killed by a letter bomb that was presumably meant for him in 1982. From 1985 he was the first white person to be part of the ANC executive. In 1986 he was appointed secretary-general of the South African Communist Party, giving up this post in 1991 after it became known that he had cancer. During the first meeting between ANC leaders and president de Klerk and other government representatives in 1990 he surprised everyone with his moderate manner and willingness to compromise. It is thanks to him that the agreeable suggestion of creating a temporary coalition of the big parties was taken on as the »Government of National Unity«. He indicated that he still held firm in his communist ideals by wearing red socks to this meeting. After the first free parliamentary elections of 1994 he became the housing minister. On 6 January 1995 Slovo died in Johannesburg of bone-marrow cancer.

»Red devil«

J. R. R. Tolkien (1892–1973)

Author His fantastic stories made him a cult figure for the »hippie generation« of the late 1960s. John Ronald Reuel Tolkien was born in

Bloemfontein, South Africa on 3 January 1892. In 1896 he came to England; after studying at Oxford and serving in the First World War he lectured at British universities. From 1920 to 1925 he taught English in Leeds, from 1925 to 1959 he was professor of Anglo-Saxon and later of English language and literature at the University of Oxford. Inspired by his studies of Old and Middle English and Celtic-Germanic myths, he wrote novels: *The Hobbit* (1937) was intended as a children's book. In this work he created a fantasy-world with human-like inhabitants who had their own language. In the *Lord of the Rings* trilogy (1954–55), which brought his international breakthrough, he expanded on the story of the hobbits. Tolkien died in Bournemouth, England, in 1973.

Five years after his death *The Lord of the Rings* was made into an animated film and released in cinemas. In 2001 it was made into an epic movie and as such conquered the international cinema charts (including China!). In 2003 the third part of the saga was released. This made *The Lord of the Rings* a cult story once and for all.

Desmond Tutu (born 1931)

Bishop The contentious bishop Desmond Mpilo Tutu was born in the mining town of Klerksdorp (Transvaal) on 7 October 1931, where his father, a Xhosa, was working as a Methodist primary school teacher. After completing his degree at the University of Johannesburg he started his career as a high school teacher in 1954. In 1957 he gave up this job in protest against a law that disadvantaged black students. He became a member of the Redemptionist order and trained to become a priest at the Anglican St Peter's Theological College in Johannesburg. After further stages in his training and teaching in London,

Alice and Lesotho he was the deputy director of the Theological Education Fund of the World Council of Churches in England; in 1975 he returned to South Africa as the Anglican Dean of Johannesburg. In 1976 he was ordained bishop of Lesotho. As the General Secretary of the South African Council of Churches (1978–84) he denounced apartheid and called on foreign countries to impose economic sanctions. Tutu's fight was respected not just amongst the black population of his country, but also outside South Africa. He was awarded the Nobel Peace Prize in 1984. Also in 1984 he became the first black Anglican bishop of Johannesburg, two years later archbishop of Cape Town, and thus head of the Anglican church of South Africa (until 1996). In 1987 he was elected president of the All-Africa Conference of Churches. Tutu also tried to mediate between the rival black groups who were increasingly willing to use violence. When de Klerk lifted the ban on the ANC and released Nelson Mandela, Tutu initially withdrew from politics. He took up his role as a mediator again when the conflict between the ANC and the Inkatha threatened the democratization process and the first free parliamentary elections in South Africa. In 1995 Tutu took over the chair of the »Truth and Reconciliation Commission«, which published its final report in 1998. His book *No Future without Forgiveness* was published in 1999.

Desmond Tutu at the first free elections of 1994 in Guguletu in Cape Town

Practicalities

WHERE ARE THE GOOD PLACES
TO STAY AND EAT IN SOUTH
AFRICA? WHAT DO VISITORS
NEED TO KNOW ABOUT
PERSONAL SAFETY? USEFUL
INFORMATION AND FACTS TO
MAKE THE TRIP SUCCESSFUL.

Accommodation

Hotels and Guesthouses

From hotels to campsites South Africa has a dense network of hotels and guesthouses that keep up with the international standard in the good to luxury class. They are officially divided into five categories, from basic accommodation (1 star) to luxury establishments (5 stars). That does not mean that the no-star accommodation or the many excellently run backpacker hostels do not offer cleanliness and comfort. Bed & Breakfasts in private households are plentiful. Note that quite a number of hotels only take in children aged 14 years and older. In Cape Town and Johannesburg hotel beds are always scarce, so book well in advance. South African Tourism (▶ Information) publishes an accommodation guide, which describes the hotels, guesthouses, etc rated by South African Tourism.

Agencies The agencies **Portfolio** and **Caraville** have an excellent choice, ranging from hotels to game lodges. Caraville also acts as tour operator and neutral agency for car rental companies.

Lodges In the »non-civilized« areas, particularly in the national parks and their surrounding area, lodges (in tents, bungalows or thatched round huts) provide accommodation; the standard ranges from basic to luxurious. This is reflected in the prices: from ZAR 2000–7000, even ZAR 10,000 per person per day, where all amenities are included: meals and drinks, safaris etc. A large proportion of the national park lodges are run by SANParks and KZN Wildlife (both ▶ p.156). **CCAfrica** (▶right) is a private organization that combines nature conservation with luxury tourism; they also run one of the biggest lodges in South Africa.

Prices and reservations As in all countries with definite holiday periods, the prices vary a lot over the course of the year (▶price categories p.9).
The absolute peak seasons when everything costs the most (and sometimes a minimum stay of several days is required) are the school holidays Dec–Jan and Easter; for accommodation in tourist areas and national parks it is necessary to book several months in advance.

Youth Hostels and Backpacker Hostels

Backpacker hostels and youth hostels are extremely popular and generally of a high standard. However they are concentrated in the more frequented parts of the country such as Cape Town and the Garden Route. Apart from inexpensive accommodation (approx. ZAR 50–80 for a bed in a dorm or ZAR 150–200 for a double room) these hos-

ACCOMMODATION ADDRESSES

► **Portfolio**
PO Box 132
Newlands 7725
Cape Town
Tel. 021 686 5400
reservations
Tel. 021 689 4020
www.portfoliocollection.com

► **Caraville Group**
PO Box 1166
ZA-3630 Westville
Tel. 031 266 0030
www.caraville.co.za

► **CCAfrica**
Private Bag X27
Benmore 2010
Johannesburg
tel. 011 809 4300
www.ccafrica.com

► **Hostelling International (HISA)**
Tel. 021 424 2511
www.hisa.org.za

► **Backpacker Tourism South Africa**
www.btsa.co.za

tels are sources of valuable tips and information. In addition the hostels act as agencies for bus companies, tours, car rental companies etc. Usually they have kitchens for self-catering travellers, internet access, a garden with swimming pool, a bar, cafeteria or restaurant. The Baz Bus (►p.176, 180) drives to a large number of hostels, and other establishments have a shuttle service. The privately run youth hostels that are part of HISA are of a standard equal to the backpacker hostels.

Camping and Caravanning

South Africa has more than 700 campsites, where visitors can stay in tents, caravans, chalets or rondavels. It is the cheapest way to get to know South Africa. Since they are also very popular amongst South Africans, most sites are guarded and very well-tended (including the sanitary facilities) and have restaurants, swimming pools, shops, sports facilities and children's playgrounds. Usually every tent site has its own barbecue. In the popular national parks and for the summer holidays (►p.184) a site should be booked several months in advance. Information in the tourist information offices of the respective provinces. The »Guide to Caravanning & Camping in South Africa« (Struik Publishers, Cape Town) is very useful.

Depending on size (2, 4, 6 people) a camper generally costs ZAR 650–1500 a day. Campers come in the form of off-road vehicles with a roof tent, but are all fully equipped. It is important to book well in advance from home. Rental companies ►p.177.

Camper rental

Arrival · Before the Journey

Arrival

By air   In addition to South African Airlines (SAA) and Air Namibia, major European airlines such as Air France, British Airways, KLM, Lufthansa and Virgin Atlantic all fly daily or several times a week non-stop from their European hubs to Johannesburg and/or Cape Town or to Windhoek. The flying time from Europe to Johannesburg is ten to eleven hours. North America: SAA flies direct from New York and Atlanta to Johannesburg; as an alternative, take a European airline, changing in Europe at that airline's hub. From the west coast of the USA, Malaysia Airlines from Los Angeles via Kuala Lumpur to Cape Town or Johannesburg is an option. From other continents there are connections with Cathay Pacific, Emirates, Singapore Airlines and Qantas, among others. It is best to fly overnight and arrive in the morning. It is advisable to book at least three months in advance for the busiest times (Dec–Jan and July–Sept), which also makes the tickets quite a bit cheaper. South African Airlines offer well-priced connecting flights. The return flight has to be confirmed around three days prior to the departure date. Make sure to ask for the name of person you are dealing with; this can avoid unnecessary trouble down the line.

By boat   Not many choices are available for cruises to South Africa. Cargo ships are an alternative for a comfortable passage to South Africa. It costs about GBP 1500–2000/€ 2000–2500 to ship a car from Europe to South Africa in a sealed container.

By car   Visitors who enter South Africa with their own car need, in addition to the vehicle registration papers, driving licence (see below) and third-party insurance, a carnet de passage en douane, which provides exemption from import duty. To obtain the carnet, contact an automobile association in your home country.

TOUR OPERATORS: UK

▶ **Dragoman Overland Adventure**
Camp Green,
Debenham, IP14 6LA
Tel. 01728-86 11 33
www.dragoman.com

▶ **Naturetrek**
Cheriton Mill, Cheriton
Alresford SO24 ONG
Tel. 01962-73 30 51
www.naturetrek.co.uk

TOUR OPERATORS: USA

▶ **Africa Adventure Company**
5353 N Federal Highway, Suite 300, Fort Lauderdale, FL 33308
Tel. 1-954-491 88 77
www.africa-adventure.com

▶ **Wilderness Travel**
1102 Ninth Street
Berkeley, CA 94710
Tel. 1-800-368 27 94
www.wildernesstravel.com

There is an almost limitless number of companies in South African and around the world that offer organized trips. There is something for everyone, from customized tours for individual travellers to all-inclusive holidays lasting several weeks. A directory can be found at South African Tourism (►p. 141); travel agents and the internet are further important sources of information. The services on offer from SAA Tours (an offshoot of South African Airways) also deserve a mention.

Organized trips

Travel Documents

Travellers from countries of the European Union and Common-wealth and from the USA need to present a passport to enter South Africa, Lesotho, and Swaziland, but do not require a visa. For South Africa it must be valid for a further 30 days past the departure date, for Lesotho for another three months, and for Swaziland an additional six months. There must be one blank page each for the entry stamp and the exit stamp. A visa is only necessary in South Africa and Lesotho for stays lasting longer than three months. You may be requested to produce a departure ticket and proof of sufficient funds (credit card is fine). When changing money it is a good idea to have some proof of home address on hand.

Personal documents

For all who wish to drive in South Africa, an English-language driving licence with a photo is essential. If your national licence does not meet these requirements, you must obtain an international driving licence.

Driving licence

Members of motoring organizations must bring their membership card for free usage of the AA's services (►p.177).

Motoring organizations

An import clearance issued by a vet is required for importing pets into South Africa. Dogs must have an implanted microchip for identification purposes. Without proof of the necessary vaccinations an animal will have to be quarantined. Information: Directorate Veterinary Services, Private Bag X138, Pretoria 0001, tel. 012 319 7414, fax 012 329 8292, www.nda.agric.za). Many hotels will not take dogs.

Animals

Visitors from most countries need no visa to enter Swaziland if the intended stay does not exceed 60 days. A multiple-entry visa is needed for repeated entries into the country. Those who need a visa can obtain it at the border post.

Entry into Swaziland

Lesotho does not require tourists from any country to have a visa if they intend to stay less than 30 days.

Entry into Lesotho

Since South Africa does not have a national health service, visitors have to pay for their own medical care. European medical cards are

Insurances

not accepted in South Africa. It is absolutely necessary to purchase travel health insurance (including cover for a medically attended return flight, ▸Health). It is also advisable to check out overseas accident insurance and travellers' baggage insurance.

Photocopies   Photocopies should be made of all documents, including passport, credit cards and flight tickets; one of these copies should be left at home with a trusted individual.

Customs Regulations

Entry into South Africa   The following may be imported into South Africa duty-free: 1 litre of spirits, 2 litres of wine, 400 cigarettes, 50 cigars, 250 g tobacco, 250 ml toilet water, and 50 ml perfume, as well as gifts worth up to R200. Further information is available at the Department of Customs and Excise, Pretoria, tel. 012-284 308 242.

Leaving South Africa   Plants and animal products (trophies for example) can only be exported with a special permit. Trading endangered plants and animals is prohibited and the prohibition is strictly enforced. Further information ▸Purchases.

Re-entry into the EU   When re-entering EU countries souvenirs up to a value of €175 are duty-free; in addition travellers over 15 years of age may bring back 500g of coffee or 200g of instant coffee, and 100g of tea, 50g of perfume and 0.25 l of toilet water. In addition travellers over the age of 17 may import 1 litre of spirits of more than 22% alcohol by volume (or 2 litres less than 22% alcohol by volume) or 2 litres of sparkling wine and 2 litres of wine, also 200 cigarettes or 50 cigars or 250 g tobacco.

Beaches

South Africa has more than 3000km/1900mi of coastline! It is no wonder that water temperatures, bathing beaches and visitor numbers all vary greatly. The cold Benguela current that flows past the west coast causes temperatures of maximum 17°C/63°F. Bathing on the east coast is much more pleasant as the warm Agulhas current coming from the Indian Ocean is responsible for warmer temperatures.

Along the Garden Route the water temperatures are good for swimming from November to April. At the northern coast of KwaZulu-Natal the water is pleasant all year round (up to 24°C/75°F). Here there are some wonderful deserted beaches. Sun worshippers and water lovers who love the quiet get what they want along the Wild Coast, quite unlike the beaches of the main seaside towns: those

Surfers find excellent waves along South Africa's coastline.

looking for a more lively atmosphere will find what they are looking for here during the peak season. Do not swim in the lagoons, as they are inhabited by hippos and crocodiles.

West coast

Strandfontein (north of Lambert's Bay) is very popular amongst swimmers. McDougall's Bay (near Port Nolloth) is sheltered by shallow reefs and is excellent for swimming.

Cape peninsula

Beautiful and popular beaches can be found west of Mossel Bay near Still Bay, Witsand, Infanta as well as near Muizenberg at False Bay and Sea Point, a suburb of Cape Town. The Cape Hangklip has nice cliff walks. Whale-watching is possible in Walker Bay between June and November (► Baedeker Special p.318). Sandy Bay is Cape Town's nudist beach.

Garden Route

The safest places for swimming are Kings Beach, Humewood and McArthur (these beaches have lifeguards).
Jeffrey's Bay and St Francis Bay are equally popular amongst surfers and swimmers (choppy sea).
Mossel Bay has many sheltered lagoons (with calm waters) such as Hartenbos and Little and Great Brak Rivers.
There is a saltwater pool at Herold's Bay (south-west of George with its sandy beaches). Swimming in the ocean is completely safe.
Sedgefield (at the Swartvlei), Buffels Bay (near Knysna), Plettenberg Bay, Nature's Valley (east of Plettenberg Bay) and the estuary regions of the Bushman's River and of the Kariega have nice and sometimes long sandy beaches. Less suitable for bathing, but all the more attractive are Tsitsikamma National Park (steep cliffs with the mouth of the Storm's River) and Morgan's Bay (steep cliff coast).

Wild Coast

At the coast of the Transkei between East London in the south and Port Edward in the north there are sharks, particularly in the river estuaries. There are no shark nets! Good places to swim between the mouths of the Umngazi and Mzamba, near Port St John, East London, between Kidds Beach and the Great Fish River, near Kei Mouth at Kei River. Saltwater pools (tidal pools) can be found near Fullar's Bay (East London) and Kidds Rock.

KwaZulu-Natal   Along the coast of KwaZulu-Natal the important beaches are protected by shark nets and monitored by trained staff.
South of Durban there are particularly beautiful beaches that have shark nets between Port Shepstone and Port Edward.
The most magnificent beaches north of Durban are near Umhlanga Rocks, Umhloti Beach and Ballito Bay. During the holiday season they get very busy. Tidal pools are very popular here (particularly in Thompson's Bay, north of Ballito Bay).

Electricity

The electricity grid carries 220/230V alternating current. The plugs take three round pins. Adapters can be obtained in department stores and electrical shops. Hotels also loan them out.

Emergency

IN SOUTH AFRICA

▶ **Police**
Tel. 10111
When help is needed as well as for medical problems.

In the event of an emergency also: tel. 083 123 2345 (Tourism Info & Safety Line)

▶ **Ambulances**
Private patient transport:
Netcare, tel. 082 911 or
E24, tel. 084 124 (nationwide)
They only service private hospitals.

▶ **Johannesburg**
Fire brigade
Tel. 011 331 2222
Johannesburg General Hospital, Parktown tel. 011 488 4911

▶ **Cape Town**
Fire brigade
Tel. 021 461 5555
Groote Schuur Hospital
Main Rd., Observatory
Tel. 021 404 9111
The telephone numbers of the regional hospitals can be found on the first pages of local telephone books.

Etiquette and Customs

Clothing   It is customary to dress casually. However, when dining in an upmarket hotel or restaurant visitors should dress more formally. Women should pack a »little black dress« or something similar and men should bring a jacket and tie. On the beach do as others do; sunbathing topless or naked is only permitted in a few places. More ▶climate p.23, when to go p.184.

Diners do not look for a table themselves, but wait at the entrance to be seated. **Restaurant**

Tips are a significant part of the income of people employed in the service industries. A tip of approx. 10% of the bill is appropriate and up to 15% in restaurants when the service is good. Often restaurants have bills with a column called »gratuity«, which diners can fill out themselves; then the staff do not get the tip directly from the guest. After a safari it is customary to thank the ranger with ZAR 20–25 a day. **Tips**

It should be self-evident to ask permission before photographing people; this is particularly true in African villages. It is best not to take pictures of the military or of military institutions. In Lesotho, the royal palace in Maseru, all government buildings and the airport are taboo; in Swaziland visitors should be careful when it comes to the military, police, government buildings and airports. **Taking pictures**

Festivals, Holidays and Events

▷ CALENDAR

HOLIDAYS

1 January: New Year's Day
21 March: Human Rights' Day, anniversary of Sharpeville 1960
March/April: Good Friday
March/April: Easter Monday (Family Day)
27 April: Freedom Day, commemorating the first free elections of 1994
1 May: Workers' Day
16 June: Youth Day, commemorating the student revolt in Soweto in 1976
9 August: National Women's Day
24 September: Heritage Day, originally the Zulus' Shaka Day
16 December: Day of Reconcilia-tion, originally Day of the Vow of the Voortrekkers
before the battle at Blood River in 1838; also the founding date of Umkhonto we Sizwe, the militant wing of the ANC in 1961
25 December: Christmas Day
26 December: Day of Goodwill
If a holiday falls on a Sunday the following Monday is also a holi-day. Jewish and the various Asian religious groups have their own holidays.

EVENTS

▶ **January**
Cape Town, 1/2 January and the

two following Saturdays: Cape Minstrel Carnival, with a big procession on 2 Jan; Coon Carnival. Jazzathon (jazz festival on the waterfront)

▶ **February**
Cape Town: art and antiques fair.
Durban:
Kavadi Festival (Hindu festival)

▶ **March**
Jeffrey's Bay near Port Elizabeth: shell festival.
Cape Town: Cape Town Festival (arts and culture, street festival)
Cape Town: North Sea Jazz Festival
Durban: Fiesta and Harbor Festival: big festival

▶ **March/April**
Johannesburg: Rand Easter Show (biggest consumer fair in South Africa)
Oudtshoorn: Klein Karoo National Arts Festival

▶ **April**
Underberg, last week in April: Splashy Fen Festival (music)

▶ **May / June**
Comrades Marathon between Pietermaritzburg and Durban

▶ **June /July**
Eshowe: Zululand Show (big Zulu show with agricultural exhibits)

▶ **July**
Grahamstown: National Arts Festival (beginning of the month, ten days of theatre, opera, dance and jazz)
Durban July: horse racing on the Greyville race course
Ekupakuneni near Durban (end of the month): Shembe religious festival of the Zulu with tribal dances
Kimberley Steam Festival: the town presents its collection of steam engines.

▶ **September**
Johannesburg, Sept/Oct: Arts Alive Festival (www.artsalive.co.za)
Johannesburg, last Saturday: Gay Pride March
Haenertsburg near Tzaneen, end of Sept/beginning of Oct: Cherry Blossom Festival
KwaDukuza near Stanger: King Shaka Day Festival (on the last Saturday thousands of Zulus come together to celebrate their hero)
Stellenbosch, end of Sept/Oct: Van der Stel Festival (mixes the Food & Wine Festival with music and art)

▶ **October**
Morija (Lesotho), first week in October: Arts & Culture Festival
Roodepoort near Johannesburg, every second year (2009 etc): international festival of song and dance
Bloemfontein Rose Festival: flower festival in the »City of Roses«
Durban Tattoo: festival in the Scottish tradition with bands and fireworks
Pretoria: Jacaranda Festival (street festival when the jacaranda trees are in bloom)
Cape Town: Cape Craft Exhibition
Johannesburg: Jazz Festival

▶ **December**
Cape Town: Rothmans Week (biggest sailing regatta in South Africa, from Cape Town to Saldanha)

Flying

The north-east of the country is the best bet for long flights because of the region's stable weather conditions and good thermals. A number of gliders' clubs allow visitors to take rides, lessons and even charter a plane themselves.

Gliders

These two sports are extremely popular in Western Cape and Eastern Cape provinces as well as in the Natal-Drakensberg mountains. For insurance purposes hang-gliders have to be members of the Aero Club of South Africa (temporary membership available). There are no companies renting out hang-gliders; but clubs help out in this aspect. A bring-back service is essential. Visitors should under no circumstances fly alone and always take along water, a GPS and a radio.

Hang gliding and paragliding

Parachuting is possible all year round in South Africa, but the summer months of December and January are considered the best time to go.

Parachuting

Information on South African aviation law and the necessary conditions for receiving a flying permit in South Africa can be obtained from the Aero Club of South Africa (►address list). It also organizes ICAO tickets. Information on learning to fly in South Africa can be obtained from the Aero Club of South Africa, on the internet at www.learn-to-fly.co.za and www.flightschools.net.

Flying yourself

▶ INFORMATION: FLYING

► **Aero Club of South Africa**
Grand Central Airport
Midrand, tel. 011 805 0366
www.aeroclub.co.za

GLIDING

► **Soaring Society of South Africa**
P. O. Box 890
Sloane Park 2152
Tel. 011 789 1328, www.sssa.org.za

► **Magaliesberg Gliding Club**
Orient Airfield Magaliesburg
P. O. Box 190
Tarlton 1749
Tel. 011 440 8315
www.mgc.org.za

► **Soaring Safaris**
New Tempe Airfield
Bloemfontein
Tel. / Fax 012 361 1761
www.soaring-safaris.com
In Bloemfontein, the gliders' mecca, the seven-time South African champion Dick Bradley organizes everything for the perfect gliding holiday, either with rented equipment or the visitor's own.

HANG GLIDING AND PARAGLIDING

► **South African Hanggliding and Paragliding Association**
P. O. Box 1993, Halfway House
Centurion 1685

Tel. / Fax 012 668 1219
www.sahpa.co.za

▶ **Cape Albatross
Hang Gliding Club**
P. O. Box 12814
Mill St., Cape Town 8010
Tel. 021 790 0296
www.hanggliding.co.za
www.flycape.co.za

PARACHUTING

▶ **The Cape Aero Club**
Cape Town International Airport
Tel. 021 934 0234
www.capeaeroclub.co.za

▶ **Western Province
Sport Parachuting**
P. O. Box 7017
Roggebaai 8012
Tel. 021 509 2665

BALLOON SAFARIS

▶ **Wineland Ballooning**
64 Main Street, Paarl
Tel. 021 863 3192
Area of operation: Paarl

▶ **Bill Harrop's Original
Balloon Safaris**
P. O. Box 67, Randburg 2025
Tel. 011 705 3201
Fax 011 705 3203
Area of operation: Greater
Johannesburg/Pretoria; trips over
the Magaliesberg mountains

▶ **Airtrack Adventures**
P. O. Box 630
Muldersdrift 1747
Tel. 011 957 2322
Fax 011 957 2322
Trips over Pilanesberg National
Park, amongst others.

Food and Drink

Price categories
▶ p.9
There is no uniform South African cuisine. There is rather a whole spectrum of delicacies that draw on African, European (British, Dutch, French, German), and Asian (Malay, Indian) elements.

Breakfast
The breakfast served in most large hotels consists of a generous buffet with typical British additions (egg, bacon, sausage, baked beans, grilled tomatoes).

Cape Town
In and around Cape Town Malay cuisine is well-represented. Delicacies include bobotie (a casserole made of minced lamb, curry, fruits and an egg-based topping), sosaties (little skewers of mutton or beef with onions) and various kinds of bredie (stew with meat and vegetables). The best-known is waterblommetjie-bredie, which is made with the petals of a plant similar to the waterlily.

Durban
The most common cuisine in Durban is Indian, with spicy curries and chutneys made with lamb, beef, chicken, or fish. Samosas, small triangular pastry shells filled with meat and/or vegetables, are very tasty. If the curry is too »hot«, chewing the coconut flakes served with the meal will help.

South Africa has a weakness for meat, particularly for braaivleis, braai for short, for outdoor barbecues (»braai« means »grill« and »vleis« means »meat«). Large amounts of game, beef, mutton, lamb, and pork are barbecued; other popular options are boerewors, a well-spiced fried sausage made of beef or mutton (not to be confused with the far less good braaiwors, which should be avoided at all costs!) and pap (or mealie pap), a more or less dry maize porridge. Many of the hotels also serve

Ostrich steak with juniper sauce

braais. Biltong, in other words air-dried beef or kudu, springbok or ostrich meat, is a particular speciality. Don't be put off by this food's appearance: it tastes delicious. Generally speaking all of the meat from native animals such as kudu, springbok, impala and crocodile is excellent. Be sure to ask for your steak »medium rare«or even »rare« rather than »medium« if that's what you want, as South Africans tend to err towards the well-done.

Seafood The coastal regions are a great place to sample some delicious seafood. Among the specialities are crayfish, grilled kingklip (a cod species with firm flesh), snoek (barracuda) and perlemoen (abalone), a hand-sized shellfish from the Atlantic Ocean, and, along the Garden Route, oysters.

Sweets Popular sweets include koeksisters (▶Tip p.137) and melktart, a kind of cheesecake from »boerekos« cuisine (literally: farmers' food).

Fruit and vegetables South Africa's different climate zones allow it to produce a lot of fruit and vegetables, which are usually served fresh. Thanks to strict controls, there is no need to worry about eating fruit, salad and vegetables. Among the fruit growing at the Cape are grapes, applies, pears and Cape gooseberries, which are little yellow fruits used in cakes and jams, while in KwaZulu-Natal and Eastern Transvaal tropical and subtropical vegetables and fruits such as bananas, pineapples, papayas and avocados are cultivated. In South Africa green asparagus is eaten, but white asparagus is becoming more popular.

Drinks The tap water can be drunk without hesitation; the water at the Cape is among of the best in the world. One of the mineral waters is Skoonspruit (»clean spring«), which is the best-known brand. The higher temperatures mean people here like to enjoy a glass of iced water with their meal. The beers brewed here under licence (Lion, Black Label, Castle, Amstel, Carlsberg) are all good; Windhoek beer

An autumnal vineyard near Stellenbosch

WINE AT THE CAPE

If South African wines have a firm place on our supermarket shelves, this is a development of the past thirty years. However, viticulture at the Cape looks back on a history of more than 300 years.

For a long time South African viticulture suffered from the low demand for high-quality table wines. The most famous wine was the legendary Constantia, a Muscat wine that the royal courts of Europe preferred even to Yquem, Tokay and Madeira in the early 19th century. England, the most important export market, was more interested in Cape sherry than in table wine, and the South Africans themselves were the world's thirstiest brandy drinkers. Only gradually did new conditions lead to a qualitative leap, and since the mid-1970s South Africa has taken its place amongst the world's leading wine-producing nations.

Some history

Napoleon loved wine from the Cape, and South African Muscadel made his banishment to St Helena a little easier to bear. Cape wines were top of the list for the Prussian king Frederick the Great. Bismarck, too, valued them. Thus it does seem a little surprising that South Africa has only recently started to love its own wines. Grapes have been grown there for more than 300 years after all. Jan van Riebeeck, who under orders from the Dutch East India Company (VOC) set up the first permanent white settlement on the Cape in 1652, had vine cuttings sent to him, which he received in 1654; unfortunately they had not been properly transported. In the following year the settlement had more luck with French, German, Spanish and Bohemian vines, and in 1659 South African wine was harvested for the first time: 15 litres of French Muscadel grapes. On 2 February 1659 Riebeeck wrote in his diary: »Today, praise the Lord, was the first day wine was pressed from Cape grapes.« It was said to have been really quite bad, because amongst the first settlers there was no-one with any wine-making experience. Professional viticulture at the Cape only began after the future governor of the VOC settlement, Simon van der Stel, founded Stellenbosch in the fertile, sunny valley east of Cape Town in 1679 and his vineyard Constantia in 1685, where he had 100,000 vines planted. The Huguenots, who were expelled from France and settled in

Franschhoek between 1688 and 1690, advanced South Africa's wine-growing efforts even more, as did the German Hendrik Cloete on Groot Constantia from 1778 onwards. Towards the end of the 19th century South Africa was attacked by phylloxera, but with resistant American rootstock the old level of production was achieved again by 1918. That same year a wine-growers' co-operative, the »Kooperatiewe Wijnbouwers Vereniging van Zuid-Afrika« (KWV), was founded with its headquarters in Paarl. 1999 was another memorable date: it was the year New Beginnings, the first vineyard run by blacks, successfully launched its first wine on to the market.

Some figures

South Africa is the tenth-largest wine producer in the world today and with approximately 112,000 ha/277,000 acres of land dedicated to growing wine, it contributes 2.5 % to the world's total production. The yield is around 8 million hl (France: approx. 50–60 million hl), of which only around 75 % is used as table wines. 30 % of the wine is exported. Domestic consumption adds up to 7.9 litres per capita per annum (Britain 18, Germany 24 litres). Besides still wines, from simple tipples to heavy late-harvested wines, there

are sparkling wines from traditional bottle fermentation, fortified wines (in the style of port wine) and spirits (brandy). South Africa has some 300 private vineyards or wine cellars and 66 co-operatives, the latter producing 75% of the country's total wine production. The grapes come from around 4500 wine-growers, and the wine industry employs approx. 350,000 workers.

Wine-growing regions

The natural conditions at the Cape and in the mountainous country further inland are excellent. The prevailing westerlies make the climate cooler and moister here than further north and east on the other side of the mountains; there large-scale irrigation is indispensable, and the bulk of the wines produced are used for fortified wines and spirits. The growing season is eight months long; there is never any frost or hail, no rain in the autumn and only very few of the common vine diseases. Cool nights alternating with hot days are the norm, so that the plant does not use up the sugar produced during the day, thus storing even more of it in the grapes.

Thus the main wine-growing region is the area around Stellenbosch and Paarl. This is also where the country's largest wine cellar (Stellenbosch

Farmers' Winery) and the Koopera-tiewe Wijnbouwers Vereeniging (KWV), the former wine-growers' central co-operative, have their seat. Further north along the coast are the areas of Malmesbury and Piquetberg. There are no mountains here to stop the rain clouds; for that reason the land is not ideal. Nevertheless the region grows reds with a port-wine character and dry whites. Further north along the Olifants River, where it is even drier, wines could not be grown without irrigation. Table wine production is still relatively in its infancy here, grapes being tradition-ally produced for distilled liquor, grape juice and sultanas.

In the mountains of Tulbagh the conditions are more favourable. This is where the best white wines grow, light Steens and Rieslings as well as

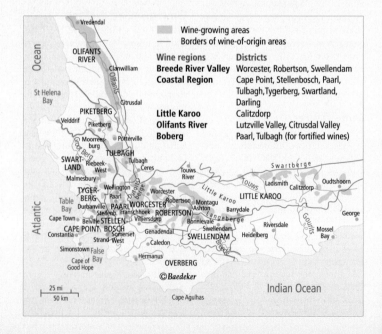

Wine-growing areas
— Borders of wine-of-origin areas

Wine regions	Districts
Breede River Valley	Worcester, Robertson, Swellendam
Coastal Region	Cape Point, Stellenbosch, Paarl, Tulbagh, Tygerberg, Swartland, Darling
Little Karoo	Calitzdorp
Olifants River	Lutzville Valley, Citrusdal Valley
Boberg	Paarl, Tulbagh (for fortified wines)

©Baedeker

25 mi
50 km

Matthewes Thabo, one of the first black wine makers, in the cellar of the »New Beginnings« vineyard

the strong basic ingredients for the (decreasing) sherry production. Tulbagh together with Paarl belongs to the appellation d'origine known as Boberg, which is reserved for »port« and »sherry« originally called Boberg. The districts of Worcester, Robertson, Swellendam and Klein Karoo specialize in desert wines and spirits, but the trend here is also towards producing table wines.

Wine of origin

In 1973 the »wine of origin« system came into effect, comparable to the »appellation contrôlée« in France. The origins of the wines are fixed in this system; every specification of origin, variety, vintage, vineyard and quality has to be affirmed by a state seal on the bottle neck. There are currently 93 private vineyards (estates) that produce their own grapes and process them into wine; »superior« on the label guarantees that the wine was pressed 100% from the grape variety indicated. These regulations have promoted new small businesses, whose success also en-

couraged the purchase of French oak barrels. In around 1975 the wine-growing businesses started to supplement their time-tested Cabernet Sauvignon plantations with other superior international varieties such as Chardonnay, Sauvignon Blanc and Pinot Noir. In 1992 the much-criticized monitoring of domestic wine production by KWV was given up, making the path clear for producers to plant their estates as they saw fit.

Grape varieties

The global trend towards red wine can also be witnessed in South Africa; while in 1990 red varieties still only accounted for one sixth of the entire cultivated area, this figure had risen to 40% in 2003. The »international« varieties saw a great increase, but the real South African grape, the Pinotage, also tripled its proportion up to 6%. This variety, first produced in 1925 by crossing Pinot Noir (from Burgundy) and Cinsaut (from southern France, previously called Hermitage in South Africa), combines the advantages of the original varieties and produces, after the difficulties of earlier times were overcome, a full-bodied, velvety, fruity wine with its own character. The best red wines come from the Bordeaux Cabernet Sauvignon grape (11.7% of the cultivated land); while Shiraz (7.7%) and Merlot (6%) have greatly caught up. In addition Cinsaut (2.7%, for a fresh table wine), Cabernet Franc (0.8%) and Pinot Noir (0.5%) are also cultivated. White wine is dominated by Chenin Blanc (17%), a grape from the Loire, which is usually called Steen in South Africa. Its naturally high acidity yields fresh, lively wines, even after very hot summers. Their greatest advantage however is their versatility. Steen provides everything: from smooth to dry table wines, from sparkling wines to »sherry«. Despite this fact its production has fallen by 40% since 1990. Semillon (0.9%) and Cape Riesling (which has nothing to do with the real Riesling; 1.2%) will most likely disappear, as will Palomino, which used to be used for »sherry«. Colombard (9.8%) is also on the decrease. The popular grapes are Chardonnay (5.9%) and Sauvignon Blanc (6.1%), while the »real« Riesling (0.3%) is still quite rare. Muscat d'Alexandrie (called »Hanepoot«, 2.7%) is cultivated for dessert wines. The Sultana variety (11%) is mainly eaten as a grape and used for making brandy.

KWV

The wine-makers' co-operative founded in 1918 was meant to counteract surplus production, organize sales and improve production methods; minimum prices and harvest quantities were regulated by law. Over time KWV however developed into a quasi state-run cartel, with which old Boer families secured their income and prevented free development of the wine economy; thus wine-growers were forbidden until 1978 to import European vines, and until 1992 new plantations had to be authorized by KWV.

Since 1997 KWV has been a large private winery, which mainly sells its wines outside South Africa; shares can be bought by anyone. The governmental task of monitoring is now done by the South African Wine Industry Trust, which is however greatly dependent on KWV in financial and personnel terms.

Wine tours

No visit to South Africa is complete without a drive through the Winelands, particularly Constantia, Paarl, Stellenbosch and Franschhoek. After exhaustive wine tasting many estates also serve good or even excellent food and have high-class accommodation. Information and suggestions for wine tours are available in the tourist information offices and at www.wine.co.za.

For further reading on the subject, see p.152

from Namibia is also popular. Beer on tap is rare. Where available, it is served in »large« (0.5 litre, which is slightly more than a US pint, slightly less than an Imperial pint) and »small« (half the size of the »large«) glasses. Bars usually serve what's known as a »Long Tom«, a bottle holding 0.75 litre (i.e. one »large« and one »small« glass). South Africa produces many spirits, such as brandy and the strong Mampoer and Witblits, the Amarula liqueur (made from the fruits of the marula tree) and the sweet Van der Hum tangerine liqueur.

Good alcohol-free choices are fruit juices in cartons (big brand names are Liquifruit and Ceres), the Appletiser and Grapetiser brands as well as the caffeine-free rooibos tea. The taste of the coffee here does not live up to European standards: it is roasted differently and mixed with chicory. However, acceptable filtered coffee is being served more and more. The top South African drinks are still the excellent wines (►Baedeker Special p.132).

Alcohol is only sold to people over the age of 18 and must not be drunk in public places (such as on the beach). Only a few supermarkets and shops sell alcohol, but usually a Bottle Store selling alcohol can be found right next door. Restaurants and bars that don't have a liquor licence allow guests to bring their own alcohol in return for a small corkage.

Alcohol

The choice of restaurants of any category is wide in the cities and holiday resorts. It is always best for visitors to make reservations if they wish to eat in an upmarket establishment. On behaviour in restaurants: ►Etiquette and Customs.

Restaurants

Health

South Africa's general hygiene standard is about the same as that in Europe or North America. Tap water can usually be drunk without hesitation (South Africa is considered one of the countries with the best water in the world). There have been increasing numbers of cholera cases in KwaZulu-Natal, Lower Umfolozi, Eshowe/Nkandla, Durban and Port Shepstone, so visitors are well advised to pay attention to good food-and-drink hygiene; this is also true of Lesotho and Swaziland. Current information can be found on the websites listed below.

Basic information

⏵ MEDICAL INFORMATION

▶ **International Association for Medical Advice to Travellers** (IAMAT)
www.iamat.org
IAMAT provides the addresses of certified, English-speaking, western-trained doctors to its members and advice on the necessary precautions.

▶ **South African Airlines**
Netcare Travel Clinics
www.travelclinic.co.za
South African Airlines (SAA) operates a travel medicine service with some clinics, the website also contains very good information.

Medical care Medical care in South Africa, including in hospitals, corresponds to European standards. Doctors are listed in telephone books under »medical practitioners« and hospitals under »hospitals«. Lesotho's remote areas are serviced by flying doctors. Good care should be taken to have a well-stocked first-aid kit, particularly when travelling to Lesotho and Swaziland.

Pharmacies Pharmacies in South Africa are also drug stores. They are called »Apteek« (Afrikaans), »Pharmacy« or »Chemist«. All of the larger towns and cities have an emergency service.

Health insurance ►Arrival, travel documents

Malaria Visitors wishing to travel to lower-lying regions in the north, east and west of Mpumalanga and Limpopo provinces (including to Kruger National Park) as well as to the coastal regions of KwaZulu-Natal north of latitude 28° should take precautions against malaria all year round; the other parts of the country are malaria-free. For these precautions and all other necessary medical measures (immunization against tetanus and maybe hepatitis A) visitors should consult their GP or a tropical doctor at least six weeks prior to the departure date. If visitors should get malaria-like symptoms despite having taken the necessary precautions (generally feeling unwell, headaches, joint pains, a temperature, chills) it is necessary to seek out a doctor immediately, self-medication could have dangerous consequences. African tropical doctors recommend not using the active agent mefloquine (e.g. Lariam) as a prophylaxis or for treatment, because of its massive side effects. The (very expensive) agent Malarone, a combination of the active agents Atovaquone and Proguanil, has fewer side effects. It should be taken 1 or 2 days before entering a malaria region until 7 days after leaving the area. Anyone suffering vague, even slight cold-like symptoms after returning home should have themselves examined for malaria.

Visitors should also protect themselves against bites from the anopheles mosquito, which transmits malaria, by taking the correct medication. Visitors should sleep under mosquito nets; otherwise the windows have to be closed firmly, the room sprayed with insecticide and/or the room has to have an active plug-in humidifier with replaceable insecticide discs. After darkness falls wear only light-coloured clothing with long sleeves and trousers, treat all uncovered skin with insect repellent. Pay attention to special treatments for children. There are smoke-emitting substances to keep mosquitoes away outside (but do not use them indoors!). Perfume, aftershave and scented cosmetics attract mosquitoes.

Mosquito protection

Bilharzia (schistosomiasis), caused by tiny flatworms, can be cured without side effects if treated early with medication such as Praziquantel (expensive!). Prevention is the best protection: do not bathe in standing water or rivers in bilharzia regions. Sea water and chlorinated swimming-pool water are safe.

Bilharzia

Hiking

The ways to get to know South Africa on foot are positively heavenly: mountains, plateaus, forests, bushland, grass steppes, beaches etc.

Giant's Castle Nature Reserve is a wonderful place to go hiking.

● OPERATORS HIKING TOURS

▶ **Drifters Adventure Tours**
P. O. Box 48434
Roosevelt Park 2129
Tel. 011 888 1160
www.drifters.co.za

▶ **Jacana Trails**
P. O. Box 95212
Waterkloof 0145
Fax 012 346 2499
www.jacanacollection.co.za

▶ **Ventures for Africa**
P. O. Box 3005
Cresta 2118
Johannesburg
Tel. 011 476 1517,
011 476 1437

▶ **Thaba Tours**
P. O.Box 1172
Maseru, Lesotho
Tel. / Fax (00266) 340 678
www.thabatours.de

The hiking opportunities are just as diverse as the landscapes; from easy day trips to hikes lasting several days that are anything but a walk in the park, with trained guides or without, past waterfalls or crystal clear streams and lakes; through game reserves with the opportunity to watch the animals close up; on to more than 3000m/ 10,000ft mountains; along never-ending sandy beaches, along the coast; with overnight stays in tents, huts, caves or replica gold digger houses. For an overview of the South African trails and further valuable information (including a bibliography), see www.hiking-south-africa.info.

Reservations The number of people setting out on the hiking trails is large and as a result accommodation is very limited; it is also best to be prepared. That's why visitors should make it the exception to set off unprepared; reservations are usually necessary and it is best to book a few months in advance, particularly during the South African holiday times. The section »Sights from A to Z« lists the reservation addresses and recommended reservation time limits.

Information

South African Detailed information is provided by the employees in the service
Tourism centre of South African Tourism.
Most places have a tourist bureau, a tourist information office, a publicity association, or something similar, where information on all kinds of topics is provided; Addresses can be found in the chapter »Sights from A to Z«. See also Embassies and Consulates ▶p.142.

TOURIST INFORMATION

SOUTH AFRICAN TOURISM

► **In South Africa**
Bojanala House, 90 Protea Road
Chislehurston, Johannesburg 2196
Private Bag X10012, Sandton 2146
Tel. 011 895 3000
Info Line: Tel. 083 123 6789

► **Australia**
Suite 301, Level 3, 117 YorkStreet
Sydney NSW 2000
Tel. 02-92 61 50 00
Fax 02-92 61 20 00
Email: info.au@southafrica.net

► **UK**
6 Alt Grove, London SW19 4DZ
Tel 08 70-155 00 44
Fax 020-89 44 67 05
E-mail: info.uk@southafrica.net

► **USA**
500 5th Avenue
20th Floor, Suite 2040
New York, NY 10110
Tel. 1-800-593 13 18
Fax 212-764 19 80
E-mail: info.us@southafrica.net

SOUTH AFRICAN PROVINCES

► **Eastern Cape Tourism Board**
King's Center, East London
PO Box 18373, Quigney 5211
Tel. 043 701 9600
www.ectourism.co.za

► **Free State Tourism**
Bloemfontein Tourist Centre
60 Park Road, PO Box 639
Bloemfontein, Tel. 051 447 1362
www.dteea.fs.gov.za

► **Gauteng Tourism Authority**
1 Central Place, Newtown,
Johannesburg
PO Box 155, Newtown 2113
Tel. 011 832 2780
www.gauteng.net

► **Mpumalanga Tourism Authority**
Mpumalanga Parks Board
Block F, Halls Gateway (N 4)
PO Box 679, Nelspruit 1200
Tel. 013 752 7001
www.mpumalanga.com

► **Northern Cape Tourism Authority**
187 Du Toitspan Road
Private Bag X 5017
Kimberley 8300
Tel. 053 832 2657
www.northerncape.org.za

► **Limpopo Tourism & Parks Board**
PO Box 2814, Polokwane 0700
Tel. 015 290 7300
www.limpopotourism.org.za

► **North West Parks & Tourism Board**
PO Box 4488
Mmabatho 2735
Tel. 018 397 1500
www.tourismnorthwest.co.za

► **Tourism KwaZulu-Natal**
Tourist Junction
160 Pine Street, Durban 4001
PO Box 2516, Durban 4000
Tel. 031 366 7500
www.zulu.org.za

► **Western Cape Tourism**
Pinnacle, Burg St. / Castle St.
Private Bag X9108, Cape Town
Tel. 021 426 5639
www.tourismcapetown.co.za

LESOTHO
▶p. 374

SWAZILAND
▶p. 484

REPUBLIC OF SOUTH AFRICA: EMBASSIES

▶ **In Australia**
Rhodes Place, Yarralumla
Canberra, ACT 2600
Tel. 02-5273 2424
www.sahc.org.au

▶ **In Canada**
15 Sussex Drive, Ottawa, Ontario,
K1M 1M8
Tel. 613-744 0330
www.southafrica-canada.com

▶ **In Ireland**
2nd Floor, Alexandra House
Earlsfort Centre, Earlsfort Terrace
Dublin 2
Tel. 01-661 5553
info@saedublin.com

▶ **New Zealand**
Refer to embassy in Australia

▶ **In UK**
South Africa House, Trafalgar
Square, London WC2N 5DP
Tel. 020-7451 7299
www. southafricahouse.com

▶ **In USA**
3051 Massachusetts Ave NW,
Washington DC 20008
Tel. 202-232 4400
www.saembassy.org
Consulates in New York, Chicago
and Los Angeles

KINGDOM OF LESOTHO

▶ **In UK**
7 Chesham Place, Belgravia,
London SW1 8HN
Tel. 020-7235 5686
www.lesotholondon.org.uk

▶ **In USA**
2511 Massachusetts Ave NW,
Washington DC 20008
Tel. 202-797 5534
www. lesothoemb-usa.gov.ls

KINGDOM OF SWAZILAND

▶ **In UK**
20 Buckingham Gate
London SW1E 6LB
Tel. 020-7630 6611
www. swaziland.org.uk

▶ **In USA**
1712 New Hampshire Ave NW,
Washington DC 20009
Tel. 202-234 5002

AGENCIES IN SOUTH AFRICA

▶ **Australia**
Embassy in Pretoria
292 Orient Street, Arcadia
Tel. 012-342 3740

▶ **Canada**
Consulate in Cape Town
19th Floor, Reserve Bank Building,
60 St George's Mall, City Bowl
Tel. 021-423 5240

▶ **Ireland**
Consulate in Cape Town
54 Keerom Street, City Bowl
Tel. 021-423 0431

▶ **Lesotho**
Embassy of Lesotho
343 Pretorius Street, Pretoria
Tel. 012 322 6090

▶ **New Zealand**
Embassy in Pretoria
Block C, Hatfield Gardens
Arcadia, tel. 012-342 8656

► **Swaziland**
High Commission
715 Government Avenue
Arcadia, Pretoria 0083
Tel. 012 344 1910

► **UK**
Consulate in Cape Town
Southern Life Centre

8 Riebeeck Street, City Bowl
Tel. 021-425 3670

► **USA**
Consulate in Cape Town
4th Floor, Broadway Industries
Centre, Foreshore
Tel. 021 421 4280

Internet

In South Africa the internet is an important source of information. There is hardly any location, means of transport, tour operator, museum, event or accommodation in South Africa that is not in some way represented online. Doing some research with one of the well known search engines always results in a large number of hits. The section »Sights from A to Z« contains relevant addresses; the following section contains a compilation of further helpful websites.

Every fair-sized town (except for Johannesburg) has internet cafés or cybershops and many hotels etc. have internet access, including for guests' personal computers, some of them via WLAN.

Internet access

THE COUNTRY AND ITS PEOPLE

► **www.gov.za**
Website of the South African government, contains a lot of information.

► **www.anc.org.za**
Website of the ruling party, press statements, facts and figures, links to interesting sites.

► **www.gov.sz**
Website of the government of Swaziland.

► **www.lesotho.gov.ls**
Website of the government of Lesotho.

PORTALS

► **www.aarvark.co.za**
Good search engine.

► **www.ananzi.co.za**
Search engine for everything from culture and entertainment to environment, industry, politics and government, science, society and people to tourism.

► **www.iafrica.com**
One of the large portals with good travel information.

► **www.saeverything.co.za**
Everything to do with South Africa, including events.

▶ **www.safrica.info**
South Africa's »official portal«.

▶ **www.southafrica.co.za**
South Africa online, good portal.

SOUTH AFRICAN MEDIA

▶ **www.iol.co.za**
The *Independent* online: news, links to daily newspapers from all around South Africa.

▶ **www.mg.co.za**
Mail & Guardian, up-to-date information (e.g. events).

▶ **www.sundaytimes.co.za**
Sunday Times online.

▶ **www.sabcnews.com**
South African Broadcasting Co.

▶ **www.africaonline.com**
Current news, including about South Africa.

TOURISM

▶ **www.aatravel.co.za**
The South African Automobile Association provides travel information and online reservations for accommodation, comprehensive search engine.

▶ **www.coastingafrica.com**
Travel magazine for backpackers.

▶ **www.dining-out.co.za**
Very informative restaurant guide, somewhat cumbersome.

▶ **www.getawaytoafrica.com**
Website of the big South African travel magazine.

▶ **www.go204co.za**
All-round travel information.

▶ **www.go2africa.com**
All-round travel information.

▶ **www.hostels.com/za.html**
Budget hostels in South Africa

▶ **www.linx.co.za**
Links and information about accommodation, camps, hiking trails

▶ **www.places.co.za**
All-round travel information.

▶ **www.routes.co.za**
Maps for even the smallest places, basic information on all larger towns.

▶ **www.shellgeostar.co.za**
Route planner by Shell, with comprehensive information for holidaymakers travelling by car, such as toll fees and fines.

▶ **www.southafrica.com**
Excellent search engine.

▶ **www.southafrica-travel.net**
Good online travel guide.

CULTURE

▶ **www.artthrob.co.za**
South Africa's contemporary art scene.

▶ **www.museums.org.za**
Portal of South Africa's most important museums, with links.

▶ **www.music.org.za**
Everything about the current South African music scene.

EVENTSAND TICKETS

▶ **www.computicket.com**
Programme information and tickets for cultural events of any kind, from music to theatre to

sports, as well as information on the overland buses.

► **www.rage.co.za**
Everything about the scene and nightlife in Cape Town, Durban, Johannesburg and Pretoria.

► **www.sacitylife.com**
Event guide, internet edition of the renowned SA Citylife magazine.

NATURE RESERVES

► **www.ecoafrica.com**
Important information about visiting game parks, reservations for parks and nature reserves.

► **www.panda.org.za**
Website of Worldwide Fund for Nature for South Africa.

► **www.peaceparks.org.za**
Peace Parks Foundation: Projects and maps.

► **www.sanparks.org**
www.kznwildlife.com
►p. 156

► **www.acts.travel.com**
Guide for the game reserves and game lodges.

Language

Recommended book: B. Donaldson, Colloquial Afrikaans, Routledge (Great Britain).

Afrikaans phrase book

AFRIKAANS WORDS AND PHRASES

Pronunciation

Vowel pairs are not pronounced as a diphthong, but as two separate sounds. a, e, i, o before an ng, n and m are often nasalized, particularly when followed by an f, g, h, l, r, s, v, w or z: kans (kās), »chance«.

aa, ae	as in »grass«
au, ou	o + u
ee	as in »deer«
ei	e + i
eu	as in French
ie	as in »brief«
oe	u
oo	as in »pause«
u	as in French
ui	as in »how«, but pronounced in the front of the mouth
y	lym, between »lame« and »lime«

g, ch	ch as in Scots »loch«
gh	g
j	y as in »yes«
ng	ng as in »sing«
r	is trilled
s	ss as in »kiss«
sj	sh
tj	ch as in »church«
sch	sk, except at end of word, then: ss
-djie, -tjie	ky + short i

Important phrases

Good morning	Goeie more
Good afternoon	Goeie middag / Goeie dag
Good evening	Goeie naand, naand
Good night	Goeie nag
Goodbye	Tot siens
yes / no / maybe	ja / nee / ja-nee
please	asseblief
thank you	dankie
excuse me	Ekskuus (tog)
excuse me please	Verskoon my
you're welcome	Plesier
Mr, Mrs (address)	Meneer, Mevrou
When is (are) … open?	Wanneer is … oop?
When does (do) … close?	Wanneer word … gesluit?
What time is it?	Hoe laat is dit?
How do I get to …?	Hoe kom ek na (by die) …?
How long will it take?	Hoe lank sal dit neem?
How far is it to …?	Hoe ver is dit na (tot by die) …?
Where can I get …?	Waar kan ek … kry?
Where is …?	Waar is …?
May I have … please	Gee my asseblief …
Do you have …?	Is daar …?
I need …	Ek het … nodig.
I would like … (to have)	Ek wil graag …
Do you have …?	Het u …?
How much does it cost?	Wat kos dit?
I like that	Ek hou daarvan
I don't like that	Ek hou nie daarvan nie
That's too expensive	Dit is te duur
Don't you have anything cheaper (better)?	Het u nie iets goedkopers (beters) nie?
Do you have change?	Kan u geld wissel?
What is that called in English (Afrikaans)?	Wat noem 'n mens dit in Engels (Afrikaans)?
Do you speak English?	Praat u Engels?

I don't speak …	Ek praat geen … nie.
I can't understand you.	Ek verstaan u nie.
Please speak more slowly.	Sal u asseblief 'n bietjie stadiger praat.
Please write that down.	Skryf dit asseblief neer.
Monday	Maandag
Tuesday	Dinsdag
Wednesday	Woensdag
Thursday	Donderdag
Friday	Vrydag
Saturday	Saterdag
Sunday	Sondag

numbers

0	nul	19	negentien
1	een	20	twintig
2	twee	21	een en twintig
3	drie	22	twee en twintig
4	vier	30	dertig
5	vyf	40	veertig
6	ses	50	vyftig
7	sewe	60	sestig
8	ag, agt	70	sewentig
9	nege	80	tag(gen)tig
10	tien	90	negentig
11	elf	100	(een) honderd
12	twaalf	101	honderd en een
13	dertien	200	twee honderd
14	veertien	330	drie honderd en dertig
15	vyftien	1000	duisend
16	sestien	100 000	honderd duisend
17	sewentien	1 million	een miljoen
18	agtien, agttien	1 billion	een miljard

Phrase books and learning material on CD (at different levels) can be obtained from African Voices (3 Arthur Road, Muizenberg 7945, tel.021 788 3954, fax 021 788 3940, www.africanvoices.co.za). Further helpful books are P. C. Taljaard, The Concise Trilingual Pocket Dictionary English / Zulu / Afrikaans, Ad Donker Publishers (Johannesburg) and A. Wilkes, N. Nkosi, Teach Yourself Zulu, Hodder Education (London, book and CD).   Zulu phrase book

ZULU PHRASE BOOK

pronunciation

Generally speaking the penultimate syllable is stressed and lengthened.

a, i, u	as in German/Italian
e	before i and u like in »meerkat«, otherwise almost like the ea in »bear«
o	before i and u like in »door«, otherwise as »toss«
bh	like the English b
b	very soft b
hl	ch a bit like the h in »huge«, the air flows from under the tongue at the side (try voicing this sound together with an l silently)
j	j as in »judge«
kh, ph, th	like k, p and t in English
k	mostly like a very soft g. At the beginning a word stem (e.g. ikati) completely without any air flow.
ng	depending on the region either as in »hunger« or as in »singing«
nk	as in »thank«
p, t	p / t without any air flow
s	s as is »kiss«
sh	like sh in English
v	like v in English
w	as w in English
y	y as in »year«
z	z as in »zone«

Click consonants

c	put the tongue at the back of the upper incisors and pull it back, like the sound made tutting.
q	put the tongue to the roof of the mouth and pull it down quickly, to make a sound like a cork popping off a bottle.
x	put the tongue to the roof of the mouth and pull one side down as if urging on a horse
ch, qh, xh	like c, q and x with a simultaneously articulated voiceless h.
gc, gq, gx	voiced variants of c, q and x, as if a g were spoken at the same time.
ngc, ngq, ngx	like c, q and x spoken with a simultaneous ng sound as in »singing«. Generally speaking it is enough to pronounce the ng separately

Important phrases

Hello! Good morning/afternoon/evening!	to one person: Sawubona!
	To several people: Sanibona!
Good night!	to one person: Lala kahle!
	to several people:
	Lalani kahle!
Goodbye!	to one person, who is staying:
	Sala kahle!
	to several people, who are stay-
	ing: Salani kahle!
	to one person, who is leaving:
	Hamba kahle!
	to several people, who are leav-
	ing: Hambani kahle!
See you later!	Sobonana!
Yes	Yebo
No	Cha
Maybe	Ingabe
Thank you	Ngiyabonga
You're welcome	as a response to »thank you!«:
	Kulungile
Please	as a request: Ngiyacela!
Yes please	Yebo, ngiyacela.
No thank you	Cha, ngiyabonga.
Excuse me	Uxolo
You're welcome	Akunkinga
Mr, Mrs (address)	baba, mama
What time is it?	Sithini isikhathi?
How do I get to ......?	Ngingafika kanjani e-...?
How far is it (to ...)?	Kukude kangakanani (e-...)?
How long will it take?	Kuthatha isikhathi
	esingakanani?
Where can I get ...?	Ngingatholaphi ...?
Where is ...?	Kuphi ...?
Please could you give me ...	Ngicela ungiphe ...
I'd like to have ...	Ngingathanda ...
I need ...	Ngidinga ...
Can I get ... here?	Kukhona ... lapha?
Do you have ...?	Unayo ...?
How much does that cost?	Yimalini?
I like that	Inhle le
I don't like that	Ayinhle le
That's too expensive	Kuyabiza kakhulu
Do you have change?	Unawo ushintshi?
What is that in English /Zuli	Yini ngesiNgisi / ngesiZulu?
Do you speak English / Zulu?	Ukhuluma isiNgisi / isiZulu?
I don't speak any ...	Angikhulumi ...
I can't understand you	Angikuzwa

Please speak slowly	Ngicela ukhulume ngokunensa
Monday	uMsombuluko
Tuesday	uLwesibili
Wednesday	uLwesithathu
Thursday	uLwesine
Friday	uLwesihlanu
Saturday	uMgqibelo
Sunday	iSonto
The day before yesterday	kuthangi
Yesterday	izolo
Today	namhlanje
Tomorrow	kusasa
The day after tomorrow	ngomhlomunye

Numbers

Since in the Zulu language the expressions for numbers already become very cumbersome when they reach double digits (e.g. 69 is: amashumi ayisithupha nesishiyagalolunye), the English number words are generally used.

Literature

History and current affairs

Gwen Ansell: *Soweto Blues: Jazz and Politics in South Africa*, 2004
The author traces the origins of South African jazz and shows its political and social significance, highlighting the influence of such figures as Hugh Masakela and Miriam Makeba.

K. Chubb, L. Van Dijk: *Between Anger and Hope: South Africa's Youth and the Truth and Reconciliation Commission*, 2001.
Report about children and young people who were entangled in the war of liberation.

Fraser, Craig: *Shack Chic: Art and Innovation in South African Shack-Lands* 2003.
Illustrated with superb photographs, a fascinating view of life in the townships.

Meredith, Martin: *Diamonds, Gold and War: The Making of South Africa*, 2007
An account of eventful times: the four decades preceding the establishment of the Union of South Africa in 1910.

Stevenson-Hamilton, James: *South African Eden*, 1993.
Reprint of a classic: the story of the Kruger National Park in the first half of the 20th century, by the man who became warden there in 1902.

Sparks, Allister: *Beyond the Miracle: Inside the New South Africa*, 2003 An excellent analysis of the country by a distinguished journalist. Less up-to-date but still full on insights is Sparks' book about the history and attitudes of the different ethnic groups that make up South Africa: The Mind of South Africa (1991)

Taylor, Stephen: *Shaka's Children: History of the Zulu People*, 1995. From the time before the rise of Shaka up to the role of the Zulu people in modern South Africa.

Sampson, Anthony: *Mandela: The Authorised Biography*, 1999.   *Biographies*
A substantial work that not only describes Mandela's rise to power and his qualities as a politician and statesman, but is also an interesting portrayal of Mandela the man.

Mandela, Nelson: *Long Walk to Freedom*, 1994. Reprinted many times and also available in an illustrated edition. A highly readable autobiography that truly sheds light on the apartheid system. The humility and greatness of the man shine through.

Brink, André: *An Act of Terror*, 1992. A tale of violent resistance to the   *Fiction and* regime by the first Afrikaans author to be banned by the apartheid   *reports* regime. Further recommended novels by Brink are *A Dry White Season* and *Praying Mantis*.

Coetzee, J.M.: *Age of Iron*, 1999. A white women who is dying of cancer forms a bond with a vagrant who has moved into her back yard. The novel examines the dilemmas of white liberals living in the apartheid system against the background of violence in the townships.

Coetzee, J.M.: *Disgrace*, 2000 A university lecturer falls into disgrace for having an affair with a student. A brilliantly written and disturbing examination of issues of race, ethics and political correctness, set in a South African society that is overshadowed by violent crime.

FitzPatrick, P.: *Jock of the Bushveld*. One of the best dog stories ever, which has been a popular book in South Africa since its publication in 1907. The hunting episodes, adventures and encounters are based on true events.

Gordimer, Nadine: *My Son's Story*, 1991. The 15-year-old son recounts the love story between his black father Sonny and a white apartheid opponent and its effect on the family.

Gordimer, Nadine: *None to Accompany Me*, 1995. Gordimer portrays a woman looking for independence in South Africa after the end of apartheid and illustrates the loneliness of exiles returning to South Africa

Hobbs, J.: *The Sweet-Smelling Jasmine*, 1993. The impossibility of love between a white woman and a coloured man during the apartheid era.

Malan, R.: *My Traitor's Heart*, new ed. 1991. The author, born in Johannesburg in 1954, comes from one of the oldest Boer-Huguenot families in the Cape. He describes everyday life during the apartheid era with its terrible outgrowths, and attempts to explain racial segregation.

Paton, Alan: *Cry, the Beloved Country*, first published 1948.
One of South Africa's great works of literature, about a black priest who comes to Johannesburg to find his son.

Wildlife
Estes, Alden: *A Field Guide to African Wildlife*, 1996.
Newman, Kenneth: *A Starter's Guide to Birds of Southern Africa*, 2004
Stuart, Chris and Tilde: *Field Guide to Larger Mammals of Africa*, 2006.

Practical travel literature
The following titles as well as others of interest by the South African publisher Struik can be obtained from Amazon:
Guide to Hotels in South Africa / Guide to Guesthouses in South Africa / Guide to Caravan Parks & Camping in South Africa / Dive Guide to South Africa
A. J. Venter: *Where to Dive in Southern Africa and off the Islands* (Ashanti Publishing, Rivonia)
R. Suchet: *A Backpacker's Guide to Lesotho* (can be purchased in Lesotho)

Wine
Hugh Johnson's Pocket Wine Book. Annually published handbook with detailed chapters on South Africa: producer, year etc.
D. Hughes, Ph. Hands, J. Kench: *South African Wine*, 2000
J. Platter: *South African Wines*
The handbook par excellence on South African wine, published annually. Lists all of the vineyards, assesses wines, addresses and maps. Platter also publishes a travel guide (Travelling in Cape Wine Country). Both books can be obtained from the Wines of South Africa (► p.136).

Maps

Resources
The most important South African map publisher is Map Studio in Cape Town (tel. 021 462 4360, www.mapstudio.co.za).
Maps Unlimited (formerly Map Office) has all kinds of maps: 95 6th Rd., Hyde Park, Johannesburg, www.mapoffice.co.za, tel. 027 11 788 6399).
The Automobile Club AA (►p.177) publishes a good series of maps and street maps, including Lesotho and Swaziland.

Road atlases
Shell Road Atlas to Southern Africa, available in Shell petrol stations in South Africa.
MapStudio, Road Atlas South Africa (1 : 1,500,000), with detailed maps.

MapStudio 1 : 250,000: Garden Route, Drakensberg mountains, Kwa-Zulu-Natal, North Coast and South Coast, KwaZulu-Natal Midlands, Kruger National Park and Lowveld.
Maps Unlimited: official topographical maps.
KZN Wildlife (▶ p.156): trail maps 1 : 50,000 Natal-Drakensberg mountains

Larger-scale maps

Media

Radio and television are run by the South African Broadcasting Cor-poration (SABC), which has its headquarters in Johannesburg. SABC produces eleven radio channels on MW and VHF. SAFM can be re-ceived nationwide and has some interesting discussions. Apart from nine private stations there are 80 local stations. SABC broadcasts three television channels. SABC 1 mainly targets young people, the second channel broadcasts family shows, largely in Afrikaans, and the third channel mainly broadcasts in English with more intellectual programming. The American influence on South African television is apparent: there are many comedy shows and soaps.
The programmes broadcast by the station etv are all entertainment. The private station M-Net can only be received via a decoder and mainly broadcasts films. Visitors can choose between many interna-tional stations in almost any accommodation.

Radio and television

There are more than 5,000 newspapers and magazines in South Africa. The newspapers are sold on the streets in the mornings and also in the afternoons. International papers are available in the larger branches of the book retailer CNA. The weekly paper *Mail & Guard-ian* is considered the best newspaper in the country, it is connected to the British newspaper *The Guardian*; its website www.mg.co.za is always worth reading, not least because of the current event listings. Other weekly national newspapers are the *Sunday Times* and the *Sunday Independent* (with links to London's *The Independent*).
The other daily newspapers *Star* and *Citizen* (Johannesburg), *Daily News* and *Natal Mercury* (Durban), *Cape Argus* and *Cape Times* are more of regional significance; they are also of interest because of their event listings. The widely available *Sowetan*, which mainly tar-gets the country's black population, is worth reading because of its look at the social and political situation.

Newspapers

The magazines of interest for tourists are *SA Citylife* (published monthly, cultural events in and around Johannesburg, Pretoria, Dur-ban and Cape Town), *Eat Out* (bi-monthly, restaurant tips) and *Get-away* (monthly, suggestions for tours, activities and accommodation covering all of southern Africa).

Magazines

Money

Currency The country's currency is the South African rand (R or ZAR). 1 rand = 100 cents. Notes available in denominations of ZAR 200, 100, 50, 20 and 10, coins in ZAR 5, 2 and 1 as well as 20, 10 and 4 cents.

Foreign currency Every visitor is allowed to import and export 1,000 R in cash. No restrictions are placed on the amount of money brought into South Africa in the form of travellers' cheques or cash in other currencies, but it has to be declared on entering the country. It is advisable to obtain some cash in small notes and coins immediately after entering South Africa (currently the moment 1,000 R per person is advised). Rand are best exchanged back into visitors' own currencies at the airport just before leaving.

Travellers' cheques Visitors are recommended to bring travellers' cheques in sterling, euros, Swiss francs or US dollars. Banks and currency exchange services are the best places to cash cheques and exchange cash. Some hotels and shops also cash travellers' cheques, but the rates are not as good.

Credit and debit cards For amounts over ZAR 20 it is best to pay with a credit card, such as Visa, Mastercard or American Express, which are accepted by most hotels, shops, restaurants, travel organizations, car rental companies etc. (but not at petrol stations). Debit cards which are part of the Maestro-Cirrus system can be used to withdraw money at ATM machines. Credit cards should not be kept in the wallet and visitors should not let them out of their sight when paying. Only use ATMs in banks, and ignore any »help« offered in operating them. Write down the number to report a lost or stolen card!

EXCHANGE RATES

ZAR 1	=	US$ 0. 16
US$ 1	=	ZAR 7.80
ZAR 1	=	GBP 0.06
GBP 1	=	ZAR 15.65
ZAR 1	=	EUR 0.08
EUR 1	=	ZAR 12.04

Banks can be found everywhere from cities to small towns, ATM machines in every bank. In the larger towns most banks are open Mon–Fri 9am–3.30pm, Sat 8.30am–11am but in rural areas they often have shorter hours and close for lunch. The bank branches and exchange bureaus at the international airports are usually open around the clock.

VAT refunds The rate of value added tax (VAT) is 14 % and is usually included in the price. From ZAR 250 (around EUR 21/GBP 16/US$ 32) upwards foreign tourists can get a refund of their VAT if they are taking the goods back home with them. The retailer has to fill out a tax invoice, on which are noted: the number of the tax invoice, the name and address of the buyer and seller, the seller's VAT number and an exact description, price and VAT of the item(s) bought. When leaving the country (at airports, shipping ports and border crossings) visitors can claim their refund at the VAT refund counter. To get the refund visitors have to show their passport, the item(s) bought and the tax invoice(s). It is best to hand over a credit card to which the refund can be credited: otherwise a cheque will be issued, which involves a high bank fee when cashing it. The whole procedure (filling out forms, having the goods inspected) should be done a day in advance or visitors should set aside at least three hours (before check-in!) on their departure day. In Cape Town there is a VAT refund office in the Waterfront tourist information office.

Krugerrand are only allowed to be taken out of the country by visitors. Visitors buying Krugerrand in the international departures terminal at Johannesburg international airport will save the VAT.

Krugerrand

Lesotho's currency is called loti (plural: maloti; 1 loti = 100 lisente) and has a fixed exchange ratio of 1 : 1 with the South African rand. Rands are an accepted currency in Lesotho.

Lesotho

Swaziland's currency is called lilangeni (plural: emalangeni; abbreviation: E) and has a fixed exchange rate of 1 : 1 with the South African rand. Rands (notes only) are accepted in larger hotels.

Swaziland

National Parks

An overview of the nature reserves and game reserves can be obtained on the website of South African Tourism (▶p.141). More detailed information is available from the organizations South African National Parks and KwaZulu-Natal Wildlife; both of these organizations also have websites with a lot of detailed information. (▶p.156).

Information

Usually visitors can explore the parks in their own cars. Often experienced rangers offer stalking and hiking tours; in the private game reserves small groups can explore the terrain in open off-road vehicles.

Activities

All of the national parks have different types of accommodation, ranging from inexpensive rustic huts or tent camps to comfortable lodges. The private game reserves usually have accommodation ranging from comfortable to very luxurious (which is reflected in the price). Visitors wanting to stay during holiday times should book at least six months in advance.

Accommodation

▶ INFORMATION NATIONAL PARKS

▶ **South African National Parks**
SANParks
P. O. Box 787
Pretoria 0001
643 Leyds St.,
Muckleneuk, Pretoria
Tel. 012 426 5000
reservations: tel. 012 428 9111
www.sanparks.org

▶ **KwaZulu-Natal Wildlife**
KZN Wildlife
P. O. Box 13053
Cascades 3202
Pietermaritzburg
Information tel. 033 845 1002
Accommodation tel. 033 845 1000
Hiking Trails tel. 033 845 1607
www.kznwildlife.com

Fees
WILD Card

Every nature park charges entry fees, which are added to the bill when booking accommodation. Foreigners can also take advantage of the WILD Card, which gives its holders a 5% discount for accommodation and free entry into 20 national parks, 38 provincial reserves, five private reserves in KwaZulu-Natal and three game reserves in Swaziland for one year. The WILD Card costs ZAR 795 per person, ZAR 1395 for couples or ZAR 1795 for families. They are available in every park and many tourist information offices.

When to go

From May to August, which is the South African winter, the bush grass is short, meaning wild animals can be spotted and watched more easily. During the dry months from August to October the animals often spend their time near easily visible watering holes. From September to March/April the birds show off their colourful feathers.

How to behave

In the wild it is the laws of nature that count! Never leave a vehicle during a stalking trip. Do not open any car doors. All animals may attack suddenly and extremely quickly. The other regulations, such as those pertaining to speed limits and the state of the tracks must also be obeyed. Feeding the animals is strictly prohibited.

The »Big Five«

Elephants are most often seen in Limpopo province and Mpumalanga province, in the north of KwaZulu-Natal and Northern Cape and Eastern Cape province. The African lion lives in Limpopo and Mpumalanga, in the north and east of KwaZulu-Natal and in the Northern Cape. The white rhinoceros and the black rhinoceros live in Mpumalanga and in North West province, in the north and east of KwaZulu-Natal, in Free State and in Northern Cape province. The leopard's territory includes Limpopo and Mpumalanga as well as the north and east of KwaZulu-Natal and the mountain regions at the Cape. The African buffalo migrates through Limpopo and Mpumalanga, KwaZulu-Natal and the Addo Elephant Park.

Major National Parks

Location: in the provinces of Limpopo and Mpumalanga, approx. 400km/250mi northeast of Johannesburg; approx. 20,000 sq km/ 7,700 sq mi with eight entrance gates. Steppe and savannah landscape; all South African animal species, including the Big Five; more than 130 mammal species, around 500 bird species, more than 100 different reptiles and up to 1,880 plant species (including 350 tree and bush species). Hiking trails and car drives with or without a guide. Reservations: SANParks. Towards the west the Kruger National Parks changes into managed savannah, where private nature and game reserves are located as well as exclusive lodges.

Kruger National Park

Location: north-east corner of KwaZulu-Natal at the border to Mozambique, 470 km/290 mi north of Durban; 10,117 ha/25,000 acres. Tropical and subtropical habitats in the flood plain of the Pongola River, thick forests, bird paradise. Hippopotamus, Nile crocodiles, nyalas, bushbucks and both black and white rhinoceroses. Reservations: KZN Wildlife.

Ndumo Game Reserve

Location: north-west corner of KwaZulu-Natal, north of Louwsburg at the border to Mpumalanga; approx. 30,000ha/74,000 acres. Mostly open bushland; interesting riparian vegetation in deep gorges. Both black and white rhinos, giraffes, baboons, cheetahs and antelope species; more than 300 bird species. Reservations: KZN Wildlife.

Ithala Game Reserve

Location: KwaZulu-Natal, around 335km/210mi north of Durban on the coastal road; 34,644ha/85,607 acres. Areas with low thorny scrubland alternating with open, park-like landscape. Klipspringer, common elands, mountain reedbucks, waterbucks, impalas, giraffes,

Mkuzi Game Reserve

A close-up of family life amongst lions

both black and white rhinoceroses, leopards, crocodiles, hippopotamuses and 413 bird species. Hiking trails (the 3km/2mi Mkuzi Fig Forest Walk leads through a fig forest), car drives. Reservations: KZN Wildlife.

Hluhluwe-Imfolozi Game Park

Location: north-eastern KwaZulu-Natal, 270km/170 mi north of Durban; 96,000ha/237,000 acres. The two parts of the park, Hluhluwe and Imfolozi, are separated by an 8km/5mi-wide strip. The park's main part is located on the catchment divide between the White and Black Imfolozi Rivers. Smaller trees and woody thickets. Both black and white rhinoceroses (around a quarter of the total number living in South Africa) live here, as do red forest duikers and common duikers, elephants, antelopes, zebras, blue wildebeests, buffaloes, giraffes, warthogs, lions, leopards, cheetahs, spotted hyenas, black-backed jackals, crocodiles, baboons and more than 300 bird species. Hiking trails and car drives. Reservations: KZN Wildlife.

Greater St. Lucia Wetland Park

Location: KwaZulu-Natal, from the mouth of the St Lucia 58km/36mi northwards along the Zululand coast. The park includes:

National Parks and Nature Reserves

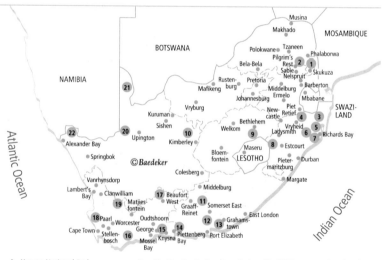

1 Kruger National Park	8 uKhahlamba Drakensberg Park	15 Wilderness National Park
2 Blyde River Canyon Nature Reserve	9 Golden Gate Highlands National Park	16 Bontebok National Park
3 Ndumo Game Reserve	10 Vaalbos National Park	17 Karoo National Park
4 Ithala Game Reserve	11 Mountain Zebra National Park	18 West Coast National Park
5 Mkuzi Game Reserve	12 Zuurberg National Park	19 Tankwa Karoo National Park
6 Hluhluwe-Imfolozi National Park	13 Addo Elephant National Park	20 Augrabies Falls National Park
7 St Lucia Wetland Park	14 Tsitsikamma National Park	21 Kgalagadi Transfrontier Park
		22 Richtersveld National Park

the St Lucia Marine Reserve (44,480ha/109,900 acres), which extends 3km/2mi out to sea; tortoises. Cape Vidal State Forest, approx. 32km/20mi north of the mouth of the St Lucia (113,313ha/280,000 acres), forested dunes along the coast with a glut of tropical plants and animals; many hiking trails. False Bay Park, on the west bank of Lake St Lucia (2,247ha/5,552 acres); hiking trails and fishing opportunities. St Lucia Park, an approx. 1km/0.5mi-wide strip of land around the lake (12,545ha/31,000 acres); subtropical coastal forest. Hippopotamuses, crocodiles, pelicans, goliath herons, flamingos. Hiking trails and walks; boat trips. Excellent fishing. Reservations: KZN Wildlife.

Giants Castle Game Reserve

Location: KwaZulu-Natal, 70km/45mi south-west of Estcourt at the foothills of the KwaZulu-Natal Drakensberg mountains; 34,638ha/85,592 acres. Bushman's River and Little Tugela River flow through the reserve with grassland, forests, thickets, and scrubland. 12 antelope species, amongst the 140 bird species is the great bearded vulture. Approx. 50km/30mi of hiking trails and bridle paths; great fishing; San museum. Reservations: KZN Wildlife.

Royal Natal National Park

Location: KwaZulu-Natal, 98km/61mi west of Ladysmith on the slopes of the Drakensberg mountains; 8,094ha/20,000 acres. Grassland, forested areas, proteas, evergreen mountain forest, thickets, fynbos and heathland. Black wildebeests, mountain reedbucks, deer, blesboks and klipspringers; amongst the birds are black eagles, bearded vultures, Cape vultures and jackal buzzards. 31 hiking trails and bridleways between 3km/2mi and 45km/28mi. Reservations: KZN Wildlife.

Golden Gate Highlands National Park

Location: KwaZulu-Natal, at the foot of the Maluti mountains near the border to Lesotho; 11,630ha/28,738 acres. Bizarre rock formations; sedges with bushes and tuberous plants. From spring to autumn lavish sea of flowers. Oribis, springboks, black wildebeests, blesboks, common elands, plains zebras, African clawless otters, baboons; 140 bird species, including bearded vultures and Verreaux's eagles. Reservations: SANParks.

Vaalbos National Park

Location: Northern Cape, near Kimberley. The park is home to both black and white rhinoceroses, buffaloes, giraffes, zebras, wildebeests, oryx and common elands. No accommodation.

Mountain Zebra National Park

Location: Eastern Cape, 27km/17mi west of Cradock; 20,000ha/50,000 acres. Mainly dry grassland with low-growing bushes, larger bushes and thick forests. Besides mountain zebras the park is home to common elands, springboks, blesboks, black wildebeests, kudus, duikers, steenboks and hartebeests as well as mountain reedbucks; amongst the more than 200 bird species there is also a colony of Verreaux's eagles. Reservations: SANParks.

Zuurberg National Park Location: Eastern Cape, 70km/45mi from Port Elizabeth and 16km/10mi north of the Addo Elephant National Park. Antelopes, mountain zebras, hippopotamuses, caracals, leopards, jackals and many bird species. Reservations: Port Elizabeth Publicity Association, tel. 041 521 3105

Addo Elephant National Park Location: Eastern Cape, 72km/45mi north of Port Elizabeth near the Zuurberg mountains; 14,754 ha/36,458 acres. The Addo bush is a bush made up of creepers, shrubs and smaller trees. More than 120 elephants as well as black rhinoceroses, buffaloes, and antelopes; at night red river hogs, old world porcupines and anteaters are out and about. 180 bird species, including goshawks, finches, willow grouses, francolins and little grebes. Reservations: SANParks.

Tsitsikamma National Park Location: Eastern Cape, between the Groot River Mouth (near Humansdorp) and Plettenberg Bay; 2,840ha/7,018 acres. This national park is 80km/50mi long and reaches up to 5km/3mi out into the ocean. The slopes are covered in evergreen forests and the mountain ridges and plateaus are overgrown with fynbos. Yellowwoods stand in the midst of heath and proteas. There are also ferns, wild orchids and many lily species. Visitors may see riverine rabbits, bushbuck, Cape grysbok, blue duiker, baboons and green monkeys as well as 210 bird species, including 35 sea birds. Hiking trails such as the 42km/26mi Otter Trail (reservations necessary, at least six months in advance). Reservations: SANParks.

Wilderness National Park Location: Western Cape, between Knysna and George, between Goukamma Nature Reserve in the east and Touw River in the west; 10,6000ha/26,200 acres. The area contains the mouth of the Touw River, known as Wilderness Lagoon, as well as Serpentine, Eilandvlei, Langvlei, Rondevlei, Swartvlei and Knysna Lagoon (»vlei« = »marshy area«). It is home to Cape clawless otters, many bat species, antelopes, sea birds, coastal birds and forest birds; the park is one of the most species-rich sea bird reserves in South Africa. Swartvlei also has good fishing opportunities. Reservations: SANParks.

Twilight at Umkhaya Lodge after an eventful day

Bontebok National Park: Location: Western Cape, 7km/4.5mi southeast of Swellendam; 3,236ha/7,996 acres. Diverse vegetation, in spring the landscape is transformed into a colourful sea of flowers. Bonteboks, roe deer, Cape grysboks, mountain zebras, steenboks, common duikers and almost 200 bird species. Fishing in the Breede River; two short hiking trails. Reservations: SANParks.

Location: Western and Northern Cape, north of Beaufort West; 32,792ha/81,031 acres. Flat hills and open plains with many tree species, perennial grasses, bushes and scrubs. 50 small and large mammal species, including mountain zebras, oryx antelopes, South African hartebeests, black wildebeests and springboks. Hiking trails; car drives. Reservations: SANParks. *Karoo National Park*

Location: Western Cape; Langebaan, around 100km/60mi north of Cape Town; 32,494ha/80,294 acres with an almost 30km/20mi-long beach. The Langebaan lagoon south of Saldanha bay is one of the big wetland biotopes and one of the most important bird sanctuaries in the world. In spring masses of flowers from the aster family, gazanias, dollar bushes and mesembryanthemums; cormorants, sea gulls, sandpipers and flamingos populate the lagoon. A stopover for many migratory birds from the Arctic. Part of the park is open to water sports; another part is only accessed by boat, and the rest is off limits. Boat trips; hiking trails (route suggestions can be obtained from the Geelbek environment centre). Reservations: SANParks. *West Coast National Park*

Location: Northern Cape, 95km/58mi south of Calvinia; 27,604ha/68,211 acres. Karoo vegetation; no tourist facilities. *Tankwa Karoo National Park*

Location: Northern Cape, on the Orange River 120km/75mi west of Upington; approx. 88,000ha/217,000 acres. The main attraction is the impressive waterfalls. Rich flora; typical is the strange kokerboom (an aloe species). Black rhinoceroses, common elands, baboons and small antelope species, particularly klipspringers. Hiking trails. Reservations: SANParks. *Augrabies Falls National Park*

Location: Northern Cape, in the north-west of South Africa, with large areas in Botswana and Namibia; South African part 959,103ha/2,369,995 acres. Semi-desert. The area between the dried-up river beds of Nossob and Auob is shaped by grass-covered Kalahari dunes. The game mostly lives along the river channels: large herds of blue wildebeests, oryx and common elands; smaller groups of South African hartebeests, steenboks and duikers; Kalahari lions, cheetahs, leopards, African wild dogs, spotted and brown hyenas, numerous smaller mammal species and 215 bird species. Reservations: SANParks. *Kgalagadi Transfrontier Park*

Location: Northern Cape; 162,445ha/401,410 acres. Mountain desert; mountains, gorges, succulents and endemic flora. Numerous bird species, otherwise a reduced fauna. In order not to threaten the sensitive ecosystem tourism is limited in this park. A tour needs to be well-prepared. *Richtersveld National Park*

Nightlife

All of the larger towns and cities have a countless number of night-clubs, jazz bars, cabarets and casinos; the chapter »Arts and Culture« lists some tips for Johannesburg and Cape Town under »Music, Theatre, Dance«. In smaller towns the nightlife is more or less limited to eating out; there is not much going on except in the hotel bars. ► Theatre, Opera, Concerts.

Sun City ► ►Sun City, two and a half hours' drive from Johannesburg, is a real entertainment mecca. This huge holiday park built in the former Bophuthatswana homeland in order to circumvent South Africa's strict racial, gambling and alcohol laws has casinos, vaudeville shows and a large concert hall.

Personal Safety

People who have travelled to South Africa have widely differing experiences: there are reports of being robbed in Cape Town in broad daylight despite having taken precautions, and also reports that visitors did not even feel threatened in Johannesburg. But even the latter reports stress that it is not possible to move around in South Africa without hesitation and in a manner that is usual at home. The crime rate remains high, although mostly in areas tourists rarely venture into. However, white South Africans tend to exaggerate the objective dangers. Many houses, even entire districts are strongly fortified and guarded. Some private individuals also carry weapons in public. The cities (including Johannesburg) have become a lot safer, at least during the day, since the centres have been monitored by video surveillance and private security companies. Paranoid fears are unnecessary, but visitors should still be realistic about the fact that there are risks.

How to behave   Generally speaking it is best to be careful. It is advisable to ask about the situation in tourist information centres and hotels etc. Big cities in particular (mainly in Johannesburg but also in »white« Cape Town) demand that certain personal safety rules are followed.
Avoid wearing expensive and conspicuous clothes. Only bring the bare essentials when it comes to money, papers, credit cards etc; don't openly carry a camera. It is good, if attacked, to be able to give some money away. After dark visitors should not go out on foot (use a taxi for evening visits to the restaurants, theatres or cinemas) and in the inner city of Johannesburg it is best not to go out on foot during the daytime either.
Keep all valuables and documents in the hotel safe. Always lock the room door even when in the room. When leaving the hotel, ask for directions and let the hotel know at what time you expect to be back.

When driving in a car, stow everything in the boot, close the windows in the cities (this is one of the reasons air conditioning is a good idea; it is not fun driving around in the heat with closed windows) and lock the doors. It is best to avoid driving at night, both in the towns and cities (take a taxi instead) or in the prairie. Red traffic lights can be used to ambush a car; in threatening situations leave the scene, if necessary by driving forwards through a red light (this is legal). Never pick up hitch-hikers and do not hitch-hike yourself, even though this is a common thing for South Africans to do.

Never, not even on the beach, leave valuables unattended. Attach car keys to your swimwear with a safety pin.

In the event of a threat remain calm and do not put up a fight. Assume the assailant has a weapon. Always bear in mind: material losses can be replaced!

Certain risks also exist in Transkei, the eastern part of Eastern Cape province, between East London and Port Shepstone (▶travel destinations, Umtata). Here visitors should not drive at night and should leave beaches while it is still light.

Transkei

▶p.182.

Parking

Photography

Photographers who do not use digital cameras will find purchasing films much more expensive in South Africa than in Europe and North America, though the films are somewhat less expensive to develop. Every shopping centre has a one-hour developing service. For photographs of animals, particularly those taken with a telephoto lens, it is best to use light-sensitive films with minimum 200 ASA, and in situations with unfavourable light conditions 400 ASA. Dust-proof containers and cleaning materials are a must for all cameras.

For your information

▶Etiquette and Customs

How to behave

Post · Telecommunication

Most post offices are open Mon–Fri 8am–4.30pm, Sa 8am–noon, with a lunch break 1–2pm (except in the main branches in some cities).

Post offices

Stamps can only be bought in post offices. Postage (for airmail) to overseas destinations is ZAR 3.80 for a postcard; letters start at ZAR

Sending mail

▶ INTERNATIONAL DIALLING CODES

▶ **From South Africa**
to Australia tel. 09 61
to Ireland tel. 09 353
to UK tel. 00 44
to USA and Canada tel. 09 1
to Lesotho tel. 09 266

to Swaziland tel. 09 268

▶ **To Africa**
South Africa tel. 00 27
Lesotho tel. 00 266
Swaziland tel. 00 268

4.50. Letters take about one week, but if you forget the airmail stickers, it will take four weeks. The postboxes are red and usually in the form of pillar-boxes.

Telephone numbers in South Africa
South African telephone numbers have ten digits, i.e. the regional code always has to be dialled. For example, anyone making a call from Cape Town to another place in Cape Town has to dial »021« ahead of the number. When calling a South African number from outside the country the zero of the regional code is not dialled. Numbers beginning with 0800 are free. Telephone information tel. 10203.

Phone booths and phone cards
Telephone booths marked as »international« can be used to call anywhere in the world with a phone card. Phone cards worth ZAR 10, 20, 50 and 100 can be bought in supermarkets, newsagents, petrol stations, bookshops and post offices.

Landline prices
A local call costs ZAR 0.40 per minute, a long-distance call ZAR 0.90 per minute; a call to Europe costs ZAR 2–2.50 per minute. Slightly cheaper rates in effect Mon–Fri 7pm–7am (inland) and 8pm–8am (calls to other countries) as well as from Friday evenings to Monday mornings. Hotels charge around twice as much.

Mobile phones
South Africa uses the GSM digital system and has a good coverage for mobile phones. The most important providers are MTN, Vodacom and Cell C. Visitors can use their own mobile phone if this was cleared for roaming in South Africa.
Those who want to use their mobile phone a lot can do this the cheapest if they rent a mobile phone (cell phone) in South Africa; some car rental places also offer these.

Prices and Discounts

Price levels
Even though the rand has become stronger, holidaying in South Africa is still fairly easy on the wallet; one rand is worth approx. GBP

HOW MUCH DOES IT COST?

Simple double room	Simple meal	3-course menu	Mineral water	Cup of coffee
from R200	from R25	from R80	R8 – 10	R6 – 8

0.06/US-\$ 0.12/EUR 0.08. Accommodation, food and transport are all equally inexpensive. Limited to the bare necessities approx. ZAR 250 per person per day will be enough (excluding transport); ZAR 400–500 per person will pay for good mid-range accommodation and a good dinner including wine; a meal in a luxury restaurant in Cape Town will rarely cost more than ZAR 300. The private lodges on the other hand are expensive and will set you back around ZAR 2000–7000 a day, all inclusive, sometimes even up to ZAR 10,000 a day.

Hotels in the well-frequented holiday towns and regions charge less outside the peak season (particularly in the winter season), when staying at least three days as well as during the week or the weekend depending on whether the clientele is mainly business travellers or tourists. Asking about discounts is often worthwhile. Many hotels offer special rates, particularly Protea Hotels (www.protea-hotels.co.za), Southern Sun (www.southernsun.com), City Lodge (www.city-lodge.co.za) and Sun International (www.sun-international.com). The cheapest types of accommodation are backpacker hostels and self-catering facilities as well as campsites. Children can stay in their parents' room (for example) either free or at a reduced rate. VAT is refunded ►money. *Ways to save*

Shopping

Opening hours are not fixed. Usually shops are open Mon–Fri 9am–5pm, Sat 8am–1pm. In smaller towns shops close for lunch (1–2pm). Most small stores are closed on Monday mornings. Many large shopping centres, supermarkets, greengrocer's and bookshops only close at 6pm, including on Saturdays. A number of shopping malls also open on Sunday mornings. *Opening hours*

Be aware that many of the plant and animal species are threatened by extinction. According to CITES, the Convention on International Trade in Endangered Species of Wild Flora and Fauna, of 1975, a *Note on animal welfare*

The African Market in Cape Town has a huge selection (Heerengracht 19).

large number of endangered animal and plant species or products made from them must not be imported at all or only with a certificate. The list of prohibited animals/products includes: all spotted cats, all rhinoceroses, various turtle species (including all sea turtles), several crocodile species and boas as well as orchid and aloe species, elephants (including ivory!), two of the three zebra species living in South Africa, but also bonteboks and scimitar oryx, cycads and tree ferns etc. Violations are punished with severe fines.

Arts and crafts Arts and crafts make for a very popular souvenir and include everything from hand-woven rugs to earthenware jugs and wood carvings. Since the various Bantu peoples have developed their own unique forms the range of arts and crafts available is very diverse. A large selection can be found in what are known as curio shops and at weekly markets in the towns.

The Ndebele are very good with pearls as well as copper and brass bracelets. Metre-high dolls, artistically embroidered from pearls, symbolize fertility and masculinity.

The Zulus are also experts in making pearl crafts; they make small rag dolls embroidered with pearls as well as containers made from pumpkins (calabash gourds) and covered in pearls. Animal carvings and sieves or grain baskets woven from reed or grass are part of their repertoire.

Typical Xhosa products include the inxhili (a traditional bag embroidered with pearls and buttons in white and orange), table cloths, the isibinquo (a three-quarter length embroidered skirt with a waistcoat and matching top) as well as the inquawe, a long pipe covered in pearls. The Venda people make pretty colourful earthenware pots; the Tsonga make mats from dyed sisal.

Clothes Visitors should pay attention to the origin of pearls and leather. Imported goods are noticeably more expensive, while local products on the other hand can be acquired for around 40% less than in Europe; Swakara reversible coats (Persian lamb on the one side, nappa leather on the other), products made from impala furs and ostrich and buffalo leather. The range of handbags and briefcases, suitcases and shoes is wide. Safari wear is relatively inexpensive in the shops in the national parks and in the curio shops.

Gold and gemstones South Africa is the land of gold and diamonds and many people expect these items to be much cheaper here. That is only rarely true, however, since the price of gold and gemstones in South Africa is also determined by the international market. It is however possible to find more inexpensive items if the jewellery (offered in a specialist shop) on sale is hand-made and was produced in South Africa, because the wages there are lower than in Europe. Imported jewellery costs almost twice as much because of the high luxury and import tax. Foreign tourist do not pay VAT (VAT refunds ▶money).

▶money, p.154; famous people, Paul Kruger.

Krugerrand

The antiques business is booming; Sotheby's and Christie's can also be found at the Cape. Most antiques (furniture, silver etc.) come from immigrants, the oldest dating from around 1820. Old jewellery in particular is quite inexpensive. The centres of the antique business are Cape Town and Johannesburg.

Antiques

The number of weekly and monthly markets is infinite. Amongst the best-known are the Johannesburg market at the Market Theatre and the Greenmarket Square in Cape Town. Bartering is not customary; visitors can try at the markets and in some curio shops (with a bit of nonchalance), but it is only a must on the Indian market in Durban, where the reductions on exotic jewellery, carvings, clothes or spices is already calculated in the price.

Markets

»Cafes« are corner shops selling newspapers, groceries, cigarettes, sweets, non-alcoholic beverages and a lot more. Often they are connected to a snack-bar; they open at 6am and close at midnight.

»Cafes«

Sport and Outdoors

Abseiling from Table Mountain or the Knysna Heads, bungee jumping from the Bloukrans Bride or a swing in the Oribi gorge, swinging from tree top to tree top 30 m/100ft above the ground (»canopy tours«), and mountain bike tours up and down mountains: the choice of modern pastimes is great.

Adventure sports

▶Baedeker Special p.168

Diving

Anglers can fish to their hearts' content in South Africa. In the interior fishing for trout is a national sport. Fishing at the coast and on the open sea are also very popular, since the coastal waters have a lavish fauna due to the two ocean currents that meet at the Cape. Information online under www.safishing.co.za, www.wildtrout.co.za, www.flyfisher.co.za., www.mcm-deat.gov.za.

Fishing

▶flying, p.129

Flying

*The coral grouper –
a »gem« of a fish*

DIVE BIG: DIVING IN SOUTH AFRICA

Dive with turtles, sea lions and thousands of fish species and drift through sunken ship wrecks, kelp forests and coral reefs: even under water South Africa holds true to the motto »a whole world in one country«.

Diving in South Africa is a widespread and usually inexpensive national sport. It is best to have good sea legs, however, because the ocean is often choppy and the boats available are small.

Coral reefs

Sodwana Bay, which is located in the north of KwaZulu-Natal, is considered the mecca of South African divers. The pleasantly warm and clear water of the Indian Ocean has Africa's southernmost coral reefs. More than 1200 fish species have been counted in the colourful underwater gardens. The spectrum is equally rich in the Maputaland Marine Reserve, further north by the considerably more tranquil Rocktail Bay. Marine angelfish, blowfish and boxfish are represented here, as are groupers and metre-long moray eels. Pleasingly often divers encounter sea turtles, which lay their eggs on the beaches between October and March, and are not very shy. There are also frequent reports of encounters with dolphin schools and harmless whale sharks that are up to 15m/50ft long.

Sharks and sardines

There is almost a guarantee that divers will see large fish if they dive at the reef of the Aliwal Shoal near Umkomaas south of Durban. Mighty mountains rise up there from great depths almost to the surface of the sea. Spotted ragged-tooth sharks, which can grow up to 3.5m/11ft long and are equipped with a scary set of teeth, have particularly helped to make this diving location world famous. Since these sharks are considered harmless, it is safe to approach them slowly, but divers should stay at arm's length. At certain times of year KwaZulu-Natal's southern coast lures divers from all around the world with the prospect of tiger sharks and large schools of hammerhead sharks. Mysterious wrecks round off the range of exciting underwater adventures. Another 90km/55mi further south divers can encounter spotted ragged-tooth sharks and Zambezi sharks off the Protea Banks, and with a bit of luck even enter barracudas and sailfish into their log books. The Sardine Run (p.201), which takes place almost every year in June or July and has its

Scared of sharks? Preparations for a cage dive

starting point here, promises even more of an adrenaline rush. A shoal of millions of sardines, united in one huge living mass, fights for survival northwards along the coast against sea birds, dolphins and various whale and shark species. The diving spots of Port Elizabeth and Mossel Bay, which are to the south of this area, are not quite as rich. Divers who think they have seen it all can experience a new highlight off the coast of Gansbaai, two hours' drive east of Cape Town: a cage protects them from the most fearsome predatory fish in the ocean, the great white shark.

Ship wrecks and sea lions

The waters around the Cape peninsula also have plenty of attractions. Besides the many shipwrecks, the great kelp forests and playful, curious sea lions make diving here an unforgettable experience. Rocky reefs flaunt an opulent display of colours. Despite modest water temperatures, every square inch seems to be populated by colourful sponges, anemones and coldwater corals, which in turn provide a habitat for sea horses, spiny lobsters and cat sharks. And those who still prefer to dive with spotted ragged-tooth sharks can do so by making a reservation in Cape Town's Two Oceans Aquarium.

Best time to dive

The best times to come for spotted ragged-tooth sharks at the Aliwal Shoal and the Protea Banks is between July and November. The months from June to September are ideal for cage diving with the great white sharks. KwaZulu-Natal has the most pleasant water temperatures of up to 27°C/80°F from October to March; around Cape Town the cold Benguela Current means the water temperatures are lower, somewhere between 8°C/46°F and 18°C/64°F. A wetsuit at least 7mm thick if not even a drysuit is recommended.

Hot tips

Eye to eye with the king of the predatory fish? Want to enjoy the ultimate kick from a boat or even from a cage? Rosemary and Jackie Smit from »White Shark Adventures« in Gaansbai near Hermanus provide this adrenaline kick. Feeling even more bold? Why not dive without a cage? Adrenaline junkies find Aliwal Shoal reef particularly thrilling during the months of April and May. Italian-born Walter from »African Watersports« guarantees maximum security: »The biggest danger is that visitors might miss this one-of-a-kind diving experience.« The addresses of the diving companies cited here as well as those of further diving operators can be found on p.170.

ADDRESSES: SPORT AND OUTDOORS

VARIOUS ADVENTURES

▶ **Abseil Africa**
Tel. 021 424 4760
www.abseilafrica.co.za

▶ **African Bikers**
Tel. Cape Town 021 465 2018
www.africanbikers.co.za

▶ **Downhill Adventures**
Tel. Cape Town 021 422 0388
www.downhilladventures.com

▶ **Face Adrenalin**
Tel. 042 281 1255
www.faceadrenalin.com

▶ **Felix Unite**
P. O. Box 2807, Clareinch
Cape Town 7740
Tel. 021 425 5181
www.felixunite.com

▶ **Hardy Ventures**
P.O. Box 2831, White River 1240
Tel. 013 751 1693
www.hardyventure.com

▶ **The River Rafters**
45 Kendal Rd., Diep River 7800
P. O. Box 314, Bergvliet 7864
Tel. 021 975 9727
www.riverrafters.co.za

DIVING BASES

▶ **Ocean Divers International**
10 Albert Road, Walmer
Port Elizabeth 6070
Tel. 041 581 5121
www.odipe.co.za

▶ **Pro Dive**
Marine Drive
Port Elizabeth
Tel. 041 583 5316
www.prodive.co.za

▶ **Sodwana Bay Dive Centre**
Sodwana Bay
Tel. 035 571 0117
www.sodwanadiving.co.za

▶ **Coral Divers**
Sodwana Bay
Tel. 035 571 0290
www.coraldivers.co.za

▶ **African Dive Adventures**
Protea Banks
Tel. 039 317 1483
www.africandiveadventures.com

▶ **Wilderness Diving Safaris**
Rocktail Bay
Tel. 011 257 5200
www.rocktailbay.com

▶ **Aliwal Dive Charters**
Umkomaas
Tel. 039 973 2233
www.aliwalshoal.co.za

▶ **African Watersports**
Umkomaas, tel. 039 973 2505
www.africanwatersports.com

▶ **White Shark Adventures**
Gaansbai
Tel. 028 384 1380
www.whitesharkadventures.com

▶ **Two Ocean Divers Int.national**
1 Central Parade, Camps Bay
Cape Town 8000
Tel. 021 790 8833
www.two-oceans.co.za

▶ **The Scuba Shack Dive Team**
Glencairn (False Bay)
Tel. 021 782 6279
Cape Town Tel. 021 785 6742
www.scuba-shack.co.za

Playing golf in Milnerton near Bloubergstrand

Golf is very popular in South Africa. The country has more than 400 golf courses; the first one was founded in 1882 and golf is even played in Soweto (Soweto Country Club, 18 holes, tel. 011 980 2326). South Africa is a favourite destination for European golf enthusiasts, as many courses are wonderfully situated: with a view of Table Mountain (Milnerton, Mowbray), in the shade of old trees (Royal Cape, Royal Johannesburg), in sand dunes (Wild Coast), in the bush with wild animals as spectators (Sabi Golf Club, Phalaborwa, Malelane Golf Club). SAA transports golf equipment up to 15kg/33lb for free. Big golf tournaments: South African Open Championships, Lexington PGA Tournament (Johannesburg, January); Sunshine Circuit on different courses (February); Million Dollar Golf Classic (Sun City, December). Further information: www.golfingsa.com, www.golfinginsouthafrica.co.za.

►p.139

River trips in canoes or rubber dinghies are very popular. Many companies offer trips lasting up to six days. These river trips are generally not »wild«: no previous knowledge is necessary and children are also allowed to participate. Accommodation in lodges or tents, cooking over camp fires.

Diverse landscapes and the warm climate create ideal riding conditions. Countless parts of the country have bridleways, and many national parks organize expeditions on horseback. Lesotho, the »Roof of Africa« with its mountains reaching elevations of more than

3000m/10,000ft offers horseback trekking over mountains and across valleys on its small, tough, native Basotho horses.

Sand boarding High sand dunes are a popular substitute for the missing snow.

Skiing South Africa is not the destination that comes to mind when thinking of winter sports; those who are interested can look at what is available under www.snow.co.za.

Beaches ▶p.124

Surfing Surfing, including the current variation of kite-surfing, is a fashionable sport in South Africa and the conditions along the country's 3000km/1900mi coastline are fantastic. There is something here for everyone: small waves for beginners (Algoa Bay and Silvic Bay near Port Elizabeth); up to 5m/16ft waves for pros (Durban, St Francis Bay, Jeffrey's Bay, the estuary of the Swartkop River, Nordhoek near Cape Town on the west coast). The water temperatures vary greatly: the Atlantic near Cape Town reaches a maximum of 18°C/64°F, the Indian Ocean near Durban on the other hand a pleasant 24°C/75°F. There are many surfboard rental shops; visitors wanting to bring their own board should compare the prices of the different airlines, as the differences are sizeable. Information online under www.waves-cape.co.za, www.zigzag.co.za.

Tennis Tennis is very popular in South Africa; it is also part of the physical education programme in schools. There are tennis clubs all over the country and many hotels also have tennis courts.

Wind surfing The best wind conditions, caused by an area of high pressure, last from October to April: force 6 on the Beaufort scale. From April to August South Africa is usually in a low pressure area, which means less wind, but waves over 2m/7ft instead. Windsurfers love the speed and can let off steam on completely calm water in the Langebaan lagoon, 100km/60mi north of Cape Town on the west coast. Bloubergstrand is another well-known wind surfing area.

Theatre · Opera · Concerts

South Africa has a rich cultural scene. Western culture is available in operas, ballets and concerts (European standard throughout), African entertainment at dance events, music performances and plays. Tickets for concerts, plays, the opera and for the cinema can simply be bought as computickets online or in the ticket shops, which many towns have (and larger towns have several offices), usually in the shopping centres.

Computicket ▶

THEATRES AND TICKETS

BLOEMFONTEIN

► **Sand du Plessis Theatre**
Markgraaff St. / St. Andrew St.
Tel. 051 477 7771

CAPE TOWN

► **Artscape Theatre Complex**
D F Malan Street
Tel. 021 421 7695
www.artscape.co.za

► **Baxter Theatre**
Main Road, Rondebosch
Tel. 021 685 7880

► **Dock Road Theatre**
Waterfront, tel. 021 419 5522

► **Theatre On The Bay**
Link Street
Camps Bay
Tel. 021 438 3301

DURBAN

► **The Playhouse**
29 Acutt Street, tel. 031 369 9444

JOHANNESBURG

► **Alhambra Theatre**
109 Sivewright Avenue
Doornfontein, tel. 011 402 6174

► **Civic Theatre**
Loveday Street, Braamfontein
Tel. 011 403 3408

► **Market Theatre**
Bree Street / Wolhuter Street
Newtown, tel. 011 832 1641

PRETORIA

► **Musion Theatre**
The Aula
both in the university
Tel. 012 420 2315

► **Piet van der Walt Theatre**
Pretoria Showgrounds
Tel. 012 216 501

► **Spoornet State Theatre**
Church St. / Prinsloo St.
Tel. 012 322 1665

► **Breytenbach Theatre**
Gerhard Moerdyk Street
Sunnyside, tel. 012 444 834

COMPUTICKET

► **Call Centre**
Information and reservations
Tel. 083 915 8000, 011 340 8000
www.computicket.com

► **Bloemfontein**
Mimosa Mall

► **Cape Town**
Cape Town Tourism Office
V & A Waterfront Shop 6182

► **Durban**
The Workshop 1st Floor
Natal Playhouse Theatre
Gateway Shopping Centre –
Umhlanga

► **Johannesburg**
Balfour Park Shopping Centre
Park Station
Rosebank Mall
Gardens Shopping Centre

► **Pretoria**
State Theatre Box Office
Menlyn Park Shopping
Centre

► **Stellenbosch**
Stellenbosch Square

Time

South Africa is in the same time zone as eastern Europe (GMT + 2). During European summer time (daylight saving time) the time is one hour ahead of the UK, in the European winter South Africa is two hours ahead.

Transport

By Air

Airlines and arrival   South African Airways (SAA; ▶ p.176), its subsidiary company SA Airlink and SA Express, British Airways (Comair, www.ba.co.za), the cheap airline kulula.com as well as some small operators fly to the nine state-run airports and to more than 200 smaller airfields. Information is available from South African Tourism (▶ p.141) and from travel agencies. Hub of the international and national air traffic is Johannesburg. It is better to arrive at Cape Town airport since the entire situation is more familiar to Europeans and North Americans, and more pleasant for those who are new to South Africa.

SAA   Many SAA prices include a free inland flight, golf equipment weighing up to 15kg/33lb is free of charge. Ask about current discounts and special price regulations.

Flights · Blue Train

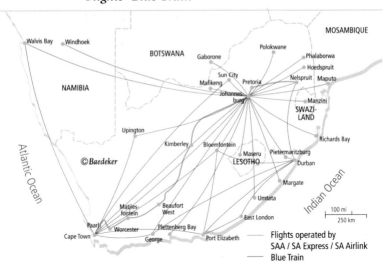

© Baedeker

Flights operated by
SAA / SA Express / SA Airlink
Blue Train

The kulula.com »no frills« airline is a very inexpensive option. It is a branch of Comair that connects Johannesburg with Cape Town, George, Port Elizabeth, Durban and Nelspruit, Cape Town with Durban Port Elizabeth and George as well as Durban with Port Elizabeth. Check in 30 to 90 minutes before departure. Reservations at the airport, under tel. 0861 KULULA (585 852) or online (www.kulula.com). In connection with Imperial kulula.com also offers inexpensive rental cars (with an outbound and return flight, no one-way fee, minimum age: 23), in addition there are some extremely inexpensive rates in a number of Protea Hotels (from approx. EUR 40/GBP 30/US$ 60 for a double room).

kulula.com

The South African Historic Flight company organizes one-hour sightseeing flights in a Junkers 53, a DC-3 or a DC-4 from Lanseria airport (northwest of Johannesburg) over Johannesburg, Pretoria and the Hartebeespoort Dam. Information at tel. 083 918 8336, www.historicflight.co.za.

Sightseeing flights

The small airfields, such as those in the national parks, are used by various charter companies and tour operators. Aeroplane safaris do not just limit themselves to South Africa, but also fly to destinations in neighbouring countries (such as the Victoria Falls for example).

Chartering aeroplanes
Safaris by aeroplane

By Rail

South Africa's largest towns are connected via the **Spoornet** railway network. The trains of the »Shosholoza Meyl« are very slow (for example, it takes 27 hrs from Johannesburg to Cape Town, compared to only 19 hrs in a coach), which always means travelling overnight when going longer distances. First class costs around the same as the coach ticket (Johannesburg to Cape Town approx. ZAR 500), second class is around a third cheaper; the very cheap third class is not recommended. There is no discount for return tickets. The sleeper cabin fee is included in the price, but bed sheets cost extra (sleeping bags are permitted). The first class has coupés for two people and cabins for four, the second class has coupés for three people and cabins for six passengers; the most pleasant and safest way to travel is in one of the well-equipped coupés. A restaurant car is available and passengers can also buy snacks and drinks in their cabin.

Spoornet

Algoa: Johannesburg – Port Elizabeth, 20 hrs, daily, except Tue and Sat
Amatola: Johannesburg – East London, 20 hrs, daily except Wed and Sat
Bosvelder: Johannesburg – Musina, 15 hrs, daily except Sat
Diamond Johannesburg – Bloemfontein, 15 hrs, Wed, Fri, Sat
Komati: Johannesburg – Komatipoort, 12 hrs, daily except Sat
Trans Karoo: Pretoria – Cape Town, 28 hrs, daily

Long-distance trains

⏵ TRANSPORT ADDRESSES

SOUTH AFRICAN AIRWAYS

▶ **South Africa**
Private Bag X13
Johannesburg Internat. Airport
Tel. 011 978 1111
www.saairlink.co.za

CHARTER COMPANIES

▶ **Kwena Air**
P O Box 475
Port Alfred 6170
Tel. 046 624 4102
www.kwenaair.com

▶ **Federal Air**
PO Box 12141
N1 City, 7463 Cape Town
Tel. 021 934 1383
www.fedair.com

▶ **King Air Charter**
PO Box 9, Lanseria 1748
Tel. 011 701 3250
www.kingair.co.za

AEROPLANE SAFARIS

▶ **Aero Safari**
Suite 456, Private Bag X1
Jukskei Park, 2153
Tel. 011 462 4521
www.aerosafari.com
This operator is something for people who want to be very close to the action, whether alone, with a pilot or professional co-pilot, in a small aircraft or on a DC-3 safari.

▶ **Big 2 Tours**
2 White Street, Cape Town
Tel. 021 689 6880
www.bigtwotours.co.za
This company offers sightseeing flights and whale-watching flights in small planes and old biplanes, departing from Stellenbosch.

▶ **Bingelela Private Travel**
P. O. Box 1033, Kloof 3640
Tel. 031 764 0288
http://bingelela-africa.co.za
Tours lasting several days in Kwa-Zulu-Natal with small aircraft and personal customer care.

▶ **Kwena Air**
▶Charter flights

HELICOPTERS

▶ **Dragonfly Helicopter**
P. O. Box 987, Northlands 2116
Tel. 011 219 5600
www.dragonfly.co.za

HOTEL TRAINS

▶ **Blue Train**
Pretoria Tel. 012 334 8459
Cape Town Tel. 021 449 2672
www.bluetrain.co.za

▶ **Rovos Rail**
Dock Road, Cape Town
Tel. 021 421 4020, www.rovos.co.za

▶ **Shongololo Express**
P.O. Box 1558, Parklands 2121
Tel. 011 781 4616
www.shongololo.com

COACHES

▶ **Greyhound**
Central reservations (24 hrs):
Tel. 011 276 8500
www.greyhound.co.za
Johannesburg tel. 011 276 8500
Bloemfontein tel. 051 447 1558
Durban tel. 031 334 9720
Cape Town tel. 083 915 9000

▶ **Translux / City to City**
Central reservations:
Tel. 011 774 3333
www.translux.co.za

Johannesburg tel. 011 773 8056
Bloemfontein tel. 051 408 4888
Durban tel. 031 361 7670
Cape Town tel. 021 449 6209

► **Intercape Mainliner**
Central reservations:
tel. 0861 287 287
From outside South Africa:
tel. (00 27) 21 380 4400
www. intercape.co.za

► **Baz Bus**
275 Main Road, Cape Town 8005
Tel. 021 439 2323, www.bazbus.com

RENTAL CARS

► **Avis (www.avis.com)**
South Africa tel. 0861 021 111
Johannesburg Airport
Tel. 011 394 5433
Cape Town Airport
Tel. 021 934 0330

► **Budget (www.budget.com)**
Johannesburg Airport
Tel. 011 394 2905
Cape Town Airport
Tel. 021 380 3140

► **Europcar (www.europcar.com)**
South Africa tel. 0860 011 344
Johannesburg Airport
Tel. 011 394 8831
Cape Town Airport
Tel. 021 934 2263/5/6

► **Hertz (www.hertz.com)**
South Africa Tel. 021 935 4800
Johannesburg Airport
Tel. 011 390 9700
Cape Town Airport
Tel. 021 935 3000

► **Imperial
(www.imperialcarrental.co.za)**
South Africa tel. 0861 13 1000
Internat. tel. (00 27) 11 574 1000

► **Rent-a-Wreck**
Apex Service Station
President St., Johannesburg
Tel. 011 402 43 91

**CAMPER RENTAL
COMPANIES**

► **Africamper**
In Cape Town, tel. 021 854 5627
www.africamper.com

► **African Leisure Travel**
Johannesburg
Tel. 011 792 1884
www.africanleisure.co.za

► **Britz Rentals**
PO Box 4300, Kempton Park 1650
Tel. 011 396 1860, www.britz.co.za

MOTORBIKES

► **Karoo Biking**
Loft 4, Five Howe Street
Observatory 7925, Cape Town
Tel. 082 533 6655
www.karoo-biking.com
Here visitors can rent BMW
motorbikes, go on tours from
afternoon expeditions to the big
round trip.

**AUTOMOBILE
ASSOCIATION**

► **Service and Emergency**
Emergency Rescue
Service Number
Tel. 083 THEAA (083 843 22)

► **Johannesburg**
Head Office, 66 De Korte Street
Braamfontein, Johannesburg
Tel. 011 799 1000

► **Cape Town**
Strand Street (corner of Burg St.,
opposite the tourist information
office)
Tel. 021 419 6914

Trans Natal: Johannesburg–Durban, 12.30 hrs, daily except Tue and Sat
Trans Oranje: Cape Town–Durban, 28 hrs, Mon departing Cape Town, Wed departing Durban

Reservations Spoornet trains have to be booked at least 24 hrs in advance (up to three months in advance), either at the stations or at Shosholoza Meyl Central Reservations, tel. 086 000 8888. Further information www.spoornet.co.za.

Hotel Trains

Blue Train The legendary and luxurious Blue Train (since 1901, named after its blue exterior) runs one to three times a week between Cape Town and Johannesburg/Pretoria (1600km/1000mi, 27 hrs); the Garden Route Cape Town–Port Elizabeth is currently closed. Sections of the line are open. The prices (from approx. ZAR 16,000 for two people) vary greatly depending on the season and the kind of suite (luxury, de luxe), including full board with excellent cuisine. There is also a dress code: during the day casual but elegant, and evening wear for dinner. Owing to high demand reservations should be made at least six months in advance.

A trip in the luxurious Rovos Rail is a real pleasure.

A trip in the »most luxurious train in the world« is a very special experience. The train, with lovingly restored wagons from the 1920 and 1930s, some of which are drawn by steam engines, offer all the comforts and excellent cuisine. The maximum number of passengers is 72, which are looked after by 14 staff members. Excursions and safaris are included. Routes: Cape Town – Pretoria (3 days, from ZAR 22,000 per person), Pretoria – Kruger National Park – Victoria Falls (2 days, flight in an old-timer from Pietersburg to the Victoria Falls); Cape Town – George (1 day), Pretoria – Durban (2 days). In addition there are some special trips such as from Cape Town to Dar-es-Salaam (Tanzania, 14 days). Reservations should be made at least six months in advance.

Rovos Rail

A comfortable hotel train for those who like to travel at less expensive prices and in a more familiar way. Choose between two 16-day tours »Good Hope Adventure« (Cape Town – Garden Route – Bloemfontein – Durban – Kruger National Park – Johannesburg) and »Southern Cross Adventure« (Pretoria – Mozambique – Zimbabwe – Victoria Falls). The price includes half-board and excursions (in Mercedes Benz minibuses that are brought along), depending on the package and the level of comfort prices range from ZAR 15,000 and ZAR 35,000.

Shongololo Express

Steam Engines and Excursion Trains

An inexpensive and popular trip amongst South African families is the Magaliesberg Express to the Magaliesburg Country Hotel at the southern edge of the Magaliesberg mountains, where passengers can picnic or dine.
On the first Sunday of the month from Johannesburg (Park Station, platform 13/14), departing at 9.15am, returning at 4.45pm. Information at SA National Steam and Railway Museum, tel. 011 888 1154 (only in the mornings), Magaliesburg Country Hotel tel. 014 577 1109.

Magaliesberg Express

The narrow-gauge Banana Express departs Port Shepstone and makes its way through banana and sugar cane plantations to Paddock, where a »braai« is served (Wed and Sat 10am, total time: 6 hrs.).
The excursion to Izotsha lasts a total of two hours (Thu 10am, Sun 11am). Information and reservations at Hibiscus Regional Tourist Association, Shelly Beach, tel. 039 315 7605, www.bananaexpress.co.za.

Banana Express

This narrow-gauge (24-inch) steam railway that runs between Port Elizabeth and Thornhill usually departs every 14 days at the weekend at 9am from Humewood Road Station in Port Elizabeth.
The trip lasts the whole day, there is time for a two-hour barbecue in Thornhill. Information tel. 041 583 2030, www.nmbt.co.za.

Apple Express

Outeniqua Choo Tjoe

Until autumn 2006 this popular historic steam train ran from George station to Knysna. A landslide close to Knysna caused serious damage and made a change of route necessary: the train now runs from the Dias Museum in ▶ Mossel Bay to the Railway Museum in ▶ George.

Departures:
April–Aug. Mon, Wed, Fri, Sept–March Mon–Sat 10am from George, 2.15pm from Mossel Bay;
mid-Dec to mid-Jan additional service 10.10am from Mossel Bay and 2pm from George.
Tel. 044 / 801 8288, www. onlinesources. co.za/chootjoe

By Bus

The overland buses are faster than the trains; they operate regularly between the larger towns. Tickets can be obtained from the bus companies and travel agencies as well as at Computicket (▶ p.173). For Translux / City to City book 24 hrs in advance, for Intercape 3 days, book even earlier during the holiday times. Translux and Greyhound offer special rates for frequent travellers.

Baz Bus

The Baz Bus is surely the most popular means of transport for holidaymakers and backpackers because it is the most comfortable. The 22-seater Mercedes Benz Sprinters connect Cape Town, Durban and Johannesburg. They drive to most of the backpacker hostels and passengers can get in and out where and as often as they want to, but it is best to book by phone as early as possible (this is usually possible from the hotel).
It is important to compare prices with other bus companies: if travellers are planning a long trip non-stop those other buses are clearly cheaper, but if visitors are planning on making several stops along the way the Baz Bus is cheaper. The drivers are a good source of information of any kind, and can also recommend accommodation.

Minibuses

Minibuses are the cheapest mode of transport and in use practically everywhere. They are the only form of transport in the places the trains and buses do not go to. Generally they are used in towns and between neighbouring places, but they can also be used to travel longer distances. The level of personal safety is adequate with the exception of Johannesburg; the main risk is posed by poorly maintained buses and bad or over-tired drivers. Minibus taxis are usually used by blacks and are generally over-crowded, and the storage space for luggage is also very limited; travellers with a lot of luggage should sit in the row behind the driver. The fare is paid in coins. If the bus is full the other passengers pass the money on to the driver and change is given back in the same way. When travellers want to get out they say »thank you (driver)!«

By Car

South Africa possesses a relatively dense and good-quality road network. The important connections are asphalted and the unsurfaced roads are generally okay to drive on. The national roads (N) range in their quality from bad main roads to six-lane motorways. Some motorways are toll roads.

Road network

Just like the British, South Africans drive on the left. It is mandatory for all occupants to wear a seatbelt and the legal alcohol limit is 0.05 % or 50mg per 100ml. Speed limits: 75mph/120kmh on motorways, 60mph/100kmh on country roads and 35mph/60kmh in built-up areas. Violating the traffic rules is an offence that is taken seriously; speed and alcohol checks are very common. No car is allowed to be driven without third-party insurance, which however need only cover personal injury. Talking on the phone while driving is permitted only when using the hands-free option.

Traffic regulations

South Africa is notorious for bad and reckless drivers, and the accident statistics are horrendous. Speed limits only seem to exist on

How to behave

PASOP VIR SEEKOEIE
_____
BEWARE OF HIPPOPOTAMUS

Beware, unusual road users!

paper. On the freeways fast drivers expect others to avoid them by driving over to the hard shoulder on the left (thanks is given by flashing the hazard lights). It is quite customary for overtaking vehicles to force oncoming traffic to avoid them. Despite the low permitted alcohol level, drunk drivers are no rarity. On narrow country roads people seem to assume that they are the only ones on the road. Travellers should generally take care in rural areas: since the fields are not fenced, livestock is to be expected on the roads; pedestrians and particularly children can appear suddenly. In certain areas the same is true for wild animals. For these reasons (apart from the reason of general safety) travellers should avoid driving at night at all costs.

Precautionary measures
When driving in sparsely populated areas it is important to completely fill up the car at every petrol station as these are often far apart. Take at least 2 litres/0.5 US gal of water per person. Bring work gloves, hand-washing paste, a safety vest, a torch and a first-aid kit, just in case.

Petrol stations
The hours of operation of petrol stations vary, but most of them are open from 7am to 6pm, while many, particularly those along the highways, are open 24 hrs. There is no self-service, the attendant gets a tip of approx. 10% for the services provided (such as cleaning the windscreen, and checking the oil and water). Petrol stations do not take credit cards, since it is not permitted to buy fuel on credit.

Parking
On public car parks beggars often offer superfluous or dubious services, such as waving drivers into the parking spot, guarding the car or putting the money into the parking meter. How you react in a case like this depends on your personal temperament and willingness to take risks. Some recommend looking at the small sum as a social service and an investment in their personal safety (it is best to hold back a portion of the fee until returning); others ignore the requests and stay in the car a little longer or notify the parking attendant. All of these problems can be avoided by making use of one of the (inexpensive) multi-storey car parks.

Automobile help
The Automobile Association of South Africa (AA, www.aa.co.za; addresses ► p.177) provides an excellent service, from information (maps etc.) to armed roadside assistance (AA Stand By You). Members of the automobile club can take advantage of the AA's service free of charge when they show their membership card. Others can become members for a month for a very small fee. ►Emergency.

Rental Cars

Car rental companies
International companies such as Avis, Budget and Hertz are represented nationwide, which makes one-way rentals easy to arrange

(however, sometimes a fee as high as the daily rate is charged to bring the car back); they also offer speedy service in the event of an accident or breakdown. It is definitely best to book from home: on the one hand it guarantees the availability of a vehicle and on the other hand the prices in South Africa are higher. The least expensive option is to take advantage of combination offers such as Fly & Drive. In addition there are many local companies, some of which have cheaper rates. Always be sure to check if there is no limit on the permitted number of miles, whether the price includes insurance etc. The minimum age is usually 21 and an international driver's licence is required.

Choose at least a category B car, because the additional space and bigger engine make longer trips more pleasant. During the hot summers air-conditioning is not a luxury. If the car has a petrol engine be sure to inquire whether it takes leaded or unleaded petrol. The »full petrol option« means the car can be returned without filling up the tank. Those wanting to visit a neighbouring country should have this noted in the rental contract so that the border control sees proof that the owner has agreed to let the car be taken out of the country. The subject of insurance is a sensitive one. When obtaining insurance it is absolutely necessary to read the small print. It could be for example that despite getting comprehensive coverage some damage is still excluded, such as anti-theft protection, or something similar.

◀ Tips for renting a car

Very cheap and unobtrusive and as a result fairly safe when it comes to theft. Rent a Wreck is a Johannesburg-based company that has existed since 1973. Their service is good and straightforward. (24-hr hotline).

Rent a Wreck

By Taxi

Taxis have to be ordered by phone or hailed at taxi stands. The rates vary from town to town. Generally there is a basic fee of ZAR 8 and an additional fee of ZAR 3 per kilometre. A fee of ZAR 10 per hour is charged for waiting. For longer distances it is best to negotiate a fixed price in advance.

Travellers with Disabilities

South African Airways (SAA) provides help for travellers with disabilities at all major airports. Many hotels, lodges in private game reserves, and most camps in Kruger National Park have adapted to the needs of physically disabled tourists. Wheelchairs and other aids can be hired in all large towns. The big car rental companies hire out cars suitably equipped for the requirements of the physically dis-

▶ **INFORMATION FOR DISABLED TRAVELLERS**

▶ **National Council for Persons with Physical Disabilities**
P. O. Box 426
Melville, 2109
Tel. 011 726 8040
Fax 011 726 5705
www.ncppdsa.org.za

▶ **Access-Able Travel**
access-able.com

▶ **Epic Enabled**
14 Clovelly Road
Fish Hoek
7975 Cape Town
Tel./fax 021-782 95 75.
www.epic-enabled.com
Organizes tours to the Kruger

National Park and other destinations.

▶ **In UK: RADAR**
12 City Forum, 250 City Road,
London EC1V 8AF
Tel. (020) 72 50 32 22
www.radar.org.uk

▶ **In USA: SATH (Society for the Advancement of Travel for the Handicapped)**
347 5th Ave., no. 610
New York, NY 10016:
Tel. (21) 4 47 72 84
www.sath.org

abled. The website of the national parks (www.sanparks) is particularly strong on information for persons with impaired mobility. Some gardens and other trails are also equipped for visitors with disabilities. The botanical garden at Kirstenbisch in Cape Town, for example, makes wheelchairs available and has a braille trail.

When to Go

A country for every season
Holidaying in South Africa is possible all year round. Generally speaking a good time is spring (mid-Sept–mid-Nov) and autumn (March–May). The **main holiday times** in South Africa are in summer between October and March. The peak of the season is from Christmas to mid-January, when most South Africans take their summer holiday. This means many holiday regions are overrun with visitors. The hottest months are January and February, the coldest is July. In winter (June–Aug) it is dry, the best months to visit game reserves, because the grass is shorter and the animals can be seen better. At this time winter sports fans can go skiing in the mountain regions. In Cape Town it rains a lot during this time of year, unlike in the country's interior: here the rain falls during the summer months from October to March, usually in short evening thundershowers. More ▶climate, p.23.

Bring clothes suitable for a country with a warm to hot climate. In summer and in KwaZulu-Natal also in the winter months of June to August light clothing and shorts are good choice. Bring an anorak, jacket and pullover too, because the evenings can become quite cool; on the Atlantic coast there is often a stiff, cool wind (in summer too). In the Cape provinces and in the higher regions real winter clothing should be worn in winter. Also come prepared for rain: although it does not rain a lot in South Africa, when it rains, it pours: so bring an umbrella, a raincoat etc.

Clothes

Tours

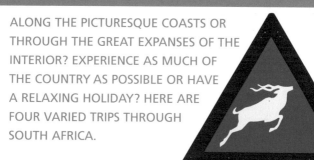

ALONG THE PICTURESQUE COASTS OR
THROUGH THE GREAT EXPANSES OF THE
INTERIOR? EXPERIENCE AS MUCH OF
THE COUNTRY AS POSSIBLE OR HAVE
A RELAXING HOLIDAY? HERE ARE
FOUR VARIED TRIPS THROUGH
SOUTH AFRICA.

TOURS THROUGH SOUTH AFRICA

However you are inclined, this section contains suggestions for routes that combine the country's most beautiful and important sights.

TOUR 1 **Cape Town and the Western Cape**
The »European« side of South Africa. The south of the country is one of the most beautiful holiday destinations in the world. ▶ **page 190**

TOUR 2 **Across the rough north**
Something for people who like to get away from civilization, at least some of the time. Apart from breathtaking scenery this tour also includes two of South Africa's capitals in its stops. ▶ **page 192**

TOUR 3 **Nature and culture in the east**
Here are some of the most significant nature reserves on earth, including the Kruger National Park. African traditions and history are particularly evident in KwaZulu-Natal. ▶ **page 194**

TOUR 4 **Great round trip**
The drive along the Wild Coast, from Durban via East London to Cradock, completes the great round trip: a kaleidoscope of very different, but always strong impressions. Take six to eight weeks to enjoy this tour in full. ▶ **page 197**

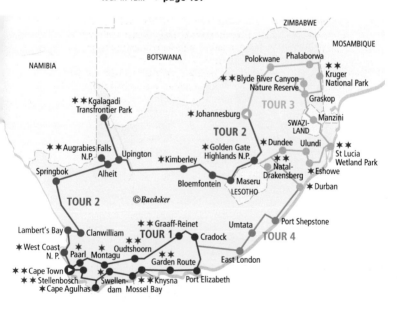

Travelling in South Africa

South Africa has become an extremely popular travel destination. Its infrastructure for transport, board and lodging is of a high standard even in remote areas. A large number of specialized operators offer very different trips, from a wine tour in the Cape to comfortable safaris, sports such as diving and surfing, and challenging tours through mountains and wilderness. Individual travellers have the same plethora of options. The best means of transport is a **personal vehicle**; many of the most beautiful regions and spots can only be reached this way. International and national rental companies offer everything from ordinary cars, motorbikes and 4 x 4 SUVs to fully equipped motor-caravans. Note that the distances are quite long (which makes greater comfort very pleasant) and certain routes can only be tackled with 4 x 4s. Longer distances within the country can quickly be covered **by air**. This allows highly individual trip configurations. Travellers who want to be more in touch with the land and have a little adventure will be happy to learn that South Africa is a very backpacker-friendly country. Options here include travel in **overland buses** and sometimes on **long-distance trains** (a trip in a luxury train, such as the Blue Train or Rovos Rail, is a special, though not exactly cheap experience).

The right means of transport

There is something here for everyone! What do you want? Classy luxury, a cosy rural guesthouse, or direct contact to nature? South Africa can fulfil all of these desires. Since South Africans prefer to do things themselves on holiday **campsites and holiday homes** are also plentiful (including in the national parks) and the majority of them are well equipped. In particularly attractive areas such as Cape Town, the Garden Route, and along the surf beaches, backpackers will find inexpensive **hostels** that are on the Baz Bus route and are real bases for touring an area. A really useful form of accommodation, not least because they offer particularly good value for money, are **guesthouses** and **Bed & Breakfasts**: whether basic establishments in the country or luxurious centuries-old houses with antique furniture and a private terrace, they are full of character, while their hosts provide insights into the country and help with travel tips. Compared with the types of accommodation mentioned so far, **hotels** take a bit of a back seat; they should be considered as an option above all in larger towns. The 19th-century Victorian hotels are especially attractive, and of course there is always the option of extremely modern accommodation that leaves no wish unfulfilled in beautiful spots. Last but not least there are the **lodges**, an African speciality. Located in state-run and private nature reserves, they take care of all of their guests' needs and provide a complete tour programme. Comfort and cost range here from good mid-range to absolute luxury. Regardless of the type of accommodation, note that certain areas and places are

Where to stay?

heavily frequented during the South African holiday periods (▶ p. 184), which means early reservations are a must; in Cape Town and Johannesburg hotel rooms are scarce all year round.

Tour 1 Cape Town and the Western Cape

Length: approx. 1400–2200km/ 870–1370mi

Duration: 2–3 weeks

This is the showcase side of South Africa with the most beautiful city in the world, the Cape of Good Hope, the breathtaking scenery of the Wineland, and the continent's southernmost point. Along Garden Route and Route 62 there are superb landscapes and old towns. This tour is ideal for those who want to have a pleasant holiday and get a first impression of South Africa.

Cape Town   Visitors to ❶ ✶ ✶ **Cape Town** at the foot of the majestic Table Mountain should reserve at least a few days for South Africa's fascinating »Mother City«. Cape Town, where the majority of the population is made up of whites and coloureds, has many sights and experiences, such as the Victoria & Alfred Waterfront, Long Street, Bo Kaap, excellent museums, and jazz bars. Another benefit of Cape Town is that plenty of excursions can be made to the surrounding area. Table Mountain (of course), the drive around the Cape peninsula, as well as to Bloubergstrand, and to the West Coast National Park (▶Tour 2) are all a must.

Winelands   The best way to discover the beautiful Wineland at the Cape is to find accommodation here and at least visit the famous sites of ❷ ✶ ✶ **Stellenbosch** and Franschhoek (Paarl is slated for the end of the tour). This is a wonderful, classic round trip: Stellenbosch – Hellshoogte Pass – Franschhoek – Franschhoek Pass – Theewaterskloof Dam – Viljoens Pass – Grabouw – Sir Lowry's Pass – Strand / Somerset West – Stellenbosch (130km/80mi).

Cape Agulhas   The tour then proceeds along the magnificent coast, passing **beaches** to Hangklip and via Kleinmond to **Hermanus** (or to Gansbaai); at the right time of year travellers will be »accompanied« by whales. A detour into the interior via Caledon to **Genadendal** is also worthwhile. Next the route goes past the Salmonsdam Nature Reserve to Bredasdorp and ❸ ✶ **Cape Agulhas**, Africa's southernmost point.

Garden Route   After visiting ❹ ✶ **Swellendam** the tour continues along the N 2 to ❺ **Mossel Bay**, where Bartolomëu Diaz landed in 1488. It marks the westernmost point of the **Garden Route** (touristically overdeveloped,

Paarl
Legendary wine town on the Cape

Ostriches
are everywhere in Oudtshoorn

★★ Graaff-Reinet   Cradock
140 km/
87 mi
9   8

240 km/ 149 mi

350 km/ 217 mi

★★ Oudtshoorn
10

120 km/
74 mi

★ Paarl   Montagu 230 km/ 143 mi
12   11

★★ 60 km/ 37 mi

Town
1

30 km/
18 mi
2

★ Stellenbosch

★★ Knysna
6   255 km/ 158 mi   7

175 km/
108 mi   105 km/
65 mi   ★★ Garden Route   Port Elizabeth

100 km/
62 mi   4   5

260 km/
161 mi   ★ Swellen-
dam   Mossel Bay

★ Cape Agulhas   3

Cape Town
The highlight of almost every South Africa visit

Plettenberg Bay
Long, sandy beaches and a beautiful hinterland along the Garden Route

but not for nothing), with its spectacular, diverse landscapes between the mountains and the sea. A particular highlight is the lagoon of ❻ ★ ★ **Knysna**. In Tsitsikamma National Park visitors can experience the jungle and spend relaxing days on the beaches. An excursion with the Outeniqua Choo-Tjoe and a trip over the Seven Passes Road are not to be missed.

Excursion to the Great Karoo

Travellers with a little more time on their hands who would also like to get to know some of South Africa's other facets should do the loop via Port Elizabeth and Cradock to Graaf-Reinet (from Plettenberg Bay to Uniondale approx. 800km/500mi). **❼ Port Elizabeth** is a lively port and university town, the centre of the automobile industry and a holiday spot with long sandy beaches; the **✳✳ Addo Elephant Park** (75km/45mi north) is one of South Africa's most attractive parks. About 160km/100mi further north lies **❽ Cradock**, a typical country town in the midst of the Great Karoo and home to author Olive Schreiner; here too there is an interesting reserve, the **✳✳ Mountain Zebra National Park**. A detour from Route 62 would also be worthwhile for **❾ ✳✳ Graaf-Reinet** 140km/90mi further west (approx. 250km/155mi from Uniondale).

Route 62

The road that runs through the back country of the N 2 from Uniondale to Cape Town, through the impressive landscapes of the Little Karoo, the Breede Valley, and the Cape Wineland, has the promotionally effective name Route 62. Prince Alfred's Pass, which links Knysna with Uniondale, is a fitting start to this tour. **❿ ✳✳ Oudtshoorn**, the famous centre of South Africa's ostrich farms, can be reached via De Rust. After a detour to the Swartberg Pass the tour leads 230km/145mi westwards (via Calitzdorp, Ladismith, and Barrydale) to **⓫ ✳ Montagu**, a pretty little town in the midst of fruit plantations, and then via the Kogmanskloof Pass into the Breede Valley (with Robertson as its centre), one of the big wine-growing areas in South Africa. Last stop before Cape Town is **⓬ ✳ Paarl**, where the Cape's food and wine culture can be experienced in all its glory.

Tour 2 Across the Rough North

Length: approx. 2300–3000km/ 1430–1865mi	Duration: 3–4 weeks

South Africa off the beaten track for travellers wanting to turn their backs on civilization for a while. Endless expanses and inhospitable semi-desert create strong impressions, as do historic Bloemfontein and Johannesburg, South Africa's »black« economic metropolis.

Along the west coast

From **❶ ✳✳ Cape Town** the road to take is the coastal road via Bloubergstrand with its impressive view of the city at the foot of Table Mountain to the **❷ ✳ West Coast National Park** at the Langebaan Lagoon, one of the most important bird sanctuaries in the world. The salty air of the Atlantic can be felt all the way to **❸ Lambert's Bay**, the fishery centre of the »Crayfish Route«. Further inland at **❹ Clanwilliam**, a pretty old town and »home« of rooibos (»red

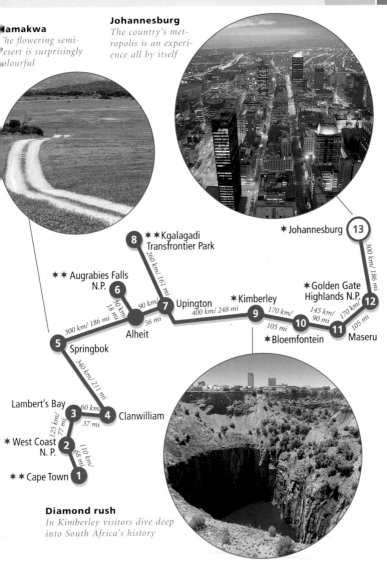

Namakwa
The flowering semi-desert is surprisingly colourful

Johannesburg
The country's metropolis is an experience all by itself

* Johannesburg ⑬

⑧ * * Kgalagadi Transfrontier Park
260 km/ 161 mi

300 km/ 186 mi

* * Augrabies Falls N.P. ⑥

* Golden Gate Highlands N.P. ⑫

50 km/ 18 mi   90 km/ 56 mi   ⑦ Upington
* Kimberley
400 km/ 248 mi

145 km/ 90 mi   170 km/ 105 mi

Alheit

300 km/ 186 mi

⑨   170 km/ 105 mi   ⑩   ⑪ Maseru

⑤ Springbok

* Bloemfontein

340 km/ 211 mi

Lambert's Bay   60 km/ 37 mi   ④ Clanwilliam
③
125 km/ 77 mi

* West Coast N. P. ②
110 km/ 68 mi

* * Cape Town ①

Diamond rush
In Kimberley visitors dive deep into South Africa's history

bush«) tea the N 7 is reached; further south are the picturesque Cederberg mountains, a popular hiking region with the Cederberg Wilderness Area. After that the route runs 340km/210mi north to the capital of the * **Namakwa**, ⑤ **Springbok**; during the rainy season in August and September this inhospitable land is transformed into a flowery paradise.

Semi-desert and diamond town

After Springbok it is a 300km/186mi drive along N 14 to the exit to ❻✳✳ **Augrabies Falls National Park**: here the Orange River, South Africa's longest, plummets into a 240m/790ft-deep gorge. The river-desert landscape and a rich and exotic flora and fauna mean a visit lasting several days is definitely worthwhile. After Kakamas and Kei-moes, two surprisingly green little towns with palm tree-lined streets and vineyards all around, the road leads to ❼ **Upington**, the centre of the wild northwest. This is the base for a visit to the ❽✳✳ **Kgala-gadi Transfrontier Parks** 260km/160mi away in the semi-desert of the Kalahari. After Upington the N 10 / R 64 roads lead past Griqua-town to the legendary diamond town of ❾✳ **Kimberley**; most of the mines have been shut down, but the Big Hole, the largest ever to have been dug by human hands, is testimony to the time of the diamond rush.

Through Free State to Johannesburg

Free State has wide, undulating grassland in the east and hilly farmland in the west where the clocks still seem to run more slowly; the gold mines around Welkom and Virginia are a world away. 170km/106mi from Kimberley is ❿✳ **Bloemfontein**, formerly a stronghold of the Boers and now judicial capital of South Africa. This place has a lively music scene and a lot of history. Those who do not want to go from here straight to Johannesburg (400km/250mi) should, after a detour to ⓫**Maseru**, visit the ⓬✳ **Golden Gate Highlands National Park**; the route via Ladybird and Ficksburg along the border to Lesotho is very attractive. The N 3 then leads to ⓭✳ **Johannesburg**, the country's great economic centre, which is worth a visit despite its problems; make time for a tour of Soweto.

Tour 3 Nature and Culture in the East

Length: approx. 2300km/1430mi　　**Duration:** 3–4 weeks

The north-east of South Africa is home to some of the greatest scenery in the world: the Kruger National Park, Blyde River Canyon, Greater St Lucia Wetland Park, and Natal-Drakensberg mountains. KwaZulu-Natal is full of traditional culture; the Battle-fields are evidence of the country's bloody past.

From ❶✳ **Johannesburg** the N 1 leads to the quieter ✳ **Pretoria**, the administrative capital of South Africa. The Voortrekker Monument recalls the time of the Great Trek and the wars against the native population. Continuing on the N 1 the tour goes past Mokopane to ❷**Polokwane**, capital of the province of Limpopo, then eastwards to Tzaneen in beautiful subtropical surroundings. At ❸ **Phalaborwa**

Stalking leopards
in the Kruger National Park, which is about the same size as Wales

Blyde River Canyon
The world's third-largest gorge and one of South Africa's most impressive landscapes

Polokwane
2

Phalaborwa
3

240 km/ 149 mi

320 km/ 199 mi

180 km/ 112 mi

★★
Blyde River
Canyon
Nature Reserve
6

35 km/ 22 mi

★★ Kruger
National Park
4

115 km/ 71 mi
5

120 km/ 74 mi

Graskop

1

240 km/ 143 mi

Manzini
(Swaziland)
7

★ Johannesburg

240 km/ 149 mi

mphitheatre
rock wall, almost 500m/1640 tall and 5km/3mi long, in the atal-Drakensberg mountains

★Dundee

Ulundi
10

★★
St Lucia
Wetland Park
8

120 km/ 74 mi
11

150 km/ 93 mi

100 km/ 62 mi

170 km/ 105 mi

12

250 km/ 155 mi

9

★★ Natal-
Drakensberg

★ Eshowe

13   ★ Durban

Durban
A cosmopolitan holiday city on the Indian Ocean

there is access to the ❹ ✳ **Kruger National Park**. It takes at least two or three days to discover all the animals the park has to offer. Accommodation can be found in state-run camps or in luxurious private game reserves. This latter type of accommodation is mainly located in the western part of the park. Leave the park by the Paul Kruger Gate and take the R 536 via Hazyview to ❺ **Graskop**, the starting place for the approx. 150km/95mi trip through the ❻ ✳ **Blyde River Canyon Nature Reserve**, one of South Africa's most terrific landscapes. Don't leave out ✳ **Pilgrim's Rest**, a little 19th-century gold-digger town that has been transformed into an open-air museum.

To get to the north-east of KwaZulu-Natal and its nature parks, drive through Sabie – here are the biggest human-planted forests in the world – and Nelspruit to Barberton, an old gold prospectors' town. At this point there are two alternatives: either go through ❼ ✳ **Swaziland** via Mbabane, Manzini and Big Bend to Golela and join the N 2, or go via Badplaas (R 33) and Amsterdam on the R 33 to Piet Retief and through the hilly Zululand to Pongola and Mkhuze, where there is a fantastic selection of several great reserves: the ✳✳ **Hluhluwhe-Imfolozi Game Park**, located on the first ridges of the back country, the ✳ **Mkuzi Game Reserve** and the ❽ ✳✳ **St Lucia Wetland Park**. Insatiable nature-lovers should definitely make a detour to the Kosi Bay and Ndumo reserves 80km/50mi north of Nkhuze (all-wheel drive required). These reserves are only a few miles from the Mozambique border and for that reason are visited less often.

The journey continues on the N 2 through Zululand, the home of South Africa's largest ethnic group. Take the R 34 from Empangeni, then the R 68 to ❾ ✳ **Eshowe**. Several open-air museums in the vicinity of Eshowe provide insights into Zulu traditions and their way of life. The next destination on this tour is **Durban**, then the Natal-Drakensberg mountains; if time is not an issue take the loop to the north through the **KwaZulu Battlefields**: first north to ❿ **Ulundi** (approx. 100km from Eshowe), then westwards to ⓫ ✳ **Dundee**; near Nqutu there are two major battlefields, Blood River and Rorke's Drift. Next travel southwest to Ladysmith and one of the absolute highlights of any South Africa trip: the amphitheatre of huge rock walls in the **Royal Natal National Park**; it is part of the uKhahlamba Drakensberg Park in the ⓬ ✳✳ **Natal-Drakensberg mountains**. From Harrismith it is possible to make a detour to the ✳✳ **Golden Gate Highlands National Park** with its bizarre rock formations. The fantastic Natal-Drakensberg mountains, the »Alps of South Africa«, are impressive. Spectacular mountains reach an elevation of more than 3000m/9840ft; lush vegetation and San rock drawings are the other attractions. Don't leave out the drive to the 2895m/9498ft-high ✳✳ **Sani Pass** on the border with Lesotho. The onward journey to Durban (on the N 3 or on back roads) has something of interest for beer-lovers (►Baedeker Tip p.431). From the main town of the province, ✴ **Pietermaritzburg**, which as the former capital of Natal still has a very British air, it is definitely worth making an excursion to the attractive Valley of 1000 Hills. And finally ⓭ ✴ **Durban** is considered »South Africa's sunshine capital«, and is clearly one of the country's most visited holiday destinations. The scene here has been shaped by a colourful mix of Zulus, British and Indians. The subtropical coasts north and south of Durban, such as Dolphin Coast and Sunshine and Hibiscus Coast, are a holiday paradise hundreds of miles long.

Tour 4 Great Round Trip

Tours 1 to 3 can be combined into one great round trip. Set aside six to eight weeks for this 6500km/4040mi-long tour. Some stretches can be completed by air. In the tour overview on p.188 the round trip is not separately marked except for the section between Durban and Cradock.

After leaving Cape Town follow Route 2 along the Atlantic and through the Namakwa into the Kalahari to Upington, not forgetting to make the detour to the Augrabies Falls. From Kimberley it is possible to visit Bloemfontein, before flying to Johannesburg (location in Johannesburg or Pretoria). Then, as in Route 3, through the Kruger National Park, the Blyde River Canyon Reserve and Swaziland to the nature parks in the north-east; spend at least two or three days each in the Mkuzi Reserve and in the St Lucia Wetland Park. After a detour to Eshowe the next stop is Durban. En route the beaches of the Dolphin Coast ensure some relaxing days. From Durban explore the Natal-Drakensberg mountains; the most important spots are the Sani Pass, Giant's Castle, Cathedral Peak and the Amphitheatre in the north. The 620km/385mi-long drive on the N 2 from Durban to East London is a chance to get to know the Wild Coast, which fully lives up to its name (alternative: by air). After East London the N 2 leaves the coast and makes its way to Fort Hare; from there the attractive Amatola mountains are well worth a visit. After that, make your way to the Great Karoo via Cradock and the Mountain Zebra National Park to Graaff-Reinet. The next major destination is the Garden Route: on the N 9 to Uniondale, then over Prince Alfred's Pass to Knysna. The »ostrich town» of Oudtshoorn in the Little Karoo can be reached via George; then onwards along Route 62 to Swellendam. The R 319 via Bredasdorp leads to Cape Agulhas, the continent's southernmost point. After Cape Town follow the picturesque coast via Gansbaai, Hermanus, the Hangklip, and Strand. The Wineland around Stellenbosch makes a pleasant end to the journey.

Sights from A to Z

FROM CAPE TOWN TO JOHANNESBURG, FROM THE KRUGER NATIONAL PARK TO THE KALAHARI: THERE IS PLENTY TO BE DISCOVERED IN SOUTH AFRICA

Amanzimtoti · Sunshine Coast

J 7

Province: KwaZulu-Natal
Population: 27,000

Altitude: 5m
Distances: Durban 30km/19mi

Amanzimtoti is a suburb of ►Durban and the first of the holiday resorts that line the 160km/100mi-long coastline of the Indian Ocean between Durban and Port Edward.

The name of this town (»Toti« for short) goes back to the Zulu king Shaka (►Famous People): after he drank the water of the Umbogintwini River in 1828, he is said to have called out: »Kanti amanza mtoti«, »The water is sweet«. The most popular part of the **7km/ 4.5mi-long sandy beach** with its rock spurs is at the Nyoni Rocks, where there is a seawater swimming pool.

What to See in Amanzimtoti

✳
Amanzimtoti Bird Sanctuary

Ilanda Wilds Nature Reserve

At the end of Umdoni Road the entrance to the Amanzimtoti Bird Sanctuary is surrounded by ilala palms (open daily 6am–6pm). The viewing platforms at the upper end of the pond are good bird-watching sites. Around 300 bird species are at home in the 14ha/32-acre Ilanda Nature Reserve, located a little outside on the Umbogintwini River. Visitors can get to know over 100 tree and shrub species along its trails.

Sunshine Coast

Popular holiday destination for South Africans

The coast between Amanzimtoti and Mtwalume, situated approx. 40km/25mi further south, is called the »Sunshine Coast«. It is adjoined by the »Hibiscus Coast« (►Port Shepstone) to the south. Together they are one of the country's **most popular holiday regions**. During the school holidays, particularly over Christmas and at Eas-

 VISITING SUNSHINE COAST

INFORMATION
Amanzimtoti Publicity Association
95 Beach Road, Amanzimtoti
Tel. 031 903 7498
http://amanzimtoti.kzn.org.za

WHERE TO STAY
► **Budget/Mid-range**
Dolphin Point
31 Wavecrest Road

Athlone Park
Tel. 031 904 3592
www.dolphinpointbnb.co.za
Small family guesthouse on the Indian Ocean with five rooms, breathtaking views, and a cordial atmosphere. The peak time for spotting dolphins and whales is between June and November. Beautiful garden with private access to the beach.

ter, many South Africans come here. There are only a few hotels of more than average comfort, but many B & Bs and countless apartment houses. This region is not particularly recommended for visitors from overseas, as the beaches further south in the Western Cape and Eastern Cape provinces are nicer and quieter. The **Aliwal Shoal** off the coast at Umkomaas (Baedeker Special ► p.168) is a well-known destination for divers, who watch **huge schools of sardines** between June and August. The sardines live in the cold waters off the south and south-west coast of Africa and move to the area warmed by the Agulhas current around Durban to spawn. The current brings them (and hungry predatory fish in their wake) close to the coast.

A few miles south of Amanzimtoti five beach resorts have been merged to form the municipality of Kingsburgh (population: 26,000). The wide, long sandy beaches (eight in total) and the lagoons are protected from sharks with nets, so that safe bathing is possible. Every district has its own unique character. The next place after Amanzimtoti, **Doonside** with its shady beach, is a good place for a restorative holiday. **Warner Beach** is a friendly coastal town on a lagoon, well-liked by yachting and motorboat enthusiasts. **Winklespruit** is a hit with sailors, and anglers also find plenty to keep them happy. The dense forest that comes all the way down to the beach is a great place to take a stroll. On **Illovo Beach** at the mouth of the river Illovo there are more good fishing opportunities; sugar cane is cultivated in the surrounding area. The area around **Karridene** is good for long walks on the beach and in the forest.

Kingsburgh

In Umgababa numerous stalls sell Zulu crafts (carvings, pottery, etc.) as well as imported kitsch.

Umgababa

Umkomaas (population: 2000) is located at the mouth of the Mkomazi River, which has its source at an altitude of 3000m/5000ft in the Drakensberg mountains. It is a centre of the pulp industry and thus not an attractive holiday spot. The **18-hole golf course** however is well laid-out. An attempt in 1861 to build a harbour in the Mkomazi estuary failed because of strong ocean currents and sandbanks. The town was only founded in 1902 and was named after the river (»place of cow whales«). In the past whales would come into the shallow water of the river mouth to give birth to their young. The Zulu chief Shaka is said to have witnessed this and given the river its name.

Umkomaas

The **crocodile farm** south of Umkomaas (4km/2.5mi north of Scottburgh), which has more than 2000 crocodiles kept for breeding purposes as well as snakes, is well worth a visit (open daily. 8.30am–3.30pm; feeding times 11am, 3pm). A glass tunnel leading through the snake house is a special attraction. Try some crocodile meat in the farm's restaurant.

Croc World

Scottburgh
The rugged coast of Scottburgh (population: 7000) is popular amongst anglers. There is a seawater swimming pool on the main beach and a golf course.

Vernon Crookes Nature Reserve
The 2198ha/5500-acre Vernon Crooks Reserve is located 15km/9mi west of Scottburgh (open daily 6am–6pm). Old-world porcupines, blue wildebeests, antelopes, gazelles, zebras and black-backed jackals are all at home in this gentle hilly landscape. Two artificial lakes attract lots of birds. The best time to go is spring because of the **fascinating vegetation**. Self-catering accommodation is available, including a tree house. Information at KZN Wildlife (►p.156), camp tel. 039 974 2222.

Ifafa Beach
This village (population: 400) at the mouth of the Ifafa River has a sheltered beach and a lagoon well-suited for fishing. It is also a good place to go water skiing. Rowers face an adverse current for a relatively long stretch.

Mtwalume
The southern endpoint of the Sunshine Coast is Mtwalume. The rocky beach is a favourite fishing area, and swimming is possible in a seawater pool.

★ ★ Augrabies Falls National Park

D 6

Province: Northern Cape   **Distance:** Upington 120km/75mi

The Augrabies waterfalls in the north-west of South Africa close to the Namibian border are considered one of the country's natural wonders. A national park was set up for their protection in 1967.

»Place of Great Noise«
The **Orange River** plummets in several cascades, the main fall being 56m/180ft high, over a width of almost 150m/165yd into an 18km/

 VISITING AUGRABIES FALLS

INFORMATION

Augrabies Falls National Park
The Warden
Tel. 054 452 9200
SANParks ►p.156

WHEN TO GO

Open from 6am (6.30am in winter) to 10pm. During the summer months and particularly in late summer the Orange River carries a lot of water; during the summer the daytime temperatures are often around 40°C/104°F. The most pleasant time to go is from March to October. During the winter months the nights can get very cold. Two days in the park are ideal, but a day trip from ►Upington (120km/75mi away) is also worthwhile.

Augrabies Falls: a fantastic natural spectacle in a desert-like landscape

11mi-long granite gorge with rock walls that can be up to 240m/750ft high. The name »Augrabies«, which means »place of great noise«, was given to the falls by the Khoikhoi in holy reverence for the great masses of water. The national park is 882 sq km/341 sq mi in area and extremely arid with an average of 107mm/4.2in of precipitation annually. The vegetation is correspondingly sparse; spurges and quiver trees in particular do well here. Only on the banks of the Orange River do the trees grow more densely. Amongst the park's fauna are antelopes, gazelles, old world porcupines, leopards, baboons and guenons as well as more than 140 bird species. The rare **black rhinoceros** has been resettled here. The African black eagle can be observed, and black storks breed in the gorge. The base for a visit to the Augrabies Falls park is ► Upington, which is 120km/75mi away, but Keimoes and Kakamas are also good places to stay.

Facilities

The camp has comfortable chalets, a campsite, a restaurant, a swimming pool and a visitor centre. A 12km/7.5mi-long, rather rough track is the access route to the national park. Several paths branch off to sights and viewpoints. Do not fail to drive to the **Ararat viewpoint**; it offers a spectacular view of the gorge. The **Klipspringer Hiking Trail** is a 40km/25mi route that runs along the gorge; it can be completed in three days (overnight stays in huts; closed from mid-October to the end of March because of the high temperatures; very low capacity, so book early).

Barkly East

G 7

Province: Eastern Cape
Population: 14,000

Altitude: 1800m/5500ft
Distances: Aliwal North 120km/75mi, Umtata 210km/130mi

Barkly East is an important centre for sheep farming and the wool industry. It is situated in the Witteberg mountains, which are praised as the »Switzerland of South Africa«.

Apart from the museum in White Street there is little to see in Barkly East. However, the town is the starting point for discovering the incredibly **beautiful mountain landscape** in the southern part of the Drakensberg mountains. The altitude means this area gets approx. 81 nights of frost a year; skiing is possible during the winter, and during the summer months it is ideal for hiking and trout fishing.

Around Barkly East

Lady Grey

Barkley East is connected to Aliwal North by a 157km/98mi railway line, the construction of which challenged its engineers from 1866 to 1869. Today enthusiasts from all around the world come here to experience the **Zig Zag Train**. The approx. 70km/45mi track between Barkly East and Lady Grey makes its way through an impressive mountain landscape and climbs with a **gradient of up to 2.8% and eight zigzags** from 1355m/4500ft to 1991m/6600ft. At the top it is even possible to ski during the winter; although the pistes are not very long they are almost as enjoyable as Alpine skiing. In the health resort of **Aliwal North** go to the Buffelsvlei Farmhouse to learn about the history of the place. The church, dating from 1864, is also a museum.

! *Baedeker* TIP

Hot springs

In Aliwal North 4.4 million litres/1.16 million US gal per day of hot mineral water at a temperature of 34°C/93°F bubbles to the surface from a depth of 1280m/4000ft, bringing relief for sufferers with rheumatism and arthritis. Around 150,000 spa visitors come here each year. Even travellers just passing through are welcome. After a long car journey a bath is a real pleasure. Information tel. 051 633 2951.

The drive from Barkly East via the **Barkly Pass** to **Elliot** (population: 12,000) 60km/35mi further south conveys magnificent impressions of the surrounding scenery. The region is known for its **San rock drawings**; the largest »gallery« was discovered on the territory of the Denorbin Farm: 32m/35yd long with more than 5000 drawings (phone before visiting: tel. 045 971 9052). During the summer months the Thompson Dam in a nature reserve and the **Gilli-Cullum Falls** are popular destinations.

WITTEBERG MOUNTAINS

INFORMATION
▶Rhodes Hotel

WHERE TO STAY

▶ Budget/Mid-range
Rhodes Hotel
Miller St. /Sauer St., Rhodes
Tel. 045 974 9305
www.rhodesvillage.co.za
A friendly house, made to look old, nine rooms with old furniture and fireplace. The hotel is the tourist base of the region.

The village of **Rhodes** east of East Barkly (60km/35mi of unpaved roads) is one of the most beautiful places on the plateau, at an altitude of almost 2000m/6500ft at the foot of the 3001m/9846ft **Ben MacDhui**, and this is also true of its only hotel. Winter visitors should make sure to bring plenty of warm clothing.
The Ben MacDhui Hiking Trail is extremely scenic (50km/30mi, three days, book by phoning 045 971 0446). Skiing is possible in **Tiffindell** (2800m/9190ft); the 4WD journey up to Tiffindell is also very attractive.

Beaufort West

E 8

Province: Western Cape
Population: 37,000

Altitude: 915m/3000ft
Distances: Cape Town 460km/285mi,
Port Elizabeth 500km/310mi

Beaufort West is located in the middle of the Great Karoo, whose impressive wide-open landscape can be experienced in the Karoo National Park.

Beaufort West lies on the N 1, the main road between Cape Town and Johannesburg in the middle of the Great Karoo, where it is the main town. The area is primarily used for animal husbandry; Beaufort West is the centre of merino sheep breeding. The town was founded in 1818. Sir John Charles Molteno, a wealthy sheep breeder and later the prime minister of the Cape province, and the famous heart surgeon **Christiaan Barnard** were born here. Some of the distinctions of the medical pioneer are on display in the museum. The **Stadhuis**, the oldest communal building, is also worth seeing.

✱ Karoo National Park

To the north-west of the town is the Karoo National Park, home to the **Nuweveldberg mountains**, which have an altitude of 825–1911m/2707–6270ft. The 80,000ha/200,000-acre area protects the unique Karoo flora and fauna. Several mammalian species have been reintroduced here, such as the mountain zebra, the springbok, the kudu and wild cats. The park is best explored by a three-day hike along its trails. Accommodation: campsite, Cape Dutch houses. The

Landscape and facilities

A splendid carpet of flowers in the Karoo

VISITING BEAUFORT WEST

INFORMATION

Beaufort West Tourism
57 Donkin Street, Beaufort West
Tel. 023 415 1488
www.tourismbeaufortwest.co.za

WHERE TO STAY

▶ Mid-range

Lemoenfontein Game Lodge
Tel. 023 415 2847
www.lemoenfontein.co.za
A comfortable 19th-century hunting
lodge in splendid surroundings, with
wildlife park. The huge terrace offers a
magnificent view over the Karoo, and
the atmosphere is magical in the
evening. The bar (with fireplace) is
self-service and the charge is put on a
tab. A good place for watching wildlife
and hiking.

▶ Budget/Mid-range

Matoppo Inn
Meintjies St./Bird St.,
Tel. 023 415 1055
Tasteful, cosy guesthouse with a gar-
den and pool. The more expensive
rooms all have antique furniture.
Candlelight dinners at pleasant prices.

WHERE TO EAT

▶ Inexpensive

Mac Young
156 Donkin Street
Tel. 023 414 4068
A friendly Scottish restaurant in the
town centre. Large selection, including
lamb chops prepared on a charcoal
grill, seafood, as well as pizza and
pasta.

41km/25mi **Springbok Hiking Trail** is only open from February to
September. The main gate, which is reached by a road leading off the
N 1, is open daily from 5am to 10pm. Book at SAN Parks, ▶p.156.

Karoo
The Karoo is a predominantly flat, semi-arid landscape with sparse
vegetation and several jagged elevations that reach an altitude of up
to 2000m/6500ft. At about 500,000 sq km/200,000 sq mi it accounts
for one-third of South Africa's total area. It begins north of the
▶Garden Route as the **Little Karoo**, becomes the **Great Karoo** and
ends in the north as the **Upper Karoo**. In the border region to Namibia and Botswana the Karoo turns into the Kalahari.
The climate is unpredictable; the temperatures range from over
40°C/104°F to -7°C/19°F. The great bulk of the small amount of precipitation falls in February and March and during this time the vegetation changes dramatically. The Karoo is covered with low, woody
scrub, interspersed by succulents (aloe, mesembryanthemum, crassu-
la, spurges and stapelia) that are able to store water in their thick
leaves and their roots. After a short shower the grasses recover and
the Karoo turns green. Several days of rainfall transform it into a
flowering paradise. The seeds of »daisies« that may have been dormant for years germinate; the result is a gloriously colourful carpet
of flowers.

The first inhabitants of the Karoo were **nomadic San**, who found grazing grounds for their herds and huntable game here. The name also originates from their language and means »great drought«. The large amount of game also attracted European hunters and farmers, who consequently had a great impact on the ecological balance: first the predators were wiped out, then large areas were fenced in. The livestock herds over-grazed the land and the fences restricted the free movement of the surviving wild animals. The Karoo's flora and fauna changed irreparably.

Bela Bela

H 4

Province: Limpopo
Population: 13,000

Altitude: 1143m/3750ft
Distance: Pretoria 100km/60mi

Bela Bela is one of the most popular domestic travel destinations for South Africans. Particularly during the mild, sunny winters it is a place where the health-conscious like to come to relax in the water of the hot springs.

Bela Bela, 100km/60mi north of Pretoria, was founded in 1921 under the name of **Warmbaths**. It is famous for its healing **hot springs**. Its modern name comes from the Tswana name for the place, meaning »boiling boiling«. Every hour 22,000 litres/6000 US gal bubble out of the springs at a temperature of 55°C/131°F; the water is used to treat

VISITING BELA BELA

INFORMATION
Tourism Association
Waterfront, Old Pretoria St.
Tel. 014 736 3694
www.belabelatourism.co.za

WHERE TO STAY
► Luxury
Mabula Game Lodge
Tel. 014 734 7000
bookings under 031 310 6900
www.mabula.co.za, 51 rooms
This exclusive lodge with pretty thatched chalets is located in the Mabula reserve 47km/29mi from Bela Bela. Experience the rich fauna from a hot-air balloon or on horseback.

► Budget/Luxury
Aventura Resort
Voortrekker Street, tel. 014 736 2200
www.aventura.co.za
Besides accommodation ranging from hotel rooms to well-equipped chalets and a campsite, this huge holiday resort has medicinal baths, restaurants and cafés, as well as tennis and squash courts and a lot more.

► Budget
De Draai Gastehuis
10km/6mi north of Bela Bela
Tel. 014 736 4379
Pleasant guesthouse (two rooms), Victorian style, with a pool and cafe.

rheumatic conditions. Adjoining the health resort is the 50ha/125-acre **Bela Bela Nature Reserve**, which is home to hartebeests, plains zebras and impalas.

Around Bela Bela

Modimolle

Modimolle (previously called Nylstroom, population: 12,000), located 27km/17mi further north, is the centre of an agricultural region; the main products of cultivation are grapes, tobacco and peanuts. The small town was given its name by the Boers, who came across a spring in 1866 and believed it to be the source of the river Nile. This assumption seemed to be confirmed by the discovery of a »pyramid«, which in fact was a San burial site. The new name comes from the Sesotho language and means »God has eaten«. The town's historic buildings include the Hervormde Kerk (reformed church) built in 1889 and the J. G. Strijdom House, the residence of the man who was prime minister from 1954 to 1958 (museum).

Naboomspruit

Naboomspruit (population: 7000), located 40km/25mi further north-east at the foot of the Waterberg range on the N 1, is another important agricultural centre (maize, peanuts, citrus fruits), but there are also productive tin mines and fluorite deposits. Excursions into the **Waterberg range** can be made from Naboomspruit. This area is hardly known as a tourist spot, but is well worth visiting for its river and lake landscapes, its deep gorges and picturesque little villages, as well as the rich fauna.

Lapalala
Wilderness

North-west from Modimolle it is a 125km/78mi drive to the Lapalala Wilderness biosphere reserve (R 517 to Vaalwater, then north-east towards Melkrivier). The reserve in the Waterberg range is home to a large number of big-game species. Accommodation is available in small camps (tel. 014 755 4395). A 50km/30mi stretch of river can be navigated by canoe; rangers accompany hikes.

Bethlehem

H 6

Province: Free State	**Altitude:** 1747m/5732ft
Population: 66,000	**Distances:** Bloemfontein 180km/110mi, Johannesburg 235km/145mi

Bethlehem is mainly of interest as a stop on the way to the Natal Drakensberg mountains or to the Golden Gate Highlands Park.

The stately main town in the eastern part of Free State, with a good selection of hotels and restaurants, lies in a fertile part of the Maluti Mountains on the banks of the Jordaan river, which has been dammed to form **Loch Athlone**. It is the centre of an **important cereal-growing region** (the Hebrew word »Bethlehem« means »house of bread«) and it is also known for rose-growing. The Voortrekkers came to the area during the 1840s as fugitives from the British who had conquered the Cape. In 1864 they founded the town on the premises of Pretoriuskloof Farm and named it after the birthplace of Jesus Christ; in the same spirit they gave the river the name Jordaan. The town rapidly developed into an economic and administrative centre of the eastern Orange Free State. There is a plan to rename Bethlehem as Dihlabeng.

What to See in and around Bethlehem

There is a limited number of sights. The civic museum in the Nazareth Mission Church that was built in 1806 has everyday items from Boer households on display (open daily). There is a steam locomotive in the garden, which ran the route between Cape Town and Mafikeng at the end of the 19th century. Also noteworthy are the Strapp Building (1894, corner of Church St. and Louw St.), the Anglican church of St Augustine, the mighty Dutch Reformed Moederkerk (1910) on Church Square and the **Tuishuis** (around 1870, has a good restaurant; ►below).

Bethlehem

The holiday village of Loch Athlone is situated on the banks of the Jordaan reservoir around 3km/2mi outside Bethlehem. Marked hiking trails lead around the reservoir; the floating restaurant is quite an attraction. The holiday village is the starting point for hikes requiring several days, such as the 36km/22mi **Houtkop Hiking Trail**. From the entrance of the holiday village the 15km/9mi **Wolhuterskop Hiking Trail** runs through the 800ha/2000-acre Wolhuterskop Nature Reserve, which is home to various species of antelope and gazelle as well as to many birds.

Loch Athlone

◄ Wolhuterskop
Nature Reserve

▶ VISITING BETHLEHEM

INFORMATION
Bethlehem Tourist Office
Civic Centre, Muller St.
Tel. 058 303 5732

WHERE TO STAY
▶ Budget/Mid-range
Fisant Guest House
10 Thoi Oosthuyse St.
Tel. 058 303 7144
A pretty house on the outskirts of town with a garden, eight tasteful

rooms and some well-equipped self-catering apartments. Very friendly service.

WHERE TO EAT
▶ Moderate
Wooden Spoon
12 Church St., tel. 058 303 2724
The food served in the Tuishuis, the oldest house in Bethlehem, is hearty and contains a lot of meat. The ambience is rustic and simple.

Bethulie

F 7

Province: Free State
Population: 13,500

Altitude: 1589m/5213ft
Distances: Aliwal North 75km/45mi,
Bloemfontein 185km/115mi

The undulating land used for grazing cattle and sheep south-west of Bloemfontein called »Gariep« is not a very touristy area. Its centre is Bethulie, which is located between two large nature reserves in the vicinity of the Gariep reservoir.

What to See in and around Bethulie

Bethulie
The small town was founded in 1829 by the London mission and taken over by the Paris mission four years later. The latter also gave the place its name, meaning »chosen by God«. **Pellissier House**, named after the first French missionary, contains an informative exhibition about the mission and the region's history.

D H Steyn Bridge
The road and railway bridge that crosses the Orange River at Bethulie is, at 1152m/1260yd, the **longest bridge in South Africa**.

Tussen-die-Riviere Game Farm
This 23,000ha/55,000-acre reserve (with a basic campsite), which is home to antelopes, gazelles, zebras and rhinoceroses, is situated around 15km/9mi south-east of Bethulie between the Orange and Caledon rivers. It is open from September to April, from sunrise to sunset; hunting is permitted during the winter to regulate the animal population.

Gariep Dam
To the south-west of Bethulie the Orange River was dammed to form a reservoir more than 100km/60mi long and 374 sq km/144 sq mi in area, known as the Gariep Dam; it offers superb water-sports opportunities (sailing, fishing). The dam which closes off the **fourth-largest reservoir in Africa** is 90m/300ft high; dam and reservoir form part of the Orange River Project, an irrigation system set up in 1966. The 82.5km/51mi Oranje Fish Tunnel, the longest water tunnel in the world, channels the water into the valley of the Great Fish River and secures the water supply of Port Elizabeth. On the lake's northern shore is a 36,500ha/90,000-acre protected area, the Gariep Nature Reserve, whose residents include wildebeests and ostriches, as well as **South Africa's largest springbok population**. At the lake's western end is the big Aventura Gariep Resort with different types of accommodation, sports facilities, shops, and restaurants.

Gariep Nature Reserve ▶

Philippolis ▶
It is well worthwhile to take a trip to Philippolis, approx. 50km/30mi north-west of Gariep reservoir: the pretty town is the oldest town in Free State (founded in 1823 as a station of the London mission); 75 of its buildings have been declared national monuments (such as the Dutch Reformed church and the library). Why not spend a night here in the **Old Jail**, the prison built in 1872? (www.philippolis.org.za).

Bisho · King William's Town

G 8

Province: Eastern Cape

Distances: East London 60km/35mi, Grahamstown 125km/80mi

»Amatola«, meaning »calf« in English, is the name of the coastal area west of ► East London together with its hinterland. A large portion of the area used to be »Ciskei», the Xhosa homeland.

Bisho (population: 10,000, 530m/1739ft), situated to the north-east of East London, was the capital of **Ciskei**, a homeland declared »independent« in 1981 in which the Xhosa made up 97% of the population. Like all homelands it was re-integrated into the Republic of South Africa with the interim constitution of 1994. The town only developed during the 1970s; the previous administrative centre had been Zwelitsha, located 15km/9mi further south. Several modern government buildings shape the look of Bisho. Befitting its role as the main town in Ciskei, Bisho has its own airport.

Bisho

Stutterheim (population: 38,000) is located 42km/26mi north of Bisho and can be reached by the R 346. Outside the town to the east is the **Bethel mission station**, which was founded by missionaries from Berlin in 1837. In 1857 more Germans settled here. They were members of the German legion who had fought for the British against Russia in the Crimean War. The town, named after the German commander Richard von Stutterheim, is the starting point for hikes to the magnificent mountain landscape and the surrounding area. Many native tree species such as the yellowwood, stinkwood and wild fig grow here.

Stutterheim

The **Amatola Mountains** span the area between Stutterheim and ► Fort Beaufort; the beautiful, mountainous landscape with its lush forests is said to have inspired Tolkien in his creation of »Middle Earth«. The demanding 105km/65mi six-day **Amatola Trail** is one of South Africa's most beautiful mountain hikes; magnificent views, deep forests, waterfalls and natural pools are just some of the rewards this hike brings. Information and bookings at Keiskamma Ecotourism.

Amatola Mountains

Bisho's neighbouring town, which was not part of Ciskei, is the region's shopping and administration centre (population: 20,000). Numerous educational institutions are located here. The economy is particularly shaped by light industry. King William's Town emerged from a mission station founded on the Buffalo River in 1826 and was destroyed by the Xhosa several times. Members of the British-German legion came here in 1857, German settlers around 1858. The **Amathole Museum** (open Mon–Fri, 9am–4.30pm, Sat 9am–1pm) developed from the collections of the Naturalist Society founded in 1884. Amongst the vast collection of mounted African

King William's Town

● VISITING KING WILLIAM'S TOWN

mammals, some of them very rare, is the famous **hippopotamus Huberta**, which travelled along the coast back and forth between St Lucia and King William's Town between 1928 and 1931 without anyone being able to capture it. The excellent cultural history collections illustrate the life and history of the Xhosa (a Xhosa gallery was set up in the former post office building) as well as of the British and Germans who settled here. **Steve Biko**, the leader of the Black Consciousness Movement, is buried in the Steve Biko Remembrance Garden on the outskirts of the town towards Port Elizabeth. He died in Port Elizabeth jail in 1977 (►p.438).

Peddie   The N 2 connects King William's Town with ►Grahamstown. There is a watchtower in **Peddie** built in 1841 on the site of a fort that was a military base during the Kaffir Wars. Numerous roads (not all of them surfaced) lead off southwards from the N 2, which can be taken to reach the coastal area, the **Shipwreck Coast** with its wonderful beaches.

Hamburg   Hamburg is situated at the mouth of the Keiskamma River, which forms a lagoon here. German settlers made a home for themselves here in 1857 and constructed a harbour, which however rapidly silted up and was abandoned. In recent times Hamburg has become a popular holiday spot, thanks to its beach, which is considered one **Kiwane Resort ►** of the most beautiful in the country. The same is true of the Kiwane resort, a small holiday village with a campsite and bungalows located 6km/3.5mi further east.

Shipwreck Hiking Trail   The coastal region of the former Ciskei can be discovered on the Shipwreck Hiking Trail, a 64km/40mi trail between Great Fish River in the south-west and the Ncera River in the north-east. The sections between Great Fish River and Bira River (23km/14mi) and between Hamburg and the Kiwane Resort (6km/3.5mi) are particularly attractive. Bookings at the Department of Water Affairs, 9 Chamberlain St., King William's Town, tel. 043 642 2571. There are no wrecks to be seen, even though many ships were damaged here.

Bloemfontein

G 6

Province: Free State
Population: 233,000

Altitude: 1392m/4567ft
Distances: Kimberley 170km/105mi,
Johannesburg 400km/250mi,
Durban 630km/390mi

Bloemfontein is situated in the middle of the country and is the main political and cultural city of the province of Free State. It is well worth getting to know this Boer stronghold, the city of roses.

As the seat of the Supreme Court of Appeal, Bloemfontein is the **judicial capital of the Republic of South Africa**. It has been a university town since 1855 and is mainly an administrative centre: more than 40% of jobholders are employed in public, semi-public or social institutions. The other central factor of Bloemfontein's economy is light industry (furniture, glass, canned food and other foodstuffs). Bloemfontein's central location has caused the town to become a transport hub and made it the home to the country's largest railway workshops. This largely modern city with a number of historic buildings and museums is a good starting point for exploring Free State and is also a suitable stop on the journey from the Cape to Johannesburg. It is not worth a long stay.

The first big Voortrekker camp north of the Orange River developed in the vicinity of what is now Thaba'Nchu around 1836. Somewhat further west the Boer Johannes Brits built his farm by a spring in 1841, which he called »Bloemfontein« (»flower spring«). By 1841 the British had decided to found a garrison and seat of administration here, thus they bought Brits' farm. The small town became the capital of Orange Free State when the latter was formed in 1854; at that time it stretched from the banks of the Bloemspruits to the Bloemfonteinberg (now Naval Hill), which rises in the north-east. During the Boer War Bloemfontein was fiercely contested. After the founding of the Union of South Africa it became the country's third capital alongside Pretoria and Cape Town. When huge gold deposits were found in the area of Welkom-Odendaalsrus-Virginia in 1946, which were amongst the richest in the world together with the ones of Witwatersrand, a huge economic boom took place. Ironically this Boer stronghold is the **birthplace of the ANC**: black leaders met here in 1912 to protest against the Union that was denying them the right to vote. They founded the South African Native National Congress, the forerunner of the ANC. **J. R. R. Tolkien** was born in Bloemfontein (► Famous People). It is planned to rename the town Mangaung (»place of the cheetah«); the wider urban area already bears that name and there is also a township of the same name too.

History

One of Bloemfontein's landmarks: Fourth Radsaal

City layout The town is situated on the central plain of the highveld, a semi-arid region; Naval Hill towers over the city in the north-east. It undoubtedly lives up to its name »flower spring»; numerous **parks and garden** line the town centre. The main shopping street is Maitland Street. In the west it joins President Brand Street, on which most of the buildings in the following paragraphs are located.

What to See in the City Centre

Hoffman Square The lively centre of the city is Hoffman Square where the main post office is located. The square, where a market used to be held and which took on its current appearance during the 1970s, is a good starting point for a one-hour city tour.

Twin-Spired Church North of Hoffman Square is the Twin-Spired Church, the only Dutch Reformed church in South Africa with two towers. It is also known as »President's Church«, because it was the site of historically significant ceremonies; several presidents of the Orange Free State were sworn in here.

★ **National Museum** The National Museum just a few steps to the west is well worth a visit (Charles St./Aliwal St., open Mon–Fri 8am–5pm, Sat 10am–5pm, Sun noon–5.30pm). It has a large collection of fossils and archaeological discoveries on display, including the famous Florisbad skull and the skeleton of one of the **largest known dinosaurs**. The ethnological department informs its visitors about the life of the San, while other exhibitions present the history of the Free State.

The city hall on the other side of Hertzog Square was built in 1935 to a design by Sir Gordon Leithe. It is decorated with Italian marble and intarsias of Burmese wood.

City hall

Now turn south into President Brand Street. The first building on the right is South Africa's Supreme Court of Appeal, a neo-classical building dating from 1929. Its halls are decorated with stinkwood panels and magnificent carvings.

Court of Appeal

One of the town's most beautiful buildings is the Fourth Raadsaal opposite. The foundation stone for this neo-classical building was laid by President F. W. Reitz in 1890; it was completed in 1893. The last session of parliament of the old republic of the Orange Free State took place in the Fourth Raadsaal, before Bloemfontein was occupied by the British in March 1900. Today it is the seat of the Provincial Council of the province of Free State. In front of the building is a monument (by Coert Steynberg) to Christian de Wet, a general in the Boer War.

★
**Fourth
Raadsaal**

Further noteworthy buildings south of the Fourth Raadsaal are the Waldorf Building, which was originally built for an insurance company in 1928 but now houses offices and flats, and the Jubileum Building & Hall, once the seat of the Dutch Reformed Church of the Orange Free State.

**Waldorf Building
Jubileum
Building**

On the other side of the road is the seat of the National Literary Museum in the Old Government Building built in 1908. It is a treasure trove of **African literature**, containing manuscripts, books, photographs, and other items that were owned by South African writers. The music and theatre museum are also housed here. (open Mon–Fri 8am–12.15pm, 1–4pm, Sat 9am–noon). In the garden there are busts of famous literary figures who wrote in Afrikaans.

★
**National
Afrikaans
Literary Museum**
🕐

A little further south on Brand Street the Fire Station of 1926 and the Supreme Court (1906) stand opposite each other.

**Fire Station
Supreme Court**

This grand building in Victorian style was built on the west side of Brand Street in 1885 and was the **residence of three presidents of the Orange Free State**. The museum in this building features P. J. H. Brand (1864–88), P. W. Reitz (1888–95) and M. T. Stein (1896–1900); it also displays paintings and furniture (open Tue–Fri 10am–noon, 1–4pm, Sat, Sun 1–5pm). In addition the Old Presidency acts a cultural centre (art exhibitions, theatre performances, music nights).

Old Presidency
🕐

Bloemfontein Map

Botanical Gardens

Jan van Riebeek

DAN PIENAAR

Harry Smith

Tempe Sports Ground
Garrison Golf Course

Brebner

General Dan Pienaar

Nettleton

Levieux

James Scott

John Weston

Clapp

R 702

Thomson

Chris Botha

Athlone

General Hertzog

Brebner

Conroy

Reyger

Brebner

Arboretum Ave.

ARBORETUM

Bompart

Haarburger

High Street

Agste

Klerck

Skool

Melville

Parfant

Klerck

Brill

Brill

WESTDENE

Britt

Signal Hill

John Chard

Poole

St. Michael's
School

Mchardy

BRANDWAG

Leisegang

Stapelberg

Kimberley

Wanner-
burg

Melville

Captain Proctor

General Dan Pienaar

Kellner

Third St.

Victoria
Square

Second Ave.

Pres. Steyn

2

Reid

President Reitz

First Ave.

Arboretum

Collins

Derde

Eerste

University, Kimberley

Springbok
Park

Donald Murray

Parfitt

Zastron

Kellner

Barnes

Kellner

Kloof

4

Grey College
High School

Nelson Mandela Drive

N 8

N 8

Second Ave.

Zastron

Nelson Mandela Drive

CENTRAL

Grey College
Junior School

Jock Meiring

Sir George Grey

Henry

King's Park

Loch
Logan

First Ave.

Charles

Markgraaf

14

15

17

Eunice
High School

Donald Murray

5

Kingsway

8

Elizabeth

13

16

Maitland

Eunice
Primary School

7

St. Andrew's

9

Pres. Brand

12

St. Andrew's

Fontein

Groenewoud

At. Horak

First Ave.

21

Selborne

President Paul Kruger

Park

6

10

Green

Douglas

Gordon

Gun

Donald Murray

Parfitt

King Edward

Etta

Park

R 706

R 700

11

18

Steven

John Knox

Coligny

R 702

WILLOWS

Victoria

Pres. Boschoff

Pres. Brand

Suid

Saltzmann

Goddard

Kazerne

19

Martin-
Luther-
Square

Haldon

Van Heerden

Faure

Harris

R
48

President
Brand Cemetery

Petrusburg, Kimberley

1

WILGEHOF

Roth

Huguenot

President

R 700

Willowpark
Ontspannungs-
terrein

National
Hospital

Oranje Hospital

R
30

Daniel van Niekerk

Rose

George Home

Kolbe

ORANJESIG

Rose

James Dick

0,25 mi

500 m

©Baedeker

Krause

Waltey

Church

Kommandant Erwee

Jagersfontein

National Woman's Memorial
Colesberg, Aliwal North

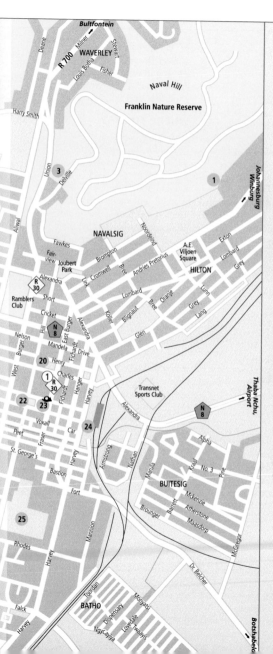

1 White Horse
2 Oliewenhuis Art Museum
3 Orchid House
4 University of the
   Orange Free State
5 Zoo
6 The Fountain
7 Sand du Plessis Theatre
8 Civic Theatre
9 H. F. Verwoerd House
10 Old Presidency
11 First Raadsaal
12 National Afrikaans
   Literary Museum
13 Court of Appeal
14 City Hall
15 Hertzog Square
16 Fourth Raadsaal
17 National Museum
18 Anglican Cathedral
19 Hertzog House
20 Twin-Spired Church
21 Supreme Court
22 Hoffman Square
23 Main Post Office
24 Railway Station
25 Queen's Fort

Where to stay
① Protea Landmark Hotel
② Hobbit Boutique Hotel

Where to eat
① De Oude Kraal
② Beef Baron

▶ VISITING BLOEMFONTEIN

INFORMATION

Tourist Centre
60 Park Road
Tel. 051 405 8490
www.bloemfontein.co.za
www.freestateprovince.co.za

TRANSPORT

The airport is 8km/5mi east of the city; there are no bus connections (taxis, car rentals). The Algoa, Amatola and Trans Oranje long-distance trains leave from the station in Maitland Street; the Diamond Express connects Pretoria and Johannesburg. Overland buses leave from the tourist centre.

WHERE TO EAT

▶ Expensive

① *De Oude Kraal*
35km/22mi south on the N 1
Tel. 051 564 0636
Top South African »boerekos« (country food) is served in the old farmhouse. Reservation is necessary. Good rooms too (luxury category; www.deoudekraal.co.za).

▶ Inexpensive

② *Beef Baron*
22 Second Ave., Westdene
Tel. 051 447 4290. Excellent steaks, good fish, and fine wines.

WHERE TO STAY

▶ Luxury

② *Hobbit Boutique Hotel*
19 President Steyn Avenue
Tel. / Fax 051 447 0663
www.hobbit.co.za
A small settlement house dating from 1925; it has been a guesthouse since 1988 and has been voted the best in South Africa several times. The decor is somewhat over-the-top; the service is very friendly. Romantic dinners for in-house guests.

▶ Mid-range

① *Protea Landmark Hotel*
Sanlam Plaza, East Burger St.
Tel. 051 430 8000
www.protea-hotels.co.za
Large four-star hotel with a pleasant atmosphere, one of the best accommodation addresses in Free State, with 115 comfortable rooms.

First Raadsaal ✱ ⊙

The city's oldest building, dating from 1849, stands in St George's Street east of Brand Street. At first the thatched house served as a school, then as the seat of the people's assembly and later as a church. Today it is a museum of the history of Bloemfontein (open Mon–Fri 10am–1pm, Sat, Sun 2–5pm).

Hertzog House ⊙

To get to Hertzog House, turn right into Saltzman Street and then into Goddard Street. The home of the Boer general and later prime minister J.B.M. Hertzog also houses a museum (open Tue–Fri 9am–noon, 1–4pm). Hertzog lived here from 1895 to 1924. During the revolt of 1914 his friends took up position in the branches of the tree that stands outside the dining room to protect him. Amongst them was a future president of South Africa: C. R. Swart.

Back in St George's Street stands the Anglican Cathedral, which is definitely worth a look (built 1850–85). The belfry had to be removed in 1964. From the church go north along Gordon Street to get back to Hoffman Square.

Anglican Cathedral

What to See outside the City Centre

A stone column at King's Park, which is decorated with the city's coat of arms, marks the spring at which Bloemfontein was founded.

The Fountain

The Sand du Plessis Theatre, opened in 1985 in Markgraaf Street, accommodates 950 spectators for opera, ballet, concerts and plays. Opposite is the H. F. Verwoerd House, whose windows are made up of over 17,000 colourfully shimmering pieces of glass.

Sand du Plessis Theatre

Towards the west **President Swart Park** and King's Park form the boundary of the city centre. The former contains the stadium of the Free State with a capacity of 35,000, as well as a heated swimming pool, tennis courts, playgrounds and a campsite. **King's Park**, opened in 1925 by the then Prince of Wales, has over 4000 rose bushes. On the first Saturday of the month a flea market takes place here. The western part of King's Park is occupied by the zoo (open daily 8am–6pm, in winter until 5pm).

Parks

In the north-east the city centre reaches almost to the summit of Naval Hill (access via Union Avenue). On the hill, which has a lovely view, is the Franklin Nature Reserve, a wildlife park with antelopes,

★
Naval Hill

Old and new times: the court of appeal and a modern administrative centre

zebras and giraffes (open daily 8am–5pm). The large **horse sculpture** (White Horse) on the hill's east side was set up during the Boer War and served as a landmark for the British cavalry. The largest orchid collection in South Africa can be seen in the **Orchid House** in Hamilton Park at the foot of Naval Hill (open Mon–Fri 10am–4pm, Sat–Sun until 5pm).

✱
Oliewenhuis
Art Gallery
⊙

The Oliewenhuis, a beautiful house built in 1941 and surrounded by wild olive trees, is a branch of the National Museum and as such houses one of the **best collections of South African art**. 16 Harry Smith St., open Mon–Fri 8am–5pm, Sat 10am–5pm, Sun 1–5pm).

Queen's Fort

⊙

The Queen's Fort in the south of the city was built in 1848 and rebuilt shortly after the Boer War broke out. The **military museum** documents amongst other things the role the South African army played during the World Wars. In addition weapons and photographs of the rebellion of 1914 can be seen (open Mon–Fri 10am–noon, 1–4pm).

National
Women''s
Memorial

✱
Anglo-Boer War
Museum

The 36.5m/120ft obelisk south of the city (Monument Road) was built in memory of the more than 26,000 women and children who died in British concentration camps during the Boer War of 1899–1902. The pedestal contains the ashes of the Englishwoman Emily Hobhouse, who stood up for the internees. The adjacent Anglo-Boer War Museum displays amongst other things weapons from the Boer War (open Mon–Fri 9am–4.30pm, Sat 10am to 5pm, Sun 2–5pm).

Around Bloemfontein

✱
Free State
Botanical
Gardens

⊙

Take the General Dan Pienaar Drive to reach the Free State Botanical Gardens located approx. 10km/6mi north-west of the city centre. On 45ha/110 acres it gives an overview of the highveld's flora and has interesting **fossilized tree trunks**, which are many millions of years old. Part of the garden is a well-tended park with a lake; in the much larger remaining area the natural vegetation has been left untouched. Open daily 8am–6pm.

Maselspoort

In Maselspoort, 22km/14mi north-east of Bloemfontein on the banks of the Modder River, there is a pleasant holiday centre with a wide range of leisure activities and different kinds of accommodation.

Soetdoring
Nature Reserve

The Soetdoring Nature Reserve is located 35km/22mi north-west of Bloemfontein, also on the Modder River. The reserve covers an area of more than 4000ha/10,000 acres and contains the Krugersdrif reservoir. It is home to waterfowl and, amongst other wild species, lions and cheetahs that were introduced here.

The Blyde River has created a magnificent canyon in the northern Drakensberg mountains.

★ Blyde River Canyon

Province: Mpumalanga

One of the most magnificent experiences of the country's landscape is the »Grand Canyon« of South Africa. A visit to Blyde River Canyon can be combined with a visit to the Kruger National Park.

The Blyde River Canyon Nature Reserve is situated at the edge of the Drakensberg plateau north of ►Pilgrim's Rest in one of the most attractive landscapes of South Africa. Here, the **highveld** falls off abruptly from its altitude of more than 2000m/6500ft to the adjoining **lowveld** to the east. The lowveld is shaped by a subtropical climate and reaches an altitude of only around 150–600m (500–2000ft).

After the Grand Canyon (USA) and the Fish River Canyon (Namibia), the Blyde River Canyon is the **third-largest canyon in the world**. It is the centre of the reserve and a popular stop on the journey from Johannesburg to the Kruger National Park; stay at least two days to really enjoy the scenery. The 27,000ha/65,000-acre nature reserve can be explored by car on an excellent **panoramic road**, from which paths lead off to magnificent viewpoints. The bottom of the canyon can be reached by rewarding, marked hiking trails.

VISITING BLYDE RIVER CANYON

INFORMATION

Mpumalanga Parks Board
Halls Gateway, N 4, Nelspruit
Tel. 013 759 5432
www.mpumalangaparksboard.com
Komatiland Ecotourism ▶Sabie

WHERE TO STAY

▶ Mid-range

Westlodge
12 Hugenote Street
Graskop
Tel./fax 013 767 1390
B & B in a small Victorian property with four elegant rooms, some of which have a view of God's Window. This establishment prides itself on its hospitality. For non-smokers.

▶ Budget/Mid-range

Aventura Blyde Canyon
Tel. 013 769 8005
www.aventura.co.za
Popular resort on the R 532 with a luxurious guesthouse at the canyon, 93 self-catering chalets, camping, pool, shop, golf, etc. Advance booking advisable.

Aventura Swadini
Tel. 015 795 5141
Situated beautifully at the northern edge of the area at the Blyde River, close to the R 531. 78 chalets for 4–6 people, campsite. 75km/47mi to the Orpen Gate of the Kruger National Park.

▶ Budget

Belvedere Guest House
Close to Bourke's Luck.
The house was built in 1915, near the old power station, magnificent views. Self-catering accommodation for 4–6 people, can only be booked en bloc (information and bookings at Mpumalanga Parks Board).

Flora and fauna The climate and the variations in altitude created a very diverse vegetation. In the areas affected by high levels of precipitation (2000mm/80in annually in Blyde River Canyon, only 500mm/20in in the lowveld) there are thick forests, which are a result of comprehensive afforestation measures. The rock, particularly dolomite and quartzite, is often covered with colourful lichen. The plants in this park include giant ferns, rare orchids, and also species of erica and protea. There are many species of animal living in the nature reserve, such as all the monkey species that can be found in South Africa and many different bird species, too.

Some history The **Blyde River** (Motlatse River) rises in the Drakensberg mountains south of Pilgrim's Rest. On its way north it joins the **Treur River** (Sefogane River) at Bourke's Luck Potholes. It flows through the canyon and then into the Olifants River. In the winter of 1844 the Boer Voortrekkers were searching for an access to the sea that was not under British control. They set off on an expedition to Delagoa Bay under the leadership of **Andries Hendrik Potgieter**. The women and children were left behind with the unwieldy wagons on the malaria-free hills of the Transvaal Drakensberg mountains. When the planned time of return came and went, those who had been left behind thought something had happened to the expedition. In their grief they called the river where they were waiting »Treur River«, »river of mourning«. Shortly after they set off towards Ohrigstad Potgieter caught up with them. He had found an access point to the sea, but needed more time than originally thought. After the happy reunion they called the river »Blyde River«, meaning »river of joy«.

Hikes

Two hiking trails lead through the nature reserve. The starting point of the 65km/40mi, five-day-long **Blyde River Canyon Hiking Trails** is God's Window; the end point is Swadini; huts provide overnight accommodation. The **Fanie Botha Hiking Trail** is almost 80km/50mi long; it takes five days to get from the starting point of Ceylon Forest 13km/8mi west of ▶Sabie to the end, God's Window. Registration is essential. Blyde River Canyon Hiking Trail: Mpumalanga Parks Board; Fanie Botha Hiking Trail: Komatiland Ecotourism.

✳ Panorama Route

Graskop

Graskop (population: 15,000), centre of the wood and forestry industry is a good starting place. Leave Graskop on the R 532 north-bound, then turn off east on to the R 534 after 3km/2mi (after 15km/9mi the R 534 joins up with the R 532 again). After 1.5km/1mi on the R 534, a 200m/220yd path on the right leads to the park above the Drakensberg cliff. The **Pinnacle**, a free-standing granite column, towers out of the forested gorge.

✳ ✳
God's Window

Next stop is God's Window. From the viewpoint at an altitude of 1829m/6000ft take in Blyde River Canyon in the north, the 1000m/3300ft lower lowveld and the Kruger National Park all the way to the border of Mozambique in the east, and forested mountains in the west. The signposted trail to the nearby rain forest is also well worth a visit.

Lisbon Falls

The R 534 leads back to the main road (R 532) in a big loop. To get to the Lisbon Falls, follow the R 532 southbound for 1km/0.6mi, then turn right on to the 2km/1.2mi-long access road leading to the falls. The river plummets to the ground in several little cascades with a total of drop of 92m/302ft.

Berlin Falls

A good 1km/0.6mi north of where the R 534 meets the R 532, a road (2km/1.2mi) leads to the Berlin Falls. The 45m/148ft-high waterfall is named after the farm on whose terrain it is sited. It is possible to swim in the pool at the bottom of the fall, and the banks are a good spot for a picnic.

Three Rondavels: three rocks whose shapes resemble the Xhosa round huts tower over Blyde River Canyon.

★★
Bourke's Luck Potholes

Now follow the R 532 northbound. Bourke's Luck Potholes can be reached on this road approx. 27km/17mi after the R 534 joins the R 532. They are located at the confluence of the Treur and Blyde rivers. Over the course of millions of years the sand and rubble carried along by the river have hollowed out the bedrock. Here a gold prospector tried his luck to no avail (hence »Bourke's Luck«). Today trails lead to points with magnificent views. A former military base has been transformed into a tourism centre with a hotel and a restaurant. Two 5km/3mi hiking trails begin at the visitor centre.

★★
Three Rondavels

This next section of the R 532 that has truly splendid views. The Three Rondavels View Site is excellent; the 3km/2mi-long access road turns off to the right from the R 532 13.5km/8.5mi past Bourke's Luck Potholes. The 700m/2300ft-deep gorge is dominated by the **Three Rondavels**, rock bastions in the shape of straw-covered round huts, and the 1944m/6378ft-high **Mariepskop**, the highest mountain in the Transvaal Drakensberg range. It was named after the Pulana chief Mariep, who fled to the top of the mountain with his tribe at the beginning of the 19th century and fended off the attacks of the Swazi there. Far below the dammed Blyde River sparkles at the confluence with the Ohrigstad River.

For a short stretch the R 532 travels along the Blyde River Nature Reserve (past the comfortable Odendaal Camp), then it veers off to the west and joins the R 36. An attractive pass road and a reptile park are located north of the crossing, but the direct route is towards the south.

On the road to the Abel Erasmus Pass opened in 1959, continue northbound towards Tzaneen. The bendy drive takes in a 700m/ 2300ft difference in altitude (head of pass 1224m/4016ft) and offers incredible views.

Abel Erasmus Pass

Approx. 50km/30mi north-east of the crossing R 532/R 36 on the R 527 is the Swadini Reptile Park. This well-kept complex is home to indigenous snakes, lizards and crocodiles as well as others from all around the world. Explanations and reptile presentations make the visit into an interesting experience (open daily 9am–5pm; cafeteria).

★
Swadini Reptile Park
⊙

The R 36 southbound towards Lydenburg leads to the »Echo Caves«, which are located 1km/0.6mi behind the crossing on the western side of the road. The Echo Caves are large dripstone caves in the dolomite rock. Discoveries have proved that they were already inhabited during the Stone Age. Rock paintings and artefacts from the caves can be seen in the **Museum of Man** (open daily 8am–5pm).

★
Echo Caves
⊙

The road continues through a rugged landscape. Fruit and vegetables, as well as tobacco are cultivated in the reddish soil. 23km/ 14mi beyond the Echo Caves lies **Ohrigstad**. The first time a village was set up here was in 1845, but it had to be abandoned again because of frequent malaria epidemics. It was only in the 20th century after the mosquito plague was removed that people started settling in the fertile valley again. Ruins still remind visitors of the early village.

Bourke's Luck Potholes: bizarre rock formations at the confluence of the Blyde and Treur Rivers

Some 18km/11mi after Ohrigstad the R 36 meets the R 533. Take this road eastbound. Soon a 4km/ 2.5mi-long path leads off to the right to the **Ohrigstad Dam**. The reservoir is surrounded by the Ohrigstad Dam Nature Reserve, a popular leisure, camping and picnic area.

A further 6km/4mi east a road turns off to the Mount Sheba Nature Reserve 10km/6mi away. This reserve still has relatively pristine forests (►Pilgrim's Rest).

Mount Sheba Nature Reserve

Definitely plan a visit to the gold-digger settlement ►Pilgrim's Rest (approx. 15km/9mi east of the access road to the Ohrigstad Dam). From here it is approximately another 15km/9mi back to Graskop.

Pilgrim's Rest

Bredasdorp · Cape Agulhas

D 9

Province: Western Cape
Population: 10,000

Altitude: 164m/538ft
Distances: Cape Town 170km/105mi

It is hardly possible to get any further south in Africa: the distance from Bredasdorp to the continent's southernmost point is only 30km/20mi.

Bredasdorp is situated in the fertile **Overberg** region; agriculture and sheep breeding are two of the main activities here. The town was named after Michiel van Breda, a merino sheep breeder, who founded this place in 1837 as the first »dorp« in South Africa. Every year in August it is host to a **Wild Flower Show**.

What to See in and around Bredasdorp

Shipwreck Museum

The Shipwreck Museum is a small but very interesting museum (open Mon–Fri 9am–4.45pm, Sat until 1pm). All kinds of discoveries from sunken ships, such as figureheads, gold and silver coins and furniture are on display in the museum's hall. The oldest exhibit comes from the *Nieuwe Haarlem*, which sank in 1647. The Independent Church, the Old Parsonage and the Old Coach House are also part of the museum.

Lonely lighthouse at Africa's southernmost point

Bredasdorp Nature Reserve encompasses an 800ha/2000-acre area at the end of Van Riebeeck road. Besides many species of protea and erica this reserve is home to the red **Bredasdorp lily**. The 368m/1207ft hill affords a nice view. The best time is from September to October, when the spring flowers are blossoming.

Bredasdorp Nature Reserve

A visit to the fishing village of Arniston (Waenhuiskrans) 24km/15mi to the south-east is a worthwhile excursion. Several of the old fishing huts have been restored. The name Arniston comes from a British ship that smashed on the cliffs nearby in 1815. 372 people lost their lives. The second name stems from a huge cave 2km/1.2mi south (only accessible at low tide).

✷ **Arniston/ Waenhuiskrans**

The De Hoop Nature Reserve is more than 40,000ha/100,000 acres in size and lies 50km/30mi north-east of Bredasdorp. Get to it via the road leading to Wydgeleë (open daily 7am–6pm). It encompasses a picturesque stretch of coastline and some beautiful backcountry with the typical Cape vegetation, **fynbos**, with 1400 plant species, of which 25 are considered very rare or endangered; 63 species of mammal (50 of which live on land and 13 in the sea), 40 reptile species, and 260 bird species can also be found in this reserve. The period between June and November, particularly August and September, is an excellent time for watching **right whales**, which come here to mate or give birth. There are cottages for rent and a campsite.

✷ **De Hoop Nature Reserve**

Cape Agulhas and not the Cape of Good Hope is **Africa's southern-most point** (latitude 34° 49' 58" S). Here, at the »Cape of Needles« (the Portuguese word »agulhas« means »needles«), the Atlantic and Indian Oceans meet. The name has several explanations: it is said that it was here that the compass needles of the first Portuguese sailors pointed directly north; another interpretation suggests that the needles refer to the sharp reefs. The scenery here is not very spectacular. The **lighthouse**, which was built in 1848 and is the second-oldest in South Africa (open Mon–Sat 9.30am–4.45pm, Sun 11am–3pm), and a radio transmitter direct the ships that pass along the horizon. The Agulhas Bank is just off the coast; for more than 250km/155mi the sea is no more than 110m/360ft deep, then the ocean floor drops off suddenly. These waters are some of the world's most fertile fishing grounds.

✷ **Cape Agulhas**

🕐

The town of L'Agulhas 5km/3mi east of the Cape consists of modern holiday homes and some shops. The stretch of coast here is rocky and not very attractive. A very nice beach for swimming, fishing and collecting shells can be found in Struisbaai, 8km/5mi north-east of the Cape. The fishing village of Hotagterklip 2km/1.2mi north of Struisbaai is a popular motif for South African artists. Some of the **old fishing huts** have been restored and are now protected heritage buildings.

L'Agulhas

◄ Struisbaai

✷ ◄ Hotagterklip

Caledon

C 9

Province: Western Cape
Population: 7000

Altitude: 324m/1063ft
Distances: Cape Town 100km/60mi

From the vineyards on the Cape the spectacular Sir Lowry's Pass leads into the farming country of the Overberg region. The springs of Caledon were already highly valued by settlers in the 17th century.

Mineral springs　The quiet rural village of Caledon is situated between Cape Town and Cape Agulhas in an area used for intensive agriculture and sheep breeding. It developed around springs that are still being used for their healing properties. Every day a total of seven springs yield 900 cu m/34,000 cu ft of water rich in iron and minerals. Six of them have a temperature of approx. 50°C/120°F; the seventh is cold.

What to See in and around Caledon

Caledon Museum　The town museum has Victorian antiques on display (Constitution Street, closed Sat afternoon and Sun). The Anglican Holy Trinity Church built in 1855 and the historic houses in Mill Street are all classified as national monuments.

✱
Victoria Wild Flower Garden　The Victoria Wild Flower Garden (open daily 7am–5pm) created in 1927 is part of the Caledon Nature Reserve at the **Swartberg**, north of the town centre. The 56ha/140-acre park-like complex has a unique diversity of flowers. There is a big wild flower show in September.

✱
Salmonsdam Nature Reserve　The 834ha/2100-acre Salmonsdam Nature Reserve spans an area 40km/25mi south-east of Caledon. It can be reached via the R 316 and R 326 towards Stanford. The **fynbos vegetation** typical of the

 VISITING CALEDON

INFORMATION

Overberg Tourism Association
22 Plein Street
Caledon
Tel. 028 214 1466
www.tourismcapeoverberg.co.za
www.viewoverberg.com
www.southernmost.co.za

HOT SPRINGS

► **Mid-range/Luxury**
Caledon Casino Hotel & Spa
Nerina St., tel. 028 214 5100
www.thecaledon.co.za
The publicly accessible bathing facilities (with sauna, massage, etc.) are part of a tastefully decorated hotel complex from 1990. There is a popular casino.

Cape grows here. It can be explored on the signposted trails (1–2 hours). With a bit of luck visitors may spot antelopes, gazelles and various bird species such as blue cranes (open daily 7am–6pm). ⊕

★
Genadendal

Nelson Mandela visited Genadendal (population: 3500; 30km/19mi north-east of Caledon) in 1995 and named his residence in Cape Town after it. This place was founded by Georg Schmidt in 1738 as **South Africa's first mission station**. He belonged to the Bohemian Brethren (Moravians) who even at that time taught the very endangered Khoi to read and write as well as baptizing them. This alienated the farmers, who were illiterate themselves, and members of the conservative Dutch Reformed Church. Schmidt had to leave the country in 1774 and it was not until 1792 that the Moravians were able to start their work again. In 1838 South Africa's first teacher training college, now the mission museum, was built (closed Sat afternoon and Sun; tel. 028 251 8582). In addition there are buildings dating back to

Genadendal: pharmacy dating from 1830 and behind it the parsonage of 1823–24

the 18th and 19th centuries. The choir of the Moravian Church is definitely worth listening to. The two-day, challenging **Genadendal Hiking Trail** allows visitors to experience the beautiful landscape of the Riviersonderendberg mountains; information and (early) booking at Vrolijkheid Nature Reserve, tel. 023 625 1621.

★
Cape Town

C 8

Province: Western Cape
Population: 3 million
(Greater Cape Town)

Altitude: 12m/39ft
Distances: Bloemfontein 1000km/620mi,
Johannesburg 1400km/870mi,
Durban 1750km/1090mi

Cape Town is considered one of the most beautiful cities in the world, particularly because of its grand, majestic backdrop: Table Mountain. Visitors should be sure to find time to drive around the Cape peninsula with its magnificent beaches and wine-growing regions.

Economic and political significance Cape Town (in Afrikaans: Kaapstad), on the south-western tip of the African continent is, after Johannesburg (excluding Soweto), South Africa's second-largest city as well as the oldest European settlement in southern Africa. In the first half of the year the parliament, otherwise located in Pretoria, resides here. As the capital of Western Cape province, »CT« is the seat of administrative institutions and also has Roman Catholic and Anglican bishops. Furthermore it is a significant cultural centre with two universities, technical colleges, and many state and private schools. Cape Town also plays a major role in the country's economy. The trading and fishing port with modern handling equipment is the second-largest in the country after Durban; from here the great majority of South African fruit is exported. Industrial activity, such as oil refineries, concrete factories, chemical plants, textile and clothing factories, as well as electronics and light industry, is mainly located in the north and east of the city. Many banks, insurance companies, as well as many printing and publishing houses have their headquarters in Cape Town.

Cape Town is the only city on the African continent south of the equator where blacks are in a minority. The Cape Malays are a special group. They are descendants of slaves who came to South Africa from Indonesia; their cultural tradition is shaped by Islam.

The **climate** is determined by the two ocean currents that come to-gether at Africa's south-west coast: the Agulhas current coming down the east coast from the equator and the cold Benguela current that originates in Antarctica and flows past Africa's west coast. The summers are warm and dry to hot; in winter the weather corre-sponds to north European April weather with low temperatures, rain, and cold winds. The summer months are marked by the ap-pearance of the »Cape Doctor«, a strong south-easterly wind that frees the town of dust and exhaust fumes. The south-easterly is also responsible for the famous »table cloth« over Table Mountain: the wind forces moist warm masses of air from False Bay onto the mountain; the moisture condenses and clouds lie over the plateau like cotton wool.

Victoria & Albert Water-front (in front of Table Moun-tain with its famous »table cloth«): idyllic during the day, tumultuous at night

The oldest human traces at the Cape were left by the Khoikhoi and San (formerly called Hottentots and Bushmen respectively) who lived here as shepherds, hunters, gatherers and fishermen. The first European sailor to circumnavigate the Cape was Bartolomeu Dias from Portugal in 1488; in 1503 his fellow countryman Antonio da Saldanha was the first European to climb Table Mountain. The colo-nization of South Africa however only began with the disembarka-

History

tion in Table Bay on 6 April 1652 of the Dutch merchant Jan van Riebeeck, who on behalf of the Dutch East India Company set up a base for the merchant ships on their way to India. The choice of location was favourable: around Table Mountain springs provided fresh water, the soil was fertile, and over time ever larger areas of cultivation were developed by settlers from the Netherlands, Germany and France. For a long time the history of Cape Town, the »Mother City«, as it is still called today, was identical to the history of the rest of South Africa. The small »Vleck van den Kaap« (»Village at the Cape«) developed into a town for merchants, administration and craftsmen, which was the capital of the British colony from 1806 to 1910. Since then, as the seat of parliament, it has been one of the country's capitals.

! **Baedeker** TIP

On two wheels

It is great fun to explore »the most beautiful city at the most beautiful end of the world«, and particularly its surroundings, on a bicycle, motorbike or a scooter. Bicycles: Rent-n-Ride (tel. 021 434 1122, also inline skates and skateboards); Downhill Adventures (tel. 021 422 0388, www.downhilladventures.com). Motorbikes: Le Cap Motor Cycle Tours (tel. 021 423 0823, www.lecapmotorcyclehire.co.za); Karoo Biking (p.177); Hire a Harley (tel. 021 424 3990, www.harley-davidson-capetown.com).

Highlights Cape Town

Victoria & Alfred Waterfront
The city's most popular leisure area with restaurants, cafés, cinemas and other attractions in old buildings and modern malls.
► page 239

City Bowl
The lively city centre around Long Street and Government Avenue with the Company's Gardens, major sights and good museums.
► page 241-245

Table Mountain
Table Mountain has a lot to offer, including fascinating scenery, cute dassies and romantic sunsets.
► page 248

Kirstenbosch Botanical Gardens
Have a picnic in the midst of a wonderful display of flowers – ideally during the popular concerts on Sunday afternoons.
► page 251

Robben Island
An insight into the not-too-distant past in the country's most notorious prison.
► page 260

Tour around the Cape peninsula
From the penguins to the stormy Cape of Good Hope, then via Chapman's Peak Drive to the wonderful beaches of Camps Bay and Clifton.
► page 250

Vineyards in Constantia
Groot and Klein Constantia, Buitenverwachting, Steenberg, Constantia Uitsig: relax in old Cape Dutch manor houses and enjoy some excellent wines.
► page 253

● VISITING CAPE TOWN

INFORMATION

Cape Town Tourism
Pinnacle, Burg St. /Castle St.
Tel. 021 426 4260

Victoria & Alfred Waterfront
Tel. 021 405 4500
www.tourismcapetown.co.za
www.cape-town.org

Western Cape Tourism (▶p.141) and
an office of SANParks are also based
in the Pinnacle.

TRANSPORT

The international airport is 22km/
14mi south-east of the centre. Bus
connections are offered by several
companies; the Backpacker Bus provides drop-offs at hotels and hostels.
Taxis are expensive. The luxury trains
Blue Train and Rovos Rail as well as
the long-distance Trans Karoo and
Trans Oranje depart from the station
(Adderley St.). The terminal for
coaches (Greyhound, Intercape,
Translux) is connected to the station
on the south-east side. Metro trains
operate between 5.30am and 6–7pm
and run to the suburbs (Cape Peninsula, False Bay, to Simon's Town,
and to Bellville in the north). They
are relatively safe, particularly during
rush hour; it is best to take the
marginally more expensive first class.
The Golden Arrow city buses have
their central stop (with an information office) at Grand Parade. The
minibus taxis are practical for getting
to the suburbs and are sufficiently safe
when the standard safety rules are
followed. Their main stop is located
on the roof of the station and is
accessible from the Golden Acre
shopping centre. Buses and minibuses
only operate until approx. 7pm.

HOLIDAYS AND EVENTS

Jan: New Year Karnaval (on the
first and following Saturdays), the
city's largest and most colourful
event; Jazzathon (jazz festival); Cape
to Rio Yacht Race (every second year:
2010, 2012 etc). March: Cape Town
Festival (theatre, film, etc.); North Sea
Jazz Festival. May: Cape Gourmet
Festival. Dec–March: Sunday afternoon open-air concerts in the Kirstenbosch Botanical Garden. Current
event listings can be found in the
daily newspapers *Cape Times* and
Argus.

EATING OUT

▶ Expensive

① *Aubergine*
39 Barnet Street, Gardens
Tel. 021 465 4909
Excellent cuisine in an elegant setting
in the former residence of the supreme judge at the Cape. Traditional
dishes such as bobotie, game, fish and
vegetables accompanied by select
wines.

② *Blues*
8 The Promenade
Camps Bay
Tel. 021 438 2040, www.blues.co.za
Great seafood restaurant, Californian-
style with a view of the ocean. The
shrimp in avocado cream with fried
vegetables, coconut and raisins is
very good. Reservations are necessary,
try to book a table on the
beachfront.

Cape Town Map

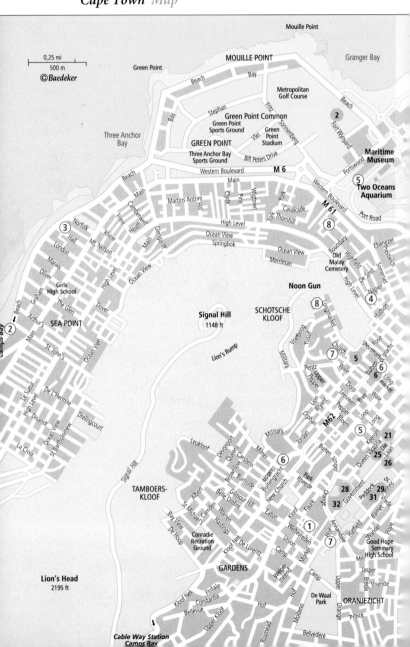

0,25 mi
500 m
© Baedeker

Mouille Point

Granger Bay

MOUILLE POINT

Green Point

Beach

Bay

Metropolitan
Golf Course

2

Stephan

Sonnenberg

Fritz

Beach

Three Anchor
Bay

Green Point Common
Green Point
Sports Ground

Bay

GREEN POINT

Green
Point
Stadium

Vlei

Portswood

Maritime
Museum

Three Anchor Bay
Sports Ground

Bill Peters Drive

Western Boulevard   M 6

Port Wynard

5
Two Oceans
Aquarium

Main

Western Boulevard

M 61

Port Road

Beach

Main

Martins Antrim

Clyde

Pine

Midtown

Cavalcade

York

3

Norfolk

Camberwell

Hall

Rhine

Frere

Health

Mt. Nelson

Glengariff

Thornhill

8

Boundary

Highfield

Ebenezer

London

Main

High Level

Ocean View
Springbok

Ocean View

Old
Malay
Cemetery

De Smit

Somerset

Napier

Hudson

Prestwich

Marais

Oliver

High Level

Ocean View

Merriman

High Level

4

Girls
High School

Dover

Noon Gun

8

Longmarket

Graham

The Glen

Voetboog

Yusuf

Church

Rose

2

Arthur's

SEA POINT

Signal Hill
1148 ft

SCHOTSCHE
KLOOF

Military

7

Wale

Shortmarket

5

6

Main

St. John's

Ocean View

Lion's Rump

Pentz

Upper
Pepper

Dorp

Leeuwen

Bree

Wale

Loop

Buitengracht

6

Long
market

Le Sueur

De L'Hermite

High Level

Disandt

Drelingcourt

Lion

Bryant

Orphan

Pepper

Bloem

Long

M62

5

Ketelm

21

La Croix

Ocean View

St. Bartholomew

Leukloof

Devonport

Queens

Carstens

Mlmer

Military

Jordan

Buiten

Singel

Queen Victoria

25

Laan

Bonnie

26

Signal Hill

Brownlow

Burnside

Upper
Buitengracht

6

Park

Rheede

New Church

28

Government

29

St.

TAMBOERS-
KLOOF

Albert

Gilmour Hill

Belle Ombre

Eaton

Faure

Orange

Paddock

31

Frede

Bay View

St. Michael's

Camden

Warren

Hastings

Weltevreden

Hof

Annandale

32

Barnet

Lion's Head
2195 ft

De Hoop

Kloof Nek

De Lorentz

Camp

Mortel

1

7

Hatfield

Good Hope
Seminary
High School

Hope

Conradie
Recration
Ground

Union

Camp

Wandel

Constantia

Frdale

Welgemeend

Mill

Jasper

Breda

Vriende

Bellevue

Kloof

Hof

Camp

Molteno

Upper
Orange

Prince

GARDENS

Cable Way Station
Camps Bay

Rosmead

De Waal
Park

ORANJEZICHT

Belvedere

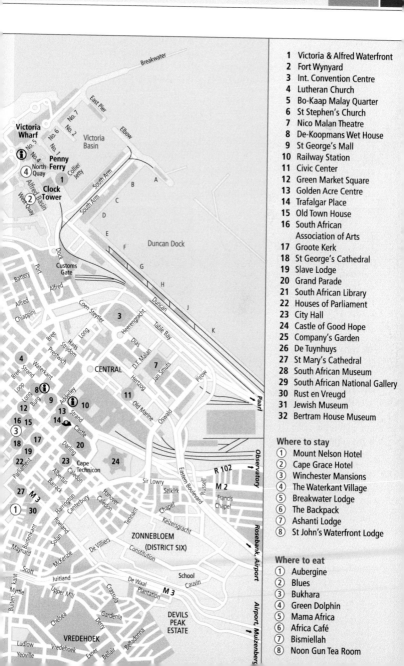

1 Victoria & Alfred Waterfront
2 Fort Wynyard
3 Int. Convention Centre
4 Lutheran Church
5 Bo-Kaap Malay Quarter
6 St Stephen's Church
7 Nico Malan Theatre
8 De-Koopmans Wet House
9 St George's Mall
10 Railway Station
11 Civic Center
12 Green Market Square
13 Golden Acre Centre
14 Trafalgar Place
15 Old Town House
16 South African
   Association of Arts
17 Groote Kerk
18 St George's Cathedral
19 Slave Lodge
20 Grand Parade
21 South African Library
22 Houses of Parliament
23 City Hall
24 Castle of Good Hope
25 Company's Garden
26 De Tuynhuys
27 St Mary's Cathedral
28 South African Museum
29 South African National Gallery
30 Rust en Vreugd
31 Jewish Museum
32 Bertram House Museum

Where to stay
① Mount Nelson Hotel
② Cape Grace Hotel
③ Winchester Mansions
④ The Waterkant Village
⑤ Breakwater Lodge
⑥ The Backpack
⑦ Ashanti Lodge
⑧ St John's Waterfront Lodge

Where to eat
① Aubergine
② Blues
③ Bukhara
④ Green Dolphin
⑤ Mama Africa
⑥ Africa Café
⑦ Bismiellah
⑧ Noon Gun Tea Room

③ *Bukhara*
33 Church St.
Tel. 021 424 000
Top-class, elegant Indian restaurant.
Dining on the veranda is particularly
nice.

► Moderate
④ *Green Dolphin*
Victoria & Alfred Waterfront
Tel. 021 421 7471
Popular upscale jazz bar (music from
8pm); good cuisine, salads, seafood
and meat, as well as sandwiches and
burgers.

⑤ *Mama Africa*
178 Long St./Pepper St.
Tel. 021 426 1017
Couscous, crocodile steak, kudu steak
or chicken, everything tastily prepared. Cosy ambience. African music
in the evenings. Make reservations for
the weekend.

► Inexpensive
⑥ *The Africa Café*
108 Shortmarket St.
Tel. 021 422 0221
Dishes from 16 African countries,
good presentation and all-you-can-eat
for one fixed price. Touristy, but still a
very good value for money. Non-
smoking restaurant.

⑦ *Bismiellah*
2 Upper Wale St.
Tel. 021 423 0850
An institution in Bo-Kaap with real
Cape Malay cuisine. No alcohol.

⑧ *Noon Gun Tea Room*
273 Longmarket Street
Tel. 021 424 0529
Cosy tea room near the Noon Gun
(good view) with wonderfully aromatic teas, but there are also Malay
fish and meat curries.

WHERE TO STAY
► Luxury
① *Mount Nelson Hotel*
76 Orange Street, Gardens
Tel. 021 423 1000
www.mountnelson.co.za
First port of call in Cape Town: pink-
coloured luxury hotel in the British
Empire style in the middle of the city.
Terrace and huge park with centuries-
old trees. All the amenities that can be
expected from one of the most
expensive hotels in the country. A cup
of tea on the terrace is a real treat.

② *Cape Grace Hotel*
Waterfront
Tel. 021 425 0012
www.capegrace.com
Top hotel in a magnificent location: in
the marina with a great view of Table
Mountain. 121 rooms and suites, high
tea is served in the library. Pool, plenty
of sports opportunities (golf, riding,
etc.) close by.

③ *Winchester Mansions*

221 Beach Rd., Sea Point
Tel. 021 434 2351
www.winchester.co.za
This hotel in Cape Dutch style has won many awards for its hospitable and comfortable atmosphere. 35 rooms and 18 suites, the expensive ones have an ocean view; brunch with jazz on Sundays. Heated pool.

► Mid-range

④ *De Waterkant Village*

1 Loader Street
Tel. 021 409 2500
www.dewaterkant.com
Located in the colourful Bo-Kaap quarter and in the hip Waterkant quarter, this organization owns around 50 small houses and apartments (for 1–6 people) as well as the guesthouse De Waterkant House; all very nice to luxurious, top service.

⑤ *Breakwater Lodge*

Portswood Road, Greenpoint
Tel. 021 406 1911
www.bwl.co.za
More than 100 years old, this establishment used to be a prison; close to the waterfront; bright white and modernized. Good value for money.

50 small houses in Bo-Kaap quarter: De Waterkant Village

► Budget

The Backpack

⑥ 74 New Church St.
Tamboerskloof
Tel. 021 423 4530
www.backpackers.co.za
Considered to be the city's best, »most fancy« and most comfortable back-packer hostel; excellent value for money. Garden with a pool.

⑦ *Ashanti Lodge*

11 Hof St., Gardens
Tel. 021 423 8721
www.ashanti.co.za
Probably the most popular back-packer accommodation in the city, not least because of its view of Table Mountain and the party atmosphere. However, it is noisy and not first class; a more peaceful and better choice would be one of the guesthouses that also belong to the lodge.

⑧ *St John's Waterfront Lodge*

6 Braemar Road, Green Point
Tel. 021 439 1404
www.stjohns.co.za
Large, well-run hostel close to the V & A Waterfront. With a garden and swimming pools.

City layout   The natural setting of Cape Town makes it one of the most impressive cities in the world, which is why the city itself takes a bit of a back seat. The grid-pattern centre can be found in the **City Bowl** between Table Bay and the harbour in the north and the 1000m/3280ft Table Mountain to the south. Many architectural witnesses to the past have survived here.

The recently constructed **Victoria & Alfred Waterfront** is a great enrichment to Cape Town; the harbour area, once unattractive, has now become a lively district, great for taking a stroll and enjoying the entertainment. The Malay quarter **Bo Kaap** has mosques and houses dating from the 18th and 19th centuries as well as from the 1950s. It is located at the north-west edge of the city centre. The **Atlantic** coast south of Green Point boasts attractive seaside towns from Sea Point to Hout Bay.

The »better« **suburbs**, almost exclusively inhabited by whites, such as Goodwood, Parow and Bellville, are situated north-east of the centre along the N1 towards Paarl. In the vicinity of the harbour are ugly 19th-century industrial and residential estates such as Saltriver and Woodstock. Most inhabitants of the **Cape Flats** are coloureds. The Flats start south-east of the city centre and go all the way to False Bay. Between the N2 and False Bay are black townships such as Athlone, slums like Crossroads and the satellite towns of Mitchell's Plain and Khayelitsha. Sprawling townships can also be found north of Table Bay near the large factories, such as Atlantis and Philadelphia.

What to See in the City Centre

Sightseeing tour   The tour of the city described below begins at the Victoria & Alfred Waterfront (parking spots). For a shorter city tour make the Castle of Good Hope your starting point; then take the »blue-waved« Waterfront Bus to the Waterfront after looking at the city centre (the bus leaves from the station from 7am to 11.30pm approx. every 15 minutes).

Table Bay, Harbour   Cape Town's artificial harbour is the fourth-busiest in South Africa (after Richards Bay, Saldanha and Durban). Since its bed consists of rocks and cannot be dug out any further it is only 12m/40ft deep at low tide. Fishing boats still land their catch in the Victoria & Alfred Basins. The harbour is also the base for the **cruise ships and ocean-going trawlers** that moor at the Duncan and Ben Schoeman docks, which were constructed in the 1930s.

Fruit is an important export product, so one of the largest cold-storage warehouses in the world was built for it. The eastern part of Duncan dock contains the largest dry dock of the southern hemisphere: the **Sturrock Dock** can easily hold two large ships. The Royal Cape Yacht Club is also located in the harbour; it is the starting point of the Cape to Rio regatta.

Several companies offer harbour tours as well as various other tours (the **sunset tours in schooners** by the Waterfront Bay Company, www.waterfrontboats.co.za, are enjoyable). The Penny Ferry takes four minutes to shuttle back and forth from one quay to the other.

Harbour tours

The Victoria & Alfred Waterfront is an entertainment area modelled on San Francisco, Boston or London. It runs along the two harbour basins that were constructed in 1860 and named after Queen Victoria and her son. In the late 1980s the area was a desolate, run-down fishing harbour; today the Waterfront is one of Cape Town's hotspots. People are out and about here day and night, drawn by the shops, bars, music bars, restaurants, hotels, theatres (one of them being the Dock Road Theatre in a former power station), cinemas and museums. Wherever possible the old fabric of the buildings was kept: a three-storey warehouse was transformed into a luxurious hotel, a pump house was made into a bar and the prison became the Business School of the University of Cape Town. The new buildings were constructed in the style of the surrounding buildings. The **Clock Tower Centre** houses a large tourist information office (open daily 9am–9pm) which not only provides information on Cape Town, but also enables visitors to book trips. There is also an office for VAT returns here (►p.154).

★ ★
Victoria & Alfred Waterfront

Beer garden at the Clock Tower on the waterfront

South African Maritime Museum

The maritime museum (Dock Road, open daily 10am–5pm) illustrates the history of the harbour, fishing, shipping companies and shipwrecks. Model ships and treasures from ships that have sunk are also on display. The museum includes several old ships in the harbour that are open to view. One of them is the »Alwyn Vincent«, a **steam tugboat of 1859**, which was launched in Venice and is used for harbour tours.

★

Two Oceans Aquarium

The aquarium, opened in 1995 (Dock Road, open daily 9.30m–6pm), is one of the best in the world. It has more than 30 tanks, which are home to 300 fish species native to the Atlantic and Indian Oceans. Among the special attractions are the **Open Ocean Tank**, which holds more than 2 million litres/500,000 gal, and in which sharks and rays can be observed, and the **Living Kelp Forest**, which reflects the coastal fauna. A sandy beach with penguins simulates high and low tide at the Cape.

Old Clock Tower

The entrance to Alfred Basin is guarded by the neo-Gothic clock tower that was erected in 1887; it was once the home of the harbour-master. Near the Clock Tower, stands the **Nelson Mandela Gateway**, from which boats shuttle back and forth to Robben Island (►p.260).

Victoria Wharf

This large shopping mall is a good place to while away time in boutiques, restaurants, cafés and good Africana shops, and find unusual souvenirs.

Van Riebeeck Statues

Follow Heerengracht into town to get to the bronze statues of Jan van Riebeeck and his wife Maria (by J. Week and D. Wolbers). They are probably close to the place where the founders of Cape Town came ashore on 7 April 1652 (at that time the sea still came this far inland).

Nico Malan Theatre

Hertzog Boulevard leads to the Nico Malan Theatre, Cape Town's most modern stage, where opera, ballet, plays and concerts are performed. The building is connected to the Civic Centre, the seat of the city council.

Adderley Street

Go down Adderley Street, one of the main shopping streets, in a south-westerly direction. It passes the **Railway Station**, which was built in 1970. The next large building complex is the **Golden Acre** shopping centre. During its construction the remains of a reservoir from 1663 were discovered. Black tiles on the ground floor mark the position of Table Bay's coastline in 1663. More shops can be found in the underground shopping arcade between Strand Concourse and Adderley Street.

★

Castle of Good Hope

The Castle of Good Hope, South Africa's oldest surviving stone building, was built between 1666 and 1679 as the seat of the gover-

Changing of the guards in the Castle of Good Hope: from this balcony governors made speeches and announced important decrees.

nor and for the protection of the first settlers. The fort never came under attack. The wing with the balcony supported by columns served the purpose of display; now it houses the **William Fehr Collection** (open daily 9am–4pm), which includes paintings, chinaware, glass, pottery and furniture from South Africa, Europe and Asia dating from the 17th, 18th and 19th centuries. Further parts of the fort can be viewed on a guided tour (11am, 12 noon, 2pm). This is a good way to see the dungeon, storage rooms (with archaeological exhibits) and one of the bastions. A larger wing is not accessible: it is the provincial headquarters of the South African army. The **Changing of the Guard** takes place Mon–Fri at noon.

The square between the castle and City Hall was built in 1710 as a parade ground. Today it serves as a car park, and one corner is reserved for flower and fruit stalls. A **colourful market** takes place here in the mornings from Monday to Saturday. The square's south-west side is occupied by the imposing City Hall (1905), whose architectural style is a mix between neo-Renaissance and British colonial style. The Cape Town Philharmonic Orchestra gives concerts in the Great Hall; the City Library here has national and international newspapers. The 60m/200ft clock tower, which has a carillon dating from 1923, was modelled on Big Ben.

Grand Parade

◄ City Hall

! *Baedeker* TIP

Jazz in Cape Town

Cape Town is also known as Jazz Town; many bars have live music and stars perform at many concerts. The big get-together is the four-day Cape Town Jazz Festival in January. At Blue Note (Cine 400 Building, College Road in the Rylands district) the stars of the future meet Tue–Sat from 8.30pm. Hip meeting places include Manenberg's Jazz Café (Clock Tower Centre, Waterfront) and the Green Dolphin (also on the Waterfront).

Groote Kerk

The Groote Kerk forms the southern end of Adderley. It is South Africa's oldest and best-known church (open Mon–Fri 10am–2pm, Sun 7pm). The church dates from 1678; it was rebuilt twice, once in 1703 and again in 1836. The belfry dates from 1703. The Groote Kerk is the mother church of South Africa's **Nederduitse Gereformeerde Kerk** (NGK). A huge organ, a pulpit of Burmese teak and a carved lectern are among its notable features.

Slave Lodge

The neighbouring building was constructed in 1679 as a hostel for slaves of the Dutch East India Company (VOC); up to 1000 slaves lived here in dreadful conditions. Thibault and Anreith converted it into a post office in 1811 and later it became the seat of the Supreme Court. Travelling exhibitions take place here. The museum rooms display various items from antiquity to the history of the VOC. The museum's courtyard has a reproduction of the tomb of Jan van Riebeeck and his wife, who are buried in Jakarta. Open Mon–Sat 9.30am–4.30pm.

St George's Cathedral

St George's Cathedral opposite is the seat of the Anglican archbishop in South Africa. From 1986 to 1996 this position was held by Nobel Peace Prize winner **Desmond Tutu**, who provided a refuge for demonstrators in the fight against apartheid here. The neo-Gothic sandstone building was constructed between 1897 and 1901 to designs by Herbert Baker.

★
Government Avenue
South African Library

The continuation of Adderley Street is Government Avenue, a popular promenade lined by tall oak trees, which connects the city centre with the suburbs at the foot of Table Mountain. The National Library, which was opened in 1812, is also situated on this street. It is the **state copyright library** (i.e. it owns a copy of every work published in South Africa).

Houses of Parliament

On the opposite side of the street are the impressive Houses of Parliament (main entrance on Parliament Road), which were first used for parliamentary meetings in 1814. Between the end of January and the end of June this is the seat of the **South African parliament**, which otherwise sits in Pretoria. The debates are public (registration at the Public Relations Office; passport necessary). When there are no meetings there are guided tours (entrance Plein Street, bookings tel. 021 403 2266). Next door is the Tuynhuis of 1751, the seat of the State President (not open to the public).

◄ De Tuynhuis

The 5.5ha/13.5-acre Botanical Garden (entrance on Government Avenue) is located where Jan van Riebeeck planted his fruit and vegetable gardens in 1652. With its exotic trees and flowers, a rose garden, an aviary, ponds and a café the park is a popular place to come and relax. A monument was erected in remembrance of Sir George Grey, who was governor at the Cape from 1845 to 1862; there is also a statue of Cecil Rhodes (1853–1902; he is pointing north and the pedestal's inscription reads »your hinterland is there«, an expression of Rhodes's dream to expand British influence from the Cape all the way to Cairo. The monument was designed by Sir Herbert Baker, a British architect who came to South Africa in 1892 and was given many commissions by Rhodes.

★
Company's Garden

At the edge of the park is the South African Museum founded in 1825 (Queen Victoria Street, open daily 10am–5pm). Its fascinating, broad collection contains archaeological finds and provides information about the native fauna as well as about extinct dinosaurs. One section is devoted to the **culture of the San and the Khoikhoi** (the Linton Panel, a rock drawing, is outstanding). Other spectacular exhibits include the Lydenburg heads (► p.89), a huge communal nest made by weaver birds, a stuffed foal of the now extinct quagga and the huge whale skeletons. A planetarium is connected to the museum (shows Mon–Fri 2pm, Tue 8pm, Sat, Sun 1pm and 2.30pm).

★
South African Museum

🕐

The South African National Gallery mostly owns works by South African artists, but also paintings by British, French and Dutch masters of the 17th to 20th centuries (open Tue–Sun 10am–5pm, pleasant café).

★
South African National Gallery
🕐

Right next door (88 Hatfield Road) is the **country's oldest synagogue**; it was built in 1862. A modern extension of note both for its architecture and content houses Jewish art as well as exhibits on the history of the Jews in South Africa. Open Sun–Thu 10am–5pm, Fri 10am–2pm. Good kosher food is served in the Riteve café.

Jewish Museum

🕐

The Georgian-style Bertram House (1820) at the south-west end of Government Avenue was built of brick. It is used by the South African Museum: old furniture, pottery, silver and other objects of art (open Tue–Thu 9.30am–4.30pm).

Bertram House Museum

🕐

St George's Mall

The best option here is to return down the shady Government Avenue, keep left in front of the Groote Kerk and then turn right again immediately into St George's Mall. This pedestrian zone with its fountains, benches and shops is an inviting place to shop and a popular place for musicians and street artists.

✶ ✶
District Six Museum

The District Six Museum is located a block further west (25A Buitenkant Street); it is **one of the country's most important apartheid museums**. District Six was a vibrant black quarter with a population of approx. 60,000, who were driven out after 1966; the quarter was torn down and today those who were displaced are slowly returning. In 2004 the first house was handed over, and over the next few years another 4000 homes will be built. Former inhabitants are adding to the moving memorabilia with their equally moving stories (open Mon–Sat 9am–4pm).

✶
Green Market Square

Old Town House ▶

From St George's Mall turn left on to Longmarket or Shortmarket Street to get to Green Market Square, the **old heart of the city**: it was built as a market square in 1710. In front of the attractive backdrop of **art deco houses** a market offers arts and crafts and junk (Mon–Sat). On the west side stands the Cape Dutch-style old town hall, built in 1755 and known as the Old Town House. This was the original home of the Town Watch. In 1804 the city council moved in

Green Market Square with Old Town House and Metropolitan Methodist Church of 1876

Baedeker TIP

Long Street

Long Street is a good 2km/1mi long, and with its Victorian, Cape Dutch and art deco houses it is not just Cape Town's most beautiful street, but also the embodiment of its atmosphere. Hip bars, second-hand shops, bistros, mini flea-markets, romantic hotels and backpacker hostels, wacky hairdressers, Africana shops, antique shops and book shops … it's easy to spend an entire day here.

and later the building became the courthouse. Today it displays a collection of paintings that was presented to the state by **Sir Max Michaelis** in 1914. It mainly contains works by Dutch and Flemish masters of the 17th century, such as Frans Hals, Jan Steen, van Ruysdael and Jan van Goyen (open Mon–Fri 10am–5pm, Sat 10am to 4pm).

South African Association of Arts

Contemporary South African art can be found one street down at the South African Association of Arts (35 Church Street, open Mon–Fri 10am–5pm, Sat 10am–1pm).

Riebeeck Square

Riebeeck Square is located where the first settlers at the Cape set up their camp. The building that is now **St Stephen's Church** initially served as a theatre and an opera. In 1839 it was converted into a Dutch Reformed Church.

★ Bo Kaap

The **Malay quarter** is situated further north-west beyond Buitengracht at the foot of Signal Hill, between Rose, Wale, Chiappini and Shortmarket Streets. The colourful, low single-storey buildings are still primarily inhabited by Malays. They are the descendants of slaves who were brought to the Cape from the East Indies during the 17th century and usually made a name for themselves as craftsmen. There are several small mosques; five times a day muezzins loudly call people to prayer from the minarets. The **Masjid Korhaanol** mosque in Longmarket Street has remained unchanged since its construction in 1886. In 1934 the convoluted houses, often displaying elements of Cape Dutch architecture, only narrowly escaped demolition. Many of the 19th-century houses have recently been refurbished. The **Bo Kaap Museum** (71 Wale Street), housed in a building from 1763, illustrates the way of life of the Cape Muslims (open Mon–Sat 9.30am–4.30pm). The quarter is best explored with a local guide. Tana Baru Tours allows visitors to learn about the traditions, including tea in a private home (tel. 021 424 0719).

Its colourful little houses and steep roads make Bo Kaap one of Cape Town's most interesting residential districts.

Lutheran Church
★
Gold of Africa Museum ▶

Strand Street leads back to the city centre. It is the site of the Lutheran Church, which was consecrated in 1787 and is one of the oldest Protestant churches in South Africa. The belfry was added in 1818; the pulpit and choir screens are by Anton Anreith. The pastor's house (**Martin Melck House**, 1782) accommodates the Gold of Africa Museum with its excellent, historically significant exhibits (open Mon–Sat 10am–5pm, nice garden with a café).

★
Koopmans-De Wet House
☉

A further noteworthy building in Strand Street is number 35: built in 1701, the façade was designed by Louis Thibault (1771). It still contains its original furniture and illustrates the lifestyle of a successful businessman of the 18th century. The antique furniture was made in European and South African workshops (open Tue–Sun 9.30am–4pm).

What to See outside the City Centre

Green Point

Green Point Common north-west of the centre is a large green space with many sports facilities, including a golf course. It belongs to the district of the same name at the foot of Signal Hill (see below). Close to the sea is the **fort** built in 1861 by R. H. Wynyard, after whom it is named. Not far south of the fort the **Cape Medical Museum** (Portswood Road, in the Old City Hospital Complex) provides an insight into medical history (open Tue–Fri 9am–4pm). Take Beach Street to get to **Green Point Lighthouse**; the lighthouse was built in 1824 and is the oldest in South Africa.

Fantastic views of the city and Table Bay can be had from the top of the 350m/1150ft Signal Hill. It is particularly delightful and popular in the evenings when the city's sea of lights sprawls out below (but avoid it at night). It can be accessed from the south via Kloof Nek and Signal Hill Street. On weekdays a cannon is fired at noon (the observatory provides the signal). In the past both seafarers on ships and Cape Town's inhabitants oriented themselves by the **Noon Gun**.

★
Signal Hill

South-east of the centre, close to the intersection of Buitenkant Street and Roeland Street, is the Rust en Vreugd, a Cape Dutch townhouse from 1778 with a magnificent façade. Parts of the **William Fehr Collection** are on display here, including watercolours, African paintings and antiques (open Mon–Sat 8.30am–4.30pm).

★
Rust en Vreugd

St Mary's Cathedral on the corner of Roeland and St John Streets is **South Africa's oldest Roman Catholic church**.

St Mary's Cathedral

In the eastern district of Ysterplaat (access via the N 1 / M 5) the South African Air Force Museum illustrates the history of the South African Air Force since the 1920s, particularly its involvement in the two World Wars. Open Mon–Fri 8am–3.30pm, Sat until 12.30pm.

South African Air Force Museum

Head south-east out of the city centre on the N 2 / M 3 or the M 4. The Groote Schuur Hospital is not far. The hospital, which was

Groote Schuur Hospital

Signal Hill is a wonderful spot, both during the day and in the evening (with Table Mountain in the background).

TABLE MOUNTAIN

✶ ✶ Cape Town's landmark is the 1087m/3566ft Table Mountain, which rises
south of the city centre. Often its plateau is covered in a »table cloth«, a
cloud layer. Since the weather changes quickly, an ascent should be started
as soon as the mountain is cloud-free. The reward is a fantastic view of
Cape Town and the Cape peninsula.

⏱ Hours of operation of the cable car:
Dec–Jan 8am–10pm (last ascent 9pm), shorter
during the rest of the year. In strong wind the
cable car shuts down. Cable Way Information,
valley station, Tafelberg Road, tel. 021 424 8181,
www.tablemountain.net

Natural history

The mountain, made up of layers of sandstone
and slate, forms the northern end of the Cape
peninsula. It is flanked in the east by the 1001m/
3284ft **Devil's Peak** and in the west by the
669m/2195ft **Lion's Head**, from which it is
separated by a wide depression. Towards the
south Table Mountain continues as a broad
plateau and finally drops steeply to the Orange
Kloof, which only rises 200m/656ft above sea
level. The Kirstenbosch botanical garden is
located on the mountain's eastern slope, and in
the west the Twelve Apostles tower over the
seaside towns of the Atlantic coast.

Thanks to its location between the west coast and
False Bay, Table Mountain has a **mountain
climate** with a lot of precipitation (1400mm/55in
annually). Most precipitation falls during the
winter between May and September. Two dams
(numerous streams have their sources here)
contribute to Cape Town's water supply.

The special climatic conditions have brought
about an **extraordinary wealth of plants**
(more than 2200 species) and animals. Soil
erosion, the loss of native plants, the encroach-
ment of alien vegetation and the large number of
visitors all threaten this picturesque mountain. For
that reason the **Table Mountain National
Park** was set up, which together with Table
Mountain itself includes the entire Cape peninsula
(www.tmnp.co.za).

Getting to the top

Since 1929 a cable car has run up Table
Mountain; the cabins of the new Swiss-made
cable car that went into operation in 1997 turn
once through 360° during the ride. The lower
station in Tafelberg Road can be reached by car
from the city centre via Buitengragt Street and
Kloof Nek Road. The most convenient bus
connection is provided by Cape Town Tourism,
leaving from the Visitors' Centre (corner of Burg
Street and Castle Street).

Table Mountain can also be ascended on foot,
and it is said there are more than 300 ways to do
this with varying degrees of difficulty. The
Portuguese explorer Antonio da Saldanha, who
was the first European to climb Table Mountain in
1503, chose the Platteklip Gorge. Depending on
the starting point, visitors should allow 2–4
hours. Some routes are extremely steep and also
dangerous because of the fog that can appear
very suddenly. The tour is a real alpine enterprise
and equipment should be chosen accordingly:
apart from alpine boots, waterproof and warm
clothing is a must as are food and 2 litres of water
per person (it can get very hot in summer, so it is
best to go early in the morning). It is also best not
to go alone and before departing to inform
someone about the chosen route and the
approximate time of return. A map is available
from the tourist information office, which also
arranges mountain guides. The »Approved Paths
of Table Mountain« brochure by the Mountain
Club of South Africa is recommended; it also
contains useful information (97 Hatfield Street,
tel. 021 465 3412). The lower station is the
starting point of the popular »Indian Windows«;
the easy trail from the Botanical Gardens in
Kirstenbosch (approx. 3 hrs) is also very pleasant.
Table Mountain not only causes climbers to break
a sweat, but also has adrenaline-filled activities in
store, such as abseiling from a 112m/122yd piste
down to the Indian Windows trail (www.abseila-
frica.co.za), as well as bungee jumping
(www.adventurevillage.co.za).

Top views

There is a café on the peak and a self-service
restaurant with a viewing platform. This is the
starting point for several short trails, from which
the fantastic backdrop can be enjoyed. Tortoise
Walk (which is also marked by a tortoise) can be
completed in 5 to 10 minutes, the Rock Dassie
Walk, along which many of the comical klipspringers can be seen, requires around 10 to 20
minutes. At the weekends Table Mountain is lit
up with flood lights after nightfall. Signal Hill
(p.247) has the best view and is also a great place
to take a picture.

Su*
Bo*

founded in 1932, became world famous when **Christiaan Barnard** (1922–2001) performed the first heart transplants here in 1967. A small museum recalls this event (www.gsh.co.za).

Observatory ▶ Not far to the east in the district of Observatory is **South Africa's oldest observatory** (1821). Since the construction of the South African Astronomical Observatory in Sutherland in the Karoo, the observatory in Cape Town has only been used by amateur astronomers.

Mostert's Mill Shortly after the N 2 leaves the M 3, the latter, now also known as Rhodes Drive, goes past Mostert's Mill. This windmill was built in 1792 and is still fully functional. Not far to the east in Cecil Road, in the friendly suburb of Rosebank, the German artist Irma Stern lived from 1928 until her death in 1966. More than 200 of her works as well as antiques and other art objects are on display here (open Tue–Sat 10am–5pm).

Irma Stern Museum ▶

🕑

University of Cape Town West of Rhodes Drive is the campus of the University of Cape Town. UCT was established in 1918 and originated as the South African College, which had been founded in 1829. Today approx. 20,000 students are enrolled here, of whom 50% are white. A path leads up to the **Rhodes Memorial**, which was created from Table Mountain granite in 1912 to a design by Sir Herbert Baker. It is a very popular spot, as it commands fantastic views and there is also a good café.

Groote Schuur Not far to the south-east, beyond Rhodes Drive, the **residence of the state president** occupies the site where a granary of 1657 once stood; it was later replaced by a prestigious country house; this latter building was destroyed in a fire in 1896. Subsequently Cecil Rhodes commissioned Sir Herbert Baker to construct a new building in the Cape Dutch style.

Woolsack This house, which Rhodes built for his friend, the author **Rudyard Kipling**, is also part of the university complex. Once again Sir Herbert Baker was the architect. Kipling and his family spent the summer months here from 1900 to 1907.

Newlands The Newlands district to the south is considered one of Cape Town's best neighbourhoods. Cape Town's only surviving watermill, the **Josephine Mill** of 1818, is in Boundary Road (open Mon–Fri 9am–4pm). Another attraction in Boundary Road is the **Rugby Museum** with its lovingly compiled collection (open Mon–Fri 9am–5pm).

🕑

✳ ✳ Drive around the Cape Peninsula

A tour of the Cape peninsula alone would justify a trip to South Africa. It is 52km/32mi long and up to 16km/10mi wide. At the

⏵ VISITING CAPE PENINSULA

WHERE TO EAT

▶ Moderate

Bertha's Restaurant
Waterfront, Simon's Town
Tel. 021 786 2138
A café and restaurant at the marina.
Seafood and satays as well as old
favourites. Very romantic in the
evenings.

Dunes Bar & Restaurant
Hout Bay, at the beach
Tel. 021 790 1876
What could be better than eating fish
while sitting under a sunshade with
your feet in the sand? Informal,
familiar atmosphere. With a bit of
luck you may even spot a whale.

WHERE TO STAY

▶ Luxury

The Cellars Hohenort
93 Brommersvlei Road, Constantia
Tel. 021 794 2137

www.cellars-hohenort.com
This winery built in 1769 is now one
of the most beautiful hotels in the
country. It is surrounded by a park
with ancient trees. 38 rooms and 15
suites with elegant, antique decor;
pool, spa and golf course as well as
fine restaurants and a wine bar.

Constantia Uitsig Country Hotel
Spaanschemat River Road, Constantia
Tel. 021 794 6500
www.uitsig.co.za
Beautifully situated vineyard with 16
luxurious summer houses and two
swimming pools. Wine tasting available in the grounds. Three excellent
restaurants: Constantia Uitsig, La
Colombe (provincial Cape Dutch
cuisine, tel. 021 794 2390) and the
relaxed, inexpensive Spaanschemat
River Café. Dine in the garden or by
the fire in the winter. Reservations are
necessary.

---

end of its coastline of long, white sandy beaches lies the famous **Cape
of Good Hope**; the nearby Cape Point is the Cape peninsula's southernmost point (however, it is not the southernmost point of the African continent, ▶ Bredasdorp). The sights are described here in the
form of a 150km/90mi round trip along the east coast to the Cape of
Good Hope and back to Cape Town along the west coast. Leave the
centre of Cape Town southbound on the M 3, Rhodes Drive, past
the university campus (▶ p.250). Take the M 6, which branches off
from the M 3, which leads to the Kirstenbosch Botanical Gardens.

The botanical garden on the eastern slope of Table Mountain is considered one of the best and most beautiful in the world. Cecil Rhodes
left the land to the state in 1902. 528ha/1305 acres (of which approx.
40ha/100 acres are cultivated) are home to around 9000 of the
22,000 plant species native to South Africa. This diversity is however
limited by the cool, moist winters. The hedge of wild almond trees
planted by Jan van Riebeeck in 1660 and an avenue lined by camphor trees and sycamores planted by Cecil Rhodes in 1898 are two

**✹ ✹
Kirstenbosch
Botanical
Gardens**

Cape Peninsula Map

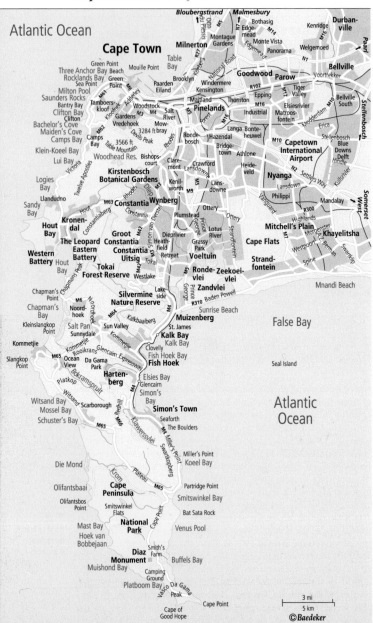

of the garden's historically significant features. Most of the plants bloom sometime between mid-August and mid-October. From January to March the **red disa**, an orchid also known as »the pride of Table Mountain«, flowers along streams and in shady gorges. The **proteas** show their wonderful colours from May to October. The fragrance and herb garden, the protea area and the rock garden are outstanding attractions. The Bird Bath, a pond created by Colonel C. Bird in 1811, is the centre of an area with yellowwoods. The restaurant has a shady terrace. The Botanical Garden is open Sept–Mar 8am–7pm, April–Aug until 6pm (tel. 021 799 8620 or 021 761 4916, www.nbi.ac.za). During the summer months visitors come here to enjoy a picnic and an open-air concert on Sunday afternoons (photograph p.249).

Groot Constantia ✹✹

Groot Constantia, South Africa's **oldest and best-known vineyard**, lies in the valley of Constantia. Take the M 63 from the Kirstenbosch Botanical Garden towards the south-west and turn onto the M 41; direct route from Cape Town on the M 3 to the Plumstead/Constantia/Hout Bay exit, then continue on the M 41.

In 1685 the Dutch East India Company gave the parcel of land to the governor, Simon van der Stel. They assigned him the task of checking which agricultural products grew best at the Cape. He had a manor house built and lived in it from 1699 until his death in 1712. The property was divided up amongst van der Stel's heirs and be-

Cape Dutch architecture at its best: the manor house of the Buitenverwachting vineyard, once part of Constantia

came run down. Hendrik Cloete, grandson of one of the first Dutch immigrants, bought the house as well as part of the land in 1778; he commissioned Louis Thibault and Anton Anreith to extend the building. In 1791 the ground-floor wine cellar was added; in addition Cloete increased the area of cultivable land, since his wines were quickly highly valued in Europe too (by Napoleon, among others). The spread of phylloxera at the Cape in 1860 ended the first golden age of viticulture. In 1885 the entire property was sold to the colonial administration.

The **manor house** has been a museum since 1926 and contains valuable furniture from the 18th and 19th centuries, as well as paintings and china. The wine cellar façade of 1791 is adorned by gable figures by A. Anreith; the building is now used for exhibitions and conventions. A small museum informs visitors about viticulture at the Cape (open daily 10am–5pm). The **Jonkershuis** is a popular, upscale restaurant (open Tue–Sat 9am–11pm, Sun and Mon until 5pm, reservations tel. 021 794 6255), the atmosphere in the **tavern** in the former warehouse is more rustic (tel. 021 794 5255). The property's wines can be tasted in the modern wine cellar (Dec–April 9am–6pm, otherwise 10am–5pm; cellar tours 10am–4pm on the hour, in the winter only at 10am, 11am and 3pm. Booking recommended (tel. 021 794 5128). At the weekends Groot Constantia is overrun.

Further vineyards
Other renowned vineyards of Constantia that do not just produce excellent wines but also have luxurious accommodation and/or fine restaurants are also well worth visiting: Constantia Uitsig (▶p.251), Klein Constantia, Buitenverwachting (Restaurant, tel. 021 794 3522, www.buitenverwachting.co.za) and Steenberg with one of the best hotels in the country (www.steenberghotel.com, tel. 021 713 2222)

False Bay
Between the Cape peninsula and Cape Hangklip lies False Bay, which is about 30km/20mi wide and still part of the Atlantic. Here are several popular destinations for excursions or holidays, such as Muizenberg and Strand (▶ Somerset West). While the water on the Cape peninsula's western seaboard is still quite nippy, the bay's sandy beaches that are frequented by the warmer Agulhas current have much more pleasant temperatures for swimming (up to 20°C/68°F). From the end of May to the beginning of December this is a good place for whale watching.

Muizenberg
Muizenberg, which is connected to Cape Town by a light railway, developed from a military post set up in 1743. It became famous when Cecil Rhodes acquired a holiday home here in 1899 (see below). Several well-off citizens did the same and Muizenberg became the **typical South African seaside town** with many holiday homes only inhabited for a few weeks every year. There are three museums worth visiting here, all of them on the southern edge of town (Main Road). The **Natale Labia Museum** with a collection of furniture and works

Colourful beach huts at St James near Muizenberg

of art (currently closed) is a branch of the South African Gallery. **Cecil Rhodes** (►Famous People) died on 26 March 1902 in his cottage, which is now also a museum and has some of this influential man's personal items on display (open 9.30am–4.30pm, Sun from 10.30am). The **Muizenberg Museum Complex** consists of a police museum, a library dating from 1910, the Posthuys of 1673, the post office (1911) and the railway station (1913). Photographs exhibited in the **Joan St Leger Lindbergh Arts Centre** (18 Beach Rd.) show what Muizenberg once looked like; the houses designed by Sir Herbert Baker contain a cultural centre with a café and a guesthouse.

A good 5km/3mi north-east of Muizenberg is the 120ha/300-acre Rondevlei Bird Sanctuary (get here via Prince George Drive, M 5). The dune landscape and saltwater lake are home to more than 200 bird species. They can be watched through telescopes. There is also an information centre and a small museum (open daily).
Rondevlei Bird Sanctuary

To the east, off the coast of Muizenberg is a 2ha/5-acre island, which is home to around 50,000 seals. Boat trips are available from Kalk Bay and Gordon's Bay during summer.
Seal Island

Beyond the south-west border of Muizenberg lies Silvermine Nature Reserve (to get here branch off onto a road at Kalk Bay or take the Ou Kaapseweg, M 64). The flora of the **impressive mountain landscape** is some of the most beautiful on the Cape peninsula. This 2158ha/5333-acre nature reserve spanning the area from the mountain ridge above Kalk Bay and the Muizenberg mountains further east to the 756m/2480ft Noordhoek Peak is home to antelopes, gazelles, caracals, porcupines and genets. Hiking trails lead to fantastic viewpoints. Open daily 8am–7pm, in winter until 6pm.
Silvermine Nature Reserve

Kalk Bay   In the lively port of Kalk Bay it is possible to watch the arrival of the fishing boats in the mornings. The town was founded in 1795 as a military outpost; from 1806 Kalk Bay was a centre of whaling for five years, after which it became a seaside resort.

Fish Hoek   Next stop is Fish Hoek, another popular seaside town that developed from a farm founded by Lord Charles Somerset in 1818. There is a pleasant walk to Sunny Cove (and further to Simon's Town).

Simon's Town   This small town with a population of 6000 was named after Governor Simon van der Stel and is the end of the line of the Cape Town light railway. Its sheltered location made it Cape Town's winter harbour in 1741, and in 1957 the **headquarters of the South African Navy**. But there are also numerous fishing boats and yachts moored in the harbour. St George's Street between the station and Jubilee Square is a **historic promenade** with pretty buildings from the 18th and 19th centuries. The governor's residence of 1777 now houses the Municipal Museum (open Mon–Fri 10am–4pm, Sat–Sun 11am–1pm). The Martello Tower was built by the British as a powder magazine in 1796. South of Simon's Town is **Boulders Beach**, which owes its name to the large granite boulders. A special attraction here is the colony of jackass penguins. These flightless birds

How about a swim in the company of penguins?

are quite trusting and are not bothered by human presence (their smell however is a deterrent from getting too close). The **boat trip to the Cape of Good Hope** is very enjoyable.

★ ★
Cape Peninsula
National Park
ⓟ

The coastal road leads to the southern end of the Cape peninsula, which was made into a nature reserve in 1939 and became a national park in 1998 (Cape Peninsula National Park; open daily 7am–6pm, in winter until 5pm). Upon entry visitors receive a map marking all the park's roads and hiking trails. The approx. 8000ha/20,000-acre park, with 40km/25mi of coast, is home to antelopes, bonteboks, ostriches, warthogs, mountain zebras, lynxes, otters and baboons. The baboons can become very importunate; under no circumstances should they be fed. Whales, dolphins and seals can be seen in the waters off the coast. Amongst the **1200 plant species typical of the Cape** are proteas and heathland vegetation. However, it is less the flora and fauna that attract hundreds of thousands of visitors to the south-west tip of Africa, but the magnificent scenery and the aware-

The often stormy Cape of Good Hope

ness of standing at a momentous spot. The main road runs through the nature reserve to **Cape Point**. From the car park (with restaurant) it is just a few minutes on foot or by cable car to the Cape's highest point. At an elevation of 249m/817ft stands the **lighthouse of 1860**, whose beam can be seen 67km/42mi away on clear days; however it often disappears in fog. For that reason the new lighthouse was constructed in 1919 on a site almost 100m/330ft lower down. It shows the way to more than 20,000 ships that use the Cape route every year.

From Cape Point a hiking trail leads to the more westerly Cape of Good Hope, which can also be reached by car. Bartolomeu Dias, who was the first to circumnavigate the rocky headland in 1488, called it the »Cape of Storms«; and it is true that there is almost always a strong wind howling here (don't forget to bring a coat). Close to the information centre a cross commemorates Dias and further east near to Buffelsbaai there is a cross for Vasco da Gama, who sailed round the Cape in search of a sea passage to India in 1497.

✱ ✱
Cape of Good Hope

Leaving the national park, the M 65 goes north-west to the fishing town of Kommetjie (20km/12mi) via Scarborough. Surfers like to come here because of the strong winds.

Kommetjie

The M 65, which initially heads inland, as well as the M 6, goes to Noordhoek on the Atlantic. The following 15km/9mi road, opened in 1922, runs beside the 592m/1942ft Chapman's Peak and is one of

✱ ✱
Chapman's Peak Drive

Shipwreck beach

Long Beach north of Kommetjie is not just of interest to surfers: on its maiden voyage in 1900 the Kakapo steamer smashed on the rocks here. Its remains still impress visitors today.

the world's **most impressive coastal roads**. (The crumbling rocks have been secured with steel nets and a toll is charged.) The mountain was named after the British sailor John Chapman, who came ashore here in 1607 in order to explore the area. The mountain road is »glued« to the cliff-face at an elevation of up to 160m/525ft above the ocean; the reddish-yellow Table Mountain sandstone layers are easily recognizable above the Cape granite. There are many car parks from which to enjoy the glorious view over Hout Bay to the 331m/1086ft **Sentinel**.

Hout Bay — At the northern end of Chapman's Peak Drive the town of Hout Bay lies on the bay of the same name. It was once covered in thick forest (»hout« means »wood«). The town is an important fishing port and a centre of spiny-lobster fishing. They are for sale on **Mariner's Wharf** (with restaurants, etc.). Boat trips leave from the harbour for »sunset cruises« from September to April. One destination is **Duiker Island**, a seal and bird sanctuary. Hout Bay Museum provides information on the town's history and its fishery (4 St Andrew's Road, open Tue–Sat 10am–4.30pm).

World of Birds — At the northern edge of Hout Bay is a tropical garden landscape, home to more than 3000 native and exotic birds, including pelicans, penguins, parrots, eagles and waterfowl. Among the bird park's special features are the large walk-in aviaries (Valley Road, open daily 9am–6pm).

Llandudno — The seaside town of Llandudno has almost merged with Hout Bay. Exclusive villas line the mountainside. A nice, relatively sheltered sandy beach also attracts day visitors. Sandy Bay south of Llandudno has a nudist beach.

Twelve Apostles — Further on the coastal road passes the »Twelve Apostles«, a picturesque rock formation off the coast of Table Mountain.

Camps Bay, Clifton — In good weather the beaches of the affluent suburbs of Camps Bay and Clifton attract a lot of visitors. The **Round House** in Camps Bay (Kloof Road) served Lord Charles Somerset (see above, Fish Hoek) as a hunting lodge; today it houses a restaurant with a good view of the coastal town (tel. 021 438 2320).

Sea Point — The round trip ends in Sea Point, a densely populated suburb of Cape Town. Between modern skyscrapers there are still some beautiful Victorian buildings. The 3km/2mi beach promenade is lined by hotels, restaurants and nightclubs.

Camps Bay with its beautiful beaches and the Twelve Apostles in the background

✳ Wine Regions at the Cape

Against the backdrop of rugged mountain ranges, vineyards stretch as far as the eye can see; dotted amongst them are white manor houses in the Cape Dutch style. Names like La Dauphinée or La Provence derive from the French settlers who, along with the Dutch, brought viticulture to the Cape. Well-drained, almost barren soils, sunny, warm summers and cool winters are the basis for excellent wines (► Baedeker Special p.132). From Cape Town several routes can be taken to visit vineyards, do some wine tasting and learn about how a good wine is made; many vineyards have excellent restaurants. Cape Town Tourism has information material for a wine excursion. **Enchanting wine landscape**

The route closest to Cape Town begins in ►Stellenbosch, a 40-minute drive. The tour, the best-known in the country, leads into the heart of the »Winelands«. A little further are the drives to Franschhoek (►Stellenbosch) and ►Paarl. Visitors in a hurry should at least visit the vineyards of the Cape peninsula (►p.250 f.). Further routes in the Cape Province can be found near Wellington (► Paarl), ►Worcester, ►Tulbagh, ►Robertson and ►Hermanus. **Wine routes**

What to See North of Cape Town

Bloubergstrand 25km/15mi north of Cape Town boasts a **magnificent view of Table Mountain and Cape Town**. The scenery is also im- ✳ ✳ **Bloubergstrand**

Blouberg beach: surely one of the world's most beautiful backdrops

pressive in the evenings, when Table Mountain is lit by the setting sun. The small town (»beach of the blue mountain«) was named after a 330m/1083ft hill in the area, which appears bluish from the sea. Once an important fishery centre, it has become a favourite and expensive residential area. Bloubergstrand is not a good place for swimming: often a fresh breeze is blowing and the temperature of the water is only for the very hardiest (around 10°C/50°F). **Surfers and windsurfers** on the other hand are in their element here. A major international surfing competition takes place here regularly.

Melkbosstrand

From Bloubergstrand a coastal road with plenty of great views makes its way through the dune landscape to the north. In spring many wild flowers bloom here. The quiet town of Melkbosstrand is a popular destination for the inhabitants of Cape Town. Wonderful shells can be found on the beach. It is not a good idea to visit in summer when there is a stiff south-easterly wind.

★ ★
Robben Island

Robben Island, the prison island in Table Bay that became a symbol of resistance to apartheid, was granted the status of UNESCO World Heritage Site in 1999. The Portuguese were the first to use the 5.4km/3.4mi-long and 1.5km/0.9mi-wide island as a **place to keep prisoners**. Over the course of time the captives here included unruly slaves, Asian princes who defied the rule of the Dutch East India Company, African chiefs and »political« prisoners. Intermittently the island was also a leper colony, a lunatic asylum and a naval base. During the apartheid era more than 3000 black resistance fighters were incarcerated here. Nelson Mandela (▶ Famous People), who spent almost 20 years of his life here, was prisoner number 466/64. His cell in block B is now Robben Island's biggest attraction. Less well-known political prisoners vegetated in block G in huge communal cells. The last political prisoners left the island in 1991, the others in 1996. Boats to Robben Island leave between 9am and 5pm from Cape Town's Waterfront (Nelson Mandela Gateway); the entire tour lasts three and a half hours (bring your own drinking water!). The tour is extremely popular, it is best to book in advance (www.robben-island.org.za, tel. 021 413 4200).

Durbanville, approx. 20km/12mi north-east of the centre of Cape Town, is one of the oldest municipalities in the Western Cape. It bears the name of Sir Benjamin D'Urban, who was governor of the Cape from 1834 to 1838. Durbanville is also the starting point of a wine route. The main object of interest is the **Rust En Vrede** (Cultural Centre, Wellington Road; tourism office) in a Cape Dutch building from 1850. Works by modern South African artists are exhibited here; the collection of African pottery art is also interesting (open Mon–Fri 9.30am–4.30pm, Sat, Sun 2–4.30pm).

Durbanville

Ceres

C 8

Province: Western Cape
Population: 13,000

Altitude: 502m/1647ft
Distances: Cape Town 100km/60mi

The mountains rising to over 2000m/6500ft around 100km/60mi north-east of Cape Town form such a picturesque landscape that they have been called »the Switzerland of South Africa« (as have other regions in the country).

Here, in the fertile valley of the Dwars River, lies the village of Ceres, which deservedly gets its name from the Roman goddess of agriculture: its economic prosperity comes from fruit plantations. The fruit is packaged or made into fruit juice in the country's biggest facility; Ceres and Liquifruit are nationally recognized brands. In the winter enough snow falls in the mountains to make skiing possible.

▶ VISITING CERES

INFORMATION

Ceres Tourism
Owen St. / Voortrekker St.
Tel. 023 316 1287, www.ceres.org.za
The tourist information office organizes guided tours through the fruit and vegetable processing facilities; long trousers and closed shoes are required.

WHERE TO STAY/EAT
▶ **Budget/Mid-range**
Belmont Hotel
Porter Street
Tel. 023 312 1150

www.belmonthotel.co.za
»The« hotel in the district was founded in 1890 and is situated in an attractive, large park on the Dwars. 40 rooms in the main building, as well as garden bungalows. The more expensive restaurant Oom Be Se Vat serves African cuisine, the inexpensive Pizza Nostra serves pizza, pasta, etc.

What to See in Ceres

Transport Rider's Museum

Ceres, a town whose appearance is characterized by many shady trees, was once a centre for the production of all kinds of **carriages**, which were used to transport agricultural products to Cape Town. The museum (Oranje Street, closed Sat afternoon and Sun) provides information about the town's history and also displays old carriages.

Ceres Nature Reserve

The 30ha/75-acre nature reserve on the western edge of the town was set up to protect the native flora. Trails lead to attractive viewpoints and to rocks with prehistoric drawings.

Around Ceres

Gydo Pass

Beautiful views set the scene for the drive over the 1018m/3340ft Gydo Pass (it may be closed in winter). It was named after a euphorbia species that covers the slopes of the Skurweberg. To the north lies **Prince Alfred Hamlet**; here too the main economic activity is fruit cultivation. On the other side of the pass the road runs through an attractive, desolate landscape; after 115km/70mi (from Ceres), of which the last 30km/20mi is dirt track, the road reaches ►Citrusdal.

Mitchell's Pass

The drive over Mitchell's Pass, built between 1846 and 1848, is also highly recommended. The route to the south-west of Ceres with the backdrop of the **Hex River Mountains**, which reach elevations of up to 2251m/7385ft, to Wolseley (population: 6700) 18km/11mi away is a good road.

! *Baedeker* TIP

Kagga Kamma

This private reserve with its bizarre rock formations, where visitors can observe bushbucks and springboks and admire San rock drawings, is located at the edge of the Cederberg range, around 90 minutes' drive north-east of Ceres (from Op-die-Berg over the Katbakkies Pass). Spend the night in the luxurious, but still relatively inexpensive Bushmen Lodge: in straw-covered round huts or in caves. Information and reservations: tel. 021 872 4343, www.kaggakamma.co.za.

Citrusdal

C 8

Province: Western Cape
Population: 2800

Altitude: 275m/902ft
Distances: Ceres 115km/70mi, Lambert's Bay 120km/75mi, Cape Town 180km/110mi

Citrusdal was founded in 1916 in the fertile valley of the Olifants River. It is a good starting point for excursions into the Cederberg mountains.

This area is South Africa's third-largest **fruit-growing region**: between May and October more than two million boxes of oranges and other fruit are picked and packaged in Citrusdal. A great many of them are meant for export. Two farms produce excellent wine. The place itself is not worth an extended stay. The local museum in Church Street has an exhibition about the town's history. The Hex River Farm north of the town has the country's **oldest orange tree**; it is said to be over 200 years old.

Tourist facilities (baths, accommodation, etc.) can be found in The Baths, 16km/10mi south of Citrusdal. This quiet town has mineral springs at a temperature of 43°C/110°F (www.thebaths.co.za).

The Baths

Citrusdal is the starting point for the Olifants River Wine Route, which leads downriver all the way to Lutzville. Goods and cooperatives that provide provisions, sometimes even picnics and lunch can be found in and around Citrusdal, Cederberg, Trawal, Vredendal (►p.399) and Lutzville.

Olifants River Wine Route

✴ Cederberg Wilderness Area

The Cederberg mountain range (also spelt Cedarberg, Sederberge in Afrikaans) is approx. 100km/60mi long; the highest point is the Sneeuberg at 2027m/6650ft. The range lies between ►Clanwilliam in the north and ►Ceres in the south. The mountains were named after

Cederberg

▶ VISITING CITRUSDAL

INFORMATION
Tourism Information Citrusdal
Tel. 022 921 3210
www.citrusdal.info

WHERE TO STAY
► Budget/Luxury
Mount Ceder
Tel. 023 317 0113
www.mountceder.co.za.
The best place to stay in the Cederberg mountains. Separate little houses with a restaurant (dinner only with reservation).

The Cederberg mountains are famous for their dramatic rocky landscape (Wolf's Arch).

the **Clanwilliam cedars** (*Widdringtonia cedarbergensis*) that originally grew here. These days only a few remain at relatively inaccessible higher elevations. The Cederberg mountains are known for their forested canyons, their **bizarre, red-coloured rocks** caused by iron oxide, their caves with San paintings, and their flora. With luck visitors who come here in March will be able to see the white snow protea, which only grows here, at the highest elevations. Most of the precipitation, much of it snow, falls between May and September.

Visiting conditions 71,000ha/175,000 acres between Citrusdal and Clanwilliam (►below) are protected (www.capenature.org.za). Admission permits are obtainable from the Algeria Forest Station (Mon–Fri 8am–1pm, 2–4.30pm; it is important to book several days in advance, tel. 026 482 2812). The Forest Station can be reached via the N 7, from which the road over the 590m/1936ft Niewoudts Pass turns off to the east 27km/17mi north of Citrusdal. The best hiking time is between Sept and April; beware of snakes (16 species, including highly venomous ones).

Clanwilliam

C 8

Province: Western Cape
Population: 3000

Altitude: 75m/246ft
Distances: Cape Town 220km/135mi, Lambert's Bay 60km/35mi

Clanwilliam is located in the fertile valley of the Olifants River and is interesting because of its pretty Cape Dutch houses and its proximity to the Cederberg mountains (► Citrusdal).

People started settling here in 1732; the town was founded in 1820 and is one of the oldest in the country. The **rooibos** (»red bush«) is cultivated around Clanwilliam; its leaves are exported as tea all around the world. Other cultivation products are vegetables, citrus fruits, cereals and tobacco. Some of the first buildings that were constructed in Clanwilliam in the early 19th century still survive today; they include the prison and the house of an Irish settler. To the south of the town the **Olifants River** was dammed into a lake and is popular for leisure activities (fishing, water sports). The river, whose

! **Baedeker** TIP

Rooibos tea

With its unique aroma, caffeine-free »rooibos« tea has won over many fans. Malay slaves discovered that a good thirst-quencher could be made from *aspalathus linearis*. Why not visit a tea factory (booking required): Rooibos Ltd., Ou Kaapseweg, Clanwilliam, tel. 027 482 2155.

water supplies the region's plantations, rises in the mountains north-west of Ceres and flows into the Atlantic near Strandfontein. The **Ramskop Nature Reserve** is known for its wild flowers.

North of Clanwilliam the R 364 winds up to the Pakhuis Pass; 37km/23mi from Clanwilliam a road turns off to the south towards Wuppertal. Keep to the left after 15km/9mi to get to the Bidouw Valley (the access road does not make for good driving), which is famous for its bizarre rock formations and its **wild flowers** in August and September.

★
Bidouw Valley

Wuppertal, approx. 18km/11mi south of the junction to the Bidouw Valley, was founded in 1830 as the first South African station of the **Rhenish Missionary Society**. The famous shoe factory set up by J. G. Leipoldt, one of the town's founders, still produces »velskoene«.

★
Wuppertal

VISITING CLANWILLIAM

INFORMATION

Tourist Information
Main Street, Clanwilliam
Tel. 027 482 2024
www.clanwilliam.info

WHERE TO STAY

► Luxury
Bushmans Kloof
Tel. 027 482 2627, www.bushmans kloof.co.za. This lodge 35km/22mi to the east combines a true experience of nature and real comfort. A game reserve with diverse fauna and flora as well as an »art gallery« of San rock paintings. Excellent cuisine, select wines.

► Mid-range
Karukareb Wilderness Reserve
Clanwilliam, tel. 027 482 1675 www.karukareb.co.za. Classily furnished accommodation with all amenities (five rooms in the lodge, five tents), an experience in the great outdoors.

WHERE TO EAT/ WHERE TO STAY

► Inexpensive
Reinhold's Restaurant
8 Main Street, tel. 027 482 1101 Best restaurant in town (make reservations), in the recommendable, comfortable Clanwilliam Hotel.

Clarens

Province: Free State
Population: 1200

Altitude: 2477m/8127ft
Distances: Bethlehem 40km/25mi,
Harrismith 60km/37mi,
Ficksburg 80km/50mi

The small town of Clarens is the base for a visit to the very attractive Golden Gate Highlands National Park, situated close to the northern border of Lesotho.

Clarens was founded in 1912. It was named after the town near Montreux on Lake Geneva where Paul »Ohm« Kruger, former president of Transvaal, died in exile in 1904. Clarens is a popular destination with a number of restaurants; artists have also settled here and now offer their products in galleries. The rivers of the surroundings are good for fly-fishing.

✷ Golden Gate Highlands National Park

The Golden Gate Highlands National Park is one of the most attractive natural parks in the country. Its 12,000ha/30,000 acres stretch along the edge of the Maluti mountains between elevations of 1892m/6207ft and 2770m/9088ft. Erosion has created bizarre formations in the sandstone, which has several different colours caused by iron oxide. The name **Golden Gate** (at the road leading through the national park) comes from two mighty rocks that are around 100m/325ft high and take on a golden glow at sunset. The San used the numerous caves in the area. During the Boer War many Boer families hid here to avoid internment in the feared British camps. The annual precipitation for this region is around 800mm/30in. It frequently falls as snow in winter. Flower lovers will find grasses and herbs, as well as lilies and irises typical of the highlands. Many kinds of antelope, along with zebra and warthog, live in the park. The number of bird species alone is 100, including the majestic lammergeier and the black eagle.

▶ VISITING CLARENS

INFORMATION

Clarens Information
Market Street
Clarens
Tel. 058 256 1542
www.clarenstourism.co.za

WHERE TO STAY

▶ Budget
Cottage Pie
Tel. 058 256 1214
www.cottagepiebb.co.za
Cosy, thatched house in the park with a double room, a holiday flat, and a log cabin at the stream

Bold sandstone bastions form the »Golden Gate«.

The national park can be accessed via Clarens or from the north-east via ►Harrismith. It is traversed by a public road (no tolls) that runs along the valley of the Caledon River. Spend the night at the Glen Reenen Camp (tel. 058 255 0000, ►SAN Parks p.156) or in the Protea Golden Gate hotel (www.proteahotels.com, tel. 058 255 1000). Several hiking trails lead through the park, which can also be explored on ponies. The peak of the 2732m/8963ft Generalskop (bookings at SANParks) can be reached via the 33km/21mi **Rhebok Hiking Trail** (2 days).

Facilities

Further Destinations around Clarens

Stay on the R 712 eastbound through the park to get to Phuthaditjhaba, the main town of the former homeland of QwaQwa. Two southern Sotho tribes live here, the Bakwena and the Batlokwa, with approx. 190,000 members. Arts and crafts products can be purchased in Phuthaditjhaba: tapestries, baskets, copper and tin, and glass.

Phuthaditjhaba

Witsieshoek Mountain Resort, 25km/16mi south of Phutaditjhaba, is a good base for those who want to stay in the area longer. The **Metsi Matso Hiking Trail** also starts here. It can be completed in two days.

Witsieshoek Mountain Resort

Fouriesburg The R 711 connects Clarens and Fouriesburg 36km/22mi to the south-west. The route runs along the border to Lesotho and there are many spectacular views of the mountains. The 72km/45mi **Brandwater Hiking Trail** (five days, some overnight stays in caves; bookings under tel. 058 223 0050) ends at the campsite of Fouriesburg.

Cradock

F 8

Province: Eastern Cape
Population: 30,000

Altitude: 1020m/3346ft
Distances: Port Elizabeth 240km/150mi

This small town in the wide, impressive landscape of the Karoo, which was once home to the author Olive Schreiner, is the starting point for a visit to the Mountain Zebra National Park.

The rural town of Cradock was founded as a military base in 1813 and named after the governor Sir John Cradock. Its location on the Great Fish River, which is now one of the country's best **white-water sports sites**, was the reason why many farmers chose to settle here; the town became the centre of the area's intensively used agricultural land.

What to See in Cradock

Dutch Reformed Church, Great Fish River Museum ⊙ The Dutch Reformed Church modelled on the London church of St Martin-in-the-Fields was built in the centre of town in 1867–68. The Great Fish River Museum located in the minister's house (1825) displays objects from the 19th century, such as furniture and household items (open Tue–Fri 8am–1pm, 2–4pm, Sat 8am–noon).

Olive Schreiner House The former home of the author Olive Schreiner is now a museum (open Mon–Fri 8am–12.45pm, 2–4.30pm). She was born in Wittebergen (Lesotho) in 1855 as the daughter of a German Methodist missionary. When she was 15 she became governess in a Boer family on the edge of the Karoo. From 1881 to 1889 she lived in England, where her novel *Story of an African Farm* was published. In her novels and stories she repeatedly addressed the problems in her country and fought against racism and imperialism. She was incarcerated during the Boer War following confrontations with Cecil Rhodes. Olive Schreiner died in Cradock in

! *Baedeker* TIP

Getting wet
on a rubber dinghy tour on the Great Fish River is a lot of fun, even if it's not done in the style of the participants of the Fish River Canoe Marathon, one of the biggest competitions of its kind in the world. Amanzi Adventures, tel. 048 881 2976, www.fishmarathon.org.za, http://home.intekom.com/amanzi.

The pretty mountain zebra, the smallest of the zebra species, has a white abdomen with no stripes.

1920 and was buried 24km/15mi south of the town on the Buffelskop. The trip there is very worthwhile, but challenging.

A popular swimming pool was set up at the sulphurous springs 4km/2.5mi north of the town. There is also a restaurant as well as inexpensive chalets and a campsite.

Cradock Spa

✱ Mountain Zebra National Park

The now 20,000ha/50,000-acre national park was opened in 1937 at the northern slope of the 2000m/6560ft Blankberg range 24km/15mi south-west of Cradock. It is one of South Africa's most interesting national parks, not just because of its unique wildlife, but also because of its attractive scenery. Many objects from the Palaeolithic era have been discovered here. San rock drawings can be viewed in one cave, accessible via a signposted trail.

Natural scenery

Mountain zebra, which reach a height of only 1.25m/4ft, have a red-brown nose and a white abdomen. In 1960 this reserve was home to only 50 mountain zebra. These days the number fluctuates between 200 and 220 and any extra animals are given to other reserves. This reserve is also home to many other savannah animals such as antelopes like springboks, bonteboks, kudus, as well as the black rhinoceros, buffalo, caracal, jackal, mongoose and more than 200 bird species. Botanists will find the typical Karoo vegetation as well as wild olive trees, sumac and acacia mellifera.

Flora and fauna

▶ VISITING CRADOCK

Visiting The ranger's house is the starting point for roads leading to many parts of the park (open Oct–April 7am–7pm, May–Sept 8am–6pm). The park can also be explored on guided hikes or on the three-day Mountain Zebra Trail. Accommodation (► SANParks, p.156), shop and restaurant available.

✶ Dundee · Battlefields

J 6

Province: KwaZulu-Natal	**Altitude:** 1442m/4731ft
Population: 28,000	**Distances:** Durban 380km/235mi, Johannesburg 330km/205mi

Dundee, the centre of KwaZulu-Natal's coal-mining industry, is located in the Midlands, the hilly landscape between the Drakensberg range and the Natal coast on the Indian Ocean. During the 19th century Voortrekkers and Zulus, Boers and British, as well as British and Zulus all fought bloody battles in the surrounding area.

History After his defeat at Blood River in 1838 at the hands of the Boers, the Zulu king **Dingane** fled to Swaziland where he was killed in 1840. Under his successor Mpane the Zulus lost land to the Europeans, both to the Boers and the British, who by then had founded the Natal colony. His son and heir to the throne **Cetshwayo** founded Ulundi in 1873. While he was in power the Boers of the Transvaal republic occupied further parts of Zululand. Although the British declared this taking of land illegal, they refused to help the Zulus; they had their own plans. In 1879 they occupied the Zulu kingdom under a pretext. At first the numerically superior Zulus were able to defend themselves and defeated the British at the **Battle of Isndlwana**. Then they were unable to take Rorke's Drift and on 4 July they suffered a devastating defeat at the **Battle of Ulundi**. Cetshwayo was locked up.

The British divided Zululand between the supporters and opponents of Cetshwayo and finally annexed it in 1887; in 1897 they handed over administration of the kingdom to the province of Natal. The current king of the Zulus is Goodwill Zwelithini, but the controversial **Mangosuthu Buthelezi** (►Famous People) is considered the more powerful man.

? DID YOU KNOW ...?

- that British soldiers wore khaki uniforms for the first time at the Battle of Talana on 20 October 1899?

Dundee

Amongst the buildings of the 19th century, the row of shops called The Mews and the Boswells Building (a theatre, 1898) are particularly interesting. 3km/2mi from the town on the road towards Vryheid is the **Talana Museum** (open Mon–Fri 8am–4.30pm, Sat 10am–4.30pm, Sun noon–4.30pm). It encompasses several buildings that are spread out over an 8ha/20-acre area. This is where the **first battle of the Boer War** took place in 1899. The farmhouse of the town's founder Peter Smith is still standing. Besides the original furnishings it also contains a collection on the region's military history. The Glass Museum, the Coalmining Museum and the Craft Market are also interesting. The museum organizes tours to the nearby battlefields.

Prince Imperial Monument

Prince Eugène Louis Napoleon, the son of Napoleon III, had joined the British army and fell in 1879 in an insignificant skirmish (one hour's drive by car east of Dundee).

Rorke's Drift

The **Shiyane Museum** in Rorke's Drift, 50km/30mi south-east of Dundee, is well worth a visit (open daily 8am–5pm). It lies at the

Blood River monument: a fort of cast-bronze wagons

scene of a battle between 110 British soldiers and 4000 Zulus that took place in January 1879, the subject of a memorable film (*Zulu*, 1964) starring Michael Caine.

Isandlwana In Isandlwana (70km/45mi east of Dundee, take the R 68 to get there) a monument commemorates the defeat of the British by 25,000 Zulu warriors on 22 January 1879.

Blood River Monument 27km/17mi north-east of Dundee a road turns off from the R 33 to the Blood River Monument, which is another 20km/12mi away. It towers in a wide, windy plain; individual farmhouses and animal herds dominate the peaceful scene. It is an unfavourable place for a big battle: on 16 December 1838 13,000 Zulu warriors attacked 464 Voortrekkers who had formed their wagons into a defensive circle. More than 3000 Zulus lost their lives in the massacre; their blood discoloured the water in the river, which has been called Blood River ever since. The Voortrekkers did not have any losses on their side. Besides the **Voortrekker Monument** there is also a replica of a wagon laager with 64 larger-than-life-size bronze wagons; one of the two museums portrays the whole event from the Zulu perspective.

Ulundi Until 1994 Ulundi (population: 8000, 155km/96mi east of Dundee) was the capital of the non-independent **homeland of Kwazulu**, which consisted of ten separate areas. Approx. three million of the total of 5.5 million Zulus, a Bantu people, lived here. Today this region together with the region of Natal forms the province of KwaZulu-

▶ **VISITING DUNDEE**

INFORMATION

Tourism Dundee
Victoria Street
Dundee
Tel. 034 212 2121
www.tourdundee.co.za

BATTLEFIELDS

The KwaZulu Battlefields encompass the area between Estcourt, ►Ladysmith, Newcastle and Volksrust, as well as in the east Vryheid, Ulundi and Stranger on the coast. The region's tourist information offices can provide detailed information and arrange tours. Information can be found in the internet under http://battlefields.kzn.org.za.

WHERE TO STAY

▶ **Budget**
Royal Country Inn
61 Victoria Street, Dundee
Tel. 034 212 2147
Nice house dating from 1886 in the town centre with 26 comfortable rooms. The dining hall and the garden are also very pleasant.

WHERE TO EAT

▶ **Inexpensive**
Miner's Rest
in the Talana Museum, Dundee
Tel. 034 212 1704
Cosy traditional restaurant in a former miner's hut. The Sunday meat buffet is very popular.

Natal; ►Pietermaritzburg and Ulundi are the main towns. This modern town does not have any places of interest. Opposite the parliament buildings in the town centre is the grave of King Mpane and a museum.

Ondini

Ondini, Cetshwayo's capital, was destroyed by the British in 1879. It lay a few miles south-east of modern-day Ulundi and can be reached via the road that leads to the ►Hluhluwe Imfolozi Game Park. Archaeologists have excavated here and reconstructed some of the huts. The **Kwazulu Cultural Museum** holds an interesting and informative exhibition on the history and culture of the Zulu people. Further Zulu museums and attractions ►Eshowe.

Vryheid

Vryheid (population: 24,000) 70km/45mi north-east of Dundee is the main town on the **Northern Natal Battlefields Route**. For a short period it was the capital of the New Republic proclaimed in 1884. This small political entity only survived until 1887, after which it was incorporated into the South African Republic. Some buildings from the time independence still survive, such as the Volksraad and the Lucas Meyer House, the former home of the state president's widow, which is now a museum.

Ithala Game Reserve

God must have had a good day when he created this landscape, the Zulus say: gentle valleys in rugged mountain ranges that reach elevations of 1400m/4600ft, marula trees with strange shapes caused by the wind, diabase rocks that sound like bells because of their iron content, a rich fauna with buffaloes, elephants, giraffes, leopards, rhinoceroses, antelopes, zebras and much more. There are several comfortable lodges in the 30,000ha/75,000-acre reserve which lies approx. 70km/43mi north-east of Vryheid; information and reservations at KZN Wildlife (►p.156).

★ Durban · Ethekwini

J 6

Province: KwaZulu-Natal
Population: 800,000
(conurbation 2.4 million)

Altitude: 5m/16ft
Distances: Johannesburg 590km/365mi, Bloemfontein 640km/400mi, Cape Town 1750km/1090mi

A modern, very lively and colourful town with African and Asian traits, a subtropical climate, miles of beaches on the warm Indian Ocean: Durban has long been the pre-eminent summer holiday place in South Africa.

Durban, South Africa's third-largest city is called eThekwini in the Zulu language. It is a significant location for industry (sugar, textiles, paints, chemicals, food) and has a big harbour as well as more than two million visitors annually, which makes it the **country's leading tourist destination**. It owes its cosmopolitan flair to its ethnic diversity: almost half the population is Asian (mainly Indians); there are also 200,000 whites. A majority of the black population were pushed into the townships surrounding the city during apartheid.

Harbour The harbour of Durban with its more than 15km/9mi-long quays is one of the continent's largest and the most important in South Africa. It supplies the mining and industrial regions on the Witwatersrand and exports a lot of goods, particularly sugar, fruits, and maize.

History Vasco da Gama discovered the bay he called Port Natal on Christmas Day 1497 (Portuguese »natal« means »Christmas«, »birth«), but it was only in 1823 that some British merchants founded a settlement here. This was located in tribal area belonging to the Zulus, who accepted the place as a trading base, particularly for ivory. Port Natal grew rapidly and in 1835 a town was founded here, which was named after the governor of the Cape at the time, Sir Benjamin D'Urban. The first Voortrekkers came to the area in 1837 and founded ► Pietermaritzburg 80km/50mi north-west of Durban. The spreading of the white population met with more and more resistance from the Zulus. Bloody massacres ensued, during the course of which Durban was abandoned. After the victory over the Zulus at Blood River (16 December 1838), the Boers founded the Natalia Republic and declared Durban a part of it. This provoked resistance by the British who initially suffered a defeat at the Battle of Congella in

Highlights *Durban · Ethekwini*

Golden Mile
This is why people come to Durban: the beach, the sun, and surfing. The atmosphere is particularly pleasant in the early morning at sunrise; then enjoy a breakfast in the beach café.
► page 280

uShaka Marine World
At the end of the Golden Mile is one of the world's largest aquariums, with entertainment on a site of more than 15ha/35 acres, fish from the Indian Ocean, and a well-known dolphin show.
► page 280

Hip living
Cafés, terrace restaurants, bars and night-clubs attract the young and beautiful in the districts of Musgrave (Musgrave Road), Morningside (Florida Road), Greyville and Berea.
► page 284

BAT Café
The marina is a place for enjoying a sundowner and some jazz.
► page 283

Gateway Shopping Umhlanga Rocks
This mall, probably one of the biggest in the world, has enough stores to tempt shoppers to spend a complete day here.
► page 287

The skyline of Durban along the Golden Mile

1842 and were besieged for over a month in their fort (now the Old Fort). After the arrival of reinforcements, which Richard Philip King had managed to bring from Grahamstown on a daring ride of over 1000km/600mi, the Voortrekkers were defeated; they moved north and settled in Orange Free State and Transvaal. In May 1843 Natal became a part of the Cape Colony, which was the start of the economic boom. In 1860 the first Indians arrived to work on the sugar cane plantations surrounding Durban; in 1883 there were already more than 30,000 Indians living in Natal. A large number of them remained in the country even after their work contracts had expired. One of the country's immigrants was Mahatma Gandhi, a young lawyer, who arrived in 1893 and worked for the rights of the suppressed in South Africa over the following years (▶Famous People). In 1860 the railway line from Durban to Cape Point was inaugurated. It was the first one in South Africa.

Orientation

Durban is a modern city with wide roads, tall office and apartment blocks and many green spaces. Only a few Victorian-style buildings remain. However, there are plenty of hotels, shopping centres, restaurants and bars; peace and quiet can be found in one of the seaside towns north or south of Durban.

A city tour through Durban could begin on the Golden Mile, the beach boulevard. The most lively area is the junction of West Street and Marine Parade. The main shopping streets are the one-way West Street and Smith Street, which run from east to west. They lead to the Indian quarter centred on Grey and Victoria Street (approx. 2.5km/1.5mi from the coast). Erskine Parade, the southern extension of Marine Parade, leads to Point. This almost derelict quarter is situated on the headland of the same name that terminates the harbour in the north-east. To the north-west of the centre the well-to-do suburbs of Berea, Greyville and Morningside spread over Berea Ridge; Pinetown, the slum, follows to the west.

Durban • Ethekwini Map

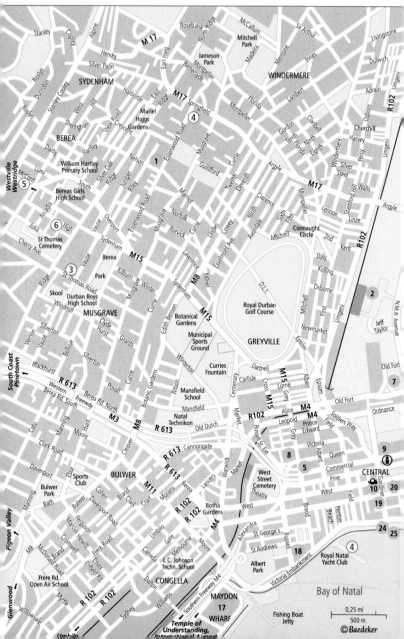

Stanley · Copley · Alpine · M 17 · Rosebank · North Ridge · McCallum · Sir Arthur · Livingstone
Hendry · Earl Haig · Jameson Park · Mitchell Park · Madeira · Mertone · Innes · Dulwich
Silver Palm · Montpelier · Benerycde · Springfield · WINDERMERE · R 102 · Umgeni
Roslyn · Durrobin · SYDENHAM · Harbottle · M17 · Florida · Lambert · Adrain
Stanley Copley · West · Hill · East · Ridge · Muriel Higgs Gardens · Gordon · Clanbell · Osborn · Churchill
Sheringham · View Road · Crescent · Currie · Tenth · Ninth · Florida · Eighth · Harvey
Rodyn · BEREA · Hartley · Nelson · 1 · Guildford · Twelfth · Eleventh · Argyle · Percy · M17 · Silver · Steel
Darby · William Hartley Primary School · Juniper · Riley · Marriot · Clarence · Sixth · Fifth · Connaught Circle · Lennon · Linze · Argyle
Westville Westridge · Lum · McCord · 5 · Bereas Girls High School · South · Ridge · Silver Oak · Musgrave · Norfolk · Ninth · Avondale · Mitchell · 2nd · Kent · R 102
Arcadia · Vause · Overport · Sydenham · Rorvick · Currie · Linden · Covey · Esselmont Ave · Daly · N.M.R. Avenue
Julia · 6 · High · St Thomas Cemetery · Berea · Lawrence · M15 · Kolling · 2
Cherry Ave · Vause · 3 · St Thomas Road · Park · Kilburn · Winter · Miller · Sydenham · M8 · DLI · Osborne · Jeff Taylor
Ridge · Skool · Durban Boys High School · Currie · M15 · Royal Durban Golf Course · First · 7 · Old Fort
Windmill · MUSGRAVE · Clyde · Hurst · Botanical Gardens · GREYVILLE · Epsom · Umgeni
Vernon · Silverton · Bellvue · Grants · Municipal Sports Ground · Newmarket · Mitchell
Vause · Blackhurst · R 613 · Silverton · Winterton · Curries Fountain · Dartnell · Carlisle · M15 · Lorne · Old Fort · Ordnance
South Coast Pinetown · Western · Berea Rd. North · Povall · Ritson · Mansfield School · Centenary · Cross · Grey · M4 · Soldiers Way
Cato · Berea Rd. South · M3 · M8 · R 613 · Mansfield Natal Technikon · Old Dutch · R102 · Alice · Leopold · M4 · Field
Clark Road · Moore · Clever · R 613 · Cannongate · Market · Russell S. Ext · Prince Edward · Victoria · 9
Davenport · East · Sports Club · R 613 · Warwick · Lancers · 8 · Albert · Queen · CENTRAL
Bulwer Park · BULWER · Cohen · Brand · Clark · Craft · Morans · Berea · 5 · Commercial · 10 · 20
Bath · Bulwer · Davenport Road · M11 · Umbla · Gale · Botha Gardens · West · Pine · Brand · 19
Manning · Ferguson · Frere Road · R 102 · Canada · M4 · Alexandra · West · Field · Ferron · Beach · 24
Pigeon Valley · Marcus Hewitt · Essex · Enfield Rd. · L.C. Johnson Techn. School · St George's · St Andrews · Russell · 18 · 25
Glenwood · Cromwell · McDonald Brand · R 102 · Dalton · CONGELLA · Albert Park · Royal Natal Yacht Club · 4
Frere Rd. Open Air School · Myrtle · R 102 · R 102 · Williams · MAYDON · Victoria Embankment · Bay of Natal
Willowvale · Sydney · Southern Freeway M4 · 17 · WHARF · Fishing Boat Jetty · 0,25 mi · 500 m
Umbilo · Temple of Understanding, International Airport · ©Baedeker

M 17 · M17 · 4 · M15 · M8 · M15

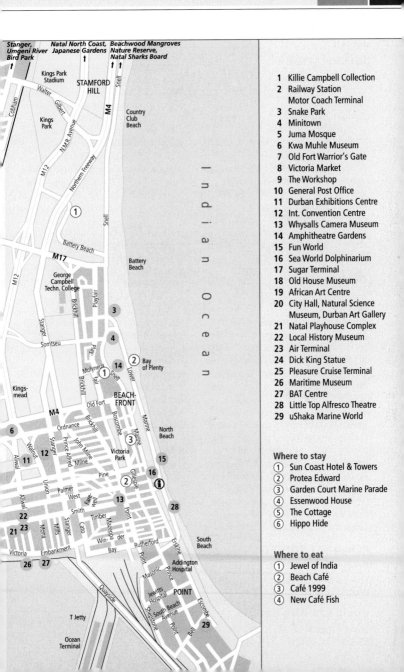

Stanger,
Umgeni River
Bird Park

Natal North Coast,
Japanese Gardens

Beachwood Mangroves
Nature Reserve,
Natal Sharks Board

Kings Park Stadium

STAMFORD HILL

Walter

Cobham

Gilbert

Kings Park

N.M.R. Avenue

M4

Snell

Country Club Beach

M12

Northern Freeway

①

Snell

Battery Beach

M17

M12

Stanger

George Campbell Techn. College

Brickhill

Playfair

Battery Beach

Indian Ocean

3

4

Somtseu

Molyneux

Play

fair

Brickhill

② Bay of Plenty

14 ①

Snell

Lower

Kingsmead

Old Fort

Brickhill

BEACH-FRONT

Boscombe

Marine

M4

Ordnance

6

Walnut

Prince Alfred

John Milne

Milne

Pine

North Beach

Victoria Park

3

Marine

Gillespie

15

11 12

Aliwal

Union

Palmer

West

Smith

Fare-

well

16 ①

②

13

Point

28

South Beach

22

Aliwal

Stanger

Cato

Timber

Mazeppa

Mora

Mills

Win- der

Rutherford

21 23

Victoria

Embankment

Bay

Point

Erskine

Addington Hospital

26 27

Quayside

Masonic

Prince

Jewitts Hospital

POINT

South Beach Avenue

Shepstone

Bell

Escombe

T Jetty

Ocean Terminal

29

1 Killie Campbell Collection
2 Railway Station
   Motor Coach Terminal
3 Snake Park
4 Minitown
5 Juma Mosque
6 Kwa Muhle Museum
7 Old Fort Warrior's Gate
8 Victoria Market
9 The Workshop
10 General Post Office
11 Durban Exhibitions Centre
12 Int. Convention Centre
13 Whysalls Camera Museum
14 Amphitheatre Gardens
15 Fun World
16 Sea World Dolphinarium
17 Sugar Terminal
18 Old House Museum
19 African Art Centre
20 City Hall, Natural Science
    Museum, Durban Art Gallery
21 Natal Playhouse Complex
22 Local History Museum
23 Air Terminal
24 Dick King Statue
25 Pleasure Cruise Terminal
26 Maritime Museum
27 BAT Centre
28 Little Top Alfresco Theatre
29 uShaka Marine World

Where to stay
① Sun Coast Hotel & Towers
② Protea Edward
③ Garden Court Marine Parade
④ Essenwood House
⑤ The Cottage
⑥ Hippo Hide

Where to eat
① Jewel of India
② Beach Café
③ Café 1999
④ New Café Fish

► VISITING DURBAN · ETHEKWINI

INFORMATION

Tourist Junction
Old Station
160 Pine Street
Tel. 031 304 4934
www.durbanexperience.co.za
The tourist offices for Durban and the province of KwaZulu-Natal, the offices of SANParks, KZN Wildlife (►p.156) and the Baz Bus as well as travel agencies can all be found in the Tourist Junction. Book city tours and excursions into the surrounding area here. Further offices are located in the airport and at the beachfront (North Beach, tel. 031 332 2595).

TRANSPORT

International airport 16km/10mi south of the city centre. Air Terminal in the city centre, corner of Smith Street and Aliwal Street (Airport Bus Service, tel. 031 465 1660, and Magic Bus). The Trans Natal and the Trans Oranje both leave from the station. The overland bus terminal is located behind the station, the main bus station (Mynah and Durban Transport) on Commercial Street opposite the Workshop shopping centre. Mynah connects the southern and northern beach area via Smith Street (back over West Street) with Albert Park between 6.30am and 7pm. Hire a three-wheeled tuk-tuk at the beachfront or the city centre. They cost about the same as taxis.

PERSONAL SAFETY

Beware of thieves on the Beach Front. Don't go out alone or on foot after nightfall.

HOLIDAYS AND EVENTS

Jan/Feb and April/May: Thai Poosam Kavady Festival (Hindu festival in honour of the god Muruga). March: fiesta and harbour festival. April–May (18 days): Draupadi Festival in honour of the goddess Draupadi. July: horse races. July–Aug: Mariammen (ten days). Nov: Diwali (Indian festival of lights). Oct: Tattoo (Scottish-style fair). Dec (five days): Ratha Yatra (Hare Krishna festival). Current dates in *What's on in Durban* (in the tourist office) and *Durban for All Seasons* (in hotels).

WHERE TO EAT

► Moderate/Expensive

① *Jewel of India*
in the Holiday Inn Crowne Plaza
63 Snell Parade
Tel. 031 337 8168
Indian cuisine at its best, in an original and luxurious setting. During special festivals there is live Indian music.

③ *Café 1999*
Silvercause Centre
Vause Road
Tel. 031 202 3406
Popular restaurant serving international cuisine. Reservations a must.

④ *New Café Fish*
Yacht Mole
Victoria Embankment
Tel. 031 305 5062
Fantastic fresh fish, lobsters and crabs in a trendy restaurant in the marina with terrace. Reservations essential!

► Inexpensive

② *Beach Café*
Bay of Plenty
North Beach
Tel. 08 2726 2627
Simple, good value meals – and the tables are right on the beach.

WHERE TO STAY

► Luxury

① Sun Coast Hotel & Towers
20 Battery Beach
Tel. 031 314 7878
www.southernsun.com
Art deco building. Only separated from the beach by a footpath, luxurious surroundings away from the hustle and bustle; safe. Many restaurants in the hotel and the nearby casino.

► Mid-range

② Protea Edward
149 Marine Parade
Tel. 031 337 3681
www.proteahotels.com
The most glamorous and the nicest hotel on Durban's beachfront; rooms with a sea view are expensive. Classy atmosphere.

③ Garden Court Marine Parade
167 Marine Parade
Tel. 031 337 3341
www.southernsun.com
Modern complex, art deco style, with 346 rooms, right on the beach. Two restaurants and a swimming pool on the top floor. (Southern Sun has further hotels at South Beach and North Beach.)

Baedeker recommendation

④ Essenwood House
630 Essenwood Road, Berea
Tel./fax 031 207 4547
www.essenwoodhouse.co.za
This elegant guesthouse from the colonial era with a view of the town and the sea is surrounded by a tropical garden with a pool and located in the well-to-do suburb of Berea.

► Budget

⑤ The Cottage
24 Palmiet Drive
Westville
Tel./fax 031 266 3082
Original cottage with individually designed rooms in a spacious garden. The owners are Jean Powell, a well known artist, and her husband Terence.

⑥ Hippo Hide
2 Jesmond Road, Berea
Tel./fax 031 207 4366
www.hippohide.co.za
Pretty »African« backpacker hostel, in a luxuriant garden with pool. Double rooms with bath and bedrooms. A good base close to Musgrave Road with its shops, restaurants and bars.

✳ Beach Front

Beaches

There is an 8km/5mi stretch of beach between the Blue Lagoon in the north, into which the Umgeni River flows, and Point in the south. The boulevard along the coast is closed to through traffic. The main beaches from north to south are: Blue Lagoon, Laguna, Tekweni, Country Club, Oasis, Dunes, Battery, Bay of Plenty, North Beach, South Beach and finally Addington Beach. The beaches are protected by shark nets and have lifeguards on duty from 8am to 5pm. Some areas are reserved for swimmers, others are used by surfers.

★★
Golden Mile

There are many hotels and apartment blocks, restaurants and bars on Marine Parade (between Snell Parade and Erskine Parade). Smartly dressed **rickshaw drivers** wait in various locations (approx. ZAR 20 per person for a five-minute ride; taking photographs costs extra). The atmosphere in the **Amphitheatre Gardens** with its sub-tropical plants is lively at weekends (flea market with Indian snacks, and knick-knacks). In **Minitown** on Snell Parade, Durban's most important buildings have been reconstructed on a scale of 1:25. **Snake Park** at the north end of the Lower Marine Parade (open daily 9am–4.30pm) is home to around 120 native snake species such as green and black mambas, cobras and puff adders. Crocodiles, iguanas, and tortoises can also be seen. Shows take place at the weekends and during the holidays. **uShaka Marine World** at the south of the Golden Mile is not only for children. The new amusement park has, amongst other attractions, Africa's largest aquarium, which is housed in the hull of a cargo ship, a dolphin stadium, a seal stadium and a penguin enclosure. The complex also includes Wet'n Wild, a flume park in tropical surroundings, a guarded beach section with plenty of watersports entertainment, as well as shops and restaurants (1 Bell St., tel. 031 382 8000, www.ushakamarine world.co.za; open daily 9am–6pm).

A young, multicultural society

City Centre

Francis Farewell Square

Francis Farewell Square by the city hall is the city's historic centre. This is where the British merchants Fynn and Farewell are said to have set up their first camp in 1824.

★
City hall

The city hall is the most impressive building in the city centre. Surmounted by a copper-covered dome, it was built in 1910 on the model of the town hall in Belfast (Northern Ireland). Besides the city administration, it also houses the public library and the Natural Science Museum (open Mon–Sat 8.30am–4pm, Sun 11am–4pm).

Durban Art Gallery ▶

Durban Art Gallery, too, **South Africa's second-largest art museum**, is housed in the city hall (opening times are the same as those of the Natural Science Museum). It has works by European and South African artists on display, and also exhibits craftwork (ceramic, ivory, silver and glass).

Behind the city hall in the courthouse built in 1863 is the Old Court-house Museum, which informs its visitors about the history of Zulu-land and the European settlement of Natal (access via Aliwal Street, open Mon–Sat 8.30am–4pm, Sun 11am–4pm).

Old Courthouse Museum

The theatre opposite the city hall (231 Smith Street) is a modern complex with five stages for opera, concerts, plays and ballet. The re-stored façades and panelling of older theatre buildings were used in its construction. Zulu crafts, jewellery, baskets, wood and stone sculptures, ceramic containers, woollen carpets and colourful fab-rics are on sale in the **African Art Centre** (8 Guildhall Arcade).

Natal Playhouse

The **main post office** completed in 1885 (corner of Gardiner Street and West Street) served as Dur-ban's first town hall. On Church Square east of the post office tow-ers St Paul's Church, built in 1909.

The **Old Station** of 1899 was used until 1980 and is now a place for exhibitions and trade fairs. The **Tourist Junction**, restaurants and a parking place are also here. Many of the attractions stem from the time of apartheid. Old business buildings on Commercial Road were transformed into the shop-ping centre called **The Workshop**, which also houses restaurants and cafés.

The **Kwa Muhle Museum** in the Old Pass Office (Ordnance Road) is probably the most interesting museum in Durban, essential for anyone interested in learning how apartheid »worked«. Opening hours: Mon–Sat 8.30am–4pm, Sun 11am–4pm.

A hot-dog stand, the African way. In the background: the Art Gallery.

The Old Fort is located in the neighbouring garden; in 1842 Dur-ban's British inhabitants took refuge from the Voortrekkers here dur-ing a siege that lasted more than a month. There is a small war mu-seum in Warrior's Gate (open Tue–Fri and Sun 11am–3pm, Sat

Old Fort

Indian atmosphere in the shops of the Madressa Arcade in Grey Street

Kingsmead
Stadium ▶

10am–noon). On the opposite side, to the east, international rugby matches and athletics competitions are held in the Kingsmead Stadium; it is also the finishing line of the Comrades Marathon.

Battery Beach

There are more amusement parks north of the Golden Mile on Snell Parade: Animal Farm has cows, goats, and ponies for riding; Waterworld has a fast river suitable for all kinds of water adventures; finally, the big attraction is the **Suncoast Casino** with a gaming house, cinemas, restaurants, bars and more.

Indian Quarter

Grey Street

Juma Mosque

Bazaar

The axis of the Indian quarter is Grey Street (»grey«: i.e. not black and not white), which runs north off West Street. The Juma Mosque on the corner of Queen Street and Grey Street is the biggest and most magnificent mosque south of the equator according to South Africans (remove shoes before entering; guided tours tel. 031 306 0026). In Albert Street (between Queen Street and Commercial Road) behind a Baroque façade a small oriental bazaar with many colourful stores invites visitors to enjoy a spot of shopping.

★
Victoria Market

After a fire in 1973 a new Indian Market (open Mon–Sat 6am–6pm, Sun until 4pm; beware of pickpockets) was opened at the west end of Victoria Street. The modern building lacks the charm of the old hall, but the colourful and quirky **mix of the Orient and Africa** is still fascinating. More than 160 stalls offer exotic spices (with names like »mother-in-law-exterminator«) piled up in colourful heaps, meat and fish, fruit and vegetables, woven and brass object, jewellery, woodwork and carvings. At the food stalls on the first floor sample the town's specialities, such as Bunny Chows, curries and samosas. Outside the door Zulu homeopaths, called inyangas, offer their medicines for sale.

Harbour Area

Port

Africa's biggest and most important port (in ninth place globally) is enclosed by two headlands: Point in the north and Bluff in the south; Bluff is a 4km/2.5mi-long built-up dune. Both of the headlands are extended by a pier. The big passenger and cruise ships all dock at the Ocean Terminal and at the Marine Terminal in the north of the port basin. The port administration is situated next to the terminals.

Dick King Statue

The ever-congested Victoria Embankment is the site of the Dick King Statue built in honour of Richard (Dick) King, who succeeded in bringing in British reinforcements when the Boers were besieging Durban in 1842 (▶ p.274). **Harbour tours** and sea trips start from here. To the east of the Dick King Statue three smaller ships have been made into navigation museums (open Mon–Sat 8.30am–3.45pm, Sun from 11am). The Vasco Da Gama Clock, a bell-shaped iron construction crowned with a clock, was a present from the Portuguese government on the occasion of the 400th anniversary of the discovery of Port Natal in 1497. The Bartle Arts Trust Centre is a popular meeting place, where people come to listen to jazz in the evening, sit in a friendly café, or enjoy a meal in the **Zansi Restaurant** on the first floor, which has a good view of the harbour.

◀ Maritime Museum

◀ BAT Centre

Old House Museum
🕐

Past the Royal Natal Yacht Club is the Old House Museum (31 Street Andrews Street), a 19th-century house with original furnishings (open Mon–Sat 8.30am–4pm, Sun 11am–4pm).

◀ Maydon Wharf

◀ Sugar Terminal

🕐

The western part of the harbour contains Maydon Wharf with the Sugar Terminal, dry wharfs and the Fishing Boat Jetty, the moorage of the open-sea fishing fleet. The Sugar Terminal is **one of the biggest sugar transhipment points** in the world; its three silos can hold more than half a million tons. Tours Mon–Fri 8.30am, 10am, 11.30am and (not Fri) 2pm; bookings at tel. 031 310 0331.

What to See outside the City Centre

✱
Campbell Collections
The residence of Dr Killie Campbell (designed by Sir Herbert Baker), situated on Berea Ridge to the north-west of the centre, houses the most significant library of documents on the history of Zululand and Natal. In addition there are paintings and illustrations by Barbara Tyrrell, Zulu craftworks and valuable furniture (220 Marriot Road; accessible Tue, Thu 8am–1pm only by reservation tel. 031 207 3432).

✱
Botanic Gardens
The Botanic Gardens on the slope of the Berea Ridge founded in 1849 is an oasis to the north-west of the city centre (open daily 7.30am–5pm). Many plant and tree species grow in the 20ha/50-acre park, including some rare species. The Palm Way is majestic, while the tropical colours of the Orchid House are a fine sight. Further attractions are the herb garden and the area for blind visitors. The café is a good place to relax.

Greyville Race Course
Greyville Race Course is South Africa's most famous horseracing venue; the sporting and social highlight is the **Rothman's Durban July Handicap**, which takes place on the first Saturday in July. The Royal Durban Golf Course is situated within the boundaries of the racecourse.

✱
Mitchell Park
Mitchell Park north of the racecourse is one of the city's oldest parks. The aviary is home to a large number of exotic and in some cases rare birds (open Mon–Fri 7.30am–4pm; restaurant). Adjoining Mitchell Park is Robert Jameson Park; more than 200 rose species flower there in September and October.

✱
Umgeni River Bird Park
The Umgeni River Bird Park is situated on the northern banks of the Umgeni in the district of Riverside (open daily 9am–5pm). Birds from south-east Asia and Australia as well as native species can be observed on the park's circular routes. The species include lorikeets, cockatoos and macaws.

! *Baedeker* TIP

Temple of Understanding
The magnificent Temple of Understanding of the Hare Krishna movement is located in the southwest of Durban (N 2 towards South Coast, exit Chatsworth Centre; accessible 9am–4pm). The stylistically curious complex was designed by the Austrian architect H. Raudner. The vegetarian restaurant has a large selection of excellent dishes ranging from snacks to curries (open 11am–8pm).

South of Durban

Approx. 15km/9mi south-west of Durban is the 253ha/630-acre Stainbank Nature Reserve (open daily 6am–6pm), which is home to zebras, antelopes, mongoose, monkeys and genets, as well as 200 bird species. Four hiking trails run through the reserve. It is the seat of the **Wilderness Leadership School**, a training facility for rangers; it was the first non-public nature conservation organization that never had any racial restrictions.

Kenneth Stainbank Nature Reserve

The approx. 160km/100mi-long south coast of the province of Kwa-Zulu-Natal between Durban and Port Edward is one of the country's most popular year-round holiday destinations (particularly amongst South Africans) as well as one of the areas most developed for tourism. This strip of coastline boasts one seaside town after the other. The section between ► Amanzimtoti and Mtwalume is called the Sunshine Coast, the section between Hibberdene and Port Edward the Hibiscus Coast (► Port Shepstone). The seaside towns are connected to Durban by the N 2 (motorway), the older coastal road, and by a railway line. They run through evergreen subtropical forests, past banana and sugar cane plantations and hills with flowering hibiscus trees.

Sunshine Coast Hibiscus Coast

Hibiscus Coast

West of Durban

In 1882 the Trappist abbot Franz Pfanner (1825–1909) founded the **Mariannhill monastery** in the slums of Pinetown 10km/6mi to the west of the city centre. In 1909 Mariannhill became an independent congregation, which was given the name of CMM (Congregation of the Missionaries of Mariannhill) in 1936. The monastery is the centre of the order's counselling, social and educational work in South Africa.

Mariannhill

The 535ha/800-acre Krantzkloof Nature Reserve is located around 25km/16mi north-west of Durban (M 13 towards Pietermaritzburg to Kloof, then east). The Umgeni River plummets into a deep, forested canyon close to the entrance.

Krantzkloof Nature Reserve

North of Durban

This landscape, which has been forming since the Mesozoic era through the retreat of the Great Escarpment, is well worth seeing. Its name of »Valley of 1000 Hills« is self-explanatory. It stretches along the Umgeni River between its estuary on the Indian Ocean north of Durban and Nagle Dam east of Pietermaritzburg. Leave Durban towards Pietermaritzburg on the M 13; take the R 103, the old road between Durban and Pietermaritzburg, approx. 10km/6mi after Kloof. It runs along the southern edge of the Valley of 1000 Hills and has

★ ★ Valley of 1000 Hills

A Zulu magician with her aide in the Valley of a Thousand Hills

impressive views (such as on Botha's Hill). The **PheZulu Safari Park** is an unpleasantly touristy folklore show; behavioural researchers will enjoy studying the busloads of day-trippers taking pictures of topless Zulu dancers. At Cato Ridge the R 103 rejoins the N 3. 4km/2.5mi before the estuary the road turns off to the north. From there it is another 18km/11mi to **Nagle Dam**. The reservoir is located at the foot of the 960m/3150ft Natal Table Mountain; there are glorious views from the top.

Dolphin Coast There are many seaside towns along the coast north of Durban; but this stretch of coastline is less developed for tourism than the Sunshine Coast and the Hibiscus Coast south of Durban. Travellers wishing to explore the region on a round trip should choose the M 4 that runs close to the coast as far as Stanger. The return drive to Durban can then be done on the R 102, which is further inland.

 VISITING DOLPHIN COAST

WHERE TO EAST

▶ **Expensive**

The Sugar Club
Beverly Hills Sun Hotel
Lighthouse Road, Umhlanga Rocks
Tel. 031 561 2211
Top restaurant in a top hotel with an exclusive atmosphere and creative French-South African cuisine. Terrace café with fabulous views of the ocean.

▶ **Inexpensive/Moderate**

Cottonfields
2 Lagoon Drive
Umhlanga Rocks
Tel. 031 561 2744
Popular restaurant with a terrace. Mainly fish, seafood, and meat; the fisherman's stew and the prawn curry are just two of their tasty menu choices.

WHERE TO STAY

▶ **Mid-range / Luxury**

Mt. Edgecombe Lodge
47 Farlane Hoylake Ville
Mt. Edgecombe
Tel. 031 502 1555
www.afrogolf.co.za. Comfortable accommodation in a safe nature reserve, only 7km/4.5mi from the beach and 15km/9mi from Durban. Excellent cuisine.

Zimbali Lodge
Ballito
Tel. 032 538 1007
www.sun-international.com
Located approx. 40km/25mi north of Durban, this exclusive lodge offers a wonderful view of the Dolphin Coast. 76 rooms in lodges, with terrace or balcony. Golf course in the neighbouring Zimbali Country Club.

The beach town of Umhlanga Rocks (pronounced »Umshlanga«) is located 18km/11mi further on the M 4. Although it is classier than Durban and less busy outside the high season, it has not been spared from ugly concrete buildings. It has comfortable hotels, good restaurants, and big shopping centres (one of them is **Gateway Shopping** with cinemas, restaurants and the largest artificial surf wave in the world). The long beaches are intercepted by rocky sections and are also protected by shark nets.

★
Umhlanga Rocks

Travellers wanting to find out more about sharks should visit the Natal Sharks Board (2km/1.2mi west of Umhlanga Rocks). Audiovisual demonstrations Mon–Thu noon, 1pm, 3pm; with the dissection of a shark (not for the squeamish) Tue–Thu 9am, Wed also at 11am and 2pm as well as at 2pm on the first Sunday of the month. It is also possible to ride along on the boat when the sharks are collected from the protective nets (tel. 031 561 1001).

★
Natal Sharks Board
🕐

Die 26ha/64-acre Umhlanga Lagoon Nature Reserve borders the north of Umhlanga Rocks. Different hiking trails run though one of the last untouched dune forests.

Umhlanga Lagoon Nature Reserve

There are wonderful sandy beaches south and north of Durban. Here the lighthouse of Umhlanga Rocks.

★
Umdloti

The beach of the holiday resort of Umdloti at the mouth of the Mdloti River is considered to be one of the most beautiful in the area. The river owes its name to the wild tobacco that grows on its banks.

Ballitoville

Shaka's Rock ▶

Ballitoville, or »Ballito« for short, 45km/28mi north of Durban is another popular seaside resort. The magnificent beach protected by shark nets justifies the resort's fame. Shaka's Rock also has hotels and a protected beach; a beautiful hiking trail runs along the coast. The seawater pool at the beach is an attraction. Tiffany's Reef and Sheffield Reef are both considered good snorkelling grounds.

Salt Rock

The atmosphere becomes more tranquil north towards Salt Rock. Accommodation can be found in the big Hotel Salt Rock on the ocean (www.saltrockbeach.co.za) and on the campsite, amongst other places. There are jetties for anglers along the coast.

Stanger

The coastal road continues to the quiet holiday towns of Sheffield Beach and Blythdale Beach. Stanger (population: 26,000) is located further inland. It is a lively trading and administration centre shaped by its Indian community, and one of South Africa's most important sugar-producing regions. The town was founded in 1873 at the site where the **Zulu chief Shaka** had his last royal kraal. A memorial in a park denotes the place where the ruler was murdered in 1828 (▶Famous People). Every year on 24 September (Heritage Day) Zulus meet here in honour of Shaka. **Albert Luthuli**, who was awarded the Nobel Peace Prize in 1960, was banished to Stanger and died here in 1967.

Tongaat

Take the R 102 southbound from Stanger. It is 30km/19mi to Tongaat (population: 50,000), also a centre of the sugar industry that takes its character from the Indian community. Some buildings from the town's founding days still survive. The conspicuous, 23m/75ft-high **Shri Jagganath Puri Temple** on the main road is well worth a visit. The golf course with its palm trees attracts players from near and far.

Verulam

Verulam (population: 30,000) is located 15km/9mi south of Tongaat (10km/6mi north-west of Umhlanga Rocks). It was founded in 1850 by Methodists and is one of the province's oldest towns. Today Indians form the majority; north of the town at the railway bridge is the **Subramanyar Temple** in a nice park, where magnificent weddings are celebrated at the weekends.

Phoenix Settlement

South of Verulam a road turns off from the R 102 westbound to Phoenix. This is where **Mahatma Gandhi** (▶Famous People) founded a farm. In Gandhi's former living quarters, which were destroyed in riots in 1985 but rebuilt by 2000, a small museum commemorates the great political leader.

East London

G 8

Province: Eastern Cape
Population: 135,000

Altitude: 36m/118ft
Distances: Cape Town 1080km/670mi,
Port Elizabeth 310km/195mi, Johannesburg
990km/615mi

The wonderful coast of the Indian Ocean with its miles of wide, solitary beaches makes East London a good year-round holiday destination, especially for surfers.

East London, situated where the Buffalo River flows into the Indian Ocean, is the only significant river port in South Africa. It mainly handles wool and other agricultural products. Besides the food and textile industries the **automobile industry** is also of significance (Daimler Benz amongst others). However, in recent decades East London has fallen behind economically because of its unfortunate location between the former homelands of Transkei and Ciskei. In the two nearby settlements inhabited by blacks, Mdantsane and Zwelitsha, more than half the people are without work, but tourists do not see much of that.

As early as 1688 a ship anchored at the mouth of the Buffalo River in search of survivors of a shipwreck. In 1752 Ensign Beutler undertook the first exploration trip into the area; he spoke about a river the natives called »Konka« (»buffalo«). This is the origin of the name **Buffalo City** for the municipality. The next time a British ship landed here was not until 1836; this time it brought supplies for the troops stationed in the region. During the Kaffir Wars the river port was of tactical significance. The British occupied it in 1848 and called it Port East London; in 1857–58 nearly 5000 disbanded mercenaries of the **British German Legion** settled in the area with their families. Many of the German place names as well as the founding of the **German Market**, which is still held on Fridays and Saturdays in the northern suburb of Beacon Bay, go back these families; however, these days it is mainly African women who sell goods there. East London received its civic charter in 1880.

History

With its historical buildings, exclusive residential areas, public parks and green spaces, East London comes across as quite a cultivated town. The actual centre is small and can be explored in one short walk. The main road is the 5km/3mi-long Oxford Street; a mile-long esplanade runs parallel to the coast.

Townscape

Between the mouth of the Buffalo River in the south and the Nahoon River in the north are **three of the town's most beautiful sandy beaches**. Orient Beach, which has a playground and a seawater

★
Beaches

East London Map

King William's Town
Queenstown

Berea

Clarendon High School

Techn. College

Selborne Park

Egerton

Cheltenham

Connaught

Lukin

M5

St David's

Fairview

Quarry

Union

M1

Oxford

King

St Andrew's

St Mark's

Gatey

Vere

Stanhope

De Villiers

Rodney

Murial

Knoll

Valley

View

Naboom

Reservoir

Park-way

Panmure Halt

Lennox

Frederick

Grange

Moir

Kenwich

Elmira

Hendon

Downie

St Patricks

St Mark's

St Luke's

Belgrave

Belgravia

Oxford

St Matthew's

St James

Wynne

Garden

Gordon

M 15

Southernwood School

Amalinda Fisheries Station, Reptileworld, Umtiza Forest Reserve, Bridle Drift Dam

Morningside,

Lilac

Tudor Rose

Lisbit

Evans

Moffat

Scott

M3

Lennox

Kimberley

De Beers

Factory

Milner

Richmond

Bayswater

Kensington

St Pauls

St George's Park

St George's

St King

Webb

St Peter's

Muller

Graham

SOUTHERNWOOD

M 15

Craig

Thorburn

Atlas

Bowls

McGrath

Southernwood School

Mdantsane

Phoenix

Strelitzia

Selago

Hibiscus

Plumbago

Acacia

Magnolia

Magnolia

North West Expressway

NORTH

END

St Johns

Chapel

Milton

Cross

Willets

Ryanes

St Johns

Park St.

Time

Walker

Ward

Porter

Wobeley

Beaconsfield

Pine

Elm

Park

Muir

Lambart

Brill

Paterson

Turnbull Park

Recreation

Ilney

Mill

Middle

Southernwood

Jan Smuts Ground

ARCADIA

Dyer

Dyer

Malcolmess

M 14

Commercial

Oxford

Current

Stephenson

North

CITY

Albert

Argyle

Buxton

Buffalo

Gladstone

Cambridge

Oxford

Caxton

Drury

CITY
CENTRE

Market Square

Quigney

Station

Lock

Chamber

Fleet

Symons

Alsont

Currie

Signal

Genadendal

Ebenezer

Cressy

Parkside

Bridge

Abdurahman

Jacaranda

Saldanha

Windy-

Phillip

Dower

Brisseket

Olive

Aloe

Euphorbia

Violet

Myrtle

Dorking

Queen's

Park

Park Gates

Gillwell

Terminus

Union

M3

Thorne

Settlers Way

R72

Princess Elizabeth

Graving Dock

Pontoon

Commissioner

Church

Hill

South

Helg Hutchinson

Prior

Gantaume

Bonanz

Signal H

R72

Settlers Way

Nuffield

Buffalo Bridge

Nuffield

Dr. Zahn

Buffalo

Port

C. W. Malan Turning Basin

Ben Schoeman Airport,
Port Alfred, Port Elizabeth

Powder Magazine, St Peter's Church
West Bank

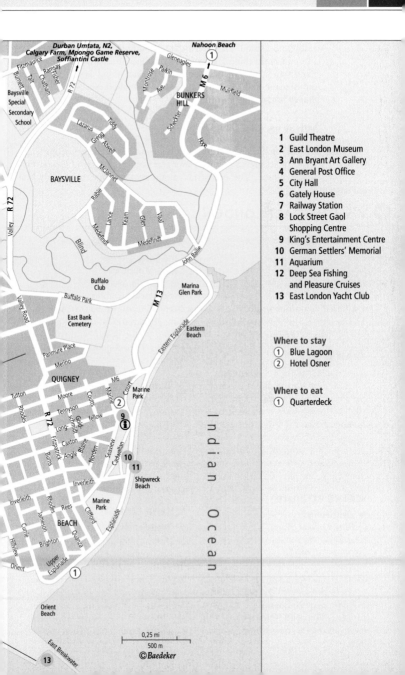

1 Guild Theatre
2 East London Museum
3 Ann Bryant Art Gallery
4 General Post Office
5 City Hall
6 Gately House
7 Railway Station
8 Lock Street Gaol
  Shopping Centre
9 King's Entertainment Centre
10 German Settlers' Memorial
11 Aquarium
12 Deep Sea Fishing
   and Pleasure Cruises
13 East London Yacht Club

Where to stay
① Blue Lagoon
② Hotel Osner

Where to eat
① Quarterdeck

pool with a slide, is closest to the town centre. Thanks to the Mozambique current, the water of the adjoining Eastern Beach, which is lit up in the evenings, is very warm. Nahoon Beach is located approx. 8km/5mi north of the town centre near a big lagoon (with an amusement park and a campsite). An offshore shelf creates **ideal waves for surfing**.

What to See in East London

City hall · The city hall is an impressive building located between Oxford Street and Argyle Street. The bell tower was built in honour of Queen Victoria's jubilee. The equestrian monument in front of the city hall

 VISITING EAST LONDON

INFORMATION

Tourism Buffalo City
King's Entertainment Centre
Esplanade, East London
Tel. 043 722 6015
www.eastlondontourism.co.za
The Eastern Cape Tourism Board is also located in the King's Centre.

TRANSPORT

Ben Schoeman Airport, 11km/7mi outside town; shuttle buses connect the town to the airport (tel. 082 569 2599). The Amatola Train goes to Johannesburg. The buses operated by Greyhound, Translux, and SA Connection leave from Windmill Park (Moore Street); Intercape buses stop at the airport and the station.

WHERE TO STAY

▶ **Mid-range**
① *Blue Lagoon Hotel*
Blue Bend Place, Beacon Bay
Tel. 043 748 4821
www.bluelagoonhotel.co.za
Modern, tasteful buildings 10 minutes north of the town at the mouth of the Nahoon, near Nahoon Reef, a surfing paradise. The good restaurant has fish, meat and pasta – something for every taste.

▶ **Budget/Mid-range**
Crawfords Cabins
Cintsa Mouth East
Tel. 043 738 5000
www.crawfordscabins.co.za
40km/25mi north-east of East London: enchanting house in a gorgeous setting on the beach, with rooms and cottages for 2–3 people. Wonderful ambience.

▶ **Budget**
② *Hotel Osner*
Eastern Beach
Tel. 043 743 3433, 0800 42 2433
www.osner-resorts.co.za
A somewhat impersonal three-star hotel on the beach. 111 rooms with sea view, a restaurant, pool, sauna and gym.

WHERE TO EAT

▶ **Inexpensive**
① *Quarterdeck*
Orient Pavillion, Esplanade
Tel. 043 743 312
Lively eatery with sea food, German beer on tap, and live music (Wed, Fri, Sat). The neighbouring more expensive Ernst's Chalet Suisse under the same management is also good.

East London's town hall with the Boer War monument in front

commemorates the lives of the people who fell in the Boer War. The central station was built in 1877; a steam engine from England (1903) is on display here.

Railway station

The aquarium is located by the sea and has many marine species from sea horses and colourful fish that live around coral reefs to great white sharks. Open daily 9am–5pm; seal show 11.30am and 3.30pm. The aquarium also has a whale deck from which whales can be watched (a blue flag signalizes when whales are around).

Aquarium

⏱

A few steps away on the esplanade, the German Settlers' Memorial by the South African sculptor Lippy Lipschitz commemorates the German settlers of 1857–58.

German Settlers' Memorial

The coast off East London holds a sad record: 82 ships have run aground here, 46 off the esplanade alone. The last was the »Oranjeland« on 13 August 1974. Commemorative plaques on the esplanade mark six of these unfortunate locations.

Shipwreck Bay

On a hill to the west of the town centre is the 34ha/85-acre botanical garden, which also has a small zoo. Children can ride ponies here (open daily 9am–5pm). at the park entrance, built for the mayor Johan Gately in 1878, is one of the oldest buildings on the Buffalo River; it still has its original Victorian furnishings (closed Mondays).

★
Queen's Park
Gately House

The Ann Bryant Art Gallery can be found in a pretty house built in a Cape Dutch-Victorian style. The collection encompasses old and modern South African art, as well as paintings by British artists (open Mon–Fri 9.30am–5pm, Sat 9.30am–noon).

Ann Bryant Art Gallery

⏱

East London Museum

The only remaining egg of the extinct **dodo**, a flightless bird, and a stuffed **coelacanth** are just two of the attractions featured in the East London Museum, which was founded in 1931 (Oxford Street, open Mon–Fri 9.30am–5pm, Sat 2–5pm, Sun 11am–4pm). Until the coelacanth was caught in 1938 in the Chalumna River near East London, it had been thought that this fish species had become extinct more than 50 million years ago. The good anthropological section provides information about **Xhosa culture**, amongst other things.

Harbour

The port extends south of the centre along the mouth of the Buffalo River. The **dolosse** are pointed out to anyone taking a guided tour. They are unusually shaped breakwaters made of concrete that were developed by Eric Merrifield in 1961 and can now be found all over the world. The East London Yacht Club is the goal of the **Vasco da Gama Regatta**, which starts in Durban. Latimer's Landing at the northern end of the Buffalo Bridge is »the« rendezvous for eating and having a good time.

Buffalo Bridge

Powder Magazine ►

The southern river bank can be reached via the Buffalo Bridge, which was completed in 1935. Nearby to the east is the Powder Magazine, a leftover from the old Fort Glamorgan. This fort was built in 1848 to protect the British troops from the Xhosa.

Around East London

The coast

Dream beaches that are almost completely deserted can be found west of East London along the coast of the former Ciskei homeland (►Bisho). They should be avoided at all costs in the evenings and at night. For the Wild Coast east of East London see ►Umtata.

Bridle Drift Dam and Nature Reserve

Approx. 25km/16mi west of East London the Buffalo River has been dammed to make a reservoir, which has been declared a nature reserve along with the surrounding land. The Bridle Drift Dam is very popular for windsurfing.

! *Baedeker* TIP

Strandloper Trail

The 60km/37mi hiking trail between Gonubie (east of East London) and Kei Mouth takes five days to complete. Sometimes the going is tough, sometimes it's plain sailing. It runs along golden beaches and rugged cliffs. It is supervised by the Ecotourism Board (P. O. Box 86, Kei Mouth 5260, www.encounter.co.za, tel. 043 841 1046), where a guide can be booked (recommended). To the left is the coast near Hagga Hagga.

The Mpongo Reserve is a small, private game reserve in the Umpongo River Valley 30km/19mi north-west of East London. Apart from many birds it is also home to various savannah animals (including lions). The terrain can be explored by car, on guided walks or on horseback (campsite, restaurant).

Mpongo Game Reserve

This small nature reserve is located approx. 20km/12mi north-east of East London near the coastal town of Gonubie (open weekdays 8.30am–4pm, on weekends by appointment 043 705 9777). Another attraction is the **garden with African medicinal plants**.

Gonubie Nature Reserve

★ Eshowe

J 6

Province: KwaZulu-Natal
Population: 15,000

Altitude: 520m/1706ft
Distances: Durban 220km/135mi

This friendly town close to the north coast of KwaZulu-Natal is a good starting point for a drive into the Zulu heartland.

Eshowe is situated in attractive countryside used for sugar-cane cultivation west of the N 2, which runs parallel to the north coast of the province of KwaZulu-Natal here. The **Zulu king Cetshwayo** settled in the region of modern-day Eshowe in 1860 before moving his kraal to Ondini (►Dundee · Battlefields Route). After Zululand had been annexed and incorporated into the province of Natal, the British built several forts, including **Fort Nongqayi** in Eshowe; in 1887 the town was made the seat of administration. In June a popular agricultural show takes place here.

Gateway to the Zulu heartland

The **Zululand Historical Museum** is currently housed in Fort Nongqayi (open daily 9am–4pm). On the outskirts of the town at the end of Kangella Street is **Dlinza Forest**, a 250ha/625-acre wooded area with smaller mammals (open daily 8am–5pm). Some of the forest trails were made by British soldiers who were stationed in Eshowe in 1879 after the end of the war against the Zulus.

What to See in Eshowe

★ Drive into the Zulu Heartland

The drive to Empangeni (► Richards Bay) is very scenic. Leave Eshowe on the R 66 northbound and turn east on to a dirt road after 6km/4mi. What is now an area for sugar cane cultivation used to be a preferred hunting territory of the Zulu. 27km/17mi outside Eshowe is a monument to KwaBulawayo, the »capital« of the legendary **Zulu ruler Shaka** (►Famous People). According to the report of an ivory merchant who went to visit it in 1824, the town consisted of several thousand huts.

KwaBulawayo

▶ VISITING ESHOWE

INFORMATION
Eshowe Tourism Bureau
Osborn St. / Hutchinson St.
Tel. 035 474 1141

WHERE TO STAY

▶ Mid-range
Protea Hotel Shakaland
Tel. 035 460 0912
www.proteahotels.com
www.shakaland.com
Nice, very comfortable accommodation in beehive-like Zulu huts that

were built in 1986 for the American television series »Shaka Zulu«. Half-board for two people including the »cultural experience« ZAR 2000.

▶ Budget/Mid-range
Stewarts Farm
KwaBhekithunga
Tel. 035 460 0644
www.zululand.co.za/kwabheki/
This accommodation also features attractive, comfortable »rondavels«. Restaurant and pool facilities.

Zulu villages

Approx. 15km/9mi north of Eshowe a road branches off from the R 66 to **Shakaland** 4km/2.5mi away, which was created for the television series »Shaka Zulu«. Today it serves as an open-air museum

staging folklore performances. An African meal is included in the admission price. Somewhat more authentic impressions are provided by the village of **KwaBhekithunga**, which is run by a Zulu family and is known for its good craftwork. To get here, take the R 66 from Eshowe to Nkwalini, then take the R 34 eastbound; after 6km/4mi take the dirt road (in total 30km/18mi). Another site well worth a visit, though it is a tourist centre, is **Dingane's Kraal**. To get here, take the R 34 from Melmoth towards Vryheid; the access road branches off the R 34 5km/3mi after the junction with the R 66. Dingane, Shaka's half-brother, founded his main settlement **Mgungundlovu** here in 1828; it consisted of more than 2000 huts for up to 20,000 warriors. Here Dingane met the Boer leader Piet Retief to negotiate a contract, but instead had him and his 70 followers murdered. Some of the huts have been rebuilt; a museum and a monument commemorate the Boers. The magnificent landscape also makes the trip worthwhile.

Interesting, despite being staged:
an insight into Zulu culture

Fort Beaufort

G 8

Province: Eastern Cape
Population: 26,000

Altitude: 486m/1594ft
Distances: Grahamstown 75km/47mi,
King William's Town 80km/50mi

This quiet, pleasant rural village is situated in the Kat River valley. Surrounded by spectacular mountain ranges, it is the starting point for lovely tours in the Amatola Mountains.

Fort Beaufort, a good 100km/60mi from the coast of the Indian Ocean on the border to the former Ciskei homeland, was founded in 1822 as a military outpost of the Cape Colony and is now the centre of the agricultural activities of the surrounding area (cultivation of citrus fruits and sheep farming).

Outpost of the Cape Colony

In 1846 a Xhosa stole an axe from a shop here. The retribution for this degenerated into the seventh border war, which lasted until 1847. Nothing can be felt of those days any longer in this quiet, pretty village. The military past comes to life in the Historical Museum (closed Sundays), in the Martello Tower of 1837, and in the Military Museum next door.

Fort Beaufort

Around Fort Beaufort

Alice, 23km/14mi east of Fort Beaufort, began as a mission and military base in 1847. The municipal museum has an exhibition of traditional Xhosa dress. Somewhat outside Alice is the **University of Fort Hare**, housed in a British fort (with an art museum and an exhibition on Black Consciousness, the ANC, etc.). It was founded in 1916 as a college for blacks and made into a university in 1970. Amongst its prominent graduates are Nelson Mandela, Oliver Tambo, Robert Mugabe, Kenneth Kaunda and Desmond Tutu. Currently 3,500 students attend the university.

Alice

A few miles east of Alice a road runs north to Hogsback (approx. 50km/30mi). The town is situated at an altitude of 1300m/4265ft in the impressive **Amatola Mountains**. Garden lovers should not miss the **Applegarth Gardens**. Hogsback and Katberg 27km/17mi further east are popular holiday destinations in both summer and winter. A few days in winter even get some snowfall; but most of the precipitation falls in summer when thunderstorms and fog are the order of the day, which creates a magical atmosphere. The forests surrounding Hogsback are good for hiking; the **Amatola Trail** (►Bisho) ends close to the town. A portion of the forest was made into the Auckland Nature Reserve; two sights of interest there are the waterfalls »Madonna and Child« and »Kettlespout«.

★
**Hogsback
Katberg**

▶ VISITING FORT BEAUFORT

INFORMATION
Publicity Association
Historical Museum, Durban St.
Tel. 046 343 1555
Mountain Escape Tourism
Tel. 045 962 1130
www.hogsback.co.za

WHERE TO STAY
► **Budget**
Savoy Hotel
53 Durban Street
Tel. 046 645 1146
Opposite the Historical Museum, with
18 good rooms, a nice garden and a
restaurant.

Tsolwana Game Reserve
A good 50km/30mi north of Fort Beaufort (west of Sada) is the 7000ha/17,500-acre Tsolwana Reserve, set at an altitude of 1300–1800m/4250–6000ft in the dry Karoo landscape south of the magnificent **Table Mountain** (1965m/6447ft). After rainfalls in this area a luxuriant flora develops; it is home to rhinoceroses, giraffes, mountain zebras and antelopes. The reserve can be explored by car on dirt roads or on guided hikes; accommodation is available in the former farmhouses. Information tel. 040 635 2115.

★ ★ Garden Route

E/F 8/9

Province: Western Cape, Eastern Cape

This famous road that runs along the rugged south coast with its wonderful white beaches and a luscious green hinterland is one of the great destinations in South Africa.

The »Garden Route« (»Tuinroete« in Afrikaans) is a 220km/140mi stretch of the 2000km/1250mi-long N 2, which mostly runs along the coast of the Indian Ocean and connects Cape Town with Swaziland. The section between Mossel Bay in the west and the mouth of Storm River in the east is probably the country's most famous travel route. It is particularly busy in December and January. The tourist facilities are excellent. It is a good idea to leave the N 2 toll road from time to time to find hidden places on smaller roads or tracks.

Outeniqua and sitsikamma Mountains
The Garden Route is sandwiched between the Indian Ocean and the Outeniqua and Tsitsikamma Mountains, which reach an elevation of 1875m/6152ft along a narrow coastal terrace, itself 200m/656ft above sea level. It runs through lush tropical forests and man-made pine forests; it often crosses wild rivers that have dug deep gorges and created lovely lagoons in the shallow coastal regions. Steep cliffs alter-

Wide sandy beaches like here at Nature's Valley, enchanting lagoons and pristine forests make the Garden Route a paradise.

nate with gently sloping, deserted beaches along this road. There are many year-round holiday resorts here; the climate is exceptionally mild, although the water is only an average 17°C/63°F . Unlike the dry savannah-like back country in the Karoo (the scenery changes dramatically within just 20km/12mi) the coastal region gets plenty of rain and as a result almost everything is able to grow here; along the Garden Route there are numerous nature reserves, national forests and bird parks, as well as marine reserves.

Drive along the Garden Route

Leave the popular holiday destination of ►Mossel Bay eastbound on the N 2 or the R 102 that runs parallel to it. 10km/6mi after Mossel Bay the R 328 branches off to the north. It crosses the spectacular **Robinson Pass** and after 80km/50mi reaches ►Oudtshoorn and its ostrich farms.

Mossel Bay
Oudtshoorn

After the Great Brak River the N 2 and the R 102 continue somewhat more inland, but the scenery remains fantastic. There are plenty of magnificent views of the **Outeniqua Mountains**. To the south roads branch off to the quiet holiday towns of Glentana and Herold's Bay. Both have nice beaches. One of the larger towns along the Garden Route is ►George. Take the N 2 from here; it soon runs along the coast again. After 10km/6mi the road reaches Wilderness, where there are good hotels, restaurants and magnificent beaches.

Glentana, Herold's Bay

George

Wilderness

Wilderness National Park

The 2600ha/6500-acre Wilderness National Park spans both sides of the N 2 between the mouth of the Touws River in the west and Sedgefield in the east. In the north it is bordered by the Outeniqua Mountains. In the south it reaches all the way to the coast in some areas. The region is simply called »The Lakes«, because there are many connecting lakes, marshes and estuaries here. The mix between salt and fresh water has created a **diverse flora and fauna**. The lakes are good for water sports (boat rentals). The park also has accommodation: Ebb & Flow Restcamp North/South, reservations at SAN-Parks (►p.156).

Goukamma Nature Reserve

A few miles east of the Wilderness National Park lies the Goukamma Nature Reserve at the mouth of the river of the same name. The reserve was set up to conserve the coast's **dune landscape** and unique bird life. It can be accessed via the road leading to Buffalo's Bay; the nature reserve itself can be explored on foot (gates open daily 8am–5pm).

Knysna

Next the N 2 passes the particularly **picturesque lagoon landscape** of ►Knysna. One of the Garden Route's most visited seaside towns is ►Plettenberg Bay.

Plettenberg Bay ►

Tsitsikamma country

Until 1868 it was impossible to get into the Tsitsikamma country. Today there is the choice between the N 2 and the R 102 from Plettenberg Bay. The N 2 crosses the Bloukrans River on a 460m/500yd-long and 216m/710ft-high bridge: if the adrenaline kick of looking down over the edge of the bridge isn't enough, it is always possible to do one of the **world's highest bungee jumps** here (tel. 042 281 1458, www.faceadrenalin.com).

Bloukrans Bridge ►

The R 102 is one of the Garden Route's nicest stretches; the road winds through old-growth forests and deep, narrow gorges with

▶ VISITING GARDEN ROUTE

INFORMATION
►George, Knysna, Mossel Bay, Plettenberg Bay
www.gardenroute.co.za

WHERE TO EAT
▶ **Moderate**
Kaaimans Grotto
Wilderness, tel. 044 877 1001
www.kaaimansgrotto.com
A cave near the famous railway bridge, which can only be reached by the George/Wilderness train.

WHERE TO STAY
▶ **Mid-range**
Lilypond Lodge
Niels and Margret Hendriks
R 102 Nature's Valley Rd., The Crags, tel. 044 534 8767
www.lilypond.co.za
A beautiful lodge in the middle of a natural paradise, 7km/4.5mi from the beach, 23km/14mi from Plettenberg Bay. Six tastefully decorated rooms; two self-catering flats. Excellent cuisine.

spectacular views of the coast. Shortly after the small town of The Crags it turns off from the N 2, towards the wonderful holiday area of **Nature's Valley** (► Plettenberg Bay). It subsequently crosses the **Bloukrans Pass** and re-joins the N 2 6km/4mi before Storms River. A good kilometre/1100yd after the hamlet of Kleinbos a road branches off from the N 2 to Storms River Mouth and to the Tsitsikamma National Park.

The name »Tsitsikamma« comes from the Khoikhoi language and means »clear water«. The national park was opened in 1964 and encompasses an 80km/50mi strip along the coast with rocky and sandy

✷ ✷
Tsitsikamma National Park

areas, as well as the waters just off the coast. The vegetation is very luxuriant, thanks to the ample year-round precipitation, which is heaviest in May and October, and lowest in June and July. The thick forest, home to metre-high ferns, orchids, and old trees that grow up to 40m/130ft tall, is **one of South Africa's last primeval forests**. Nature-lovers will enjoy the species-rich bird life, monkeys and smaller antelopes. Snorkellers and divers can explore the diverse marine fauna. Dolphins and whales are frequently spotted from the coast. The park is open daily all year round; there are different types of accommodation, shops and one restaurant. Several shorter trails start at Storms River Mouth Restcamp. Two must-sees are the **mouth of the Storm River** reached via a long boardwalk at the end of the road and a view point accessed via the suspension bridge.

A swaying suspension bridge over Storms River

There are two famous hiking trails in the national park: the Otter Trail and the Tsitsikamma Trail. The former (41km/25mi) begins in Storms River Mouth and ends in Nature's Valley, the latter (64km/40mi) runs in the opposite direction through the country's interior, which means they can be combined to make a round trip. Each can be completed in five days. The Otter Trail must be booked at least one year in advance on account of its great popularity (SANParks, ► p.156). The Tsitsikamma Trail is not much frequented, except during the holiday seasons (book at: MTO Ecotourism, George, tel. 044 874 4363, www.mtoecotourism.co.za).

✷ ✷
Otter Trail
Tsitsikamma Trail

! *Baedeker* TIP

Adventures at Storms River

Would you like to experience the jungle way up high, suspended from steel ropes? Or abseil into the 100m/330ft-deep Storms River Canyon and drift down the river on a lorry tyre? The choice of adventures at Storms River is immense (in Storms River Village, tel. 042 281 1836, www.stormsriver.com).

Approx. one kilometre (1100yd) east of Storms River, close to the N 2, is the **Big Tree** (Groot Boom): a yellowwood said to be 800 years old and thus South Africa's oldest and largest tree. It is 37m/121ft tall, and eight people are needed to encircle its trunk (girth: 8.5m/ 25ft). The eastern end of the Garden Route is marked by the **Paul Sauer Bridge** 3km/2mi east of the Big Tree. A 190m/200yd-long arch spans the Storms River at a height of 130m/430ft (restaurants, picnic sites). There is a beautiful view of the **Tsitsikamma State Forest** north of the N 2 from a view point to the west of the bridge; the outstanding feature of this reservie is its virgin rainforest; many trees are 50m/160ft or higher. Fungi, mosses and lichens testify to the high precipitation. A 4km/2.5mi hiking trail to the Big Tree starts at the Paul Sauer Bridge.

George

E 8

Province: Western Cape
Population: 106,000

Altitude: 226m/741ft
Distances: Mossel Bay 45km/28mi,
Knysna 90km/55mi,
Cape Town 410km/255mi

George is nicely situated close to the south coast on a plateau at the foot of the Outeniqua Mountains. It is the main town along the ►Garden Route (with an airport). Since it is not directly on the ocean, it mainly attracts visitors because it is the end point of the famous »Outeniqua Choo tjoe« and because it is a mecca for golfers.

George was originally called Georgetown; founded in 1811, it took its name from the reigning English king, George III. In 1878 the English novelist Anthony Trollope lauded George as the »most beautiful village in the world«; these days the town is more interesting as a stop along the Garden Route. The surrounding area is used for intensive agriculture; one of the crops here is hops.

What to See in George

George Museum   York Street (the continuation of the N 2 from Mossel Bay) is the main road. It has a junction with Courtenay Street. There the George Museum is housed in the **Old Drostdy**, which dates from 1813 (exhibitions of the history of the region, particularly about the lumber trade and the mission stations; open Mon–Fri 9am–4.30pm, Sat 9am–12.30pm).

The Dutch Reformed Church at the top of Meade Street (1842) has a pulpit made of the wood of a stinkwood tree; the columns and the dome are made of yellowwood. The church of St Peter and Paul (1843) is the oldest Catholic house of worship in South Africa.

Dutch Reformed Church

Next to the station is a 25,000 sq m/270,000 sq ft hall where the historic trains and carriages of the **Transnet Heritage Foundation** based in Johannesburg are housed (closed on Sundays). It is thus the only »official« railway museum in the country. Good information, including on the Choo-Tjoe, can be found at www.transnetheritagefoundation.co.za.

★ **Outeniqua Railway Museum**

Around George

A trip in the Outeniqua Choo-Tjoe, a **narrow-gauge railway with steam engines** that operates on a particularly attractive stretch between the beautifully restored station of George and ► Mossel Bay (►p.395), is an unforgettable experience.

★ ★ **Outeniqua Choo-Tjoe**

From George the N 12 crosses the Outeniqua Mountains and reaches ► Oudtshoorn after 60km/40mi. Approx. 15km/9mi north of George from the top of the Outeniqua Pass at 799m/2621ft there are many magnificent views of the still fertile landscape. North of the head of the pass the picture changes instantly; this is the semi-arid region of the **Little Karoo**.

Outeniqua Pass

Golfer's paradise: Fancourt Golf Resort near George

▶ VISITING GEORGE

INFORMATION

George Tourism Bureau
124 York Street
Tel. 044 801 9295
www.georgetourism.co.za
Garden Route Marketing
Tel. 044 873 6314
A lot of information all about the Garden Route.

WHERE TO STAY

▶ Luxury
Fancourt Hotel
Montagu Street, Blanco
Tel. 044 804 0010; www.fancourt.co.za
This complex with its glorious view of the Outeniqua Mountains radiates old elegance; it is probably one of the pleasantest of all golf estates. It has four 18-hole golf courses and a private lounge at George airport.

▶ Mid-range / Luxury
The Waves
7 Beach Road
Victoria Bay

Tel. / fax 044 889 0166
Victoria Bay is a small, tranquil beach town situated near steep cliffs approx. 20km/12mi south-east of George. The house of 1906 (▶photograph p.118–119) is right by the sea. Warm, unpretentious hospitality. Watch the whales from the terrace.

WHERE TO EAT

▶ Expensive
Le Pecheur
Montagu St., Blanco
Tel. 044 804 0010 (in the Fancourt Hotel)
Fresh fish excellently prepared. A unique eating experience.

▶ Moderate
The Old Townhouse
Corner of York Street and Market Street.
Tel. 044 874 3663
South African-inspired cuisine, lovingly prepared.

Outeniqua Hiking Trail
The 108km/67mi hiking trail through the Outeniqua Mountains, one of the most beautiful at the Cape, starts in Beervlei in the Bergplaas State Forest and ends at the Harkerville Forestry Station near ▶ Knysna; seven days are required to complete the whole trail (it is possible to do individual sections of it). Information and registration at the Department of Forestry in the Denmar Shopping Centre, Main Road, Knysna, tel. 044 382 5466.

✳ Seven Passes Road
A trip into another world: away from the sea and the busy N 2. The road over the plateau between George and ▶ Knysna was once the only road along the coast. Like many passes it was built by Thomas Bain by 1867. The road is partially unsurfaced and even falling apart in places. For two hours it winds through thick forests, past green meadows and old farms. The »seven passes« – Swart River, Kaaimans, Touw River, Hoogekral, Karatara, Homtini and Phantom – are river valleys or gorges with a bridge at the lowest point.

Magnificent Cape Dutch architecture in Graaff-Reinet: the Reinet House

✳ Graaff-Reinet

Province: Eastern Cape
Population: 37,000

Altitude: 663m/2175ft
Distances: Cape Town 675km/420mi,
Port Elizabeth 250km/155mi

The small provincial town of Graaff-Reinet, the »pearl of the Karoo«, is a real must-see: a real treasure trove of old architecture, surrounded by the wild beauty of the Karoo landscape.

Graaff-Reinet is one of the most beautiful towns in the country. It is situated at the foot of the Sneeuberg range in a meander of the Sunday River, between the foothills of the Great Escarpment and the open expanse of the Great Karoo. The town centre has more than 200 lovingly restored, protected houses and is a veritable museum of the architecture of the past two centuries, ranging from simple Karoo flat-roof style to the proud gables typical of Cape Dutch, and Victorian wedding-cake architecture. This town is a significant centre of animal husbandry: merino sheep, Angora goats and ostriches.

The town was founded in 1786 by Boer settlers and is thus one of the oldest European settlements in the Cape provinces. It was named after the governor Cornelis Jacob van de Graaff (1785–91) and his wife Cornelia Reinet. Since the Cape government did not provide the settlers with sufficient protection from the tribes that lived in this

History

area, the inhabitants deposed their governor in 1795 and proclaimed the town an independent republic. One year later the Cape government took over the governance again, but Graaff-Reinet remained a trouble spot. In the mid-19th century many English and German settlers made their homes here.

What to See in Graaff-Reinet

Groote Kerk The striking building in the town centre is the Dutch Reformed Church (1886) that was modelled on **Salisbury Cathedral**. Two different types of stone create an attractive design.

✱
Old Library The library of 1847 (Church Street/Somerset Street) houses the tourist information office and a small museum exhibiting 19th century costume, photographs by W. Roe, who travelled around South Africa during the second half of the 19th century, paintings, and fossils
⊙ from the Karoo. Open Mon–Fri 9am–12.30pm, 2–5pm, Sat, Sun 9am–noon.

Hester Rupert Art Museum The art museum with works by contemporary South African artists is housed in the mission church that was built in 1821 further down Church Street. Opening times: as Old Library.

✱
Drostdy The building diagonally opposite the Hester Rupert Museum was designed in 1806 by the French architect Louis Thibault as the seat of local government. It now houses a wonderful hotel; the adjoining Stretch's Court has pretty little houses that were built during the mid-19th century for emancipated slaves (►below).

● VISITING GRAAFF-REINET

INFORMATION
Publicity Association
Church Street, Graaff-Reinet
Tel. 049 892 4248
www.graaffreinet.co.za
www.graaffreinet.com

WHERE TO STAY AND EAT
► **Mid-range/Luxury**
Andries Stockenstroom Guest House
100 Cradock Street
Tel. 049 8924575
www.stockenstrom.co.za
This nicely decorated house dating from 1819 with only six rooms is also

known for its excellent cuisine with Karoo specialities (only for hotel guests).

► **Mid-range**
Drostdy Hotel
30 Church Street, tel. 049 892 2161
www.drostdy.co.za
An elegant hotel in a building that was once the seat of government; it has comfortable rooms with antique furniture. The pool overlooks the Valley of Desolation. Excellent cuisine, romantic candlelight dinners can be had in the »De Camdeboo« restaurant.

Bizarre rock formations in the Valley of Desolation

The old residence of the governor to the east in Parsonage Street was built in 1820. Today it houses a weapons collections (opening times as for the Old Library). **Old Residency**

The minister's house, built between 1806 and 1812 in the Cape Dutch style on the opposite side of the street on the corner of Murray Street, is now a museum (opening times as for the Old Library). It has attractive furniture from the 18th and 19th centuries, household items and vehicles on display; in the garden behind the building there is a **huge vine** that was planted in 1870. **★ Reinet House**

★ Karoo Nature Reserve

The town is surrounded by the 16,000ha/40,000-acre Karoo Nature Reserve, which contains Spandau Kop and the Nqweba (Van Ryneveld) Dam on the Sunday River, and the Valley of Desolation. The semi-desert of the **Great Karoo** has expanded further and further over the past 100 years and today takes up a third of the country. Overgrazing by sheep has had a significant impact on the landscape; predators have become extinct and the plant diversity has drastically diminished. The Karoo Nature Reserve was established in an attempt to stop this development in a small area at least (▶Beaufort West). Various animals have been reintroduced to the area, such as mountain zebra, white-tailed gnu and springbok. Since the larger mammals are not harmless, visitors are not allowed to leave their cars. **Migrating semi-desert**

Valley of Desolation The most impressive sight is the Valley of Desolation to the west of the town (drive 5km/3mi towards Murraysburg; the entrance is signposted and the gates always open). The Valley of Desolation is more of a gorge than a valley. The steep road that climbs up to 1500m/5000ft above sea level ends at a car park, from which trails lead to several viewpoints. There are fantastic views of the Great Karoo to the south, the plain of Graaff-Reinet to the east, and the Sneeuberg range to the north.

! Baedeker TIP

Desolation Nature Walks

Visitors should definitely take the time to do the 1.5km/1mi round trail that starts at the car park opposite Spandau Kop and affords fantastic views. Those who have more time can choose trails from the Eerstefontein Day Walks varying in length between 5km/3mi and 14km/9mi, where mountain zebras, kudus and klipspringers can be seen. The exhausting Drie Koppie Trail (two days, reservations at Karoo Nature Reserve, tel. 049 892 3453, or Karoo Connections in Graaff-Reinet) is much less frequented and makes its way through the eastern part of the nature reserve.

Nieu Bethesda, 55km/34mi north of Graaff-Reinet, is also well worth a visit (31km/19mi on the R 51, then north-west). For one the **Sneeuberg** (2504m/8215ft) is a very picturesque backdrop, and in addition the pretty village is a good example of rural life. It became famous through the eccentric artist **Helen Martin** (1898–1976), who lived as a recluse in her »Owl House« at the edge of the Great Karoo and created a fantasy world of strange figures made of concrete and glass (open daily 9am–5pm).

★ Grahamstown

G 8

Province: Eastern Cape
Population: 56,000

Altitude: 540m/1772ft
Distances: Port Elizabeth 130km/80mi, East London 160km/100mi

Grahamstown, located between Port Elizabeth and East London, and approx. 50km/30mi away from the coast, is a lively, well looked-after university town. Many historical buildings give the town centre a British air.

Grahamstown is the capital of the Settler Country, where white settlers and Xhosa came into contact. As the seat of Rhodes University Grahamstown has become one of South Africa's significant cultural centres; in addition it is the seat of an Anglican bishop. Grahamstown is also known as »the city of saints« because of its **many churches**; it is said to have more than forty. The humble **Xhosa townships** with their poor infrastructure on the other riverbank form a stark contrast to the Victorian atmosphere of the city centre.

Attractive Victorian houses shape the centre of Grahamstown.

In the 18th century Dutch settlers from the Cape Province headed east to find new settlement land. At the Great Fish River they came across the Xhosa, a Bantu people, who were also in search of land. After the Cape Colony had been occupied by the British in 1806, there was an increased influx of British immigrants, who mainly settled along the east coast. By 1857 there had been eight wars in less than a century in frontier land between the Great Fish River and the Bushman's River. The British erected a chain of forts to secure the border between the black and the white population; Grahamstown, named after Colonel John Graham, was one of these military bases, set up in 1812. By 1831 it was the second-largest town in the Cape Colony after Cape Town.

What to See in Grahamstown

The main road is the High Street that runs between the station and the university. The Cathedral of St Michael and St George, begun in 1824, forms an island in the High Street. After Grahamstown became a diocese in 1853, the cathedral was enlarged; the 53.6m/176ft spire is **South Africa's tallest church spire**. The city hall behind the cathedral was built around the belfry of 1870.

By the city hall Bathurst Street branches off the High Street towards the south. This is the location of the Observatory Museum (open Mon–Fri 9.30am–1pm, 2–5pm, Sat 9am–1pm). From 1850 to his death, this house was home to Henry Carter Galpin, a watchmaker, goldsmith and amateur astronomer. In 1882 he built a **camera**

obscura in the tower. It is the only one in South Africa. When the air is clear a mirror on the roof reflects views of the city. The Victorian rooms also have furniture, everyday objects and telescopes on display.

Eastern Star Gallery

Return to the High Street and follow it in a south-westerly direction towards the university. In Anglo-African Street the building in which the *Eastern Star* was once printed is now a museum. This paper later became *The Star*, which is the daily newspaper of Johannesburg and has the highest circulation of any newspaper in the country.

Rhodes University

At the south-western end of the High Street is Rhodes University (www.ru.ac.za), named after Cecil Rhodes (► Famous People), and founded in 1904. The only surviving building of the Cape government from the 19th century is the gate (Drostdy Gate) through which the university campus is accessed; many of its buildings were designed in the office of the famous architect Sir Herbert Baker at the beginning of the 20th century. Approx. 6000 students attend this university; their presence makes itself felt in the town in the form of a diverse and **lively bar and café scene**.

Baedeker TIP

Edwardian Shopping

One of the town's prettiest English houses is that of the gentlemen's outfitter T Birch & Co. on Church Square (www.birchs.co.za), which supplies all the relevant institutions in South Africa, such as churches and universities, with gowns and the like. The shop still uses a curious cable system to transport the customer's money to the central cash register and receive the change.

Next to the entrance to the university in Somerset Street is the **Natural Science Museum** of 1902. It has a lot of interesting information about the early history of humans in Africa, as well as geology and ornithology. Opening times are the same as the Observatory Museum.

The **History Museum** next door has focused on the political and cultural history of the Eastern Cape: furniture and everyday objects, weapons, paintings, and photographs. The archaeological department has one of South Africa's three Egyptian mummies. Opening times are the same as the Observatory Museum.

Botanical Garden

The Botanical Garden was laid out in 1850 and is one of the oldest in the country; it can be accessed from Lucas Avenue, which branches off from Somerset Street. The area stretches out over the slope of Gunfire Hill up to Fort Selwyn (1835), which is one of the military signalling stations that reach all the way to the Fish River (not accessible).

Fort Selwyn

1820 Settler's Monument

A few steps away from Fort Selwyn this not very attractive office building and **cultural centre** was opened in 1974. It houses an art gallery, conference rooms and a theatre. The bronze monument at the entrance shows a settler family in typical dress.

This project was founded by the ANC in the Dakawa refugee camp in Tanzania in 1987 and brought to South Africa after the abolition of apartheid. It gives artists the opportunity to establish themselves professionally; several of them have become famous. Drawings, sculptures, paintings and woven goods can be acquired here (4–11 Froude Street, www.geocities.com/dakawaart).

Dakawa Art and Craft Project

It is definitely worth getting to know the townships, particularly on foot. Tours are offered by the Egazini Outreach Project (tel. 046 637 1500, www.grahamstown.co.za/egazini.htm) and the Umthathi Project (tel. 082 784 1458 or 046 622 4450, www.umthathi.co.za).

Township tours

Around Grahamstown

The 1000ha/2500-acre Baines Reserve, through which the Palmiet River flows, can be accessed 15km/9mi south of Grahamstown from

Thomas Baines Nature Reserve

► VISITING GRAHAMSTOWN

INFORMATION
Makana Tourism
63 High St., Grahamstown
Tel. 046 622 3241
www.grahamstown.co.za

FESTIVALS AND EVENTS
End of June and early July: National Festival of Arts. One of the most significant cultural events in South Africa; the town turns into a huge stage (www.nafest.co.za). Accommodation must be booked one year in advance for this period.

WHERE TO EAT / WHERE TO STAY
► Moderate
The Cock House
10 Market Street, tel. 046 636 1287
www.cockhouse.co.za
This luxurious guesthouse, a property dating from 1826, has an excellent restaurant with country cooking. The accommodation comprises eight rooms in which people like Nelson Mandela and Andre Brink have stayed.

► Inexpensive/Moderate
Calabash
in the Protea Hotel in Grahamstown
123 High Street, tel. 046 622 2324
Famous for its good African food, including delicious Xhosa hotpots. The hotel is quite unattractive from the outside but has inexpensive, tasteful and almost luxuriously furnished rooms.

WHERE TO STAY
► Mid-range
Protea Evelyn House
115 High Street, tel. 046 622 2366
www.albanyhotels.co.za
A pretty guesthouse dating from the 19th century in a quiet garden in the town centre. Six rooms/suites, pool, barbecue.

► Budget
The Hermitage
14 Henry Street, tel. 046 636 1503
An English villa from the 1820s with a nice garden. Bea Jaffray, a well-known ceramic artist, provides comfortable accommodation in two rooms.

Endless beaches near Port Alfred

the R 343. Since it is home to wild animals (the rare Cape buffalo and rhinoceros amongst others), visitors are not allowed to go hiking here; the reserve can be explored by car on a 15km/9mi-long track as well as by boat (open daily 7am–5pm).

Bathurst From Grahamstown the R 67 goes to Bathurst 40km/25mi to the south-west. The small town (population: 5200) was founded in 1820 and is one of South Africa's centres of **pineapple cultivation**. Dutch settlers brought the fruit with them in the mid-19th century and by 1860 it was grown in Natal. St John's Church, the oldest surviving Anglican church in South Africa, was consecrated in 1832 and is well worth a visit, as is the »British« **Pig & Whistle Hotel** with its popular pub (Kowie Road), which were opened in 1831.

✱ Port Alfred Port Alfred (population: 25,000), 58km/36mi south of Grahamstown, where the Kowie River flows into the Indian Ocean, is a popular destination for holidays and weekend trips. The wonderful beaches of the surrounding area, the opportunities for water sports, and the attractive **18-hole golf course** all justify the reputation of a town that was founded as a port in 1820 and later renamed after Queen Victoria's second son. During the high season it is very busy and prices are considerably higher than at other times.

Kenton-on-Sea The small coastal town between the mouth of the Bushman's River and the Kariega River is ideal for visitors who want to spend some quiet days and have few other needs; during the holiday season the beaches are also used by South African holidaymakers. There are rewarding trips on the **scenically attractive rivers**, where it is possible to rent a boat and go fishing on a 40km/25mi or a 22km/14mi stretch (houseboat charter in the marina, tel. 046 648 1223).

The Kowie Nature Reserve begins 5km/3mi north of Port Alfred (accessible via the road to Bathurst; open daily 7am–5pm). The hiking trail (approx. four hours) through the reserve and the 24km/15mi canoe trip from Port Alfred up the Kowie River (or the other way around) are justifiably popular. Canoes can be rented. It is best to book as early as possible at Cape Nature Conservation, Port Alfred, tel. 046 624 2230.

★
Kowie Nature Reserve

! *Baedeker* TIP

Kwandwe Private Game Reserve

20 minutes north of Grahamstown the wilderness has returned to the malaria-free area at the Great Fish River. Accommodation is available in luxurious lodges; why not go on the prowl for some wildlife? The Upland Homestead is a little gem. It is a Cape Dutch house built in 1905, which can accommodate groups of up to six people. Day visitors are also welcome. Information and reservations at CCAfrica (see p.167).

Harrismith

H 6

Province: Free State
Population: 38,000

Altitude: 1615m/5300ft
Distances: Johannesburg 285km/175mi,
Durban 310km/195mi,
Bloemfontein 330km/205mi

Harrismith, situated between Johannesburg, Durban and Bloemfontein, is a good starting point for a visit to the Natal-Drakensberg range and the Golden Gate Highlands National Park.

This quiet, pleasant rural town is an important hub with petrol stations, hotels and restaurants: here the N 5 from Bloemfontein joins the N 3, which connects Johannesburg with Durban on the Indian Ocean. Apart from the Botanical Garden, Harrismith does not really have any sights.

Harrismith was founded in the vicinity of Vrededorp in 1849, but it kept growing in the direction of the Wilge river as a reaction to the water supply problem. The town was named after the governor of the Cape Colony (1848–52) Sir Harry Smith. During the diamond rush of the 1860s a post station was set up here, which greatly accelerated the town's growth.

Some history

▶ VISITING HARRISMITH

INFORMATION

Harrismith Marketing Bureau
City Hall
Pretorius Street
Tel. 058 622 3525

WHERE TO STAY

▶ **Mid-range**
Huize Sandwijk
91 Wardne Street
Tel. 058 622 2809
Mobile tel. 082 372 9362

www.sandwijk.com
A very pleasant bed & breakfast with a
personal atmosphere.

WHERE TO EAT

▶ **Moderate**
Pringles
at the N 2 entrance to Harrismith
Tel. 058 623 0255
South African family cooking with an
emphasis on beef and fish dishes.

Berg Marathon A big sporting event that takes place in Harrismith every year on 10
October is the **Berg Marathon**. The 2377m/7799ft-high Platberg near
Harrismith was snidely called »that little hill of yours« by a British
major. An angry inhabitant bet him that he would not be able to
make it to the top in one hour. The major did however achieve the
feat, and donated a prize for future winners of the race.

What to See in Harrismith

Town Hall The town hall is a sandstone building dating from 1907. It stands in
a park in the city centre. At the entrance is a 27m/30yd-long fossilized tree that is estimated to be around 150 million years old.

★
**Drakensberg
Botanic Garden** At the foot of the Platberg 5km/3mi south of the city is the Botanic
Garden (open daily) with plants native to the Drakensberg moun-
tains. Only the parts of the park near the reservoirs are maintained
by gardeners.

Around Harrismith

**Sterkfontein
Dam** The Sterkfontein Dam 25km/16mi south of Harrismith is a popular
area for water sports fans and anglers (trout). The road from Harrismith to the ►Natal Drakensberg mountains passes the lake.

**Mount Everest
Game Reserve** The 1000ha/2500-acre Mount Everest Game Reserve 20km/12mi
north-east of Harrismith (R 722 towards Verkykerskop) is hilly
country that provides a habitat for more than 20 species of game.
The animals can be observed from off-road vehicles or on horseback.
Accommodation is in holiday homes and round huts. Trout fishing,
climbing.

Hermanus

C 9

Province: Western Cape
Population: 13,000

Altitude: 233m/764ft
Distances: Cape Town 120km/75mi

Hermanus is a popular holiday destination on the Atlantic east of Cape Town, with beautiful sandy beaches and good conditions for water sports and fishing. The whales that come to Walker Bay are the big attraction between June and November.

The town bears the name of the Dutch itinerant teacher Hermanus Pieters who set up camp with his flock of sheep at a nearby spring in 1830. The original name of the place was Hermanuspietersfontein. It was fortunately shortened in 1904 when the town was given municipal status. The beginnings of tourism go back to the 19th century; the first hotel was opened in Hermanus in 1891. In the early 20th century the first holiday homes were built around the harbour.

A little history

Hermanus is a conspicuous sea of holiday homes; the town centre around the **old harbour** is fairly small. Here some restored fishing huts now house restaurants, bars, and shops. The 15km/9mi Cliff Path that leads from the new harbour to Grotto Beach has some good views.

Townscape

★

◄ Cliff Path

»Whale watching« near Hermanus

▶ VISITING HERMANUS

INFORMATION
Hermanus Tourism
Mitchell St., Old Station Building
Tel. 028 312 2629
www.hermanus.co.za

FESTIVALS UND EVENTS
Whale Festival, Sept: cultural festival
with theatre, music, and arts and crafts
(www.whalefestival.co.za)

WHALE HOTLINE
Call tel. 028 312 2629 to find out when
and where whales can be seen between
Betty's Bay and Gaansbai.

WHERE TO EAT
▶ Moderate
Bientang's Cave
Marine Drive, tel. 028 312 3454
www.bientangscave.co.za
In the cliffs below Market Square, with
a veranda: the »best whale watching
restaurant in the world«. Excellent
seafood. Reservations essential.

Burgundy
Marine Drive, tel. 028 312 2800
One of the best and most popular
restaurants in Hermanus (reservations
essential), located in cottages from
1875 at the old harbour. Excellent fish
and seafood, but also dishes such as
chicken Portuguese style. Opposite the
Auberge Burgundy.

▶ Inexpensive
The Harbour Rock
New Harbour
Tel. 028 312 2920
Magnificent view of Walker Bay and
the mountains. Enjoy dishes such as
smoked salmon pancakes or mussels
in coconut cream outside on the
terrace.

WHERE TO STAY
During the high season (Dec–Jan)
Hermanus is overrun and accommo-
dation must be booked well in advance.

▶ Luxury
The Marine Hermanus
Marine Drive, tel. 028 313 1000
www.marine-hermanus.co.za
One of the country's most beautiful
hotels in a building dating from 1890
perched on the cliffs over the sea.
Watch the whales from your hotel bed!
47 rooms, two restaurants and a pool.
Golf course, diving excursions, hikes,
horse riding, sailing, etc. Unfortunately
children under 14 are not welcome.

▶ Mid-range/Luxury
Auberge Burgundy
16 Harbour Road, tel. 028 313 1201
www.auberge.co.za
Despite its name, this wonderful villa
makes you feel you're in Provence
rather than Burgundy. 17 luxurious
rooms; the penthouse (for up to six
people) is an absolute dream. Inner
courtyard with a pool, a wonderful
view of the bay from the verandas and
balconies.

▶ Mid-range
Whale Cottage Guest House
38 Westcliff Drive, tel. 028 313 0929
A small, modern villa close to the new
harbour in a maritime design. Garden
with pool.

▶ Budget
Hermanus Backpackers
26 Flower Street, tel. 028 312 4293
www.hermanusbackpackers.co.za
A highly praised hostel, friendly management, with small bedrooms as well
as double rooms. Garden, pool, bar,
and a large choice of activities.

What to See in and around Hermanus

The Old Harbour Museum (at the old harbour, open Mon–Sat 9am–1pm, 2–5pm, Sun noon–4pm) has numerous exhibits on the history of fishing and whaling in Hermanus. The collection includes some of the old fishing boats that were used between 1855 and 1961. They can be seen in the harbour outside. In September and October the strangely clad »Whale Crier« calls out when there are whales in sight.

Old Harbour Museum

North-east of Hermanus along the Mossel River is the 1446ha/3615-acre Fernkloof Nature Reserve, which also includes the Platberg in its territory; the difference in altitude (60–840m/200–2760ft) means there is a wide variety of **fynbos and proteas** in the reserve. More than 40 species of erica can be admired all year round. Amongst the many bird species in the reserve the black eagle is worth mentioning. From the visitor centre a 50km/30mi long network of trails traverses the reserve (picnic places).

✷ Fernkloof Nature Reserve

! Baedeker TIP

Hermanus Wine Route

A few miles north of Hermanus on the road to Shaw's Pass the stunning Hemel-en-Aarde Valley has acquired a reputation for producing excellent wines from the Burgundy grape varieties of Pinot Noir and Chardonnay. Hamilton Russell (tel. 028 312 35 95, closed on Sundays) and Bouchard Finlayson (tel. 028 312 515, www.bouchardfinlayson.co.za, closed on Sundays) are two of the most renowned vineyards in South Africa.

The small village of De Kelders and the simple, still relatively authentic **fishing village** of Gansbaai to the south-east on Walker Bay are much less overrun than Hermanus. Several factories process the catch landed in the modern deepwater port. This is another good location for whale watching. At Danger Point (9km/5.5mi from Gansbaai) a ship ran aground in 1852, at the cost of 443 lives; but it was only in 1895 after yet more accidents that a lighthouse was built. The 7km/4.5mi-long, interesting **Duiwelsgat Trail** that runs along the coast can be completed in three hours. Information available from the Gansbaai Tourism Bureau, Berg Street/Main Street, tel. 028 384 1439.

De Kelders Gansbaai

Southern right whales can live as long as 100 years and weigh as much as 80 tons. Whalers called them »southern right« because they were the »right« whales to catch and brought them a rich return.

WHALES OFF SOUTH AFRICA

To see these giant, primeval beasts without venturing into choppy seas, South Africa is just the right place, particularly between False Bay near Cape Town and Plettenberg Bay along the Garden Route.

In South Africa it is possible to watch whales over breakfast on the terrace or even from bed (but the whales do »sing« and grunt all night long, which can interfere with the sleep of anyone whose accommodation is close to the water). Near **Hermanus**, which the WWF considers one of the best whale-watching spots in the world, the cliffs drop so steeply into the crystal-clear ocean that it almost seems as if the whales are within stroking distance. Of course the whales are intensively exploited as a tourist attraction; there is a whale hotline and in September and October the world's only »whale crier« gets not a moment's rest.

About the whales

Between June and the end of November 18m/60ft-long **southern right whales** (Eubalaena australis) come to Walker Bay in order to have their young (in August and September the 6m/20ft-long whale calves are born in shallow, secluded bays) and to mate. These whales can be recognized by their horny calluses in the head area and their V-shaped blowhole. In

Walker Bay and off the west coast visitors can see the 14m/45ft-long, 20t **Bryde's whale** (Balaenoptera edeni) from the rorqual family. Another whale from the rorqual family is the 15m/50ft-long **humpback whale** (Megaptera novaeangliae) with very long flippers, which are usually white on the underside. The **pygmy right whale** (Caperea marginata), confined to the southern hemisphere and up to 6m/20ft in length, surfaces off the coast of South Africa. These species are all members of the baleen whale suborder (Mysticeti). They have baleen plates for filtering food from the water. The second sub-order, the **toothed whales** (Odontoceti), is also represented along the South African coastline: this sub-order includes Layard's beaked whale, the Chinese white dolphin, True's beaked whale, the dusky dolphin, Heaviside's dolphin, the common dolphin and the bottlenose dolphin. The most spectacular and striking of the toothed whales is the orca (Orcinus orca), which also attacks other whales, and was called the killer whale by whalers because of its hunting technique.

✳ Hluhluwe-Imfolozi National Park

J/K 6

Province: KwaZulu-Natal
Distances: Richards Bay 80km/50mi,
Durban 280km/175mi

Altitude: 60–600m/200–2000ft

This two-part national park in the north-east, in the heart of the Zululand, is one of the oldest and most interesting in South Africa. The diverse landscape provides a home to many wild animals, particularly to the »Big Five«.

The Hluhluwe (pronounced »shlu-shlu-wee«) and Imfolozi (previously Umfolozi) reserves in the north-east of KwaZulu-Natal province are separated by an 8km/5mi-wide corridor through which the R 618 runs; they are amongst the continent's oldest reserves. Hluhluwe was founded as far back as 1895. The two reserves together with the corridor have an area of 960 sq km/370 sq mi, which makes them South Africa's third-largest game preserve. Its establishment was not well received by the white settlers in the area. They blamed the wild animals, as the hosts for the tsetse fly, for the spread of an epidemic amongst their cattle herds and therefore shot a large proportion of the game in the area. In two decades, between 1930 and 1950, 100,000 animals are said to have been killed. From 1945 DDT was used to combat the tsetse fly, which eventually led to its eradication.

Buffaloes are not the only animals that like oxpeckers to look after their fur.

▶ VISITING HLUHLUWE-IMFOLOZI

INFORMATION
KZN Wildlife, ▶p.156
Hluhluwe Tourism Association
Bush Road, Hluhluwe
Tel. 035 562 0353, www.hluhluwe.net

WHEN TO GO
The reserve can be visited all year round, but it gets very hot and muggy in summer (temperatures can exceed 35°C/95°F) and there are also frequent thunderstorms. The temperatures are more pleasant in winter (May–Oct). Anti-malaria measures are necessary.

WHERE TO STAY
▶ **Mid-range/Luxury**
Zulu Nyala Game Lodge
Msinene Road, Hluhluwe
Tel. 035 562 0169, www.zulunyala.com

Very nice, stone-built thatched lodge 15km/9mi from Hluhluwe. 40 tasteful rooms, Zulu-style. Guided tours, wildlife exploration drives, pool and tennis.

▶ **Budget/Mid-range**
Hilltop Camp
Hluhluwe Park
Camp Tel. 035 562 0848
Reservations at: KZN Wildlife, ▶p.156.
In a hilly location with fantastic views. The complex is well looked after and has different types of accommodation, from the luxury lodge to more basic self-catering chalets and rondavels. With a bar and a good restaurant. It is best to book early, because bus tours frequent this place too.

Animals in the reserves

The reserves are home to 50 species of mammal, including buffaloes, blue wildebeests, zebras, giraffes, elephants, dwarf antelopes, klipspringers, nyalas, bohor reedbucks, red river hogs, lions, leopards, cheetahs, spotted hyenas, black-backed jackals, baboons and crocodiles. There are a large number of rhinoceroses in the reserves. Most of them are white rhinoceroses; in 1895 the number was estimated to be only 50, while it is thought today that 50% of the world's rhinoceroses live here. The bird fauna comprises 400 species.

Hluhluwe Region

How to get here

The main gate of the north-eastern part (Memorial Gate) is reached via the N 2. Where it approaches the town of Hluhluwe a surfaced road turns off to the reserve 15km/9mi away. An alternative access route is the R 618; turn right on to a track 17km/10mi beyond Mtubatuba.

Landscape

The Hluhluwe reserve has an area of only 230 sq km/89 sq mi and is thus less than half as big as the Imfolozi section. The hilly terrain has particularly thick forests in the north and along the rivers and gives a tropical impression. The area can be explored on a 40km/25mi track network.

Imfolozi Region

The R 618 leads to the main gate of the south-western part. A further access route exists from Ulundi and leads to the western border of the reserve (Cengeni Gate). A 70km/45mi round trip (Mosaic Auto Trail, four to five hours) leads through the northern part of Imfolozi.

How to get here

The prevailing landscape in Imfolozi is savannah with occasionally thick scrubland and semi-desert. Taller trees line the Mfolosi Emnyana (»black«) and Mfolosi Emhlope (»white«) rivers, which meet in the reserve. Around half of the area may be explored by car. A 240 sq km/93 sq mi area in the south (Wilderness Area) is only accessible on guided hikes. It is necessary to be in good shape for these three-day keeper-led excursions, even though all the equipment (including food, everything provided by the KZN) is transported on donkeys; on the four-day **Primitive Trails** everything must be carried by the participants. Early booking necessary.

Landscape

★

◄ Wilderness Trails

★ Johannesburg · Egoli

G/H 5

Province: Gauteng
Population: approx. 2 million (Greater Johannesburg 5 million)

Altitude: 1752m/5748ft
Distances: Bloemfontein 400km/250mi, Cape Town 1400km/870mi

Despite the problems that continue to exist even after the end of apartheid, African life in South Africa can be experienced best in Johannesburg, the country's largest city and main economic centre.

Johannesburg, for the local whites simply »Jo'burg«, for the blacks »eGoli« (»city of gold«), is Africa's third-largest city after Cairo and Alexandria. It is situated on the highveld, the plateau in the centre of South Africa at the end of the **Witwatersrand** (this 80km/50mi ridge rich in natural resources towers 300m/1000ft above the surrounding area). Johannesburg is gradually merging with Pretoria in the north and the industrial settlements of Vanderbijlpark and Vereeniging in the south. They make up the **province of Gauteng**, which encompasses only 2% of South Africa's total area, but contains 25% of its total population. The actual population of Johannesburg cannot be stated exactly. For years the number of whites living in the city has been going down (approx. 400,000); the figures for the black population fluctuate between four and five million, not including the neighbouring black township of **Soweto** (incorporated into the mother city in 2000), which in itself is home to a further 1.5 to 2 million, maybe even 4 million, people. Even though many of the gold mines in the city and its surroundings have been closed down, Johannes-

South Africa's economic metropolis

burg has remained the **country's financial and industrial centre**. Most of South Africa's significant companies have their headquarters here and almost 70% of the country's industrial production comes from the Witwatersrand area. The city's stock exchange is active all around the world. There are three universities: the University of Witwatersrand (English-speaking) founded in 1922, the Rand Afrikaans University created in 1966, where classes are taught in Afrikaans and English, and Vista University in Soweto, which has students of all skin colours. Further educational institutions are the Technical College and a teacher training college.

Climate
Thanks to Johannesburg's altitude the city has a very pleasant climate. On average the city receives 8.7 hours of sunshine a day. In summer the temperatures are high and afternoon downpours are frequent. The winters are relatively cool and dry; sunny days are followed by freezing nights.

History
In July 1886 the Australian adventurer George Harrison discovered the gold deposits of the Witwatersrand. Although the rapidly growing gold prospectors' camps maintained their makeshift character for a long time, the first public buildings were opened in 1888: a school, a hospital and a theatre. That same year the famous Wanderers' Club, a sports and entertainment centre for miners, opened; ten

Highlights Johannesburg · Egoli

Newtown Cultural Precinct
An attempt to fill the inner city with life: with new venues for the cultural scene, cafés and good museums.
► page 330

MuseuMAfrica
Excellent museum in Newtown, presenting the lives of blacks in Johannesburg and Gauteng.
► page 331

Constitution Hill
Also part of the city redevelopment project and a symbol of the rainbow nation: the new constitutional court in the area of the Old Fort.
► page 332

Shopping malls
Another experience of Johannesburg's contrasts: a visit to one of the elegant suburban shopping malls, particularly in Rosebank, Sandton and Hyde Park as well as in the Randburg Waterfront.
► page 333

Old Melville
7th Street in Melville has become a trendy area with restaurants, cafés, and nightclubs.
► page 333

Apartheid Museum
Gold Reef City is on the agenda for most visitors to Johannesburg. This museum is however a must-see; it vividly presents the nightmarish atmosphere of the apartheid era.
► page 333

Soweto
No South Africa trip would be complete without a tour through the notorious »South West Township«.
► page 335

The view of the vibrant city of Johannesburg from the Carlton Centre is absolutely breathtaking.

years later it had 1500 members engaged in six different sports. The Turffontein racecourse was opened in 1887. Towards the end of the 19th century the owners of the gold district, the »Randlords« like Barney Barnato, the Beit brothers, Cecil Rhodes and the Wernher family had already established small financial empires.

The population grew very quickly. A mere six years after the first gold was discovered, 40,000 whites were living in the area. In 1905 the number had risen to 150,000. The black population grew from approx. 60,000 inhabitants in 1904 to 112,000 in 1911; in addition there were another 300,000 who lived outside the city boundary. Most of the blacks were employed as seasonal workers. By the end of the 19th century the infrastructure did not match the population. This was mostly due to **Paul Kruger** (►Famous People), who did not want to accept an English-speaking town so close to Pretoria. Kruger refused to grant Johannesburg municipal status, even though it had overtaken Pretoria in less than two decades both in population and economic significance. The building boom only began after the Boer War (on 31 May 1900 British troops occupied Johannesburg). Johannesburg received the right to elect a municipal council in 1904. The inhabitants had to wait until 1905 for a sewerage system. During the 20th century the gold mines reached ever new depths (3581m/ 11,749ft near Carletonville). At the beginning of the 1990s there were still more than 50 mining corporations, mostly operating smaller shafts where manganese, iron, asbestos, and uranium were mined in addition to gold. Today no more mines are active in the Johannesburg area.

Johannesburg · Egoli · Centre *Map*

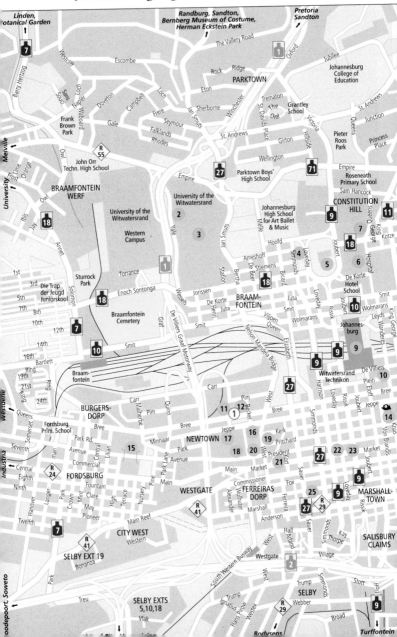

1 Hillbrow Tower
2 Planetarium
3 University Museums
    and Galleries
4 Civic Theatre
5 Civic Centre
6 Adler Museum of
    the History of Medicine
7 Old Fort
8 Johannesburg Art Gallery
9 Railway Station/
    Park Station
10 St Mary's Cathedral
11 MuseumAfrica
12 Market Theatre Complex
13 Diamond Cutting Works
14 Supreme Law Courts
15 Oriental Plaza
16 Turbine Hall
17 Worker's Museum
18 Sci-Bono Centre
19 Former Exchange
20 SAB World of Beer
21 KwaZulu Muti Museum
22 City Hall
23 Rissik Street Post Office
24 Carlton Centre
25 Chamber of Mines

Where to stay
All recommended hotels
are outside the city centre.

Where to eat
① Gramadoela's
The other recommended
restaurants are outside
the city centre.

▶ VISITING JOHANNESBURG · EGOLI

INFORMATION

Johannesburg Tourism Company
195 Jan Smuts Ave., Parktown North
Tel. 011 214 0700
www.joburg.org.za

Gauteng Tourism Authority
Rosebank Mall, Rosebank
Tel. 011 390 3614
www.gauteng.net

South African Tourism
Airport, International Arrivals Hall
Tel. 011 970 1669

TRANSPORT

O. Tambo International Airport is a
hub for all of southern Africa and is
located 25km/15mi east of the centre.
Most of the planes arrive early in the
day; for night-time arrivals it is
important to organize a pick-up;
otherwise it is best to take one of the
airport taxis to the hotel. The Magic
Bus goes every half-hour or hour to
the biggest hotels in the northern
districts. Most hotels will also have or
arrange a shuttle. The central station
(Park Station) is also the station for
coaches. Taxis are expensive, but
indispensable; some reliable companies are Maxi, Rose's, International
and Midway (negotiate prices in
advance). City buses and minibus-
taxis should be avoided, as well as the
suburban trains to Pretoria.

PERSONAL SAFETY

▶p.328

FESTIVALS AND EVENTS

End of Aug: Joy of Jazz Festival
(African and international musicians,
www.joyofjazz.co.za). Beginning of
Sept: Arts Alive (cultural festival in
Newtown, mainly music, www.artsa-
live.co.za). Current event dates in the
Mail & Guardian (Fridays), in the Star
(»Tonight«) and in »SA City Life«.

TOURS

The best way to get to know the city is
by taking a tour. Some organizers that
have proven to be good are: Expedi-
tionary Force (tel. 011 667 2833),
Lords (tel. 011 791 5494), A'Zambezi
(tel. 011 462 6620), Karabo (tel. 011
880 5099), Jimmy's Face to Face (tel.
011 331 6109). A tour of a gold mine is
very interesting; registration at the
Chamber of Mines,
tel. 011 498 7100, www.bullion.org.za.

WHERE TO EAT

▶ Expensive

Leipoldt's
Rivonia Rd./Kelvin Rd., Morningside
Tel. 011 339 2765
Restaurant with tradition in the Pavilion Centre. Popular South African
buffet: ostrich fillets in port and
pepper sauce, fish bobotie (casserole)
and sosaties (skewers).

Linger Longer
58 Wierda Road
Wierda Valley, Sandton
Tel. 011 884 0465
For years a top-class restaurant in a
beautiful old house with a garden.
Unusual menu, e.g. lemon pepper
fillets with mushroom sauce.

Moyo Restaurant
Melrose Square, Melrose
Tel. 011 684 1477, www.moyo.co.za
Extravagant African restaurant with
the typical ambience and cuisine.

▶ Moderate

① *Gramadoela's*
Bree Street, Newtown

Tel. 011 838 6960
In Cape Dutch ambience, serving a good selection of South African dishes, such as sosatie, bobotie, mel-kart, or »mopani worms« (deep-fried caterpillars). Moderate prices, despite illustrious guests such as Queen Elizabeth, Nelson Mandela and Hillary Clinton.

► Inexpensive
Bistro 277 on Main
Cramerview Centre
277 Main Road, Bryanston
(north of Sandton)
Tel. 011 706 2837
Excellent restaurant with French-inspired cuisine. Very family-oriented.

Bushveld Pub and Diner
Valley Ventre – Corner of Jan Smuts and Buckingham Road
Tel. 011 326 0170
South African cuisine. Here, in the suburb of Craighall Park north of Johannesburg, the best steaks and T-bones are served. Cosy.

WHERE TO STAY
► Luxury
Saxon Hotel
36 Saxon Road, Sandhurst
Tel. 011 292 6000, www.thesaxon.com
The modern villa of an insurance magnate who let Nelson Mandela write his autobiography here and later transferred his business headquarters to London, now a hotel for people who value absolute luxury and absolute security. Suites range in price from ZAR 4200 to 16,000 to be paid in advance.

Michelangelo
Nelson Mandela Square, Sandton
Tel. 011 282 7000
www.michelangelo.co.za
One of the world's leading luxury

hotels (242 rooms), in magnificent Italian neo-Renaissance style. Located above Sandton Square; an escalator leads directly to the restaurants, shops, etc.

Rosebank Hotel
13 Tyrwhitt Ave., Rosebank
Tel. 011 447 2700
www.rosebankhotel.co.za
Comfortable, relatively inexpensive hotel in the vicinity of the Rosebank shopping district; restaurants and cinemas in walking distance, five minutes to Sandton. 294 rooms and 24 suites with 24-hour service.

► Mid-range
City Lodge Sandton Morningside
Hill Rd./Rivonia Rd.
Morningside, Sandton
Tel. 011 884 9500
www.citylodge.co.za
Inexpensive hotel near the shopping district. The hotel company owns several comparable properties in Johannesburg.

► Budget
Mercure Inn
Republic Rd./Waterfront Rd.
Randburg
Tel. 011 326 3300
Located close to the Randburg Waterfront. Small, but inexpensive and well-equipped rooms (fridge, internet, etc.).

The Melville House
59 Fourth Avenue, Melville
Tel. 011 726 3503
www.themelvillehouse.com
Pleasant guesthouse in Melville, the artists' and nightlife district. The owner of Melville House is the author Heidi Holland (*Born in Soweto*).

The Cottages
30 Gill Street, Observatory
Tel. 011 487 2829
Very nice, inexpensive rooms in former farmhouses built in the English style, near the African district of Yeoville, 5km/3mi from downtown.

Backpackers Ritz
1 A North Road, Dunkeld West
Tel. 011 325 7125
www.backpackers-ritz.co.za
The best backpacker hotel in Johannesburg, in an impressive old building with a garden, restaurant, pool, etc. Fantastic view of the city.

Cityscape Johannesburg is a town of extreme opposites, of great wealth and great poverty. While the black population, who over the past 100 years were pushed out into the overflowing townships in the periphery, has, with Hillbrow, reclaimed the inner city, the majority of whites live in the northern suburbs. Luxurious villas with lovely gardens, swimming pools and other amenities are concealed behind high walls guarded by barbed wire. In Sandton, Parktown, or in super-rich Houghton guarded barriers secure entire residential

At the Arts Alive Festival in Newtown

streets around the clock. The shops in the shopping centres can easily match with boutiques in Berlin, Rome, Paris or London. The exodus of hotels, companies, institutions and shops from downtown into the outskirts continues.

The architectural appeal of the city is limited. The centre, the **Central Business District** (CBD), arranged in a grid pattern, is relatively small and with its skyscrapers reminiscent of American cities. Historic façades and glass skyscrapers, many of which stand empty, stand side by side. After hours and at the weekend almost everyone out and about in the city centre is black. During the day the city belongs to African street traders; the atmosphere is a unique mix of modern business life and traditional everyday life.

Personal safety Often Johannesburg is inevitably the first stop on a South Africa trip. Many stay for only one or two days and flee the city with its formidable problems as quickly as possible. Others who stay a bit longer (while following the rules of personal safety▶p.162) find their stay in the city interesting and conducive to their understanding of the country. In any case visitors should be prepared for the high likelihood of crime and violence. In the evenings and at weekends the city centre turns into a ghost town, but even during the day the risk of being mugged in the centre and the neighbouring districts, particularly in Hillbrow, is real. It is best not to walk around with cameras; sightseeing buses (like the City Slicker) are good places from which to take pictures.

What to See in the City Centre

Carlton Centre

After the Hillbrow Tower the Carlton Centre (152 Commissioner St.) is the city's tallest building. From the 50th floor at a height of 202m/663ft, from the »Top of Africa« the **view is fantastic**; it can also be enjoyed from the Marung restaurant. The Carlton Hotel next door was once one of the best hotels in the country, but at the end of 1998 it closed its doors.

Mobile City

In the north tower of the ABSA Bank (180 Commissioner St.) a **gigantic mobile**, a portrait of the old and the new Johannesburg, takes up five floors of the atrium. To view it, ask the security staff in the building.

Post Office
City Hall

Two of the few older buildings in Johannesburg stand opposite each other at the intersection of Rissik Street and Market Street. The former post office, a brick building dating from 1897, gained its tower in 1902. Only a small part of the city administration is still located in City Hall, which was built between 1910 and 1915 in a neo-Renaissance style.

Johannesburg skyline: in the foreground MuseuMAfrica, with the Hillbrow Tower behind

Diagonal Street A skyscraper in Diagonal Street, which is the only street to break through the city centre's grid pattern, used to be the address of the stock exchange during the 1970s; in 2001 it was transferred to Sandton. The conspicuous De Beers **Diamond Building**, reminiscent of the facets of a diamond, was designed by Helmut Jahn.

✴

KwaZulu Muti Museum The KwaZulu Muti Museum (14 Diagonal Street) is stuffed full of fearsome objects spreading strong smells, such as roots, animal skins, bones and fertility symbols. The shop, which has been in business since 1897, is a **mecca for medicine men** and all those who believe in the power of healing herbs (muti). Whatever cannot be found here, will be available on the Mai Mai market on Anderson Street.

World of Beer In the World of Beer (15 President St., west of Diagonal St.) the **South African Breweries** (SAB) give an insight into the manufacture of the barley or sorghum beverage in a 90-minute tour; two glasses are included in the admission price.

✴✴

Newtown Cultural Precinct In the »shadow« of the 295m/968ft-high **Nelson Mandela Bridge** (it too a sign of the new economic boom) the Newtown district around the Mary Fitzgerald Square has been transformed into a cultural quarter. To name the most important buildings: after the Market Theatre Complex (see below) the huge Turbine Hall is now being made into an event venue; to the west of it parts of the electricity plant now house the **Workers' Museum** (closed on Sundays) and to the south is the interesting **Sci-Bono Discovery Centre** (modern natural sciences, open daily, www.sci-bono.co.za).

Colourful life on the Theatre Square Market

The vegetable market in Bree Street, built in 1913, now acts as a cultural centre, housing the Market Theatre, cafés and restaurants, book and music shops, as well as art galleries. The four stages of the Market Theatre have been the venues for South Africa's best productions; the musical **Sarafina**, which later became very successful on Broadway, had its world premiere here. Gramadoel's restaurant is famous. (►p.326).

Market Theatre Complex

The MuseuMAfrica next door (121 Bree Street, open Tue–Sun 9am–5pm) takes its visitors on a realistic trip through the events of the past: learn about the fight for equality, experience mines and slums, and find out about the life of the South African peoples in the ethnological department. The **Rock Art Museum** does a good job of explaining the significance of the San rock drawings (► Baedeker Special p.90). The collections of the **Bensusan Museum of Photography** have also been integrated into the museum.

★ ★ **MuseuMAfrica**

Kippie's Bar, opposite the Market Theatre Complex, which developed from a Victorian-age public lavatory, has become an institution in Johannesburg and is one of the most important stages of the South African jazz scene (www.kippies.co.za).

★ **Kippie's Bar**

The central station, the largest railway station in Africa, which has been newly designed as the city's hub (Park Station), is located at the northern edge of the city centre. The old part houses the Heritage Library and the Documentation Centre of the **Transnet Foundation**; it is the most important documentation centre in South Africa on the subjects of land development and transportation.

Railway Station Park Station

The Johannesburg Art Gallery in Joubert Park east of the railway station displays works of African and European artists. One room has more than 200 exhibits dating from the 15th to the 20th century. Various sculptures can be seen in the courtyards and in Joubert Park (open Tue–Sat 10am–5pm). Restaurant and museum shop.

Johannesburg Art Gallery

The Anglican St Mary's Cathedral towers over the Hoek Mall, which can be accessed via the De Villiers Street. The impressive building was constructed in 1926 to a design by Sir Herbert Baker.

St. Mary's Cathedral

What to See outside the City Centre

The Civic Centre (1978) is located between Loveday and Joubert Street. The **Civic Theatre** across the street is one of the city's leading stages for ballet, opera, and theatre (www.showbusiness.co.za).

Civic Centre

East of Joubert Street is the Hillbrow district with a **269m/883ft tower**. Hillbrow was »in« until the end of the 1980s; here it seemed possible for blacks and whites to live side by side. Today this is definitely

Hillbrow

Constitution Hill ►

a dangerous area. The quarter is bordered by an old and a new land-mark of Johannesburg, Constitution Hill: the **Old Fort** (1892) was a notorious prison, in which Gandhi and Mandela were incarcerated, to name but two; the »Number Four« for blacks had the most brutal conditions (guided tours, open 9am–5pm, www.constitutionhill.co.za). Next door the new **Constitutional Court** was built, a highly symbolic act, but that is not all: the entire block is to become a top-class shopping and residential quarter with hotels. The Old Fort by the way affords excellent views.

University of the Witwatersrand

Several interesting institutions are located on the campus of the University of the Witwatersrand (in the district of Braamfontein). The **planetarium** has a 22m/72ft-high dome (www.wits.ac.za, shows tel. 011 717 1392). The **Bleloch Geological Museum** has 50,000 types of minerals and stone and is thus the most significant museum of its kind in Africa (open Mon–Fri 8am–4.30pm, guided tours tel. 011 717 6665). In the **Studio Gallery** in the senate (open Tue–Fri 10am–4pm) valuable African tribal art of the Ndebele is on display.

Herman Eckstein Park / Zoological Garden

Herman Eckstein Park is located at the north end of Jan Smuts Avenue. Part of it is taken up by Johannesburg zoo (open daily 8.30am–5.30pm). Over 400 species live here; the lake is good for boating. The Museum of Rock Art in the east of the park has replicas of prehistoric rock paintings.

Botanical Garden

A further park with more than 30,000 trees lies to the west of the Eckstein Park in the district of Emmarentia. In summer, when over 4500 roses are in bloom here, visitors can admire bridal couples in their wedding outfits having their pictures taken here on Saturdays.

Pioneers' Park

Pioneers' Park 3km/2mi south of the city centre is a popular destination (accessible via Rosettenville Road). Show fountains accompanied by music in the south of the park are in operation daily 10am–4.30pm. Santarama Miniland in the north of the park (the same hours) shows models of the best-known buildings in the country at a scale of 1 : 25 as well as miniature railways. The James Hall Transport Museum (open Tue–Sun 9am–5pm) exhibits carriages, cars, steam engines and trams.

Gold Reef City

There are no surviving buildings in Johannesburg from the time when the first gold deposits were discovered. Gold Reef City is designed to give an impression of what the city used to look like (6km/4mi south of the city centre, on the M 1, open Tue–Sun 9.30am–5pm). Besides Disneyland-like replicas of residential and shop buildings, the theatre, brewery, etc. all kinds of entertainment businesses, souvenir shops and over-priced restaurants attract many visitors; it is definitely a tourist trap. However, the tour down a 220m/727ft shaft in the **Crown Mines** (extra charge) is interesting; it

Gold-digger atmosphere in Gold Reef City

was once one of the richest gold mines in the world. The tribal and **Gumboot dances** are also worthwhile. It is possible to make reservations for tours, theatre productions and historical shows. The **Gold Reef City Hotel** is a comfortable hotel; the casino is not just a good place to gamble, but also to eat. In the pub of the gold-digger town beer-lovers can make in-depth comparisons between Windhoek Lager, Mitchell's, Beck's, Jever and the house brew (free entry after 5pm).

Opposite Gold Reef City is the modern **Apartheid Museum**, which Nelson Mandela opened in 2002; it is definitely worth a visit (Gold Reef Road, open Tue–Sun 10am–5pm). The atmosphere of racial segregation becomes oppressively real here. The photographs by Ernest Cole are particularly moving.

The Melville Koppies Nature Reserve in the **trendy district** of the same name (Judith Road) is home to approx. 80% of the plant species of the Witwatersrand. The reserve has an important bird watching centre, where more than 150 bird species have been registered (open Sep–April from sunrise to sunset).

Melville Koppies Nature Reserve

Northern Periphery of Johannesburg

Roads number 9 and number 27 lead from the city centre to the northern suburb of Rosebank. Besides its fine shops and galleries it has restaurants, bars, and clubs. The Rosebank Mall (with the office of Gauteng Tourism) in Cradock Avenue is the suburb's centre; on Sundays there is a good and large flea market on its roof from 10am to 5pm.

✶
Rosebank

Sandton at the north end of Johannesburg, approx. 20km/12mi from the centre, is synonymous with pleasant living in attractive surroundings. Beautiful villas, all guarded like Fort Knox, stand on tree-lined streets. Many tourists wishing to escape the unsafe inner city choose one of the luxury hotels in Sandton as their place to stay. Plenty of fine boutiques and designer shops can be found in the

Sandton

! *Baedeker* TIP

Lipizzaner Horses in Africa

A worthwhile destination on the northern border of Sandton is the Lipizzaner riding school (1 Dahlia Road, Kyalami; to get here, take the N 1 to the Alan Dale Road exit, then take the R 561 westbound). The stud farm founded in 1965 is the only approved Spanish riding school outside Vienna. The first horses came here in 1944 from war-torn Austria. Shows on Sundays at 10.30am (www.lipizzaners.co.za).

Sandton City shopping centre; **Nelson Mandela Square** (with a 6m/20ft-high statue) makes it quite clear that this is an affluent area.

Bordering Sandton to the west is **Randburg**, a district formed in 1959 by combining 13 suburbs; it rapidly developed into a shopping and commercial centre. It contains **37 parks** and a gallery (parish hall, Hendrik Verwoerd Drive) exhibiting contemporary South African art. The **waterfront** with an artificial lake south of Republic Road (daily 7.30pm, 8.30pm trick fountains) and the Harbor Flea Market (Tue–Sat) are pleasant and popular spots.

East of Johannesburg

Kempton Park

Near Kempton Park, an industrial centre with a population of 90,000, is **Johannesburg International Airport**. In the **Madiba Freedom Museum** Nelson Mandela's career is illustrated (in the Erikson Diamond Centre, Monument Road, open Mon–Fri 8am–5pm).

South of Johannesburg

Suikerbosrand Nature Reserve

Approx. 50km/30mi south-east of Johannesburg, at the foot of the 1903m/6243ft Suikerbosrand (»sugar ridge«), is **Heidelberg**. The 13,400ha/33,500 acre Suikerbosrand Nature Reserve (open daily 7am–6pm) is home to zebras, black wildebeests, several species of antelope and more than 200 bird species. The Diepkloof farmhouse built in 1850 functions as a visitor centre and museum. It is the starting point of several hiking trails and there is also a surfaced road leading through the highveld landscape.

Vereeniging

Vereeniging (population: 170,000) lies approx. 60km/40mi south of Johannesburg on the River Vaal. The town was founded in 1892 and came to fame ten years later when the peace treaty ending the Boer War was signed there. Vereeniging became a major centre of heavy industry (coal, steel) and the processing industry (mechanical engineering). The trigger for this came from the construction of a large power station in 1909 as well as the building of the Union Steel Corporation's steelworks in 1913. The high-quality coal reserves around Vereeniging are still estimated at four billion tons.

Vaal Dam Nature Reserve

South-east of Vereeniging the Vaal River was dammed to a huge lake in 1938. The Vaal Dam, which is almost 700m/770yd long, holds

back a lake that can be as deep as 50m/165ft and supplies Johannesburg with drinking water. The reservoir is a popular place to come
and relax; willows grow around the shore, which has some nice picnic places and barbecue areas.

Potchefstroom, located 120km/75mi south-west of Johannesburg, **Potchefstroom**
was the first capital of the Transvaal Boer republic. Even after this
role was taken over by Pretoria in 1860, it remained culturally and
economically significant. Today the town has a university. The climate, with its cool, dry winters and warm, wet summers, means the
agriculture in this area is quite profitable. Historic buildings such as
the Dutch Reformed Church (1866) and the fort near the station, in
which a British unit was besieged by Boers for three months in
1880–81, are reminders of bygone days. Besides the town museum
and the museum in the house of President Marthinus Wessel Pretorius, the Totius Museum is worth mentioning; it houses personal pos-
sessions as well as the library of the Afrikaans author and poet Totius.

On the banks of the Vaal, 130km/80mi south-west of Johannesburg, **Parys**
the town of Parys was founded in 1876. A German called Schilbach,
who had participated in the siege of Paris, named this town thus, because it reminded him of the French capital. These days Parys (population: 46,000) is a popular holiday destination. In Parys the Vaal is
well over half a mile wide and there are numerous little tree-studded
islands in the river, which makes it an ideal location for fishing and
boating. Otherwise the cultivation of maize, peanuts and cereals is of
significance.

West of Johannesburg

The outskirts of Soweto, which is short for »South Western Town- **Soweto**
ships«, lie around 15km/9mi south-west of Johannesburg's city
centre. 50 smaller settlements have grown together to create this
huge suburb. With an estimated population of three to five million
(official population 900,000), almost exclusively made up of blacks
and coloureds, it is South Africa's largest township. It became famous worldwide in 1976, when students protested against the introduction of Afrikaans as the teaching language, thereby causing a
countrywide wave of resistance. The unrest was violently suppressed;
the photograph of the dead 13-year-old Hector Peterson went
around the world at the time (►p.82). Soweto is an endless sea of
small houses with two or three rooms, a kitchen and a bathroom.
Many of the less privileged live in huts made of corrugated-iron
sheets. The lowest level is made up of the men's hostels, whose inhabitants live far away from their families. In Soweto the different
black peoples of South Africa live together in a small space; the largest group are Zulus, who make up 33% of the inhabitants. In recent

times signs of change have become apparent: there are tidy streets with nice houses, a very successful BMW trader, allegedly the highest density of millionaires in South Africa, and a golf course on which golfers play with great enthusiasm and ability. Although hundreds of kindergartens and schools have been built, there are nowhere near enough and the only hospital is the huge Chris Hani Baragwanath Hospital (5000 beds, the biggest in the world). Vista University gives blacks the opportunity to complete higher education. Like everywhere else in the country the social divide between black and white has shifted to becoming a divide between rich and poor; the large ma-

A never-ending sea of huts and small houses: nobody knows exactly how many people live in Soweto.

jority have to make do with meagre housing. Only a few have a regular income. The unemployment rate ranges between 50% and 90%. There are almost no jobs in Soweto; most of the working population commute to Johannesburg. A large part of Soweto is supplied with electricity and some roads are surfaced; the lack of sanitation infrastructure (drinking water, toilets) is blatantly obvious in many areas.

Guided tours
Soweto has become a tourist attraction that has created more than 1400 jobs to date. More than 1000 visitors a day are driven through Soweto by well-organized tour companies. The pioneer was Jimmy Ntintili, who was doing guided tours through Soweto under the name »Jimmy's Face to Face« as far back as 1985. The programme usually includes a visit to the museum in Mandela's residence (in the same street in which Archbishop Desmond Tutu lives), a look at the Chris Hani Baragwanath Hospital, the Hector Peterson Museum and the Catholic Regina Mundi church. Anyone wanting to get to know Soweto a bit better can find somewhere to stay in friendly guesthouses and private accommodation, ranging from simple B & Bs to five-star guesthouses complete with pool and sauna. It is not advisable to go to Soweto alone because the maze of streets makes it easy to get lost; the danger of falling victim to criminal assault is low. In addition to the operators listed on p.326, KDR Travel (tel. 011 326 1700, very informative website www.soweto.co.za) is also very good.

Abe Bailey Nature Reserve
Carletonville is situated between Johannesburg and Potchefstroom in one of the world's most important gold-mining areas. The 300ha/ 750-acre reserve 7km/4.5mi north of Carletonville has the typical highveld landscape. It is known for its birds of prey and its water birds; it is also home to zebras, springboks, black wildebeests and South African hartebeests. Guided day tours.

10km/6mi west of Johannesburg is Roodepoort, an industrial settlement (population: 350,000) that developed in just a few years. Leisure activities are concentrated around Florida Lake. A portion of the lake shore is a bird sanctuary that can be enjoyed from the 3km/2mi trail leading through it. In the **National Botanical Garden** in Malcom Street (open Mon–Fri 7.30am–4.30pm, Sat and Sun 8am–5pm) the remaining original vegetation of this region is protected. The collection of succulents contains 2500 species which are native to southern Africa and the Middle East. The **Roodepoort Museum** illustrates the living conditions of the first pioneers at the Witwatersrand and also shows how the gold is mined (open Tue–Thu 9.30am–4.30pm, Fri 9.30am–4pm).

Roodepoort

Krugersdorp (population: 230,000), approx. 15km/9mi north-west of Johannesburg bears the name of Paul Kruger, the president of the former Transvaal republic (**Famous People**). The town was founded on a farm in 1887 after gold had been discovered close by; it has some fine buildings. The **South African Railway Society Museum** is also worth seeing; it has around 90 steam engines (Tweelopies Road Junction, open daily 9am–4pm). The Paardekraal monument outside the town refers to the place where Boers came together in 1880 to protest against the annexation of Transvaal by the British.

Krugersdorp

The 1400ha/3500-acre Krugersdorp Game Reserve (5km/3mi from Krugersdorp on the road to Rustenburg) gives an idea of what the Witwatersrand may have looked like in the past. The animals living here include lions, giraffes, rhinoceroses, common elands, blue wildebeests, kudus, buffaloes, impalas and baboons. The reserve is approx. 40 minutes' drive from Johannesburg and is one of the most visited reserves in Transvaal; accommodation in huts or on the campsite. Several shorter hiking trails run through the game reserve (open daily 8am–5pm).

★
**Krugersdorp
Game Reserve**

The Sterkfontein Caves located 8km/5mi north of Krugersdorp consist of six chambers and a lake 40m/130ft under ground. After their discovery in 1896 the caves were initially used as a chalk-pit, so that they no longer have any attractive stalactite/stalagmite formations. They have however become famous as the **Cradle of Humanity**; in 1999 UNESCO declared them a World Heritage Site (www.cradleofhumanity.co.za). During the digs started in 1936 archaeologists found the skull of an Australopithecus in 1947; it is estimated to be 2.6 million years old (»Mrs. Ples«). In 1997 an almost complete skeleton of another fossil hominid (»Little Foot«) who lived 3.5 million years ago was found. Guided tours Tue–Sun 9am–4pm, tel. 011 956 6342.

**Sterkfontein
Caves**

Between Krugersdorp and Randburg, near Honeydew (take the M 5 from Johannesburg) is the Heia Safari Ranch, situated in an attractive hilly landscape (www.heia-safari.co.za, reservations tel. 011 901

**Heia Safari
Ranch**

5000); it's a touristy but certainly pleasant place to visit. Stay in luxurious rondavels or in simpler Zulu huts. On Sunday afternoons a »braai« takes place, after which Zulus perform dances. Day-trippers can also take part in the excursions to spot wild animals.

Lion Park

Lion Park 23km/14mi north of Johannesburg (on the R 55) is another popular destination. The animals can be observed from inside a car; it also has a restaurant, a swimming pool, and a barbecue area (open daily 8.30am–5pm, avoid Sundays because it get too crowded).

Lesedi Cultural Village

Visitors who are in the mood for a further demonstration of African heritage can go and see the Lesedi Cultural Village (on the R 512, 12km/7mi north of the Lanseria airport). Zulu, Xhosa, Pedi, and Sotho villages have been reconstructed here. The shows last two and a half hours and include singing and dancing as well as an African meal. It is possible to stay overnight in beautifully decorated, comfortable huts that are part of the Protea hotel chain (www.lesedi.com).

★ ★ Kgalagadi Transfrontier Park

D 4 / 5

Province: Northern Cape

Distances: Johannesburg 580km/360mi, Upington 250km/155mi

Deserts have their own incomparable beauty. The Kalahari, with its endless, blistering expanse of terrain, white and red sand dunes, fantastic sunsets and stunning night sky, is no exception. In addition a tour still has a touch of adventure.

In 1999, in line with the programme of the South African **Peace Parks Foundation**, the 9591 sq km/3703 sq mi Kalahari Gemsbok National Park in the extreme north-west of South Africa and the approx. 28,400 sq km/11,000 sq mi Gemsbok National Park in Botswana became the first transnational park in which no more border fences exist and the animals were able to start their ancestral migrations again. Further projects of the Peace Parks Foundation followed, such as the Great Limpopo Park, which connects the Kruger National Park with reserves in Mozambique and Zimbabwe.

Springboks at a watering hole

Arid savannah in the Kalahari

The Kalahari desert is located in a basin that extends over more than 1 million sq km/386,000 sq mi and has no outlet to the sea. The greater part of the Kalahari is in Botswana, the western area is in Namibia and only the southern tip is in the Republic of South Africa. The wide plains are on average 800–1200m/2600–3900ft above sea level and are covered by layers of red sand, which was created by the erosion of huge rocks. The coloration comes from iron oxide. The **dune landscape** glows in various shades of colour and alternates with **arid savannah**. Great areas of the Kalahari remain untouched because of the inhospitable living conditions. Only the San occasionally roam through its great expanses. The Kalahari is not a complete desert. The South African part receives approx. 200mm/8in of precipitation annually, which allows sparse vegetation to grow here. Chamaephyte, hairgrass and succulents are adapted to this arid climate. Among the few tree species growing here is the shepherd's tree or matoppie, whose leaves provide shade all year round and are a popular food because of their high protein content. Camel thorns can grow more than 15m/50ft and are mainly found in the dry river valleys. After rainfall the semi-desert is brought to life; for a short while it becomes a carpet of flowers.

There is no permanent surface water. Although the Auob and Nossob riverbeds cross the nature reserve, they have only carried water three times in the past 100 years. Nonetheless they have formed im-

VISITING KGALAGADI

INFORMATION

Park Office, Twee Rivieren
Tel. 054 561 0021
www.peaceparks.org
SANParks, ►p.156
Green Kalahari Information
►Upington

ARRIVAL

Very good roads from ►Upington (260km/160mi); the last 60km/35mi from Andriesvale (last petrol station) consists of sand roads. Alternatively from ►Kuruman via Hotazel (385km/240mi, of which 325km/200mi are dirt tracks).

WHEN TO GO

The hottest time is between October and March with daytime temperatures of more than 40°C/104°F. A more pleasant time of year is May to September, when it is still warm during the day and at night cools down dramatically, sometimes down to -10°C/14°F. The best time to watch animals is February to May; however, the park is also most crowded during that period.

AMENITIES

Open all year round from sunrise to sunset. Camps: Twee Rivieren at the south end, Mata Mata in the west on the border with Namibia (it is not possible to cross the border) and Nossob in the north. Book well in advance for visits during holiday times; at all other times it is a good idea to inquire about the park's vacancies. The camps have chalets and huts, campsites, a petrol station and shops selling basic items. Guided tours. Tracks that can be driven on by cars (4WD is recommended) criss-cross the park, they follow in part the dry valleys of Auob and Nossob. The park roads in Botswana can only be driven on with 4WDs; accommodation has to be arranged with the Botswana Department of Wildlife & National Parks in Gaborone (tel. 00267 3 918 0774, dwnp@gov.bw).

pressive valleys over the centuries. Approx. 80 wind pumps in the river valleys secure the animals' water requirements. The tsamma melon also provides refreshment. The fruit consists of 90% water and is valued by the animals and the nomadic San alike.

Fauna The national park is named after the gemsbok that used to live here. Blue wildebeests, elands and hartebeests are also common; more rarely visitors will spot black-backed jackals, spotted hyenas, brown hyenas, caracals, leopards, impalas and kudus. The Kalahari lions are not a separate species; they are just well-adapted to their surroundings and can survive without water for weeks. Their main food consists of porcupines. Amongst the 215 registered bird species are 50 raptor species such as the martial eagle, pygmy falcon and the long-legged secretary bird. Game is most often seen in the dry valleys and at watering holes.

Kimberley

F 6

Province: Northern Cape
Population: 150,000

Altitude: 1198m/3930ft
Distances: Bloemfontein 180km/110mi, Johannesburg 480km/300mi, Cape Town 970km/600mi

Kimberley has the reputation of being the world's diamond capital, even though only a few mines are still working. The town's extraordinary past, where the foundation for South Africa's wealth was laid, attracts many visitors.

Kimberley is located on the highveld at the border with Orange Free State and is a popular stop between Cape Town and Johannesburg. Besides diamond mining, animal husbandry is also a significant source of income and in addition Kimberley is the administrative centre of Northern Cape province.

Some history

The first diamonds were found here in 1869–70, which caused an unprecedented diamond rush; in 1873 the settlement initially called »New Rush« was renamed after the British colonial secretary of the time. The town's ascent was dramatic: by 1900 it had become a flourishing municipality, and electric street lighting already existed in 1882. The first trams came into operation in 1887.

Orientation

Unimaginable riches were generated in Kimberley, but not much of that can be seen in the town centre with its streets that are narrow by South African standards. Several jewellers have shops on Jones Street. The most important administrative buildings and department stores can be found around the market square. From here the Big Hole can be reached on foot or by the museum tram that leaves from the town hall. The affluent residential area of Belgravia southeast of the centre has a quite different feel. It is home to some of the museums worth visiting in Kimberley.

Town Centre · Big Hole

town hall

The neo-classical town hall inaugurated in 1899 is considered a national monument. The lanterns on the forecourt are replicas of the first electric lamps to be installed in South Africa.

Kimberley Mine Museum

At the Big Hole (► 3 D p.346) a museum village with 48 original buildings has been set up. It illustrates what things looked like here at the time of the diamond rush. Many of the houses decorated with antique furniture are open to the public. The first church was the German **Lutheran Church of St Martini**, consecrated in 1875; the oldest house in Kimberley dates from 1877. Its individual wooden

Kimberley Map

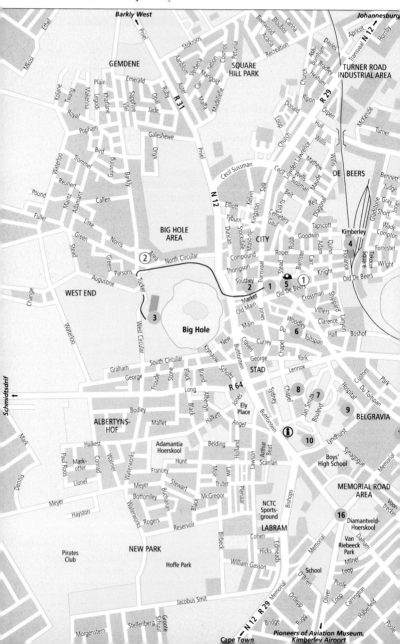

1   City Hall
2   De Beers Consolidated
    Mines Ltd. Head Office
3   Big Hole
    Kimberley Mine Museum
4   Railway Station
5   General Post Office
6   Africana Library
7   Oppenheimer
    Memorial Gardens
8   Harry Oppenheimer House
9   William Humphrey
    Art Gallery
10 Civic Centre
11 Sister Henrietta
    Stockdale Chapel
12 Rudd House
13 Dunluce
14 Duggan Cronin Gallery
15 McGregor Museum
16 Honoured Dead Memorial

Where to stay
① Edgerton House
② Milner House

Where to eat
① Tiffany's
② Star of the West
③ Halfway House

▶ VISITING KIMBERLEY

INFORMATION

Diamantveld Visitors Centre
121 Bultfontein St./Lyndhurst St.
Kimberley, tel. 053 832 7298
www.bdb.co.za/kimberley
Northern Cape Tourism Authority ▶
p.141

TRANSPORT

The airport (7km/4.5mi south-west,
can be reached by taxi) has flights
from Johannesburg and Cape Town.
The Diamond Express, Trans Karoo
and the Trans Orange trains as well as
Greyhound, Intercape and Translux
coaches also all stop in Kimberley.

WHERE TO EAT

▶ Inexpensive

① *Tiffany's*
15 Old De Beers Road, tel. 053 6211
In the pretty Savoy Hotel from 1892
(inexpensive and recommendable) the
food is good and the selection is
ample.

② *Star of the West*
North Circular / Barkly St.
Tel. 053 832 6463, ▶below.

③ *Halfway House Pub*
229 Du Toitspan Road
Tel. 053 831 6324
▶p.348. On Friday and Saturday
evening there is live music on the roof
terrace. Large, basic, very inexpensive
rooms.

WHERE TO STAY

▶ Mid-range

① *Edgerton House*
5 Egerton Road, Belgravia
Tel. 053 831 1150
This is Kimberley's most luxurious
place to stay, located in Belgravia
opposite the McGregor Museum.
Thirteen very comfortable rooms
with a fantastic historic ambience.

Baedeker recommendation

▶ Budget

② *Milner House*
31 Milner Street, Belgravia
Tel. 053 831 6405, www.milnerhouse.co
Charming Victorian house in a quiet
location with six nicely furnished rooms
well as a garden and pool.

parts were brought to South Africa from Great Britain and reassembled here (an extraordinary luxury, since the mine workers used
to live in tents at the time). The **Digger's Rest** is a reconstruction of
one of the 128 bars that existed in Kimberley's early days. A cobbled
street is lined by further homes, shops and workshops. The **Mining
Hall** has photographs and documents from the time of the diamond
rush on display. Diamonds themselves can be admired opposite in
the **Diamond Hall**; it has a 616-carat diamond, one of the largest un-
cut diamonds in the world, and the approx. 21-carat Eureka, which
was the first diamond to be discovered in South Africa.

Star of the West Kimberley's **oldest pub** can be found north of the open-air museum.
The bar has been restored and given the status of national monu-

ment; it has been made to look like a bar that would have existed during the first days of the diamond rush in the early 1870s. One of the bar's proud mementoes is a bar stool that was allegedly made for Cecil Rhodes.

The Africana Library in Du Toitspan Road documents the town's history, particularly the early contacts between the missionaries and the Tswana, and diamond mining. Its great treasures are the translation of the Old Testament into the Tswana language by Robert Moffat and a copy of the **Nuremberg Chronicle**, a world history published in Nuremberg in 1493. Open Mon–Fri 8am–4.30pm.

Africana Library

🕐

Belgravia

The first houses in the district of Belgravia south-east of the city centre were built in 1873. Its inhabitants, who had become extremely wealthy, surrounded their luxurious villas with large gardens. To this day Belgravia has remained Kimberley's preferred residential area. Besides works by South African artists, the William Humphreys Art Gallery on Jan Smuts Boulevard, **one of South Africa's most important collections of paintings**, also exhibits works by Dutch, Flemish, English and French masters (open Mon–Sat 10am–5pm, Sun 2–5pm). The 13-storey **Harry Oppenheimer House** (Hentrich Street) was built in 1974 to blueprints by the German architect H. Hentrich.

★
Humphreys Art Gallery

🕐

Here all the diamonds found in South Africa are graded. Since this can only take place under artificial light, the windows on the building's southern side have been constructed in such a way that no direct sunlight can enter (not open to the public). **Rudd House** (5–7 Loch Road) belonged to the mining magnate H. P. Rudd, whose father had been a friend and business partner of Cecil Rhodes. It is attached to the McGregor Museum. Guided tours ► McGregor Museum. Lodge Road also has some beautiful old villas. No. 7, **Oppenheimer House**, was built in 1906 for Kimberley's first mayor, and later chairman of De Beers Consolidated Mines Ltd., Ernest Oppenheimer. In 1908 his son Harry, who took over the company leadership from his father in 1957, was born in this house. At the time De

Magnificent villas like Dunluce House are testimony to old wealth.

Beers controlled 80% of the diamonds mined in the world. **Dunluce** House (no. 10) is a magnificent example of late-Victorian architecture; it was built in 1897 and in 1903 came into the possession of John Orr. It belonged to his family until 1975. Guided tours ▶McGregor Museum.

Duggan Cronin Gallery

✱

This gallery displays a unique collection of photographs of South Africa's native population taken by A. M. Duggan Cronin between 1919 and 1939. Many of the customs captured in the pictures have since died out. The gallery also exhibits African art as well as several rock drawings on the original (open Mon–Fri 9am–5pm, Sat 9am–1pm, Sun 2–5pm).

McGregor Museum

A stone's throw away is the McGregor Museum, which is housed in a former nursing home. **Cecil Rhodes** had it built in 1897. During the siege of Kimberley by the Boers in 1900, Rhodes inhabited two rooms on the ground floor, which still contain their original furniture. The McGregor Museum has occupied this building since 1971. It is devoted to natural history, religious history and the history of the town, with a particular emphasis on the time of the diamond rush (open Mon–Sat 9am–5pm, Sun 2–5pm, tel. 053 842 0099, www.museumsnc.co.za).

Half Way House Kimberlite Hotel

Take Du Toitspan Road to get back to the town centre. On the corner of Edgerton Street and Main Street are the Half Way House of 1880 and the Kimberlite Hotel. The Half Way House and the pub in the hotel were the only **ride-in pubs** in Africa at the time: thirsty riders were served their beer in the saddle.

What to See outside the Town Centre

Honoured Dead Memorial

The Honoured Dead Memorial is Kimberley's first object of interest for visitors coming from the airport. Sir Herbert Baker designed the memorial, which is dedicated to those people who lost their lives when Kimberley was besieged during the Boer War (1899–1900).

Pioneers of Aviation Memorial

South Africa's first flying school was founded in Kimberley in 1913. Replicas of the first hangar and of a biplane that was used for training can be seen in Alexandersfontein 3km/2mi from the airport (open Mon–Fri 9am–5pm).

Bultfontein mine

The Bultfontein diamond mine in Molyneux Road at the southeast end of town is still working. Tours of the above-ground facilities Mon–Fri 9am and 11am, starting in the De Beers Visitor's Centre. Tours through the underground mines (minimum age 16 years) Mon 9.30am, Tue–Fri 7.45am, book the day before on tel. 053 842 1321.

Around Kimberley

A good 30km/20mi south of Kimberley the British army suffered a huge defeat in the Boer War in December 1899 in what was called the Black Week. Take a look at the battlefield and the trenches from a viewpoint and see weapons and uniforms in the museum (open daily 7am–5pm). **Magersfontein Battlefield**

The **first diamonds** were found in the gravel of the Vaal in Barkly West (population: 11,000, 35km/22mi north-west of Kimberley) in 1866. It was not long before severe conflicts broke out over the valuable riverbed: the resident Griqua, a Khoikhoi tribe, as well as the Tswana, the Boers and the British all laid claim to it. Initially the British left the area to the Griqua, but in 1870 bought the land from them and founded a new colony, Griqualand West. Klipdrift, as the town was originally called, became the capital and in 1873 it was renamed after Sir Henry Barkly, the governor at the Cape. From June to September the police issue prospecting permits; however these days there are many more semi-precious stones than diamonds. At the market on Saturday mornings there is still a touch of the old atmosphere, when buyers and treasure-hunters haggle about the spoils of the week. Next to Barkly Bridge, built in 1885, the town museum can be found in the Toll House and just a few steps away in the old pump house is a pub. **Barkly West**

Approx. 10km/6mi north-west of Barkly West and south of the Vaal is the Vaalbos National Park. It is more than 22,500ha/55,500 acres in size and has plenty of interesting vegetation. The name goes back to the camphor tree, which is very prevalent here. Currently the park does not yet have any tourist infrastructure. **Vaalbos National Park**

Griquatown (population: 5000; 1476m/4843ft), 160km/100mi south-west of Kimberley, was once the capital of an independent state with its own money and flag. In 1801 The London Missionary Society set up a station here, which subsequently became the centre of Griqualand. This is where **Robert Moffat** (1795–1883) worked, whose daughter Mary married the British explorer David Livingstone (1813–73). After the first diamonds were discovered in the area (► above Barkly West) Griqualand became a British colony in 1871 and in 1874 it was incorporated into the Cape Colony. The residence of the Moffat family is now the **Mary Moffat Museum**; it shows the family's personal effects and there also is an exhibition on the history of the London Missionary Society, particularly on the activities of Robert Moffat. The other sights here are the Raadsaal, the administrative seat of Griqualand, the execution tree, which was used to hang cattle thieves, and the grave of Andries Waterboer, one of the leaders of the Griqua. In Pannetjie, 5km/3mi from Griquatown, surviving San rock drawings can be seen. **Griquatown**

Roaring Sands

A special natural phenomenon can be experienced in the **Witsand Nature Reserve** approx. 125km/80mi north-west of Griquatown. The dry heat that is normal here makes the shifting sand dunes, which can reach a height of 100m/330ft, produce a strange sound in extreme heat that can develop into a howl as if a storm were raging. The light sand dunes form a stark contrast to the otherwise reddish sand of the Kalahari. Refer to ►www.witsandkalahari.co.za for information on accommodation and other travel practicalities.

Kleinmond

C 9

Province: Western Cape
Population: 2400

Altitude: 15m/50ft
Distances: Cape Town 105km/65mi

Kleinmond is a small, not too attractive holiday town with a fishing harbour on Walker Bay south-east of Cape Town. The surrounding area however is extremely pleasant. It is considered the »flower paradise on the Cape«.

Kleinmond Coastal Nature Reserve

West of Kleinmond at the mouth of Palmiet River a reserve has been set up to protect the delicate ecosystem between the mountains and the coast. The 400ha/1000-acre reserve is home to many native tree species (the milkwood is particularly common) including rare species of erica and protea. Several hiking trails run through the reserve; the 18km/11mi **coastal trail** is particularly worthwhile; whales and dolphins can also be spotted from this trail. The nature reserve is open all year round from sunrise to sunset. The lagoon formed by the Palmiet River is just as good for swimming as it is for canoeing and windsurfing.

 KLEINMOND

INFORMATION

Kleinmond Tourism Bureau
Main Road
Tel. 028 271 5657
www.ecoscape.org.za

Betty's Bay

Betty's Bay 7km/4.5mi west of Kleinmond was named after Betty Youlden, the daughter of an estate owner who lived during the Second World War. The charmingly situated town consists almost exclusively of private holiday homes. West of Betty's Bay on Stony Point is a colony of the rare African penguins.

Harold Porter National Botanical Garden

North of Betty's Bay at the foot of 917m/3009ft Platberg lies a 200ha/500-acre botanical garden that is known for its **magnificent wild flowers**. Only 10ha/25 acres are cultivated, the remaining area being made up of the typical Cape vegetation (fynbos). January is the flowering time of the rare red disa, an orchid, and in March the nerine comes into bloom. During the flowering period from October to February the reserve attracts many birds (88 species have been identified), such as the olive thrush, several species of woodpecker and cuckoo and the rare Cape canary. Old-world porcupines, mongooses, baboons and, albeit rarely, leopards also live here. The park is open daily all year round from 8am to 6pm.

✱ The road to Gordon's Bay

The R 44, which connects Betty's Bay with Gordon's Bay (►Somerset West) approx. 40km/25mi further north, is incredibly scenic. Sandy beaches that extend for miles are interspersed with rugged rocks. The route offers views of the wide **False Bay** (►Cape Town), and on the horizon visitors can see the Cape peninsula. A small road that leads to **Cape Hangklip** branches off from the R 44. The mighty 454m/1490ft Hangklip forms the eastern point of False Bay. There are a lighthouse, holiday homes and the basic, cheap Hangklip Hotel here. Picturesque **Kogel Bay** has an excellent campsite and a luxury hotel.

✱ Knysna

E 9

Province: Western Cape
Population: 38,000

Altitude: 0–150m/0–500ft
Distances: Cape Town 470km/290mi

The lagoon that reaches far inland on the famous ►Garden Route along the south coast is a special place: as a holiday area it could hardly be more beautiful.

Knysna – pronounced »nice-nah« – is beautifully situated between the forest and the sea **by a large lagoon** that offers a wide choice of leisure activities. The attractive landscape of saltwater lakes and marshes has been declared the »National Lake Area«. Holiday homes, hotels and guesthouses line the lagoon, whose exit to the sea is guarded by two rocks, the **Knysna Heads**. The two islands in the lagoon are connected to the mainland via bridges. More than 200 fish species and marine creatures are said to live in the lagoon, including a rare sea horse, *Hippocampus capensis*. The popular Outeniqua Choo Tjoe train which travelled between Knysna and George had to change its route after a landslide in 2006. It now runs from ►Mossel Bay to ►George.

From history

The name of George Rex (1765–1839) comes up repeatedly in Knysna. Rex, who came to the area in 1803, is said to have been the son of the English king George III. He owned a huge farm property and turned out to be an all-round businessman. His alleged royal origin attracted numerous further settlers, and in 1825 Knysna was officially

Fantastic scenery: the view from the Knysna Heads over the lagoon

founded by the Cape governor Lord Charles Somerset. The harbour instigated by Rex created an economic boom for the town during the 19th century. However, trains replaced ships as the preferred form of transport, and in 1954 the port was closed.

What to See in and around Knysna

Town centre The most important public buildings, restaurants and shops are all located close to the lively **Main Road**. Good shopping and restaurants can be found in the attractive Woodmill Lane Shopping Centre in Long Street off Main Road. The **Millwood House Museum** in Queen Street occupies a beautiful little house that once stood in nearby Millwood (see below), where gold was discovered in 1876; but by 1895 the deposits were exhausted. One of the houses was taken apart and reassembled in Knysna as a national monument. The exhibits focus particularly on the town's founder George Rex and the gold discoveries in Millwood (open Mon–Fri 9.30am–4.30pm, Sat 9.30am to 12.30pm).

Pledge Park Close to the town is this 10ha/25-acre nature reserve (to get to it turn into Gray Street from Main Street, then left into Bond Street). The park grounds stand out for their beautiful native vegetation and many magnificent views.

Belvidere Church Visitors leaving Knysna to the west and turning off to Brenton-on-Sea after crossing the river pass the »church at the good view« built in 1855. A son-in-law of the legendary George Rex had this private

Knysna Oysters

The oysters farmed in the lagoon are said to be amongst the best in the world. Try them yourself, maybe in the tavern of the Knysna Oyster Co. (Long St., Thesen's Island, tel. 044 382 6941, www.oysters.co.za), in the fancy La Loerie (57 Main Road, tel. 044 382 1616) or in Crabs Creek, a basic eatery with a pretty terrace (Brenton Road, tel. 044 386 0011).

chapel built for himself. Approx. 6km/4mi south of the church is the attractive holiday town of Brenton-on-Sea with its **gorgeous long sandy beaches**.

★
◄ Brenton-on-Sea

The Featherbed Nature Reserve on the **Western Head** can only be reached by ferry from Knysna town centre. The tour includes a drive in a Unimog, a large lunch buffet and a guided tour. Reservations under tel. 044 382 1693, www.featherbed.co.za.

Featherbed Nature Reserve

A spectacular road leads over Prince Alfred's Pass (built between 1864 and 1867) from Knysna through the Outeniqua Mountains to **Avontuur** in the Langkloof Valley. Set aside at least four hours for the 85km/55mi stretch of road, because it is in bad condition and the beautiful landscape is worth several stops.

★
Prince Alfred's Pass

◄ Knysna Forest

Knysna is surrounded by an extensive forest landscape. Between George in the west and Humansdorp in the east are 80,000ha/200,000 acres of forest, which makes this area **South Africa's largest woodland region** (only 1% of the country's total area is forested, compared with, say, 25% of the United States). Much of this consists of new plantations of pine and eucalyptus. However, there are also still some primeval forest regions with an original tree population, including huge yellowwoods that are 400 to 800 years old. There are also stinkwoods and pink-blossoming Cape chestnuts. The fauna is mainly limited to a few species of antelope and many bird species. At the end of the 19th century this forest was still home to 400–500 **elephants**; in 1994 a few animals were settled here. It is said that they can sometimes be seen on the Terblans Walk. There are many hiking trails on which to explore Knysna Forest; driving through it by car is also a good way to get an impression. One drive that is worthwhile is the R 339 to the King Edward Tree (20km/12mi north-east of Knysna; see below Elephant Walk); for the way back the road running past the Gouna Forest Station is a good choice.

South Africa's largest forested area

► VISITING KNYSNA

INFORMATION

Knysna Tourism
40 Main St. (by the elephant skeleton)
Tel. 044 382 5510
www.knysna-info.co.za

WHERE TO EAT

► Moderate

O'Pescador
Brenton Road, Belvidere
Tel. 044 386 0036
Good Portuguese-Mozambican cuisine; pleasant, familiar atmosphere, very good value for money. Reservations necessary during the busy season.

► Inexpensive

The Old Oak Tavern
26 Gray Street, tel. 044 382 5439
The family-run restaurant offers a large selection of dishes: crocodile and springbok steaks, shrimp and mussels, pastas and curries.

WHERE TO STAY

► Mid-range/Luxury

Falcon's View Manor
2 Thesen Hill
Tel. 044 382 6767
www.falconsview.com
Victorian house built in 1899 with modern amenities; wonderfully situated with a superb view of the lagoon, ocean and town. Breakfast on the terrace, lunch under jacaranda trees by the pool, the bar has an open fireplace.

► Mid-range

Knysna Hollow
5 Welbedacht Lane
Tel. 044 382 5401
www.knysnahollow.co.za Comfortable complex with thatched chalets close to the lagoon and rooms in the main building, all tastefully decorated with an open fireplace. Good, homely restaurant. Pool in the garden.

Elephant Walk The extremely attractive, approx. 20km/12mi Elephant Walk begins at the Diepwalle Forest Station (to get here from Knysna, take the R 339 towards Uniondale, 20km/12mi; maps are available at the forest station). For proficient hikers this walk should not be a problem and it can also be broken down into shorter sections. The trail goes past the **King Edward VII Tree**, a 46m/150ft yellowwood estimated to be at least 600 years old.

Kranshoek Walk Kranshoek Walk begins at Kranshoek picnic place 27km/17mi east of Knysna. After approx. 2km/1mi this trail reaches the Indian Ocean, after which it runs parallel to the coastline towards Plettenberg. After 5km/3mi the path turns back inland and ends after a total of 9km/6mi back where it started.

Terblans Walk This hiking trail is named after a tree endemic to this coastal area. The starting point for this 6.5km/4mi walk is the old forest station of Gouna 17km/10.5mi north of Knysna. The route, marked by wild-boar symbols, is lined by several attractive yellowwood giants.

The Harkerville Trail makes its way through an attractive coastal region that should only be attempted by experienced, fit hikers. The two-day tour begins at the Harkerville Forest Station. Overnight accommodation in huts. Registration is required, information is available at the tourism office in Knysna. **Harkerville Trail**

A further hiking trail leads to the scanty remains of the small settlement of Millwood. After gold was discovered in the Knysna forest in 1876, a town with a post office, court, three daily newspapers and six hotels sprang up. All that remain are a few reminders of the gold-mining activity, as well as the cemetery. A museum houses mementoes; from here there is a 5.5km/3.5mi hiking trail to the remains of the gold-mining past. To get to the museum, take the road towards Rheenendal that branches off from the N 2 west of Knysna. **Millwood Walk**

Further destinations in the area are described under Garden Route, George and Plettenberg Bay. Seven Passes Road ►George. **Garden Route**

★ Kruger National Park

J 3/4

Provinces: Limpopo, Mpumalanga
Distances: Johannesburg approx. 450km/280mi

Altitude: 200–900m/650–3000ft

Kruger National Park in South Africa's extreme north-east is the largest, oldest and most famous of the country's national parks. The enjoyable drive through the entire length of the park reveals impressive changes in the landscape.

Every year 1.5 million people visit the park; however only 5% of the entire area is affected by tourism directly, although this area is at the limit of the capacity it can handle. The Kruger National Park is 350km/220mi long and up to 90km/55mi wide; its area of 19,485 sq km/7523 sq mi is approximately that of Wales. Two rivers form natural borders to the park: the Limpopo in the north and the Crocodile River in the south. The park's eastern border coincides with that of Mozambique; in the west it is bordered by an artificial barrier. Most of the area is at an altitude of 200–300m/650–1000ft, is almost flat and largely covered by grass and scrub; the river channels are frequently lined by riparian forests. In the south the landscape changes into a very bio-diverse hilly tree savannah. In South Africa such an alternation between grassland, bushes and trees is called »bushveld«. Overall a total of almost 2000 different plant species have been recorded in the national park, including approx. 500 tree and scrub species. Many trees have an extremely thick and sometimes cork-like bark protecting them from the fires in the savannah. The park's life- **Landscape and nature conservation**

A meeting with mixed feelings

lines are the five rivers flowing through it from west to east, carrying water almost all year round (Crocodile, Sabie, Olifants, Luvuhu and Letaba Rivers). On their way to the national park they are polluted by industrial and agricultural effluent and in addition a large proportion of the water is used for irrigation. Thus the Letaba no longer carries water all year round. The national park's ecosystem however is critically dependent on these water channels. There are almost 400 artificial watering holes that do not go dry even during extremely arid periods. In previous centuries the animal herds migrated onwards when there was a water shortage; the opening of the Great Limpopo Transfrontier Park is meant to help solve this problem.

Some history The park owes its name to the Boer president of Transvaal, Paul Kruger (►Famous People). Kruger was interested in creating a game preserve in Transvaal as early as 1884. Until that time eastern Transvaal had been a popular hunting ground for Europeans. The first step was taken in 1898, when a small area between the Sabie and Crocodile rivers was declared a protected area. The National Park was officially opened in 1926. In 2002 South Africa, Mozambique and Zimbabwe founded the Great Limpopo Transfrontier Park, which, with its total area of approx. 100,000 sq km/40,000 sq mi – the equivalent of the total area of Portugal – gives the animals an almost endless expanse for their migrations.

Fauna Kruger National Park has an incredibly rich fauna. The best times for watching animals are the early hours of the morning and the late afternoon. The park's population of larger animals includes 1500 lions, 900 leopards, 12,890 elephants, 1500 rhinoceroses (most of them »white rhinos«; there are only 200 of the slightly darker »black rhinos«), 32,000 zebras, 5000 giraffes, 30,000 buffaloes and 125,000 impalas (one of the 17 antelope species represented in the national park). In addition there are 114 reptile species, more than 500 bird species (15 alone are different species of eagle), many butterflies and other insects. For many endangered species such as the black rhinoceros, the scimitar oryx and the African wild dog, the national park is one of the last places of refuge.

The animal population in the park has to be artificially regulated. The elephants in particular pose a problem, since they are reproducing at a too rapid rate (on average an elephant consumes approx. 300kg/650lb of plant matter per day and can destroy 1000 trees a year). Up until 1995 gamekeepers shot a certain number of elephants. When this practice met with growing international criticism for misconceived reasons of nature conservation, other ways of controlling the population were looked for. Resettlement programmes as well as supplying the elephants with a contraceptive pill were only of limited success. For that reason elephants continue to be shot. High hopes have been put in the park's expansion into the Great Limpopo Transfrontier Park.

! Baedeker TIP

Bush Drives
Where the roads stop the art of four-wheel driving begins. The »KNP 4 x 4 Adventure Trails« offer a fun way for visitors with their own vehicles to experience this for themselves. There are four different trips leaving from Pretoriuskop, Satara, Phalaborwa and Shingwedzi / Punda Maria, where they also must be booked. Information at SANParks.

Climate

The climate is subtropical. The summer months see the most rainfall, the south of the park with 700mm/28in getting significantly more than the north of the park with 400mm/16in. During those times the vegetation is very lush, but during the day the temperatures are intolerably hot (up to around 40°C/104°F). Many of the mammals bear their young during the summer months. The best time of year for hiking and watching animals is the winter (March–July). During that time most days are sunny and warm (up to 30°C/86°F); the nights get quite chilly, and sometimes temperatures drop to freezing. Many of the trees and bushes have then shed their leaves, giving animals fewer places to hide.

Hikes, guided tours

The camps organize trips in off-road vehicles that go out in the mornings and the evenings. Knowledgeable rangers explain what can be seen (sometimes with difficulty). Several camps take bookings for bush hikes accompanied by an armed gamekeeper; hikes lasting several days are also available (»Wilderness Trails«, with starting locations): Bushman Trail and Wolhuter Trail (Berg-en-Dal), Napi Trail (Pretoriuskop), Metsi-Metsi Trail (Skukuza), Nyalaland Trail (Punda Maria), Olifants Trail (Letaba) and Sweni Trail (Satara). The nights are spent in simple huts.

▶ VISITING KRUGER NATIONAL PARK

INFORMATION

Information and reservations for accommodation (except private camps) and Wilderness Trails at SANParks (▶p.156) and Lowveld Tourism (▶Nelspruit). Links to all the camps at www.safari-portal.de.

WHEN TO GO

Kruger National Park is a destination that attracts masses of visitors. If you really want to experience a little bit of wilderness, avoid the South African holiday times: all the accommodation is booked out, access can be denied (max. 5000 visitors a day) and it is more likely that visitors will be stuck in a traffic jam rather than behind an elephant. The climate (▶p.357) is also better during the winter months. Malaria prophylaxis and protection against mosquitoes are essential.

ARRIVAL

By car from Johannesburg in 5–6 hours; the most popular gates are the Numbi Gate or the Paul Kruger Gate a bit further north (quickest route via the N 4, take the R 40 and the R 538 from Nelspruit). Kruger Mpumalanga International Airport is located 22km/14mi north-east of ▶Nelspruit (www.kmiairport.co.za) with scheduled incoming flights from Johannesburg, Cape Town and Durban. Kruger Park Gateway Airport in ▶Phalaborwa and the airfield in Hoedspruit are connected to Johannesburg. Car rentals in Nelspruit and Phalaborwa. Skukuza is used for charter flights.

DRIVING IN THE PARK

Of the approx. 2600km/1600mi of roadway, 1000km/600mi are surfaced, but even the unsurfaced tracks can generally be used by regular passenger cars without any difficulty. Open vehicles and motorbikes are not permitted. All the roads are well signposted; detailed maps can be acquired on entering the park. The roads and tracks are checked regularly. The speed limit on the surfaced roads is 30mph/50kmh, and 25mph/40kmh on the tracks. Petrol is available at the camps; like everywhere else in South Africa fuel can only be paid for in cash.

Depending on the season the eight entrance gates open between 5.30am and 6.30am; in the evenings they close between 5.30pm and 6.30pm. These times also apply to the camps in the park. Make sure to have enough time to get to the camps. Delays caused by big game, traffic jams or a breakdown should be planned for. There are fines for speeding and for feeding the animals. Except in specially marked areas it is strictly prohibited to leave the vehicle; accidents with wild animals are mainly caused by visitors who do not adhere to these regulations.

WHERE TO STAY

SANParks maintains twelve rest camps (some with outside camps), five bushveld camps (self-catering) and two bush lodges (the whole lodge has to be booked); in addition there are some private camps (direct reservations), most of them very luxurious. Early reservations are necessary for stays during the school holidays, particularly around Christmas and Easter (up to 13 months in advance is possible). Otherwise it is also possible to go from camp to camp, where visitors should book directly with the camps no more than 48 hours ahead of time.

Rest Camps and What to See in the National Park

Most visitors to the park stay in the village-like rest camps; day visitors are also welcome there. The accommodation ranges from luxurious little houses to simple huts for 2–5 people. Most of the houses have air-conditioning, almost all have a bathroom, a place to cook and a barbecue area. Well-equipped campsites are available as well as restaurants, shops, a petrol station, first-aid facilities and park information centres (these latter are located in Letaba, Skukuza and Bergen-Dal). The following section describes the rest camps from north to south.

Bases in the park

Punda Maria at the foot of Dimbo Mountain is a small, simple hut camp (tel. 013 735 6873). It is considered one of the most beautifully situated camps. It has a great view of the Mopane plain. The camp was set up in 1919 for the forestry authorities. Since then it has been modernized several times. The sandveld near Punda Maria is an extension of the Kalahari basin. In the north along the Luvuhu River the dry savannah gives way to riparian forests that look tropical. This area is not much frequented and is perfectly suited for bird-watching; there are good spots along the S 99 on a 25km/15mi round trip beginning close to the camp. Near Klopperfontein approx. 20km/12mi northeast of the camp there are large baobab trees next to a water basin; big game is often spotted in this location. 23km/14mi further

Punda Maria

A view over the river landscape from Olifants Camp

is the bridge over the Luvuhu River (picnic site), which is known as a bird-watching site. From here a track leads eastwards along the riverbank to the Pafuri picnic site. This is the starting point for the path to the Iron Age ruins of Thulamela.

Shingwedzi Camp (tel. 013 735 6806), 73km/45mi south-east of Punda Maria, is the largest camp in the north with a restaurant over the river. There are good places for observation along the road connecting Shingwedzi with Punda Maria. A few miles north of the park, elephant, buffalo and baboons are often spotted, as are wild dogs and leopards, although less often. 10km/6mi north of Shingwedzi the S 56 turns off to the west, follows the course of the Mphongolo and rejoins the main road at the Babalala picnic area after a good 30km/20mi. A side road leads from Shingwedzi south-east to Kanniedood Dam, which also has observation posts.

Shingwedzi

Mopani
A good 60km/35mi south of Shingwedzi is the modern and quite luxurious Mopani Camp (tel. 013 735 6536). This camp also has different kinds of accommodation available as well as a restaurant, a cafeteria, a petrol station, a shop, a pool and an information centre. One excellent observation spot is approx. 17km/10mi east of Mopani, Nshawu Dam. Particularly after rain, elephant herds frequent this place.

Letaba
This extremely well-equipped camp approx 65km/40mi south of Mopani (tel. 013 735 6636) is situated by a large meander of the Letaba River. The information centre there provides interesting facts about elephants; amongst other things they have huge tusks on display. Those of the elephant bull Shawu are 3.17m/10ft 5 in long, which makes them the longest tusks ever to have been found in southern Africa. The savannah is home to many antelopes and cheetahs. Shady watering holes are good places to see elephants, buffaloes, zebras and gazelles. The S 46 or rather the S 93 and the S 44 are considered the most attractive routes south-east along the Letaba River. In addition Engelhard Dam in the east and Mingerhout Dam are also excellent viewing locations.

Masorini-Museum
After approx. 50km/30mi westbound, the road connecting Letaba with the Phalaborwa Gate leads to the Masorini open-air museum. The remains of a prehistoric settlement and an iron smelting facility

Eye to eye with a leopard: a really unusual experience

have been uncovered. The area of the national park was home to hunters and gatherers thousands of years ago. The earliest human traces date from around 1700 BC; besides clay shards and copper works, gold ornaments have also been discovered.

Olifants

For many Olifants Rest Camp (tel. 013 735 6606) with its magnificent old trees is one of the most beautiful in the park. The camp (photograph p.359) itself, situated 100m/330ft above the Olifants River, affords fantastic views and wonderful observation opportunities; animals can be seen on the river with telescopes from the terrace of the comfortable huts. The sunrises and sunsets are spectacular. Around 10km/6mi west of the camp is the Nwamanzi Lookout, one of the national park's best observation sites.

Balule

Balule Camp 11km/7mi south of the Olifants is a small, basic camp for guests who appreciate closeness to nature (no electricity, no day guests; tel. 013 735 6306).

Satara

The distance between Olifants Camp and Satara Camp further south is almost 50km/30mi. This camp (tel. 013 735 6306) is located in an area with particularly large numbers of big game. This abundance is explained by the many watering holes in the surrounding area. At the Nsemani Dam 9km/6mi to the west there are hippopotamuses, waterbucks and also lions. The S 100 leads to the Gudzani Dam (16km/10mi east). Herds of buffalo can be seen here, as can herds of zebra numbering 300–400 animals, and giraffes. A popular destination is the Marcoela picnic site 25km/16mi north-west of Satara on the banks of the Timbavati. Visitors leaving Satara southbound should turn off to the right towards Nkayapan after 15km/9mi; particularly in winter this watering hole attracts many animals. Further along the road are bizarre baobab trees. It eventually leads to the Kumana Dam east of the road. This is a regular gathering place for storks.

> ## ! *Baedeker* TIP
>
> ### Noah's Ark
>
> The Hoedspruit Endangered Species Foundation 20km/12mi south of Hoedspruit (R 40) breeds endangered animal species, particularly cheetahs, and reintroduces them to the wild. Open Mon–Sat 8am–4pm, hourly guided tours; (tel. 015 793 1633). Injured animals are nursed back to health in the Moholoholo Wildlife Rehabilitation Centre. Here visitors can get especially close to the animals. North-west of Klaserie, R 531 near the turnoff to the Blydepoort Dam; tours 9.30am (except Sun) and 3pm, tel. 015 795 5236.

Orpen

Orpen Rest Camp (tel. 013 735 6355) by the park gate of the same name only provides basic accommodation without electricity (no restaurant).

Skukuza

Skukuza (tel. 013 735 5611) is the largest camp and also the park administration centre with two small museums, restaurants, a supermarket, a petrol station, a police station, a surgery, a golf course, airfield, bank, post office and a car rental facility; it is almost a small town. There is accommodation in bungalows, thatched huts and a campsite with a total capacity of 1000. A viewpoint overlooks the banks of the Sabie River, where hippopotamuses and elephants can be seen. The road from Skukuza north-east to Tshokwane is quite busy. Despite this fact big game is often spotted here and lions are sometimes seen at the Manzimahle Dam; the Olifantsdrinkgat provides drinking water and is mainly frequented in winter by elephants, baboons, zebras and lions. The water lilies on the Lionpan make it worth a stop. One of the park's largest hippopotamus herds is at home by the Silolweni Dam. A little further along the road is Tshokwane, a popular picnic site.

Lower Sabie A road from Skukuza along the Sabie River leads to the Lower Sabie Camp (tel. 013 735 6056). Large grassy areas and an abundance of trees make this a very pleasant camp. The dammed Sabie River is home to many waterfowl.

Crocodile Bridge Crocodile Bridge Rest Camp (tel. 013 735 6012) approx. 30km/19mi further south has bungalows and a campsite, a shop, a restaurant and a petrol station. The grassland here is considered one of the park's best game stomping grounds: zebras, wildebeests, impalas, kudus, gazelles and large buffalo herds. During the winter the Crocodile River dries out except for small water basins, but it remains an important drinking site. Approx. 6km/4mi away from the camp visitors can observe hippopotamuses pleasurably wallowing in the mud.

Plains zebras with their black and grey stripes at a watering hole

The wilderness has become very comfortable: dinner in Ulusaba Lodge, which belongs to entrepreneur Richard Branson (in the Sabi Sands Reserve).

Pretoriuskop

In the south-west of the park, approx. 9km/6mi from the Numbi entrance, lies the park's oldest camp and one of the three largest (tel. 013 735 5128). It has more than 400 guest beds, a campsite, a restaurant, a shop, a natural rock swimming pool and a post office. The land is set on a picturesque granite hill on which 67 tree species and 21 bush species grow, including the coral tree that flowers blood red in August and September. In the surrounding area rare animal species such as wild dogs, cheetahs, leopards and antelopes can be spotted.

Berg-en-Dal

Berg-en-Dal Camp, approx. 60km/35mi south-east of Pretoriuskop (tel. 013 735 6016, with approx. 600 guest beds, a campsite, a restaurant, a shop, a swimming pool, an information centre and a petrol station), is very comfortable. There are magnificent views of the hilly landscape.

Private Reserves around Kruger National Park

Adjoining the national park at its south-west border is an area of 2000 sq km/770 sq mi with several private reserves, which are also home to most of the animal species living in the national park (the fences to the Kruger National Park were removed in 1994). These reserves have exclusive game lodges that distinguish themselves from the camps in the national parks through a lot more luxury (and prices to match: per person per night around ZAR 2500–7000); almost all of the lodges have a swimming pool. They all offer an exciting mix of adventure and relaxation; here visitors will be away from the masses. Guests are driven through the reserve in off-road vehicles for animal observations. There are also night-time tours; a »dinner in the bush«

is particularly atmospheric. Many of the reserves or lodges have a landing strip. Be aware: there are varying minimum ages for children.

Timbavati Game Reserve

The Timbavati Game Reserve with its approx. 75,000ha/185,000 acres borders on the central part of Kruger National Park. This bushveld region is home to numerous bird species and big game. Visitors can go on a 24-hour safari (day and night) to experience Africa in close-up, accompanied by a ranger. **Ngala Lodge** provides first-class accommodation for 40 guests, with a pool, landing strip and a conference centre (reservations at CCAfrica,► p.121). The small, exclusive **Tanda Tula Camp** (reservations: tel. 021 794 6500, www.uitsig.co.za) is also located in the Timbavati Game Reserve. Thatched cottages arranged around the swimming pool have enough space for 14 people. Further comfortable accommodation in the Timbavati Game Reserve can be found in the **Motswari** and **M'bali** lodges (reservations for both: tel. 011 463 1990, www. Motswari.co.za).

Klaserie Nature Reserve

West of Timbavati is the Klaserie Reserve. It is 30km/20mi long and 25km/16mi wide, and has three pleasant camps; access from Hoedspruit (reservation: tel. 015 793 2208, http://klaseriecamps.com).

Thornybush Game Lodge

Although this reserve located 30km/20mi west of the Kruger park's Orpen Gate is small (11,500ha/28,500 acres), it is an excellent safari area. Besides the luxury lodges owned by Inzalo (tel. 011 883 7918, www.thornybush.co.za) the incredibly inexpensive, small Kwa Mbili Lodge is also a good place to stay (www.kwambili.com, tel./fax 015 793 2773).

Manyeleti Game Reserve

The Manyeleti Game Reserve neighbours Timbavati in the southeast. It can be accessed via the road that connects Acornhoek with the Kruger Park's Orpen Gate. The **Khoka Moya Lodge** places a greater emphasis on closeness to nature than to luxury and is therefore relatively inexpensive (approx. ZAR 2500 per person; tel. 015 793 1729).

! *Baedeker* TIP

Sabi Sabi

This small, private reserve is situated on the Sabi River. There are two exclusive lodges and two camps providing top comforts such as butlers, spa facilities, a pool, etc.; the underground Earth Lodge is an extraordinary experience (including the price). www.sabisabi.com.

There are several lodges in the 60,000ha/150,000-acre Sabi Sand Game Reserve. The **Londolozi Game Reserve** at the centre of Sabi Sand is the most exclusive facility in the lowveld; the guest list reads like a who's who of international high society. There are six different camps to choose from here (reservation: CCAfrica, ► p.121). It is a few minutes' drive from Londolozi to the **Mala Mala Reserve**, the oldest private lodge of the lowveld and next to Londolozi also the most exclusive; it has three camps. Many wild animals live by the Sand River: there are leopards, lions, elephants, rhinoceroses and buffaloes. Reservations tel. 011 442 2267, www.malamala.com. South of the Mala Mala Reserve is the elegant **Kirkman's Camp**. The verandas of the guesthouses afford magnificent views of the river landscape. The centre is a 1920s farmhouse, which now functions as a lounge and restaurant. **Inyati Game Lodge** provides pleasant accommodation on the Sand River with small, thatched houses for 20 guests, luxurious, but significantly less expensive than Mala Mala for instance. Reservations tel. 011 880 5907, www.inyati.co.za.

Sabi Sand
Game Reserve

Kuruman

E 5

Province: Northern Cape
Population: 10,000

Altitude: 1315m/4313ft
Distances: Vryburg 150km/90mi,
Kimberley 215km/135mi,
Upington 260km/160mi

The Kalahari: semi-desert in the central north of South Africa. It is both a threatening and overwhelmingly fascinating landscape. In Kuruman, the main base in this region alongside ► Upington, the »Eye« and the Moffat Mission are of interest.

Kuruman, an unattractive small town, is considered the oasis of the Kalahari; it owes its creation to the source of the Kuruman River, the **Eye of Kuruman**, which provides, almost like a miracle, 18–20 million litres (about 500,000 US gal) of water every day year in, year out, enough to supply the town with water. Some of the water is siphoned off into canals that irrigate a 6km/4mi-long valley. Kuruman's economy is based on mining and rearing livestock. Tourists can stock up on supplies in the town's supermarkets.

What to See in and around Kuruman

The park with the Eye of Kuruman is very pleasant; the water gushes out of a gap in the dolomite rock and fills a small pond. The park with its shady trees is a popular spot for picnics. Some houses dating from the early days of the mission station have survived. The **Oude Drostdy**, the old town hall, houses the tourist information and a nice café.

Town

▶ VISITING KURUMAN

INFORMATION
Tourist Office
Main Road, Kuruman
Tel. 053 712 1001
www.kalahari.org.za

WHERE TO STAY

▶ Luxury
Tswalu Private Reserve
P.O. Box 1081, Kuruman 8460
Reservations tel. 053 781 9234
www.tswalu.com
At the foot of the Korannaberg (near Sonstraal north-west of Kuruman) this lodge, owned by the Oppenheimer diamond family, provides absolute luxury, starting with its own airfield (planes from Anglo American departing from Johannesburg fly here). Trips and safaris are included in the price, but French wine from the Oppenheimer Collection costs extra.

▶ Budget
Riverfield Guest House
12 Seodin Road
Tel. 053 712 0003
www.riverfield.co.za
The best place in Kuruman in a lavish, green garden with a spring water pool. Twelve well-equipped rooms, large breakfasts. From Mondays to Thursdays guests can eat à la carte.

Janke Guest House
16 Chapman St.
Tel. 053 712 0949
Friendly guesthouse on the road to the mission (painted in bright colours) with seven pretty rooms.

★ **Moffat Mission**   In 1824 **Robert Moffat** from Scotland took over the station of the London Missionary Society (4km/2.5mi north on the road to Hotazel), which was to become the most famous in South Africa. In 1829 he baptized members of the Tswana tribe living in this area; he translated the Bible into their language and printed 1000 copies on a basic press. It was the first on the African continent, the first in a hitherto unwritten African language. It was from here that **David Livingstone** (1813–73) set off on his expeditions into Africa's interior; in 1838 he married Moffat's daughter in the church that had been completed in 1831. The simple, thatched building with space for 800 people, together with the Moffats' house and a school now form a museum. These days the mission is under the management of the United Congregational Church of South Africa and also has accommodation (tel. 053 732 1352).

Wonderwerk Cave   The Wonderwerk Cave approx. 45km/28mi south of Kuruman features rock drawings by the San, some of which are more than 10,000 years old.

Ladybrand · Ficksburg

G 6

Province: Free State
Population: 17,000

Altitude: 1612m/5289ft
Distances (Ladybrand): Bloemfontein 145km/90mi, Maseru 16km/10mi

The land west of the Maluti Mountains (in Lesotho) was already populated in prehistoric times, as numerous rock drawings confirm. Ladybrand and Ficksburg are two pretty little towns in this pleasant cereal and fruit-growing area.

Ladybrand (population: 17,000; 1612m/5289ft) is located on the western border of Lesotho at the foot of the Platberg. The town, which was founded in 1867, was named after Lady Catharina Brand, the mother of J. H. Brand, president of Orange Free State. The town is characterized by **attractive sandstone buildings**, examples of which are the town hall, the Dutch Reformed Church and the grammar school. The **Catharina Brand Museum** has a collection of interesting archaeological finds and rock drawings on display. In Rose Cottage Cave 3km/2mi outside the town **San rock drawings** were discovered, as was ash from a fire that burned here 50,000 years ago. A good 10km/6mi from Ladybrand is **Modderpoort Cave Church**, where

Ladybrand

> ! *Baedeker* TIP
>
> **Rustler's Valley Festival**
> In the hill country at the foot of the Maluti Mountains between Fouriesburg and Ficksburg visitors can experience the South African pop and folk scene at the beginning of spring (around the 23 September) and at New Year (29 Dec–2 Jan). Good choices of accommodation in the town are the Rustler's Valley Lodge (www.rustlers.co.za) and the Franshoek Mountain Lodge (www.franshoek.co.za).

services have been held since 1869. Initially the Anglican Society of St Augustine also used the cave as a dwelling; today it belongs to the Anglican Society of the Sacred Mission. **Leiehoek Holiday Resort** not far from Ladybrand is the start of the Steve Visser Hiking Trail, a worthwhile two-day hike.

The green town (population: 30,000; 1884m/6181ft) is 75km/45mi north-east of Ladybrand in the middle of **cherry tree plantations and asparagus fields**. When the trees are in blossom in September and October it is a very beautiful sight (the Cherry Trail leads through the plantations) and in November there is a cherry festival. Ficksburg has kept its **original appearance** with pretty old sandstone buildings, parks and gardens. Many San rock drawings in nearby

Ficksburg

 ▶ LADYBRAND

INFORMATION
Maloti Tourist Information
Brand Museum, Kerk St.
Tel. 051 924 5131

caves confirm that the surrounding area was settled early on, probably because of the region's favourable climate. The museum informs visitors about the town's eponym, General Johan Fick, the town's history and the history of the Sotho people.

Meulspruit Dam Meulspruit Dam 5km/3mi from Ficksburg is a good place for fishing and water sports; there is a picnic place and a campsite. Meulspruit Dam is the starting point of the **Imperani Hiking Trail**, a two-day round trip leading to Imperani Mountain and to numerous San drawings in caves and rock shelters.

Ladysmith

H 6

Province: KwaZulu-Natal	**Altitude:** 1015m/3330ft
Population: 115,000	**Distances:** Johannesburg 365km/ 225mi, Durban 235km/145mi

The name of this rural town in the savannahs between Johannesburg and Durban became famous all around the world because of the musicians of Ladysmith Black Mambazo. As one of the locations of a long siege in the Boer War it is a stop on the Battlefields Route.

History European settlers founded this place in 1847 and declared it the capital of the Klip River Republic. However, this republic only existed for a few months, after which the area came under British rule. It was raised to municipal status and renamed after Lady Juana Maria de los Dolores de Leon, the wife of governor Sir Harry Smith, in 1850. During the Boer War from 1899 to 1902 Ladysmith was besieged for 118 days by Boer troops before it was liberated by General Sir Redvers Buller. Several major battles were fought in the surrounding area, such as Spioenkop, Colenso, Wagon Hill, Caesar's Camp, Lombard's Cop and Umblawana Hill. Today maize, soy, barley, fruit and vegetables are cultivated here; stockbreeding is another significant economic activity.

▶ LADYSMITH

INFORMATION

Ladysmith Tourism
Siege Museum, Murchison St.
Tel./fax 036 637 2992
www.ladysmith.co.za

BATTLEFIELDS

►Dundee. The tourism office provides information and arranges tours.

What to See in and around Ladysmith

Ladysmith The **Siege Museum** next to the town hall shows what life was like in the town while it was under siege (open Mon–Fri 9am–4pm, Sat un-

Ladysmith town hall

til 1pm). The nearby **Cultural Museum** (25 Keate St., open Mon–Fri 🕐
9am–4pm) is housed in a Victorian building; there are rooms dedicated especially to **Ladysmith Black Mambazo**, a band that has its roots in Ladysmith, and the Drakensberg Boys' Choir. Visitors can live and dine in an old-world atmosphere in the Royal Hotel or in the Crown Hotel (Murchison St.). Follow Murchison Street towards the north-east to get to the **old Indian quarter**; the NGR Institute (1903) and the Central Mosque (1922) with a pretty courtyard still survive today. The new Indian quarter Rose Park in the south on the other side of Klip River contains the **Sufi Mosque** built in 1969; locally it is praised as the »most beautiful mosque south of the equator«.

This nature reserve 35km/22mi west of Ladysmith is situated in a beautiful hilly landscape around the dammed Tugela River and was the scene of a battle in the Boer War; a hiking trail leads to the Spioenkop Battlefield. The reserve also has a 400ha/1000-acre game park with blue wildebeests, blesboks, impalas, hartebeests, rhinoceroses, giraffes, etc. The terrain can be explored in the company of a guide. The **Spioenkop Discovery Trail** (it takes 2–4 hours to complete) gives visitors an insight into the region's ecology. Accommodation is available in the form of chalets, which are somewhat rustic, and on campsites.

Spioenkop Dam & Nature Reserve

The area around Colenso (approx. 25km/15mi south of Ladysmith), named after John William Colenso, the Anglican bishop of Natal from 1853 to 1883, was also the scene of several major battles of the Boer War. Countless monuments and the **Robert Stevenson Museum** were set up in memory of these events. The battlefield of Colenso can be seen from the small Tugela Drift Nature Reserve. The **Bloukrans Monument** 18km/11mi south of Colenso (to get here take the R 74) on the other hand is not connected with the Boer War. It commemorates a bloody confrontation between Zulus and Boers in 1838.

Colenso

Lambert's Bay

C 8

Province: Western Cape
Population: 3600

Altitude: 50m/164ft
Distances: Cape Town 290km/180mi

Lambert's Bay, a fishing port on the Atlantic almost 300km/200mi north of Cape Town, has become a popular, though not altogether attractive destination for day visitors and holidaymakers.

Lambert's Bay is situated along a 30km/18mi-long strip of coastline with very sandy ground on which plants adapted to arid conditions grow; in the spring months the **sandveld** is transformed into a sea of blooming wild flowers. Many South Africans appreciate the atmosphere at the port and enjoy the fresh fish. An event taking place in March is the **Crayfish Festival**. The town owes its name to Sir Robert Lambert, who was the naval commander at the Cape around 1820. The bay was the scene of the only naval battle in the Boer War; the fleet under General Hertzog opened fire on the British cruiser *Partridge* and in 1901 the British warship *Sybille* ran aground.

What to See in and around Lambert's Bay

Lambert's Bay

The **Sandveld Museum** has an interesting documentation of the town's history. From the harbour a mole leads out on to **Bird Island** with large, breathtakingly smelly colonies of cormorants, Cape gannets and African penguins. The best time for bird watching is September to February in the early mornings or the late afternoons.

At the harbour of Lambert's Bay

A dirt road leads southwards from Lambert's Bay to Eland's Bay **Eland's Bay** 27km/17mi away. During the summer months it is a **mecca for surfers**. The town boasts a wonderful beach, a hotel, good shopping and a campsite.

In **Graafwater** 30km/20mi east of Lambert's Bay the agricultural produce from ► Clanwilliam and the seafood from Lambert's Bay are marketed. A cave, called the **Heerenlogement** (»Gentlemen's Lodgings«), 22km/14mi north of Graafwater, is worth a visit. More than 170 travellers who stayed here in the 17th and 18th centuries carved their names into its walls. The cave was a popular place to spend the night because there was a nearby spring.

 **LAMBERT's BAY**

INFORMATION
Tourist Office
Sandveld Museum, Church St.
Tel. 027 432 1000
www.lambertsbay.info

Lesotho

G/H 6/7

Area: 30,335 sq km/11,712 sq mi   **Capital:** Maseru
Population: approx. 2.2 million

»Roof of southern Africa«, »kingdom in the sky« are two names for this independent country, which is completely surrounded by South Africa. Wonderful treks, either on foot or on ponies, allow visitors to get to know a wonderful mountain landscape.

It is not just the landscape that make a detour to Lesotho worthwhile, despite or especially because of the undeveloped infrastructure. The friendly, peaceful atmosphere also leaves a lasting impression; visitors are often asked where they have come from and where they are going, and a greeting (at least »lumela« meaning »hello«) is considered good manners. The independent state of Lesotho, officially Kingdom of Lesotho/Mmuso wa Lesotho, has an area of 30,355 sq km/11,712 sq mi and is thus approximately the same size as Belgium. The official languages are English and Sesotho, which is a Bantu language. The plateau is at least 1000m/3300ft above sea level, and over 80% of the country is more than 1800m/6000ft above sea level. This plateau is traversed by the Oranje and its tributaries, which have carved out gorges up to 800m/2600ft deep; countless waterfalls plummet over their edges. The **Maletsunyane Falls** thunder 192m/630ft to the ground and are the highest in southern Africa. The uplands are bordered in the east by the **Drakensberg mountains** with **Thabana Ntlenyana**, the highest mountain in southern Africa

Lesotho – here a look at the valley of the Makhaleng River in the southwest – enchants visitors with its impressive mountain landscapes.

(3482m/11,424ft), in the west by the **Maluti** (up to 3277m/10,751ft) mountains and the **Thaba Putsoa** (up to 3096m/10,157ft) mountains further south. Towards the west the land descends into hilly lowlands with altitudes of 1200–2000m/3900–6600ft, traversed by the Caledon riverbed, which forms the border to the South African province of Free State. This area, approximately a quarter of the country's total area, is where most of the economic activity takes place and where the greatest number of people live.

Climate and vegetation

The climate of the lowlands is temperate, with average temperatures of 8°C/46°F in July and 21°C/70°F in January. 85% of the mean annual rainfall of 700–800mm/28–32in falls in summer. In the mountain area the temperatures drop below freezing in winter (May–Sept) and then Lesotho gets snow. Mountain pastures are prevalent at higher altitudes, while grassland is dominant at lower elevations. Only protected valleys have trees, such as oleas.

Population

The majority of Lesotho's 2.2 million inhabitants (72 persons per sq km, 188 per sq mi) live in the western lowlands, particularly in the Caledon Valley, while large parts of the highlands are either unsettled or very sparsely populated. Four fifths of the Sotho people still live in country areas, but more and more are flooding into Maseru, the capital. Lesotho has an annual population growth of nearly 3%, which has led to over-population. Lesotho has one of the most uniform population structures of all African countries: almost 100% are Sotho of the southern Bantu group (Basotho). In addition the country is home to 2000 whites and Indians. 43% of the population are Catholic, 30% are Protestant and 12% are Anglican; there is also a minority of Muslims as well as followers of traditional religions. Almost a third of the inhabitants are infected with HIV; in Maseru the figure is as high as 40%.

Lesotho's economy is mainly agricultural. It is one of the poorest **Economy** countries in the world. The extremely limited job opportunities (around half the population do not have a job) mean that around 40% of the employed men work in South Africa, mainly in mining. Nearly 80% of the population work in the **agricultural sector**, which contributes only a fifth of the country's GDP. Most are subsistence farmers. The land is the property of the state. In contrast to pasture there are individual usage rights for agricultural crop land, which are determined anew each year. The most important agricultural products are maize, millet, sorghum, wheat and vegetables. The yields have been dropping as a result of soil erosion and outdated cultivation methods and are not enough for subsistence, so that the urban population in particular requires imported food, mainly from South Africa.

The raising of angora goats for **mohair wool** is of great significance for export; Lesotho is the world's fourth-largest producer of mohair. Raising sheep is also important for Lesotho's export trade. In recent years cut flowers and strawberries have also become significant. Since the majority of the population owns livestock, overgrazing has become a major problem.

In the processing industry South African and Far Eastern companies are prevalent; they are attracted by the availability of labour and the state subsidies. In recent times Lesotho has become a **jeans centre**: every year Taiwanese companies produce approx. 25 million pairs of jeans that are bought by American department stores such as Walmart. Lesotho's main imports are food, machines and petroleum products. The country imports much more than it exports.

Lesotho is a member of the Southern African Customs Union, which is its most important trading partner besides Switzerland and the European Union. Besides money transfers by Lesotho's migrant labourers, tourism, which is concentrated on Maseru, and development aid are also of great economic significance. It is hoped that the **Lesotho Highland Water Project** (www.lhwp.org.ls), the world's biggest water supply project, will bring about an improvement of the economic situation. Water from the snow-covered Maluti mountains secures the water supply of the industrial areas around Johannesburg. South Africa naturally has to pay for this drinking water, and

► VISITING LESOTHO

INFORMATION

Lesotho Tourist Board
Victoria Hotel Building
209 Kingsway, Maseru
Tel. 2231 2896
www.lesotho.gov.ls
www.seelesotho.com
The Maloti Tourist Information in ►
Ladybrand is also helpful for Lesotho.

GETTING THERE AND ROADS

Moshoeshoe I International Airport
21km/13mi south of Maseru has
planes arriving from Johannesburg.
The border crossings Maseru Bridge
(N 8 from Bloemfontein) and Ma-
putsoe Bridge (near Ficksburg) are
open around the clock, the ten others
are only open during the day and
some of them only until 4pm. A large
part of the country can only be
reached via dirt roads and visitors
should enquire about their condition
at the border or at the Tourist Board.

FESTIVALS AND EVENTS

17 July: the King's Birthday. End of
Sept–beginning of Oct: Morija Arts &
Cultural Festival (music, dancing,
horse racing, arts and crafts and food;
www.morijafest.com). 4 Oct: Independence Day. Nov: Roof of Africa
(www.roofofafrica.org.ls), one of the
hardest motorbike rallies in the world

WHERE TO STAY

► Mid-range

Lesotho Sun
Hilton Road, Maseru
Tel. 2231 3111
Comfortable hotel on a hill above the
town with a casino and a good
restaurant: large selection of dishes,
including German home-style cooking (!).

Maseru Sun
12 Orpen Road, Maseru
Tel. 2231 2434, 115 rooms.
Modern, comfortable rooms. The
restaurant has a buffet with fish, meat
and vegetables dishes, but it also
serves à la carte.

► Budget

Lancer's Inn
Kingsway /Pioneer Rd., Maseru
Tel. 2231 2114
Maseru's oldest hotel. Cosy living in
comfortable round houses and chalets, self-catering optional. Good restaurant; try the delicious trout from
the mountains of Lesotho.

New Oxbow Lodge
Oxbow, contact South Africa:
tel. 051 933 2247
www.oxbow.co.za
Comfortable chalets modelled on the
chalets in the Alps by Malibamatso
River, popular hostel for (winter)
sports enthusiasts. Pony trekking,
4 x 4 trails, trout fishing, etc.

Sani Top Chalet
Mokhotlong / Sani-Pass, contact
South Africa: tel. 033 702 1158
www.sanitopchalet.co.za
Mountain-climber chalet in a fantastic setting with double rooms, dor-
mitory and a campsite. Africa's
highest bar (2874m/9429ft) serves
hearty food.

Malealea Lodge
Mafeteng
Contact South Africa:
tel. 082 552 4215
www.malealea.co.ls
Familiar accommodation in the rustic
buildings of an old farm and in round
huts. Ideal for pony and hiking tours.

in addition Lesotho is no longer dependent on electricity supplied by its neighbour, thanks to the hydro-electric power plant at the Katse Dam. The planned further extension of the project is not considered wise by environmental organizations.

History

The area was first settled by the San who lived here as hunters and gatherers from 3500 BC and left countless rock drawings behind. From the 17th century they were pushed westwards by tribes wanting to use the land for agricultural and pastoral purposes. In around 1820, refugees took shelter in the mountains of modern-day Lesotho from military persecution by the Zulu under Shaka. Almost all of them were members of the Sotho group, whom King Moshoeshoe I united into one nation around 1830. This state, which alongside Lesotho encompassed large parts of modern-day Free State, came under pressure from the Boers leaving the Cape province (Great Trek). When it became evident that his army would be defeated, Moshoeshoe asked for British protection in 1867, and after valuable land had been lost to the Boers, the remaining area was governed as part of the Cape colony after 1868 and incorporated into the colony in 1871.

After several revolts the British at the Cape returned the region to the crown as the protectorate of Basutoland in 1884. In 1903 a Na-

A traditional Sotho group

! *Baedeker* TIP

Not on your high horse

There is no need to be an experienced rider to experience Lesotho's mountains on horseback. The Basotho ponies are sure-footed and incredibly patient. Tours lasting anything from several hours to up to six days are offered by: Basotho Trekking Centre (tel. 2231 7284, see p.379), Malealea Lodge (see p.374), Semonkong Lodge (www.placeofsmoke.co.ls, tel. South Africa 051 933 3106). A day-long expedition on horseback costs around LSL 100–150.

tional Council was formed as an advisory body for the colonial administration. After the introduction of democratic principles in 1944, the reformist Basutoland Congress Party won the majority in 1960, but lost at the first direct election in 1965 to the conservative Basotho National Party. On 4 October 1966 (national holiday) Lesotho became independent as a constitutional monarchy under King Moshoeshoe II, but remained in the Commonwealth. Moshoeshoe II demanded great political powers, which again led to crises and confrontations with the army. After a national strike in 1970 the king had to go into temporary exile; between 1990 and 1995 he was again deposed by the army. After he became king a second time in 1995 Moshoeshoe II promised to keep out of current affairs and party politics. He died in 1996 when his off-road vehicle drove off a cliff in the Maluti mountains. His son Letsie III became his successor. After the elections of 1998, which were not declared invalid despite irregularities, there was unrest, and troops from South Africa and Botswana marched into Lesotho. These »peace-keeping troops of the Southern African Development Community« (SADC) got the situation under control and were withdrawn again in 1999.

Drives through Lesotho

Particularly in winter visitors should be careful when undertaking car and mountain tours. A drop in temperature, fog and sudden snowfall are not unusual. The Tourist Board offers organized round trips; early booking is recommended.

Maseru – Mafeteng – Moyeni (180km/110mi)

Maseru   Maseru, meaning »red sandstone«, Lesotho's capital and the country's **only large urban settlement** (population: 150,000), is situated by the Caledon River in the western lowlands. Initially the place was mainly inhabited by merchants. As early as 1869 the British chose it as the administrative centre of the Basutoland protectorate. Maseru is a good starting point for tours into the country.

At first this route to the south follows the main road leaving Maseru though a landscape shaped by erosion. Further on the road leads through the sunny plain of a maize-growing region with herds of livestock, villages, waterfalls and the **Sotho Castles**, the relics of a former sandstone plateau.

Approximately 40km/25mi south of Maseru a turnoff to the east leads to the Morija mission station, named after the biblical Mt Moriah, and founded by the Paris Evangelical Missionary Society in 1833. The Basuto cultural objects and archaeological finds that have been collected by the missionaries since the beginning of the 20th century are on display in the country's only museum, the **Morija Museum & Archives** (open Mon–Fri 8am–5pm, Sun 2–5pm).

Morija

Further east is Matsieng, where the royal family lives. The round-hut settlement above the village was inhabited by Letsie I, who had chosen the location because erosion had formed stones here that were used for eating. Thus there was a »soup stone« and a »meat plate«. Recommended alternative route: around 50km/30mi south of Maseru the eastern turnoff towards Mphaki via the **Matelile Pass** leads to the wonderfully situated **Malealea Lodge**.

Matsieng

Mafeteng (»place of the fat spinster«), a small industrial and commercial town with a population of 13,000, is rather bleak. From here the main road continues in a south-easterly direction through a rocky plain and after 40km/25mi crosses the **Makhaleng River**. From the bridge the Thaba Tsoeu (»white mountains«), which are famous for their stone forest, can be seen in the east. The pretty town of Mohale's Hoek is a good starting point for tours into the surrounding area, to the Makhaleng Gorge. Information is available in the recommended, small **Hotel Mount Maluti** (tel. 2278 5224).

Mafeteng

◄ Mohale's Hoek

The main road runs southbound through an increasingly rugged landscape to the Mesitsaneng Pass (»place of the wild beans«) from which there are beautiful views. From the top of the pass the road descends into the valley of the **Maphutseng River**, before crossing a gorge and then the Oranje/Senqu River via the Seako Bridge, which at 191m/209yd is the longest in Lesotho.
Around 8km/5mi from Moyeni/Quthing is the Masitise Mission with a large church that was founded by the missionary D. F. Ellenberger. Cave House is sheltered by a rock. Here just as at other places in the region visitors can admire some of the famous San rock drawings. Past the Catholic mission Villa Maria the road climbs up to the **Moorosi's Mountains**.

Mesitsaneng Pass

◄ Masitise Mission

The double name of the settlement (population: 6000), which was founded in 1877 and is the main town in the district of Quthing, is due to the fact that the first coaching inn was called Quthing. Moyeni means »place of wind«, because there is always a strong wind blowing in this area.
From Moyeni visitors should go on the day-long tour to the border town of Qacha's Nek (a total of approx. 320km/200mi) through very impressive mountain landscape. On the way there are **dinosaur tracks** and a **San cave** near the village of Pokane.

Moyeni/Quthing

◄ Qacha's Nek

Maseru – Maletsunyane Falls (115km/70mi)

Thaba Bosiu East of Maseru a track turns off from the A 2 that leads to the historically significant Thaba Bosiu (»mountain of the night«), which was **founded by Moshoeshoe I as a fort** in 1824 and was the capital of the country for a long time. From the mountain with remains of the settlement there are good views of the Berea plateau and Qiloane Mountain.

Roma Further south along the A 5 is the university town of Roma, founded by Moshoeshoe in 1862. A few years later a **Catholic mission station** was built here, which became a college in 1945 and later the university. At first the road is still surfaced as it runs south-east (the distance from Roma to Semonkong is 85km/53mi) but after Ngope it turns into an dirt track. Along the extremely picturesque route there are villages, fields, herds of cattle and flocks of sheep. In March cosmoses and wild peach trees are in bloom. The caves here also have San rock drawings, in the village of **Ha Mpotu** for example. There are many large reed-covered areas in this region, which find expression in the name of the Malehlakana (»mother of the reed«), the main river here.

Mapeshoane The Helekokoane Cave near Mapeshoane 3km/2mi south of the road also has San drawings. 3km/2mi after the turnoff to Mapeshoane a path leads eastbound through the Raboshabana Gorge past the Mohomeng Cave to the 200m/650ft **Raboshabane Rock**. Subsequently the dirt road climbs steeply and at the top makes its way over a grass plateau. The nearby town of Motlepu is the base for the ascent of the impressive **Thaba Telle** (2533m/8310ft). Next the road descends and crosses the Makhalaneng River (»place of the small crabs«) after which it reaches **Nkesi's Pass** (2012m/6601ft), from which there are magnificent views of the 3096m/10,157ft **Thaba Putsoa** and the **Ramabanta** ▶ neighbouring mountains. Ramabanta is the start of an unforgettable mountain route with spectacular views; the scenery displays a large array of colours.

✳
Maletsunyane An hour and a half's walk away from Semonkong (»place of smoke«)
Falls the Maletsunyane Falls, the highest in southern Africa, plummet 192m/630ft to the ground. They carry the most water during summer, and in winter they are frozen, which is a spectacular sight.

Into the Blue The route into the Blue Mountains, which branches off to the east
Mountains on the Maseru–Roma road, at first climbs over sandstone rocks up to the grass plateau at the foot of the Maluti mountains, which, together with **Machache** mountain (2884m/9462ft), create a beautiful view. The road (A 3) then descends through a hilly plateau, where maize, sorghum and other grains are cultivated. In the small town of **Ha Nhatsi** a track turns off towards the north to the excellent rock

A large part of Lesotho's population lives in villages.

drawings of **Ha Boroanna** (»place of the small San«). After the small town of Machache (with a campsite) the road climbs steeply to the **Bushmann Pass**, then leads into the Makhaleng Valley and up to the 2328m/7638ft **Molimo Nthuse** (»God help me«) Pass with the lodge of the same name. After a few miles the road reaches the **Basotho Pony Trekking Centre**; it is definitely worth taking a three to four-hour pony ride to the Qiloane Falls. Just a little further along the road crosses the Blue Mountain Pass (2621m/8599ft) and then descends into the Likalaneng Valley. After it crosses a further pass the road reaches the large valley of the **Senqunyane River**; the town of Marakabei has a lodge for self-catering guests. The track then leads onwards to **Thaba Tseka**, which was founded as an administrative centre in 1980, and then further to the Katse Dam (see below).

Maseru – Oxbow – Sani Pass (365km/225mi)

The main road runs northwards past high sandstone rocks with interesting caves that tower over Teyateyaneng River. Teyateyaneng (»quick sand«, population: 14,000) is the bustling centre of commerce of the Berea district and is known for its **knotted carpets**. Beyond the town the road crosses the wide plain between the Caledon River and the Maluti Mountains. The landscape is dominated by large fields of maize.

Teyateyaneng

The small town of Leribe/Hlotse (population: 10,000) with some industry was founded in 1876. The name Hlotse (»dead meat«) is said to have come from travellers crossing the river who threw meat into

Leribe / Hlotse

it to distract the crocodiles. The oldest building is the Anglican church of 1877. The **Leribe Crafts Centre** was founded by Anglican nuns who taught the Basuto women how to weave. Good-quality arts and crafts products, such as ponchos, are for sale here.

Katse Dam ► Visitors should definitely take the time for an excursion through the beautiful landscape (on a very well-surfaced road) to the Katse Dam a good 120km/75mi away; overnight stays in the Katse Lodge (tel. 910 202).

Butha-Buthe The road from Leribe in a north-easterly direction runs through a breathtaking **sandstone landscape**. Butha-Buthe (population: 7000) is a collection of administrative buildings and shops; the small, picturesque market is in the shape of a typical Sotho straw hat. The name (»place where people settled«) was probably given to the town because it was here that Moshoeshoe united the Basuto people in 1823.

Joel's Drift Until Joel's Drift the road never falls below an altitude of 2300m/ 7500ft. The next part of the journey is along one of the **most impressive routes in Africa**, along the original route of the »Roof of Africa« Rally to Oxbow. It runs through the valley of the Hololo River and is lined with many bizarre sandstone formations. An altitude difference of 760m/2500ft and a gradient of up to 35% have to be overcome to reach the 2835m/9301ft **Moteng Pass**. 65km/40mi beyond Butha-Buthe lies New Oxbow Lodge (3000m/9840ft, ►p.374), a good base for fishing trips, hiking, pony trekking and skiing.

Onward journey to Mokhotlong The road from Oxbow to Mokhotlong (115km/70mi) is asphalted. Those who choose to continue reach the almost deserted Letseng-la-Terae. Since **diamond mining** was abandoned here by a South African company, the search for diamonds has been continued by a few private individuals under incredibly tough conditions (visitors are strongly warned not to buy diamonds here, as it would be both illegal and otherwise very risky). Mokhotlong (»place of the bald-headed ibis«), still very remote, is a base for hikes and rides into the ►Natal-Drakensberg mountains or along the Mokhotlong River. Visitors are strongly recommended to find themselves a guide (information in the hotels).

Mokhotlong

✶✶
Sani Pass The breathtakingly steep, winding track from Mokhotlong south-east to the Sani Pass (48km/30mi), the only crossing into **KwaZulu-Natal** (► Natal-Drakensberg mountains), is only open for 4 x 4s. On the way the road passes the 3240m/10,630ft **Kotisephola Pass**. From the Sani Top Chalet at 2874m/9429ft (► p.374), from which there are magnificent views, **Thabana-Ntlenyana**, at 3482m/11,424ft Africa's second-highest mountain, can be climbed in a day. In the Sani Top Chalet, South Africa's highest bar, visitors can refresh themselves with an exotic, home-brewed beer.

Lydenburg

J 4

Province: Mpumalanga
Population: 22,000

Altitude: 1381m/4531ft
Distances: Johannesburg 300km/185mi,
Phalaborwa 175km/110mi

This quiet town on the western slope of the Transvaal Drakensberg mountains is a good stop on the journey from Johannesburg to Blyde River Canyon.

The town was founded in 1849 by Boers who had settled in Ohrigstad 45km/28mi further north but had to flee from a devastating malaria epidemic. Here, on the highveld in a malaria-free area, they founded a new town, which they named »town of suffering« in remembrance. Today Lydenburg has numerous shops and service facilities and is a centre of the predominantly agricultural surrounding area; the main products are maize, grains and soy. The school built in 1851 in Church Street is the oldest school building in the province. The building of the Dutch Reformed Church also dates from this time. The rich fish stocks in the waters around Lydenburg (particularly trout) make it an angler's paradise.

Lydenburg past and present

A little outside the town on the road to Long Tom Pass, the local museum displays the significant **Lydenburg Heads** (replicas, originals in the South African Museum in Cape Town). In the nearby Sterkspruit Valley seven of these terracotta heads were found, six of them having human traits and one the traits of a wild animal. At first the heads were dated to the 6th or 7th century BC but recent research suggests they were not made until around AD 1500.

★ Lydenburg Museum

For a short time Lydenburg was the capital of a Boer Republic.

▶ VISITING LYDENBURG

INFORMATION
Lydenburg Tourism Bureau
Jock's Country Stalls
Viljoen Street, tel. 013 235 3076

WHERE TO STAY
▶ **Budget/Mid-range**
The Manor Guest House
43 Viljoen Street

Tel./fax 013 235 2099
www.lydenburgmanorhouse.com
Stylish house from the end of the 19th
century close to the museum. Twelve
comfortable rooms/suites with separate garden entrance, small bar. Dinner for house guests.

Around Lydenburg

**Gustav Klinkbiel
Nature Reserve**

East of Lydenburg, close to the R 37, is the Gustav Klinkbiel Nature
Reserve. The 2200ha/5400-acre terrain with a native flora and its
own species of antelope contains the remains of an Iron Age settlement. A small museum informs visitors about the first settlers in this
region.

Long Tom Pass

East of Lydenburg the R 37 crosses the 2,149m/7,051ft Long Tom
Pass and after 53km/33mi reaches the town of ▶Sabie (more about
the Long Tom Pass there). Further sights of interest in the area are
described under ▶Blyde River Canyon and ▶Pilgrim's Rest.

Makhado · Louis Trichardt

H 3

Province: Limpopo
Population: 11,000

Altitude: 901m/2956ft
Distances: Johannesburg 440km/270mi,
Polokwane 110km/70mi, Musina 95km/
60mi

**In the far north-east of South Africa Makhado (Louis Trichardt) lies
in a beautiful valley at the foot of the Soutpansberge mountains.
Some nature reserves in its surroundings are worth a visit.**

The pleasantly warm climate, relatively high precipitation (940mm/
37in annually) and fertile soils make intensive agriculture possible in
this region. Large farms raise livestock and cultivate citrus fruits,
pears, avocados, pistachios and vegetables. Makhado itself does not
have any sights worth seeing, but tours into the area's impressive
mountains more than make up for that with their rich flora and fauna. The northern part of the ▶Kruger National Park (Punda Maria)
is approx. 145km/90mi away.

In 1836 the Boer leader Louis Trichardt set up his camp here. In **History**
1847 the founding of the settlement of Zoutpansbergdorp followed
and attracted ivory and livestock traders. However, the Venda who
lived in the area resisted so ferociously that the Europeans temporarily gave up the place in 1867, after which it was destroyed. Only in
1898 did the government of Transvaal manage to get the area under
control and a year later Louis Trichardt was re-founded as an administrative centre. As part of the general policy of renaming, Louis Trichardt was given the name Makhado, which came from a Venda
king, but as a result of a court ruling in 2007 it has reverted (temporarily?) to Louis Trichardt.

Around Makhado · Louis Trichardt

The region's mountain landscape can be explored on the 91km/57mi **Soutpansberg**
Soutpansberg Hiking Trail, which can be broken down into shorter
segments. Five days should be set aside for the entire trail; accommodation in huts for up to 30 people (information at the Tourist Office
in Makhado).

This reserve (open daily 6am–7pm) 12km/7mi south-east of Makha- **Ben Lavin**
do is a good place for a stop. Giraffes, impalas, wildebeests and ze- **Nature Reserve**
bras inhabit the green plains of the reserve famous for its large number of bird species. There are fully equipped huts and a campsite
along the 18km/11mi trails.

❯ VISITING MAKHADO · LOUIS TRICHARDT

INFORMATION

Soutpansberg Tourist Office
on the N 1 at the northern edge of
town
Tel./fax 015 516 0040
www.tourismsoutpansberg.co.za
www.makhadomunicipality.co.za

WHERE TO STAY

► Mid-range
Adam's Apple
14km/9mi south on the N 1
Tel. 015 516 3304
A low house situated in well-tended
gardens with a view of the Soutpansberge. 16 individually designed
rooms, swimming pool. Good restaurant with Portuguese specialities,
as well as shrimps and spare ribs.

► Budget
Clouds End Hotel
3km/2mi north on the N 1
Tel. 015 517 7021
Quiet country hotel in the style of the
1970s, with 37 rooms, a large lounge
with an open fire (for the winter), a
garden, a pool and a tennis court.
Very good restaurant.

WHERE TO EAT

► Inexpensive/Moderate
Country Cuisine Restaurant
Koraalboom St.
Tel. 015 516 4452
African-style restaurant with large
tables; meat is plentiful here.

Wyllie's Poort
The northbound road from Makhado winds up the Soutpansberg mountains for 10km/6mi to the 1524m/5000ft pass, which has some spectacular views. The mountains take their name from a large **salt pan** in the western area, which already provided the region's inhabitants with salt in prehistoric times. The road then makes its way through a fertile valley and finally reaches the town of Wyllie's Poort.

Thohoyandou
East of Makhado after 90km/55mi the R 524 reaches the capital of the former **Venda homeland** (population: 44,000). It has an area of 7410 sq km/2860 sq mi and a population of half a million, making Venda the smallest of all the homelands. The town, named after a legendary leader of this people, was founded only after the creation of the homeland in 1973 and has the appearance of a modern city with a university and an airport. A small museum has exhibits on the history of the Venda people. There is a hotel and a casino; Venda arts and crafts can be purchased in the Ditike Craft Centre. The market is also worth seeing.

Lake Fundudzi
Thohoyandou is a good base for trips into this region, which is almost entirely inhabited by Venda (guided tours through the Soutpansberg Tourist Office in Makhado; Kuvona Tours and Face Africa are recommended). Away from the flocks of tourists, visitors can experience fantastic and still largely untouched landscape. Most of the Venda people still live in **traditional villages** where a chief and a shaman dictate the order of the day. Many locations are associated with myths. **Lake Fundudzi** north-west of Thohoyandu is considered holy, because it is the home of the python god who is worshipped as a symbol of fertility (not open to tourists). The Thate-Vondo Forest close to the lake is also sacred and not open to tourists.

Mabudashango Hiking Trail
This very attractive route takes four days to complete and is 50km/30mi long. It makes its way through some magnificent landscape and comes quite close to the sacred sites. Very basic accommodation, starting point at the Thate-Vondo Forest Station. To book contact the Department of Tourism, Private Bag X50008, Thohoyandou, Limpopo, tel. 015 962 4724.

Dzata Ruins
A road leaving Thohoyandou in a north-westerly direction leads to Wyllie's Poort (see above). Take this road to get to the Dzata Ruins in the Nzhelele Valley. Here there are some surviving ruins of the **600-year-old wall** that the Venda built to fortify Dzata, their first headquarters.

Nwanedi National Park
Nwanedi National Park is almost 80km/50mi north of Thohoyandou. The access road is not very good; a better road leading to the reserve goes through the town of Tshipise. The national park established in 1981 has a small population of giraffes, zebras and antelopes. Accommodation is available.

Malmesbury · Darling

C 8

Province: Western Cape   **Distances:** Cape Town 70km/45mi

On the way from Cape Town northwards to the West Coast National Park, a small detour through the hinterland is particularly rewarding when the wild flowers are in bloom in the spring months of August and September.

Malmesbury (population: 16,000; 140m/460ft) is the centre of South Africa's most significant wheat-growing region. The small town is located north of Cape Town in an area called **Swartland**, which owes its name to the fertile, dark soils (»swart« means »black« in Afrikaans). It is not just wheat that does well here. This region also produces some excellent wines; in the Swartland Cellars 4km/2.5mi outside the town visitors can taste full-bodied red wine and the famous **Hanepoot**, an alcoholic, honey-sweet dessert wine made from the grape of the same name.

The 32°C/90°F sulphurous **spring** was a significant reason for the development of the town. The first settlers made a home for themselves near this spring in 1744. The hamlet was given the name of Malmesbury in 1829 when the British governor came for a visit and named it after his father-in-law, the Earl of Malmesbury. Today the spring is no longer used for medicinal purposes. The imposing Reformed Church (1751, after which it was extended several times) has an **impressive pulpit** dating from the time the church was originally built. The synagogue of 1911 houses a museum.

Malmesbury

 Baedeker TIP

Evita se Perron

»Evita se Perron« (»Evita on the railway platform«) is the punning title of a satirical show at the old railway station: with his wacky stage figure of Evita Bezuidenhout (somewhat like Dame Edna) the satirist and actor Pieter-Dirk Uys makes fun of everything that is wrong in the state. Shows Sat and Sun, tel. 022 492 2831, www.evita.co.za.

The theatre restaurant is a must in itself; the menu features good African cuisine.

Darling (population: 3600; 79m/259ft) was founded in 1853 and named after the Cape governor of the time. It is situated in the sandveld, a strip along the coast north of Cape Town ranging in width from 20 to 30 kilometres (12–20mi). It is known for its wealth of wild flowers in spring, when the fields turn into carpets of flowers. A real highlight of the year is the **Wild Flower Show**, which takes place in the third week of September; the town is also worth a visit when the flowers are not in bloom, because of Evita se Perron (►Baedeker Tip). The flower fields are the property of farms and can only be visited at certain times; information is provided by the Tourist Office

Darling

(Pastorie St., www.darlingtourism.co.za). The Darling Museum informs visitors about everything to do with the manufacture of butter (open Sat–Sun 10am–3pm).

Mamre Mamre, 17km/11mi south of Darling, was founded in 1808 as a mission station of the **German Moravian community**. The small town with its old houses in Cape Dutch style is a real gem. A watermill can be visited (Mon–Sat 9am–5pm and Sun 2–5pm).

✳ Matjiesfontein

D 8

Province: Western Cape
Population: 1200

Altitude: 732m/2402ft
Distances: Cape Town 240km/150mi

This inconspicuous little town half way between Cape Town and Beaufort West in the Little Karoo is a national monument thanks to its past as a Victorian health resort.

The small town, pronounced »my-keys-fon-tain«, is a popular weekend destination; foreign visitors should definitely stop here on their trip through the country's interior (the Trans Karoo that connects Cape Town with Johannesburg, Rovos Rail and Blue Train all stop here). The bare region only allows sheep farming, and some farms are larger than English counties.

Lord Milner Hotel, relic of a hopeful time

The young Scotsman James Douglas Logan initially worked for the **History** railway and earned a lot of money with his licence to run all railway restaurants between Cape Town and Bulawayo (Zimbabwe). At 36 years of age he was a member of parliament. In 1880 he settled in modern-day Matjiesfontein. Since early childhood he had suffered from a lung disease that got better in the arid climate, so he decided to open a health resort here. In the late 19th century many famous people came here, such as the Sultan of Zanzibar, Lord Randolph Churchill (father of Sir Winston) and the author Olive Schreiner. They expected to be provided with the luxuries of the day, and as a result Matjiesfontein was the first place in South Africa to get electricity and running water. From 1899 to 1902 Matjiesfontein was the headquarters of the Cape commander and his 12,000 soldiers.

Some buildings from Victorian times still survive, for instance the **What to See** **Lord Milner Hotel** opened in 1889, a magnificent building in which guests feel they have travelled 100 years into the past, the **country house of Olive Schreiner**, the post office and the old warehouse. The chaotic Mary Rawdon Museum in the station has equipment dating from Victorian times and exhibits on the Boer War on display.

Around Matjiesfontein

The R 354 connects Matjiesfontein with Sutherland (population: **Sutherland** 2000; 1456m/4777ft) approx. 120km/75mi further north. The road runs through the impressive **Great Karoo** (► Beaufort West); the sunrises and sunsets are a special treat. Sutherland, which still has some Victorian buildings, is one of the coldest places in South Africa. In winter temperatures of -6°C/21°F are no rarity. The altitude and the clear air in the Karoo make the region ideal for astronomical observations, for which reason the **South African Astronomical Observatory** was built (visitor programme) 14km/9mi outside Sutherland.

VISITING MATJIESFONTEIN

INFORMATION
Tourist Office
Tel. 023 5613011
www.matjiesfontein.com

WHERE TO STAY
► Budget/Mid-range
Lord Milner Hotel
Logan Road, tel. 023 551 3011
A wonderful hotel furnished with antique furniture (photograph opposite). 58 rooms, some of them have a balcony; pool. The staff of the inexpensive restaurant serve in lace caps.

► Budget
Kambrokind Guest House
Sutherland, tel. 023 571 1405
Comfortable, familiar, personally run bed & breakfast, lounge with an open fireplace. Good local food is served in the café.

Austere, wide-open landscape near Middelburg

Middelburg

H 4

Province: Mpumalanga
Population: 100,000

Altitude: 1447m/4747ft
Distances: Johannesburg 145km/90mi, Pretoria 130km/80mi

Middelburg is located halfway between Pretoria and Lydenburg: hence the name. The town, a significant centre of agriculture, industry and coal mining, is not very interesting, but there are worthwhile sights in its vicinity.

Middelburg   Some buildings survive from the time after the town was founded in 1866, such as the White Church (1890), the station and Meyer's Bridge (1896).

Around Middelburg

✷
Fort Merensky,
Botshabelo Open
Air Museum

In 1865 Alexander Merensky was asked by the Berlin Missionary Society to found the Botshabelo Mission Station (»Botshabelo« means »place of refuge«) north of Middelburg. Members of the Sotho nation were commissioned to build the fort, resulting in an interesting mixture of African and European ingredients. The fort and some further buildings along with an Ndebele village form an open air muse-

🕑   um (open daily 9am–5pm) that documents the **colourful look of the houses** amongst other things (▶Baedeker Special p.460). Several hiking trails start at the museum. On the Botshabelo Trail (approx. three hours) visitors see baboons, antelopes and gazelles. Six hours are needed for the Klein Aavoelkrans Trail, eight hours for the Baboon Trail.

45km/28mi north along the R 35 is the Loskop Dam on the Olifants River. A viewpoint close to the reservoir offers magnificent views over the forested hilly landscape. The surrounding reserve is home to rhinoceroses, ostriches, giraffes, zebras, buffaloes, kudus and wildebeests. Accommodation is available in holiday homes or on a campsite.

Loskop Dam Nature Reserve

★ Mkuzi Game Reserve

K 5

Province: KwaZulu-Natal
Distances: Hluhluwe 60km/35mi, Durban 350km/215mi

Altitude: 60–150m/200–500ft

The Mkuzi Game Reserve in the far north-east of South Africa has become part of the Greater St Lucia Wetland Park (►p.467). It has a fascinating fauna, and particularly many bird species.

This 34,644ha/85,607-acre reserve (also spelt »Mkhuze«) established in 1912 is not much visited, but is interesting because of its different habitats and rich bird life. The area extends in the plain between the Lebombo mountains in the west and the thick forests along the Mkhuze River in the east. Coastal dunes alternate with woodland steppes, riparian forests and open savannah. More than 410 bird spe-

► VISITING MKUZI

INFORMATION
KZN Wildlife (►p.156)
Maputaland Tourism
Kingfisher Road, Mkuze
Tel. 035 573 1439

FACILITIES
KZN maintains the comfortable Nhlonhlela Lodge, the Mantuma camp with cottages ranging from basic to comfortable, the Tented Safari Camp (with a swimming pool) as well as campsites. There is a petrol station at the entrance gate.

WHEN TO GO
This region near the east coast gets very hot and clammy in summer. The weather conditions are better in winter, which is also the best time to see animals because the vegetation is less dense. The reserve is open all year round from sunrise to sunset. It is always necessary to take the right malaria precautions.

cies are represented here, including heron species, cormorants, Pel's fishing owls, the rare Senegal lapwing and saddle-billed storks. The main mammals here are two species of rhinoceros (black and white rhinoceros), large populations of elephants and antelopes (particularly impalas), gazelles, blue wildebeests, giraffes, zebras, hippopotamuses and crocodiles. To get to the reserve from Durban take the N 2 (turnoff 35km/22mi north of Hluhluwe).

Drives and hikes Approx. 100km/60mi of track criss-cross the reserve. Guided tours are available, particularly guided bird-watching tours. At Nsumo Pan birds can be watched at close range. This lake is also the starting point for the 3km/2mi **Fig Forest Trail**. After crossing a suspension bridge visitors enter one of South Africa's last fig forests. Many of the **wild fig trees** (sycamore figs) have trunks 12m/40ft in girth, and some reach a height of 25m/80ft. The figs on every tree ripen at different times, making them a popular food source all year round.

Mmabatho · Mafikeng

F 4

Province: North West
Distances: Johannesburg 280km/175mi,
Bloemfontein 460km/285mi

Population: 50,000

The central north of South Africa, close to the border with Botswana, is largely flat, bare Kalahari landscape with agricultural areas dotted around. In the 19th century Boers settled here after their Great Trek.

Mmabatho, formerly the main town of the Bophuthatswana homeland, forms a closed settlement area together with its neighbouring town Mafikeng. Mmabatho was first founded in 1977 when the Republic of South Africa declared the homeland to be an independent republic; Mafikeng on the other hand was part of Western Transvaal. The region's traditional economic activities include agriculture (wheat, maize, millet, peanuts, sunflowers) and cattle farming, while mining and industry have become more significant over the past decades.

History Before the first whites crossed the Vaal River in the 1830s the Bantu Tswana people controlled large parts of what are now the provinces of Mpumalanga and Limpopo. They fought against the advances made by the Boers and asked the British for assistance. The British however only reacted when their own interests came under threat, at which point they established the protectorate of Bechuanaland (modern-day Botswana); Mafikeng (formerly Mafeking), a British settlement founded in 1857, was made the administrative centre, even though Mafikeng was not actually in the protectorate. Until 1965 Mafikeng kept this status. When the town was besieged by Boers for 217 days in 1899–1900, the British under the command of Colonel **Robert Baden-Powell** resisted. To this end Baden-Powell trained a cadet corps made up from boys from the town so they could deliver messages and run errands; this was the birth of the **Boy Scout movement** that Baden-Powell started in England in 1907.

The centres of Mafikeng and Mmabatho are approx. 4km/2.5mi apart. Wide roads and some representative buildings shape Mmabatho's townscape; the name means »mother of the people«. Administrative institutions are located here as well as a university established in 1979. The **sports stadium with 60,000 seats** and the airport are also worth mentioning. Mafikeng has some historic buildings, like the Anglican church designed by the famous architect Sir Herbert Baker. The **Mafikeng Museum** (open Mon–Fri 8am–4pm, Sat 10am–1pm) explains the eventful local history. The relics from the time of the siege are particularly interesting.

What to See

! **Baedeker TIP**

Mafeking Road

The stories by H. C. Bosman, one of the great South African authors, entitled *Mafeking Road* are well worth reading but not very well known; it is also not widely known that the Marico district is one of South Africa's biggest fruit-growing regions. Peaches, apricots, etc. are made into a very strong liquor called Mampoer; in Zeerust there is a Mampoer Festival. Groot Marico Information Centre, tel. 083 2722 958, www.marico.co.za.

Zeerust (population: 25,000), approx. 70km/45mi north-east of Mafikeng, is a significant agricultural centre (fruit, citrus fruit, tobacco, maize and wheat); together with Groot Marico and Ottoshoop it forms what is known as the **Marico District**. For tourists this lively little town is important as a station on the way to Botswana. A reservoir 5km/3mi to the east is used for water-skiing and fishing (holiday village). The Marico Trail runs along the river of the same name.

Zeerust

▶ VISITING MMABATHO

INFORMATION

Mafikeng Tourism
Information Centre
Nelson Mandela Drive
Cookes Lake
Mafikeng
Tel. 018 381 3155
www.mafikeng.co.za
www.tourismnorth-west.co.za

WHERE TO STAY/ WHERE TO EAT

▶ **Budget/Mid-range**
Ferns Guest House
12 Cook Road, Mafikeng
Tel. 018 381 5971
www.ferns.co.za
Well-kept little house (17 rooms) with a pool; the restaurant is considered one of the better ones in Mafikeng.

The hike lasts two days; the night is spent in a refuge. **Kaditshwene** (36km/22mi north-west of Zeerust), once centre of a rich culture, was destroyed by the Zulus in the 19th century; only ruins remain. The **Tswana Museum**, where craftspeople can sometimes be watched at work, is worth a visit.

⭑ Montagu

D 8

Province: Western Cape	**Altitude:** 223m/732ft
Population: 7500	**Distances:** Cape Town 170km/105mi

Anyone travelling east from Cape Town to the valley of the Breede River should definitely pay a visit to Montagu. The Langeberge range rises south of this wonderful, quiet little town along the famous Route 62 (▶Robertson), and to the north the arid landscape of the Little Karoo unfolds.

The area around Montagu is a wine and fruit-growing region: apples, pears, apricots and peach plantations as far as the eye can see. The nearby hot springs (43°C/109°F) have been in use for 200 years. It is easy to forget the time and feel transported back into the 19th century: the small town founded in 1851, named after the Cape governor John Montagu (1842–53), has many pretty houses in Cape Dutch and Georgian styles. Fourteen buildings on **Long Street** alone, parallel to the main road (Bath Street), have been declared national monuments, and a further nine in the town share this honour.

What to See in Montagu

Montagu Museum

Joubert House

The old mission church in Long Street houses the Montagu Museum (open Mon–Fri 9am–1pm, 3–5pm, Sat 10am–noon, Sun 10.30am–12.30pm). It informs visitors about everything worth knowing about the town's history and displays some old furniture. Joubert House from 1853 to the west of the museum is considered one of the town's most beautiful buildings (opening hours the same as the Montagu Museum).

Montagu Hot Springs

Lovers' Walk, an attractive walk along the Keisie River (and one of the best climbing walls) connects Montagu with the **hot springs** 2.5km/1.5mi away. Here there is a comfortable hotel (Avalon Springs) with several pools, which are very busy at weekends and during the holidays, and many holiday homes.

Wine Route

Montagu is known for dessert wines from the Muscadel grape. The Montagu Wine Route connects vineyards in the town and the surrounding area; in April a **wine festival** takes place here.

▶ VISITING MONTAGU

INFORMATION
Tourism Bureau, 24 Bath St.
Tel. 023 614 2471
www.montagu.org.za

WHERE TO EAT
▶ Moderate
Jessica's
47 Bath St., tel. 023 614 1805
Excellent South African dishes, ostrich and springbok steaks amongst other things. Exquisite domestic wines.

Preston's
17 Bath St., tel. 023 614 3013
Traditional South African dishes such as bobotie, ox tail and steaks of course. Pretty garden terrace.

WHERE TO STAY
▶ Mid-range/Luxury
Montagu Country Hotel
27 Bath St., tel. 023 614 3125

www.montagucountryhotelco.za
Pleasant, modern building in the centre with large rooms, a pool and a good restaurant; in winter there is a wood fire burning in the fireplace.

Mimosa Lodge
Church St., tel. 023 614 2351
This guesthouse is considered the nicest in Montagu; it has lounges, a bar, a library, a garden (with a pool) and an excellent restaurant. The Orchard Suite is particularly romantic.

▶ Mid-range
Kingna Lodge
11 Bath St., tel. 023 614 1066
www.kingnalodge.co.za
Elegant Victorian building, surrounded by a garden, vineyards and an impressive mountain landscape. Famous 5-course dinner.

Mossel Bay

E 9

Province: Western Cape
Population: 35,000

Altitude: 76m/249ft
Distances: Cape Town 360km/225mi,
George 55km/35mi,
Oudtshoorn 95km/60mi

Attractive beaches make Mossel Bay, the western end of the ▶Garden Route, a popular holiday destination. Attractive old buildings in the town centre speak of its long history.

Mossel Bay owes its name to the many mussels the first Europeans found here. Unfortunately the scenery is blighted by ugly facilities processing the crude oil that was discovered off the coast in the 1980s. However, well-kept villas and holiday homes are the other side of the coin and in December alone approx. 1 million guests come here.

On the beaches of Mossel Bay

History Many of the seafarers who circumnavigated the Cape of Good Hope anchored in Mossel Bay. The first of them was Bartolomëu Dias, who set foot on South African soil here in 1488. He was followed by Vasco da Gama in 1497 and by the Portuguese admiral João da Nova in 1501. João da Nova had a chapel built (it has not survived). It was the first European-style building in South Africa. However the Bay was not colonized until 1787; Mossel Bay developed into a significant port of the southern Cape and the Little Karoo.

What to See in Mossel Bay

✳

Bartolomëu Dias Museum Complex The large museum complex was built for the occasion of the 500th anniversary of Dias' landing (open Mon–Fri 8.15am–5pm, Sat–Sun 9am–4pm). The granary of 1786 serves as the information centre. The building opposite, which was a flour and lumber mill from 1901, now houses the Maritime Museum. The museum's pride and joy is a replica of **Dias' caravelle**; this incredibly tiny ship was built in Portugal and sailed to Mossel Bay in 1988. The Shell Museum is also worth a visit. The **Munrohoek Cottages** built around 1830 are amongst the oldest buildings in Mossel Bay (arts and crafts shop).

✳

Post Office Tree The great milkwood tree next to the Shell Museum was used by seafarers in times gone by on their journey to the east as a **post box**; ships sailing in the opposite direction picked the letters up. They restocked with water from the spring that still exists today.

Local History Museum The nearby Local History Museum (Market Street, closed Sundays) is also part of the Bartolomëu Dias Museum. It is housed in a building dating from 1858 and a larger extension of 1879.

Boats leave the port for excursions to Seal Island off the coast of the mainland; it is home to thousands of seals and penguins; it is common to see sharks hunting for seals on the way.

Seal Island

On the rocky headland called The Point east of the centre stands the lighthouse of 1864. This is a good place for watching whales and dolphins. From Bat's Cave below the lighthouse the spectacular **St Blaize Trail** leads to Dana Bay 13km/8mi further west.

Lighthouse of St Blaize

The Outeniqua Choo Tjoe, a narrow gauge steam railway, travels through the magnifiscent landscape between Mossel Bay and ▶ George (see also p.180).

Outeniqua Choo Tjoe

◗ VISITING MOSSEL BAY

INFORMATION
Mossel Bay Tourism Bureau
Church St./Market St.
Tel. 044 691 2202
www.gardenroute.net/mby
www.mosselbay.co.za

WHERE TO EAT
▶ Inexpensive
Café Gannet
Tel. 044 691 1885
Restaurant with nice décor at the Dias Museum. Good fish, pizza made in wood-burning stoves, terrace with a wonderful view of the bay. Part of Protea Mossel Bay (see below).

Jazzbury's
11 Marsh Street, tel. 044 691 1923
Good African/Cape Malay cuisine, also ostrich and seafood. On the town's main street.

WHERE TO STAY
▶ Mid-range
Protea Mossel Bay
Market St., tel. 691 3738
www.oldposttree.co.za
This hotel is part of the Dias Museum: elegant, modern rooms in one of the town's oldest buildings.

Eight Bells Mountain Inn
Tel. 044 631 0000
www.eightbells.co.za
Situated in beautiful mountain scenery, very pleasant hotel 35km/22mi north of Mossel Bay at the foot of the Robinson Pass. Nice garden, pool, tennis, riding.

A replica of the tiny Dias caravel

▶ Budget
Allemans Dorphuis
94 Montagu St., tel. 044 690 3621
Nice old-fashioned Victorian building in the town centre, with a view of the bay.

Musina

J 3

Province: Limpopo
Population: 20,000

Altitude: 538m/1765ft
Distances: Johannesburg 530km/330mi

As South Africa's northernmost town, Musina, on the border to Zimbabwe and at the centre of an important mining region, gives the impression of a small American town, where shops, banks and fast food restaurants line the main street.

Mining and horticulture

Until the 1990s this region produced most of South Africa's copper. Since 1992 De Beers has been operating the country's largest diamond mine 80km/50mi west of Musina. The name Musina currently in use, which replaced the malapropism »Messina«, comes from the Sotho language and means »copper«. The subtropical climate allows not just lavish vegetation to grow here, but also fruit and vegetables. The farms in the surrounding area mainly focus on intensive livestock farming. The large cattle markets are major events in the region.

History

Numerous finds confirm that this region was already populated in prehistoric times. The Europeans who came here at the beginning of the 20th century found traces of previous mining activity everywhere. They started mining the vast copper deposits on a grand scale in 1905. After the road from ► Makhado (95km/60mi) was completed in 1907, the town experienced a boom.

Around Musina

Baobab trees

Musina is known for the numerous **baobab trees** here. This tree was made famous by Saint-Exupéry's *The Little Prince*; it is a broad-leafed tree with a thick stem that can grow to have a girth of 30m/330ft and a few short branches, and is a protected species in all of South Africa. A particularly beautiful specimen along the road to Malala Drift is called »Elephant's Trunk«; there is another one 5km/3mi further on the road to Makhado.

Musina Nature Reserve

This reserve on the edge of Musina stretches over an area of 3700ha/9100 acres (open daily 7am–5pm; no accommodation). It is known for its many baobab trees; approx. 12,000 have been counted. The largest is 25m/82ft tall. 350 tree and shrub species flourish here. The animal population is limited to giraffes, wildebeests, antelopes and gazelles.

Tshipise

In Tshipise 40km/25mi south-east of Musina there is a **sulphurous spring** that supplies a few pools and bathing facilities. This town has a hotel, holiday homes and a campsite. Tshipise is the starting place for guided tours into the **Honnet Nature Reserve**, but visitors can also explore the terrain on foot by themselves. The 10km/6mi **Baobab Trail** traverses the reserve; besides magnificent baobab trees, with some luck giraffes, zebras, antelopes and gazelles can also be seen.

★ **Mapungubwe**

In the region of the Mapungubwe Hills, a flat hill rising up from the plains east of Musina, there was a town until AD 1290, which was the **centre of the powerful kingdom** of southern Africa and even traded with India. The remains of an 11th-century stone fort have been discovered here, as well as rock drawings, clay containers and gold objects such as the famous rhinoceros (►p.457). In 2003 Mapungubwe, which is located in a savannah landscape with baobab trees, was declared a World Heritage Site and in 2004 Mapungubwe Hill became the centre of the 28,000ha/70,000-acre **Mapungubwe National Park**. The entrance gate is 85km/53mi from Musina; accommodation in camps and lodges by SANParks (►p.156). The creation of a Transfrontier Park covering an area of 800,000ha/2 million acres is planned.

★ Namakwa

Provinces: Northern Cape, Western Cape

Distances: Cape Town 300–600km/190–370mi

Namakwa is the name of the extremely arid hinterland on the Atlantic between Lambert's Bay and Namibia. During the spring months the bizarre semi-desert is transformed into a wonderfully colourful sea of flowers.

The Namakwa, formerly Namaqualand, is a 48,000 sq km/18,500 sq mi strip of semi-desert in the north-west of South Africa. It reaches from Vanrhynsdorp (on the N 7) in the south to the Orange River, which forms the border to Namibia in the north; it stretches to Pofadder in the west. The flat southern part changes into a hilly landscape in the north. The amount of precipitation is very low in all parts of this area. The coastal region, past which the cold Benguela current flows, gets no more than 50mm/2in of rain annually; east of the N 7 the amount is somewhat higher at 200mm/8in per year.

★★ **Wild flowers**

The lack of precipitation only allows very sparse vegetation to grow here. In summer the searing heat eradicates everything green. No-one driving through the bare strip of land at that time of year could imagine what a magnificent sight it becomes after the winter rains: between mid-August and October the land is covered in a **carpet of flowers**. The most prevalent flowers are the differently coloured asteraceae. The region around Springbok is said to be the centre of this

This is a semi-desert: covered in a carpet of flowers.

fabulous display of flowers, but there are also colourful carpets along the N 7. When and where the flowering season is at its peak depends on the year's weather. Before travelling from Cape Town to Springbok visitors should inquire at the MTN Flowerline about the current flower situation. A tip: since the flowers turn towards the sun it is a good idea to drive in a southerly direction (at least for a while).

Economy   When the first whites came to the Namakwa during the mid-19th century they encountered San, who were using the copper deposits. Around 1852 Europeans opened the first copper mine near Springbok. Today Okiep and Nababeep are the centres of copper mining. Since the first diamonds were found between Port Nolloth and the mouth of the Orange River near Alexander Bay in 1926, the Namakwa has also become an important diamond region. Diamonds were also found on the ocean floor off the coast; today **diamond divers** work here, going out on boats and vacuuming the seabed with hoses (many roads between Hondeklipbaai and Alexander Bay are closed to regular traffic). Further sources of income in the sparsely populated region are fishing and sheep farming.

Vanrhynsdorp   The gate to the southern Namakwa is Vanrhynsdorp (population: 16,000), which can be reached from Cape Town on the N 7 after around 300km/185mi. This is where the railway line from Cape Town ends – and it feels like the end of the world. High-quality marble is quarried in the surrounding area.

The area around Nieuwoudtville 50km/30mi further north-east (population: 1000, 719m/2359ft) is used for sheep farming and the cultivation of cereal crops and rooibos tea. A visit to the **Wild Flower Reserve** is particularly impressive in spring, when approx. 300 species of wild flowers are in bloom. The drive from Nieuwoudtville towards Loeriesfontein is very attractive. On the way the 100m/328ft **Nieuwoudtville Falls** provide an interesting natural spectacle. The **Kokerboom Forest** along the way is a bizarre sight.

Nieuwoudtville

A dirt road leads from Nieuwoudtville to Oorlogskloof Nature Reserve 10km/6mi further south. **San rock drawings** and several rock formations constitute the main attractions in the 5070ha/12,530-acre reserve. An approx. 150km/95mi trail traverses the reserve. It is possible just to walk sections of it or do the whole hike in seven days. Register at: Oorlogskloof Nature Reserve, Nieuwoudtville 8180, tel. 027 218 1159, www.nieuwoudtville.co.za.

Oorlogskloof Nature Reserve

The R 27 leaves Vanrhynsdorp westbound via Vredendal, which is surrounded by fruit plantations and vineyards thanks to an irrigation system to Strandfontein (80km/50mi). The coastal town is esteemed by the farmers of the surrounding area as a holiday resort. The wine from Vredendal is dark, earthy and very aromatic; visitors can have a bottle filled in one of the wine cellars.

Vredendal, Strandfontein

▶ VISITING NAMAKWA

INFORMATION

Namakwa Tourism Information
Voortrekker St., Springbok
Tel. 027 712 8035
www.northerncape.org.za
www.namakwa.com

MTN FLOWERLINE

Tel. 083 910 1028,
027 718 2985

WHERE TO EAT

▶ **Inexpensive**
Titbits
Voortrekker St.
Springbok
Tel. 027 718 1455
Cosy eatery, a vision in pink. Mainly pizza and pasta as well as chicken and meat from the barbecue.

WHERE TO STAY

▶ **Budget/Mid-range**
Mountain View Guest House
2 Overberg Ave.
Springbok
Tel. 027 7121438
www.mountview.co.za
Ten luxurious, comfortably furnished suites with views of the town.

▶ **Mid-range**
Naries Guest Farm
27km/17mi from Springbok along the R 355 towards Kleinzee
Tel. 021 930 4564
www.naries.co.za
Variously equipped accommodation (B & B; self-catering, etc.) in a wonderful and romantic lodge in the Namakwa with good service.

Kamieskroon The N 7 runs northwards from Vanrhynsdorp through a landscape that becomes more and more bare; after 190km/120mi it reaches Kamieskroon. The area surrounding this town at the foot of the **Kamies Mountains** (grass mountains) is also known for its colourful fields of flowers in the springtime.

Springbok From Kamieskroon it is another 70km/45mi to Springbok (population: 8000), the Namakwa's main town at an altitude of 1000m/3280ft. The eponym was the springbok, a species of antelope that was once very common in this area. Sights of interest in the modern town and centre of the copper and diamond mines of the surrounding area are the **Blue Mine**, the first commercial copper mine in South Africa, and the museum of the former **synagogue**. Springbok is a good location for viewing the wild flowers in bloom; during this period accommodation is expensive and should be booked well in advance.

✳
Goegap Nature Reserve Even outside the flower season, Goegap Nature Reserve 15km/9mi south-east of Springbok is worth a visit (to get here take the R 355). In the 15,000ha/37,000-acre **Hester Malan Wildflower Garden** the vegetation typical of the Namakwa grows: succulents, shrubs, the bizarre kokerboom and in spring a lavish display of flowers. Larger mammals living here are antelope and mountain zebras. There is no accommodation; there are three round trails (4–7km/2.5–4.5mi).
🕑 Open daily 8am–6pm.

Port Nolloth In Steinkopf 52km/32mi north of Springbok a road turns westwards to Port Nolloth, which is another 95km/60mi from the junction. On the way there is a great view of the coast and the ocean from the **Annienous Pass**. Today the harbour town is home to about 6000 people, attracted by the diamonds that were found here. (Under no circumstances should visitors be talked into buying diamonds »under the counter«; firstly it would be illegal and secondly it might not be diamonds that these black-market traders are selling.) Fishing for spiny lobsters and tourism are the other economic activities; the Benguela current »warms« the water only to 16°C/61°F.

✳
Richtersveld Transfrontier National Park The 185,000ha/455,000-acre national park north of Port Nolloth was named after a German missionary who came to this region in 1830. The park is the property of the Nama people and contains a mountainous semi-desert landscape that has a certain rough beauty. It is only accessible with an all-terrain vehicle. In summer the temperatures rise to more than 50°C/122°F. A tour in the Richtersveld Park has to be well prepared (information: www.richtersveld.net and at SANParks ▶ p.156). Entrance and park office in Sendelingsdrift (from Springbok via Port Nolloth and Alexander Bay 320km/200mi); there and in the park there are basic camps. Tours by Richtersveld Challenge and other operators (tel. 027 712 1905), richtersveldchallenge@kingsley.co.za).

! **Baedeker TIP**

Pofadder Hiking Trail

Grey-brown semi-desert in the blistering heat... Pofadder is the start and finish of a trail for fit hikers: 72km/45mi in four days through surreal landscape, past the mission stations of Onseepkans and Pella, the Ritchie Falls on the Orange River and the Coboob Farm with Africa's largest koker-boom forest. The high summertime temperatures mean the trail is open only from May to September and only for groups of three people or more. Information in the Pofadder Tourist Office (tel. 054 933 0066) and in the recommended Pofadder Hotel (tel. 054 933 0063, www.pofadderhotel. co.za).

»Pofadder« is a »puff adder« in English, but in actual fact the town is named after Klaas Pofadder, a Koranna chief who was shot in 1860 by the farmers for stealing cattle. The town is the only base along the N 14 from Springbok to Upington for hundreds of kilometres of flat semi-desert. 40km/25mi to the north-west (dirt road) is the Pella mission station, founded in 1814. It has a cathedral that was built in seven years by amateur builders: the priests themselves. Refreshments are available in a »desert café«; accommodation is also on hand.

Pofadder

◄ Pella

⋆ Natal-Drakensberg

Provinces: Limpopo, Mpumalanga, KwaZulu-Natal

Neighbour state: Lesotho

The Natal-Drakensberg range east of Lesotho is among the most fantastic natural beauties in South Africa. A magnificent mountain landscape, rich flora and fauna and San rock drawings make this UNESCO World Heritage Site into a popular all-year-round destination.

Drakensberg is the name of the approx. 1000km/620mi-long mountain ridge that rises between the Kruger National Park in the north and the eastern border of the kingdom of Lesotho in the south. It forms the eastern and **most impressive part of the Great Escarpment**, which separates the interior from the coastal region. It has nu-

Drakensberg

merous peaks over 3000m/10,000ft, which makes the Drakensberg the highest elevation on the African continent after Mount Kilimanjaro. It was formed at the end of the Palaeozoic era around 300 million years ago, when the powerful deposits of the Karoo formation were established all over southern Africa. When the continent of Africa was created during the Mesozoic era, vast masses of lava pushed out the earth's interior and subsequently solidified as black basalt to form a blanket over the light sandstone, up to 1400m/4600ft thick in places and reaching to South Africa's east coast. Since then this layer of basalt has been eroded through the constant influence of water and wind. As a result the Great Escarpment has moved further and further inland.

Transvaal-Drakensberg

In the north of South Africa west of Kruger National Park the Transvaal Drakensberg range rises to an altitude of up to 2286m/7500ft. It separates the highveld from the fertile lowveld, which is approx. 1000m/3200ft lower and only reaches altitudes of 150m/500ft to 600m/2000ft. This mountains consist of older rocks (particularly dolomite and quartzite). The Transvaal Drakensberg mountains are also an area of incredible natural beauty; they are described under ▶ Blyde River Canyon.

✶ ✶ Landscape

Gigantic dragon mountains

Originally the name »Drakensberg« only referred to the 180km/110mi-long mountain range in the south in KwaZulu-Natal and Lesotho between Mont-aux-Sources in the north and Sehlabathebe National Park in the south; today this part is called Natal-Drakensberg. This mountain range reaches an elevation of 3377m/11,079ft at **Champagne Castle** and no less than 3482m/11,424ft at **Thabana-Ntlenyana** in Lesotho. Towards the east the mountains drop almost vertically to 1000m/3300ft. The bizarrely shaped hilly zone in front of this cliff, with altitudes between 1800m and 2000m (5900–6600ft) is known as **Little Berg**. The Boer settlers gave the Drakensberg mountains this name because their shape reminded them of the back of a dragon. In the language of the Zulu people the mountain range is called »uKhahlamba«, meaning »wall of the raised spears«, which is equally fitting.

uKhahlamba Drakensberg Park

The area is divided into three parts: the Royal Natal National Park in the north, the central mountain range (Champagne Castle, Cathedral Peak, Giant Castle, Castle Game Reserve) and the southern mountain range (Loteni Nature Reserve, Kamberg Nature Reserve, Mzimkulwana Nature Reserve). The term covering all twelve nature reserves with a total area of almost 2,500 sq km/965 sq mi is **uKhahlamba Drakensberg Park**. The renaming took place after it was awarded the status of a UNESCO World Heritage Site in 2000, after more than 35,000 San rock drawings were discovered in approx. 600 locations.

The magnificent Amphitheatre in the Royal Natal National Park

In the winter months from April to September the precipitation often falls in the form of snow. The driest months are June and July. Even though the nights are cold (temperatures can drop to -20°C/ -4°F!) the sun still often shines during the day and in sheltered valleys daytime temperatures can reach 20°C/68°F and be quite mild. In summer the weather tends to be warm with temperatures ranging from 15°C/59°F to 35°C/95°F; there are almost daily thundershowers; it also hails frequently. The majority of the total annual precipitation of 1000mm/40in to 1700mm/67in falls between January and March. After heavy downpours the rivers and streams swell and often the roads can quickly become difficult to pass. **Climate**

The slopes of the Drakensberg mountains are covered with grass; below about 2000m/6500ft the landscape is interspersed with tussock grasses, sclerophyllous evergreens and proteas. Above 2800m/9200ft low-growing plants such as heather and strawflowers do well. In sheltered valleys there are thick forests with mountain cypress, tree ferns and yellowwood trees. More than 800 different species of flowering plants have been recorded, including 63 kinds of orchid. **Flora**

Numerous caves and rock overhangs that once gave shelter to the San have more than 20,000 rock drawings on their walls, depicting wild animals as well as hunting and fighting scenes (particularly in Giant's Castle Game Reserve). The oldest rock drawings date back 2000 years; the last San in the Drakensberg mountains lived at the end of the 19th century (►Baedeker Special p.90). **San drawings**

There are various accommodation options: either in the places listed here (p.404) or in the more attractive holiday resorts in the mountain landscape. Various camps let their huts; comfortable accommodation can be found in the Thendele Camp, the Giant's Lodge, the Cathedral Peak Hotel or in the Sani Pass Hotel. Most hotels and camps offer an extensive programme, including guided tours, riding trips, car drives and climbing excursions and a lot more. **Accommodation**

▶ VISITING NATAL-DRAKENSBERGE

INFORMATION

KZN Wildlife (▶p.156)
Midmar office: tel. 033 239 1500

Drakensberg Tourism Association
Sunbird Nursery, Bergville 3350
Tel. 036 448 1557
www.drakensberg.kzn.org.za

Southern Drakensberg Publicity
P.O. Box 169, Himeville 3256
Tel./fax 033 702 1158
www.drakensberg-tourism.com

ARRIVAL

The main way to get here is via the N 3, which connects Johannesburg (approx. 400km/250mi) with Durban on the Indian Ocean (approx. 150km/95mi). Roads branch off from the N 3 leading westwards into parts of the mountain landscape. The bases for the northern mountains are ▶Harrismith and Bergville. The central mountain range is reached from Winterton, Estcourt and Mooi River. The southern part can be accessed from ▶ Pietermaritzburg via Underberg.

GUIDES AND MAPS

D. Bristow: *Guide to the Drakensberg*. *Best Walks in the Drakensberg*. Both books are published by Struik (Cape Town).
KZN Wildlife: topographical maps on a scale of 1 : 50,000 with marked hiking trails.

WHERE TO STAY
▶ Mid-range/Luxury
① *Cathedral Peak Hotel*
Tel. 036 488 1888
www.cathedralpeak.co.za
Luxurious complex in a fantastic setting in the central mountain range. It has 90 rooms, several restaurants, three pools, a golf course, etc. as well as a large selection of outdoor activities.

② *Little Switzerland Resort*
Royal Natal National Park
Tel. 036 438 6220, www.lsh.co.za
Reed-covered self-catering houses and chalets with views of the mountains. Activities to choose from are riding, fishing, boat trips, tennis and much more. Near Oliviershook Pass, sign posts at the petrol station on the R 74.

▶ Mid-range
③ *Thendele Camp*
Royal Natal National Park
Tel. 036 438 6310
Wonderful view of the Amphitheatre. 26 cottages and bungalows, some of them with their own kitchen, some with cooks, all with terraces and barbecue sites. It is important to book early, as the camp is very popular. Approx. 50km/30mi west of Bergville.

④ *Sani Pass Hotel*
Sani Pass Road, Himeville
Tel. 033 702 1320
www.sanipasshotel.co.za
Large complex with luxuriously furnished cottages situated at the foot of the pass, the spectacular crossing into Lesotho, in a wonderful mountain landscape. A pool, tennis and riding etc. are on offer as are tours of the pass. The English-style food is rather poor. Somewhat too expensive.

▶ Budget
⑤ *Sandford Park Lodge*
Tel. 036 448 1001
www.sandford.co.za
Farmhouse dating from 1850 with mountain views; antique furniture in the 52 rooms.

Natal-Drakensberg Map

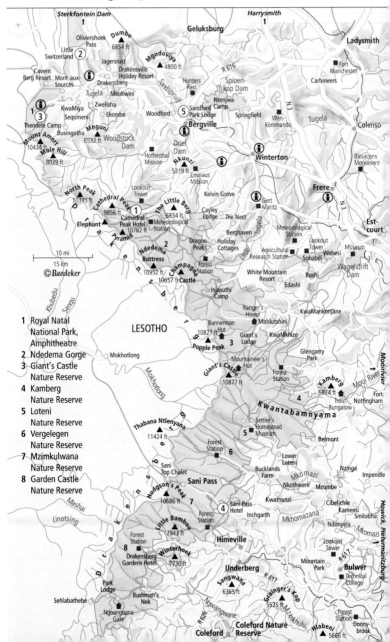

Sterkfontein Dam

Harrysmith

Geluksburg

Ladysmith

Oliviershoek Pass

Dumbe
6854 ft

Little Switzerland (2)

Jagersrust

Mgodoviya
4800 ft

R 616

Fort Manchester

Cavern Berg Resort

Mont-aux-Sources

Drakensville Holiday Resort

Carbineers

Drakensberg

Hunters Rest

Spioen-kop Dam

Tugela

Mkukwini

Sandspruit

Ntenjwa Camp

Springfield

Wen-kommando

N 3

KwaMiya

Zwelisha

Ekombe

Woodford (5)

Sandford Park Lodge

Bergville

Tugela

Colenso

Seqomeni

Thendele Camp

Busingatha

Mnguni
6532 ft

Woodstock Dam

Hoffenthal Mission

Driel Dam

Nkunzi
5319 ft

Emmaus Mission

Winterton

Bloukrans Monument

Mount Amery
1043 ft

Mole Hill
8029 ft

Kelvin Grove

Gert Maritz

Frere

North Peak
10345 ft

Lookout Tower

The Little Berg

Cathedral Peak
9856 ft

Cathedral Peak Hotel
10762 ft

Cayley Lodge

The Nest

Meteorological Station

Est-court

Elephant

Pyramid

Meteorological Station

Berghaven

Lookout Tower

Webesi

Museum

Dragon Peaks

Holiday Cottages

Sobabili

Wagendrift Dam

10 mi

Ndedema Buttress
10952 ft

Champagne Castle
10657 ft

Forest Station

Agricultural Research Station

Boshi

15 km

©Baedeker

White Mountain Resort

Edashi

Injasuthi Camp

Ranger's House

Mahlutshini

KwaMankonjane

Khubedu

Senqu

1 Royal Natal National Park, Amphitheatre

LESOTHO

Bannerman Hut
10877 ft

Popple Peak

3

Giant's Lodge

KwaMkhize

Glengarry Park

2 Ndedema Gorge

3 Giant's Castle Nature Reserve

Mokhotlong

Mountaineer's Hut

Giant's Castle
10877 ft

Forest Station

Kamberg
6874 ft

Trout Bungalow

Fort Nottingham

4 Kamberg Nature Reserve

5 Loteni Nature Reserve

Mokhotlong

Kwantabamnyama

6 Vergelegen Nature Reserve

Thabana Ntlenyana
11424 ft

Settler's Homestead Museum

Belmont

7 Mzimkulwana Nature Reserve

Forest Station
6

Nzinga

Impendle

8 Garden Castle Nature Reserve

Mashai

Sani Top Chalet

Hodgson's Peak
10686 ft

Sani Pass

Lower Loteni

Bucklands Farm

Mkomazi

Nkothweni

Mzumbe

Kwathunzi

Mkhomazana

Cibelichle

Kamensi

Smilobha

Howick, pietermaritzburg

Linotsing

Little Bamboo
7943 ft

Forest Station

(4) Sani Pass Hotel

Inchgarth

Ndonyela

Mkomazi

Lookout Tower

8

Forest Station

Winterhoek
7730 ft

Himeville

Mountain Park

R 617

Bulwer

Drakensberg Gardens Hotel

Underberg

Technical College

Park Lodge

Bushman's Nek

Sangwana
6365 ft

R 617

Grainger's kop
5525 ft

Mkhulu

Forest Station

Sehlabathebe

Ngoangoana Gate

Igwangwane

Rozo

Coleford

Coleford Nature Reserve

Hlabeni
5666 ft

Donny-brook

| Tours on foot | The landscape can be explored on hiking trails of varying degrees of difficulty. Most of them do not require any mountaineering experience. Despite the relatively well-developed infrastructure this is still the edge of civilization, so visitors should be properly prepared when undertaking trips on foot or by car. Visitors wanting to go on longer tours should put their names down in their camp's »walk register«. The best months for longer tours are the autumn months of April and May; in summer many streams turn into raging rivers making them impossible to cross. Some hikes have become so frequented that erosion and rubbish have become a problem and the number of hikers allowed per day has to be restricted. |

Destinations in the Natal-Drakensberg Mountains

| Mont-aux-Sources | The name Mont-aux-Sources refers to a 3282m/10,768ft mountain and a popular holiday resort close by in the northern Natal-Drakensberg mountains. It means »mountain of springs«; many tributaries of the Orange and the Tugela rivers rise here. |

| ✶ ✶ Royal Natal National Park | The Royal Natal National Park with the neighbouring Rugged Glen nature reserve takes up an area of 8800ha/21,750 acres. The magnificent high mountain landscape was put under protection in 1907 and in 1916 declared a national park. The »royal« was added to the name on the occasion of a visit by the British royal family in 1947. The scenic highlight is the mountain face in the south of Royal Natal Park (photograph p.403) known as the **Amphitheatre**. It is 5km/3mi long and in places the rocks drop vertically for more than 500m/1600ft. The 3165m/10,384ft Sentinel borders the rock wall in the west, the Eastern Buttress (3047m/9997ft) in the east. The waters of the Tugela River plunge a total of 948m/3,107ft in several cascades. This makes it **South Africa's highest waterfall** and the world's fourth-highest. The vegetation comprises more than 1000 plant species; visitors can often see black wildebeests, mountain reedbucks, grey rheboks, blesboks, klipspringers and baboons. More than 180 bird species have been documented, including black eagles, bearded vultures, Cape vultures and jackal buzzards. |

Information is available in the visitor centre on the road into the park area (1km/0.6mi beyond the gate, tel. 036 438 6411). There are more than 30 marked hiking trails on which to explore the park. A good trail for a walk is the 4km/2.5mi Otto's Walk. The longest trail with a total of 45km/28mi is the **Mont-aux-Sources Trail**, for which visitors will need to be in good shape. It starts at the Mahai River Camp, follows the valley of the Mahai River upwards past the Witsieshoek Mountain Resort and the car park at the 3165m/10,384ft Sentinel, before it reaches the ridge of the amphitheatre via 30m/100ft chain ladders. The hike to the **Tugela Gorge** is particularly enjoyable (14km/9mi from Thendele Camp); on the way visitors can bathe in the natural rock pools. Later it is necessary to cross the river or clamber over a chain ladder. The payoff is the view of Eastern Buttress and the Tugela Falls.

Around 45km/28mi west of Winterton the **Cathedral Peak Hotel** is beautifully situated in the Mlambonja valley at the edge of the Cathedral Peak State Forest, which is a great place to go hiking and climbing. The hotel complex is surrounded by several peaks, the 3004m/9856ft **Cathedral Peak**, the 2930m/9613ft Bell, the 3006m/9862ft Outer Horn and the 3005m/9859ft Inner Horn. From the hotel a trail leads up Cathedral Peak (10km/6mi, some parts quite demanding and exhausting); the views from the top are stunning. Also recommended, but only with a 4 x 4, is the drive up to **Mike's Pass**, which also has wonderful views. To get here from the hotel, take the Winterton road and turn right after 3km/2mi.

✴ **Cathedral Peak**

Hikers and riders can get to the 5.5km/3.5mi-long Ndedema Gorge via Mike's Pass. The Sebayeni cave alone has around 4000 surviving San rock drawings. The oldest date back to between 970 and 1230, the more recent ones to between 1720 and 1820. Without a guide these rock drawings are incredibly hard to find; information is available in the hotels.

✴ **Ndedema Gorge**

South of Cathedral's Peak rise Cathkin Peak (3181m/10,436ft), which is set somewhat outside the main mountain chain, and Champagne Castle (3377m/11,079ft). There are plenty of trails and climbing routes leading through Monk's Cowl State Forest. The hotels offer further sports and entertainment activities.

✴ **Cathkin Peak**

The 34,600ha/85,500-acre nature reserve is one of the most impressive destinations in the southern Natal-Drakensberg mountains (fastest access from Estcourt or Mooi River). It is located below a 35km/22mi-long basalt cliff with an average elevation of 3000m/9800ft between **Champagne Castle** in the north and the 3315m/10,876ft **Giant's Castle** in the south. The reserve is traversed by the Bushman's River, which has rich fish stocks, and the Little Tugela. The north and south of the reserve in particular have remains of the mountain rainforest. Otherwise the vegetation is mainly grassland. In spring and summer there are also wild flowers here. The reserve was established in 1903 to protect the last herds of the common eland. The

✴ ✴ **Giant's Castle Nature Reserve**

! *Baedeker* TIP

Drakensberg Boys' Choir

The wonderfully situated school in Monk's Cowl with views of Cathkin Peak and Champagne Castle is famous for its boys' choir, which is one of the best in the world. Its repertoire includes everything from classical to African, to jazz and folk. Concerts are held on Wednesdays at 3.30pm during term time (reservations necessary: tel. 036 468 1012; www.dbchoir.co.za). The nearby Dragon Peaks Mountain Resort provides accommodation ranging from a campsite to a comfortable, thatched cottage. On the R 600 approx. 30km/19mi south of Winterton.

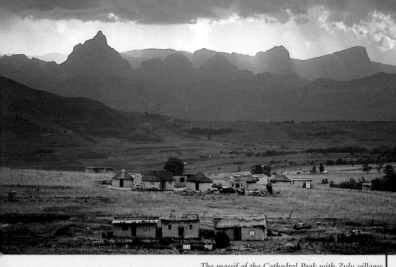

The massif of the Cathedral Peak with Zulu villages

reserve is also home to bushbucks, blesboks, hartebeests, klip-springers and baboons. One of the park's main attractions are the numerous **San rock drawings**. Around 500 have survived in the Main Cave 2km/1mi south of Main Camp (can be accessed via a comfortable path); the museum organizes tours. Battle Cave near Injasuti Camp has 1000 rock drawings.

There are several camps providing accommodation in and at the edge of the reserve: Giant's Camp (► KZN p.156), Injasuti, Mount Lebanon. They are starting points for hikes of varying degree of difficulty. A 30km/19mi round trail goes to the peak of Giant's Castle (3315m/10,876ft). The »Roof of South Africa« has stunning views. Tours on horseback can be booked at KZN Wildlife.

Kamberg Nature Reserve

The 2230ha/5510-acre Kamberg Nature Reserve is located south-east of Giant's Castle at the foot of the Drakensberg mountains (to get here take the N 3, then turn west either in Mooi River or at the height of Nottingham Road). The Mooi River flows through a varied landscape that is home to several species of antelope. It is popular with anglers for its plentiful fish. More than 30 orchid species grow here; their flowering period is between December and March. Accommodation can be found in Kamberg Camp and in Stillerus Camp (both KZN Wildlife) amongst others.

Loteni Nature Reserve

Adjoining the reserve in the south-west is the Mkhomazi State Forest, which is in turn adjoined by the 3984ha/9845-acre Loteni Nature Reserve (accommodation in huts; self-catering). The Loteni River, rich in trout, is a mecca for anglers. The Settlers' Homestead Museum displays agricultural tools, furniture and household objects from the time of colonization by Europeans.

Not far to the south where the Umkomaas River rises at 1500m/4900ft lies the remote and not much visited Vergelegen Nature Reserve (accommodation in huts, self-catering).

Vergelegen Nature Reserve

Mzimkulwana Nature Reserve can be reached via Himeville 14km/9mi to the south-east. The 22,750ha/56,200-acre reserve is home to numerous endangered plants and animals, such as Verreaux's eagles, martial eagles, Cape vultures and side-striped jackals.

Mzimkulwana Nature Reserve

A road lead through the Mzimkulwana Reserve to the 2895m/9498ft Sani Pass. This, the only pass over the Natal-Drakensberg mountains, is **spectacular and sometimes horrendously steep**. The pass, which got its name from the San, is also the border to ►Lesotho (opening times etc. check there; only open to 4 x 4s, motorbikes, mountain bikes and pedestrians). To the north of the pass towers **Thabana Ntlenyana**, at 3482m/11,424ft the highest peak in southern Africa. On the South African side at the foot of the pass the Sani Lodge and the Sani Pass Hotel provide comfortable accommodation, information and tours to the Sani Pass Top Chalet for example (► p.374). The hotel is the starting point for the 68km/42mi **Giant's Cup Hiking Trail** to Bushman's Nek, which is easy walking and considered one of the most beautiful and popular excursions of its kind (five days, accommodation in well-equipped huts, reservations up to nine months in advance at KZN, ►p.156).

✶ ✶
Sani Pass

The base for exploring the southern Natal-Drakensberg mountains is Underberg (population: 1000). Himeville Nature Reserve 6km/4mi further north is a mecca for trout anglers.

Underberg Himeville Nature Reserve

Ndumo · Tembe · Kosi Bay

K 5

Province: KwaZulu-Natal   **Distances:** Durban 470km/290mi

Three nature reserves in South Africa's tropical north-east, on the border with Mozambique, are considered to be amongst the wildest and most beautiful in the country.

The 10,000ha/25,000-acre Ndumo Game Reserve is located on the flood plain of the **Pongola River**, a wetland with tropical and subtropical biotopes. The river channels are lined by thick riparian forests. The more than 200 tree species include huge specimens of marula trees, sycamore figs and fever trees. The 115m/377ft **Ndumo Hill** is covered by an acacia forest. The sometimes swampy forests are inhabited by numerous mammals, including hippopotamuses, rhinoceroses, antelopes, cheetahs and zebras. In addition the reserve is home to many crocodiles, insects, snakes and birds (approx. 400 spe-

Ndumo Game Reserve

Traditional fishing in Kosi Bay: with reed fences and a spear

cies). For many tropical birds of eastern Africa the reserve is their southernmost habitat. The game is hard to spot in the forest so it is best to observe the animals at the rivers or one of the many flood lakes. Accommodation in the rest camp of KZN Wildlife and in the private wilderness camp (reservations: Wilderness Safaris, tel. 011 807 1800, www.wilderness-safaris.com).

Tembe Elephant Park Adjoining the reserve to the east is the Tembe Elephant Park, home to approx. 140 elephants. Visitor numbers are limited, and only 4 x 4s are permitted. Every group is accompanied by a ranger. Tembe Lodge has luxurious tents on platforms. Information at KZN Wildlife, bookings for the lodge tel. 031 267 0144, www.tembe.co.za.

Kosi Bay Nature Reserve A dirt road leaves from Ndumo village first southbound then eastbound to Kosi Bay Reserve approx. 70km/45mi away on the coast of the Indian Ocean. Mangrove marshes and swampy woodlands surround one **fresh-water and several salt-water lakes**. Hippopotamuses, crocodiles and the critically endangered leatherback turtles like it here just as much as the 250 bird species to which this place is home. The sandy and marshy area and the access to Kosi Mouth require an off-road vehicle. Accommodation in the luxurious Kosi Forest Lodge (tel. 011 463 3376, www.zulunet.co.za), Kosi Bay Lodge (tel. 031 266 4172, www.hluhluwe.net)

 NDUMO

INFORMATION
KZN Wildlife, ►p.156

WHEN TO GO
The tropical climate make the months between November and March murderously hot and humid; it is best to come between July and September. Malaria prophylaxis and mosquito control are necessary.

or in Lake Nhlange Camp, which is run by KZN Wildlife. Why not participate in one of the guided tours, such as the 44km/27mi, four-day **Kosi Hiking Bay Trail** (except for tents participants have to bring their own equipment and food). Information and reservations at KZN Wildlife.

Nelspruit

J 4

Province: Mpumalanga
Population: 63,000

Altitude: 671m/2201ft
Distances: Johannesburg 355km/220mi, Barberton 45km/30mi, Sabie 65km/40mi

Nelspruit, the friendly capital of Mpumalanga province, is situated on the Crocodile River in the subtropical lowveld. It is the hub for visits to Kruger National Park and can also be reached by bus, rail and air.

Nelspruit is a significant agricultural centre. The good soils and the temperate climate (warm to hot in summer and pleasantly cool and frost-free in winter) allows the cultivation of tobacco, lychees, mangoes, avocados, papayas, bananas and nuts; in addition a third of South Africa's oranges for export are grown in this region. Livestock farming is becoming more and more important. Nelspruit does not have any particular sights, but its tree-lined streets give it a friendly atmosphere and the surrounding area is also attractive. There is a large selection of guesthouses and restaurants.

Some history

When the railway line of the Eastern Line, which follows the valley of the Crocodile River, was completed in 1892, a railway station was set up on the farm of the Nel family. Soon there were shops, a hotel and a police station here; in 1905 Nelspruit was given municipal status. It is planned to rename it Mbombela.

What to See in and around Nelspruit

★
Lowveld National Botanical Garden

At the northern edge of Nelspruit (take the R 40 to get here) is the 154ha/380-acre botanical garden (open daily 8am–6pm, in winter until 5pm). The Crocodile River is responsible for the impressive **Nelspruit Falls**. A path runs along the course of the river. Only a small part of the garden has been landscaped; the remaining area is covered by 500 of the plant species growing in this region.

★
Sudwala Caves

24km/15mi west of Nelspruit the R 539 turns off from the N 4 towards the north (quite nearby the Crocodile River plummets 12m/39ft into Schoemanskloof at the **Montrose Falls**), which leads to the Sudwala Caves, the oldest in the world. A 600m/650yd section of the

▶ VISITING NELSPRUIT

INFORMATION
Lowveld Tourism Association
Crossing Mall, Louis Trichardt St.
Tel. 013 755 1988
www.lowveldinfo.com

Mpumalanga Tourism (▶p.141)
5km/3mi west on the N 4

TRANSPORT
Kruger Mpumalanga International
Airport 22km/14mi north-east
(car rentals). The Numbi Gate into
the Kruger park is approx. 50km/
30mi away. Baz Bus, Intercape,
Greyhound and Translux buses all
stop in Nelspruit, as does the
Komati Express.

WHERE TO EAT
▶ Moderate
Timbuctoo Restaurant
30 Alie van Bergen St.
White River
(19 km von Nelspruit)
Tel. 013 751 3353
Delicious game dishes, African
ambience.

▶ Inexpensive
Ristorante Italiana
Riverside Mall
Tel. 013 757 0347
In the shopping centre 5km/3mi
north of the town. Large selection of
fish, pasta and pizza. Try the seafood
pasta or the filet mamma with a
brandy and mushroom sauce.

WHERE TO STAY
▶ Budget/Mid-range
Bee Eaters Guest House
P. O. Box 3913
Freidenheim Rd.
Tel./fax 013 755 3225
Unique location outside the town.
3 suites, a pool, friendly
atmosphere.

Shandon Lodge
1 Saturn St.
Tel./fax 013 744 9934
www.shandon.co.za
Pretty little colonial-style house with
a veranda on to the garden. Seven
comfortable non-smoking rooms.

⊙ dripstone caves is accessible (open daily. 8.30am–5pm). Humans already inhabited these caves in prehistoric times; the temperature is a constant 17°C/63°F. Only fit people with a sense of adventure should attempt the six-hour **Crystal Tour**, which leads into a crystal chamber made of aragonite. The tour goes through narrow tunnels, water channels and steep shafts. On the last Saturday of every month, not for children under the age of 13. Registration two months in advance, tel. 013 733 4152. A visit to the caves is also worthwhile for their lush green surroundings. Visitors can get a good impression of

⊙ the vegetation on a walk through **Dinosaur Park** (open daily 8am–5.30pm), which has life-sized replicas of these extinct animals by the famous South African sculptor Jan van der Zyl. Not far away is the **Sudwala's Kraal Complex** with a large arts and crafts market and typical Ndebele, Zulu and Xhosa huts.

From Nelspruit the R 40 goes to Barberton (population: 25,000) 50km/30mi further south. The town experienced a brief boom when gold was found here in the late 19th century. However, by 1888 the boom was over and the gold-seekers focused their attention on the Witwatersrand (► Johannesburg). Some pretty houses still attest to the town's »golden« past; some of them are open to the public. Visitors to the Barberton Museum learn about history, geology, archaeology and the ethnology of religion.

Barberton

The green-blue **Hlumu Hlumu mountains** are a fantastic backdrop to Badplaas, the »bath farm«, a well-known **hot spring**. The complex 75km/47mi south-west of Barberton has bungalows, a campsite and nice pools (www.aventura.co.za) The 35,000ha/85,500-acre **Badplaas Nature Reserve** (the access road turns off from the Barberton road) is home to many antelopes. Many hiking trails and bridleways traverse the park (open all year round, horses for hire).

Badplaas

Oudtshoorn

E 8

Province: Western Cape
Population: 84,000

Altitude: 335m/1099ft
Distances: Cape Town 510km/315 km, George 60km/35mi

Oudtshoorn, the largest town in Little Karoo, is proud of its role as the global centre of ostrich farming. Its classy, calm atmosphere of the 19th century makes this town a good base for excursions into the attractive surrounding area and the Great Karoo.

From the ►Garden Route visitors should definitely take the time to see Oudtshoorn 70km/45mi inland. It became famous around 1900 when ostrich plumes were sent out all around the world. Although these times are over, ostrich farming still allows people to earn a decent living; ostrich leather and meat are coveted and the antistatic feathers are used by the computer industry. Oudtshoorn is located in a fertile valley (cultivation of tobacco, fruit, vegetables and grains) surrounded by the chains of the Groot Swartberge and the Outeniqua Mountains.

The small town was founded in 1847 and experienced a great boom during the 1870s when ostrich feathers became fashionable in Europe. Between 1880 and 1915 up to 750,000 ostriches were kept in Oudtshoorn. They flourished in the warm dry climate and brought the »feather barons« great wealth. A number of attractive **ostrich palaces** still remind visitors of those days. After the First World War broke out the feathers were no longer en vogue and demand

History

● VISITING OUDTSHOORN

INFORMATION

Tourism Bureau
Baron van Rheede Street
Tel. 044 279 2532
www.oudtshoorn.com

WHERE TO EAT

► **Moderate**

Jemima's
94 Baron van Reede Street
Tel. 044 272 0808
One of the best restaurants in the
country, but still has a cosy family
feel. Home-cooked South African fare
with fresh produce; excellent saddle of
lamb, and curries.

► **Inexpensive/Moderate**

The Godfather
61 Voortrekker Road
Tel. 044 272 5404
Good pasta and pizza from the wood
stove, some of the dishes prepared in
interesting South African or Oudtshoorn style (e.g. tagliatelle with
ostrich fillet, smoked mussels and
bacon in sherry cream).

WHERE TO STAY

► **Mid-range**

Queen's Hotel
Baron van Reede Street
Tel. 044 272 2101

www.queenshotel.co.za
Historic hotel in the town centre,
tastefully renovated. 60 rooms, nice
garden with a pool, good restaurant.

Oulap Country House
15km/9mi from De Rust (signposted)
Tel. 044 241 2250
oulap@mweb.co.za
One of the finest guesthouses in the
country. The owner is Jans Rauten-
bach, a film-maker and patron of the
South African art scene. Artists styled
the house in the middle of the
Swartberg mountains: Gordon Voster
did the dining room, André Brink the
guest bathroom, Breyten Breytenbach
and Nadine Gordimer each did a
room, and so on. The master of the
house is a fund of fascinating stories.
Dinner in the house.

► **Budget/Mid-range**

Oakdene Guest House
99 Baron van Reede Street
Tel. 044 272 3018
www.oakdene.co.za
One of the oldest houses in Oudtshoorn (national monument), a pretty
mix of Karoo and Victorian architecture. Six nice, comfortable rooms.

collapsed; however, the realization that the nutritious meat had an
excellent taste and the great demand for ostrich leather by the fash-
ion industry have made farming of *Struthio camelus* worthwhile
again.

**Ostrich
cuisine** During a blind taste test conducted by Slow Food the ostrich fillet
won out over top-class roast beef. »De Fijne Keuken« (114 Baron
van Reede Street, tel. 044 272 6403) is known for ostrich meat in all
of its varieties; lamb and other regional delicacies are also delicious.

What to See in Oudtshoorn

The C. P. Nel Museum on the main road is housed in a sandstone building of 1907 with a striking belfry. The collections range from San culture to fashionable items of clothing and utility objects made of ostrich feathers (open Mon–Sat 9am–5pm). The **Le Roux Town-house** of 1908 is also part of the museum; it is one of the magnificent »ostrich palaces« (146 High Street); in summer the garden is a fine place to enjoy a cup of tea.

C. P. Nel Museum

A number of ostrich farms offer visitor programmes lasting one to two hours. Visitors can see the breeding facilities, test the hardness of the eggshells are and can watch ostrich chicks hatch. A further, not exactly tasteful attraction is a ride on the back of an ostrich. Programmes like this are offered by Highgate Ostrich Show Farm and Safari Show Farm amongst others, which are located near the R 328 approx. 10km/6mi south-west of the town as well as by Cango Ostrich Farm between Oudtshoorn and the Cango Caves (see below).

★
Ostrich farms

This wildlife ranch is located at the edge of town on the R 328 heading towards the Cango Caves. Crocodiles, snakes, different species of wild-cat, ponies and hippopotamuses are kept here. Petting a cheetah costs extra (open daily from 9am to sunset).

Cango Wildlife Ranch

Around Oudtshoorn

These impressive, though commercialized **dripstone caves** lie 39km/ 24mi north of Oudtshoorn at the foot of the Groot Swartberg mountains. Tours daily on the hour 9am–4pm; since they are very busy during the holidays it is best to come in the morning. There are dif-

★
Cango Caves

An ostrich farm in Oudtshoorn

AN ANIMAL OF SUPERLATIVES

At the centre of Oudtshoorn an oversized ostrich egg is a testament to the source of the local wealth. Initially a supplier of sought-after feathers, the ostrich has embarked on a new career with its meat and leather.

Initially the ostrich, called »mhou« in Africa (its scientific name is *Struthio camelus*), was widespread in Africa and the Middle East. Today only a few wild ostriches are left in the hot and arid savannas south of the Sahara. **Ostrich breeding** started in 1860, after the incubator for ostrich eggs was invented. Since the 16th century the ostrich had been so heavily persecuted for its **sought-after feathers** that it was threatened with extinction. Until the end of the First World War South African farmers earned a fortune with ostrich feathers, as the villas of the »feather barons« in Oudtshoorn testify. After the war they were no longer en vogue, but following decades of stagnation the business with these huge birds has been revitalized. Although feathers continue to bring in little money, the meat is becoming ever more popular. One ostrich, which is ready for slaughter at the age of 14 months, delivers around 15kg/33lb of **high-quality steak meat**. In colour, structure and taste it resembles top-quality beef and can also be prepared in the same way, but it has the advantages of poultry: it is very lean (less than 1% fat), and low in cholesterol and calories, but still tender and tasty. During a blind tasting that **Slow Food** conducted in Italy in 1997, the ostrich meat beat roast beef! The skin with its characteristic texture is made into expensive leather jackets, belts, handbags and more.

High achievers

An ostrich can grow up to 3m/10ft tall, weigh up to 160kg/350lb and live for 40 years. When it sprints it can reach a speed of 80kmh/50mph, which makes the mhou, the »great runner«, the fastest animal on two legs. Its stride when running can reach a length of 4m/13ft. On the other hand it cannot fly. An ostrich egg is 16cm/6in long with an approximate weight of 1.6kg/3.5lb; the shell is 2 mm thick and its contents corresponds to **two dozen chicken eggs**. When the ostrich chicks hatch they weigh more than 1kg/2lb. The male ostrich has a foldout penis (in most bird species the males as well as the females, like the female ostriches, only have what are known as cloacas.)

Surprising birds with a large number of uses

Ostriches are not aggressive, except when they feel threatened: first an intruder will hear a kind of howling, not unlike that of a lion. If that has no effect, the ostrich will show its tae kwon do skills: it kicks with one of its feet, which can break a opponent's bones.

Strange family life

There is room for between 21 and 25 eggs under the brooding bird. The male and only his favourite female brood for 45 to 46 days. Sometimes a nest can contain 30 eggs or more; during cold nights the eggs at the edge die. Lions, hyenas and vultures like to get their paws and claws on such a protein-rich meal. Now and then a herd of buffalo will trample a nest of eggs. Statistically only 0.9 chicks per nest survive, and up to six hens may have contributed eggs to that nest. This probably explains the ostriches' **interesting partnerships**. During the breeding season the male has two to four females besides his main female (there is a surplus of females). He inseminates all of them, and they all lay up to six eggs in a single nest. However, the females also stray and lay further eggs in neighbours' nests. This means that if disaster strikes the main nest, a few eggs in neighbouring nests may still survive. The ostrich daddy is a **very caring father**. He spreads his wings like a parasol over the chicks. The ostrich mother has nothing to do with raising the chicks: once the young have hatched she is chased away by the father. He does not need to feed the chicks, because just one day after hatching they can peck their own seeds and insects. What is important is that they are led to places where there is food and that they are protected from enemies. Here too the protector instinct does not limit itself to the father's own genes. If an ostrich with its young comes across another male with his chicks, he will try to chase away the other male and adopt his young. Fathers with one hundred chicks have been witnessed.

Another alternative is for several fathers to join together with their chicks to form a **crèche**. And what about the popular myth that an ostrich will stick its head in the sand at the sight of danger? In reality the ostrich wants to protect its nest. In order to do that it presses its body flat on to the nest, spreads its wings and presses its long neck and its head on to the ground in order to look like a dead branch. It would be more accurate to use the expression »sticking one's head in the sand« to describe the behaviour of a person who makes a personal effort to protect others.

ferent tours lasting 30 minutes, 1 hour or 90 minutes (participants on this last tour need to be quite thin because it involves crawling through 45cm/18in tunnels), which allow visitors to explore 2km/1.5mi of the cave system. In past centuries the caves, which are a constant 18°C/65°F, were inhabited by San. Hardly anything can still be recognized from their drawings. The 70m/230ft-long, 35m/115ft-wide and 17m/56ft-high **Van Zyl's Hall** was named after the man who was the first to advance into the darkness in 1780. Further caves (Cango II–IV) that are more than 2.5km/1.5mi long were found in 1972. In order not to destroy their ecosystem they are only open to scientists.

★★
Swartberg Pass

Beyond the Cango Caves the R 328 climbs to the 1568m/5144ft Swartberg Pass. The Swartberg mountains, which form the border between the Little Karoo and the Great Karoo, have a length of more than 200km/125mi and reach elevations of up to 2326m/7631ft. Of the three pass roads over the mountain range the Swartberg Pass (constructed between 1881 and 1888) is the most spectacular. The road is not asphalted throughout, but can be navigated with a regular passenger car in dry weather; however, it is very steep with tight blind bends. Magnificent views are guaranteed and the vegetation with its many proteas is no less fascinating.

Die Hel

Approx. 3km/2mi beyond the top of the pass a dirt road branches off to »The Hell« (Gamkaskloof), a narrow, fertile valley that was inhabited by descendants of Boers who had settled here around 1840. Until 1962 it could only be reached on donkey tracks and in 1991 the last »hell-dweller« left this remote place. It takes at least 90 minutes to complete the 60km/35mi drive to Die Hel.

Prince Albert

A good 70km/45mi from Oudtshoorn the road reaches the town of Prince Albert (population: 9000), founded in 1762 and later named after **Queen Victoria's husband**. The mountain streams of the surrounding area supply the fruit plantations around the town with water. January is the harvest month for peaches, and in March the grapes are picked. The museum in Church Street was once the residence of the Haak family and now houses a Bible collection, furniture, household objects, weapons as well as old vehicles and tools.

Baedeker TIP

In Abraham's Bosom

The authentic ambience of Bergkant Lodge matches the magical Victorian atmosphere in Prince Albert. The lovingly restored Cape Dutch mission station has huge rooms and a garden with a pool. 5 Church Street, tel. 023 5411 088, www.princealbert.org.za.

Meiringspoort is the lowest (716m/2349ft) and quickest of the three passes over the Swartberg mountains. The N 12, which connects Oudtshoorn with ► Beaufort West, runs parallel to a 20km/12mi gorge with sandstone fold formations.

✳ Paarl

Province: Western Cape
Population: 88,000

Altitude: 145m/476ft
Distances: Cape Town 60km/35mi

This beautifully situated, pretty little town in Cape Town's hinterland is known all around the world as the nucleus and centre of South African viticulture.

Paarl is located in a wide, fertile valley on the banks of Berg River. The 729m/2392ft Paarl Mountain towers above it. It was given its name (»pearl«) from three massive granite rocks above the town that shine like pearls after rain. Fruit and vegetables are cultivated in the surrounding area and processed in the canning factories. Paarl's six vineyards, of which the best-known is probably Nederburg, and ten winemakers' cooperatives make it one of the most important centres of South African wine industry. This is also where the KWV wine cooperative, founded in 1918 under the name of **Kooperatieve Wijnbouwers Vereniging van Zuid-Africa** has its headquarters.

History

The first Europeans settled here as early as 1687. They were soon followed by Huguenots fleeing from France, who introduced wine-growing. Officially the town was founded in 1717, which makes it

Fantastic view from the terrace of the Grande Roche Hotel

▶ VISITING PAARL

INFORMATION
Tourist Office
216 Main St. (entrance on Auret St.)
Tel. 021 872 3829
www.paarlonline.com

Paarl Wine Route
Tel. 021 872 3841
www.paarlwine.co.za

WHERE TO EAT
▶ Moderate
Laborie Restaurant
Taillefert Street, tel. 021 807 3095
www.kwv-international.com
Stylish restaurant in a Cape Dutch
building, traditional South African
dishes such as waterblommetjiebredie
and Mediterranean specialities. Open
10am–5pm, reservations required for
the evenings.

Bosman's in the Grande Roche Hotel

Kontreihuis
193 Main Road, tel. 021 872 2808
Charming country house restaurant.
In summer diners can eat outside and
on cooler days there are cosy nooks
near the fireplace. Traditional dishes
such as boerewors (farmer's sausage)
and ox tongue in a green pepper sauce
on polenta.

▶ Inexpensive
Kostinrichting
19 Pastorie Ave., tel. 021 871 1353
Nice café in a Victorian building
between the museums.

WHERE TO STAY
▶ Luxury
Grande Roche Hotel
Tel. 021 863 2727, closed June–Aug.
www.granderoche.com
Exclusive five-star hotel, romantic
location at Paarl Rock Mountain.
Besides the Manor House there are
two historic buildings with 35 suites;
the 300-year-old chapel is popular for
weddings. »Bosman's« is one of the
country's finest restaurants. Wonderful view of the vineyards.

▶ Mid-range/Luxury
Roggeland Country House
Dal Josaphat Valley, tel. 021 868 2501
www.roggeland.co.za
Comfortable guesthouse, run in a
personal, Cape Dutch atmosphere.
Excellent lunch and dinner menus.
Near the R 303 towards Wellington.

Palmiet Valley
Tel. 021 862 7741, www.palmiet.co.za
Nice, small place to stay east of the
town in the manor house of an old
vineyard, with a garden and pool
(photograph p.95).

▶ Mid-range
Goedemoed Country Inn
Cecilia Street, tel. 021 863 1102
www.goedemoed.com
This is another attractive Cape Dutch
house on a vineyard, in a beautiful
setting; luxurious but still quite inexpensive. Part of the Best Western hotel
chain.

one of the oldest European settlements in Cape Town's hinterland. At that time **Afrikaans**, the second official language alongside English, was being written down for the first time, and in 1876 the first Afrikaans newspaper, *Die Patriot*, was printed in Paarl.

What to See in Paarl

The town's oldest street, the oak-lined Main Street, was built in 1720 and is around 11km/7mi long. It has a number of historical buildings. The **Strooidakkerk** (»straw roof church«) built in 1805 is one of the oldest churches still in use in South Africa. The pastor's house from 1787 (Oude Pastorie) houses a **museum of cultural history** (303 Main Street; open Mon–Fri 10am–5pm, Sat 10am–noon). It mainly exhibits Cape Dutch antiques and textiles of French-Huguenot origin.

Main Street

Next door in the Gidoen Malherbe House is the **Afrikaans Language Museum**. It was here that the »Genootskap van Regte Afrikaners« was founded in 1875 and the first Afrikaans newspaper *Die Patriot* was founded one year later. In the museum (open Mon–Fri 9am–1pm, 2–5pm) the development of the language is explained.

Afrikaans Language Museum

The Kooperatieve Wijnbouwers Vereniging van Zuid-Afrika is South Africa's most important winery (►Baedeker Special p.132). The large

KWV

The Cathedral Cellar of KWV

> ! *Baedeker* TIP

Bird's-eye view

A spectacular way to enjoy the beautiful land-scape around Paarl is from a hot air balloon. The Wineland Ballooning company specializes in trips early in the morning at 5am, after which a champagne breakfast awaits in the Grande Roche Hotel. From November to April, tel. 021 863 3192, 64 Main Street.

Cape Dutch-style cellar buildings with the **five largest wine barrels in the world** (no longer used) are located in Kohler Street. Wine tasting daily 9am–4.30pm, guided tours Mon–Sat 10am, 10.30am and 2.15pm (English), information at www.kwv-international.com (under »Wine Emporium«), tel. 021 807 3007. Taillefert Street is the site of the wonderful **Laborie winery**, KWV's »gem«; why not sample some wine here in the Cape Dutch buildings surrounded by roses (daily 9am–5pm, May–Sept, closed Sundays); the food here is both excellent and inexpensive. There is also a smart guesthouse.

Around Paarl

Paarl Wine Route

A signposted wine route leads to a number of vineyards, some of them famous, such as Nederburg, Rheboksklof, Fairview and Landskroon (information is available in the office of the wine route, address the same as the tourist office). Wine tasting takes place at fixed times or by arrangement. The adjoining shops sell wine and other delicacies for enjoyable picnics.

Afrikaans Taal Monument ⏲

At Paarl Mountain west of the town centre (to get here take the Jan Philips Mountain Drive) is the 57m/187ft **Afrikaans Language Monument**, which can be seen from far away (open daily 9am–5pm). The design was provided by the architect Jan van Wyk as well as the poets C. J. Langenhoven and N. P. van Wyk Louw. The monument, which was dedicated in 1975, is supposed to symbolize the different influences of Africa, the Netherlands and England in the creation of the Afrikaans language, which caused to some controversy. There is a fine panorama from the café.

Paarl Mountain Nature Reserve

A visit to the Afrikaanse Taal Monument can be combined with a walk in the 2000ha/5000-acre Paarl Mountain Nature Reserve. There are good views from the 649m/2129ft **Britannia Rock**. The small adjoining **Meulwater Wild Flower Reserve**, which is an impressive sight on the mountain slopes, is home to around 200 native plant species. The flowers are absolutely stunning in late spring.

★ **Nederburg**

The large and well-known vineyard of Nederburg is 7km/4.5mi east of Paarl at the edge of the small district municipality of Drakenstein. In the month of March it is the scene of an important social event: the **auction of top-class South African wines by Sotheby's**. The tradition of viticulture in this region goes back the German immigrant

The manor house of the Nederburg estate

Philip Wolvaart, who acquired the land in 1792. Around 1800 the Cape Dutch-style manor house was built. Wine tasting Mon–Fri 8.30am–5pm, Sat 9am–1pm; it is necessary to book in advance for a tour of the vineyard and the winery (www.nederburg.co.za, tel. 021 862 3104). In the Paarl Rock Brandy Cellar visitors can enjoy a demonstration of how brandy is produced (tours tel. 021 862 6159).

Wellington

Wellington (population: 26,000) is located approx. 20km/12mi north of Paarl at the foot of Bain's Kloof; with its fruit plantations it is the South African centre of the **production of dried fruit**. Along the **Wellington wine route** several good wineries offer wine tasting (BoVlei, Onverwacht, Wamakersvallei, Wellington Wynboere). Huguenots settled here in 1688. They called the area »Limiet Vallei« (»border valley«). In 1840 the town was given its modern name in honour of the Duke of Wellington. The **Wellington Museum** is dedicated to the history of the town and the valley. The Huguenot University College has an excellent collection of Egyptian artefacts on display. The Victoria Jubilee Park is also pleasant; the Old Blockhouse, a national monument, was built during the Boer War.

Bain's Kloof Pass

The drive along the R 303 towards Ceres is quite wonderful. It crosses the 595m/1952ft Bain's Kloof Pass. The 30km/20mi road was built in 1853 and is still considered to be a masterpiece amongst the passes of South Africa. It offers a fantastic view of Paarl, Wellington and Swartland.

Phalaborwa

J 3

Province: Limpopo
Population: 11,000

Altitude: 445m/1460ft
Distances: Johannesburg 710km/440mi,
Polokwane 210km/130mi

Phalaborwa, a modern mining town, is the gateway to the central part of the ▶ Kruger National Park. When the camps within the park are booked out, which is increasingly the case in the high season, visitors can still set up base here.

The average maximum temperature in summer is 38°C/100°F and together with approx. 460mm/18in of precipitation annually this makes Phalaborwa a real garden town. It is the trading and administration centre of a mining area with huge phosphate, copper and iron deposits; gold mining also takes place here. 2 billion years ago magma was pushed to the earth's surface, which is why this place is so rich in natural resources. They were already being used in prehistoric times, as an excavation in the Kruger National Park confirmed.

The town
The wide streets are lined by trees and gardens, but that is just one side of the story; the mines on the edge of town resemble a lunar landscape. An artificial crater, which is larger than Kimberley's Big Hole with its 2km/1.5mi diameter, reaches far below sea level. One of the by-products of copper mining is sulphur, which gives the soil a yellowish hue.

Hans Merensky Golf Course
The golf club is legendary for its unofficial members, such as monkeys that steal the balls and warthogs that ambush the golfers on the course. The club has some luxurious chalets at pleasant prices and an excellent restaurant. Tel. 015 781 3931, www.hansmerensky.com.

 VISITING PHALABORWA

INFORMATION
Phalaborwa Tourism Association
Wildevy St. (by the Impala Inn)
Tel. 015 781 6770
www.phalaborwa.co.za

TRANSPORT
The Kruger Park Gateway Airport (2km/1mi) has planes arriving from Johannesburg. The gate to the Kruger National Park is 3km/2mi east of the town.

WHERE TO STAY

▶ **Mid-range**
Steyn's Cottage
67 Bosvlier Street, tel. 015 781 0836
Very pretty, award-winning guesthouse in Victorian style with a garden; the good La Werna restaurant is next door, which is only 1km/1,100yd from the entrance to the national park. On offer are night trips and river safaris, to name just two of the choices.

Pietermaritzburg

Province: KwaZulu-Natal
Population: 133,000

Altitude: 613m/2011ft
Distances: Johannesburg 510km/315mi, Durban 80km/50mi

Old England in Africa: Pietermaritzburg was once the main town of the colony of Natal. With its Victorian brick buildings it is reminiscent of a British provincial town. However, it also has a large Indian community, which throws some Asian colour into the mix.

»Maritzburg« is located in a fertile landscape. It is the capital of Kwa-Zulu-Natal province, the seat of the Supreme Court and the **University of Natal** as well as a significant centre of industry and trade. It has been dubbed »City of Flowers«; numerous great jacaranda trees, parks and gardens shape the look of the city. In addition it boasts the **best-preserved Victorian city centre in South Africa** and is considered the centre of British conventions: even very conservative English people call it »more British than the United Kingdom«.

The city hall of Pietermaritzburg

Pietermaritzburg was founded in 1838 after the Battle of Blood River in which the Boers defeated the Zulus. It was named after the leader of the Voortrekkers, Pieter Mauritz Retief; only in 1938, after the »u« in »Mauritz« had disappeared, was it decided that the name should also honour another Boer leader, Gerrit Maritz. When the republic was founded in 1839, Pietermaritzburg became the **capital of Natal**. After the British had annexed the republic, they relocated their administration to Pietermaritzburg and built Fort Napier. The town became the capital of the British Colony of Natal and in 1910 it became the seat of government of the province of Natal. In 1839 a young lawyer from India, **Mohandas Karamchand Gandhi**, was thrown out of a train here because he was not white; the consequences of this event shaped world history (►Famous People).

Pietermaritzburg Map

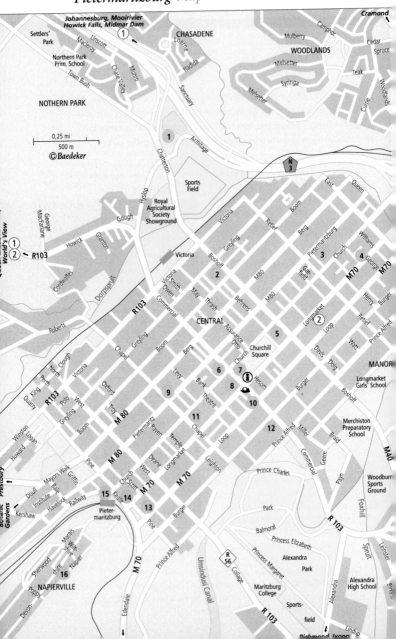

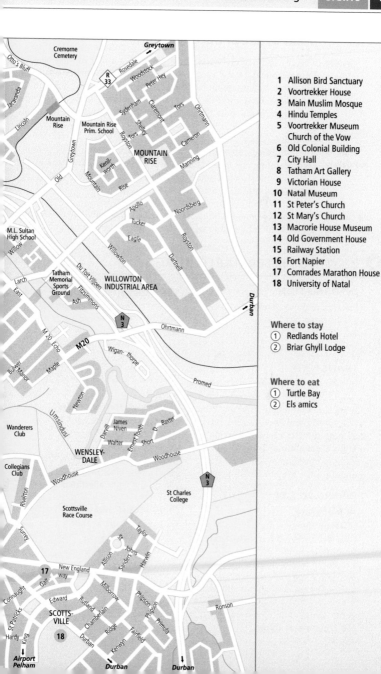

1   Allison Bird Sanctuary
2   Voortrekker House
3   Main Muslim Mosque
4   Hindu Temples
5   Voortrekker Museum
     Church of the Vow
6   Old Colonial Building
7   City Hall
8   Tatham Art Gallery
9   Victorian House
10   Natal Museum
11   St Peter's Church
12   St Mary's Church
13   Macrorie House Museum
14   Old Government House
15   Railway Station
16   Fort Napier
17   Comrades Marathon House
18   University of Natal

Where to stay
①   Redlands Hotel
②   Briar Ghyll Lodge

Where to eat
①   Turtle Bay
②   Els amics

What to See in the City Centre

City hall The city hall makes a good starting point for a tour of Pietermaritzburg (Publicity House is next door, it houses the tourism office and the stylish bar/restaurant Da Vinci's). The city hall, a national monument with its 47m/154ft belfry and magnificent lead crystal windows, is thought to be the largest brick building south of the equator.

Tatham Art Gallery The art gallery opposite the city hall (open Tue–Sun 10am–6pm) owns paintings by Degas, Corot, Sisley and Sickert, drawings by Picasso, Braque, Chagall and Moore and an extensive, interesting collection of South African art.

Old Colonial Building The Old Colonial Building (1899) west of Churchill Square is a real eye-catcher. It housed some of Natal's colonial government offices.

► **VISITING PIETERMARITZBURG**

INFORMATION

Pietermaritzburg Tourism
177 Commercial Road
Tel. 033 345 1348
www.pmbtourism.co.za

TRANSPORT

Airfield 6km/4mi south-east, connection to Johannesburg. Durban airport is approx. 45 minutes' drive away. Baz Bus, Greyhound and Translux buses all stop in Pietermaritzburg, as do the Trans Natal and the Trans Oranje. Visitors travelling by rail should organize a pick-up.

WHERE TO EAT
► **Moderate**
① *Turtle Bay*
Cascades Centre, Mc Carthy Drive
Montrose, tel. 033 3471555
Excellent cuisine, ranging from Cape Malay to Cape provincial, good value for money and a pleasant ambience.

② *Els Amics*
380 Longmarket Street
Tel. 033 345 6524

This restaurant in a Victorian building serves tasty Catalan cuisine (particularly fish) as well as more exotic fare such as warthog meat. The daily specials always include a curry.

WHERE TO STAY
► **Mid-range**
① *Redlands Hotel & Lodge*
1 George McFarlane Lane
Wembley
Tel. 0331 943 333
Modern, luxurious hotel with antique furnishings, quiet location. Eight rooms and eight apartments.

② *Briar Ghyll Lodge*
George MacFarlane Lane
Tel. 033 345 2514
Fax 033 342 9796
www.bglodge.co.za
There are eight tastefully and individually decorated suites in this Victorian homestead dating from 1865. The house is beautifully situated in a park and still belongs to the family that built it.

The Natal Museum dating from 1905 (Loop Street, open Mon–Sat 9am–4.30pm, Sat 10am–4pm, Sun 11am–3pm) is one of South Africa's five national museums. The exhibitions feature various African animals, palaeontological and geological treasures as well as objects from different regions of Africa; the room on **the history of Natal** contains historical documents. A reconstructed Victorian street with houses and shops can also be seen.

★
Natal Museum

Loop Street runs south-west to the elegant **Macrorie House** built in 1862. Bishop William Macrorie lived here from 1869 to 1891 and set up a tiny chapel. Today furniture and other objects from Victorian times are on display (open Mon 11am–4pm, Tue–Fri 9am–1pm). The neighbouring **Old Government House** from 1860, the former residence of the governors of Natal, is also an impressive building. The station, a Victorian brick building, is at one end of Church Street, a pedestrian zone with many shops, including a famous book-shop. Church Street leads back to Churchill Square. The alleyways between Church Street and Longmarket Street have lots of atmosphere.

Loop Street

🕒

Church Street

North-east of Churchill Square the Voortrekker Museum (open Mon–Fri 9am–4pm, Sat 9am–1pm) in the **Church of the Vow** is interesting. The Church of the Vow was built by the Boers in 1841 in fulfilment of a promise after their victory over the Zulus at Blood River. The exhibition features items from the history of the Voortrekkers and a carved seat belonging to the Zulu king Dingane. The

Voortrekker Museum

The Tatham Gallery was the seat of the supreme court from 1906 to 1983.

museum also has on display exhibits of Zulu culture and relating to **Louis Napoleon**, the last Bonaparte, who was killed in the Anglo-Zulu War in 1879. The modern Memorial Church with the vow of the Boers and the reconstructed reed-covered house of **Andries Pretorius**, the commander at the Battle of Blood River, are also part of the complex. The statues in the courtyard commemorate Pieter Retief and Gerrit Maritz, the men who gave the city its name.

Voortrekker House ⏲
Around 600m/650yd further north-west (Boom Street 333) is the city's **oldest two-storey building**; it was built in 1847 and features old furniture and fine ceilings made of yellowwood (open Mon–Fri 9am–4pm, Sat 8am–12.30pm).

What to See outside the City Centre

Main Mosque Hindu Temples
The mosque north of the city centre (Church Street) is open daily to the public 9am–1pm and 1.30–5pm. The two Hindu temples east of the mosque (Longmarket Street), Sri Siva Soobramoniar and Mariammen, are the **religious centres of the Indian community**. Every year on Good Friday a festival with fireworks takes place here.

Alexandra Park
Adjoining the city centre to the south is the Alexandra Park with a fine music pavilion from 1890. The **Art in the Park** event in May each year is a platform for South African artists to display their work, and on the first Sunday of every month a flea market takes place here.

In KwaZulu-Natal the fields are still tilled with oxen

In a Victorian house in the district of Scottsville visitors can learn about the history of South African marathon running. It is the seat of the Comrades Marathon Association, which organizes the **Comrades Marathon** between Pietermaritzburg and Durban every year in June (89km/55mi, www.comrades.com).

Comrades Marathon House

This botanical garden about 2km/1mi south-west of the city centre (Mayor's Walk) founded in 1870 has plants from the native subtropical vegetation and from all around the world. The **Zulu Muti Garden** is interesting. It has a beehive hut of a sangoma (healer); here visitors can find out about traditional medicinal plants. Courses for experts are also held. There is a tea-room at the lake.

KwaZulu-Natal Botanical Gardens

Around Pietermaritzburg

The park 8km/5mi north of the city (open in summer 5am–7pm, otherwise 6am–6pm) has lavish vegetation with aloes and proteas as well as pretty picnic sites. **KwaZulu Natal Wildlife** has its headquarters (information centre, ►p.156) in the park.

Queen Elizabeth Park

This viewpoint can be reached on the old Howick road (8km/5mi). From the top (1083m/3553ft) there is a great view of the city. The remains of the old **Voortrekker road** that winds up the hill can still be made out.

★ World's View

The impressive **Howick Falls** near the town of the same name 25km/16mi north of Pietermaritzburg are, with a drop of almost 100m/330ft, the largest attraction in the **Umgeni Valley Nature Reserve**. In addition visitors can see more than 200 bird species, giraffes, zebras, wildebeests and numerous antelope species. Hiking trails run along the river; accommodation is available.

West of Howick is the 2844ha/7028-acre Midmar Nature Reserve in the Inhluanza Hills (always open). The **Midmar Dam** is a popular destination for water-sports enthusiasts and anglers. In addition visitors can watch rhinoceroses, zebras, wildebeests, antelopes and waterfowl and go riding, hiking and swimming; there are campsites and a restaurant. Accommodation in chalets and huts. Not far away is the **Midmar Historical Village** with relics of the days of the pioneers, a Zulu village and steam engines.

> ! **Baedeker TIP**
>
> ### Pickled Pig
>
> The N 3 leads from Durban through the midlands, open country of rolling hills with wheat fields. The German influence in this region is evident in the fact that beer is brewed here in line with the German purity law. There is a beer route taking in, for example, the Wartburger Hof brewery in the German village of Wartburg approx. 45km/28mi north-east of Pietermaritzburg and the Nottingham Road Brewery in the town of the same name (30km/19mi north-west of Howick). This is the home of the Pickled Pig, a powerful brew with 5.5% alcohol. More information under www.beer.kzn.org.za.

✶ Pilgrim's Rest

J 4

Province: Mpumalanga
Population: 1600

Altitude: 1255m/4117ft
Distances: Lydenburg 55km/35mi,
Nelspruit 90km/55mi

The time of the gold rush comes alive in Pilgrim's Rest. Gold was prospected between 1873 and 1972 close to this small town, which now houses a much-visited open air museum.

Do not miss the detour to Pilgrim's Rest on the way to the Transvaal Drakensberg mountains in Mpumalanga province (► Blyde River Canyon). The buildings in this small town situated at the foot of 2115m/6939ft Mauchberg are all listed; the town has an air of the old gold-digger »romance«. During the day and particularly during the weekends the town is populated by bus-loads of tourists.

History

Alec Patterson and William Trafford found gold in Pilgrim's Creek in 1873, and it was not long before many adventurers in search of fortunes settled here. Bit by bit companies bought up the prospectors' mining rights, and finally the Transvaal Gold Mining Estate was founded. Pilgrim's Rest developed into a town with its own church, school and daily newspaper. Mining was discontinued only in 1972.

✶
Open-air museum

The town and the mining company was bought and restored by the provincial administration. The gold-mining town has originally furnished homes and shops, the Royal Hotel (the hotel bar contains the remains of a church pew from Lourenço Marques, now Maputo in Mozambique), the bank and the printing press of the »Pilgrim's Rest & Sabie News«. Many of the houses are open to the public, while others can only be admired from the outside. The tourist office on the main road provides maps (open daily 9am–12.45pm, 1.15–4.30pm). These are also the opening times of most of the museums in the town.

 ► VISITING PILGRIM'S REST

INFORMATION
Tourism Information
Main Street
Tel. 013 768 1060

WHERE TO STAY
► **Mid-range**
The Royal Hotel
Tel. 013 768 1100

www.saftour.co.za/royal
A little bit of gold-digger romance can be felt in this hotel built in 1883; it is a pretty building full of character: wood and iron decor adorns the Victorian-style former mining huts. Hearty stews are served on the veranda.

The general store in a former gold-miners' village

Around Pilgrim's Rest

A good 10km/6mi west of Pilgrim's Rest a road branches off from the R 533 southbound to Mount Sheba Nature Reserve. After a further 10km/6mi the road reaches the Mount Sheba Hotel in the 1500ha/3700 acre nature reserve that surrounds the 1958m/6424ft Mount Sheba. Hiking trails run through the forested mountain landscape. Besides the flora the nature reserve boasts impressive waterfalls and beautiful views.

Mount Sheba Nature Reserve

One of the highlights of a trip to South Africa is a drive through ► Blyde River Canyon north-east of Pilgrim's Rest. On the way to ►Sabie the road passes the Mac Mac Falls, which definitely warrant a stop.

Blyde River Mac Mac Falls

★ Plettenberg Bay

E 9

Province: Western Cape
Population: 10,000

Altitude: 73m/240ft
Distances: Mossel Bay 145km/90mi,
Port Elizabeth 210km/130mi

Its beautiful coast with its long sandy beaches and crystal clear ocean together with magnificent mountain ranges in the hinterland make Plettenberg Bay one of the most popular seaside towns along the ► Garden Route.

The sun shines an average of 320 days a year and the water temperature is 20°C/68°F all year round. This and the splendid coast attracts

Plettenberg Bay with the beaches of Beacon Island

many South Africans, who have built luxurious holiday homes here. In addition there are numerous hotels, guesthouses and campsites in and around »Plett«. During the high season in summer, particularly around Christmas, the town's 10,000 inhabitants are joined by around 50,000 visitors (which means higher prices, busy beaches and restaurant queues). There are far fewer visitors here between February and April, the time when the weather is best in this area.

Some history The Portuguese seafarer Mesquita da Perestrelo anchored in the bay in 1576 and called it »Bahia Formosa«, »beautiful bay«. The town owes its modern name to Governor Joachim van Plettenberg, who visited this region in 1778.

Around Plettenberg Bay

Beacon Island Beacon Island, a headland jutting out into the Indian Ocean outside the town centre was set up in 1912 by a Norwegian whaling station, but it was abandoned again in 1920; some of the buildings are still standing. The comfortable Beacon Isle Hotel, albeit a painful eyesore, has a spectacular location. It offers magnificent views of the bay and the ocean; between the months of July and September visitors can see many whales who give birth to their young in the sheltered bay.

✳
Robberg
Nature Reserve Robberg Nature Reserve is located south-east of Plettenberg Bay on a 4km/2.5mi peninsula, over which the Mountain of the Seal towers. The reserve is the breeding area of many waterfowl, while dolphins

and whales play in the coastal waters. Information is available in the visitor centre at the car park. It is the starting point for hikes of between 2km and 9km (1–5.5mi); picnic areas can be found along the way (open daily 7am–6pm).

Another nature reserve is located 7km/4.5mi north-east of Plettenberg Bay near the N 2 (open daily 8am–6pm). Its centre is the Keurboom River, whose shores are lined by thick forests; fynbos grows on the cliffs and in the dramatic canyons. Besides many birds, this reserve is home to wild pigs, monkeys and antelopes. A hiking trail (approx. 1 hour) runs along the riverbank. A more attractive option is to explore the reserve by canoe (canoe rental available).

**Keurbooms River
Nature Reserve**

VISITING PLETTENBERG

INFORMATION
Plettenberg Bay Tourism
Mellville's Centre, Main Street
Tel. 044 533 4065
www.plettenbergbay.co.za

WHERE TO EAT
► Inexpensive
Moby Dick's Grill
Tel. 044 533 3682
This very informal restaurant on
Central Beach (veranda) serves
delicious fish dishes.

Lookout Deck
Tel. 044 533 1379
A popular beach restaurant above
Lookout Beach. Enjoy some oysters,
fish and cocktails while watching
dolphins and surfers in the sea?

WHERE TO STAY
► Luxury
The Plettenberg
40 Church Street
Tel. 044 533 2030
www.plettenberg.com
One of the best hotels on the Garden
Route with 38 rooms furnished in an
elegant Mediterranean style. Dream
location with views of Lookout Bach.

Pool, tennis court, golf course, fishing.

► Mid-range/Luxury
Hunters Country House
Pear Tree FarmTel. 044 532 7818
www.hunterhotels.com
Five-star hotel in a country house-
style 10km/6mi west of Plett. Tasteful
atmosphere, excellent restaurant.
Ideal for riding and hiking.

Milkwood Manor
Tel. 044 533 0420
www.milkwoodmanor.co.za
Classy house in a magnificent location
near Lookout Beach, 12 very nice
rooms, some with ocean-view. Private
pool and a Thai restaurant »The
Lemon Grass«.

► Mid-range
Cottage Pie
16 Tarbet Ness Ave.
Tel./fax 044 533 0369
www.cottagepie.co.za
Very friendly, luxurious and comfortable B & B south of the town,
100m from breathtaking Robberg
Beach.

Baedeker TIP

Monkeyland

The forest of the 12ha/30-acre reserve is home to lemurs, squirrel monkeys, baboons and guenons released into the wild from zoos, private households or pharmaceutical laboratories. A highlight here is a 118m/130yd suspension bridge. 16km/10mi east of Plettenberg, along the N 2, exit Forest Hall, daily 8am–6pm.

Nature's Valley   Adjoining the reserve in the east is Nature's Valley, an idyllic holiday town set between the mountains and the sea. The entire surrounding area is a nature reserve. Here is the starting point of the **Tsitsikamma Hiking Trail** as well as the end of the **Otter Trail** (▶Garden Route).

Polokwane

H 3

Province: Limpopo
Population: 105,000

Altitude: 1280m/4200ft
Distances: Johannesburg 320km/200mi, Makhado 120km/75mi, Phalaborwa 205km/125mi

Polokwane, the largest town and the main community in Limpopo province, is located along the northbound N 1 to Johannesburg. This is a good place to stop on the way to the ▶ Kruger National Park and to the scenic area around ▶Tzaneen.

The town, founded in 1884 under the name of **Pietersburg**, after the Voortrekker general Pieter Joubert, quickly developed into a commercial and administrative centre of a region used intensively for agriculture, which also has one of South Africa's largest cattle farms.

▶ VISITING POLOKWANE

INFORMATION

Limpopo Tourism Board
Grobler/Kerks St., tel. 015 290 7300
www.limpopotourism.org.za

WHERE TO STAY

▶ Mid-range
The Ranch
22km/14mi south along the N 1

Tel. 015 290 5000, www.theranch.co.za
Three-star country house situated on a large plot of farmland with attractive rose gardens. Riding opportunities and one of South Africa's best golf courses are close by. Two restaurants (»The Armoury« presented with an award by the Chaîne des Rôtisseurs) and swimming pools.

The town is a typical farming centre with a large supermarket, cinema, bars and a campsite.

Two museums are worth a visit. Located in the Irish House, a cast-iron construction from Germany with an interesting history, the **Polokwane Museum** has collections about the region's cultural history. The neighbouring Dutch Reformed church was converted into a museum of photography; the **Hugh Eston Glass Negative Collection** is here (closed Saturdays). Besides their artistic value Hugh Eston's photographs are also of historical interest.

What to See in Polokwane

Around Polokwane

The 3200ha/7900-acre reserve 5km/3mi south of the town centre has a diverse flora and fauna, including rhinoceroses, zebras, antelopes and gazelles (open daily in summer 7am–6pm, in winter 8am–5pm). The reserve is bordered by Union Park with a lake (fishing allowed), picnic sites and a campsite.

Pietersburg Nature Reserve

◄ Union Park

North of the town along the N 1 towards Makhado there is an exhibition of a different kind: sculptures made of industrial waste, railway cars, turbines and railway tracks.

Industrial Art Exhibition

This open air museum 9km/6mi south of Polokwane (take the R 37 to get here) is a traditional Northern Sotho village. Arts and crafts are for sale and archaeological finds can be viewed, such as remains of iron and copper smelteries as well as rock drawings (around 1000 BC; open Tue–Fri, only in the mornings on Mondays).

★
Bakone Malapa Open Air Museum
🕓

Along the N 1 to Makhado the road passes the Tropic of Capricorn 60km/35mi beyond Polokwane. A stone column marks the area. At latitude 23°26' south the sun is exactly overhead at noon on the summer solstice (21 or 22 December).

Tropic of Capricorn

Around half way between Polokwane and Mokopane north of the N 1 is a breeding station for antelope species threatened by extinction (such as the tsessebe, roan and sable). The 3462ha/8550-acre nature reserve can only be visited in the company of a staff member.

Percy Fyfe Nature Reserve

Mokopane (previously **Potgietersrus**), 43km/27mi south-west of Polokwane, is the centre of a mining and agricultural area. Large quantities of chromium, platinum, tin and asbestos-bearing ores are mined here. The pretty little town owes its old name to the commander Pieter Potgieter, who was killed in a battle with the followers of Chief Tlou Makapan in 1854. The town was abandoned for some years and has been inhabited again since 1890. The **Arend Dieperink Museum** has good cultural and historical collections (Voortrekker Road, open Mon–Fri 8am–4.30pm, Sat 9am–1pm, Sun

Mokopane

🕓

2–5pm). The **Mokopane Nature Reserve** at the northern edge of the town is home to antelopes, gazelles, blue wildebeests, plains zebras, impalas, the Hartmann's zebra and white rhinoceroses as well as to the relatively rare pygmy hippopotamus. Open daily 8am–6pm, in winter until 5.30pm.

Port Elizabeth

F 8

Province: Eastern Cape
Population: 850,000

Altitude: 60m/197ft
Distances: Cape Town 770km/480mi, East London 310km/190mi

Cars, students, beaches: although the largest coastal town between Cape Town and Durban is not a must-see, it does have a pretty Victorian centre and long, wide sandy beaches on the ocean. Nelson Mandela Bay is a mecca for water sports enthusiasts.

Port Elizabeth, usually just called »PE« for short, is South Africa's fifth-largest city and third-largest port. Together with Uitenhage, Despatch and Coega it forms the **Nelson Mandela Bay Municipality**, the commercial and industrial centre of Eastern Cape province. In the »Detroit of South Africa« automobile manufacturing (Ford, GM; VW and Audi in neighbouring Uitenhage) is the most important economic activity, while the textile industry is also important. From a cultural perspective PE is easily capable of keeping up with the country's other large cities. The students of the university and the Institute of Technology create a lively bar and pub scene. Port Elizabeth is also a popular holiday destination with a cosmopolitan, colourful, albeit unattractive cityscape and endless beaches.

History Originally the Khoikhoi used the area for grazing. The first Europeans to discover Algoa Bay were Portuguese seafarers; Bartolomeu Dias landed on the bay's eastern beach in 1488. However, Port Elizabeth was only founded in 1820 when the British arrived in Algoa Bay. Rufane Donkin, the Cape's vice-governor, named the settlement after his wife Elizabeth, who had died very young. The town, which developed slowly, received municipal autonomy in 1861. In 1977 **Steve Biko**, a young leader of the Black Consciousness movement, died of the consequences of torture in the Sanlam Centre after being in police custody for 26 days.

! **Baedeker TIP**

Going out in Port Elizabeth

Despite its conservative reputation PE has an unparalleled restaurant and pub scene. Nowhere else in South Africa are there more bars per capita, particularly in the Boardwalk Casino and Entertainment Center. This »Rimini of Africa« on Hobie Beach is weather-proof: it is covered by a glass roof.

Beach and skyline of Port Elizabeth

The centre stretches along the coastal lowlands and the hill rising in the west with the Donkin Reserve. Overall the city does not look very attractive, even though some pretty Victorian buildings survive in the city centre. Despite PE marketing itself as a »friendly city« visitors wanting to go out in the evenings would be well advised to take a taxi (►p.162). There are 47 things to see along the 5km/3mi **Donkin Heritage Trail** from the city hall to St George's Park, where cricket is played. Information available from the Tourist Information Centre.

Orientation

Why not go on one of the boat trips leaving from the harbour? An excursion to Santa Cruz Island, which is home to a large penguin colony, is particularly interesting. The diving expeditions to shipwrecks are also an attraction; they are organized by Ocean Divers International, Pro Dive and other operators (►p.170).

Boating and diving excursions

What to See in Port Elizabeth

The view from the 52m/171ft Campanile near the coast (at the station) offers visitors a first impression of the city (open Tue–Sat 9am–12.30pm, 1.30–5pm, Sun 2–5pm). The tower with its chimes (daily 8.32am, 10.32am, 6.02pm) was built in 1923 in memory of the first settlers.

Campanile
⏲

Pass under the expressways to get to the market square, the city's historic centre. Opposite the city hall of 1858 is a replica of the **Dias Cross**, which Bartolomeu Dias erected in Kwaahoek in 1488.

City Hall, Market Square

Port Elizabeth *Map*

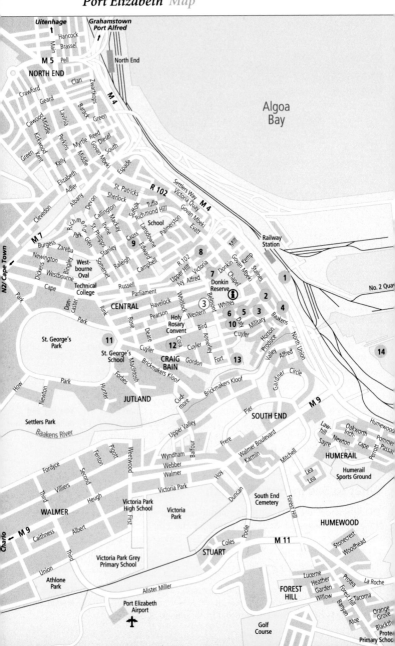

Uitenhage
Grahamstown
Port Alfred

Hancock
Brassel
Main
Pell
North End

M 5

NORTH END

Crawford
Geard
Clan
Zwartkops
Barack
Green

Cawood
Middle
Kirkwood
Kent
Lavinia
Perkins
Myrtle
Reed
Govan Mbeki
Diesel
South

Green
Kelly
Elizabeth
Adler
Albany
Clevedon
Middle
Espode

R 102

Settlers Way
Victoria Quay

Algoa
Bay

M 4

St. Patricks
Sherlock
Devon
Richmond Hill
Tufta
School

M 7

Burgess
Zareba
Newington
Dickens
Westbourne
Cape
Westbourne
Oval
Technical
College

Westbourne

Doncaster
Park

St. George's
Park

CENTRAL

Russell
Parliament
Havelock
Pearson

Holy
Rosary
Convent

11

St. George's
School
Brickmakers Kloof

CRAIG
BAIN

JUTLAND

Settlers Park
Baakens River

Cudmore

Brickmakers Kloof

Upper Valley

SOUTH END

M 9

WALMER

Victoria Park
High School

Victoria
Park

Victoria Park Grey
Primary School

STUART

M 11

Athlone
Park

Alister Miller

Port Elizabeth
Airport

Golf
Course

Railway
Station

No. 2 Quay

1

8
7
Donkin
Reserve
2
4
3
6
5
10
13
12

14

HUMERAIL

Humerail
Sports Ground

HUMEWOOD

FOREST
HILL

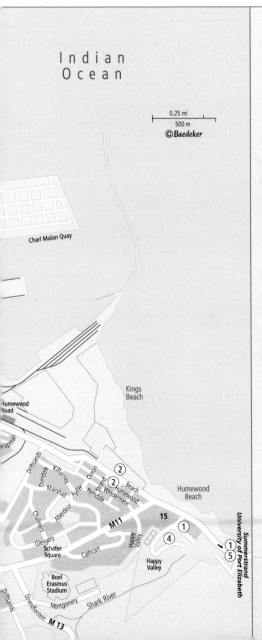

Indian
Ocean

0,25 mi
500 m
©Baedeker

1 Campanile
2 City Hall
3 Feather Market Hall
4 White House
5 Castle Hill Museum
6 Drill Hall
7 Donkin Street Houses
8 Upper Hill Street Houses
9 Jewish Pioneer's
  Memorial Museum
10 Sterley Cottages
11 Mandela Art Museum
12 Cora Terrace
13 Fort Frederick
14 Pleasure Cruises
15 Bayworld

Where to stay
① The Beach Hotel
② The Humewood Hotel
③ Protea Hotel Edward
④ The Chapman
⑤ Margate Place

Where to eat
① Piccolo Blackbeard's
② Sandpiper

Charl Malan Quay

Humewood
Road

Kings
Beach

Humewood
Beach

Driftsands
Dundalk
Killarney
Marshall
Aberdour
Ayliff
Strand
Ferndale
Windermere
Ocean
Beach
Humewood
Chalmers
Glengary
Schafer
Square
Cathcart
Happy
Valley
Happy
Valley
Boel
Erasmus
Stadium
Montgomery
Shark River
Driftsands
Standfontein

M11

M 13

15

④

① Summerstrand
University of Port Elizabeth

①
⑤

⊙ VISITING PORT ELIZABETH

INFORMATION

Tourist Information Centre
Donkin Lighthouse Building
Tel. 041 585 884
www.pecc.gov.za
www.nmbt.co.za

TRANSPORT

Airport 4km/2.5mi south-west of the centre. No public bus service. Taxis and free hotel buses are available. From the station by the harbour the Algoa train goes to Johannesburg. PE is on the routes of Baz Bus, Greyhound, Translux and Intercape buses.

WHERE TO EAT
▶ **Moderate**

① *Piccolo Blackbeard's*
Brooke's Pavilion
Tel. 041 585 5567
Spin-off of the Blackbeard's Tavern in The Chapman Hotel (▶right) and like the original good for seafood; it also serves good meat dishes and Italian cuisine.

▶ **Inexpensive**

② *Sandpiper*
37 Beach Road, Humewood
Tel. 041 585 8961
Beach restaurant of the Humewood Hotel with a large buffet: fish, steaks, chicken and salads.

WHERE TO STAY
▶ **Mid-range**

① *The Beach Hotel*
Marine Drive, Summerstrand
Tel./fax 041 583 2161
www.pehotels.co.za
Considered PE's best hotel. Large, comfortable rooms with an ocean view (expensive) or with a view of the garden. A stone's throw away from

Hobie Beach and the Boardwalk Casino. Diving, surfing, gold and tennis are available.

② *The Humewood Hotel*
33 Beach Road, Humewood
Tel./fax 041 585 8961
www.humewoodhotel.co.za
Attractive building dating from 1920, it has remained in the possession of the same family ever since. Charming house with modern standards, located behind Kings Beach. 67 individually furnished rooms.

③ *Protea Hotel Edward*
Belmont Terrace
Tel. 041 586 2056
www.proteahotels.co.za
A showpiece of the Edwardian period at the Donkin Reserve. Nice view of the city and the port. 110 comfortable rooms, which are however in need of an update. Good restaurant.

▶ **Budget**

④ *The Chapman*
Brooke's Hill Drive
Tel. 041 584 0678
www.chapman.co.za
Modern building at Brooke's Hill, behind Humewood Beach, very tasteful, simple and elegant rooms with balconies; wonderful view of the ocean.

⑤ *Margate Place*
5 Margate St, Summerstrand
Tel. 041 583 5799
www.margateplace.co.za
Cosy apartments (with a kitchen and barbecue site) for 2–4 people, quiet, close to the beach. With a swimming pool.

The city hall of Port Elizabeth on Market Square

To the north-west of the Market Square is a small park, which was commissioned by Rufane Dunkin in 1820. The lighthouse of 1861, which is no longer in use, now houses the tourist information office. The pyramid is a reminder of Elizabeth, Donkin's wife. In the north the Donkin Street Houses form the park's boundary; they were built between 1860 and 1870 in the Victorian style (national memorial, not accessible to the public).Upper Hill Street somewhat further north also retains some of its 19th-century atmosphere.

Donkin Reserve

★
◄ Donkin Street
Upper Hill Street

The Historical Museum (Castle Hill 7, open Mon 2–5pm, Tue–Fri 10am–1pm, 2–5pm, Sat 10am–1pm) is housed in **the city's oldest building**, which was initially built to be the vicarage in 1827 and was later converted. It has historical furniture, household objects and dolls on display.

Castle Hill Historical Museum

Further south is Fort Frederik, a national memorial, which can be reached via Belmont Terrace; it was built in 1799 to defend the mouth of the Baakens River. From the fort visitors should retrace their steps along Belmont Terrace a little and then turn left into Bird Street to see some pretty little houses in the Regency style, which are collectively called »Cora Terrace« (private ownership).

Fort Frederik

◄ Cora Terrace

Further west is the 73ha/180-acre St George's Park with green zones and sports facilities. Within the park is the **Nelson Mandela Metropolitan Art Museum** (open Mon–Fri 9am–5pm, Sat, Sun 2–5pm), which displays British works from the 19th and 20th centuries, South African art and Asian arts and crafts.

St. George's Park

⊙

Bayworld

Bayworld on the coast (open daily 9am–4.30pm) provides entertainment for children. The main building contains archaeological and anthropological collections, while the Oceanarium has marine creatures. The main attraction is the **dolphin show** (daily 11am, 3pm); Bayworld also has a snake house and a tropical area with a luxuriant flora and free-flying birds.

Jewish Pioneers' Museum

The synagogue built in 1912 and in use until 1954 houses the Jewish Pioneers' Museum, which documents the history of the Jews in the city (Raleigh Street, open Sun 10am–noon).

Around Port Elizabeth

✳
Apple Express

Steam-engine romantics should not miss a trip on the narrow-gauge railway, which used to transport fruit from the producing areas west of the town to the port (▶p.179). Crossing the Van Stadens Gorge on the **highest narrow-gauge railway in the world** is a spectacular experience.

Cape Recife Nature Reserve

This 370ha/915-acre nature reserve near the old Cape Recife lighthouse (1851) is a must for bird-lovers. The 9km/5.5mi **Trail of the Roseate Tern** can be completed in 3–4 hours. Game passes cross the trail allowing sightings of red river hogs and antelopes. At locations such as the Bird Hide visitors can observe rare bird species such as the roseate tern, from which the trail gets its name.

Uitenhage

Uitenhage (population: 207,000) 35km/20mi north of Port Elizabeth is a modern, unattractive industrial town; the automobile and mechanical engineering industry has located here, including a Volkswagen plant, **Africa's largest automobile factory**. The station in Market Street, built in 1875, houses a railway museum; the Drostdy Museum (50 Caledon St.) contains pre-colonial cultural historical collections as well as a VW museum.

✳ ✳
Greater Addo Elephant National Park

Greater Addo Elephant National Park, today covering an area of almost 500,000ha/1.2 million acres, includes four further reserves between the Little Karoo and the Indian Ocean along with the original Addo Elephant Park. The Addo Park, located a good 70km/45mi north of Port Elizabeth between the Zuurberg mountains and the Sundays River valley, was set up in 1931 in order to save the last eleven **Cape elephants**; today it is home to more than 300 (do not bring any citrus fruits: the elephants were fed with them for a long time and are still mad about them). The Big Five as well as many species of antelope, bushbuck, kudu, Cape grysbok and duiker live here; amongst the 185 bird species there are exotic kinds such as spotted thick-knees, emerald-spotted wood-doves, Pacific swifts, wattled starlings and Cape glossy starlings. The vegetation is shaped by climbing plants and spekboom bushes, the elephants' main food source. Besides various camps there is a camp-site, a restaurant and a shop. Day visitors are also welcome. Visitors can explore the terrain in their own vehicles. Information and book-ings at SANParks ▶ p.156); park tel. 042 233 0556.

Over time the Cape elephants have developed some special characteristics; the cows do not have tusks for example.

The 20,777ha/51,341-acre **Zuurberg National Park** lies 12km/7mi north of Addo in the Winterhoek mountains. The hilly terrain is home to numerous spe-cies of antelope and ga-zelle as well as to ba-boons, caracals and jackals. Mountain zebras and hippopotamuses have been re-settled here. There is a guesthouse. The region can be explored on hiking trails (approx. 1 or 5 hours) or on horseback.

This 20,000ha/50,000 acre private game reserve, in which wild ani-mals once native here (including the Big Five) have been reintro-duced, is around 30km/20mi east of the Addo park. Amongst the luxurious places to stay, the most noteworthy are **Long Lee Manor**, an Edwardian manor house of 1910, and 19th-century settlers' houses (tel. 042 203 111, www.shamwari.com).

Shamwari Game Reserve

▶ VISITING ADDO ELEPHANT PARK

WHERE TO STAY
▶ Mid-range
Hitgeheim Country Lodge
Addo
Tel. 042 234 07780583
www.hitgeheim-addo.co.za
Located along the R 336 north of Addo towards Kirkwood, close to Addo Elephant National Park. Com-fortably furnished, thatched lodge with a fantastic view of Sunday Valley.

Very good cuisine. The farm cultivates citrus fruits and also keeps ostriches, game and buffalo.

Chrislin B & B
Tel. 042 233 0022
www.africanhuts-addo.co.za
Thatched clay cottages on a citrus farm, with swimming pool. Approx. 3km/2mi west of Addo.

Port Shepstone · Hibiscus Coast

J 7

Province: KwaZulu-Natal
Population: 29,000

Altitude: 17m/56ft
Distances: East London 500km/310mi,
Durban 130km/80mi

Fantastic long sandy beaches and some scenic attractions make the Hibiscus Coast, the southernmost coastline of KwaZulu-Natal province, a popular holiday spot.

Angling and golf paradise
Port Shepstone at the mouth of the Umzimkulu River is the main town and the commercial and administrative centre of the Hibiscus Coast. The presence of marble attracted the first settlers in 1867. They built a port and founded the town in 1882. Until 1901, when the railway line from Durban reached Port Shepstone, all agricultural products were transported to Durban via the port. Port Shepstone has a particularly nice golf course, fishing and water sports opportunities in the sheltered estuary and attractive beaches nearby.

★
Banana Express
The Banana Express, a **steam engine**, runs from Port Shepstone on a 39km/24mi narrow-gauge line opened in 1907 to Paddock (▶p.179)

Beautiful beaches make the Hibiscus Coast a favourite destination for South African holidaymakers.

at an elevation of 550m/1800ft. One possible excursion on the railway is to explore the Oribi Gorge Reserve (see below) in the company of a ranger from the Plains stop, before enjoying a Braai and travelling back to the coast.

★ ★
Oribi Gorge
Nature Reserve

One of the south coast's most attractive destinations is the 1837ha/4539-acre Oribi Gorge Nature Reserve, at the centre of which is a 24km/15mi-long, 5km/3mi-wide **impressive gorge** (21km/13mi west of Port Shepstone, N 2). The Umzimkulwana River, which has dug its way 300m/1000ft down through the sand stone layers, is lined by thick forests; leopards, long-horned beetles, bohor reedbucks, baboons, samango monkeys, green monkeys, blue duikers and common duikers are at home here. The oribi, from which the reserve takes its name and which has a shoulder height of only 60cm/24in, is no longer very numerous here. The gorge has 260 bird species, making it the region's best bird watching location. Accommodation in chalets and huts (KZN Wildlife, ► p. 156); the **Oribi Gorge Hotel**, built in Fairacres in 1870 (tel. 039 687 0253) has wonderful views of the gorge, but not for free. The area is made accessible by an approx. 30km/20mi surfaced road as well as several hiking trails varying in length between 1km and 9 km (0.5–5.5mi).

Hibiscus Coast

The Hibiscus Coast is made up of the towns between Hibberdene and Port Edward 50km/30 km to the south. The Sunshine Coast adjoins the Hibiscus Coast in the north (► Amanzimtoti). The main season is the time around Christmas, when many South Africans spend their holidays here; accommodation is hard to get during this period. Evergreen tropical forests line the coast, countless rivers and streams flow into the ocean and create sheltered lagoons at the estuary. Information available at Hibiscus Coast Tourism (►p.448).

Hibberdene

Hibberdene, 80km/50mi south of Durban, is a pretty holiday town with long sandy beaches and facilities for many different sports. The summer climate here is more pleasant than it is around Durban; the temperatures and the humidity are lower. To the south is Umzumbe with equally good opportunities for swimming and fishing.

Bendigo

This name subsumes the four holiday towns of Sunwich Port, Anerley, South Port and Sea Park. The coast off South Port is protected by shark nets; in Sunwich Port there is a bathing zone surrounded by rocks and also protected by nets; Domba Bay and Sea Park are popular fishing spots and Anerley has a seawater pool.

Shelly Beach

South of Port Shepstone the R 61 follows the coastline. The coastal resort of Shelly Beach is known for its many **shells** and its shopping mall, which is the region's largest.

Margate

Margate is one the largest and most-visited holiday towns along this strip of coastline. The town, founded in 1919, is named after the seaside resort in the south-east of England. The predominantly young-ish visitors enjoy the restaurants, nightclubs and bars. Margate has a amusement park, boccia courts, bowling alleys, an 18-hole golf course and good fishing.

Southbroom

Southbroom has not just one, but two lagoons. The beach is protected by shark nets and is ideal for surfers; Southbroom also has a seawater pool. The nearby **River Bend Crocodile Farm** (open daily. 8.30am–5pm) breeds crocodiles, which were wiped out in the region as early as the mid-19th century.

Marina Beach
Trafalgar
Port Edward

Marina Beach is relatively quiet, and outside the peak season the long sandy beach is almost deserted. Trafalgar is a **good surfing area**. The **Trafalgar Marine Reserve** protects the unique underwater world. Port Edward, close to the border to the former Transkei homeland, is the southern end of the Hibiscus Coast.

Umtamvuna
Nature Reserve

Approx. 1,300 plant species, including 25 kinds of orchid, have been counted in this 3257ha/8048-acre reserve west of Port Edward on the Umtamvuna (on the road towards Izingolweni, 8km/5mi). Narrow paths lead to fantastic viewpoints. Cape vultures, falcons and eagles live in the gorge's rock walls. No overnight accommodation.

▶ VISITING HIBISCUS COAST

INFORMATION

Hibiscus Coast Tourism
Panorama Parade, Margate
Tel. 039 682 2455, 039 312 2322
www.hibiscuscoast.kzn.org.za
www.thehibiscuscoast.co.za

WHERE TO STAY

▶ **Luxury**
San Lameer Resort
Tel. 039 313 0011
www.sanlameer.co.za
Nice resort with elegant hotel rooms and luxurious villas. Idyllic location in Southbroom south of Margate. Four-star comfort and many sports facilities, including a private beach more than 1km/0.6mi in length and an 18-hole golf course that belongs to the resort.

▶ **Mid-range/Luxury**
The Estuary Country Hotel
Port Edward
Tel. 039 311 2675
www.estuary.de
Cape Dutch house, built by Sir Herbert Baker, magnificent location on an estuary 4km/2.5mi north of Port Edward. The »Fish Eagle« restaurant serves South African and international dishes.

▶ **Budget/Mid-range**
Beach Lodge Hotel
Marine Drive, Margate
Tel. 039 312 1483
www.beachlodge.org.za
Pleasant building near the beach with a nice garden, a pool and a good restaurant.

Pretoria · Tshwane

H 4

Province: Gauteng
Population: approx. 1.1 million
(Tshwane Municipality 1.8 million)

Altitude: 1370m/4495ft
Distances: Johannesburg 50km/30mi

Any picture of South Africa would be incomplete without a visit to its government capital, which has almost merged with nearby ►Johannesburg. Deeply rooted in Voortrekker history, it has maintained a serious, calm atmosphere.

The city of Pretoria has the largest area (632 sq km/244 sq mi) of any South African city; it is situated at the foot of the Magaliesberg mountain range in the fertile valley of the Apies River. It is an important industrial centre (iron and steel, automobiles, cement), the seat of **parliament** (alternating with Cape Town every six months), and an educational and cultural centre. The **university** of Pretoria was founded in 1930; since 1951 Pretoria has been the seat of the UNISA (University of South Africa), with more than 100,000 students one of the largest distance-learning institutions in the world. The subtropical climate with 360 days of sunshine annually is pleasant; the summers are hot and the average daytime temperature in winter is 19°C/66°F in winter.

The region now occupied by Pretoria was settled by the Ndebele whose houses are decorated vibrantly by the women (► Baedeker   **History**

Church Square with the Paul Kruger monument by Anton van Wouw

special p.460). The Voortrekkers advanced into an area that was only sparsely settled in 1827. The Boer general Marthinus Wessel Pretorius founded the town in 1855 and named it after his father Andries, who, with his victory over the Zulus at Blood River, had created the prerequisites for a self-sufficient white settlement in Transvaal. From 1860 Pretoria was the capital of Transvaal, from 1910 the seat of government of the Union of South Africa. It was agreed in 2005 to rename the city **Tshwane**.

City character Even though this **city of civil servants and diplomats** lies only about 50km/30mi north of Johannesburg, the contrast between the two cities is stark. Pretoria did not develop in a positive manner after the end of apartheid; its historic buildings (with the exception of the Union Buildings) seem grim, the city and its parks unkempt. The centre and Sunnyside are the worst affected, and also the city's least safe areas; hotels, restaurants, bars and jazz bars have relocated further east to Arcadia, Hatfield and Brooklyn, into the quarters where the embassies, colleges and universities are located. The prestige mansions in the »better« districts are guarded like military bases. A more attractive picture is evident in October and November, when the **70,000 jacaranda trees** bloom violet-blue. In order to view the city centre's main sights visitors have to travel considerable distances.

What to See in the City Centre

✷ The **26km/16mi-long Church Street** is the city's main axis. It is the
Church Square longest straight road in the world. Interrupted by Church Square, where the settlement first took shape, it is lined by significant buildings such as the Palace of Justice and Sir Herbert Baker's building for

Highlights Pretoria · Tshwane

Violet Pretoria
In spring blooming jacaranda trees turn the city into a sea of violet.
▶ page 450

Union Buildings
Nelson Mandela took his oath of office in the impressive parliament building built by Sir Herbert Baker.
▶ page 456

Burgers Park
An oasis in the city centre. The English garden is a popular spot to spend the lunch hour.
▶ page 456

Paul Kruger Museum
The modest house of the most famous and powerful of all Afrikaners.
▶ page 456

Mapungubwe Museum
Some of the country's most significant treasures are on display here.
▶ page 457

Voortrekker Monument
A powerful symbol of the Boer pioneering spirit, it remains a shrine for many Afrikaners, even after the end of apartheid.
▶ page 458

One of the most beautiful historic buildings in Pretoria: Melrose House

the South Africa Reserve Bank in the north, and the neo-Renaissance **Republikeinse Raadsaal**, the former seat of government, in the south. The pretty Café Riche (open 6am–midnight) is a nice place to stop and rest.

The Pierneef Museum (open Mon–Fri 8am–4pm, Vermeulen Street) in a residential house dating from the late 19th century exhibits works by Jacob Hendrik Pierneef (1886–1957), one of South Africa's leading landscape painters.

Pierneef Museum

The Post Office Museum (Proes Street, open Mon–Fri 7.30am–4.30pm) documents the history of the South African Post Office. Further north the Jansen Collection of Africana (Struben Street) has an exhibition of antiques and silver.

Post Office Museum
◀ Jansen Collection of Africana

The 60ha/150-acre zoo north of the city centre (Boom Street, open 8am–5.30pm in summer, 8am–5pm during the rest of the year) has 3,500 animals, making it **one of the largest zoos in the world**. Around 140 mammal species and 320 bird species can be seen here; the aquarium has 300 fish species and the reptile park is home to reptiles from all around the world. The zoo has also rendered outstanding service to the survival of the Mongolian Przewalski's horse, the bison and the Père David's deer.

★
National Zoological Gardens

The State Theatre dating from 1981 (Church Street) hints at Japanese architectural influences. Six stages are available for operas, ballets, plays and concerts. For information tel. 012 322 1665.

State Theatre

Pretoria • Tshwane Map

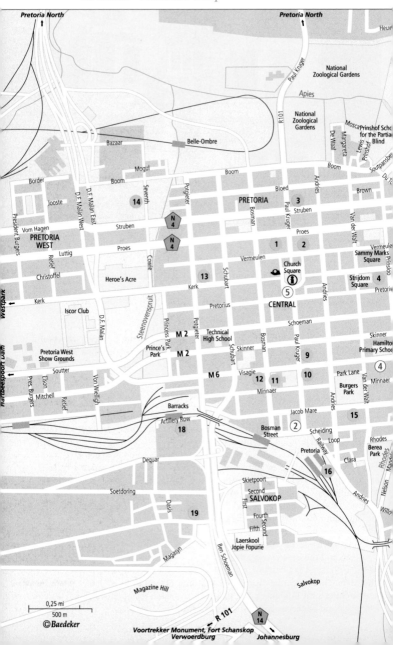

Pretoria North

Pretoria North

Heu

National
Zoological Gardens

Paul Kruger

Apies

R 101

National
Zoological
Gardens

Mosca

De Waal

Margareta

Lewis

Prinsho

Prinshof Scho
for the Partia
Blind

Sourpansbee

Du Tc

Bazaar

Belle-Ombre

Mogul

Boom

Boom

Boom

Border

Boom

Bloed

Andries

Brown

Jooste

D.F. Malan East

Seventh

14

PRETORIA

3

Paul Kruger

Struben

President Burgers

Vom Hagen

D.F. Malan West

Struben

Bosman

1

2

Proes

Van der Walt

Vermeule

Prinsloo

PRETORIA
WEST

Luttig

Proes

Cowie

Vermeulen

Sammy Marks
Square

Relief

Church
Square

N
4

N
4

Christoffel

Heroe's Acre

13

Schubart

ℹ

Strijdom
Square

4

Pretoria

Westpark

Kerk

Kerk

Steenovenspruit

Andries

5

CENTRAL

Iscor Club

D.F. Malan

Pretorius

Schoeman

Pretoria West
Show Grounds

Princess
Park

Potgieter

M 2

Technical
High School

Schubart

Skinner

Bosman

Paul Kruger

9

Skinner

Hamilto
Primary Schol

Soutter

Prince's
Park

M 2

Park Lane

Minnaer

4

Pres. Burgers

Elton

Mitchell

Von Wielligh

Relief

M 6

Visagie

12

11

10

Burgers
Park

Van der Walt

Hartbeespoort Dam

Minnaer

Jacob Mare

Andries

15

Barracks

Artillery Row

18

Bosman
Street

2

Scheiding

Loop

Railway

Rhodes

Berea
Park

Rhodes

Maré

Dequar

Pretoria

Clara

16

Nelson

Soetdoring

Skietpoort

Second

Andries

Willo

Oasis

Magasyn

19

SALVOKOP

Fourth

Fifth

Second

First

Laerskool
Jopie Fopurie

Salvokop

Magazine Hill

0,25 mi

500 m

©Baedeker

R 101

N
14

Voortrekker Monument, Fort Schanskop
Verwoerdburg

Johannesburg

1 Post Office Museum
2 Pierneef Museum
3 Jansen Collection of Africana
4 State Theatre
5 Engelenburg House
6 Union Buildings
7 Pretoria Art Museum
8 University of Pretoria
9 South African Museum
   of Science and Technology
10 Transvaal Museum
11 City Hall
12 African Window
13 Paul Kruger House Museum
14 Mariammen Temple
15 Melrose House
16 Railway Station
17 UNISA
   University of South Africa
18 Historic buildings
19 Correctional Service Museum

Where to stay
① Colosseum
② Victoria Hotel
③ La Maison
④ Protea Manor
⑤ Mutsago Guest House
⑥ Rozenhof
⑦ The Farm Inn

Where to eat
① Ritrovo Ristorante
② Villa di Amici
③ Brasserie de Paris
④ Safika
⑤ Café Riche

▶ VISITING PRETORIA · TSHWANE

INFORMATION

Tshwane Tourism Information
Old Nederlandsche Bank Building
Church Square, tel. 012 337 4337
www.tshwane.gov.za

TRANSPORT

Metro trains connect Pretoria and
Johannesburg. Visitors are strongly
advised not to use them; alternative
methods of transportation include the
buses operated by Greyhound, Intercape and Translux. Airport Link
(www.airportlink.co.za, tel. 011 792
2017, 083 625 5090) and Magic Bus
(www.magicbus.co.za, tel. 011 548
0822) go to Johannesburg International Airport on request. Larger
hotels provide a shuttle service. Trains
to Cape Town (including the Blue
Train), Komatipoort and Musina
leave from the railway station. The
municipal buses between Church
Square and the suburbs are safe
enough during the day. The best way
for visitors to complete a sightseeing
tour of the city is in their own car or
by taking a tour, e.g. with Expedi-
tionary Force or Ulysses.

WHERE TO EAT

▶ Moderate/Expensive
Ritrovo Ristorante
103 Club Avenue, Waterkloof Heights
Waterkloof Heights Shopping Centre
Tel. 012 460 4367
Award-winning restaurant with spec-
tacular views of Pretoria. Good ice
cream.

② *Villa di Amici*
1065 Arcadia St., Hatfield
Tel. 012 362 7677
Italian restaurant of the sophisticated
kind. An excellent breakfast is served
on the terrace on Sundays.

③ *Brasserie de Paris*
525 Duncan St., Hatfield
Tel. 012 362 2247
French ambience and French cuisine
prepared with fresh products.

▶ Inexpensive
④ *Safika*
Idasa Building, 357 Visagie St.
Tel. 012 320 0274
Buffet with delicacies from every
country in Africa. It is also a hotspot
for jazz lovers.

⑤ *Café Riche*
Church Square, tel. 012 328 3173
Nice art nouveau café , probably the
oldest in Pretoria. Lavish breakfast.

WHERE TO STAY
▶ Mid-range
① *Colosseum*
410 Schoeman/Du Toit Street
Tel. 012 320 5120
www.colosseum.co.za
Centrally located, modern round
building, comfortable rooms in the
classical style with marble floors and a
glass exterior. Houses an Indian-
Pakistani restaurant.

② *Victoria Hotel*
Scheiding/Paul Kruger St.
Tel. 012 323 6054
Building dating from 1892 in the
centre, tastefully decorated in the
Victorian style. Ten rooms with an
upmarket standard. Used to be the
»station« (opposite the railway station) for the Rovos Train.

③ *La Maison*
235 Hilda St., Hatfield
Tel. 012 430 4341
www.lamaison.co.za
Victorian building in the diplomatic

quarter, with a wonderful garden and a pool. 6 nice rooms and an excellent restaurant.

④ *Protea Manor*
Burnett / Festival St., Hatfield
Tel. 012 362 7077
www.proteahotels.com
Very well situated hotel in the English club style. 42 air-conditioned rooms. The nearby Protea Hatfield Lodge is also fairly good.

⑤ *Mutsago Guest House*
327 Festival Street, Hatfield
Tel. 012 430 7193
www.mutsago.co.za
A stone's throw from Hatfield's restaurants and shopping centre, this African guesthouse is situated in a

wonderful garden with a pool. Run by a musician couple.

⑥ *Rozenhof Guest House*
525 Alexander St., Brooklyn
Tel. 012 468 075
In the historical district of Brooklyn, this attractive house with its 7 rooms provides a mix of Cape Dutch, Huguenot and British tradition. Tasteful designer furnishings. Large veranda, framed by purple-flowering jacaranda trees.

⑦ *The Farm Inn*
Lynnwood Rd. East, Die Wilgers 0041
Tel. 012 809 0266, www.farminn.co.za
Approx. 12km/7.5mi east of the city centre, near the M 6. ►Baedeker Tip p.456.

Strijdom Square in front of the theatre once contained a large bust of the prime minister J. G. Strijdom (1954–58), which collapsed very symbolically in 2001. The square is used for a market on Saturday mornings.

Strijdom Square

The Police Museum (Volkstem Ave., Compol building; open Mon–Fri 7.30am–3pm, Sat 8.30am–12.30pm, Sun 1.30–4.30pm) south of Church Square brings to life the police state of the apartheid era.

South African Police Museum

The Museum of Science and Technology is located in the south of the city centre (Skinner Street; open Mon–Fri 8am–1pm, 2–4pm), displaying exhibits from space flight, science and technology.

Museum of Science and Technology

A little further south the City Hall with its **huge bell-tower** (32 bells) is a conspicuous feature on Paul Kruger Street. There are statues of Andries Pretorius and his son Marthinus Wessel Pretorius, the founder of Pretoria, outside the entrance.

City Hall

The National Cultural History Museum west of the City Hall (149 Visagie Street, open 8am–4pm) has San rock drawings, an ethnological documentation on Gauteng and archaeological finds, amongst other things.

★
National Cultural History Museum

This museum opposite the city hall (open Mon–Sat 9am–5pm, Sun 11am–5pm, café) houses an exceptional collection of stuffed mam-

★
Transvaal Museum

! Baedeker TIP

The Farm Inn

Many of Pretoria's guesthouses seem somewhat sterile, quite unlike this farm with its
rustic, thatched main building and varied
terrain, which merges with the Silver Lakes golf
course. Visitors immediately feel at home in
the Farmers Inn; riding, fishing, swimming and
golfing are all excellent ways to spend the days
(adress see p.455).

mals, amphibians and fossils as well
as geological and archaeological
finds. The remains of »Mrs Ples«,
the *Australopithecus robustus* from
the Sterkfontein Caves (▶ Johannesburg) are kept here. The Austin Roberts Bird Hall contains information
about all the 875 bird species native
to South Africa. Next door the **Museum of Geological Survey** (open
Mon–Sat, public holidays 9am–5pm,
Sun 11am–5pm) contains pretty
gemstones and fossils.

Burgers Park

Burgers Park (open 6am–10pm in summer, 6am–6pm in winter)
was opened in 1892 and named after Th. F. Burgers, Transvaal's second president. It has a pleasant café.

✳
Melrose House

Melrose House (south of Burgers Park, open Tue–Sun 10am–5pm,
photograph p.451, café), built in 1866, is a fine example of Victorian
architecture. Here the **Treaty of Vereeniging** was signed after the
Boer War in 1902, whereby the Boer republics became British pos-
sessions. The building, complete with old furniture, hosts exhibitions
and concerts.

Paul Kruger Museum

⊙

This simple Victorian house (Church Street), the oldest in the city,
was the home of **Paul Kruger** (▶Famous People) between 1883 and
1900. Personal effects of the former president of Transvaal and the
state carriage are on display here (open Tue–Sat 8.30am–4pm, Sun
11am–4pm).

✳
Mariammen Temple

A few streets of houses further north is the Mariammen Temple, the
oldest Hindu temple in Pretoria (1905). Visitors are welcome if they
remove their shoes.

What to See outside the City Centre

✳
Union Buildings

The majestic Union Buildings, surrounded by beautiful gardens, are
sited on the Meintjieskop hill in the east of the city (1913, not open
to the public). The sandstone buildings designed by Sir Herbert
Baker are the seat of government. In the grounds arranged in the
form of terraces descending towards Church Street, the Delville
Wood Memorial commemorates the South African soldiers who
fought in the First World War and statues pay tribute to the prime
ministers Louis Botha, J. B. M. Hertzog and J. C. Smuts.

Pretoria Art Museum

The Pretoria Art Museum (open Tue 10am–5pm, Wed 10am–8pm,
Thu–Sun 2–5pm), south of the Union Buildings in the Arcadia Park

The Union Buildings on the Meintjieskop hill are the seat of the South African parliament.

has **works by South African artists** such as Pierneef, F. Oerder and Anton van Wouw as well as the well-known **Michaelis collection** of old Dutch and Flemish paintings.

★ **Mapungubwe Museum**

The famous golden rhinoceros and many other national treasures from Mapungubwe, the royal city near Musina discovered in 1933 (►p.61, 397) are on display in the Old Arts Building on the university campus. To get there take Park St./Burnett St., then turn right to the entrance in University Road. Open Tue–Fri 10am–4pm.

🕐

★ **National Botanical Gardens**

The botanical gardens 10km/6mi east of the city centre (to get here take Church St./Cussonia Ave.; open daily 6am–6pm), the country's largest (77ha/190 acres), are divided into biospheres: Karoo-savannah, coastal forests and Namibia's grassy plains. A total of 5000 plant species grow here, including 300 native tree species.

Magnolia Dell

The magnificently designed garden (Queen Wilhelmina Ave.) south of the University of Pretoria is particularly pretty in springtime when the magnolias are in bloom. During the first and last Saturday of the month the »Art in the Park« exhibition takes place here.

Austin Roberts Bird Sanctuary

To the south-east of Magnolia Dell, the 11ha/27 acre Austin Roberts Bird Sanctuary (Boshoff St.; open 7am–4pm) was named after a South African ornithologist who wrote a **bird book that achieved international fame**. More than 100 native bird species and numerous other animals can be seen here in their natural environment. At the edge of the reserve there is a reservoir, where hides have been set up for bird watching.

Anton van Wouw House The home of the South African sculptor Anton van Wouw is located east of the sanctuary at 299 Clark Street and is now a museum (open Tue–Fri 10am–4pm, Sat 10am–noon).

Faerie Glen Nature Reserve The beautiful Faerie Glen Nature Reserve can be found in the easternmost part of the city. It is home to a large number of plant species, such as the umbrella tree, as well as to many animals. It is part of the **Moreleta Spruit Nature Trail**, an 8km/5mi hiking trail from Menlyn Drive to Hardekool Avenue, which meanders along a wild stream through a diverse landscape.

Fort Klapperkop Fort Klapperkop 6km/4mi south of the city can be reached via Johan Rissik Drive (which offers great views of Pretoria). It is one of the city's four defensive structures, but it never had to fulfil this function. It now documents South Africa's military history from 1852 to the end of the Boer War (open daily 10am–3.30pm).

✱ Voortrekker Monument Around 6km/4mi south of the city centre is the Voortrekker Monument, which can be seen from far and wide (open Mon–Sat 8am–5pm, Sun 11am–5pm). It was built between 1938 and 1949 to commemorate the Boers who advanced into unknown territory in the 19th century, and particularly in remembrance of the battle at Blood River fought on 16 December 1838. It consists of a 40m/130ft granite structure on a base measuring 40 x 40m/130 x 130ft. The Hall of Heroes depicts the Great Trek of the 1830s on 27 marble reliefs. At noon on the 16 December the sun shines through an opening in the roof on to a granite cenotaph in the hall below, whose inscription reads: »Ons vir jou, Suid-Afrika« (»We for thee, South Africa«). An informative small museum complements the monument.

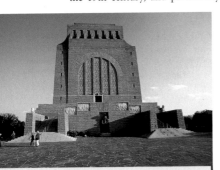

Testament to heroic Boer self-confidence

Around Pretoria

Wonderboom Nature Reserve At the northern edge of the city, Wonderboom Nature Reserve (open daily 10am–5pm) protects a **fig tree** (*Ficus salicifolia*) which is more than 1000 years old and whose stem has a diameter of 5.5m/18ft. New roots formed on branches that touched the ground, which subsequently grew into new trees. It is said that the »wonder tree«, a national monument, is able to provide shade for more than 1000 people. There are picnic sites and barbecue areas; a trail leads up to a small fort from the time of the Boer War.

At the Cullinan diamond mine, 40km/25mi east of Pretoria, the world's **largest rough diamond**, the 3106-carat »Cullinan«, was found. It was given to King Edward VII for his 66th birthday. He commissioned experts from Amsterdam to cut and polish it. After months of inspection the diamond was split into 105 pieces in 1908; the two largest pieces are now in a sceptre and crown among the British crown jewels. The **Premier Diamond Mine** in Cullinan mines approx. 1 million carats of diamonds a year. Guided tours through the mine are available on registration (tel. 012 734 0081). The Willem Prinsloo Agricultural Museum portrays the hard rural life of the 19th century.

★
Cullinan Mine

Life on the **Doornkloof Farm** owned by Jan Smuts, a general and the prime minister of the Union of South Africa, was simple, and the atmosphere of the suburb of Irene, 16km/10mi south of Pretoria, remains so to this day. The unpretentious iron and timber house is equipped with furniture from Smuts' period. Twice a month an art market takes place here. Open Mon–Fri 9.30am–4.30pm, Sat–Sun 9.30am–5pm. Campsite, cafeteria and tea garden.

Smuts House Museum

The 1883ha/4653-acre Hartbeespoort Dam a good 30km/20mi west of Pretoria provides water for tobacco, wheat and flower fields as well as for orchards via a 544km/338mi irrigation system. It is a popular leisure destination (open Mon–Fri 8am–6pm, Sat 8am–10pm) with accommodation, campsites and an amusement park. Hiking trails in the nature reserve south-east of the lake provide good opportunities for bird and antelope watching. Steam boats take visitors on round trips. The large aquarium is worth seeing.

Hartbeespoort Dam

The small town of Rustenburg at the foot of the Magaliesberg mountains west of Hartbeespoort (105km/65mi from Pretoria) is another popular destination. The Rustenburg Nature Reserve close to the town is situated in an attractive mountain landscape and is ideal for hiking. A visit to Boekhoutenfontein, Paul Kruger's (►Famous People) farm at the northern edge of the town is also worthwhile. Some of the historic buildings have survived, including Kruger's home built in 1863.

Rustenburg

◄ Boekhouten-
fontein

VISITING RUSTENBURG

WHERE TO STAY
▶ Luxury
Mount Grace Country House
Old Rustenburg Road, Magaliesburg
Tel. 014 577 1350, www.grace.co.za
Reservations tel. 011 280 4300
A smart refuge one hour's drive away from Johannesburg and Pretoria.

80 rooms in different buildings, some of them with magnificent views. Two good restaurants with interesting cuisine; on Saturdays there is a large buffet in the garden. Pools and a spa; classical music concerts are staged. The access road branches off from the R 24 2.5km/1.5mi north of Magaliesburg.

The Ndebele way of painting is derived from their artful pearl embroidery.

Right: the artist Esther Mahlangu with her mother

THE PAINTING NDEBELE WOMEN

Despite their unfortunate history and despite the fact that fate was even tougher on them than it was on other peoples in South Africa, the Ndebele women have still not lost their love of cheerful colours.

It was the women of the Ndebele people who gave back an identity to their homeless people with traditional painting, which represents an important part of the »collective memory of a people who had been in hiding for generations« (Randolph Braumann).

Colourful world

Everything in their lives is colourful: festivals, rituals, jewellery and homes. It is not just for ceremonial occasions that the women wear gilt brass rings around their necks, which are »stocked up« over the years, and on their arms and legs. Children also adorn their necks, but only with pleated straw; it is however woven so tightly that it can only be removed with the help of a saw. The pearl strings and embroidery for little girls also differs from the jewellery worn by the women, and by the older girls being prepared for their initiation for their life as a woman. When the people settled, the patterns in the pearl embroidery they had developed over centuries became the starting point for an activity unique in all of Africa: the wall painting of the Ndebele. The

umuzi, a main house with a number of free-standing single houses or double houses with forecourts, is characteristic of their settlements. Some Ndebele still live in polygamous marriages, and every woman is entitled to her own little house. The men and the women build the umuzi together. First they hammer wooden pegs into the ground, then they weave thick branches, thin twigs and straw into walls between the pegs, which are coated in a mixture of clay and cow dung; at the end the hut is covered with a thatched roof. When the walls are dry, they are painted. The colours red, brown, ochre, blue, white and black are made from clay and mud. Today they prefer to buy acrylic paints in the supermarket, which are not so easily washed off by the rain. For the traditional pastel shades they are also mixed with clay. Linear, geometric elements are prevalent on the painted house walls. The women draw on the patterns of the much older art of pearl embroidery with its **threading technique**. Achievements of modern society such as aeroplanes and cars are also represented. The

reasons for painting the façades vary considerably: weddings, initiation ceremonies or simply just the pleasure of decorating. One of the most important representatives of Ndebele art is **Esther Mahangu**, who became famous far beyond the borders of South Africa when, for the 75th anniversary of the car manufacturer BMW, she painted a 520i in the typical Ndebele style.

Almost genocide

The Ndebele suffered the worst fate amongst the South African Bantu peoples, and they are now amongst the most widely scattered tribal communities in the country. Little is known about the Ndebele's history. They have no written records: everything was handed down orally, including the techniques for painting façades. What is certain is that they settled in two groups in the northern and the southern Transvaal from the 16th century; they are distantly related to the Matabele in Zimbabwe. Their fateful hour came in 1883. After the founding of the British colony at the Cape, the Boers moved away into the country's interior and founded the Transvaal republic on Ndebele land. In 1882 they undertook their fourth

attempt to wipe out the Ndebele, who retreated to the **Mabhogo Caves** near Nomtjarhelo. The Boers blew up parts of the cave system with dynamite, but were not successful in flushing them out. In 1883 the Ndebele surrendered after a nine-month siege. Of the 15,000 men, women and children who had retreated into the caves, only 8,000 were alive. The Boers sent their king, Nyabela, to prison for 15 years. The members of the tribe were scattered to work on the farms and for decades spent their lives as farm labourers with no rights.

In 1977 the South African government set up **KwaNdebele**, the tenth homeland. The Ndebele hoped for a reunification of their people and a renaissance of their culture. KwaNdebele was not however their old settlement land, and was also too meagre and small to feed its population. Thus the Ndebele had to go outside KwaNdebele to earn a living. In 1986 Pretoria sought to force KwaNdebele to become independent. The 400,000 Ndebele successfully resisted, 200 of them losing their lives in the process: Independent status would have made them foreigners inside their own home country without the right to work.

Richards Bay

K 6

Province: KwaZulu-Natal
Population: 17,000

Altitude: 47m/154ft
Distances: Durban 200km/125mi

Richards Bay, in the far north-east of South Africa, where the Mhlatuze flows into the Indian Ocean, is one of the country's most important ports.

The deep water harbour that began operating in 1976 initially served to export coal; these days almost half of South Africa's total trade goes through this port. A 660km/410mi railway line connects it with the coal-mining region around Witbank. After it was opened industry developed rapidly; an oil refinery, a fertilizer production plant and an aluminium factory are noteworthy examples. Richards Bay and Empangeni 18km/11mi away have merged into a single municipal area known by the name of **Umhlathuze**. The town, with the exception of the port, does not have any sites of interest; there are however some attractive destinations nearby.

Industry in Richards Bay

A look behind the scenes of the industry located in Richards Bay is interesting, not least for the attention given to environmental protection. **Richards Bay Minerals** is open to visitors. Reservations no later than a day in advance, tel. 035 901 3444 (www.richardsbayminerals.co.za).

Around Richards Bay

✱
Umlalazi Nature Reserve

To the south-west of the town between the coast and the N 2 is the Umlalazi Nature Reserve, which was founded in 1948. It is a dune and marsh area with mangrove forests. Lakes and the lagoon of the Umlalazi River intersperse the coastal vegetation. Red river hogs, red

 VISITING RICHARDS BAY

INFORMATION
Umhlatuze Tourism Association
Pearce Singel / Turnbull St.
Empangeni

WHERE TO EAT
▶ **Inexpensive**
Thai Wok Food House
Tuzi Gazi Waterfront
Tel. 035 788 0525
Fish and seafood feature on the menu

in Richards Bay, here in interesting Asian versions.

WHERE TO STAY
▶ **Budget/Mid-range**
Bay View Lodge
24 Davidson Lane, Meerensee
Tel./fax 035 753 3065
www.bayviewlodge.co.za
Pretty little lodge with a pool. The beaches are within walking distance.

forest duikers, blue duikers and common duikers, long-horned beetles and a small crocodile colony make up the animal population. In
addition many bird species find refuge in the thicket. Two hiking
trails traverse the reserve. Accommodation through KZN Wildlife, ►
p.156.

Empangeni, 20km/12mi inland from Richards Bay is situated in a   **Empangeni**
picturesque hilly landscape, the centre of the sugar industry in Zululand (►Ulundi). Nearly 15km/9mi north-east of Empangeni lies the   **Enseleni Nature**
293ha/724-acre Enseleni Nature Reserve in a bend of the Enseleni   **Reserve**
River. Various hiking trails up to 5km/3mi in length meander
through terrain that is home to hippopotamuses and crocodiles.

Robertson

C 8

Province: Western Cape   **Altitude:** 209m/686ft
Population: 35,000   **Distances:** Cape Town 170km/105mi

**Just like the nearby towns of ►Montagu and ►Swellendam, Rob-
ertson, at the centre of Breede River Valley, is known for its wines.**

Along the **Robertson wine route**, the oldest in the country, there are
27 vineyards, including famous ones such as Graham Beck and De
Wetshof. Dark, heavy wines are cultivated here on chalky soil, which
is rare in South Africa; another excellent wine from this region is the
Sauvignon Blanc; dessert wines and brandy are also produced here.
The Cape Dutch town possesses a good infrastructure, but ►Monta-
gu and McGregor (►p.464) are more attractive bases. Like all settlements along Breede River the town is bedded in roses and callas.
The roses display vine diseases long before the vines themselves are
attacked. There are some pleasant hikes in the Langberg mountains
and the Riviersonderendberg mountains.

► VISITING ROBERTSON

INFORMATION

Robertson Tourism Bureau
Voortrekker Street
Tel. 023 626 4437
www.robertsonr62.com
www.robertsonwinevalley.com

FESTIVALS AND EVENTS

Around 20 Oct:
Food & Wine Festival

WHERE TO STAY

► **Budget/Mid-range**
Green Gables Country House
Voortrekker Rd.
McGregor
Tel. 023 625 1626
Pretty »English« townhouse from the
late 19th century, which was once a
corner shop. 5 rooms with separate
entrances. Good restaurant.

! **Baedeker TIP**

Route 62

Unlike the busy Garden Route, Route 62 is a
very peaceful drive from Paarl to Port Elizabeth
(via Worcester, Robertson, Montagu, Ladismith, Oudtshoorn, De Rust, Avontuur):
through the wine country, through the Little
Karoo, the Outeniqua Mountains and
picturesque little towns. Information at
www.route62.co.za.

What to See in and around Robertson

Robertson Museum Apart from numerous exhibits about the town's history, this museum has some beautiful lace on display (open Mon–Sat 9am–noon).

✳ **McGregor** McGregor, 20km/12 km south of Robertson, is an attractive town;
here, at the northern border of the **Riviersonderendberg mountains**,
time seems to have stood still. Countless Cape Dutch houses built in
the mid-19th century are still standing, surrounded by lush orchards
and vegetable gardens. Appealing accommodation is available, making it a nice place for visitors to spend one or two relaxing days. This
is a good base from which to explore the Breede River valley. The
popular 14km/9mi **Boesmanskloof Trail** is very scenic; it makes its
way over the Riviersonderendberg mountains through a fynbos landscape to Greyton. It begins 16km/10mi south of McGregor at a place
called »Die Galg« and can be done in approx. 6 hours; a swim at
Oak Falls on the way is a good way to cool off. Hikers can either return the way they came or take a bus back. Reservations at Cape Nature Conservation (Vrolijkheid Nature Reserve), on the Robertson –
McGregor road, tel. 023 625 1621.

Sabie

J 4

Province: Mpumalanga
Population: 11,000

Altitude: 1109m/3638ft
Distances: Lydenburg 50km/30mi,
Nelspruit 65km/40mi

**Sabie is the place to stop on the way to the ▶Blyde River Canyon
and the ▶Kruger National Park. The pleasant climate, absence of
malaria and extensive forests planted by humans make this area a
popular holiday destination amongst South Africans.**

Surrounded by thick forests (a rarity in South Africa), Sabie is situated on the slope of the 2285m/7497ft Mount Anderson and the 2115m/6939ft Mauchberg . Sabie's economic significance stems from its status as the regional **centre of the timber industry** and the seat of the country's largest paper mill.

At the site now occupied by Sabie was a farm, which H. T. Glynn bought in 1880. During a party the host organized an event where the participants had to shoot empty bottles lined up in front of a rock. The bullets caused the rock to splinter, which in turn uncovered a gold vein. Between 1895 and 1950 gold was mined here. In 1913 Sabie gained a railway connection to Nelspruit.

Sabie's history

What to See in and around Sabie

The Komatiland Forestry Museum (Ford St./10th Lane) is the place to find out about the history of the forestry industry and the different tree species; Komatiland Ecotourism (trails) has its office here.

Forestry Museum

There are several fantastic waterfalls around Sabie, such as the **Horseshoe Falls** (1km/0.6mi north), the Bridal Veil Falls (8km/5mi west) and the 68m/223ft Lone Creek Falls (12km/7mi west). 11km/7mi towards Graskop (R 532) is a lookout point that has a fabulous view of the **Mac Mac Falls**. The twin waterfalls plummet 65m/213ft into a forested gorge; approx. 2km/1.2mi to the south-east the river forms a crystal-clear lake. For a short while gold was prospected here; there were many Scots amongst the prospectors – hence the name.

★
Waterfalls

► VISITING SABIE

INFORMATION
Tourist Office
Market Square
Sabie
Tel. 013 764 1125
www.panoramainfo.co.za

Komatiland Ecotourism
Tel. 013 764 1292
www.komatiecotourism.co.za

WHERE TO EAT
► **Inexpensive**
Loggerhead Restaurant
Main Road
Tel. 013 764 3341

Popular, cosy steakhouse, the speciality here is trout prepared in several different ways.

WHERE TO STAY
► **Budget**
Villa Ticino
Louis Trichardt St.
Tel. 013 764 2598
www.villaticino.co.za
Near the town centre, situated in a pretty garden, 10 rooms; breakfast on the terrace with gorgeous views. Good restaurant called Wild Fig Tree next door.

Long Tom Pass   The R 37 connects Sabie with ►Lydenburg to the west. The well-developed road that crosses the 2149m/7051ft Long Tom Pass follows the old Voortrekker route over the Transvaal Drakensberg mountains. The name dates back to the Boer War, when the Boers defended the pass against the British with two Long Tom cannons in 1900 (today visitors can see replicas). On the other side of the summit of the pass is a view of the wide, undulating farmland of the highveld.

St Francis Bay

F 9

Province: Eastern Cape   **Distances:** Port Elizabeth 100km/60mi

This wide bay on the Indian Ocean west of ►Port Elizabeth is a real paradise for beach lovers, surfers and boating enthusiasts.

The Portuguese seafarer Manuel Perestrelo named the town after the patron saint of seafarers, St Francis, in 1575. Several seaside resorts (almost all of them collections of holiday homes that are only inhabited for a few weeks a year) line the bay. The bay's attractions are the beautiful beaches and the waves; the bay's west beaches in particular boast huge super-tubes, attracting surfers from near and far (in 1966 the film *Endless Summer* was filmed here). Shell collectors can find some wonderful specimens here.

 VISITING ST FRANCIS BAY

INFORMATION

St. Francis Tourism
Lime Rd South /St Francis Drive
Tel. 042 294 0076
www.stfrancistourism.co.za

WHERE TO STAY

► Mid-range
Stratos
11 Uys St.
Jeffrey's Bay
Tel. 042 293 1116
www.stratos-za.com
Modern building right on the sea, eight rooms decorated in a tasteful »African« style (the ocean side is expensive). Under Swiss management.

Super Tubes Guesthouse
10 Pepper St., Jeffrey's Bay
Tel. 042 293 2957
www.supertubesguesthouse.co.za/
The name says it all. 30m/33yd from the sea, 6 very nice rooms with balconies facing the beach. Has a self-catering kitchen.

WHERE TO EAT

► Moderate
Breakers
Ferreira St.
Jeffrey's Bay
Tel. 042 293 1801
Gorgeous view over the ocean, fantastic cuisine with both original and traditional fish dishes.

What to See in St Francis Bay

The up-and-coming, upmarket holiday town of St Francis Bay at the mouth of the Krom River is a meeting place for sun lovers, surfers and also anglers, whose preferred fishing grounds are 12km/7mi up-river. The west end of the bay is **Cape St Francis**, a headland with a 28m/92ft lighthouse, which has been guiding the way for ships since 1876. Whales can be seen between July and October.

St Francis Bay

Jeffrey's Bay (»J'Bay«, population: 7000) is considered **the best place to surf in South Africa**; winter is the peak season, when consistent waves up to a height of 3m/10ft crash into the bay. A pretty 3km/2mi trail meanders through the **Noorskloof** nature reserve along the river into the valley. With a bit of luck visitors can spot antelopes and green monkeys.

Jeffrey's Bay

The Seekoei River Nature Reserve, to the south of Jeffrey's Bay near the holiday town of Aston Bay, was set up to protect the water birds living in the estuary. It is also home to some smaller antelope species (open daily 7am–5pm).

Seekoei River Nature Reserve
🕐

St Lucia Wetland Park · Isimangaliso

K 5/6

Province: KwaZulu-Natal   **Distances:** Durban ca. 200km/125mi

Far in the north-east of South Africa by the Indian Ocean around Saint Lucia Lake lies a globally significant ecosystem with a unique vegetation and an extraordinarily rich bird life.

Several nature reserves merged at the northern coast of KwaZulu-Natal province to form the **Greater St Lucia Wetland Park**. At the centre of this wetland region is Lake Saint Lucia, South Africa's largest natural inland lake. At the end of the 1980s a South African mining company attempted to get the right to mine titanium here; 450 environmental organizations from all around the world fought against this project and were finally successful in 1999, when the 2500 sq km/965 sq mi park was granted **UNESCO World Heritage** status.

Lake Saint Lucia is 40km/25mi long, up to 10km/6mi wide and only 1–2m/3–6.5ft deep. It spans the area parallel to the coast and is separated from the sea by a 180m/200yd wooded belt of dunes. More than 400 plant species have been counted here. The lake, into which the Imfolozi, Mkhuze and Hluhluwe rivers flow, is connected to the

Landscape

Sodwana Bay's sandy beaches make it a popular year-round holiday destination.

sea via a 20km/12mi canal. Thus **salt and fresh water** mix in Lake Saint Lucia, creating the perfect habitat for fish and water fowl. An endless sandy beach runs along the ocean's coastline. The 5.6km/3.5mi of ocean immediately offshore are also part of the nature reserve. **Colourful coral reefs** grow in the warm Agulhas current, providing a habitat for many exotic fish. Adjoining the dune landscape are marshy areas and grassland, which give way to bush savannah and arid savannah further inland.

Rich animal population

Around **530 (!) bird species** nest in the nature reserve. Thousands of flamingos and pelicans inhabit the shallow waters of Lake Saint Lucia. Hippopotamuses and crocodiles are also in their element here. Leatherback turtles and loggerhead sea turtles come to the coast to deposit their eggs between October and February. In addition the area is home to several antelope species; there is also the occasional leopard, buffalo and rhinoceros.

Drives and hikes

The drive from St Lucia to Cape Vidal (35km/22mi, only 100 vehicles permitted per day) conveys a good impression. All of the camps are starting points for hiking trails and nature trails through the **forested dune landscape** and the hinterland. The Crocodile Centre about 2km/1mi north of St Lucia is well worth a visit. The 6km/4mi **Mpophomeni Nature Trail** starts and ends in Camp False Bay. A number of operators offer further tours of all kinds. Boat rentals in St Lucia; boats set off on 2-hour round trips from here.

St Lucia

St Lucia, where the lake/river and the ocean meet, has become a holiday town and is particularly popular with 4 x 4 and motorboat lovers from mid-December to mid-January. Thankfully driving has been prohibited on the **stunning beaches** that run all the way to Cape Vidal; anyone swimming here does so at their own risk as there are neither shark nets nor life guards present.

Around St Lucia Wetland Parks

North of the Greater St Lucia Wetland Park the 413ha/1021-acre Sodwana Bay National Park stretches along the coast of the Indian Ocean. The coastal landscape is forested. Huge fig trees grow from the marshes and strelitzias create a splash of colour. The fauna here includes many bird species, red river hogs, antelopes and snakes. There are unspoilt coral reefs off the coast, for which reason the area is considered a **divers' paradise**; in 2002 a coelacanth, a »primordial fish«, was caught here. To get here, turn off from the N 2 towards Mbazwana 10km/6mi behind Hluhluwe; from there it is another 25km/16mi to Sodwana. After heavy rainfall the last stretch is impassable in a normal car. Accommodation in chalets and on campsites (►KZN Wildlife, p.156).

★
**Sodwana Bay
National Park**

► VISITING ST. LUCIA WETLAND PARK

INFORMATION
KZN Wildlife, ►p.156

Advantage Cruises & Charters
Dolphin Supermarket
McKenzie St., St Lucia
Tel. 035 5901259
www.zululink.co.za

ARRIVAL
Take the N 2 from Durban to Mtubatuba, after which it is another 28km/17mi to the town of Saint Lucia. The parts located further north (Fanie's Island, Charter's Creek) leave the N 2 approx. 20km/12mi north of Mtubatuba.

WHEN TO GO
The summer is very hot and rainy. Winter temperatures are more pleasant, but it can be quite windy. The ideal time to come is between April and June. Malaria precautions are indispensable.

FACILITIES
Several camps and campsites, particularly Charter's Creek, Fanie's Island, Mapelane, Cape Vidal, False Bay

(►KZN Wildlife). There are quite a large number of guesthouses, restaurants and bars in Saint Lucia.

WHERE TO EAT
Alfredo's
McKenzie St., St. Lucia
Tel. 035 590 1150
Pizza, pasta and salads, as well as occasionally music. Tables both inside and out.

Lagosta
McKenzie St.
St Lucia
Seafood diner (dishes such as fish pies, fish & chips, paella), good and inexpensive.

WHERE TO STAY
Seasands Lodge
135 Hornbill St.
St Lucia
Tel. 035 590 1082
www.seasands.co.za
Modern, well-kept house, secluded but close to the town centre. Big garden and pool. The restaurant (only for hotel guests) is considered the best in St Lucia.

Further interesting nature reserves can be found further north along the border to Mozambique: Kosi Bay Nature Reserve and ►Ndumo Game Reserve, to name two of them. Visits to ►Mkuzi Game Reserve or to ►Hluhluwe-Imfolozi Game Park are also worthwhile. In addition this part of the country has some private game reserves with luxurious lodges, such as the 17,000ha/42,000-acre **Phinda Private Game Reserve** west of the N 2 between Hluhluwe and Mkhuze (information and reservations at CCAfrica, ►p.121).

Somerset West

C 9

Province: Western Cape
Population: 29,000

Altitude: 8m/26ft
Distances: Cape Town 35km/22mi

On the round trip from Cape Town through the wine country around ►Stellenbosch and ►Paarl visitors should definitely make a stop in the small town of Somerset West, which is beautifully situated at the foot of the Helderberg mountain range.

Somerset West developed around a Dutch reformed church in 1822; it owes its name to the Cape governor Lord Charles Somerset. Pretty, well-tended exclusive residential areas with a lot of green dominate the townscape. Most notable amongst the older buildings are the police station, the old rectory and the **church dating from 1820**.

Around Somerset West

★ ★
Vergelegen

The region's best-known vineyard and one of the best and most attractive in the country is Vergelegen, once the residence of the governor Willem van der Stel, who acquired the property in 1700 (but was ordered back to the Netherlands on a charge of corruption). Apart from the Cape Dutch manor house the **ultra-modern wine**

 VISITING SOMERSET WEST

The renowned Avontuur vineyard with the Helderberg mountains as a backdrop

cellar is impressive. From it visitors have a wonderful view of False Bay. Wine tasting daily 9.30am–4pm, wine cellar tour Mon–Sat 10.30am, 11.30am, 2.30pm; the tea garden is open daily 10am–5pm. Classy, relatively inexpensive restaurant »Lady Phillips«. To get here take the road to the Helderberg Nature Reserve, tel. 021 847 1334, www.vergelegen.co.za.

The 245ha/605-acre nature reserve on the south-east face of the 1138m/3734ft Helderberg (open daily 7.15am–6pm) is famous for its large number of proteas and rich bird fauna. Hiking trails traverse the area. The ascent through the Disa Gorge (the red disa, an orchid, flowers from December to early February) to the **Helderberg Dome** is particularly attractive. The view from the peak is magnificent.

★ Helderberg Nature Reserve

Strand, which was intended to be a coastal suburb of Somerset West, soon outstripped the original town and today it is home to 50,000 people. The wonderful sunny beaches of **False Bay** make Strand a popular holiday town and day-trip destination for the inhabitants of Cape Town.

Strand

The fishing village of Gordon's Bay (population: 3,500) 8km/5mi to the south-east is quieter. However, the coastline in this area is also rocky and is better suited for fishing than for swimming. The drive along the coastal road towards ►Kleinmond is extremely scenic.

Gordon's Bay

Southeast of Somerset West the N 2 makes its way up to Sir Lowry's Pass. From the top of the pass (452m/1483ft) there is an **impressive view** of False Bay and the Cape peninsula. Approx. 30km/20mi from Somerset West are Grabouw and Elgin, the centre of **South Africa's largest fruit growing region**.

Sir Lowry's Pass

Grabouw

Stellenbosch

C 8

Province: Western Cape
Population: 67,000
(as well as 17,000 students)

Altitude: 114m/374ft
Distances: Cape Town 50km/30mi

This university town situated in a beautiful wine and fruit growing region is one of the prettiest towns in South Africa. Thanks to its proximity to Cape Town and many attractive destinations nearby, Stellenbosch is definitely worth a longer stay.

After Cape Town, Stellenbosch is the second-oldest European settlement on the Cape. Governor Simon van der Stel founded the town in 1679. The first farmers planted wheat, but they soon realized that the soil and climate was perfect for viticulture. Today this region is one of the country's **most important and best-known wine growing regions**. In addition the town has been a university town and economic centre for more than a century; since 1995 the university has also allowed non-whites to enrol.

History

Stellenbosch is one of the best-preserved towns from the time of the Dutch East India Company (VOC). The historic core around Die Braak and along Dorp Street has a large number of wonderful Cape Dutch buildings. The many old buildings have caused Stellenbosch to be nicknamed »town of oaks«. The town is colourful all year round and is marked by a wonderfully relaxed and cheerful atmosphere.

Townscape

What to See in Stellenbosch

The central square, called Die Braak (»The Fallow«), was the site of military parades and festivals – and is still used in this way from time to time today. The small church of **St Mary on the Braak** was consecrated in 1854 and in 1884 the belfry was added. The square is lined by significant historic buildings, such as the **VOC Kruithuis** (munitions magazine), built by the Dutch East India Company in 1777 (military museum, open Mon–Fri 9.30am–1pm). Next door is the **Burgerhuis** (Fick House) of 1797, seat of the »Historical Houses of South Africa« society (open Mon–Fri 9am–12.45pm, 2–5pm, Sat 10am–1pm, 2–5pm).

★
Die Braak

⏱

The Rhenish Church at the southern end of the Braak was built in 1823 as a school for coloureds and slaves. The pulpit is very attractive. The church complex also includes the **Rhenish Corner** with several buildings from the 19th century: the rectory of the Rhenish Mis-

★
Rhenish Complex

← *Wine landscape at the Cape: Dieu Donné estate near Franschhoek*

sion houses a toy museum (Toy & Miniature Museum; open Mon–Sat 9.30am–5pm. Sun 2–5pm), another building is used as the tourist office.

Stellenbosch University

The neo-classical Old Hoofgebou (1886) is the main building of South Africa's oldest university. It can be accessed via Beyers Street and Andringa Street. It was founded in 1866 as a grammar school and in 1887, Queen Victoria's jubilee year, was renamed Victoria College in her honour. In 1918 it was given university status. Here the Boer intellectual elite, the originators of the apartheid system, studied and taught, including later heads of government and ministers such as Jan Smuts, Daniel Malan, Hans Strijdom and H. F. Verwoerd. The university's main sport is rugby; 50 teams fight for the title.

Botanical Gardens

Not far to the east is the university's botanical garden (Neethling Street, open Mon–Fri 9am–4.30pm, Sat 9am–11am) with native succulents, orchids, cycads and welwitschias, which are native to the desert of Namibia.

Erfurt House

Take Ryneveld Street southbound to get to the Victorian Erfurt House built for Johan Beyers in 1876 (seat of the Stellenbosch Museum). The name of the elegant villa is a reference to the family's home town in Germany. The neo-Renaissance building (1907) across the street houses the university art collection (Eben Donges Centre, open Mon–Sat 9am–4pm, Sun 2–5pm).

Stellenbosch Map

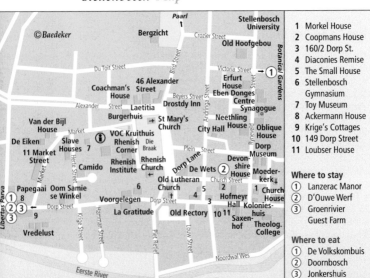

©Baedeker

1 Morkel House
2 Coopmans House
3 160/2 Dorp St.
4 Diaconies Remise
5 The Small House
6 Stellenbosch Gymnasium
7 Toy Museum
8 Ackermann House
9 Krige's Cottages
10 149 Dorp Street
11 Loubser House

Where to stay
1 Lanzerac Manor
2 D'Ouwe Werf
3 Groenrivier Guest Farm

Where to eat
1 De Volkskombuis
2 Doornbosch
3 Jonkershuis

The Rhenish Corner, founded by the Lutheran Rhenish Mission

The complex of the Dorp Museum (Village Museum, open Mon–Sat 9.30am–5pm, Sun 2–5pm) consists of four houses that still have their original furniture; the gardens have been landscaped in the style of that time. The **Schreuderhuis**, built around 1709 for the German summoner Sebastiaan Schröder, is South Africa's oldest townhouse. In 1789 the »Landdrost« (governor) **H. L. Bletterman** commissioned a building for himself that can be considered the textbook example of a Cape Dutch house with an H-shaped floor plan. The oldest part of the neo-classical **Grosvenor House** was built by the rich farmer C. L. Neethling in 1782. To the left of it are the former slave quarters, to the right a coach house. The **O. M. Bergh House** got its name from Oloff Martinus Bergh, who lived here until his death in 1866.

★ Dorp Museum

The Dutch reformed church opposite the museum is the fourth on this site. The first, built in 1722, had a thatched roof. The current one was built by the German architect Carl Otto Hager in the Gothic style in 1863. Visitors should definitely take a look at the pulpit and the very thick stained glass windows.

Moederkerk

Towards the south Drostdy Street joins with Dorp Street, the town's old tree-lined main road with its pretty white houses and artistic gables, romantically unkempt gardens and wrought-iron fences. The **Lutheran church** of 1851 now houses the University Art Gallery. No. 95 (La Gratitude), built as a rectory in 1798, has the »all-seeing eye« on the gable. It is now privately owned. **Oom Samie se Winkel** has been an emporium for all sorts of things since 1791.

★ Dorp Street

▶ VISITING STELLENBOSCH

INFORMATION

Stellenbosch Tourism Bureau
36 Market Street
Tel. 021 883 3584
www.stellenbosch.org.za

Franschhoek Tourist Office
68 Huguenot Road
Tel. 021 876 3603
www.franschhoek.org.za

FESTIVALS AND EVENTS

Beginning of Aug: Wine Festival
(South African wine lovers take this
opportunity to sample their way
through the 400 different wines at the
festival). End of Sep to beginning of
Jan: Stellenbosch Music Festival (from
classical to African). End of Oct:
Franschhoek Festival (classical music)

WHERE TO EAT

It is always advisable to make reservations over the phone. Restaurants
and vineyards are often booked by
business groups at the weekends.

▶ Expensive

① *De Volkskombuis*
Old Strand Road
Stellenbosch
www.volkskombuis.co.za
Tel. 021 887 2121
Traditional Cape Dutch cuisine in a
building designed by Sir Herbert
Baker. Light food with pizzazz, such
as deer steak stuffed with chicken liver
pate. The somewhat less expensive De
Oewer next door is also very nice.

Le Quartier Français
16 Hugenot Rd.
Franschhoek
Tel. 021 876 2248
www.lequartier.co.za
Small, but top notch. One of the best

restaurants in South Africa, in the
world even. Dishes inspired by Cape
Malay or Provençal cuisine. Accommodation comprises 15 rooms and
two luxurious apartments.

Boschendal Restaurant
Pniel Rd. (R 310),
Groot Drakenstein
Boschendal
Tel. 021 870 4272/3/4/5
www.boschendal.com
Stylish restaurant in an old wine
cellar. Great buffet at lunchtime with
French and South African specialities.
Or enjoy an inexpensive picnic in the
garden.

Haute Cabrière Cellars Restaurant
Franschhoek, am Franschhoek Pass
Tel. 021 876 3688
www.cabriere.co.za
The wines of this excellent vineyard
are best tasted during a meal in the
wine cellar.

▶ Moderate

② *Doornbosch Chez Axel*
Old Strand Road (R 44)
Stellenbosch
Tel. 021 887 5079
Very inviting restaurant with French-
Italian cuisine. Dining outside on the
veranda during the summer.

③ *Jonkershuis Restaurant*
Stellenbosch
6km/4mi south-west (R 310)
Tel. 021 809 1100
www.spier.co.za
150-year-old farmhouse in the Spier
vineyard. Nice terrace shaded by old
oak trees. Serves traditional Cape
cuisine; lavish buffet for a fixed
price.

WHERE TO STAY

► Luxury

① *Lanzerac Manor*

Lanzerac Road, Stellenbosch
Tel. 021 887 1132
www.lanzerac.co.za
Cape Dutch building on a vineyard
4km/2.5mi east of Stellenbosch. 40
luxurious rooms all furnished with a
personal note and all with their own
terrace. Three good restaurants. Golf,
hiking, wine tours.

► Mid-range/Luxury

② *D'Ouwe Werf Country Inn*

30 Church Street
Stellenbosch
Tel. 021 887 4608
www.ouwewerf.com
Classy house from 1802, allegedly the
oldest in South Africa. 31 rooms,
restored and comfortably furnished.
The good restaurant serves traditional
fare.

Auberge Clermont

Robertsvlei Road
Franschhoek
Tel. 021 876 3700
www.clermont.co.za
This magnificent redesigned old
winepress stands between 150-year-
old oak trees on a vineyard and fruit
farm. Surrounded by vines with a
view of the Franschhoek mountains.
A villa with space for six. Very
upmarket accommodation, associated
with the Haute Cabrière Cellars
restaurant.

L'Auberge Chanteclair

Middagkrans Road
Franschhoek
Tel. 021 876 3685
www.chanteclair.co.za
Victorian farmhouse near to the road
leading to the Franschhoek Pass in the
wine country, furnished in a stylish
and romantic manner.

► Budget/Mid-range

③ *Groenrivier Guest Farm*

Annandale Road, Stellenbosch
Tel. 021 881 3767
Apartments on a rose farm in a house
built in 1786, at the foot of the
Helderberg mountains 8km/5mi
south of Stellenbosch (R 44). Hiking,
swimming in the reservoir, ideal for
family holidays.

Libertas Parva, a wonderful house built in 1783 (31 Dorp Street),
houses a fine collection of South African art, including works by Irma Stern, J. H. Pierneef and A. van Wouw (open Mon–Fri
9am–12.45pm, 2–5pm, Sat 10am–1pm, 2–5pm). The gallery owes its
name to its sponsor, the Rembrandt tobacco company. The cellar of
Libertas Parva is devoted to the museum of the Distillers Corporation of SA (open Mon–Fri 9am–12.45pm, 2–5pm, Sat 10am–1pm,
2–5pm). It informs visitors about the development of viticulture by
means of tools and wines. In front of the building is an impressive
German wine press from the late 18th century.

◄ Rembrandt Van
Rijn Art Gallery
🕐

◄ Stellenryck
Wine Museum
🕐

In order to get back to the round trip's starting point, it is best to
walk back up Dorp Street and turn left into Herte Street; the slave
houses were built by former slaves after the slave liberation of 1838.

Slave houses

Around Stellenbosch

✱ Stellenbosch Farmers' Winery Centre

South Africa's largest winery operates a visitor centre along the road to Cape Town. It stages events on the history of the Cape wine as well as wine-tasting sessions (Sun–Fri 8am–5pm, Sat 10am–1pm) as well as tours through the wine cellar (Mon–Fri 10am, 2.30pm; tel. 021 808 7569). Opposite the winery the Oude Libertas Amphitheatre hosts concerts ranging from jazz to classical as well as stage performances.

✱ Stellenbosch Wine Route

The wine route (symbol: a white winding road in a green field, above it a green grape in a red field) leads to dozens of vineyards and five cooperatives, including such illustrious names as Morgenhof, Simonsig, Blaauwklippen, Neethlingshof and Overgaauw. The vineyards situated in the idyllic wine country offer wine tasting and their restaurants serve excellent food. Further information under tel. 021 886 4310, www.wineroute.co.za.

Neethlingshof

The R 310 leads south-west to the venerable Neethlingshof vineyard, which is particularly famous for its Noble Late Harvest Riesling. The Cape Dutch manor house built in 1814 is the location of the classy »Lord Neethling« restaurant; the »Palm Terrace« next door is rustic

Dining in the »Lord Neethling« is informal, but stylish

(wine tasting and sale Mon–Fri 9am–5pm, Sat, Sun 10am–4pm; reservations for the restaurants tel. 021 883 8988).

A nice outing to the south-east of Stellenbosch is the Jonkershoek Valley with its 168ha/415-acre Assegaaibosch Nature Reserve (open Mon–Fri 8.30am–4pm, Sat, Sun 9am–6pm), which is traversed by a good 2km/1mi round trail. This trail also leads to a 5ha/12-acre wildflower garden.

Assegaaibosch Nature Reserve ⏱

It is possible to hike from Jonkershoek Valley to the Hottentots Holland Nature Reserve. This reserve of almost 25,000ha/62,000 acres cannot be reached by car, but only via the **Boland Hiking Trail** (it can also be accessed at Sir Lowry's Pass, ►Somerset West). The nature reserve has an unusually rich flora; besides antelopes such as grey rehboks, springboks and duikers, visitors can also occasionally spot leopards, caracals and jackals here.

Hottentots Holland Nature Reserve

The drive to Franschhoek, around 30km/20mi to the east (R 310), should not be missed. Beyond Stellenbosch the road rises to the **Helshoogte Pass** (336m/1102ft), from which there are some magnificent views; on the other side of the pass is the Boschendal vineyard. The manor house of 1812 is a wonderful example of Cape Dutch architecture (accessible daily 11am– 1pm, 2–4pm). The vineyard's products can be tasted at the wine bar, or with a delicious meal in the »Taphuis« restaurant; the best thing to do however, is to picnic on the lawn. Wine tasting Mon–Sat 8.30am–4.30pm, Nov–Apr, also Sun 9.30am–12.30pm. Reservations for the restaurant and the picnic. ►p.476.

Boschendal

> ! **Baedeker** TIP
>
> **Tokara**
>
> The setting of the modern buildings of the Tokara vineyard at the Helshoogte Pass (on the way to the top class Thelema vineyard) is absolutely breathtaking. Etienne Bonthuys, the chef who combines old-world tradition with new-world innovation creates equally stunning highs in the kitchen, which can be seen through a glass wall. www.tokararestaurant.co.za, tel. 021 808 5959. Very upscale prices.

From the junction The R 310 with the R 45 drive to the town of Franschhoek (population: 4000), a town in the midst of wine country that was founded by Huguenots in 1688. The name means **French corner**, and this wine town still has a noticeably French air. Amongst the immigrants were numerous winemakers, who soon realized that the soil and the climate made it possible to produce top-quality wines in this region. Franschhoek is also the starting point of a wine route that makes it way through some lovely landscape (information ►p.476).

Franschhoek

At the southern end of Franschhoek is the Huguenot Monument, which was designed by C. Steynberg in 1938 in memory of the 250th

Huguenot Monument

anniversary of the valley's settlement. The central figure is a woman holding a Bible and a broken chain, a symbol of liberation from religious oppression. The museum (open Mon–Sat 9am–5pm, Sun 2–5pm) documents the history of the Huguenots in South Africa.

✱
Franschhoek Pass

Beyond the monument the road ascends again; from the Franschhoek Pass (701m/2300ft) the view over the wine country and vineyards is truly stunning. To get back to Stellenbosch visitors should take the road to Grabouw via **Viljoen's Pass** (525m/1722ft), which joins the N 2, the same road that leads to ▶ Somerset West. From there it is another 18km/11mi to Stellenbosch.

✱ Sun City

G 4

Province: North West　　　　**Distances:** Johannesburg 180km/110mi

The »Las Vegas of southern Africa« is set in a luxuriant green landscape, in the territory previously occupied by the Bophuthatswana homeland. During the apartheid era Sun City was a destination for mixed-race couples and white gamblers; at the time it was referred to as »Sin City«.

Sun City, a vast amusement complex north-west of Johannesburg, has up to 25,000 visitors a day who come here by air (Sun City Airport) or by car (approx. 2 hours' drive from Johannesburg). Sun City consists of hotel complexes, of which the Palace of the Lost City is the most exclusive. Everything imaginable is done to entertain the guests: this town boasts the world's largest casino, cinemas, night-

 VISITING SUN CITY

INFORMATION
Tel. 014 557 1000
www.suninternational.de
bookings Tel. 011 780 7800

WHERE TO STAY
The hotels all belong to the luxury category; the Palace is the most expensive of them all. It is necessary to book well in advance for stays during the holiday seasons.

The Palace
This hotel offers visitors incredible

pomp and kitsch with a view of the artificial »valley of the waves« and the golf course.

The Cascades
Nicely situated hotel with a view of the water cascades in the tropical garden. Princely rooms.

Sun City Hotel
Rooms with a view of the swimming pool and lake. In-house Sun City Casino, nightclub, restaurants etc.

The »Palace« of the Lost City: fairytale pomp

clubs, a huge variety of water sports and a world-famous golf course. The stadium hosts sporting events and pop concerts. The concept of Sun City as an amusement park is a successful one: the hotels have 80% occupancy rates, which is something other luxury establishments can only dream of.

What to See in and around Sun City

In 1992 the fantastical Lost City hotel and leisure complex was opened. The Lost City is meant to remind visitors of a legendary African culture, which however never existed in that form; it is a technologically perfect illusion. The centre of the complex is The Palace, a luxury hotel with 338 rooms, an architectural mix of styles that nevertheless seems relatively harmonious. A 70m/230ft tower rises above it, and the 25m/82ft-high hotel lobby feels more like a cathedral: in Lost City everything is somewhat oversized. Below the hotel is a 25ha/62-acre tropical rainforest. Trees weighing up to 40 tons were brought here. Watercourses form waterfalls that plummet up to 16m/52ft to the ground. The sand for the »Roaring Lagoon« beach also had to be brought to The Lost City from far away. Mechanically produced waves that are suitable for surfing break on the white sand. In order to create a »real« feeling of Africa, animal sounds can be heard through loudspeakers day and night, and computer-operated machines occasionally create the illusion of an earthquake. Visitors have to decide for themselves whether this is enjoyable or just Disneyland kitsch. Access to the Lost City from the other hotel complexes in Sun City is only possible with limitations.

✶
The Lost City

Those who want to escape this artificial world can go on a safari through Pilanesberg National Park north of Sun City (open approx. 6am–6pm, depending on the time of year; park office tel. 014 555 5356). Visitors not coming from Sun City can reach the main en-

✶
Pilanesberg National Park

trance via the R 510, which connects Rustenburg with Thabazimbi. The 58,000ha/143,000-acre malaria-free terrain is situated where **the arid Kalahari turns into the humid lowveld** in a hilly landscape, the site of the Pilanesberg (1687m/5535ft) mountain. At its centre is the caldera of a **dormant volcano** with the Mankwe Dam; the Lenong Lookout has the best view of the crater. Wild animals from other regions were settled in the area, including elephants from the Kruger National Park. The park is home to plains zebras, rhinoceroses, leopards, giraffes, buffaloes and many antelope species amongst others, as well as 350 bird species that visitors can watch from their own cars (150km/95mi of good roads and tracks) or on guided walks. Visitors wanting to stay the night in the park have the choice between luxurious lodges (www.legacyhotels.co.za) and inexpensive chalets with camping (www.goldenleopard.co.za).

Swaziland

J/K 4/5

Area: 17,364 sq km/6704 sq mi		**Altitude:** up to 1862m/6109ft	
Population: 1.1 million		**Capital:** Mbabane	

The second-smallest state of the African mainland, which borders South Africa in the north-east, is an impressive country with a varied flora, which can be explored in well-run reserves, and a friendly, relaxed atmosphere.

Swaziland (the Swazi name for their country is Ngwane), located in the south-east of the African continent, borders on South Africa in the north, south and west and on Mozambique in the east. Its total area of 17,364 sq km/6704 sq mi makes it somewhat smaller than Wales and after Gambia it is the second-smallest state on the African mainland. It is a monarchy, with the king as head of state. The job of the parliament is mainly limited to advising the king, who also appoints the head of government. Political parties are prohibited. The official language is Swazi (siSwati), and occasionally English is used as an administrative and educational language. Game reserves and the highveld mountain landscape are the most important attractions in tourism. Most of the foreign visitors to Swaziland come from South Africa.

Swaziland's natural environment

The mountains in the west of the country (in the Mlembe reaching an altitude of 1862m/3796ft) are part of the Great Escarpment of the South African interior plateau (highveld). This mountainous region receives a lot of precipitation and is traversed by many rivers. Thanks to afforestation efforts it has thick forests and is also the country's most important economic region, as iron ore is mined here. Adjoining the highveld in the east is a fertile hilly landscape (middelveld),

Small farmstead in the rocky landscape of the Happy Valley

which in turn borders the flat, equally fertile lowveld (200–300m/ 650–1000ft) in the east. For 150km/90mi the Lebombo Mountains (around 600m/2000ft) form the natural border to Mozambique in the east. This basalt mountain range, which is geologically related to the Drakensberg mountains of South Africa, runs from the northern Zululand 600km/370mi northwards to the Limpopo. The main river system, the Usutu with its tributaries, flows into the Pongola beyond the eastern border; its valley is the main settlement region of the Swazi people.

Climate and vegetation

The mountain regions have a temperate, subtropical climate and receive a lot of rainfall. The middelveld also receives a fair amount of rain annually at 1000mm/40in and is the country's main agricultural region. The lowveld is hot and dry, extensive irrigation cultivation takes place here, particularly of sugar cane. The eucalyptus and pine forests mainly arose by afforestation and are mainly to be found in the highveld, which is otherwise dominated by grassland. The middelveld has some umbrella thorn acacias, while the arid lowveld is a savannah with thorn bushes.

Population

95% of the population are Swazi; in addition there are a few thousand people of mixed descent, Europeans, Indians and Pakistanis, as well as 50,000 refugees from Mozambique. The country's population growth at more than 3 per cent a year is very high. The population density is 49 inhabitants/sq km. The eastern parts of the country are more densely populated and also continue to attract more and more people. More than two thirds of the population live in rural areas. Animistic Bantu religions and the African Apostolic Church are the main religions.

▶ VISITING SWAZILAND

INFORMATION

Swazi Tourist Board
Swazi Plaza, Mbabane
Tel. (00268) 404 2531
www.mintour.gov.sz
www.welcometoswaziland.com
www.visitswazi.com

Tourism Information
Ngwenya Border Post, tel. 442 4206
Mantenga Craft Centre
Ezulwini Valley, tel. 416 1136

ARRIVAL AND ROADS

The twelve border crossings into
South Africa are open only during the
day; Oshoek/Ngwenya, Mahamba and
Lavumisa/Golela are open until 10pm.
Planes from Johannesburg fly to
Matsapha airport near Manzini; connections to Mbabane (35km/22mi)
via taxi, rental car or hotel bus. The
Baz Bus runs through Swaziland. The
most important roads are surfaced,
but all roads and tracks are in bad
condition. Visitors wanting to go to
remote areas should inquire about the
state of the roads, particularly during
the wet season from October to
March. Malaria precautions are necessary.

FESTIVALS AND EVENTS

19 April: birthday of King Mswati III.
End of Aug/beginning of Sept: Umh-
langa Festival. 06 Sept: national hol-
iday. Dec–Jan: approx. 3 weeks:
Incwala Festival (▶p.486). 25 Dec:
Independence Day.

WHERE TO EAT
▶ Moderate
Calabash
Ezulwini Valley, tel. 416 1187
The leading restaurant in Swaziland
(near the Timbali Lodge) serves

specialities from Austria and Germany.

▶ Inexpensive
The Mediterranean
Gwamile St., Mbabane, tel.404 3212
Good Indian cuisine with curries and
seafood; South African and Portu-
guese wines.

WHERE TO STAY
▶ Luxury
Royal Swazi Sun
Ezulwini Valley, tel. 416 5000
www.suninternational.com
Luxury hotel, colonial style with an
elegant casino, three good restaurants
(inexpensive buffet restaurant), golf,
swimming pool, tennis etc., the view
from any one of the 149 rooms is
magnificent. Two further Sun Hotels
in the area.

▶ Mid-range
Lugogo Sun
Ezulwini Valley, tel. 416 4000
Large hotel complex (202 rooms) of
international standard. With a res-
taurant, bar and swimming pool.

Phophonyane Lodge
Pigg's Peak (14km/9mi north)
Tel. 437 1429, 437 1319
Thatched cottages and a luxury tent
camp, gorgeous location above the
cascades of Phophonyane River. Self-
catering is possible, but there is also
an excellent restaurant.

▶ Budget
City Inn
Gwamile St., Mbabane, tel. 404 2406
Centrally located »classic« hotel with
28 rooms in the old and the new part.
Choose a room after viewing what is
available.

The Swaziland economy is greatly dependent on its neighbour South Africa. In addition many thousands of migrant workers are employed in South Africa too. The service sector is the most important. Even though agriculture employs two thirds of the population, it makes the smallest contribution to the country's GDP. Most agricultural land is used for subsistence farming; the king leases the land via local authorities. The rest belongs to farmers of European origin or to companies. The prestige that livestock farming brings makes it more important to the Swazi than arable farming. As a result the livestock population is very large, causing overgrazing and soil erosion. The government has been trying to use cooperatives to get farmers to produce more for the market and more staple crops. Artificial irrigation is used in the lowveld to cultivate citrus fruits, rice and sugar cane. Sugar is the most important agricultural export. Other important export crops are cotton and citrus fruits, while corn and millet, the traditional staple foods, are grown for home consumption. Forestry is particularly prevalent in the highveld and is of great significance following major efforts at afforestation. Coniferous wood (mostly pine) dominates.

Economy

The industrial sector is responsible for almost a third of the country's total GDP. The main economic activities here are the food and drink industries, particularly sugar-cane processing, as well as the timber processing and paper industries. In addition there are textile and metal-working companies as well as chemical plants. Apart from the coal mines in Mpaka, there are known deposits at the country's eastern border. Further natural resources include kaolinite, diamonds, gold and tin. The country's imports, mainly from South Africa, include machines, vehicles, fuel and food, while the exports, mainly to South Africa and the EU, are food, animals and wood. Swaziland meets almost half of its energy requirements through electricity imported from South Africa and it also has smaller coal-fired power plants and hydroelectric power stations.

The Swazi came to this region during the Nguni migrations around 1750. In the 19th century important kings (Sobhuza I, c1780–1839; Mswati II, c1820–68) formed the Swazi (»people of the Mswati«) nation from the Swazi upper class, old-established Sotho and other Nguni groups who had migrated to the area. At the beginning of the 19th century the first whites came into the country, including adventurers, hunters, merchants, missionaries and farmers. Since the pressure from the new arrivals, particularly from the Boers coming from Transvaal, was getting greater and greater, Mswati asked the British for protection, which they granted with some conditions attached. His grandson and successor Mbandzeni sold large parts of the land. In addition he transferred all mining rights to South Africa. After the British had annexed Transvaal, they dictated Swaziland's independence from Transvaal and its modern borders. From 1894 to 1899 the country had been a protectorate of Transvaal. Until the legendary

History

king Sobhuza II (1899–1982) ascended the throne, the country was ruled by his grandmother, who requested her subjects to buy back Swaziland. Under her government the country became a British protectorate in 1903. The land distribution conducted by the British gave the Swazi mainly agricultural land. Despite growing problems between the colonial administration and the regents, the Swazi participated on the side of the British in the Second World War. In return, the British bought land from the whites and gave it back to the indigenous people. After achieving independence on 6 September

(the national holiday) in 1968, King Sobhuza II remained the head of state. In 1972 he nullified the democratic constitution because of political differences and prohibited all parties. In 1978 a new constitution came into effect, which granted only an advisory role to the two-chamber parliament. After the death of Sobhuza II and the regency of his two widows, his son Mswati III succeeded him in 1986 and has kept absolute power to this day, even though a commission to reform the constitution was set up in 1996; and in 2001, as a result of domestic and foreign pressure the suppression of the press and of trade unions was relaxed and the judiciary was made more independent.

On the way to school in the Ezulwini Valley

Traditional festivals

The **Incwala**, a kind of fertility ceremony, is impressive. To start, during the new moon delegates of the Bemanti people are sent to get water from all of Swaziland's large rivers as well as spray from the ocean. Young men gather branches of the lusekwana tree and plants for the royal kraal in Lobomba. The central festival begins there in the night of the next full moon and lasts six days. On the »Day of the Bull« a bull is killed and sacrificed. The following »Great Day« is the climax of the festival: the king, dressed in his best robes, symbolically tastes the first fruits of the harvest and there is dancing and singing. On the last day all the ceremonial objects are burned, an action connected to the hope for rain. Visitors are welcome during the ceremony, except during certain parts, but photographs and audio recordings are prohibited. Every two years the **Umhlanga** is celebrated in Lobamba. It is a reed dance in which only girls of marriageable age are allowed to participate. They go out for several days collecting reed, and dance in front of the king's mother; on this occasion the king chooses a new wife.

Mbabane – Siteki – Bhalekane – Mbabane (300km/185mi)

Mbabane (population: 60,000), the capital, was founded by European pioneers. In 1888 a shop was opened around which a village soon developed. After Swaziland became a British protectorate in 1903, the administrative seat was moved from Bremersdorp (modern-day Manzini) to Mbabane because of the pleasant climate. The resulting town has developed into far-flung districts with pretty gardens and shady streets. The only thing of interest to tourists is the **Swazi Market** at the southern end of Gwamile Street (formerly Allister Miller St.), the main shopping street. Besides the country's agricultural products, arts and crafts such as masks, basket goods and pottery can be obtained here.

Mbabane

The picturesque landscape makes a trip to Pine Valley north of Mbabane an attractive proposition. The tour makes its way along the Umbeluzi River and its waterfalls. It is an excellent area for hiking and riding, and also has pleasant temperatures during the summer.

Pine Valley

The »Valley of the Sky« goes from Mbabane towards Manzini in the south-east. As it is the home of the royal family it is also known as the **Royal Valley**. The steep road through the picturesque valley was considered one of the most dangerous in the world; today there is a highway to Manzini, which has an international airport. All along the valley are most of the country's big (and relatively expensive) hotels as well as a casino and further establishments such as stables, hot springs and shops with good arts and crafts (the **Mantenga Craft Centre** is particularly good).

Ezulwini Valley

Approx. 20km/12mi from Mbabane in the Ezulwini Valley is the **Royal Village**, which has the royal kraal, parliament buildings, a national museum and further government buildings. The king holds audiences in the **Embo State Palace**, the huge royal palace (it had to house Sobhuza II's 600 descendants), while the magnificent **State House** of 1978 mainly has a representative function (neither of them are accessible to the public, taking pictures is prohibited). The **parliament** of 1979 can be visited. The **national museum** (open Mon–Fri 8am–4pm, Sat, Sun 10am–4pm), located in a pretty garden, has interesting archaeological and historical exhibits illustrating every era of Swaziland's history and culture. Next to the museum there is a Swazi kraal.

✱ Lobamba

The Somhlolo Stadium in Lobamba, a place for cultural and sporting events as well as state celebrations

Mlilwane Wildlife Sanctuary

 4km/2.5mi from Lobamba is the Sangweni Gate to the Mlilwane Wildlife Sanctuary, the best-known sanctuary in Swaziland (very busy during the South African holiday times). Ted Reilly, a contentious animal rights activist transformed his Mlilwane (»small fire«) farm into a sanctuary with the help of King Sobhuza II and gave it to the state in 1964. Together with the land destroyed by tin mining the reserve grew to 4560ha/11,270 acres. Bushes and grasses dominate the land surrounded by the **Nyonyane mountains** (»place of the small bird«). This place is home to 470 bird species and many native mammals such as zebras, rhinoceroses, crocodiles, giraffes, hippopotamuses and antelopes. Visitors definitely should not miss the **Mantenga Falls**. Overnight accommodation in Swazi huts and on the campsite. Guided tours on horseback or by car. Information and reservations at Big Game Parks, P. O. Box 311, Malkerns, tel. 528 3943, www.biggameparks.org.

! **Baedeker TIP**

Malkerns Valley

To experience a more original atmosphere in the Ezulwini Valley, take time to visit Malkerns south of Mlilwane Wildlife Sanctuary. After a sundowner in the Ekuthuleni bar, dine in the Mangozeni or the Malandela's Homestead (famous for its shrimps). The atmosphere on Friday and Saturday evenings is jolly.

Manzini

A good 15km/9mi east of Lobamba is Manzini (population: 52,000), the country's economic centre. A shop and a hotel formed the core of the town at the Mzimneni River at the end of the 19th century, which was renamed Manzini (»located near water«) in 1960. In 1890, as Bremersdorp, it became the administrative seat of the British and the Boers, but it lost this status to Mbabane just a few years later. The town possesses cotton and meat processing plants, a brewery and electronic industry. In the spring its streets turn into a sea of purple and red when the **jacaranda and royal poinciana** are in bloom. There is much to see and experience at the market on the road to Mbabane on Friday and Saturday mornings. Besides fruit, vegetables and everyday necessities the market also sells good arts and crafts.

Beyond Manzini the drive eastwards from the last elevations of the middelveld affords a great view of the **lowveld** with the Lebombo mountains in the distance. The road runs through extensive pasture land. Afterwards the road climbs steeply into the mountains and the views of the lowveld become more and more spectacular.

Siteki

Siteki (population: 1500), located in a park landscape with jacaranda and tulip trees, is a small commercial and administrative town in the Lebombo district. Its name means »place of the many weddings«, which gives rise to speculation as to how the town was formed.

Hlane Royal National Park

Take the same road back from Siteki for 13km/8mi and then take the northbound road to the Hlane (»wilderness«) Royal National Park.

This national park was set up in 1967, and with its 30,000ha/74,000 acres is the country's largest. It belongs to the king, who organized a hunt here every year. It is a mecca for nature lovers. Besides the impressive bush vegetation it the park boasts elephants, giraffes, water buffaloes, zebras and crocodiles. Accommodation in two romantic self-catering camps (reservations at Big Game Parks, see above Mlilwane).

The small, surprisingly pleasant town of Simunye (population: 5000) at north-eastern border of Hlane Royal National Park was built for the workers of the large, modern **sugar factory**. East of the town, all the way to the Lebombo mountains is the 18,000ha/44,500 acre Mlawula Nature Reserve; the diverse landscape, ranging from thorn bush savannah to mountain forests, is home to an equally diverse fauna, particularly noteworthy for the approx. 350 bird species (best during the months of September and October).

Simunye

Mlawula Nature Reserve

From the junction at the bridge over the Mbuluzi River the route carries on westwards through sugar cane and citrus plantations. The road passes Mhlume, which has the country's largest sugar factory, and then reaches **Tshaneni** (»near the small stone«). In this region dams for irrigating the fields were built. Beyond the town of Bhalekane visitors can either take the southbound road via Croydon back to Manzini or the track to Pigg's Peak (76km/47mi from Tsaheni) to the north-west. The landscape along this route climbing up towards the mountains is enchanting.

Mhlume, Bhalekane

Mbabane – Bhunya – Nhlangano (190km/120mi)

Usuthu Forest (mainly pine trees) is 65,000ha/160,500 acres, making it one of the largest artificially created forest areas in the world. Visi-

Usuthu Forest

Stalking game in the Mlilwane Sanctuary

Bhunya

tors can drive through it from Mbabane on the southbound road via Mhlambanyatsi to Bhunya. Along the way visitors can enjoy many impressive view of the forest landscape. The quietly and beautifully situated **Forester's Arms** hotel approx. 12km/7mi outside Bhunya is famous for its Sunday lunch and highly recommendable (www.forestersarms.co.za, tel. 467 4177). Bhunya itself has a paper factory whose environmental impact is an output of more than 200,000 tons of paper a year.

Mankayane ►

Nhlangano ►

Hlatsikhulu ►

After leaving Bhunya the road goes east. At Loyengo visitors should take the southbound road to Mankayane through an attractive, primeval landscape. It passes the **Ngabeni mission** as well as the Mtimani Forest before reaching Mankayane, which has a few shops. The road then continues in a south-westerly direction to Sicunusa and subsequently south-east towards Nhlangano through the picturesque **Grand Valley**, which is also used for agricultural activities and was the settlement area of the Swazi during the mid-18th century. The name »Nhlangano« (»meeting place«) goes back to the meeting between King Sobhuza II and King George VI in 1947. The wonderfully situated **Nhlangano Sun Hotel** (tel. 207 8211) has a popular casino. From Hlatsikhulu, 27km/17mi north of Nhlangano, there is a great view of the Grand Valley. The road via Manzini goes back to Mbabane.

Mbabane – Pigg's Peak (70km)

Motshane

Leave Mbanabe in a north-westerly direction. After 15km/9mi the road reaches the settlement of Motshane (Motjane). From here the unsurfaced road runs north through wonderful undulating grassland with rocky hills; in the west are the Ngwenya and Silotwane Mountains.

✳
Malolotja
Nature Reserve

The 18,000ha/44,500-acre Malolotja Nature Reserve (»river with many rapids and waterfalls«) has some of the world's oldest rock formations, many reptiles and more than 280 bird species as well as an unusual flora. The **Ngwenyamine** is located in the south of the park (open to visitors Sat–Sun, book a day in advance); it is probably **the oldest mine in the world**. Hematite and smectite were mined here 45,000 years ago. More recently iron ore was extracted (this was discontinued in the 1970s). There are more than 200km/125mi of hiking trails, each of which can be completed in one to seven days. Camps and campsites provide accommodation. A tour to the San rock drawings or to the 95m/312ft **Malolotja Falls** in the Nkomati Valley are both recommendable. Information/bookings in the Tourist Office Ezulwini or at the National Trust Commission (National Museum, P. O. Box 100, Lobamba, tel. 416 1178, www.sntc.org.sz).

Nkaba

From the small market town of Nkaba it is 22km/14mi to valley of the fast-flowing Nkomati River, whose scenery of unusually beautiful shapes and colours is enchanting. The road climbs up on the valley's north side and goes past the plantations of Swaziland Plantation Ltd. and a sawmill.

Pigg's Peak

The town of Pigg's Peak owes its existence to the gold found here in 1881. Three years later William Pigg started a gold mine that remained in use for 70 years. In the town itself, a centre of the lumber industry, there are shops, administrative buildings and a market selling arts and crafts.

★
Phophonyane Nature Reserve

A detour to the imposing waterfalls on the Phophonyane River 13km/8mi north-east of Pigg's Peak is definitely worthwhile. The area, which has been used as a backdrop for films, boasts lush vegetation and a rich bird population. 3km/2mi off the MR 1 is the very nice, luxurious **Phophonyane Lodge** (►p.484).

Havelock Mine

BulembuA mine 21km/13mi west of Pigg's Peak was named after Arthur Havelock, a governor of Natal. It was one of the world's largest **asbestos mines** until its closure in 2001. Gold was found here in 1886, which attracted people from all around the world for three decades. A 20km/12mi-long freight cable-car ran from the mine to Barberton (►Nelspruit and around).

Manzini – Big Bend – Lavumisa (155km/95mi)

This route, the main route into the South African province of Kwa-Zulu-Natal, leaves Manzini and makes its way through the lower middelveld. The town of Siphofaneni (»yellow-brown place«) with its hot mineral springs is on this road. The **Usuthu**, the country's largest river with fig trees lining its picturesque banks, flows along here. It is well suited for fishing. Soon after is the turning to the 6250ha/16,550-acre private Mkhaya Game Reserve, one of the most interesting reserves in southern Africa. It is necessary for visitors to register in advance (Big Game Parks, see above Mlilwane); day visits are possible, accommodation in the house of Mickey Reilly, built at the beginning of the 19th century, in tents or in thatched cottages made of dolerite stone.

★
◄ Mkhaya Game Reserve

Big Bend

Big Bend, site of a large factory owned by Ubombo Sugar, is located in a bend of the Usuthu River in a region that produces sugar cane. A visit to the Emoya Crafts Centre is worthwhile; it sells arts and crafts from all around Swaziland. The road along the **Lebombo Mountains** is particularly scenic. It goes past the town of Nsoko (the nearby private Game Lodge Nisela's Safaris makes for a pleasant stop) and after approx. 80km/50mi it finally reaches the border town of **Lavumisa**, which completely lives up to its name (»hot place«) during the summer months.

★ Swellendam

D 10

Province: Western Cape	**Altitude:** 122m/400ft
Population: 8500	**Distances:** Cape Town 240km/150mi

Below the towering peaks of the Langberg mountains, the attractive town of Swellendam east of Cape Town was the third European town to be founded in South Africa and has many Cape Dutch, Georgian and Victorian buildings.

Swellendam, situated in a wet valley along the Langberg mountains, acts as the centre for the surrounding agricultural area. The pretty townscape is shaped by many historical buildings, including wonderful villas, the Drostdy and the church, old oak trees and countless rose bushes.

History   The Hasekwa, a Khoikhoi tribe, settled in this region and lived off the rich game population. The graves of the last two chiefs Klaas and Markus Shababa can be seen in Bontebokskloof. Swellendam was founded in 1745 as an outpost of the Dutch East India Company; it owes its name to the governor Swellengrebel and his wife Helena ten Damme. In the first half of the 19th century the town, being a centre of the wool industry, developed into a commercial and administrative centre.

What to See in and around Swellendam

Oefeningshuis   The only surviving old building in the centre is the mission of 1838, now the tourist office. One of the two clocks is permanently set at 12.45, the time of the daily religious service. Inhabitants who were unable to tell the time only needed to compare the two dials to avoid

The Drostdy, one of the country's most beautiful Cape Dutch houses

coming late. Diagonally opposite is the grand Dutch Reformed Church of 1910, built in a pretty mix of styles.

The Drostdy (1747) was the seat of the Cape government district official. Nice old furniture and personal effects are on display here (open daily). The old prison (with a good café), the house of the prison official and the Mayville house of 1853 are also part of the complex.

★
Drostdy Museum Complex

There are some nice walks in the 14,123ha/34,899-acre reserve located 5km/3mi north at the foot of the Langberg mountains. The trails vary in length between 5km/3mi and 11km/7mi and there is also the 74km/46mi Swellendam Trail (6 days). Reservations with the Marloth Reserve manager at the entrance, tel. 028 514 1410 (www.capenature.org.za).

Marloth Nature Reserve

The original habitat of the bontebok (*Damaliscus dorcas dorcas*), an antelope species, was the 56km/35mi-wide plain between Bot River in the west and Mossel Bay in the east. Until the late 18th century it was the grazing ground for large bontebok herds, but in the 19th century the population dropped to just 17. The park, approx. 3000ha/7500 acres (entrance 7km/4.5mi south-east of Swellendam), was set up to protect these animals. Lang Elsieskraal, a former Khoikhoi encampment, is an excellent location from which to watch the bontebok. The park is also home to grey rehboks, mountain zebras, Bates's pygmy antelopes and common duikers as well as to 200 bird species. The park has more than 470 plant species, which unfold a sea of colour during spring. Visitors can watch the animals from their own car; in addition there are two short hiking trails. Breede River is good for swimming and fishing. Picnic sites and campsites are available. Information SANParks, ►p.156.

★
Bontebok National Park

► VISITING SWELLENDAM

INFORMATION
Swellendam Tourism
Oefiningshuis, 36 Voortrek St.
Tel. 028 514 2770
www.swellendam.org.za

WHERE TO STAY
► Mid-range
Adin & Sharon's Hideaway
10 Hermanus Steyn St.
Tel. 028 514 3316, www.adinbb.co.za
Friendly B & B in a 100-year-old house with large, lovingly furnished suites. Garden with hundreds of rose bushes. The breakfast includes homemade jam and muesli.

WHERE TO EAT
► Moderate
Roosje van de Kaap
5 Drostdy Street, tel. 028 514 3001
www.roosjevandekaap.com
This restaurant is considered the best in town: Cape Malay cuisine and the best wood-stove pizza, romantic ambience, candlelight dinners in the evenings. Very nice guesthouse.

★ Tulbagh

D 9

Province: Western Cape
Population: 3000

Altitude: 200m/656ft
Distances: Cape Town 130km/80mi

This pretty little town in front of the dramatic backdrop of Witsenberg mountain is one of the best examples of Cape Dutch settlements and is also one of the famous wine towns around Cape Town.

History

The first settlers came into the valley of the Little Berg River in 1699. Since the land is very fertile, they founded numerous farms and in the mid-18th century built a church. It became the centre of the town of Tulbagh, named after a governor of the Cape province. Besides viticulture the soil and the climatic conditions also favour the cultivation of fruit, and sheep farming is also of significance.

Townscape

The magnificent Victorian and Cape Dutch houses that were destroyed in an earthquake in 1969 were rebuilt in their original form. The 32 gabled houses on Church Street dating from the 18th and 19th centuries are extremely attractive. »De Oude Herberg«, the first hotel (1885), is still a guesthouse with lots of atmosphere (▶below).

Wine & Sherry Route

Tulbagh is the starting point for the Wine & Sherry Route. Wine tasting and sales are offered by the Tulbagh Winery and the Drostdy-Hof Wine Cellar 3km/2mi north of the town, amongst others; the Twee Jonge Gezellen (with South Africa's first underground cellar for sparkling wine) and Theuniskraal estates also organize guided tours. More detailed information in the tourist office (www.tulbaghwineroute.com).

 VISITING TULBAGH

INFORMATION
Tourist Information
14 Church St., tel. 023 230 1348
www.tulbagh.com

WHERE TO STAY
▶ **Budget/Mid-range**
De Oude Herberg
6 Church Street, tel. 023 230 0260
www.portfoliocollection.com
Atmospheric Bed & Breakfast in Cape Dutch style with five rooms, a pool, a good restaurant (reservations advised) and an art gallery.

Hunter's Retreat
Tel. 023 230 0582
www.safarinow.com
1.5km/1mi north
This farm is situated in the vineyards with a view of the magnificent mountain landscape. Seven comfortable rooms and luxury suites in typical cottages built in the Cape Dutch style. A church and a swimming pool are also part of the property.

What to See in Tulbagh

The Dutch Reformed Church (1743) is now a museum, the old pulpit and pews being among the exhibits. Also part of the museum are three little houses in Church Street. In no. 4 historical and geological collections are on display. The Victorian House (no. 14) has exhibits from the time the town was built (1892) and no. 22 is a typical Cape Dutch house with a herb garden. All open Mon–Fri 9am–5pm, Sat 9am–4pm, Sun 11am–4pm.

✷
Oude Kerk
Volksmuseum

⊙

North of the town (3km/2mi) is the Oude Drostdy, built in 1806 by the French architect L. M. Thibault. It was once the seat of the Cape government district official. It has attractive Cape Dutch furniture and utility objects on display. In the old prison visitors can try Tulbagh sherry (open Mon–Sat 10am–12.30pm, 2–4.30pm, Sun 2.30 to 5pm).

De Oude Drostdy

⊙

Tzaneen

J 3

Province: Limpopo
Population: 5500

Altitude: 884m/2900ft
Distances: Polokwane 90km/55mi,
Phalaborwa 115km/70mi

Tzaneen is the centre of a large horticultural region in the far north of the country situated in a wonderful subtropical landscape near the Kruger National Park.

Tzaneen, at the foot of the northern Drakensberg mountains in the valley of the Letaba River, has become a popular tourist destination as a station on the way to the Kruger National Park; the range of activities includes an 18-hole golf course and an Olympic-sized swimming pool. Besides exotic fruit for teas (tours through the plantations), nuts, flowers, many different kinds of vegetables and potatoes are grown here. The climate is very pleasant in winter, warm during the day with rain rare. In Tzaneen the **Tzaneen Museum** is a must (Agatha St., closed on Sundays), it has a small, excellent ethnological collection.

Harvesting tea leaves in the plantations around Tzaneen

▶ VISITING TZANEEN

INFORMATION
Tourism Centre
23 Danie Joubert St.
Tel. 015 307 1294
www.tzaneeninfo.co.za

WHERE TO STAY
▶ Luxury
Coach House Hotel
Old Coach Road, Agatha
Tel. 015 306 8000
www.coachhouse.co.za
Excellent hotel with tasteful rooms in
a great scenic setting 15km/9mi south
of Tzaneen on the mountain, spectacular views. Nice pool, 18-hole golf
course nearby. The hotel produces
delicacies such as macadamia nuts,
macadamia oil and white nougat on
the premises, which can be sampled
and bought in the restaurant. Exter-
nally applied but equally good are the
services provided by the hotel's
Agatha Spa.

Around Tzaneen

Fanie Botha Dam and Nature Reserve

The Fanie Botha Dam is located north of Tzaneen. The dam is a popular water sports and fishing spot with prettily situated picnic sites. A 300m/330yd-wide forested strip around the dam is a nature reserve. There is no danger from big game; it is only home to antelopes and more than 150 bird species.

Duiwelskloof

Duiwelskloof, 18km/11mi from Tzaneen (R 36), is another destination. The subtropical climate allows the cultivation of avocados, mangoes and citrus fruits. In spring this place turns into a sea of flowers. The Duiwelskloof Resort is the base for hikes in this area.

★ Modjadji Nature Reserve

The drive from Duiwelskloof to the Modjadji Nature Reserve 28km/17mi further north is an attractive one. The reserve was set up in 1985 to protect a cycad species called the **Modjadji palm**. It usually reaches a height of 3–4m/10–13ft, at most 8m/26ft. The reserve can be explored on hiking trails and with a bit of luck visitors will spot impalas, blue wildebeests, nyalas and kudus.

Rain Queen

The Modjadji Reserve is located on the land of the Lobedu tribe, which is ruled by the Rain Queen. This matriarchal dynasty (in 2003 Mmakobo Modjadji VI was crowned) can be traced back to the 16th century. It is said that a princess who possessed the art of rainmaking fled here with some followers. She and her successors were asked for rain again by other tribes. The romantic story inspired Sir H. Rider Haggard's novel *She*, published in 1887. Tours into the realm of the Rain Queen are organized by the Limpopo Tourism & Parks Board (▶Polokwane), reservations at least one week in advance.

Unlike most other reserves in South Africa the Hans Merensky Reserve 70km/43mi north-east of Tzaneen does not permit visitors to explore it in their own vehicles. Bus tours start at the **Eiland Mineral Spa Complex** (spa with hot spring) near the reserve. Hikes are also possible. The 5185ha/12,812-acre territory, which is bordered by the Letaba River in the west, is home to sable antelopes, roan antelopes, zebras, giraffes and kudus. In the **Tsonga Kraal** open-air museum visitors can see how this tribe lived a hundred years ago.

★
Hans Merensky Nature Reserve

Leaving Tzaneen the R 71 heads south-west up to the Magoebaskloof. At first the road runs parallel to the Magoebas River valley, but after approx. 18km/11mi a path branches off to the right to the **Debegeni Falls** 3km/2mi away. The cascades plummet 80m/260ft and form a small lake (swimming permitted). The road climbs upwards and reaches the top of the pass (1432m/4698ft) at the Magoebaskloof Hotel. Beyond the pass the road runs past the Ebenezer Dam, a popular destination for boating and fishing. From here it is another 5km/3mi to Haenertsburg, which is known for trout and the cherry blossom festival that takes place in spring. The forest area around the Magoebaskloof can also be explored on hikes lasting several days. Accommodation is available in refuges (information at the tourist office in Tzaneen).

★
Magoebaskloof

◄ Haenertsburg

The high mountains and deep valleys of the Wolkberg Wilderness Area south of Tzaneen are part of the Drakensberg mountain range. This nearly 20,000ha/50,000-acre area is still almost untouched. By car from Tzaneen it can be reached via the New Agatha Forest Station (N 589); from there the Wilderness Area is accessed on foot.

Wolkberg Wilderness Area

View of the Ebenezer Dam

Umtata

H 7

Province: Eastern Cape
Population: 86,000

Altitude: 720m/2362ft
Distances: East London 230km/145mi

»Wild Coast« is the name of a section of South Africa's east coast that is indeed very picturesque. The largest and most important town on this 300km/186mi stretch is Umtata, the capital of Transkei; the country's great man, Nelson Mandela, comes from this area.

Umtata was the capital of the of the **Transkei** homeland, which was granted independence in 1976; since 1994 it has been part of South Africa again. The majority of the people living in this area are members of the **Xhosa people**, whose tribal communities have maintained their traditions and dialects. Umtata lies approx. 50km/30mi from the coast in hilly landscape mainly used for grazing; farming is only possible in a small area. The first inhabitants of this region, San and Khoikhoi, were pushed out by the Xhosa who migrated to this area in the 17th century. At the end of the 18th century and during the 19th century Boer, British and Xhosa interests clashed. After the bloody **Xhosa Wars** (▶p.68 f.) the British incorporated the area into the Cape colony in 1879. Transkei was given domestic autonomy in 1963.

Umtata

Umtata, founded in 1879 and situated by the river of the same name, has some imposing government buildings, including the **Bunga** (parliament, see below) and the town hall of 1907. The **Anglican cathe-**

VISITING UMTATA

INFORMATION

Eastern Cape Tourism
64 Owen St., Umtata
Tel. 047 532 2572
www.ectourism.co.za
www.wildcoast.org.za

PERSONAL SAFETY

Before a drive through Transkei visitors should inquire about the current security situation. Driving at night should be avoided, and Umtata is also considered unsafe at night. Shell Ultra City, 6km/4mi west of the town on the N 2, is a stop for overland buses and supply centre for all tourist needs.

WHERE TO STAY

▶ **Budget/Mid-range**
Umngazi River Bungalows
Port St. Johns
Tel. 047 564 1115/6/7/8/9
www.umngazi.co.za
One of the best hotel complexes at the beach near Port St Johns. Diverse possibilities to take a trip. Excellent cuisine, particularly seafood.

A particularly picturesque spot along the Wild Coast: the »hole in the wall« near Coffee Bay

dral is also striking. Otherwise the town seems run down. 6000 students are enrolled in a branch of Fort Hare University founded in 1976. Two attractive reserves are close to the town, Luchaba (5km/3mi north) and Nduli (3km/2mi south). Two arts and crafts businesses can be reached via the R 61 to Queenstown: the Hilmond weaving mill processes mohair and the Izandla pottery is attached to an arts and crafts school.

The Nelson Mandela Museum dedicated to the great statesman was opened in the Bunga building in 2000 (open Mon–Fri 9am–4pm, Sat 9am–12.30pm). The Heritage Centre in Qumu where Mandela grew up, and a memorial in Mvezo, the town where he was born, both nearby, are also part of the museum.

Nelson Mandela Museum ⏲

Wild Coast

The Wild Coast, the 280km/175mi-long rugged coastline between **Qolora Mouth** in the south and **Port Edward** in the north is a pleasure to visit thanks to its quiet bays and lagoons, bizarre rocks and caves and its many dream beaches. However, it was not the landscape that gave the Wild Coast its name, but rather the fact that the coast's cliffs and shallows brought many ships to a bad end here. The summers are hot and clammy, but it is still possible to swim in the ocean in winter. The towns along the coast can only be reached by roads branching off form the N 2, most of which are not surfaced. The drive to the coast is very attractive: evergreen **rainforests and mangrove swamps** are interrupted by open, hilly grassland covered in Xhosa round huts.

The Wild Coast has a number of tours that can be completed on foot, on horseback or in a canoe. The entire 280km/175mi could even be completed in 14 days. The section between Port St John's and Coffee Bay is considered particularly attractive. Information and tour bookings with native Xhosa guides at Wild Coast Trails, tel. 039 305 6455, www.wildcoast.org.za.

Wild Coast Trails

✳
Mkambati Nature Reserve

This reserve in the north of the Wild Coast (which can be reached via Port St John's or Flagstaff) is considered an insider tip. All the landscapes of this coastline are united here: thick forests, mangrove swamps, wide open grassland and lonely sandy beaches. The Msikaba River forms an impressive gorge, which can be explored from a canoe (rental). Campsite and shop present.

Port St John's

The largest town along the Wild Coast is Port St John's, 95km/60mi east of Umtata. The mouth of the Umzimvubu River, which forms a lovely lagoon, has luxuriant subtropical vegetation. It is an idyllic spot popular amongst young and young-at-heart »hippies« (tourism office tel. 047 564 1187).

Hluleka Nature Reserve

The road from Umtata to Port St John's has a junction near Libode with the access road to the Hluleka Nature Reserve. Evergreen forests line the estuary lagoon of the Mnenu River.

Coffee Bay

An equally attractive destination is Coffee Bay further south. It can be reached via a surfaced road that branches off from the N 2 18km/11mi south of Umtata. Several spots have a wonderful view of the spectacular coastal landscape. Safe bathing is possible in a sheltered lagoon. Cowrie shells can be collected on the beach; in the past they were used as currency. The explanation of the place name is somewhat obscure. A ship is said to have run aground here and lost its cargo (coffee beans). The beans were washed ashore and some coffee plants grew but soon died again.

✳
Hole in the Wall

The famous Hole in the Wall, an offshore rock 8km/5mi south of Coffee Bay, can be reached from there by car or via a delightful walk. Caution is advised when swimming, because the currents and depths are unpredictable.

✳
Dwesa Nature Reserve

The natural environment of the Dwesa Nature Reserve (access from the N 2 by Idutywa) is almost untouched. The larger mammals introduced here are rhinoceroses, buffaloes and zebras. Crocodiles are also part of the reserve's population. The actual attraction however is the tropical coastal forest along with the **lonely coast** with its wonderful shells. Accommodation is available in holiday houses and on the campsite.

Butterworth

Following the N 2 further south the road reaches Butterworth, the oldest (founded in 1827 as a mission station) and with 37,000 inhabitants the second-largest town of the former homeland of Transkei. The town is an industrial and commercial centre; its huts, covered by corrugated iron sheets, give it a bleak appearance.

Mazeppa Bay

After Butterworth the road makes its way through Kentani to Mazeppa Bay. In August this place is popular amongst open-sea anglers, who come here to hunt sharks. Others relax on the **long sandy beaches**. A small island off the coast is connected to the mainland via a suspension bridge; those daring enough to make their way across are rewarded with a splendid view of the coastal landscape.

The southernmost point of the Wild Coast is Qolora Mouth, which is another popular holiday destination as it too has subtropical vegetation and endless sandy beaches. A 4km/2.5mi walk along the Gxara River leads to the place where **Nongqawuse** had her visions about the resurrection of the Xhosa people; however, unlike Joan of Arc, she caused an immeasurable catastrophe (►p.68).

Qolora Mouth

Upington

D 6

Province: Northern Cape
Population: 62,000

Altitude: 805m/2641ft
Distances: Kuruman 260km/160mi,
Springbok 380km/235mi,
Kimberley 410km/255mi

After a long drive through the Kalahari the wheat fields and fruit plantations around Upington in the north of Northern Cape province come as a surprise. It is the obvious stop on the way to the ► Kgalagadi Transfrontier Park and the ►Augrabies Falls.

Upington is located on the west bank of the Orange River (Gariep) and is the centre of South Africa's northernmost viticultural region. Towards the north the landscape becomes the Kalahari desert. It gets very hot in summer; the best time to come is from April to October.

The journey is its own reward: on the R 27 towards Upington.

History A mission station was set up in 1871; the first missionaries created an irrigation system, which formed the foundation needed for the community to flourish. The town owes its name to Thomas Upington, the Cape Colony's prime minister from 1884 to 1886.

What to See in and around Upington

Upington Upington is a green town with wide streets and well-tended residential areas. **Olyfenhoutdrift**, an island in the Orange River (with a holiday centre, campsite, accommodation and sports facilities), can be reached via an avenue lined with date palms. Despite the inhospitable surroundings the town is completely geared to agricultural products. The Orange River never runs dry, thus permitting an irrigation culture; cotton, along with grapes and many other fruits, is cultivated here. A large part of the fruit is sold as dried fruit. The **South African Dried Fruit Cooperative** is the second-largest facility

Strange-looking kokerbooms

of its kind in the world (tours Mon–Thu 9.45am and 2pm, Fri 9.45am, tel. 054 337 2300). The statistics of the **Orange River Wine Cellars** are just as impressive; it is the country's largest wine-making co-operative and the second-largest in the world. The tasting bar can be found west of the centre. During the harvest between January and April viewings are also possible (tel. 054 337 8800). In the missionary building of 1883 the **Kalahari Oranje Museum** documents the region's natural and cultural history (closed Sat/Sun).

Spitskop Nature Reserve A conspicuous granite hill (»koppie«) rises 13km/8mi north of the town. It is a refuge for antelopes, gazelles, wildebeests, ostriches, plains zebras and feral dromedaries, the descendants of animals used as beasts of burden by troops in German South West Africa (open 7am–7pm).

Keimoes After Upington the R 359 follows the Orange River in a south-westerly direction. After a good 50km/30mi it reaches the town of Keimoes (population: 8,500). Don't miss the drive up the to **Tierberg**, a nature reserve above the town, for a great view of the fields and plantations surrounding Keimoes.

Kakamas Approx. 40km/25mi west of Keimoes is Kakamas with 5,500 inhabitants. The Khoikhoi name means »meagre pastureland«. Thanks to irrigation the agricultural activity in this area is flourishing in fields, vineyards and cotton plantations. The region is known for semi-precious stones such as onyx, amethyst and tiger's eye. They can be gathered during a walk. From Kakamas it is another 36km/22mi to the spectacular ▶Augrabies Falls.

Leaving Keimoes the R 27 towards Cape Town comes to a **kokerboom forest** (nature reserve) 10km/6mi south of Kenhardt. The kokerboom is a huge species of aloe that can be found in the entire north-western Cape and in southern Namibia; it can store water in its trunk and bears yellow flowers in July. In this forest there are around 700 of these bizarre trees that can grow up to 4m/13ft tall. The San use the wood to make containers for arrows, for which reason the tree is also knows as the quiver tree.

✳ **Kokerboom Forest**

VISITING UPINGTON UND KALAHARI

INFORMATION

Tourist Office
in the Kalahari Oranje Museum
Schröder Street, Upington
Tel. 054 332 6064
http://kharahais.gov.za

Green Kalahari Information Centre
Siyanda District Building, Upington
Tel. 054 337 2826
www.greenkalahari.co.za

TRANSPORT

Planes from Cape Town and Johannesburg fly to Upington's modern airport. The hotels take care of the transfer. Intercape buses connect Johannesburg, Cape Town and Windhoek (Namibia).

WHERE TO STAY

▶ **Mid-range**
Le Must River Manor
12 Murray Ave., Upington
Tel. 054 332 3971
www.lemustupington.com
Very nice, luxurious hotel in Cape Dutch style on the Orange River, with a lot of South African art, books and a music collection. The charming restaurant is considered to be one of the

best in South Africa. Neil Stemmet not only cooks excellent food, he also knows everything about the country. Trips to the ▶Augrabies Falls as well as canoe and fishing tours can be booked.

Stylish oasis in the Kalahari: Le Must

La Bohème Guesthouse
172 Groenpunt Rd., Upington
Tel. 054 338 0660
www.labohem.com
Classy accommodation in the Green Kalahari, elevated location with a wonderful view. Evelyne Meier from Switzerland has created a very private paradise here (only 2 double rooms and one cottage).

Welkom

G 5/6

Province: Free State
Population: 186,000

Altitude: 1338m/4390
Distances: Bloemfontein 150km/95mi

A third of South African gold production comes from Free State, particularly from Welkom, Virginia and Odendalsrus, which are located between Bloemfontein and Johannesburg.

Welkom, now Free State's second-largest town, was founded in 1947 and was designed on the drawing board as a garden city. The modern commercial centre is surrounded by parks; on the outskirts artificial lakes are filled with the water pumped out of the mines. They have become an **important biotope for waterfowl**. Visitors can participate in the tours through the gold mines. There is a gold museum and a town museum in the library. The town's most unusual attraction is the **wine cellar of the St Helena mine**, 857m/2812ft underground! A visit to this wine cellar is part of the also interesting general tour.

WELKOM

INFORMATION
Publicity Association
Clock Tower
at the Stateway
Tel. 057 353 3094

WHERE TO STAY

▶ **Budget**
Welkom Inn
Stateway / Tempest Rd.
Tel. 057 357 3361
Decent three-star hotel in the town centre with 148 rooms and a restaurant.

In **Virginia** (population: 77,000) almost 20km/12mi south-east of Welkom on the Sand River, has some disused gold mines open to the public. Visitors can also enjoy some tribal dancing.

50km/30mi beyond Virginia the south-east road via Ventersburg reaches the **Willem Pretorius Game Reserve** around the Allemanskraal Dam. The wide grassy plains in the south are populated by springboks, black wildebeests and other antelope species; the chances of spotting a rhinoceros, giraffe, buffalo or impala are higher in the northern hills. The remains of a prehistoric settlement have been found here. There are chalets, a campsite, a restaurant, a golf course and a swimming pool.

Winburg　　Winburg (population: 15,000) approx. 90km/55mi south-east of Welkom is the province's oldest town (founded in 1842) and was the first capital of Orange Free State. The leaders of five Voortrekker groups met in the still extant **Ford's Hotel** (on the central square, now a big shop), where they founded Free State. This event is commemorated by the Voortrekker monument (3km/2mi outside the town) and a small museum. South-west of Winburg is the **Erfenis Dam Nature Reserve** (more than 3300ha/8155 acre). The dam is good for water sports; camping and picnic sites available.

★ West Coast National Park

B / C 8

Province: Western Cape　　　　**Distances:** Cape Town 120km/75mi

The area around the Langebaan lagoon north of Cape Town with four small offshore islands has been made into a national park. Its unique bird fauna makes the approx. 18,000ha/44,500-acre area internationally significant.

The cold Benguela current determines the region's rough, dry climate. Almost all of the low amount of precipitation (270mm/11in per year) falls in winter, and morning fog is not uncommon. The vegetation is sparse, low bushes and succulents are prevalent. In spring however, between August and October, the bare land is transformed into a **sea of flowers**. The main entrance with an information centre is located south of the town of Langebaan, and a second entrance can be found 20km/12mi south of Langebaan (signposted from the R 27).

Fascinating bird life

Amongst the large and diverse bird world are cormorants, sea gulls, spotted redshanks, sandpipers, plovers, gannets and flamingos. The park is a refuge for African penguins, the only penguin species of the African mainland. In summer the resident birds are joined by tens of thousands of migratory birds, some with their home within the Arctic circle, while around 80% come from eastern Europe. Mammals living in the reserve include the bontebok, common eland, springbok, kudu and blue wildebeest.

Animal population

The lonely Jacobs Baai at Cape Columbine

VISITING WEST COAST NATIONAL PARK

INFORMATION

Parks Board
Tel. 022 772 2144

Tourist Office Langebaan
Oostewal St./Bree Street
Tel. 022 772 1515
www.langebaan.info.com

WHERE TO STAY

► Mid-range

The Farmhouse
5 Egret Street, Langebaan
Tel. 022 772 2062
www.thefarmhouselangebaan.co.za
Nice country house in Cape Dutch
style with a view of the lagoon.
Rooms with a fireplace and garden.
Excellent, very inexpensive restaurant.

Langebaan Beach House
44 Beach Road, Langebaan
Tel. 022 772 2625
www.langebaanbeachhouse.com
Small guesthouse right on the beach
with a great view of the lagoon.
Breakfast on the beach terrace.

► Budget

Paternoster Hotel
Main Road, Paternoster
Tel. 022 752 2703
www.paternosterhotel.co.za
Basic but sound hotel near the beach,
10 rooms, easy-going atmosphere.
Known for excellent spiny lobster.

WHERE TO EAT

► Moderate

Die Strandloper
Langebaan, at the beach
Tel. 022 772 2490
Popular open-air restaurant with
good fish dishes ranging from mussels
to kingklip. »All you can eat« in the
evenings. Bring your own alcohol.
Reservations a must.

► Inexpensive

Slipway Waterfront
Saldanha Bay, at the harbour
Tel. 022 714 4235
This restaurant serves fresh fish as
well as steaks and filets.

Visitor facilities It is possible to drive around the lagoon (approx. 35km/22mi) on a surfaced road, on the way there are some viewpoints from which bird watching is possible (bring binoculars). An information centre has been set up in the old Geelbek farmhouse at the southern end of the lagoon. It is the starting point of several nature trails and boating trips are also on offer. Open daily in summer 6am–8pm, in winter 7am–7.30pm.

Around the West Coast National Parks

Langebaan The town of Langebaan at the lagoon's northern end is becoming an ever more popular holiday destination with a great choice of accommodation and restaurants. There is a casino in the Club Mykonos. The lagoon is good for sailing and windsurfing. The sunsets are spectacular.

Further north the approx. 10km/6mi-wide Saldanha Bay connects to the town of the same name. It is not an overly attractive place; the harbour and industry dominate the scene. After Richards Bay and Durban, Saldanha is South Africa's third-largest port, measured by tonnage. The port mainly ships iron ore brought here from Sishen; in addition it is a centre of the fishing and lobster-catching industry. Hoedjies Bay near the centre is a popular beach for swimming. In the first week of September the Festival of the Sea takes place here: fish dishes plus folklore.

Saldanha

The fishing village of Paternoster has been discovered by the inhabitants of Cape Town as a weekend destination, but has managed to hold on to a bit of atmosphere. Old cottages are let to holiday visitors.

Paternoster

Cape Columbinewest of Paternoster is a nature reserve. Its 263ha/ 650 acres are covered by the typical fynbos vegetation. The best time to come is spring, when landscape is transformed into a real sea of flowers.

Columbine Nature Reserve

Worcester

C 8

Province: Western Cape	**Altitude:** 221m/725ft
Population: 87,000	**Distances:** Cape Town 110km/70mi

Worcester is the largest town in the fertile Breede River Valley east of Cape Town. Wine and fruit are cultivated in this valley, which is surrounded and sheltered by mountain ranges reaching elevations of more than 2000m/6500ft.

Worcester was founded by Governor Lord Charles Somerset in 1822 and owes its name to his brother, the earl of Worcester. The town is surrounded my vast vineyards that need to be irrigated due to the low level of precipitation. They yield a good 20% of South Africa's entire wine production. A well-known product is the **Hanepoot**, a sweet dessert wine from the grape of the same name, which is internationally known as Muscat d'Alexandrie.

What to See in Worcester

In Church Street and its side streets there are some pretty homes dating from the 19th century. **Beck House** (1841) is a museum open to the public (open Mon–Fri 8am–12.30pm, 2–4.30pm); its exhibits consist mainly of furniture made of yellowwood and stinkwood. There is a surviving bath-house and boxroom in the garden. **Stofberg House** built in 1920 (now the tourist office) is also worth looking at. An impressive building immediately north of Beck House

Church Street

contains the Pear Tree restaurant. The **Naudé Gallery** (113 Russell St.) is definitely worth a visit. It has paintings and sculptures by South African artists on display.

Old Drostdy

One of the most beautiful buildings on the Cape is the building of the district official built in 1825 (Somerset Street, at the south-west end of Church Street), which is used by the institute of technology.

KWV Brandy Cellar ⏱

East of Church Square is the huge brandy factory owned by KWV, with production in 120 copper stills. Open Mon–Fri 8am–4.30pm, guided tours in English at 2pm.

★ Kleinplasie Farm Museum

The **open-air museum** on the eastern outskirts of Worcester has a Khoikhoi kraal, a camp of the Trek Boers and an 18th-century farm (open Mon–Sat 9am–4.30pm, Sun 10.30am–4.30pm). Historically knowledgeable staff show how wool was spun, corn was milled, bread was baked and spirits were distilled. There is a good restaurant and several chalets, and the wine shop carries a good selection of

 VISITING WORCESTER

INFORMATION

Tourism Bureau
23 Baring Street, Worcester
Tel. 023 348 2795
http://worcesterweb.co.za
www.worcesterwinelands.co.za

Breede Valley Bureau
Tel. 023 347 6411
www.breederivervalley.co.za

WHERE TO EAT

▶ **Moderate**

The Pear Tree
21 Baring Street, Worcester
Tel. 023 342 0936
Classy restaurant in an attractive Cape Dutch house built in 1825. Good traditional South African cuisine or snacks, served in a historical ambience or by the 150-year-old pear tree.

WHERE TO STAY

▶ **Mid-range**

Merwida Country Lodge
35km/22mi west, 3km/2mi from

Rawsonville
Tel. 023 349 1435
www.merwida.com
Magnificent, luxurious building in American colonial style in the wine fields of the vineyard of the same name. Wonderful view from the balconies of the gardens and the mountains. With a pool and restaurant. Book early!

▶ **Budget**

Nuy Valley Guest House
15km/9mi east, on the R 60
Tel. 023 342 7025
www.nuyvallei.co.za
A very nice bed & breakfast on the vineyard, with 18 rooms (and a backpacker room for 27 people) in the building dating from 1871. Visitors can cook for themselves or enjoy a nice meal in the restaurant.

Spring in the idyllic valley of the Breede River near Worcester

local products (such as the »Witblits«, with 60% alcohol). The office of **Worcester Winelands** (tel. 342 8710) provides tips for discoveries around the town.

The botanical garden 2km/1mi north is home to succulents and other plants from South Africa's arid environments. Only a part of the 154ha/380-acre site has been landscaped into a garden; the rest has been left in its natural state (open daily 8am–5pm).

★
Karoo National Botanic Garden

Armed with the information provided by Worcester Winelands, visitors can tour the vineyards of the Worcester wine route. The oldest, De Wet, was only founded in 1946; as a results there are not picture-postcard vineyards, but this also means they do not have the commercial character of the other vineyards at the Cape. Some of the vineyards worth mentioning are Nuy Winery (also a very nice place for overnight stays and dining), Bergsig, Merwida and Du Toitskloof.

Worcester Wine Route

The Hex River Valley is picturesque all year round; from Worcester it runs north-east (N 1) and is covered by huge wine fields. Some of the Cape Dutch houses dating from 1770 to 1815 can be visited, while others have been transformed into atmospheric guesthouses. Rose and garden lovers should visit the **Sonskyn Rose Garden** in De Doorns, a huge rose-growing enterprise with a selection of 400 varieties; in the tea garden visitors can enjoy fresh scones and rose tea. The sweet Hanepoot Jerepigo, which can be tasted in the **De Doorns Wine Cellar** (closed Sundays), is made from grape juice and alcohol. The autumn festival is celebrated at the end of May. Information: Hex River Tourism Bureau, De Doorns, www.hexrivervalley.co.za, tel. 021 356 2014.

Hex River Valley

INDEX

Places in Lesotho are marked (L), in Swaziland (S).

LIST OF MAPS AND ILLUSTRATIONS

PHOTO CREDITS

JBLISHER'S INFORMATION

trations etc: 234 illustrations, 31 maps
diagrams, one large city plan
: Dr. Bernhard Abend, Birgit Borowski,
Schliebitz
contributions by Achim Bourmer, Carsten
ler, Carmen Galenschovski, Robert von
s, Harald Mielke, Dr. Reinhard Paesler,
homas Rößner
updates: Peter Zangerle
ing: Baedeker editorial team
 Sykes)
slation: Michael Scuffil
ography: Christoph Gallus, Hohberg;
RDUMONT/Falk Verlag, Ostfildern (map)
llustrations: jangled nerves, Stuttgart
gn: independent Medien-Design, Munich;
rin Schemel

or-in-chief: Rainer Eisenschmid,
eker Ostfildern

1st edition 2009
Based on Baedeker Allianz Reiseführer
»Südafrika«, 6. Aufl. 2008

Copyright: Karl Baedeker Verlag, Ostfildern
Publication rights: MAIRDUMONT GmbH & Co;
Ostfildern

Printed in China

DEAR READER,

We would like to thank you for choosing this Baedeker travel guide. It w
reliable companion on your travels and will not disappoint you.
This book describes the major sights, of course, but it also recommends
interesting events, as well as hotels in the luxury and budget categorie
includes tips about where to eat or go shopping and much more, helpi
make your trip an enjoyable experience. Our authors ensure the quality
information by making regular journeys to South Africa and putting all
know-how into this book.

Nevertheless, experience shows us that it is impossible to rule out errors a
changes made after the book goes to press, for which Baedeker accepts no
liability. Please send us your criticisms, corrections and suggestions for
improvement: we appreciate your contribution. Contact us by post or e-m
phone us:

▶ **Verlag Karl Baedeker GmbH**
  Editorial department
  Postfach 3162
  73751 Ostfildern
  Germany
  Tel. 49-711-4502-262, fax -343
  www.baedeker.com
  www.baedeker.co.uk
  E-Mail: baedeker@mairdumont.com

Baedeker Travel Guides in English at a glance:

▶ Andalusia
▶ Bali
▶ Barcelona
▶ Berlin
▶ Brazil
▶ Budapest
▶ Dubai · Emirates
▶ Egypt
▶ Florida
▶ Ireland
▶ Italy
▶ London

▶ Mexico
▶ New York
▶ Paris
▶ Portugal
▶ Prague
▶ Rome
▶ South Africa
▶ Spain
▶ Thailand
▶ Tuscany
▶ Venice
▶ Vienna